A History of the Classical Greek \
478–323 BC

Blackwell History of the Ancient World

This series provides a new narrative history of the ancient world, from the beginnings of civilization in the ancient Near East and Egypt to the fall of Constantinople. Written by experts in their fields, the books in the series offer authoritative, accessible surveys for students and general readers alike.

Published

A History of the Ancient Near East
Marc Van De Mieroop

A History of Byzantium
Timothy E. Gregory

A History of the Classical Greek World
P. J. Rhodes

In Preparation

A History of Ancient Egypt
David O'Connor

A History of the Persian Empire
Christopher Tuplin

A History of the Archaic Greek World
Jonathan Hall

A History of the Hellenistic World
Malcolm Errington

A History of the Roman Republic
John Rich

A History of the Roman Empire
Michael Peachin

A History of the Later Roman Empire, AD 284–622
Stephen Mitchell

A History of the Classical Greek World

478–323 BC

P. J. Rhodes

Blackwell
Publishing

BLACKWELL PUBLISHING
350 Main Street, Malden, MA 02148-5020, USA
9600 Garsington Road, Oxford OX4 2DQ, UK
550 Swanston Street, Carlton, Victoria 3053, Australia

First published 2006 by Blackwell Publishing Ltd

5   2008

Library of Congress Cataloging-in-Publication Data

Rhodes, P. J. (Peter John)
    A history of the classical Greek world: 478–323 B.C. / P. J. Rhodes.
      p. cm.—(Blackwell history of the ancient world)
    Includes bibliographical references and index.
    ISBN 978-0-6312-2564-5 (hard cover: alk. paper)
    ISBN 978-0-6312-2565-2 (pbk.: alk. paper)

    1. Greece—History—To 146 B.C. I. Title. II. Series.

    DF214.R49 2006
    938—dc22   2004028425

A catalogue record for this title is available from the British Library.

Picture research by Kitty Bocking

Set in 10.5 on 12.5 pt Plantin
by SNP Best-set Typesetter Ltd, Hong Kong
Printed and bound in Malaysia
by KHL Printing Co Sdn Bhd

The publisher's policy is to use permanent paper from mills that operate a sustainable forestry policy, and which has been manufactured from pulp processed using acid-free and elementary chlorine-free practices. Furthermore, the publisher ensures that the text paper and cover board used have met acceptable environmental accreditation standards.

For further information on
Blackwell Publishing, visit our website:
www.blackwellpublishing.com

Contents

List of Illustrations   vii

List of Figures   viii

List of Maps   ix

Preface   x

Note on References   xi

1   Introduction   1

2   The Formation of the Delian League   14

3   The Peloponnese in the Early Fifth Century   22

4   Athens After the Persian War   31

5   The Athenian Empire in the Mid Fifth Century   41

6   Periclean Athens   54

7   The Greeks in the West: The Rise of Syracuse   71

8   The Peloponnesian War: Origins   81

9   The Peloponnesian War: Resources and Strategies   90

10 The Peloponnesian War: 431–421   101

11 The Athens of Cleon   116

12 The Peloponnesian War: 421–413   124

13 The Peloponnesian War: 413–404   142

14   Athens in the Late Fifth Century   155

15   The Athenian Empire: Retrospect   172

16   Introduction to the Fourth Century: The Common Peace   189

17   Sparta's Imperialism and Collapse   204
     Appendix: Persia and its Rebels   221

18   The Second Athenian League   226

19   Thebes and Northern Greece   244

20   Athens After the Peloponnesian War   257

21   The Western Greeks from Dionysius I to Timoleon   273

22   Philip II of Macedon   294
     Appendix: Persia and the Greeks in the Reign of Artaxerxes III   323

23   Demosthenic Athens   328
     Appendix: Sparta   344

24   Alexander the Great: Sources and Outline   347

25   Alexander the Great: Topics   359

26   Epilogue   384

     Bibliography   388

     Index   396

Illustrations

1	Athens: owl and Athena	11
2	Aegina: turtle and tortoise	42
3	The first *stele* of the Athenian tribute lists: arrangement of lists	48
4	The first *stele* of the Athenian tribute lists: reconstruction of fragments	49
5	Reconstruction of the Athenian acropolis	63
6	Polyzelus' bronze charioteer at Delphi	74
7	Syracuse: 'Demareteum'	77
8	The bay of Pylos: aerial photograph	107
9	Syracuse: aerial photograph	137
10	The prospectus of the Second Athenian League	231
11	Delphi: the temple of Apollo and the stoa of the Athenians	303
12	Reconstruction of Philip's skull	322
13	Reconstruction of the Mausoleum at Halicarnassus	324
14	The Alexander Sarcophagus (*c.*320)	363
15	Treasury relief at Persepolis	379

Figures

1 Fifth-century Spartan kings and regents   26
2 Thucydides the opponent of Pericles and Thucydides the historian   66
3 Tyrants of Gela/Syracuse, Acragas, Rhegium   73
4 Fourth-century Spartan kings and a regent   206
5 The electoral units of the Boeotian federation in the late fifth and
   early fourth centuries   245
6 Tyrants of Pherae   250
7 The family of Dionysius I   278
8 Amyntas III of Macedon and his descendants   298
9 Satraps of Caria   323

Maps

1 Greece and the Aegean   xiii
2 Carthage, Sicily, Southern Italy   xiv
3 The bay of Pylos   106
4 The vicinity of Argos   128
5 The vicinity of Mantinea   129
6 Syracuse   136
7 Boeotia   246
8 The Persian campaign of Alexander the Great   350

Preface

This book gives an account of the 'classical' period of Greek history, from the aftermath of the Persian Wars in 478 to the death of Alexander the Great in 323. I have tried to make it a straightforward account, but one which combines analysis with narrative, which combines other aspects of Greek life with political and military matters, and which shows clearly the evidence on which it is based and the considerations which have to be borne in mind in using the evidence. In the course of writing it I have on particular topics consulted works by many people, including other histories comparable with this one, but I have deliberately not directly compared my treatment of the period with any other.

The book will be published about the time of my retirement after teaching Greek history in the University of Durham for forty years. I am enormously grateful to the colleagues who supported me in that, and in particular to Dr O. T. P. K. Dickinson, who helped with the opening paragraphs of chapter 1 (but who is not to be blamed for what I have finally chosen to say there); to the generations of students who listened to the lectures and participated in the tutorials out of which the book has grown, and in particular to Mr S. English, who as an undergraduate attended the lectures and tutorials and afterwards as a research student read the whole book in draft and identified many points at which it needed to be improved; and to Dr L. Rubinstein, who likewise has read the whole book and helped me to improve it. I am grateful also to Mr A. Bertrand of Blackwell Publishing, who invited me to write the book, and to everybody who has been involved in its production; and to those who have given permission for the use of copyright illustrations.

Note on References

Ancient Authors and their Works

There are four major collections of Greek and Latin texts:

1. the Budé series (also known as the Collection des Universités de France) (Paris: Les Belles Lettres): texts with French translations and short notes;
2. the Loeb Classical Library (Harvard University Press): texts with English translations and short notes;
3. the Oxford Classical Texts (Oxford University Press): texts;
4. the Bibliotheca Scriptorum Graecorum et Romanorum Teubneriana (originally Leipzig: Teubner; now Munich: Saur): texts.

There are various English translations of the more popular works, in particular in the Penguin Classics series.

The abbreviations used here are mostly those used in the third edition of the *Oxford Classical Dictionary*, but speeches are given both number and title, and where the title is centred on a person the personal name is given in full (e.g. Aeschin. III. *Ctesiphon*); notice also that *Ath. Pol.* without indication of author denotes the work of that title attributed to Aristotle.

For shorter abbreviations used in part of chapter 22 see p. 309; and in chapters 24–5 see pp. 347–8. For some works by some authors alternative forms of reference are current. For the *Hellenica Oxyrhynchia* I use the chapter numbering of the most recent Teubner text, ed. M. H. Chambers (on older systems see p. 12 n. 1 and p. 146 with n. 1 in chapter 13). Otherwise the instance most relevant to this book is Plutarch's *Lives*: here citations are by the chapters and sections of the Budé and Teubner texts; the Loeb texts use the same chapters but divide them into fewer, larger sections; there are no Oxford texts.

Collections of Inscriptions and Papyri

The abbreviations used here are mostly those used in the third edition of the *Oxford Classical Dictionary* (*OCD*), but notice: M&L for *OCD*'s ML, and R&O = P. J. Rhodes and R. Osborne, *Greek Historical Inscriptions, 404–323 BC* (Oxford University Press, 2003); also:

C. Delphes: *Corpus des Inscriptions de Delphes*
IK Placename: volumes in the series *Inschriften griechische Städte aus Kleinasien*

In multiple references to texts, the symbol ~ precedes a reference to an English translation.

Periodicals and Standard Books

Publication details of books cited will be found in the Bibliography on pp. 388–95. Titles of a few standard books are abbreviated as in the third edition of the *Oxford Classical Dictionary*, e.g. *CAH* = *Cambridge Ancient History*. Titles of periodicals are in general abbreviated as in *L'Année Philologique*, but in accordance with normal anglophone practice I use *TAPA* etc. where *L'Année Philologique* uses *TAPhA* etc., and I abbreviate some single-word titles, e.g. *Hist.* = *Historia*. Superior figures denote the second and subsequent series of periodicals (e.g. CQ^2), the second and subsequent editions of books (e.g. CAH^2).

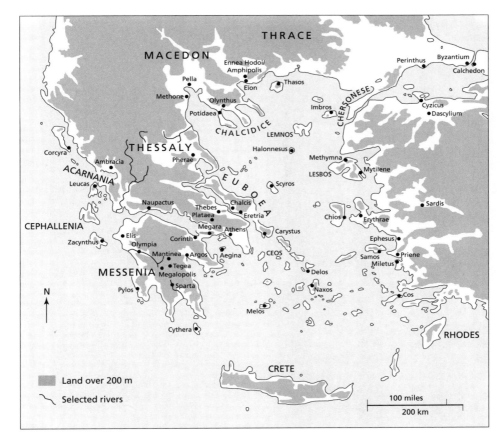

Map 1 Greece and the Aegean

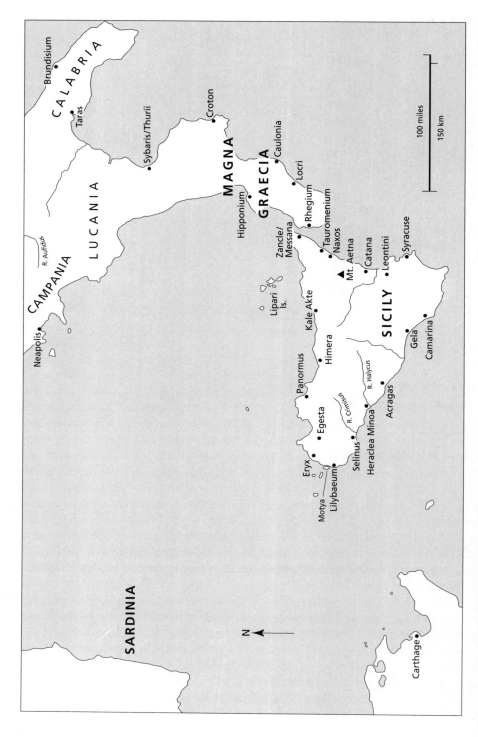

Map 2 Carthage, Sicily, Southern Italy

1

Introduction

Two large peninsulas project into the Mediterranean from Europe: Italy, dividing the whole into a western half and an eastern half, and Greece, subdividing the eastern half. What was to be the Greek world until the end of the fourth century BC comprised mainland Greece, with the islands off the west coast; and also the Aegean Sea, between mainland Greece and Asia Minor (present-day Turkey), with the coast of Asia Minor to the east, the coast of Thrace (part of present-day Greece) to the north, and the island of Crete (part of present-day Greece) closing it to the south. Mainland Greece is divided by mountains into many, mostly small, habitable areas, and by sea inlets (the Gulf of Corinth on the west and the Saronic Gulf on the east) into northern and central Greece and the southern part known as the Peloponnese, linked by the Isthmus of Corinth (where there is now a canal from one side to the other). Advanced civilisations developed earlier to the south and east of this area, in Egypt and the near east, than to the north and west; and in Greece the most important settlements were towards the south and east, and there was a tendency to look for outside contacts to the civilisations to the south and east and to absorb influences from them.

The first advanced civilisations in the Greek region arose in the bronze age of the second millennium: the Minoan civilisation of Crete (from *c.*2000: given its modern name after the legendary king Minos), the Cycladic civilisation of the Aegean (already important before *c.*2000 and flourishing after: named after the Cyclades, the large group of islands in the southern Aegean) and the Mycenaean civilisation of the mainland (from *c.*1600, with palaces from *c.*1400: named after Mycenae, near Argos, one of the main centres); from *c.*1400 Crete and the Cyclades came under the influence of the Mycenaeans. Life was based on substantial kingdoms, centred on large and rich palaces and served by bureaucratic administrations. The language of the Minoans was not Greek (their Linear A texts have not yet been deciphered); the language of the Mycenaeans was Greek (their Linear B texts were deciphered in the 1950's); the Cycladic civilisation has not left texts of its own. This was the world in which the classical Greeks' legends of their heroic past were ostensibly set (the Trojan War, the Oedipus story and so on).

That world broke up, in a period of destructions and population movements whose causes are still disputed, about 1200–1000. The classical Greeks believed that the Dorians, perceived as a separate strand of the Greek people, invaded from the north and drove out the earlier inhabitants to the islands and the coast of Asia Minor (e.g. Thuc. I. 2. vi, 12. iii). It is now thought unlikely that there was a phenomenon which deserves to be called the Dorian Invasion, but it does seem to be true that the Dorians were comparative newcomers in the Peloponnese and that the Greeks began migrating from the mainland to the islands and the coast of Asia Minor – from north to south, the Aeolians and Ionians from c.1000 and the Dorians slightly later.

Thucydides wrote of a continuous progress from the earliest and most primitive condition of Greece to the climax of the fifth century (I. 1–19), but modern scholars have thought in terms of a dark age between the end of the bronze-age civilisations and the 'archaic' period from c.800 to c.500: dark both in the sense that the size of the population and the level of civilisation were lower than before and after and in the sense that we know less about it than about the periods before and after. There is still some justice in that view, though the dark age now seems less dark in both those respects than it did half a century ago.

By c.800 the revival was well under way; but, in contrast to the bronze age, there developed a large number of separate, small communities, which often, and particularly towards the south and east, took the form of *poleis*, 'city states', which comprised a town and the farm land around it and which aspired to a high degree of independence and self-sufficiency. If these communities were originally ruled by kings, the kings were not grand rulers like the oriental monarchs but more like the chief aristocrats depicted by Homer, and before long kings gave way to officials mostly appointed annually from within the aristocracy of families which had emerged from the dark age owning the largest quantities of good land.

Rising prosperity brought complications. The population was growing once more, over time not dramatically but significantly (though occasional bursts of more rapid increase are not to be ruled out), and even after extending the land which they controlled and cultivated communities reached the point where the population (even though it was later to become still larger) seemed too large to survive a run of bad years, or by comparison with a generation earlier. The Greeks therefore took to trading on a larger scale, with one another and with the outside world, to import what was not available in sufficient quantities locally, and they also started founding colonies around the Mediterranean and the Black Sea (sometimes joining with the pre-existing population) – in convenient places for gaining access to what they wanted to import, and in places where men under pressure at home could make a new life and grow their own food. Most of the colonies became, technically, independent *poleis*, though they had familial and religious links with their mother states and the mother states hoped to retain influence over the colonies.

This process contributed to the pressures for political change. It was easier in a trading world than in self-sufficient agricultural communities for some men to become richer and others to become poorer, and for those who had become richer to think themselves as good as the established aristocracy. However, the citizen farmer was still a common ideal, and in many states many citizens continued to own some land and to live at least partly off the produce of their land. Coinage, convenient as a medium of exchange and of reckoning and storing non-landed wealth, was not invented until the sixth century, and it is in Athens in the second half of the fifth that we first find a monetary economy in which the average citizen is likely to possess coins and engage in monetary transactions on a regular basis. There was a change in fighting (though how great and sudden a change is disputed), as cities took to relying on the heavy infantry known as hoplites, organised in a phalanx whose success depended on the cohesion of the whole body rather than the prowess of individual stars, so that all who could afford the equipment and fight in the phalanx might think that they were equally important to their city. The invention of the alphabet, a system of about two dozen characters (in contrast to the scripts with much larger numbers of characters used in bronze-age Greece and in the near east), made it possible for literacy to become an accomplishment of citizens in general rather than of a specialised class of scribes, and for laws to be written down and placed in the public domain – a development which at first may have been as valuable to aristocrats afraid that one of their number would step out of line as to lower-class people afraid of unfair treatment by the aristocrats. In some places there may have been tension between inhabitants perceived as belonging to different racial groups, for instance between Dorians and others in some cities in the Peloponnese. And within the aristocracy or on the fringes of the aristocracy there will have been ambitious or disaffected individuals who thought that they did not do well enough out of the principle of holding office when their turn came round.

Different factors were of differing importance in different places, but in many states in the seventh and sixth centuries power was seized by a *tyrannos* ('tyrant'), trading on whatever grounds for discontent and groups of discontented people there were locally. The position of tyrant was not a formal office with defined powers: some tyrants ruled autocratically, others by manipulating the existing framework; some ruled cruelly, others mildly (it is only with Plato and Aristotle in the fourth century that a tyrant was automatically seen as a cruel autocrat). Tyrants were bad for the aristocrats, since they, like the lesser citizens, became subject to the tyrant. Periods of tyrannical rule tended not to last longer than two or three generations, as the original discontents were dealt with or forgotten and the dominance of the tyrant came to be a new cause of discontent; by the end of the sixth century most states had régimes in which basic political rights had been extended to all rich enough to fight as hoplites, and in several places pseudo-kinship organisations (tribes, phratries ['brother-hoods'] and the like) through which the aristocrats had controlled the popu-lace had been supplanted by new organisations.

Two cities developed in unusual ways, so as to become much larger than most, and in the fifth century to become rivals for supremacy in Greece.

Sparta, in the south of the Peloponnese, had not one king but two, probably a result of the amalgamation of neighbouring communities; it retained these into the classical period and beyond, though many of their powers were trans-ferred to an annually appointed board of five ephors ('overseers'). By the eighth century it had conquered the whole of its region of Laconia, making some of the inhabitants *perioikoi* ('dwellers-around', independent within their own com-munities but dependent on Sparta in foreign policy) and others helots (a word which probably means 'captives', a serf class working the land of its Spartan owners: they are the best-known but not the only instance of a serf class in early Greece). In the late eighth and seventh centuries it expanded westwards into Messenia, making *perioikoi* and helots of its inhabitants too, and thus coming to control an area of about 2,400 sq. miles = 6,200 km^2. It thus did not need to found colonies overseas, apart from Taras in Italy, to accommodate men judged not entitled to a share in the conquered land at home.

Probably early in the seventh century, after the first round of conquests in Messenia, tension led to the core of a settlement attributed to a man called Lycurgus. The aristocrats came to an arrangement with the Spartan citizens to maintain solidarity and preserve their superiority over the *perioikoi* and helots: politically, the *gerousia* (council of elders, comprising twenty-eight men plus the two kings) and assembly were given defined roles in the running of the state; economically, the conquered land and helots to work it were apportioned among the citizens (but, despite what scholars used to believe, it now appears that the distributed land became ordinary private property); socially, the exis-tence of the lower orders made a full-time military life for the citizens both pos-sible and necessary. For a long time this seemed to be a success: Sparta avoided tyranny and became the strongest state in Greece, and people who lived else-where professed admiration for its disciplined life.

In the sixth century Sparta's attempts to expand northwards into Arcadia were unsuccessful, and in the middle of the century there was a change of policy: instead of setting out to be a Dorian conqueror Sparta set out to be a Greek leader, binding other states to it by alliances. By the end of the century nearly all the Peloponnesian states (but not Argos, which could never accept Spartan leadership, and not Achaea, which had more to do with the north side of the Gulf of Corinth than with the rest of the Peloponnese) were linked to Sparta in an organisation for foreign policy which scholars call the Pelopon-nesian League, in which they were consulted about joint action and bound to accept majority decisions.

Originally Sparta's culture had been like its neighbours'; but owing to the conquest of Messenia and the need to keep the subject population under control, and perhaps also to the failure to conquer Arcadia, austerity came to be prized as a Spartan virtue. It was perhaps more that Sparta did not participate in developments enjoyed elsewhere than that Sparta became more austere, but when Sparta and Athens became rivals in the fifth century each was proud to emphasise that it was not like the other.

Athens itself was never totally abandoned during the dark age, and was one of the first places to recover, but in the eighth and seventh centuries it was overtaken by cities in the Peloponnese. Like Sparta it did not need to found colonies but was able to expand into its own region, Attica (about 1,000 sq. miles = 2,600 km²); but the other inhabitants were not made subject to a ruling body of Athenians but all became Athenian citizens.

Athens rose to prominence in the sixth century. In the late seventh century an unsuccessful attempt at tyranny by Cylon was followed by Draco's publication of written laws. In 594/3 Solon tried to mediate between the advantaged and the disadvantaged: he liberated a class of dependent peasants; made wealth the sole qualification for office, enabling a wider range of rich men to challenge the landed aristocrats; formalised the decision-making process by creating a new council to prepare business for the citizens' assembly; revised the laws, and modified the judicial processes to make it easier for underdogs to obtain justice. But his compromise was more than the rich aristocrats had feared yet less than the discontented had hoped for. After two earlier attempts, from 546/5 to 511/0 Athens was subjected to the tyranny of Pisistratus and his sons, who on the whole ruled constitutionally and mildly. During the sixth century Athens prospered, welcoming trade rather than trying to remain self-sufficient, and becoming the Greek world's leading producer of fine pottery.

The tyranny was ended when the Alcmaeonid family, sometimes collaborating with but at other times opposed to the tyrants, put pressure on Sparta to intervene. Rivalry between the Alcmaeonid Cleisthenes and another aristocrat led to the victory of Cleisthenes (and a quarrel with Sparta): Cleisthenes gave the Athenians a new, locally based articulation of the citizen body, in ten tribes, thirty *trittyes* ('thirds' of tribes) and 139 demes; and this supplanted the older organisations as the basis of Athens' public life, so that (for instance) the army was organised in tribal regiments and the council which prepared the assembly's business became a council of five hundred, comprising fifty members for each tribe, with the individual demes supplying members in proportion to their population. He also introduced the institution of ostracism, first used in the 480's, by which each year the citizens had the opportunity to send one man into a kind of honourable exile for ten years without finding him guilty of any offence.

In the course of the archaic period, as they had increasing contact with the outside world, the Greeks became conscious of what they had in common as Greeks in contrast to the barbarians (*barbaroi*, foreigners whose languages sounded to Greeks like *bar-bar*). Of the civilised barbarians to the east and south, those who impinged most on the Greeks were those who controlled

western Asia Minor, inland from the Greek cities on the coast. For most of
the archaic period, these were the Lydians, whose capital was at Sardis: they
acquired a kind of overlordship over the Asiatic Greeks, but though foreign
were sympathetic, and made dedications at Greek temples. But Cyrus II
of Persia, who had begun as a minor king to the east of the Persian Gulf,
in 550 conquered the Medes to his north (with the help of Babylon to his
west, but in 539 he was to conquer Babylon too), and then c.546 conquered
Croesus of Lydia, and with him the Asiatic Greeks; the islands near the coast
perhaps made token submission at this point and were actually subjected
c.520–515.

In 525–522 the Persians conquered Egypt, which was a part of the Greeks'
world in the sense that Greek traders had operated there and Greek soldiers
had been employed there as mercenaries since the seventh century. About 514
they penetrated Europe, going north of the Danube to campaign unsuccessfully
against the Scythians (whom they believed to be a part of the same people that
had troubled their northern frontier further east), and they established a rather
insecure presence in Thrace, between the Aegean and the Danube. In 498–493
Miletus in Asia Minor (whose Persian-backed tyrant had incited the Persians
to an unsuccessful attack on Naxos, in the middle of the Cyclades) led the
Asiatic Greeks in the Ionian Revolt against Persia, and asked for support from
mainland Greece. Sparta, which had solemnly forbidden Cyrus to harm the
Asiatic Greeks but had taken no action against him, refused; but Athens,
perhaps already regarding itself as the mother city of the Ionian Greeks in the
Aegean and Asia Minor, did send help, and so did Eretria in Euboea. The
Greeks started well, but were defeated when they failed to work together and
the Persians brought in large forces.

The Persians wanted to expand anyway, and now had the excuse of revenge
on Athens and Eretria for attacking Greece. In 492 an expedition sent into
Thrace as the first stage of an attack on Greece from the north was abandoned
when its ships were wrecked off Mount Athos. In 490 the Persians sailed
through the Cyclades, captured Naxos and captured Eretria, but when they
landed at Marathon in the north-east of Attica the Athenians, almost alone,
defeated them. In 480 a full-scale force under King Xerxes invaded, once more
around the north of the Aegean, and many but not all of the Greeks united to
resist: Sparta acted as leader, and Athens, which had spent the profits from its
silver mines on new warships, provided more than half of the Greek navy. The
Persians proceeded successfully through Thrace, Macedon and Thessaly;
attempts to halt their advance at Thermopylae on land and at Artemisium by
sea were heroic but unsuccessful; but the Greek navy defeated the Persian in
the strait between Attica and the island of Salamis. The Persians then withdrew
their navy and most of their army; in 479 the remnant of the army was defeated
at Plataea, while the Greek navy landed on Cape Mycale in Asia Minor and
defeated the Persians there. Greece had been saved, but the Greeks must have
assumed that the Persians would now be even more eager for revenge and would
in due course return.

Classical Greece

This book covers the classical period of Greece, from 478 to 323, in which the Greeks (and particularly the Athenians and others living in Athens: Athens in this period was culturally dominant, as it was not earlier or later) produced exceptionally good work in literature, philosophy and the visual arts. Politically, it is the period in which the concept of democracy appeared, as the culmination of what had been developing in the archaic period, and there was serious thought and discussion about how states ought to be governed and how states and individuals ought to behave.

In the half-century after the Persian Wars Sparta withdrew into the Peloponnese while Athens in an alliance known as the Delian League took over the continuing struggle against Persia but increasingly turned that League into an Athenian empire. There was an increasing polarisation between Athens, innovative, a naval power, democratic and cultured, and Sparta, conservative, a land power, a champion of oligarchy and becoming self-consciously uncultured. For a time it seemed that there might be room for the two leading states in Greece; but Athens became too powerful for Sparta to coexist with it, and so the years 431–404 saw the Peloponnesian War, in which Sparta and its allies set out to break the power of Athens. They did so, but only by enlisting the help of the former enemy Persia, which in return wanted to recover domination over the Greeks of Asia Minor.

After the Peloponnesian War Athens made a remarkable recovery. In the first forty years of the fourth century Sparta, Athens and an increasingly ambitious Thebes manoeuvred around one another and around the Persians, who finally regained the Asiatic Greeks in 387/6 and otherwise aimed for a Greece in which no state would be powerful enough to threaten Persia, and in which there would be peace so that Greek soldiers would be available to fight for Persia in its western provinces. Sparta was defeated by Thebes in 371, in fact irreversibly though it still hoped to recover its former power. But the Greek world was transformed by the rise of Macedon, a kingdom on its northern edge. Between 359 and 336 Philip II made Macedon a power to be reckoned with, and incorporated almost all of mainland Greece in a league of allies under his leadership; and between 336 and 323 Alexander the Great, with the forces of Macedon and of that league, conquered the Persian empire and brought it into an extended Greek world.

The survival of evidence for historians to work from was transformed by the invention of printing in the fifteenth century AD: there is a good chance that at any rate one copy will survive somewhere of work printed since then (but it will be for future generations to discover how much is retrievable of texts generated on and transmitted by computers in our own age). From the ancient world there survives only a fraction of the material which we know was written, and much more must have been written of which we know nothing. But, by the standards of antiquity, the world of classical Greece is a world about which we are comparatively well informed.

The histories survive of three men writing in successive generations. Herodotus, the western world's first surviving serious historian, wrote in the third quarter of the fifth century a history culminating in the Persian Wars at the beginning of the century: he provides a continuous narrative from 500 to 479, with a fair amount of material on the second half of the sixth century, a certain amount on earlier history, and a few allusions to later events down to 430. Thucydides in the last quarter of the fifth century wrote a history of the Peloponnesian War from the incidents of 435 and after which led up to the war, including also a short account of events from 478 onwards, designed to illustrate the growth of Athenian power; though he lived beyond the end of the war, his history breaks off abruptly in the autumn of 411. Xenophon, active in the first half of the fourth century, was one of the historians who deliberately started where Thucydides ended, and his *Hellenica* (Greek history) runs from 411 to 362. Later historical works include the *Athenian Constitution* written in the 330's–320's in the school of the philosopher Aristotle, drawing on a range of now-lost sources including local histories of Athens. There is the *Library of History* of Diodorus Siculus (Diodorus of Sicily), written between 60 and 30, of which not all survives but the portion from 478 to the end of the fourth century does: for this period it was based on fourth-century sources which no longer survive, particularly an Asiatic Greek, Ephorus; for 431–411 it is ultimately dependent on Thucydides, but after that it provides an account which is independent of Xenophon and derived from reputable sources, and which therefore deserves to be taken seriously. Many leading figures of the fifth and fourth centuries are among those given biographies in Plutarch's series of *Parallel Lives* of famous Greeks and famous Romans, written around AD 100; and the career of Alexander the Great generated many accounts, though none of those which survive is earlier than that of Diodorus.

Other kinds of literature are useful to historians too. Athenian fifth-century drama is important: tragedies written throughout the century, and comedies written in and after the 420's. In the century between about 420 and 320 many speeches for the Athenian lawcourts, and some speeches for the assembly, were written up and put into circulation, and they provide a valuable body of material. Some 'speeches', notably those of the long-lived Isocrates, are in fact political pamphlets written in the form of speeches; and other pamphlets were written too, of which a surviving specimen is the *Athenian Constitution* preserved with the works of Xenophon.

In a world which lacked printing, broadcasting and the Internet, if texts were to be publicised they had to be displayed in a prominent place. Temporary notices tended to be written in charcoal on whitewashed boards, which have not survived but are known about from literary references; permanent texts were inscribed on stone slabs (*stelai*) or on bronze plates, and, conveniently for historians, Athens took to publishing documents of various kinds on stone in large quantities from the 450's onwards. Coins – in the classical period the 'owl' coinage of Athens was the hardest currency of the Greek world – carried images but not much in the way of text: they usually identify the issuing state but not the date of issue, and linking changes in a state's coinage with political changes is tempting but often dangerous. It is indeed true of archaeological finds in general that dates derived from purely archaeological criteria cannot be precise, and that buildings can be dated precisely only when we have evidence of other kinds, for instance dated accounts of expenditure, as with the buildings erected on the Athenian acropolis in the 440's–430's. Archaeologists are studying the same world as historians, but both sides have to be careful not to misapply material of one kind when interpreting material of another kind.

Greek communities, both cities and other kinds of state formation, were communities of citizens, free adult males of local parentage: women were excluded from political participation (as was universal until 1893 in New Zealand; in Europe Liechtenstein in 1984 finally allowed women to vote on national issues but still not on local issues), and so were children (as is still universal, though there were then and are now disagreements over the age at which adulthood begins). Unless a state was short of citizens, when it might be more generous, immigrants had no right to acquire citizenship of the state to which they had migrated, though individuals might be given citizenship as a reward for major services; unless elevated to a more privileged status, free non-citizens were usually not allowed to own land or a house in the state in which they lived. There were also various non-free categories: chattel slaves, commonly non-Greek, who were the possessions of their owners, and Greeks in various conditions of servitude, of whom Sparta's helots are the best-known but not the only instance. Quantitatively, the gap between the richest and the poorest was enormous; but, although horse-breeding was a sign of wealth and there were some luxury items, there was not a very wide range of expensive goods, and to some extent the richest tended to have more possessions than the poorest rather than better possessions. A man who owned a large quantity of land would own a number of separate fields rather than a single large estate. Because there were slaves available for menial work, it tended to be thought degrading for a free man to work for another (though nearly all our evidence comes from the rich end of the spectrum, and we do not know how many poor men did in fact have to endure that degradation). There was no large-scale 'industry': on building projects, citizens, free non-citizens and slaves worked side by side, as sub-contractors rather than employees; there were workshops in which tens of men, mostly slaves, worked together, but not larger units; and a typical overseas trader was a man who owned one ship, and took other traders with him as passengers.

A typical city was governed by an assembly of citizens (which in an oligarchic as opposed to a democratic state would have its membership limited by a property qualification, and would have fewer matters referred to it and less freedom of debate), for which business would be prepared by a smaller council; officials were appointed annually, often (in oligarchies as well as democracies) with limits on reappointment to prevent a few men from becoming too powerful; there were no professional administrators and no professional lawyers, but administration and justice were included in the responsibilities shared among the citizens.

Religion was polytheistic, and religious correctness was more a matter of performing the correct rituals, in the community and in the household, than of holding the correct beliefs or being in a healthy spiritual state. There were not many (but there were some) professional religious specialists: religion was one aspect of the state's life; priesthoods were among the state's offices (though some were hereditary in particular families); the state regulated temples, their treasuries and so on (and could borrow from the temple treasuries for other purposes in times of need). Major religious festivals were important occasions for the whole community: they included not only what we should think of as religious ceremonies but also competitions in athletics, drama and the like.

Schools existed, but education was a private matter in which the state was not involved. Athens had institutions (the publication of documents; in the fifth century ostracism, where one voted against a man by handing in a potsherd with that man's name written on it; in the fourth century the requirement for all 59-year-old men on the military registers to serve as arbitrators in private lawsuits in which evidence was submitted in writing) which presupposed that the average citizen had a basic functional literacy, more so in the fourth century than in the fifth. It is likely that that presupposition was justified for the citizens who played an active part in politics; but we do not know what proportion of the citizens had that degree of literacy, and we know even less about places other than Athens. At the highest level, by the classical period there were skilful writers of literature in both verse and prose (but no prose literature survives from earlier than 450), and there were philosophers of great intellectual accomplishment.

In the wider world, a man was identified by his own name, his father's name (patronymic) and his state, e.g. the historian Thucydides son of Olorus, of Athens. Within his state, if it was a larger one, he would be identified by a smaller unit to which he belonged, in Athens the deme (demotic): e.g. Thucydides son of Olorus, of Halimus.

Each state had its own calendar, with its own irregularities (so that it was hard to establish that an event on a particular date in one place occurred on the same day as an event on a particular date in another place). Usually the year consisted of twelve lunar months of 29–30 days, c. 354 days in all, and from time to time a thirteenth, 'intercalary' month had to be added to keep the calendar in step with the seasons. Years were not numbered but were identified by an annual, 'eponymous' official, in Athens the archon, or by the year of reign/office of a ruler or priest. Many states, including Athens, began their year in midsummer: a date in the form 478/7 denotes the Athenian (or other) official year which by our reckoning began in 478 and ended in 477 (at Athens this was the archonship of Timosthenes), and underlining, e.g. 478/7, is a convention to indicate the earlier or later part of that year.

Likewise different states had different standards of measurement, weight and currency (coins were of silver or, less often, gold or the alloy of gold and silver known as electrum, and took their names from the weight of precious metal

Ill. 1 Athens: owl and Athena (reverse and obverse of two coins, c.480; 4 dr.). Department of Ancient History and Classics, Trent University, © Michael Cullen, Trent Photographics

which they contained). The main unit of distance was the stade, usually in the range 165–220 yards = 150–200 metres, and in Athens 193 yards = 176 metres (but usually estimated rather than precisely measured). As a measure of capacity the Athenian *medimnos* was about $11\frac{1}{2}$ UK gallons = 14 US gallons = 52.5 litres. The Athenian scale of weights and coins was: 6 obols = 1 drachma, 100 drachmae = 1 mina, 60 minas = 1 talent (there were no coins of as high a value as the mina or the talent; sums of money are often expressed in drachmae and talents without the use of minas); a standard 4-drachma silver coin (cf. ill. 1) weighed about 0.6 oz. = 17.2 grammes, implying a talent of about 57 lb. = 25.8 kg., but by the fourth century Athens' general weights were slightly heavier, with a talent of about 60 lb. = 27.6 kg. The difference in circumstances is so great that ancient currency cannot meaningfully be translated into modern, but the following will give some idea of the value of money in Athens. In the late fifth century an unskilled worker could earn $\frac{1}{2}$ drachma a day and a skilled 1 drachma; in the late fourth century an unskilled worker could earn $1\frac{1}{2}$ drachmae and a skilled $2–2\frac{1}{2}$. In the fourth century an invalid was entitled to a maintenance grant if his property was worth less than 300 drachmae; a man was considered rich enough to be liable for the burden of liturgies (cf. pp. 331–2) if his property was worth about 4 talents; one of the largest fifth-century estates is said to have been worth 200 talents, but there cannot have been many worth more than 20 talents. In the fourth century the total valuation of the property of all Athenians or else of all liable to the property tax called *eisphora* was about 6,000 talents (cf. p. 330). At the beginning of the Peloponnesian War in 431, the total annual revenue of Athens, including the tribute paid by member states of the Delian League, was about 1,000 talents; at that time the largest annual tribute paid by an individual member state was 30 talents.

NOTE ON FURTHER READING

In the second edition of the *Cambridge Ancient History*, vol. v, entitled 'The Fifth Century BC', covers the period 478–404; vol. vi, entitled 'The Fourth Century BC', covers 404–323, and also includes regional surveys spanning the fifth century and the fourth. Of the standard histories from an earlier generation, the most reliable is J. B. Bury, rev. R. Meiggs, *History of Greece*. V. Ehrenberg, *From Solon to Socrates* [sixth and fifth centuries], makes the greatest effort to integrate political and cultural history. Hornblower, *The Greek World, 479–323 BC*, is the volume corresponding to this in a series comparable to that to which this book belongs. Sealey, *History of the Greek City States, ca. 700–338 BC*, has a political emphasis. Buckley, *Aspects of Greek History, 750–323 BC*, is not a systematic history but covers a series of topics. Davies, *Democracy and Classical Greece*, is a good stimulus to further thought on the fifth and fourth centuries for those who already know the basic outline.

De Ste. Croix, *The Origins of the Peloponnesian War*, ranges more widely over the fifth century and even the fourth than its title might lead one to expect. The four volumes by Kagan – *The Outbreak of the Peloponnesian War*, *The Archidamian War*, *The Peace of Nicias and the Sicilian Expedition*, *The Fall of the Athenian Empire* – together provide a detailed history from 478 (and on some topics before) to 404 which usefully surveys the work of earlier scholars. Powell, *Athens and Sparta*, is of general relevance to the fifth century.

For the fourth century, Buckler, *Aegean Greece in the Fourth Century BC*, is a detailed diplomatic and military history. Tritle (ed.), *The Greek World in the Fourth Century*, contains chapters by different authors on the main fourth-century themes.

As for the source material, the main collections of Greek and Latin texts are the Oxford Classical Texts (texts), the Bibliotheca Scriptorum Graecorum et Romanorum Teubneriana (texts), the Collection des Universités de France, often referred to as the Budé series (texts, French translations, short notes), and the Loeb Classical Library (texts, English translations, short notes). The more popular texts are translated into English in the Penguin Classics series and in various other series; some texts which are less popular but of particular use to historians are translated with commentaries in the Clarendon Ancient History Series (Oxford University Press). On the problems of using texts of different kinds as historical sources Pelling, *Literary Texts and the Greek Historian*, provides a discussion based on test cases from the fifth century.

Commentaries on literary texts include: those on Thucydides by Gomme, Andrewes and Dover, and by Hornblower; that on the *Hellenica Oxyrhynchia* (lacking the most recent, Cairo fragments) by Bruce, and an edition of all the fragments with translation and commentary by McKechnie and Kern;[1] a now elderly commentary on Xenophon's *Hellenica* by Underhill; that on Diod. Sic. XV by Stylianou; that on the Aristotelian *Athenaion Politeia* by Rhodes; that on Arrian's *Anabasis* by Bosworth.

There are collections, with commentaries, of Greek inscriptions of particular historical importance – Meiggs and Lewis, *A Selection of Greek Historical Inscriptions to the*

---

[1]   In this book I number the chapters as in the most recent Teubner text, ed. M. H. Chambers. However, McKechnie & Kern use the numbering of the previous Teubner text, ed. V. Bartoletti, in which Chambers' ch. 4 is their ch. 1 and his chs. 6, 7, 8 are their chs. 5, 3, 4; Bruce has chs. 1–5 as in McKechnie & Kern and then (following the oldest editions) starts again from ch. 1 = 6 McKechnie & Kern = 9 Chambers.

End of the Fifth Century BC; Rhodes and Osborne, *Greek Historical Inscriptions, 404–323 BC* (the latter including translations) – and the two volumes by Fornara (to the end of the fifth century) and Harding (fourth century) in the series *Translated Documents of Greece and Rome* provide translations, with a few notes, of inscriptions and some other texts. Osborne, *The Athenian Empire*, translates and discusses inscribed and other texts relevant to that subject; and the revised edition of Hill, *Sources for Greek History, 478–431 BC*, provides a well-indexed collection of Greek and Latin texts. Bodel (ed.), *Epigraphic Evidence*, is an account of the uses of inscriptions, based largely on Roman material but relevant to Greek history too; Woodhead, *The Study of Greek Inscriptions*, is the standard handbook on that subject. The standard handbook on Greek coins is Kraay, *Archaic and Classical Greek Coins*.

The largest-scale and most authoritative classical atlas, of an austere kind showing topography and locating sites, is Talbert (ed.), *Barrington Atlas of the Greek and Roman World*. Smaller and cheaper, and containing in addition some thematic maps and plans of battle sites, is Hammond (ed.), *Atlas of the Greek and Roman World in Antiquity*.

2

The Formation of the Delian League

500	475	450	425	400	375	350	325	300

478	Pausanias in Cyprus and Byzantium
478/7	foundation of Delian League
476	capture of Eïon
469 (?)	battle of Eurymedon
465/4–463/2	siege of Thasos

Sources

For the Persian Wars of 490 and 480–479 we have a detailed account from Herodotus; for the Peloponnesian War (chapters 8–13) we have detailed accounts from Thucydides to 411 and thereafter from Xenophon; but for the Pentecontaetia, the (not quite) fifty years between the Persian Wars and the Peloponnesian War, we are much less well informed. Thucydides includes in I. 89–118. ii a sketch of the growth of Athenian power, to justify his view of the truest reason for the Peloponnesian War. He remarks that this period was not treated by his predecessors except in the Athenian history of Hellanicus, whose account was brief and not chronologically precise (I. 97. ii): Hellanicus' account has not survived, but that comment is certainly applicable to Thucydides' own account. Two later writers are particularly important for this period: Diodorus Siculus and Plutarch in his *Parallel Lives* (cf. p. 8). For the Delian League, usually they and other writers give more information, of varying reliability, on episodes mentioned by Thucydides rather than information on episodes not mentioned by him. Diodorus' narrative is organised in an annalistic framework, but where it can be checked his assignment of episodes to years is unreliable; we should take more seriously for dating (but still not believe uncritically) those sentences, apparently from a chronological table, which briefly mention events other than the main episode of a year. Inscriptions will become important for the history of the Delian League from the 450's (cf. pp. 45–51).

The Origins of the League

Various stories told in connection with the battle of Plataea in 479, the battle in which the Persians invading Greece were finally defeated, seem to point forward to later developments. Plataea was one of the Greek states which had sworn to resist the Persians (e.g. Thuc. II. 72. i, 74. ii); and after the battle the commander Pausanias made the allies swear to respect Plataea's independence and neutrality in return for which Plataea would tend the graves of the fallen Greeks (Thuc. II. 71. ii, III. 58. iv, 68. i). But more than that is found in later sources. An oath claimed to have been sworn before the battle was inscribed on stone in the fourth century as an oath of the Athenians (R&O 88. 21–51), and is quoted as an oath of the Greeks by the fourth-century orator Lycurgus (*Leocrates* 80–1) and by Diodorus (XI. 29. ii–iii), but was rejected as a fabrication by the fourth-century historian Theopompus (*FGrH* 115 F 153). The literary versions include an undertaking to leave temples destroyed by the Persians in ruins as a war memorial (known also to Isocrates, as a ʹresolution of the Ionians: IV. *Paneg.* 156). This is one of a number of alleged fifth-century documents for which there is no fifth-century evidence but which were known from the fourth century onwards (the two best known are the alleged decree of Themistocles, of 480, and the alleged Peace of Callias between Athens and Persia, on which see pp. 47–8). The texts which were current later were probably not essentially authentic texts (which had undergone some editing) but later reconstructions, made (not irresponsibly but on the basis of some genuine tradition) to present vividly the achievements of the glorious past. It is likely that there were one or more occasions in 479 when an oath of solidarity was sworn, but it is not likely that the text was preserved, or that there was an undertaking to leave the temples of the gods in ruins.

Diodorus also mentions a vow to celebrate a festival of freedom at Plataea (XI. 29. i), and Plutarch writes of an annual meeting with games every fourth year, a Greek contribution (*syntaxis*, a fourth-century term: cf. pp. 233, 367) to make war on the Persians, and the Plataeans to be sacred and inviolable, sacrificing on behalf of Greece (Plut. *Arist.* 21. i–ii). The games are not attested until the hellenistic period, and all this looks like later elaboration.

The origins of the League are better sought in the naval campaign of 479. When the Greek fleet was at Aegina in the spring, the Ionians appealed to it to liberate them (Hdt. VIII. 132). After the battle of Mycale a council was held at Samos, at which the Peloponnesians, thinking it impossible to protect the

Ionians indefinitely, wanted to transport them to Greece and give them land taken from those who had supported the Persians, but Athens, which claimed to be the mother city of the Ionians, successfully objected. Then Samos, Chios, Lesbos and the other islands were admitted to the Greek alliance (Hdt. IX. 106. ii–iv). After that, the Greeks sailed north to the Hellespont. When they found that the Persians' bridges had been broken up, the commander, Sparta's king Leotychidas, and the Peloponnesian contingents returned home; but others, perhaps including some from the Asiatic mainland, stayed on under Athenian leadership and besieged Sestos, on the European side of the Hellespont (Hdt. IX. 114–21, Thuc. I. 89. ii).

Herodotus ends his history there. We think of the Persian Wars as ending there, and we now know that the Persians would never invade Europe again; but nobody knew at the time that the Persian Wars were at an end. The Persians had been defeated and had withdrawn from Greece; but they had been defeated and had withdrawn from Greece in 490, only to return with a larger force ten years later. The Greeks could not believe that the Persian threat had been eliminated.

In 478 the two Spartans who had commanded the Greek alliance in the previous year exchanged commands. Leotychidas took an army to Thessaly to punish those who had supported the Persians (cf. pp. 25–6); and Pausanias, regent for his cousin Plistarchus, took command of the fleet. He campaigned successfully, first outside the Aegean in Cyprus, which was important both as a Persian naval base and as an island some of whose inhabitants were or at least regarded themselves as Greek; then he returned to the Aegean and went through the Hellespont to Byzantium, still occupied by the Persians, and captured that (Thuc. I. 94, cf. 128. v, Aesch. *Pers.* 891–2). But Pausanias made himself unpopular with the allies. At Plataea he had mockingly contrasted Persian luxury with Spartan austerity (Hdt. IX. 82). Now, Thucydides tells us, he wore Persian costume, he went into Thrace with a 'Median' and Egyptian bodyguard (the Greeks frequently referred to the Persians as the Medes), he feasted in the Persian manner and became unapproachable. Thucydides also has him secretly releasing prisoners who were relatives of the Persian King, and exchanging letters with the King, offering to marry his daughter (I. 128–30, cf. 95. i). It is hard to be sure how much of this is true, and, if true, how much belongs to this occasion rather than to Pausanias' later period in Byzantium (cf. pp. 26–7): on this occasion there can hardly have been time for the exchange of letters, and the offer to marry the King's daughter looks suspiciously like an improvement on the rumour reported by Herodotus, that he married a satrap's daughter (V. 32).

But we can accept that his conduct made him unpopular, and that complaints reached Sparta. He was recalled, and we shall look at his further career in a Spartan context (Thuc. I. 95. iii, 128. iii: cf. pp. 26–8). A new alliance was then formed under the leadership of Athens, which had taken the lead against Sestos earlier. According to Thucydides, it was the allies who took the initiative in approaching Athens (I. 95. i–iv, cf. 75. ii, 96. i); other texts suggest that the

Athenians took the initiative (Hdt. VIII. 3. ii, *Ath. Pol.* 23. iv): there must at any rate have been willingness on both sides. By the time the Spartans had sent out a successor to Pausanias, a man called Dorcis, the new arrangements had been made, and Dorcis was rejected. According to Thucydides the Spartans were willing to acquiesce and let the alliance go ahead under Athenian leadership (I. 95. vi–vii), and that is probably true of the majority of the Spartans if not all (cf. pp. 26–7).

Ath. Pol. 23. v writes of a full offensive and defensive alliance ('to have the same friends and enemies'), for all time (symbolised by dropping lumps of metal in the sea), made for the Athenians with the Ionians by Aristides in 478/7. Thucydides writes that a *proschema* ('pretext', which might imply a contrast either between professed and real intentions or between original intention and later development) was to get revenge for what they had suffered by ravaging the King's land (I. 96. i, cf. VI. 76. iii). Not all the allies had had their own land ravaged, as the Athenians had, and few scholars have felt able to believe that the purpose of this permanent alliance was simply raiding to obtain revenge. Thucydides elsewhere has speakers referring to the liberation of the Greeks (III. 10. iii, VI. 76. iv), and that theme occurs in Herodotus' account of 479: it is very likely that both that and defence against further Persian attacks were intended when the alliance was formed, and why Thucydides wrote only of revenge and ravaging in I. 96 is an unsolved problem.

There are many other problems in Thucydides' account of the organisation of the new alliance (I. 96. i–97. i). The Athenians (specifically Aristides: V. 18. v and the later sources) 'determined which of the cities were to provide money against the barbarians and which ships. . . . This was when the office of Greek Treasurers (*hellenotamiai*) was first established for the Athenians, to receive the tribute (*phoros*) – for that was the name given to the payment of money. The first assessment of tribute was 460 talents.' The likelihood is that at first the larger states all provided ships, as in other alliances the participants contributed their own forces; but it has been argued that more than half of the eventual members were so small that they could not man even one trireme for a long campaigning season, and most of the smaller states are likely from the beginning to have paid tribute. Aristides will have assessed the obligations of the different members, probably imposing a burden comparable to that imposed by the Persians when they reassessed the tribute of their Greek subjects after the Ionian Revolt of the 490's (Hdt. VI. 42). But how were obligations in ships and in tribute balanced? And can the first assessment, even if it included a cash equivalent for ships, have amounted to as much as 460 talents, given that in 453, when there were more members and nearly all paid tribute, the total seems to have been under 500 talents? There have been various attempts to reject or explain Thucydides' figure; he has another surprisingly high figure for 431 (cf. p. 91); the one inscribed assessment list which survives, that of 425, is an optimistic list (*IG* i³ 71: cf. p. 92), and one possible explanation is that Aristides drew up an optimistic list in cash terms which included both actual and potential members, and that that list did indeed total 460 talents. Collecting the tribute, like commanding expeditions, could well have been accepted as a responsibility of the leader, and we need not doubt that the *hellenotamiai* were Athenians from the beginning.

Thucydides says that Delos, the small island in the southern Aegean with a major Ionian sanctuary of Apollo (whence the alliance's modern name, Delian League), 'was their treasury, and the meetings took place at the sanctuary. The Athenians were leaders of allies who were at first autonomous and deliberated in common meetings.' We know that the treasury was moved from Delos in 454/3 (the first of the 'Athenian tribute lists' is that of 453: cf. p. 45). We have no direct evidence for what became of the meetings, but after 454/3 we find Athens taking decisions which ought to have been taken by meetings of the whole alliance if there were any, and we have no positive evidence that there were any, so probably when the treasury was moved the meetings were discontinued. The Mytilenaeans in a speech say that originally the Athenians led on an equal basis, and that the allies were equal in votes (*isopsephoi*), but the large number of votes (*polypsephia*) made it impossible to resist Athens (Thuc. III. 10. iv–v, 11. iv). Two scenarios have been proposed: that Athens on one side was balanced by a council of allies, so that the allies together were equal in voting power to Athens (somewhat as in Sparta's alliance, the Peloponnesian League, and in Athens' fourth-century alliance, the Second Athenian League); or that there was a single body in which each member including Athens had one vote (as in the recent Greek alliance under Spartan leadership to resist the Persians). The recent alliance is the more relevant precedent, and it is easier to accept the claim that Athens led on a basis of equality if there was a single body in which Athens had one vote like the other members.

When Naxos was coerced, after a few years, Thucydides writes of its being 'enslaved contrary to what was established' (I. 98. iv: cf. p. 19). States which join an alliance always give up the total freedom to decide their own policy with no reference to others which they might otherwise enjoy, but it was probably not thought necessary to spell out any guarantees of autonomy at the League's foundation. No previous combination of states in Greece had seriously reduced the members' freedom; and after the Ionian Revolt, in which strong leadership had been lacking and Athens had supported the Asiatic Greeks for the first year but not afterwards, it must have seemed more likely that the Athenians would withdraw from the war against the Persians than that they would interfere with the allies' freedom. (The actual word *autonomia* may have been coined in connection with the allies' later attempts to retain as much freedom as they could when Athens did start encroaching.)

How large did the League become, and how quickly? The League was represented as a patriotic Greek alliance to fight against the barbarians, formed when the barbarians were on the defensive: support may have been widespread, but we cannot be sure that every single state in and around the Aegean will have been eager to join such an alliance (we happen to have evidence that Adramyttium, on the Asiatic coast facing Lesbos, was still in Persian hands in 421: Thuc. V. 1). Thucydides and other writers refer to the allies as Ionians, a word which could be applied to the eastern Greeks generally, but which attached more strictly to one strand of the Greek people, who could be distinguished from the Aeolians (to the north of them in the Aegean and Asia Minor) and the Dorians (to the south). Delos was Ionian in the strict sense, and it no doubt eased Athens' relations with Dorian Sparta if it stressed its position as alleged mother city and as leader of the Ionians; but, of the likely early members, the cities of Lesbos were Aeolian and Byzantium was Dorian, and the League can never have been limited to those who were Ionian in the strict sense. Indeed, its members eventually included Carians, in south-western Asia Minor, who were not Greeks though their history had for a long time been bound up with that of the Asiatic Greeks.

The League's Early Years

Thucydides gives a catalogue of episodes in the early history of the League (I. 98–101). Under the command of Cimon (son of the Miltiades who commanded at Marathon in 490) they captured from the Persians Eïon, on the Thracian coast at the mouth of the River Strymon. The area was important for silver and for ship-building timber, and Plutarch adds the information that Eïon was settled as an Athenian colony (*Cim.* 7. iii). They captured and the Athenians settled the north Aegean island of Scyros, occupied by a non-Greek people called Dolopians, and situated on the grain route from the Black Sea and the Hellespont to Athens – and Plutarch adds that in response to an oracle Cimon found and brought back to Athens what were said to be the bones of the hero Theseus (*Thes.* 36. i–iii, *Cim.* 8. iii–vii). Carystus, at the south end of Euboea and again on the route from the Hellespont to Athens, had been sacked by the Persians in 490 and had supported them in 480: it was attacked and forced to join the League. The Aegean island of Naxos revolted from the League, and was taken by siege and (metaphorically) enslaved: the best indication of what that is likely to mean is what happened to Thasos a little later (below). Thucydides does not say why Naxos revolted, but he attaches to this episode the comment that the Athenians were strict in exacting the allies' contributions – they were using a permanent alliance to fight a permanent war – and that more and more members lessened their ability to resist by choosing to pay tribute rather than contribute their own forces.

Next came a major victory over the Persians by land and sea, attributed to Cimon again, at the mouth of the River Eurymedon, on the south coast of Asia Minor not quite as far east as Cyprus. To have gone there the Athenians must have felt safe in the Aegean, but Thucydides next mentions the revolt of the north Aegean island of Thasos – because of a dispute with Athens over its trading posts and a silver mine on the mainland. The Athenians besieged Thasos (later sources indicate that Cimon was again in command), and it was only in the third year that Thasos submitted: it had to demolish its city walls, surrender its warships, pay tribute in cash and give up its mainland possessions. The

Athenians had tried to found a settlement at Nine Ways, where the Strymon could be crossed, at the time when they occupied Eïon (scholiast [ancient commentator] on Aeschin. II. *Embassy* 31); they tried again now, but the settlers were defeated and killed by the Thracians when they ventured further inland.

'In the third year' is Thucydides' first indication of time; a later passage (IV. 102. ii–iii) and a probable emendation of schol. Aeschin. will make the three years of the siege 465/4–463/2. There are texts giving 476/5 as the date of the colony at Nine Ways coinciding with that at Eïon (schol. Aeschin.) and of the oracle leading to the capture of Scyros (Plut. *Thes.* 36. i): some scholars have used other texts to place Thucydides' whole series of events in the 460's, but probably we should date Eïon 476 and Scyros 475, and Carystus and Naxos not long after. It is possibly in response to success at the Eurymedon in 469 that Cimon and his fellow generals were invited to judge the tragedians' competition in the spring of 468 (Plut. *Cim.* 8. vii–ix). Into this period we have also to fit the reappearance of Pausanias and his occupation of Byzantium until he was dislodged by the Athenians (Thuc. I. 128. ii–131. i): some have placed this before Eïon, on the basis of texts which take Cimon there from Byzantium (e.g. Diodorus XI. 60. ii), but it is easier to make sense of his and Themistocles' careers if we rely on a text which has Pausanias in Byzantium until *c.*470 (Just. *Epit.* IX. 1. iii: cf. p. 27). Just before and overlapping with the siege of Thasos, there was fighting involving Cimon against Persians and Thracians in the Chersonese, the tongue of land on the European side of the Hellespont (Plut. *Cim.* 14. i, cf. the casualty list *IG* i^3 1144).

Thucydides has written a selective account to illustrate the growth of Athenian power: he does not include the last episode mentioned above, and there may well have been many other episodes which he does not include and which we do not know of. At Eïon, at the Eurymedon and in the Chersonese the League fought against the Persians; at Carystus it attacked a city which had earlier supported the Persians; in preventing Naxos from withdrawing it upheld the permanence of a permanent alliance. On the other hand, Eïon was settled by the Athenians; Scyros had nothing to do with the Persians but was of particular interest to Athens and again was settled by the Athenians; the location of Carystus gave Athens a particular interest in that city; at Naxos Athens was using force against a League member (the appearance of Carystonicus and Naxiades, in an Athenian casualty list of the 440's, *IG* i^3 1162. 27, 79, shows that these were seen as achievements to be proud of); and Athens coveted the mainland possessions of Thasos. In that case it is hard to understand how the attack can have been justified to the League, since the large islands off the coast of Asia Minor had similar *peraiai*, mainland dependencies, which they would not want to lose to Athens. This episode, to which Diodorus attaches his comment on Athens' growing imperialism (XI. 70. ii–iii), was the most blatant case yet of Athens' using the League to further its own interests.

It is clear that from the beginning the Athenians found ways of advancing their own interests through the League, but that does not prove that they had sinister intentions from the beginning: more probably the anti-Persian intentions were genuine, and continued to be acted on, but opportunities presented themselves and were accepted, and what was decided on one occasion set the pattern for what might be decided on others.

NOTE ON FURTHER READING

On the Delian League as a whole Meritt et al., *The Athenian Tribute Lists* (with a general narrative in vol. iii part 3), was the major study of the mid twentieth century, showing great boldness in the restoration of fragmentary inscriptions. McGregor, *The Athenians and Their Empire*, gives a very uncritical account by one of Meritt's collaborators; Meiggs, *The Athenian Empire*, is the best single-volume treatment; Rhodes, *The Athenian Empire*, is a booklet which focuses on the main problems.

Different views of the League's origin and organisation are given by J. A. O. Larsen, 'The Constitution and Original Purpose of the Delian League', *HSCP* li 1940, 175–213 (which I follow); N. G. L. Hammond, 'The Origins and Nature of the Athenian Alliance of 478/7 BC', *JHS* lxxxvi 1967, 41–61, revised as 'The Organization of the Athenian Alliance against Persia', in his *Studies in Greek History*, 311–45.

The chronology of the Pentecontaetia is full of uncertainties: there are similar but not identical date tables in Gomme, *Historical Commentary on Thucydides*, i. 394–6; Meritt et al., *The Athenian Tribute Lists*, iii. 175–9; *CAH*² v. 506–11; there is a review of the problems in Rhodes, *The Athenian Empire*, ch. 3; chronologies widely divergent from those of Gomme, *The Athenian Tribute Lists* and *CAH*², v, have from time to time been canvassed but have not gained much support.

3

The Peloponnese in the Early Fifth Century

500	475	450	425	400	375	350	325	300

c.494	Sparta defeats Argos at Sepeia
479	battle of Plataea: Tegea prominent but Mantinea and Elis absent
478	Pausanias in Cyprus and Byzantium; same year (?) Leotychidas in Thessaly
470's–460's	Sparta fighting against enemies in northern Peloponnese
c.465/4–456/5	Sparta's Messenian War

Elis, Arcadia and Argos

By the beginning of the fifth century most of the Peloponnese was linked to Sparta through the set of alliances which we refer to as the Peloponnesian League. In Arcadia, in the middle of the Peloponnese, whatever the exiled Cleomenes may have done in the 490's to create an anti-Spartan union (Hdt. VI. 74. i) had not lasted: the cities of which we hear most are Mantinea and Tegea, in the south-east, competing as often as they cooperated, Mantinea being the smaller of the two. In 480 all the Arcadians contributed to the Greek force resisting the Persians. In 479 Tegea as Sparta's oldest ally disputed Athens' claim to take second place, but (despite the delay before the battle of Plataea was fought) the contingent from Mantinea did not arrive until afterwards. Elis at the beginning of the fifth century controlled the north-west of the Peloponnese as far south as Olympia: in 480 it was not represented at Thermopylae but did contribute to the force assembled afterwards at the Isthmus of Corinth; but in 479 its contingent, like that of Mantinea, did not arrive at Plataea until after the battle. Most if not all of what was later called Triphylia, the region south of Olympia and north of Messenia, was at this time still independent, and a force from Lepreum fought at Plataea. From the north-east of the Peloponnese, Megara, Corinth, Sicyon and Phlius are mentioned at various points in 480–479, as are the cities beyond Argos: Troezen, Epidaurus and Hermione. Argos itself, which had never acknowledged Spartan supremacy, stayed out of the war and was suspected of sympathising with the Persians; but dissidents in Mycenae and Tiryns (cf. pp. 24–5) did fight on the Greek side. Argos' abstention from the war was certainly a result of its traditional hostility to Sparta, unaffected by a change of régime in the 490's. Mantinea and Elis subsequently punished their generals (and Elis got itself included in the inscribed lists of patriotic states, though Mantinea did not): they may have been motivated primarily by fear of finding themselves on the losing side.

For the twenty years or so after the war we have to make the best of a jigsaw puzzle of evidence from which far too many pieces are missing. There are two themes which can be traced: political change, in Elis, Mantinea and Argos; and wars in which different states fought unsuccessfully against Sparta on different occasions. A synoecism (a word which denotes either political amalgamation or physical amalgamation or a combination of the two) of Elis is dated after the Persian Wars by Strabo (336–7. VIII. iii. 2) and in 471/0 by Diodorus' chronological source (XI. 54. i). There already existed both a town of Elis and an Elean state before, and some at least of the other towns in the region continued to exist afterwards: there may have been a greater concentration of political power in the town of Elis, and some movement accompanied by a change in the balance of power within the citizen body, but the evidence does not point to a dramatic change. Elis may already at this time have dominated as *perioikoi* (subordinate 'dwellers around') some communities to the east, and some near Olympia: in the middle of the fifth century it extended its influence over the whole of the later Triphylia (Hdt. IV. 148. iv: cf. pp. 98–9, 125–7, 198, 205).

Mantinea could be referred to as a *polis* at the time of the Persian Wars, and indeed in the mid sixth century (Hdt. IV. 161. ii), and it is said by Strabo (cited above) to have been synoecised by the Argives: it was to be split into its component villages by Sparta in 385, and reunited in 370 when Sparta was no longer strong enough to prevent it (cf. pp. 212, 217). A date around 470 for the physical synoecism is acceptable but not demonstrable: this will have involved the construction of an urban centre, and the migration of some of the population to it, but not the total abandonment of the old villages. In 421 Mantinea is described as democratic (Thuc. V. 29. i), and the aristocrats are said to have been pleased when in 385 the synoecism was undone (Xen. *Hell.* V. ii. 7). Tegea was a political entity in the first half of the sixth century, when it for a time resisted Sparta but eventually became Sparta's first ally (Hdt. I.

65–8); despite that alliance, it harboured Spartan exiles both before the Persian Wars and after (Hdt. IX. 37. iv, VI. 72. ii); we do not know when its synoecism (Strabo) took place.

Argos had been defeated at Sepeia by Cleomenes c.494, but he had not followed up the victory by bringing it into alliance with Sparta. As a result of the losses in the battle, 'their slaves had control of all their affairs, ruling and administering, until the sons of the fallen grew up' (Hdt. VI. 83. i). The Greeks' chattel slaves came from various sources, commonly outside Greece, and it is hard to think of them as a body of men capable of taking over the running of the state after Sepeia. Argos had a serf class of *gymnetes*, and some have thought of them; but more probably we should regard 'slaves' as aristocratic abuse rather than literal truth, and follow Aristotle, who says that the Argives were obliged to take in some of their *perioikoi* (*Pol.* V. 1303 A 6–8): in other words, there will have been a synoecism, political if not physical, with men from the outlying communities coming to enjoy a measure of power. The new régime continued the policy of not submitting to Sparta; but Mycenae, to the north, and Tiryns, to the south, remained independent, and fought under Spartan leadership against Persia when Argos did not. It is possible, though not certain, that some members of the old aristocracy found the new régime uncongenial, migrated there, and were content to follow a policy opposed to that of Argos (Pausanias' account of the Persian War memorial set up at Olympia refers to 'the Tirynthians from the land of Argos' and 'those of the Argives occupying Mycenae': V. 23. ii).

Herodotus (IX. 35. ii), echoed by Pausanias, gives in what should be chronological order a list of five Spartan victories: at Plataea, in 479; at Tegea, against Tegea and Argos; at Dipaea, against all the Arcadians except Mantinea; against the Messenians at 'the Isthmus'; at Tanagra against Athens and Argos (cf. p. 44). Diodorus, after narrating the earthquake at Sparta and the Messenian War under 469/8 (cf. pp. 28–9), reports under 468/7 that after the Persian Wars Argos and its allies besieged Mycenae; Sparta because of the earthquake and the Messenian War could not help Mycenae; and the city was captured and destroyed (XI. 65). Strabo names Cleonae and Tegea as Argos' allies on this occasion (377. VIII. vi. 19). After referring to the rule of the 'slaves' in Argos, Herodotus reports that the sons of those who died at Sepeia recovered control of Argos; the 'slaves' were driven out, and after a battle occupied Tiryns; after a period of balance they were incited by a seer from Phigalea, in Arcadia, to attack Argos, but after a long war Argos was victorious (VI. 83). And it may be relevant that, when the Athenians ostracised Themistocles (who after the Persian Wars showed signs of hostility to Sparta), he at first lived in Argos and visited other places in the Peloponnese, but fled from there when the Spartans produced accusations against him (Thuc. I. 135. iii–136. i: cf. p. 34).

Certainty is impossible, but the way in which the pieces were fitted together by Forrest makes as good sense as any. There had been a form of synoecism – I should say producing not democracy but the admission to a share in power of men who had previously been excluded from power – in Argos after Sepeia.

In the late 470's there were synoecisms in Mantinea and in Elis; Mantinea was encouraged by Argos; and there grew across the Peloponnese an anti-Spartan alliance, which will have been encouraged by Themistocles. To this phase can be assigned Herodotus' battle of Tegea and Diodorus' war of Argos against Mycenae (his explanation of Sparta's inability to help Mycenae may be a mistaken inference from his own order of narration). Then came the counter-revolution in Argos, by which the old dominant families recovered control, and Themistocles no longer felt safe in the changed Argos. After that belong, certainly, Argos' war against the 'slaves' in Tiryns, and probably Herodotus' battle of Dipaea, in which Mantinea was not fighting alongside the other Arcadians (Mantinea was to support Sparta against the Messenians: Xen. *Hell.* V. ii. 3). This could belong in the early 460's. At Dipaea, according to Isocrates (VI. *Archidamus* 99) the Spartans fought with a single line of soldiers rather than a full phalanx: this has been seen as an indication that the battle was fought after the great earthquake and the outbreak of the Messenian War, but Dipaea is to the north-west of Tegea, and we may wonder whether the Spartans would have gone there at all then.

As for what happened in Argos, it may well be the case that those who had been in control for a generation, and who had welcomed Themistocles, lost power; and what happened next may even have been the work of the returned aristocrats, hoping to do well under the new dispensation. There seems to have been introduced either at this time or shortly afterwards a new articulation of the citizen body, with four tribes each subdivided into twelve phratries, and some public land (taken from individuals and from destroyed towns such as Mycenae) assigned to them – a reform which points in a democratic rather than an aristocratic direction; and this makes it easier to understand why, at the end of the 460's, a self-consciously democratic Athens on breaking with Sparta formed an alliance with Argos (cf. p. 41). Certainly Argos could be described as democratic in 421–420 (Thuc. V. 29. i, 31. vi, 44. i).

Sparta

In Sparta the Agid king Leonidas had been killed at Thermopylae in 480: his son Plistarchus was too young to rule, so first Leonidas' brother Cleombrotus acted as regent, and after Cleombrotus' death in winter 480/79 his son Pausanias. Leotychidas had been Eurypontid king since the late 490's. In 479 Pausanias commanded the Greek army which defeated the Persians at Plataea, Leotychidas commanded the naval force which was victorious at Mycale. They probably exchanged commands in 478. It was certainly in that year that Pausanias led a naval expedition first to Cyprus and afterwards to Byzantium (cf. p. 16); and we may guess that it was in the same year that Leotychidas went north with an army to punish the Thessalians for supporting the Persians. Herodotus reports that he accepted bribes when in a favourable position, and was found sitting on a glove full of money; he was brought to trial in Sparta,

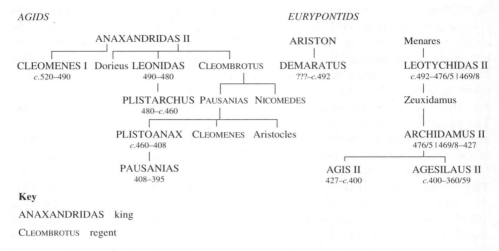

Fig. 1 Fifth-century Spartan kings and regents

he was exiled and his house was demolished, and he ended his life in Tegea (VI. 72). Plutarch includes in a list of tyrannies overthrown by the Spartans one put down by Leotychidas in Thessaly (*Her. Mal.* 859 D); and among the stories of Themistocles' opposition to Sparta after the war he has a (dubious) plan of Themistocles to destroy the Spartan fleet at Pagasae, in Thessaly, and a proposal of Sparta that states which had supported Persia should be expelled from the Amphictyony, the league of largely northern and central Greek states which controlled the sanctuary of Apollo at Delphi (*Them.* 20: cf. p. 32). Diodorus, from his chronological source, records the death of Leotychidas in 476/5 (XI. 48. ii), but his dates for fifth- and fourth-century Eurypontids seem to be seven years too early: possibly the explanation of his confusion is that Leotychidas was exiled in 476/5 and died in 469/8, or that immediately the throne was left vacant and it was not until 469/8 that his grandson Archidamus II was recognised as the next Eurypontid king.

Pausanias found himself in trouble too, and Thucydides gives an account in which he insists on the truth of charges which were never proved (I. 95, 128–135. i). When he made himself unpopular with the Greeks at Byzantium, he was recalled and put on trial, and convicted on some lesser counts but acquitted of medism, treasonable support of the Persians, although that 'seemed very clear'. To succeed him the Spartans sent out a man called Dorcis, but by the time he arrived the new alliance had been founded under Athenian leadership, and his attempt to take command was rejected. According to Thucydides the Spartans were happy to acquiesce in Athens' new alliance (I. 95. vii, cf. Xen. *Hell.* VI. v. 34); *Ath. Pol.* 23. ii, if we accept the papyrus' text and give it its natural interpretation, says they were not happy; Diodorus (XI. 50) has a debate, in which it seemed likely that they would decide to fight to recover their leadership, but unexpectedly a member of the *gerousia* called Hetoemaridas persuaded them not to do so. Sparta was a notoriously secretive state, and this story, at odds with Thucydides, of a debate which resulted in no action is more likely to represent later invention, from a time when the Spartans were afraid of Athens and were asking how they had allowed it to become so powerful, than authentic tradition. No doubt there were some Spartans who supported Pausanias and his policy of involvement in the wider world; but when he and Leotychidas had both shown that they could not be trusted away from home, when the Athenian league was led by the pro-Spartan Cimon (cf. p. 32), and when Sparta's control of the Peloponnese was insecure, it is not surprising that the majority was willing to leave the Aegean to Athens.

Pausanias, Thucydides tells us, returned to Byzantium in a private capacity, with a ship from Hermione in the Argolid, 'allegedly for the Greek war but in fact in order to pursue his business with the Persian King'. He clearly did not collaborate with the Athenians, and in that situation collaboration with the Persians is likely enough. Eventually (perhaps c.470: cf. p. 20) the Athenians drove him out of Byzantium, and he moved to Colonae, in Asia Minor inland from the Hellespont. The Spartans sent a messenger to summon him home, and, having avoided serious trouble before, he obeyed; he was at first placed under arrest, but released when he undertook to stand trial.

The story then becomes increasingly hard to believe. The Spartans were suspicious of him, but lacked the evidence that would justify them in punishing a regent. It was apparently at this stage that they had removed from the memorial set up at Delphi (from which the 'serpent column' survives in Istanbul) the inscription in which Pausanias claimed personal credit for the defeat of the Persians, and substituted a simple list of the allied Greek states (M&L 27 ~ Fornara 59; according to [Dem.] LIX. *Neaera* 96–8 the change resulted from a prosecution of Sparta before the Amphictyonic Council). He was said to be in league with the helots, promising them citizenship if they would support him – and Thucydides insists that this was indeed the case. He was also still in touch with Artabazus, the Persian satrap in the Hellespontine province. One of his messengers, realising that previous messengers had never returned, opened the letter he was given and found that it included an instruction to kill the messenger. He showed this to the ephors, who set up an encounter in which the messenger reproached Pausanias for his lack of trust while some of them were hidden as witnesses. Even after that the ephors did not act immediately. When they were about to arrest him, one of them warned him, and he fled to the sanctuary of Athena of the Bronze House; he was blockaded there and starved to death, but dragged out before he died to avoid polluting the sanctuary.

The story has surely been improved in the telling, and Thucydides' certainty about what cannot have been proved is suspicious. Not long afterwards the helots did revolt (cf. below): that might confirm the charge against Pausanias, but it might be that as a suspect figure who was safely dead he was a convenient scapegoat to whom blame could be attached. On the other hand, it is likely that he had been in touch with Artabazus while in Byzantium and Colonae, and it is credible that he remained in touch. But his chief offence was a greater degree of individualism than Sparta liked to see in its leading figures: his father had been half-brother of an earlier individualist king, Cleomenes, and Pausanias gave the name Cleomenes to one of his own sons (Thuc. III. 26. ii). Thucydides was perhaps so confident because his information came from a 'good' source, i.e. after Pausanias' death the official account of him in Sparta was thoroughly hostile. In spite of that Thucydides pronounced Pausanias and Themistocles to be the two most distinguished men of their generation (I. 138. vi).

Thucydides claims in connection with Athens' war against Thasos, of 465/4–463/2, that the Thasians asked Sparta to support them by invading Attica. 'They promised, hiding it from the Athenians, and intended to invade', but were prevented by an earthquake (which killed a large number of the citizens) and the revolt of the helots and some of the *perioikoi*, particularly in Messenia (Thuc. I. 101. i–103. ii). Here again we have a story which ends in Sparta's not taking action. Perhaps Thasos asked for Spartan help; but Athens and Sparta had not yet quarrelled, the Athenians were still fighting under the leadership of Cimon, and Sparta was shortly to ask Athens for help. Probably this like the story of Hetoemaridas is a later invention.

The rebels occupied Mount Ithome, in the centre of Messenia, and the Spartans tried to capture their stronghold. (We do not know what the Spartan victory at 'the Isthmus' [p. 24] was.) As the war dragged on they appealed to their allies, including Athens (still an ally by virtue of the Greek alliance of 481 against the Persians, and, says Thucydides, skilled in siege warfare). Cimon went, with a force of four thousand hoplites according to Aristophanes (*Lys.* 1138–44). But, perhaps because of the success of Cimon's opponent Ephialtes in Athens (cf. p. 35), the Spartans 'grew afraid of the Athenians' daring and revolutionary nature', suspected that they might change sides and support the rebels, and sent them home. Ephialtes had already been opposed to helping Sparta, and Athens now broke off its alliance with Sparta, made alliances with enemies of Sparta, and began building up its power in mainland Greece as well as the Aegean (cf. pp. 41–5). The rebels on Ithome finally came to terms with Sparta, were allowed to leave the Peloponnese, and were settled by the Athenians at Naupactus, on the north side of the Corinthian Gulf.

Thucydides dates the end of the war 'in the tenth year' (I. 103. i). There was a time when scholars used to infer from his criticism of Hellanicus (cf. p. 14) that every incident in his own account of the Pentecontaetia must have been recorded in its correct chronological sequence, to realise that it is impossible to find as many as ten years between the events mentioned before this war and those mentioned after, and to emend the text to obtain a smaller number. But Thucydides does not use temporal expressions when moving from one area of activity to another, and it is far more likely that in the interests of tidiness and intelligibility he has allowed a measure of overlap. Diodorus gives his main narrative of the war under 469/8, and like Thucydides says that it lasted ten years (XI. 63–4); but from his chronological source he reports the end of the war under 456/5 (XI. 84. viii). Philochorus seems to have dated the earthquake

468/7 (*FGrH* 328 F 117 ~ Fornara 67. A), but Pausanias dated it 464/3 (IV. 24. v ~ Fornara 67. C, cf. Plut. *Cim.* 16. iv). Some scholars have opted for the earlier date, supposing that Thucydides mentions the war at the point when it ended; but Diodorus' chronological source is more likely to be right than his narrative date (cf. p. 15), and it is easier to believe that Thucydides mentions the war at the point when it began, and that the Athenians settled the rebels at Naupactus in the mid 450's (cf. p. 44). The ten years of the war should be *c.*465/4–456/5.

Maintaining control of the helots was always a high priority for Sparta (cf. Thuc. IV. 80. iii). This war, and the fact that it ended in a compromise, will have distracted Sparta's attention from the wider Greek world. There were young and inexperienced kings on both thrones: Archidamus had succeeded his grandfather (cf. p. 26); by the early 450's Plistarchus was dead and Pausanias' brother Nicomedes was acting as regent for Pausanias' son Plistoanax (Thuc. I. 107. ii). It is no surprise that in the years which follow we do not find Sparta pursuing active policies. But on one count the Spartans seem not to have been sufficiently worried. In the Persian Wars there were about 8,000 adult Spartan citizens, not far short of the notional 9,000 of the archaic period. By 418 there were significantly fewer, though it is not certain how many fewer; at the beginning of 371 there were perhaps 1,300, of whom 400 were killed in the battle of Leuctra (cf. pp. 216–17). The earthquake caused heavy losses among the citizens; the Peloponnesian War, a generation later, impeded the recovery which might otherwise have occurred; but, although they attempted some devices to stimulate the citizen birth rate, the Spartans did not promote significant numbers of non-citizens to citizen status, or relax those features of the citizens' way of life which must have made the fathering of children harder.

NOTE ON FURTHER READING

The best general accounts of Spartan history are Cartledge, *Sparta and Lakonia*, and Forrest, *History of Sparta*. On the distinctive aspects of Sparta Michell, *Sparta*, gives a traditional account. There are collections of articles embodying newer approaches in Cartledge, *Spartan Reflections*; in Whitby (ed.), *Sparta*; and in a series of volumes edited by Hodkinson and Powell (some naming Hodkinson first, others naming Powell first: see Bibliography). Hodkinson, *Property and Wealth in Classical Sparta*, shows that a number of long-held beliefs were unjustified. Kennell, *The Gymnasium of Virtue*, warns against projecting back to archaic and classical Sparta all that is found in the late sources. Luraghi and Alcock (eds.), *Helots and Their Masters in Lakonia and Messenia*, re-examines that notorious institution.

On Peloponnesian history in the 470's and 460's see particularly W. G. Forrest, 'Themistokles and Argos', *CQ*[2] x 1960, 221–41 at 221–32; A. Andrewes, 'Argive *Perioikoi*', in *'Owls to Athens'. . . Sir K. Dover*, 171–8.

On Elis see J. Roy, 'The Synoikism of Elis', in Nielsen (ed.), *Even More Studies in the Ancient Greek Polis*, 249–64; and other articles by him in that volume, 229–47, and in

Hansen (ed.), *The Polis as an Urban Centre and as a Political Community*, 282–320. On Arcadia see Nielsen and Roy (eds.), *Defining Ancient Arkadia*; Nielsen, *Arkadia and Its Poleis in the Archaic and Classical Periods*. On constitutional change in Argos see M. Piérart, 'L'Attitude d'Argos à l'égard des autres cités d'Argolide', in Hansen (ed.), *The Polis as an Urban Centre* (above), 321–51, esp. 332–4.

In connection with Sparta, on the downfall of Pausanias see P. J. Rhodes, 'Thucydides on Pausanias and Themistocles', *Hist.* xix 1970, 387–400. On the helot revolt of the 460's it is no longer fashionable to emend the 'tenth' year of Thuc. I. 103. i (e.g. Gomme, *Historical Commentary on Thucydides*, i. 401–11): I follow D. W. Reece, 'The Date of the Fall of Ithome', *JHS* lxxxii 1962, 111–20 (ten years, beginning where Thucydides mentions it), against N. G. L. Hammond, 'Studies in Greek Chronology of the Sixth and Fifth Centuries BC', *Hist.* iv 1955, 371–411 at 371–81 = his *Collected Studies*, i. 355–95 at 355–65, and R. Sealey, 'The Great Earthquake in Lacedaemon', *Hist.* vi 1957, 368–71 (different versions of ten years, ending where Thucydides mentions it).

4

Athens After the Persian Wars

| 500 | 475 | 450 | 425 | 400 | 375 | 350 | 325 | 300 |

480	Themistocles commands in Persian War
479	Aristides and Xanthippus command in Persian War
478/7	Aristides organises Delian League
472	Aeschylus' *Persians*
463 (?)	Aeschylus' *Suppliant Women*
462/1	Ephialtes' reform of Areopagus; Athenian help rejected by Sparta
458	Aeschylus' Oresteian plays

Themistocles and Others

In 480 Themistocles commanded Athens' forces against the Persians; and, it is alleged, when the Greek generals voted to choose a 'man of the campaign', everybody voted for himself first and Themistocles second, and in Sparta he was honoured like no other foreigner (Hdt. VIII. 123–5). Yet in 479 Themistocles is not heard of, but the Athenians at Plataea were commanded by Aristides and the Athenians in the Greek navy by Xanthippus: perhaps the Athenian attitudes to competition and taking turns had led to the conclusion that other men should be given their chance to do well.

Xanthippus is not heard of again: he was presumably dead when his son Pericles, born in the 490's, acted as *choregos*, the rich citizen given the duty of overseeing and financing the dramatic production, for Aeschylus' tragedies in 473/2 (cf. p. 39). *Ostraka* reveal the existence of another son of Xanthippus, Ariphron (named after Xanthippus' father, but perhaps not the eldest son), who is otherwise attested only as a guardian in the 430's (Pl. *Prt.* 320 A).

For Themistocles after the war we have a number of stories in which he falls foul of Sparta. The story of rebuilding Athens' walls is to be found in Thucydides (I. 90–93. ii) as well as the later sources. Sparta urged that, in case the Persians returned, it would be better to have no fortified cities north of the Isthmus of Corinth; Themistocles had himself sent to Sparta to temporise, while Athens' walls were rebuilt as quickly as possible; when rumours reached Sparta, Spartans were sent to Athens to see what was happening but the Athenians did not let them return; when the walls had reached a sufficient height, Themistocles was joined by colleagues (one of whom was Aristides), and informed the Spartans that Athens was safely fortified and was fully capable of judging what was the best policy for itself and for all. Themistocles was also responsible for fortifying the harbour at Piraeus, whose building he had instigated earlier. Elsewhere we read of a plan of Themistocles to burn the Spartan fleet (at different locations in different sources), and of his opposing a Spartan plan to exclude from the Delphic Amphictyony states which had supported the Persians (cf. p. 26); the motif of his having a plan which cannot be made public but is revealed to Aristides floats suspiciously between stories. As Thucydides remarks (I. 93. ii), and as the surviving remains confirm, Athens' walls were certainly rebuilt in great haste; how much of that story is true and how much is an improvement on the truth, it is hard to tell. A plan by Sparta to reform and to give itself a stronger position in the Delphic Amphictyony is easier to accept than a plan by Themistocles to destroy the Spartan fleet (on which cf. p. 44).

It can be accepted that Themistocles envisaged a future for Athens in which Sparta would be a rival rather than an ally; and in that he stands in contrast to Cimon, son of the Miltiades who had commanded the Athenians at Marathon in 490. Cimon in the 470's and 460's was to command a Delian League with which the Spartans were content; he gave the name Lacedaemonius to a son born in the 470's; against the opposition of Ephialtes he took forces to help the Spartans against the Messenians at the end of the 460's (cf. p. 28).

In various other respects too Themistocles and Cimon can be seen as opponents or rivals. By the time of Thucydides (I. 20. ii, VI. 53. iii–59) it had become a matter of controversy whether the ending of the Pisistratid tyranny in Athens was due to the murder of Hipparchus by Harmodius and Aristogiton (in fact, in 514) or to the expulsion of Hippias by the Spartans prompted by the Alcmaeonid family (in 511/0). Cimon married an Alcmaeonid *c.*480; but statues of Harmodius and Aristogiton were set up in 477/6, allegedly as a replacement for earlier statues taken to Susa by the Persians (to be returned in the fourth century by Alexander the Great), and the epigram on the base may have been by the poet Simonides, who can be linked with Themistocles. Another matter for controversy was which was Athens' greater achievement against the Persians, the battle of Marathon, won by the hoplites and Cimon's father Miltiades, or the battle of Salamis, won by the navy and Themistocles (cf. Pl. *Leg.* IV. 707 A–D): Aeschylus' *Persians* is, among other things, a play championing Themistocles in that controversy (cf. below).

Themistocles had interpreted a Delphic oracle as encouraging the abandonment of Athens and fighting at Salamis (Hdt. VII. 140–3): Cimon was to interpret an oracle and bring back the alleged bones of Theseus from Scyros (Plut. *Cim.* 8. v–viii). Themistocles and Cimon are both associated with building projects: Themistocles (in addition to his involvement with the city walls) with a sanctuary belonging to his family, the Lycomidae, and with a temple of Artemis Aristoboule, 'of best counsel'; Cimon not only with the Theseum but also with the walls of the acropolis (Plut. *Cim.* 13. v, Paus. I. 28. iii) and with the Painted Stoa, where one of the paintings depicted the battle of Marathon (Plut. *Cim.* 4. vi–vii). We should not make too much of these things; and we should remember, for instance, that in the early campaigns of the Delian League Cimon was commanding naval forces; but there is enough evidence to justify a view of Themistocles and Cimon as rivals, and Cimon as the more successful of the two. After the rebuilding of Athens' walls we do not hear much more about Themistocles before his ostracism. He was *choregos* for the tragedian Phrynichus in 477/6 (cf. p. 39); he went to the Olympic games, probably in 476, and is alleged to have received a hero's welcome, to have urged the exclusion of the tyrant Hieron of Syracuse (but that suspiciously prefigures Lysias' urging of the exclusion of Dionysius, a century later: cf. p. 283) – and to have rivalled Cimon in the lavishness of his lifestyle (Plut. *Them.* 17. iv, 25. i, 5. iv).

Aristides is harder to place. The main tradition makes Aristides and Themistocles opponents, with Aristides aristocratic where Themistocles was democratic, and upright where Themistocles was wily. But there are traces of an alternative version in which both were on the same side – for instance the stories of Aristides' involvement with Themistocles' anti-Spartan plans – and after organising the Delian League and its first assessment of tribute Aristides like Themistocles disappears from prominence, though he seems to have lived until the mid 460's. The ostracisms of the later 480's are best seen as a three-cornered battle, as a result of which Xanthippus and Aristides were ostracised but Themistocles was not; after the Persian Wars, despite the main tradition, Aristides and Themistocles were probably on the same side, in opposition to Cimon.

Personalities were an issue in the 470's; attitudes to Sparta were an issue; recent history could be slanted in different ways. But there is no good evidence that how Athens should be governed had yet become an issue. There are stories about Aristides – that he hushed up an oligarchic plot at the time of the battle of Plataea; that after the war he proposed that the constitution should be made 'common' and officials appointed from all Athenians (Plut. *Arist.* 13, 22. i): the first may have a basis in truth if we regard the plotters as pro-Persian rather than oligarchic; it is hard to know what to make of the second beyond the fact that somebody thought it appropriate to attribute democratic sympathies to him. When the constitutional issue did surface, Cimon was on the anti-democratic side and men who can be linked with Themistocles were on the pro-democratic – but by then Themistocles himself was no longer in Athens.

The Ostracism and Exile of Themistocles

The men who had been ostracised in the 480's were recalled at the time of Xerxes' invasion: Hipparchus did not return, and was condemned as a traitor (Lycurg. *Leocrates* 117), but the others did, and Aristides and Xanthippus were generals in 479. In the 470's the practice of ostracism was resumed: the Alcmaeonid Megacles was ostracised a second time (cf. Lys. XIV. *Alcibiades i.* 39); there were some votes against Ariphron, apparently an elder brother of Pericles, who presumably soon died; and Themistocles, who had survived in the 480's, was now ostracised.

As with the rebuilding of Athens' walls, we have a story which looks as if it had already undergone embellishment before it was recorded by Thucydides (I. 135. ii–138). First Themistocles was ostracised, and went to Argos (cf. pp. 24–5). After the downfall of Pausanias, the Spartans alleged that Themistocles had been involved in medism with him, and persuaded Athens to recall him to stand trial (further embellishments in the later sources include a first stage in which he defended himself in letters and/or was acquitted, and a suggestion that he should be tried not by the Athenians but by the Greeks). Without waiting for the summons to reach Argos he fled – first to Corcyra, off the north-west coast of Greece, of which he was a benefactor (there are a few other signs that he was interested in the west); when Corcyra was afraid to harbour him, to king Admetus of the Molossi on the mainland opposite (holding on to the king's young son in an act of supplication). After that he crossed northern Greece and the Aegean (where he had to avoid the Athenian navy) to Asia, wrote to the Persian King, and, after taking time to learn 'Persian' (Aramaic?), went to the court and was greatly honoured. He was given three cities in Asia Minor, Magnesia for his bread, Myus for his sauce and Lampsacus for his wine – a reflection of the Persian custom of paying subordinates in kind rather than in cash – and seems actually to have lived in Magnesia. Coins were issued in Magnesia bearing his name and portrait, the earliest known portrait coins.

The downfall of Themistocles is bound up with several of the chronological problems of the 470's and 460's, and a great deal of effort has been devoted to the search for solutions. Diodorus narrates the whole story under 471/0 (XI. 54. ii–59. iv), but in this period he assigns one major story to each year and his assignments cannot be relied on. If Aeschylus' *Persians*, of 473/<u>2</u>, is among other things a defence of Themistocles, defending him cannot yet have become a lost cause; but the play could have been performed either before his ostracism or between that and his condemnation. According to Thucydides (I. 137. iii) the King whom he met was Artaxerxes, who had recently succeeded after the death – in August 465 – of Xerxes. Plutarch (*Them.* 27. i–ii) says that some fourth-century writers had him meet Xerxes, the King whom he had defeated at Salamis; but that would be so much more effective dramatically that, if it were true, the less effective story would hardly have been invented. We should accept that Themistocles did not arrive in Asia before *c*.465.

Some scholars have tried to exploit Themistocles' flight across the Aegean. According to Thucydides (I. 137. ii) he set out in a merchant ship from Pydna in Macedon; he was travelling incognito, but when they came close to Naxos while the Athenians were besieging it he revealed himself to the captain and asked to be kept safe; and he eventually reached Ephesus. Plutarch (*Them.* 25. ii–26. i) claims to be following Thucydides, but takes Themistocles from Pydna past Thasos (probably: the manuscripts are divided between Thasos and Naxos) to Cyme. If we knew which siege Themistocles had to avoid, that would help us to date his crossing of the Aegean – but I suspect that the two versions of the story are rival embroideries on the fact that, when crossing the Aegean, he had to take care not to fall into the Athenians' hands. It will fit what we can reconstruct of Peloponnesian history if Themistocles was out of Athens by *c*.470; his ostracism may well have preceded his flight to Asia by several years, and the Thasos version of the story is chronologically the more plausible – but that does not mean that it must be true.

Themistocles was one of a series of distinguished Greeks who ended their lives as exiles in the Persian empire. The expelled Athenian tyrant Hippias had accompanied the Persians when they invaded Greece in 490, and so had the deposed Spartan king Demaratus in 480; but there was never another invasion in which Themistocles could accompany the Persians. Ironically, he was guilty of medism after the Athenians condemned him but not, as far as we know, before. Thucydides considered him with Pausanias to have been one of the most distinguished Greeks of his generation (cf. p. 28).

Ephialtes' Reform of the Areopagus

Cimon's supremacy remained unchallenged until the war against Thasos of 465/4–463/2 (cf. pp. 19–20), at the end of which he was accused of taking bribes not to attack Macedon. On this occasion public prosecutors were appointed: one of them was the young Pericles, and it is alleged that he was persuaded by Cimon's sister Elpinice not to press the case hard (Plut. *Cim.* 14. iii–15. i, *Per.* 10. vi). Cimon was acquitted. When Sparta asked for help against the Messenians (cf. p. 28), he wanted to help, Ephialtes did not, and again Cimon was successful (Plut. *Cim.* 16. viii–x). It was probably while he was away (cf. Plut. *Cim.* 15. ii) that Ephialtes gained a winning position in Athens and enacted his reforms. The Spartans, suspicious of their Athenian allies, sent them away; Cimon on his return tried to reverse the reforms, but he was unsuccessful, and was ostracised, his opponents objecting both that he was pro-Spartan, *philolakon*, and that he was anti-democratic, *misodemos* (Plut. *Cim.* 15. iii, 17. iii, *Per.* 9. v), and Athens turned to an anti-Spartan foreign policy.

This was clearly an important turning-point in Athenian history, but our sources tell us disappointingly little about it. Thucydides mentions Cimon's help for Sparta and Athens' change in foreign policy but not the internal reform. Diodorus records the reform under the year 460/59 (XI. 77. vi): it is not his main episode for the year, but if it comes from his chronological source that source was on this occasion mistaken: there is no other reason to doubt the slightly earlier date of 462/1 given by *Ath. Pol.*

Ath. Pol. and Plutarch seem respectively to give favourable and unfavourable accounts of the reform:

> For about seventeen years after the Persian Wars the constitution in which the Areopagus was dominant persisted, though it gradually declined. As the masses increased, Ephialtes son of Sophonides became champion of the people, a man who appeared to be uncorrupt and upright in political matters. He attacked the council of the Areopagus. First he eliminated many of its members, bringing them to trial for their conduct in office. Then in the archonship of Conon he took away from the council all the accretions which gave it its guardianship of the constitution, giving some to the council of five hundred and some to the people and the jury-courts. (*Ath. Pol.* 25. i–ii)

> When [Cimon] sailed out on campaign again, finally the many were unleashed, and overturned the established order of the constitution and the traditional observances which they had previously followed; and with Ephialtes as leader they took away from the council of the Areopagus all but a few of its judgments; and, making themselves masters of the lawcourts, they pitched the city into undiluted democracy. Pericles was already powerful and thinking on popular lines. (Plut. *Cim.* 15. ii: cf. *Per.* 9. v)

The council of the Areopagus (named after the hill on which it met, south of the agora and west of the acropolis) was the body of which those who had served each year as the nine archons became members for the rest of their lives: when Ephialtes 'brought its members to trial for their conduct in office', he perhaps prosecuted archons on their retirement, to discredit the council which they were to join. Powers taken away from the Areopagus might well have been represented as 'accretions', additions to its original and proper powers, by the reformers and as part of the established order by their opponents.

But what were those powers? They were clearly, at least in part, judicial; and they gave the Areopagus a 'guardianship of the constitution', already alluded to in connection with its punishment of offenders in earlier chapters of *Ath. Pol.* Probably the expression referred to the Areopagus' general position in Athens rather than to some specific power; possibly (and this would explain the rival campaigning slogans) the Areopagus had at times taken to guarding the constitution in new ways, perhaps by instituting new judicial processes, without being explicitly authorised to do so by a decree of the assembly.

Two powers in particular seem likely candidates for removal from the Areopagus by Ephialtes. *Eisangelia*, often translated 'impeachment', a procedure for charges of major offences against the state (treason, attempting to overthrow the constitution), had been in the hands of the Areopagus in the time of Solon (*Ath. Pol.* 8. iv) but in later Athens was dealt with by the council of five hundred, the assembly and the jury-courts: here is a power which was taken from the Areopagus at some time, and this may well have been that time. Athenian officials were subject to various checks on their conduct: a validation, *dokimasia*, before they entered office; a vote of confidence each prytany during their term of office; and a financial/general accounting, *logos/euthynai*, at the end of their term. We are on less firm ground here, but there are indications that validation and accounting procedures already existed in Athens before Ephialtes' reforms, and it is credible though not demonstrable that they had been in the hands of the Areopagus and were taken from it by Ephialtes. If this is right, the Areopagus will in *eisangelia* and in the procedures for scrutinising officials previously have possessed, and now have lost, powers of considerable political importance. It retained judicial powers in connection with homicide and wounding, and some religious offences (*Ath. Pol.* 57. iii–iv, 60. ii).

Some other changes which have been suggested ought to be mentioned. By the late fifth century there existed a 'prosecution for illegality', *graphe paranomon*, which could be used to overturn a decree of the assembly as being either illegal or inexpedient (first securely attested in 415: Andoc. I. *Myst.* 17): it has been suggested that this was a democratic replacement for a right of the Areopagus to veto decisions of the assembly, but there is no evidence that such a right ever existed. One power was lost about this time not by the Areopagus but by the archons. Originally they had personally decided many lawsuits; Solon had created a right of appeal against their decisions, to a body probably called (*h*)*eliaia*, perhaps a judicial session of the assembly (*Ath. Pol.* 9. i, using the word *dikasterion*); by the later fifth century appeal had, as it were, become automatic, and the archon merely conducted a preliminary enquiry before referring a case to a jury-court (*dikasterion*), in which he presided (but he could still impose very small fines on his own authority). Here it is perhaps better to think of a gradual development, as men against whom archons ruled exercised their right of appeal increasingly often; but there may well have been legislation standardising the new procedures, and it may well have been enacted about this time. Philochorus (*FGrH* 328 F 64. b. α) seems to credit Ephialtes with the creation of a board of seven law-guardians, *nomophylakes*: there is no other reference to such officials before the late fourth century, and if they existed in the century of the Attic orators we should expect to hear of them, so probably Philochorus was wrong or has been misreported.

As a result of Ephialtes' reforms the council of five hundred and the jury-courts were to become busier, and Athens' increasingly active control of the Delian League was to make them busier still. In 453/2 the smaller private lawsuits were transferred to travelling justices (cf. p. 55). It is arguable that, although since its creation by Cleisthenes the council had comprised fifty members from each tribe, it was only after Ephialtes that the tribal contingents acted as the *prytaneis*, a standing committee of the council, each taking a tenth of the year. There is no clear evidence for *prytaneis* of this kind before Ephialtes, and the *tholos*, the circular building on the west side of the agora which was used by the *prytaneis*, was probably built about 460.

Why should the Areopagus have been deprived of power at the end of the 460's? *Ath. Pol.*'s period of domination by the Areopagus after the Persian Wars looks like a fourth-century attempt to answer the question: the last major change in the constitution, that of Cleisthenes, had been in a democratic direction; if in the 460's the Areopagus needed to be reformed, there must after Cleisthenes have been an Areopagite resurgence (*Ath. Pol.* 41. ii, cf. 23. i). But that resurgence is hard to credit. More importantly, Cleisthenes had created a political system which required and must have been eliciting a high degree of participation by the ordinary citizens; since 487/6 the archons, who were to become members of the Areopagus, had been appointed by lot, while increasingly the elected generals were becoming the most important officials in Athens. As a particular provocation, it was probably the Areopagus that had condemned Themistocles, on an *eisangelia* (*eisangelia* Craterus, *FGrH* 342 F 11 ~ Fornara 65. B. 11), and had acquitted Cimon, in his *euthynai* (*euthynai Ath. Pol.* 27. i). Citizens who were ready to take more control of the city's affairs might well ask by what right a body of ex-archons, no longer necessarily the most respected men in Athens, but serving for life, who were consistently taking the side of Cimon, should enjoy such a powerful position.

Self-interest was involved, foreign policy was involved, personalities were involved; but members of Solon's third class, the *zeugitai*, stood to gain as much as members of the fourth, the *thetes*, and although in general terms we may see the influence of Athens' growing League and of the poorer men who rowed the ships, we should not see this specifically as a victory of the oarsmen over the hoplites. This can, however, be seen as a defining moment in Athenian history, when a constitutional change was made on democratic principle (cf. p. 39, on Aeschylus). Within a few years, a self-consciously democratic Athens would be encouraging and sometimes imposing democratic constitutions in the member states of the Delian League (cf. pp. 46–7). It is probably no accident that, soon after this reform, Athens took to inscribing on stone decrees of the assembly, accounts of expenditure and other public documents on an unparalleled scale: the leaders of the new democracy seem to have believed that, to do its job properly, the *demos* should be kept well informed.

The reform is attributed to Ephialtes, of whom we know only that he had commanded an expedition to the south coast of Asia Minor (Plut. *Cim.* 13. iv) but is said by a late source to have been poor (Ael. *V.H.* XI. 9). Plutarch mentions Pericles as a supporter of his, and the attribution of a subsequent reform of the Areopagus to Pericles (*Ath. Pol.* 27. i, with no details) is probably a garbled version of that. When his laws were repealed by the régime of the Thirty, in 404/3, *Ath. Pol.* 35. ii refers to the laws of Ephialtes and an unidentifiable Archestratus. Ephialtes himself was murdered not long afterwards – by Aristodicus of Tanagra according to *Ath. Pol.* 25. iv, but it was a notoriously unsolved crime according to Antiph. V. *Herodes* 68: perhaps it was assumed that there must have been Athenians behind Aristodicus but they were never identified.

Tragedy and Politics

Most surviving Athenian tragedies have plots set in the heroic past of Greece. It has become fashionable, however, to focus on the civic aspects of the festivals of Dionysus at which tragedies and comedies were performed, and on themes in the tragedies (such as the conflict between family and *polis*, or between divine law and man-made law) which were of contemporary concern to citizens of a fifth-century *polis*. An older question, but one which still needs to be addressed, is how far particular plays are concerned with the particular political situation at the time of their first performance.

In fact some early tragedies took their plots from recent history. Perhaps in 493/2, when Themistocles was archon, Phrynichus produced a play on *The Capture of Miletus* by Persia at the end of the Ionian Revolt, which distressed the Athenians, who had helped the Ionians in the first year but not afterwards (Hdt. VI. 21. ii); and probably in 477/6, when Themistocles was his *choregos* (Plut. *Them.* 5. v), Phrynichus produced his *Phoenician Women*, which is said to have treated the recent defeat of the Persians. Those plays do not survive, but Aeschylus' *Persians* does. It was produced in 473/2, with Pericles as *choregos*, and it focuses on the Persian defeat at Salamis, or rather on the receipt first of the news and then of King Xerxes himself at the Persian court. At one level it is a patriotic Greek play, celebrating a Greek success; at another level it is a patriotic Athenian play, since the Athenian navy played the largest part in the victory. At yet another level, because it focuses on Salamis and on Themistocles, it can be seen as a play in support of Themistocles and in opposition to Cimon (cf. p. 34). Aeschylus' *Suppliant Women* is perhaps to be dated 464/3, shortly before Ephialtes' reforms. It is set in Argos in the heroic past, but the king of this Argos is a very unkingly king, and the play emphasises very strongly that the decision to receive the suppliants rests not with him but with the mighty hand of the citizen assembly lifted up to vote – *demou kratousa cheir*, juxtaposing the two halves of the word *demokratia* (l. 604). We do not have to suppose that Aeschylus was indulging in crude political propaganda, but he was at any rate engaging sympathetically with the democratic idea, about the time when that idea was first being explicitly formulated.

It is therefore interesting to read that in 469/8, when the younger Sophocles was competing, allegedly for the first time and against Aeschylus, the archon called on Cimon and his fellow generals to take the place of the normal judges, and they awarded first prize to Sophocles (Plut. *Cim.* 8. vii–ix). The story may have been improved in transmission; Sophocles may have presented what were unquestionably better plays; but it looks as if we can link Aeschylus with democracy and its supporters, in opposition to Cimon.

Shortly after Ephialtes' reforms, in 459/8, Aeschylus produced his Oresteian plays. The last of them, *Eumenides*, is centred on the trial of Orestes by the Areopagus for killing his mother Clytemnestra (N.B. ll. 681–710, Athena's speech instituting the council). Aeschylus' featuring the Areopagus, with a function which it retained, so soon after the reform cannot be unconnected with it; but, while some have seen him as endorsing the reform (as we should expect from his earlier record), others have seen him as regretting it, or at any rate fearing trouble in the future. The play also stresses unnecessarily the friendship between Athens and Argos, which by the time of the play had become allies. Aeschylus himself ended his life in Sicily; but it is not certain when or why he left Athens.

NOTE ON FURTHER READING

On Themistocles after the Persian Wars see W. G. Forrest, 'Themistokles and Argos', *CQ*² x 1960, 221–41 at 232–41; Lenardon, *The Saga of Themistocles*; P. J. Rhodes, 'Thucydides on Pausanias and Themistocles', *Hist.* xix 1970, 387–400. On ostracism the most up-to-date catalogue of surviving *ostraka* is by S. Brenne, in Siewert (ed.), *Ostrakismos-Testimonien I*, 43–71 (suggesting on p. 48 that Ariphron, though named after his grandfather, may not have been the eldest son); the most comprehensive study in English, now somewhat dated, is Thomsen, *The Origin of Ostracism*.

On the reforms of Ephialtes, the most recent presentation of my views is in *CAH*² v, ch. 4. ii; the most recent presentation of the minimalist views of R. Sealey is his 'Ephialtes, *Eisangelia* and the Council', in *Classical Contributions . . . M. F. McGregor*, 125–34, reprinted in Rhodes (ed.), *Athenian Democracy*, ch. 13; see also T. E. Rihll, 'Democracy Denied: Why Ephialtes Attacked the Areopagus', *JHS* cxv 1995, 87–98.

On Athenian tragedy and politics in this period there is a convenient presentation of older views in Podlecki, *The Political Background of Aeschylean Tragedy*, esp. chs. 2, 4, 5. More recent approaches include Pelling, *Literary Texts and the Greek Historian*, ch. 9; Sommerstein, *Aeschylean Tragedy*, ch. 12.

5

The Athenian Empire in the Mid Fifth Century

500	475	450	425	400	375	350	325	300

460 or 459	beginning of First Peloponnesian War and Egyptian campaign
c.457	battles of Tanagra and Oenophyta
455 or 454	end of Egyptian campaign
454/3	treasury of Delian League moved to Athens
451	five-year truce between Athens and Peloponnesians
c.449	Peace of Callias between Athens and Persia (?)
446/5	Thirty Years' Peace between Athens and Peloponnesians

The First Peloponnesian War and the Egyptian Campaign

After the dismissal of Cimon and his hoplites (cf. p. 28), the Athenians broke off their alliance with Sparta, and instead made alliances with enemies of Sparta, Argos in the Peloponnese and Thessaly in the north of Greece. There followed a period in which they accepted an invitation to take the war against Persia to Egypt, and at the same time, in what is known as the First Peloponnesian War, built up their power in mainland Greece (Thuc. I. 102. iv–112. iv).

Megara, on the Isthmus of Corinth linking the Peloponnese to central Greece, and involved in a border dispute with Corinth, broke with Sparta and joined Athens: Athens set an example which was to be followed in the next few

Ill. 2   Aegina: turtle (c.480) and tortoise (fourth-century) (2dr.). Ashmolean Museum, Oxford

years in Athens itself and in Corinth by building long walls to join Megara to Nisaea, its harbour town on the Saronic Gulf, in a single fortified area; and Megara's other harbour, Pegae, gave Athens access to the Corinthian Gulf. Athens campaigned against Argos' enemy in the Argolid, Epidaurus (which was supported by Corinth and Sicyon), and was defeated on land at Halieis but victorious in a naval battle off Cecryphalea, in the Saronic Gulf. An on-going dispute between Athens and the island of Aegina had been settled at the time of Xerxes' invasion, but now the Athenians resumed the offensive, winning a naval battle and landing on the island. Corinth sent some hoplites to support Aegina, and also moved into the Megarid. Athens did not withdraw from Aegina, but sent a reserve force (the oldest and youngest) to the Megarid: these first had the better of a closely fought battle, and a few days later, when the Corinthians claimed victory, defeated them more decisively. Thucydides mentions at this point the beginning of work on the long walls linking the city of Athens to the coast at Piraeus and Phalerum; but at least the idea and perhaps the formal decision and the first work should be earlier than the building of the long walls for Megara. Eventually Aegina submitted to Athens and joined the Delian League: until the outbreak of the Peloponnesian War it paid 30 tal. a year, a rate matched only by Thasos. (About the middle of the century the design on Aegina's coins changed from a sea-creature, a turtle, to a land-creature, a tortoise – see ill. 2 – but the suggestion that that is a sign of submission to the naval power of Athens is fanciful.) Corinth had supported Athens against Aegina in the 490's, and we have no information on it in the 470's and

460's. Presumably it was provoked by Megara's joining Athens; while for Athens Megara represented an important gain, providing security against attacks from the Peloponnese. In these campaigns there is no mention of Sparta, which presumably was still kept busy by the rebels in Messenia.

Athens had not given up the war against the Persians. A League force (one inscription, M&L 34, commemorates a Samian achievement) of two hundred ships was sent to Cyprus, where Pausanias had campaigned in 478 (cf. p. 16), and while there accepted an invitation to go to Egypt, where a Libyan king called Inaros had raised a revolt against Persia, killing the satrap Achaemenes (cf. Hdt. II. 12. iv, VII. 7). Egypt could not be represented as Greek, as Cyprus could, but it was part of the Greeks' world – Greeks had been there as traders and as mercenaries for two hundred years – and could reasonably be included in a Greek war against Persia. They got control of the Nile delta, and of most of the city of Memphis, and settled down to besiege the remainder. An Athenian casualty list gives the names of men who died in six places in one year: Cyprus, Egypt, Phoenicia; Halieis, Aegina, Megara (M&L 33 = *IG* i³ 1147: beginning and end Fornara 78): without it we should not have known that this campaign embraced Phoenicia as well as Egypt. It is conceivable, but far from certain, that a place called Dorus, said to have been assessed for tribute (Craterus, *FGrH* 342 F 1), was near Mount Carmel in Palestine; and that it was in 458 that the Persians sent Ezra to Jerusalem, perhaps in response to Athenian activity (Ezra vii. 7–8 – but it is disputed whether Ezra was sent by Artaxerxes I, king at this time, or Artaxerxes II or III); it is more certain that Nehemiah was sent to Jerusalem in 445, when Egypt was still or again in touch with Athens (Nehemiah ii. 1–8; Athens and Egypt 445/4 Philochorus, *FGrH* 328 F 119).

A Persian envoy called Megabazus failed to bribe the Spartans to distract Athens by invading Attica – the first time the Persians are known to have tried intervening in Greece in this way. One of the alleged fifth-century documents for which we first have evidence from the fourth century (cf. p. 15) is an Athenian decree outlawing from Athens and the League Arthmius of Zelea, a Greek city near the Propontis, for bringing Persian gold to the Peloponnese (e.g. Dem. XIX. *Embassy* 271, IX. *Phil. iii.* 41–3, Aesch. III. *Ctesiphon* 258, Din. II. *Aristogiton* 24–5): if that has a basis in truth, it may belong a few years later than this, to the time of Cimon's return to Athens (cf. p. 45). In due course the Persians sent Megabyxus to Egypt with a large army. He expelled the Greeks from Memphis, besieged them for eighteen months in Prosopitis (the southwestern part of the delta), and eventually drained a canal and captured them. Most of the Greeks were killed; a relief expedition arrived in time to join in the disaster; a man called Amyrtaeus, 'king in the marshes', held out for a while, but Inaros was betrayed and crucified. 'Thus the Greeks' affairs were ruined after six years of war' (Thuc. I. 110. i): if we may trust Thucydides' narrative, this was a disaster on a very large scale, though some have used Ctesias (*FGrH* 688 F 14 §36 [32] ~ Fornara 72) to argue that the Greek force was much smaller than Thucydides claims, either from the beginning or after the initial success.

The Spartans had not been roused against Athens by Persia; but in central Greece, when Phocis invaded Doris, alleged to be the original home of the Dorians of the Peloponnese, Sparta sent a Peloponnesian army which drove the Phocians out of Doris. They had gone by sea, across the Corinthian Gulf; but when they were ready to return the Athenians took advantage of their alliance with Megara to block both that route and the land route through the Isthmus. The Peloponnesians moved into Boeotia, and Athens sent an army (including Thessalians – who went over to the Peloponnesians – and Argives and also Delian League allies: M&L 35 records Argive casualties; M&L 36 ~ Fornara 80, at Olympia, commemorates Sparta's victory over Argives, Athenians and 'Ionians'). In a battle at Tanagra there were heavy losses on both sides, but the Peloponnesians did well enough to be able to return via the Isthmus. Two months later, however, the Athenians returned, defeated the Boeotians at Oenophyta, and gained control of much of central Greece (this is probably the context to which an Athenian treaty with the Delphic Amphictyony, *IG* i³ 9 ~ Fornara 82, belongs).

Thucydides mentions that some Athenians hostile to the democracy made contact with the Peloponnesians at Tanagra. According to Plutarch (*Cim.* 17. iv–vii, *Per.* 10. i–iii), however, the ostracised Cimon tried to rejoin the Athenian army; he was rejected, but he urged his friends to fight valiantly and demonstrate their loyalty, and they did so and were killed in the battle. Plutarch and other writers then claim that Pericles had Cimon recalled to Athens, without waiting for the end of his ten years of ostracism (*Cim.* 17. viii–18. i, *Per.* 10. iv); but despite their allegation the war was not ended at this point, and the early recall of Cimon is probably a fiction.

An Athenian naval force under Tolmides sailed round the Peloponnese, burned the Spartan dockyard at Gytheum (the basis for the plan [cf. p. 32] attributed to Themistocles?), sailed into the Corinthian Gulf and won victories there. It is probably now that the Athenians acquired Naupactus, where they settled the Messenians allowed to leave the Peloponnese (cf. pp. 28–9; an unpublished inscription shows that they shared it with the previous inhabitants). After this, however, Athens' expansion ran out of steam. An expedition into Thessaly, to restore an exiled ruler called Orestes, was unsuccessful; an expedition from Pegae into the Corinthian Gulf, commanded by Pericles, won a battle against Sicyon, near Corinth, but failed to capture Oeniadae, on the north side of the mouth of the Gulf. After that Thucydides moves directly to the making, three years later, of a five years' truce between Athens and the Peloponnesians.

If the Spartan invasion of Attica which led to the Thirty Years' Peace of 446/5 came shortly after the expiry of that truce, the truce can be dated to 451, and the Thessalian campaign and Pericles' expedition to 454. Also in 451 a thirty-year peace was made between Argos and Sparta (Thuc. V. 14. iv). The end of the six-year Egyptian campaign, mentioned by Thucydides before those expeditions, should be 455 or 454; its beginning should therefore be 460 or 459; and the Athenian casualty list enables us to put the beginning of the First Peloponnesian War in the same year. Dates of 458/7 for Tanagra

(Theopompus *FGrH* 115 F 88 ~ Fornara 76) and of 456/5 for Tolmides' expedition (schol. Aeschin. II. *Embassy* 75 ~ Fornara 84) are compatible with that; Diodorus narrates Tanagra under 458/7 and Oenophyta under 457/6 (XI. 80, 82. iv–83. i), and since the battles were two months apart this could be correct (but probably by accident).

Some scholars have thought that, in addition to their combining war against Persia with expansion in Greece, this is the time when the Athenians began acquiring interests in the west. M&L 37 = *IG* i³ 11 ~ Fornara 81, on the swearing of oaths to an alliance with Egesta, an inland city in the west of Sicily, has the older style of Athenian lettering (cf. p. 46), and its preamble included the archon's name but only the last two letters of the name were read uncontroversially: -*on*, which unfortunately is the ending of many archons' names. Claims to detect further letters and identify either [Ha]bron (458/7) or [Ant]iphon (418/7) have finally been settled by the reading of [An]tiphon: there is evidence for Athenian involvement in the west before long, but this inscription belongs not long before Athens' Sicilian expedition of 415, which was theoretically in support of Egesta (cf. pp. 68–9, 132).

If he was not recalled early, Cimon will have returned to Athens in 451, and his return may have had an effect on policy. The five-year truce was made, and after that 'the Athenians held off from the Greek war', and Cimon with a League force returned to Cyprus. Some ships went on to Egypt, where Amyrtaeus was still holding out. The rest besieged Citium, but Cimon died and the siege was abandoned; the Persians were defeated on both land and sea, but the League forces then returned home.

Athens, the League and the Persians

Thucydides moves on to further events in Greece: a Sacred War for the control of Delphi; and the revolt of Athens' mainland possessions and the campaign leading to the Thirty Years' Peace (cf. pp. 51–2). For developments in the Delian League about the middle of the century we are dependent on inscriptions, and a few passages in the later sources.

Originally the treasury of the Delian League had been at Delos, but in 454/3 the 'Athenian tribute lists' begin in Athens, a numbered series of lists (lists 1–15 on one large block of stone: a long series was clearly envisaged) of $\frac{1}{60}$ of the tribute, given as an offering to the treasury of Athena, calculated not on the annual totals but on the individual payments (*IG* i³ 259–90: extracts from 259 = list 1 M&L 39 ~ Fornara 85): there is no evidence for it, but probably an offering had previously been given to Delian Apollo. The move is generally attributed to Pericles (e.g. Plut. *Per.* 12. i), but in one text to the Samians (Plut. *Arist.* 25. iii, apparently envisaging an earlier date): after the disaster in Egypt there may have been genuine fear of a Persian resurgence (cf. p. 43, on Arthmius), and although the move has commonly been seen as a sign of Athenian imperialism it may not have appeared like that at the time. The advantage for historians is that, in so far as the lists are preserved or can be restored by comparison with adjacent lists, we can see which states paid tribute in which years, and how much they paid.

If a doctrine formulated more than a century ago could be accepted, developments in the middle of the century might also be seen in a number of decrees of the Athenian assembly. The Athenians did not make a regular practice of naming the archon of the year in preambles until *c.*420, though there are some earlier instances, and in some cases where the archon was named the relevant part of the text is lost or damaged (cf. p. 45, on Egesta). Often, therefore, other ways of dating fifth-century decrees have to be found: for instance, by finding a context in which the content makes sense, or by relying on the style of lettering used. In the course of the century the Athenian form of some of the letters of the Greek alphabet changed: in particular, *sigma* (*s*) from ⌇ to Σ, *beta* (*b*) and *rho* (*r*) from ﬔﬔ to BP, *phi* (*ph*) from Φ or Θ to Φ. The newer forms of these letters can be found in dated public documents (e.g. tribute lists) before 450; older and newer forms can coexist in the same inscription; but in documents which could be dated on other grounds the old *beta* and *phi* seemed not to be found after *c.*445; later than that there was one inscription with the old *sigma* (*IG* i³ 440, of 443/2), and there were two with a transitional *rho* (*IG* i³ 445 and 460, both of 438/7). It therefore seemed that older forms in documents which happen not to be datable on other grounds ought not to be significantly later. For many years a campaign against this doctrine has been fought by H. B. Mattingly, who has argued for dating after *c.*430 many texts which according to the doctrine ought to be dated before *c.*445, and if he were right many signs of strong imperialism would first appear not in the time of Pericles but in the time of Cleon. His view that old-style lettering could persist much longer seems now to have been vindicated since others have confirmed on the stone the reading of [An]tiphon in Athens' alliance with Egesta. This means not that all his suggestions of lower dates are necessarily right but that they cannot be ruled out on the ground of letter-forms and that the arguments for individual texts must be considered individually on their merits. I shall cite in this chapter, with due warning, texts for which I think the early date still is or could be correct.

The early tribute lists show considerable fluctuation between years: in 454/3 about 137 members paid about 350 tal. (and 18 payments from small Carian states, totalling about 7 tal., at the beginning of the next year's list are probably late payments for this year), in 453/2 (not counting the 18) about 144 paid, in 452/1 about 143, in 451/0 about 152 (including the small Carian states, so without them only about 134), in 450/49 about 163, with an appendix of late payments and second payments from states which had not originally paid in full. Athens seems to have had particular difficulties in 453, the first year of collection in Athens, and 450, but to have succeeded in exerting more pressure (or perhaps in a few cases in converting ship-providers to tribute-payers) in 449.

A decree for Erythrae, in Asia Minor (M&L 40 = *IG* i³ 14 ~ Fornara 71), now known only from a printed facsimile based on a lost copy of a lost stone, dealt with offerings at the Athenian festival of the Panathenaea (Erythrae as an Ionian city in the strict sense could be represented as a colony of Athens), made arrangements for a council of 120 appointed by lot, to be established by *episkopoi*, Athenian 'overseers', and a *phrourarchos*, 'garrison commander', prescribed for this council an oath of allegiance to the people of Erythrae, Athens and the allies, which included undertakings not to revolt and (perhaps) not without permission from Athens to take back those who had fled to the 'Medes' or to exile others; anybody exiled for murder in Erythrae was to be exiled from 'the whole Athenian alliance'; there is a reference to 'tyrants'. It appears that Erythrae, under a régime which could be described as a tyranny, had revolted with Persian support; Athens had recovered control, installed a garrison, and had sent a commission of overseers who established a democratic constitution. The facsimile shows strongly old-style lettering; attempts to restore an archon's name are unsafe, but the tribute record would justify a date at the end of the 450's: the name of Erythrae first survives in 450/49, with the bulk of its payment in the second instalment.

From Miletus itself a decree of uncertain date (M&L 43 ~ Fornara 66) outlaws certain men and their descendants; a decree probably of 434/3 (*Klio* lii 1970, 163–73, dating it three year earlier) displays constitutional machinery on the Athenian model. A pamphleteer mentions Miletus as a city where Athens supported an oligarchic régime but without success ([Xen.] *Ath. Pol.* iii. 11). Miletus paid tribute in 454/3 and 452/1, and is perhaps to be restored in 453/2; the whole of its payment in 450/49 was late. It seems likely that Miletus was in revolt *c.*450; there may have been a second revolt later; the democratic constitution may have been imposed either *c.*450 or later. However, an Athenian decree for Miletus (*IG* i³ 21 ~ Fornara 92) which has been dated 450/49 more probably belongs to 426/5: in that a commission of five Athenians aged over 50 (?) was to be sent to Miletus in connection with a series of trials; there was an Athenian garrison there.

Sigeum, at the mouth of the Hellespont, was praised for its loyalty under an archon perhaps still to be restored as that of 451/0 (*IG* i³ 17): this suggests that neighbours had been disloyal and/or that there had been a risk that Sigeum would be disloyal. And the late 450's is probably the time to which we should assign a decree for Phaselis, on the south coast of Asia Minor (M&L 31 = *IG* i³ 10 ~ Fornara 68), making favourable arrangements for lawsuits involving citizens of Athens and citizens of Phaselis.

After the death of Cimon in Cyprus *c.*450 regular fighting against Persia seems to have come to an end; in 447/6 Athens began an elaborate building programme on the acropolis, which was ultimately to include a temple of Athena Nike, 'Victory', and Plutarch reports complaints that tribute which should have been spent on fighting the Persians was being spent on beautifying Athens (cf. pp. 62–5). This involves us in a major cluster of problems.

From the fourth century onwards everybody knew of a 'Peace of Callias' by which Athens bound the Persians to keep away from the Aegean and the west coast of Asia Minor; there was an inscribed text in Athens – but Theopompus

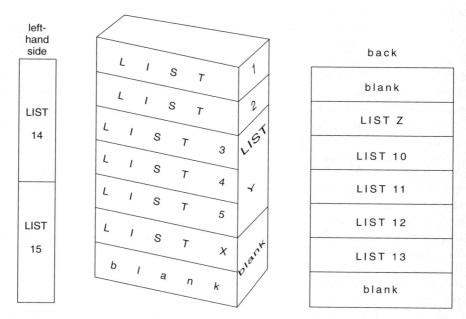

III. 3 The first *stele* of the Athenian tribute lists: arrangement of lists

denounced it as a forgery because it used the Ionian version of the Greek alphabet, not the local version which the Athenians used to the end of the fifth century (evidence collected *Staatsverträge* 152 ~ Fornara 95). But this is another alleged fifth-century document for which there is no fifth-century evidence. It is not mentioned by Herodotus (unless it lies behind his reference to Callias' presence at Susa 'on some other business': VII. 151), though it would be highly relevant to his theme of conflict between Greece and Persia; and it is not mentioned by Thucydides, though it would be highly relevant to his sketch of the growth of Athenian power, and when Persia supports Samos against Athens (cf. pp. 67–8) he does not suggest that a treaty is being broken. Most scholars have been sufficiently impressed by the later evidence to believe in a treaty. It is clear that the fears of the late 450's were no more and that Athens stopped prosecuting the war against Persia; there may even have been some kind of understanding with the Persian satraps in western Asia Minor; but the formal treaty was probably invented after 386, when the Greeks of Asia Minor had been handed back to Persia (cf. pp. 185, 193–5), to illustrate how much more glorious the past had been than the shameful present.

But if the war was, even without a treaty, at an end, what was to become of the Delian League, which had been formed to fight against the Persians? Almost certainly, there was one year in which no tribute was collected (cf. M&L 50 ~ Fornara 95. M). Lists 1–15 (*IG* i³ 259–72: 454/3–440/39) were inscribed on a

Ill. 4 The first *stele* of the Athenian tribute lists: reconstruction of fragments, inv. nos. EM6647, 12453 and 13454. Epigraphical Museum, Athens. Photo: Archaeological Receipts Fund/TAP Service, Athens

single large block of stone, but between 5 (263: 450/49) and 10 (267: 445/4) there seem to have been not four lists but three (cf. ills. 3 and 4: in ill. 3 these lists are labelled X, Y and Z). The first of these (264 = X: about 150 members paying) was not numbered; either 7 or 8 could be restored in the second (265 = Y: about 162); 9 can probably be restored in the third (266 = Z: about 156). Various explanations have been attempted, but the best suggestion is that in 449/8 no tribute was collected; in 448/7 collection was resumed, but met with some resistance, and the *hellenotamiai* were not sure whether to designate the list 6 or 7 so they omitted the number; in 447/6 collection was more effective, and that list was designated 8 as if there had been no interruption. A decree of Cleinias, with the newer forms of some letters but a curved *upsilon* (*u*), lays down procedures for the collecting and sending to Athens of the tribute, which assumes that Athenian *episkopoi* are widespread and threatens harsh justice in Athens for offenders; it also regards the sending of offerings to the Panathenaea as standard and threatens harsh justice in connection with that (M&L 46 = *IG* i³ 34 ~ Fornara 98). Cleinias is a common name, but a possible identification would be Cleinias the father of Alcibiades, who was killed at Coronea in 447/6 (cf. p. 51), so the champions of early dates placed this in 448/7; but resemblances to the decree about weights, measures and coinage (M&L 45 = *IG* i³ 1453 ~ Fornara 97), for which a later date seems more probable, suggest that this should be placed in the 420's (cf. pp. 92–3).

There is another alleged document which may be relevant here. We know only from Plutarch (*Per.* 17) of a decree proposed by Pericles, inviting all the Greek states to send representatives to a congress in Athens to discuss the rebuilding of temples destroyed by the Persians (a specifically Athenian concern), sacrifices to the gods on behalf of Greece and the preservation of peace at sea; but Sparta declined the invitation, and the congress never met. This too has been suspected of being a later invention, but it is hard to see why an unsuccessful invitation should have been invented. If it is authentic, Athens will have considered expanding the Delian League into a league of all the Greeks, and have remitted the tribute for a year while this was being planned, but when thwarted by Sparta's opposition will have decided to continue with the League that it had.

The building programme on the acropolis started in 447/6, and it was alleged that this was financed from the tribute. A papyrus fragment of a commentary on a passage of Demosthenes which refers to that programme (most recent reconstruction reprinted Meiggs, *The Athenian Empire*, 515: Fornara 94 translates that and two earlier reconstructions) seems to refer to a proposal of Pericles in the archonship of Euthydemus (450/49? 431/0?) and to a sum of 5,000 talents connected with Aristides (an accumulation of unspent tribute collected in accordance with his assessment?). This could conceivably allude to a decree to transfer to an Athenian treasury an accumulation of unspent tribute; but 450/49 looks slightly early for such a decision, and the uncertainties are so great that no theory which depended on this text could be safe.

Even though some texts formerly dated now are to be moved to the 420's, this appears to be a time when the nature of the Delian League was transformed (cf. the discussion of Athenian imperialism, p. 173). The League was kept in existence, but no longer in order to fight an unending war against Persia. All the members were required to send offerings to the Panathenaea, as if they were colonies of Athens. Democracies led by friends of Athens could be imposed on states which under other régimes had opposed Athens. Another treatment meted out to troublesome states was the confiscation of some of their land to be given to Athenian settlers, who would both benefit economically at the other state's expense and serve as an informal garrison: Diodorus (XI. 88. iii) attributes settlements in Euboea and Naxos to Tolmides, who died at Coronea in 447/6. Decisions were taken for the whole League by Athens, and it is likely that when the treasury was moved to Athens the meetings held at Delos were discontinued (cf. p. 18). The language of the League changes: in the decree for Erythrae we found an oath of allegiance to Erythrae, Athens and the allies, and a reference to 'the . . . Athenian alliance'; but there are some decrees with the older style of lettering which refer to 'the cities which Athens rules' (*IG* i³ 19, 27), and in settlements with Colophon (M&L 47 = *IG* i³ 37 ~ Fornara 99: in l. 49 *demos*, implying a democratic constitution at Colophon, or even *demokratia*, is probably to be restored), Eretria (*IG* i³ 39 ~ Fornara 102) and Chalcis (M&L 52 = *IG* i³ 40 ~ Fornara 103; the last two are still best dated 446/5, even if the first is later) allegiance is simply to Athens.

The Thirty Years' Peace

After the Cypriot expedition in which Cimon died, Thucydides concentrates on events in Greece (I. 112. v–115. i). Delphi, with the surrounding region of Phocis, had come under Athenian control after Oenophyta (cf. p. 44). In a Sacred War the Spartans invaded and gave control of the sanctuary to the city of Delphi, but after they had left the Athenians invaded and restored control to the Phocians. Plutarch (*Per.* 21) names Pericles as the Athenian commander; a fragment of Philochorus (*FGrH* 328 F 34. b) puts the Athenian response 'in the third year', and there is no reason why that should not be right. Since Athens and Sparta did not fight against each other, this will not have broken the five-year truce.

A revolt against Athens began in Boeotia, centred on the north-western cities of Orchomenus and Chaeronea, with support from Euboea. The Athenians sent an army under Tolmides, which recovered Chaeronea but during its return was attacked and defeated at Coronea, after which Athens withdrew from Boeotia (and presumably from the rest of central Greece). This was followed by a revolt in Euboea. Pericles took an army there, but returned on learning that Megara also was in revolt and the Peloponnesians were about to invade Attica. The Peloponnesians did invade, under the Spartan king Plistoanax, but they withdrew without advancing beyond the plain of Eleusis. Pericles then returned to Euboea and regained control of the island, expelling the inhabitants of the northern city of Histiaea (who had killed the crew of an Athenian ship: Plut. *Per.* 23. iv). A thirty years' peace was made between Sparta and Athens: in addition to its losses in central Greece, Athens gave up its possessions in the Isthmus and the Peloponnese, but apart from that the division of the Greek world into an Athenian bloc and a Spartan bloc was recognised (cf. Thuc. I. 35. ii, 40. ii; also 144. ii). Argos, which had made a thirty-year peace with Sparta in 451 (cf. p. 44), was well disposed to Athens but technically neutral (Paus. V. 23. iv).

From Thucydides (II. 2. i, 21. i) we can calculate that the peace was made in 446/5: the revolts of Euboea and Megara will have been in 446, that of Boeotia late in 447 or early in 446.

It was believed both in Sparta, which exiled Plistoanax (Thuc. II. 21. i, V. 16), and in Athens, where there was a story that Pericles included in his accounts a large sum for 'necessary expenses' (Ar. *Nub.* 859 with schol. ~ Fornara 104, Plut. *Per.* 23. i–ii), that Pericles had bribed Plistoanax. All too often in Greece when a leader failed to press an advantage it was assumed that he must have been bribed. On this occasion, there was little likelihood that Sparta could have taken the well-fortified city of Athens; whether or not the deal was eased by money, there must have been an understanding that Athens would agree to the terms of the thirty years' peace, and, although there was enough anger in Sparta for Plistoanax to be exiled, the peace was made. It was not a bad deal for Athens, which did not have the manpower to hold on to extensive mainland possessions against widespread opposition (cf. p. 140, on Sicily) in addition to its Aegean empire; and its possession of that empire was confirmed.

Inscriptions concerned with Athens' recovery of Euboea show it taking a tough line: allegiance is sworn to Athens alone (cf. p. 51); Chalcis (M&L 52 = *IG* i³ 40 ~ Fornara 103) gave hostages; it promised to obey and to denounce any plans for further revolt; major lawsuits were to be transferred from local to Athenian courts – and some landowners were exiled (Plut. *Per.* 23. iv). Hestiaea was resettled by the Athenians (Theopompus *FGrH* 115 F 387, Diod. Sic. XII. 22. ii; the inscription *IG* i³ 41 is very fragmentary). There seems to have been further trouble in Eretria a little later, resulting in the taking of hostages in 442/1 (Hesychius, Photius, Ἐρετριακὸς κατάλογος). We shall see that Athens remained unchastened, and the peace was to last only until 431 (cf. pp. 81–9).

NOTE ON FURTHER READING

For general books on the Delian League see the note at the end of chapter 2.

On the background to the First Peloponnesian War see D. M. Lewis, 'The Origins of the First Peloponnesian War', *Classical Contributions . . . M. F. McGregor*, 71–8 = his *Selected Papers in Greek and Near Eastern History*, 9–21. That Athens began its own long walls before those of Megara is argued by Salmon, *Pnyx and Parthenon* (forthcoming).

Against the idea that the change from turtle to tortoise coins in Aegina was imposed by Athens see Figueira, *The Power of Money*, 116–27. On Dorus, Ezra and Nehemiah see R. J. Littman, 'Dor and the Athenian Empire', and C. Ehrhardt, 'Athens, Egypt, Phoenicia, *c.*459–444 BC', *AJAH* xv 1990 [publ. 2001], 155–76 and 177–96. On the alleged Athenian decree against Arthmius of Zelea see Meiggs, *The Athenian Empire*, 508–12.

On the dating of fifth-century Athenian decrees from letter-forms, against the old orthodoxy, see a series of studies by H. B. Mattingly, beginning with 'The Athenian

Coinage Decree', *Hist.* x 1961, 148–88; that (at pp. 5–52) and many others are collected in his *The Athenian Empire Restored.* The most thorough defence of the old orthodoxy was M. B. Walbank, 'Criteria for the Dating of Fifth-Century Attic Inscriptions' in Φόρος... *B. D. Meritt*, 161–9; revised as 'Criteria for Dating' in his *Athenian Proxenies of the Fifth Century* BC, ch. 2. The orthodoxy was finally undermined by work on Athens' decree for Egesta (*IG* i³ 11): [Ha]bron (458/7) was suggested by A. E. Raubitschek, 'Athens and Halikyai', *TAPA* lxxv 1944, 10–14 at 10 n. 3; [Ant]iphon (418/7) was first suggested by Mattingly, 'The Growth of Athenian Imperialism', *Hist.* xii 1963, 257–73 at 268–9 (=*The Athenian Empire Restored*, 87–106 at 99–101), and gained more adherents after the attempts to apply modern technology by M. H. Chambers et al., 'Athens' Alliance with Egesta in the Year of Antiphon', *ZPE* lxxxiii 1990, 38–57; the reading of [An]tiphon on the stone was finally confirmed by A. P. Matthaiou, 'περὶ τῆς *IG* i³ 11', in Matthaiou (ed.), Ἀττικαὶ Ἐπιγραφαί... *Adolf Wilhelm*, 99–122.

On the mid-century changes in the Delian League see in general R. Meiggs, 'The Crisis of Athenian Imperialism', *HSCP* lxvii 1963, 1–36. Among many discussions of the alleged Peace of Callias see H. T. Wade-Gery, 'The Peace of Kallias', *HSCP* Supp. i 1940, 121–56 = his *Essays in Greek History*, 201–32 (believing); D. L. Stockton, 'The Peace of Callias', *Hist.* viii 1959, 61–79 (disbelieving), A. J. Holladay, 'The Détente of Kallias?', *Hist.* xxxv 1986, 503–7 = his *Athens in the Fifth Century*, ch. 5 (informal agreement). On Pericles' congress proposal see R. Seager, 'The Congress Decree: Some Doubts and a Hypothesis', *Hist.* xviii 1969, 129–41 (disbelieving); G. T. Griffith, 'A Note on Plutarch *Pericles* 17', *Hist.* xxvii 1978, 218–19 (believing). For a new study of Athens' coinage decree, supporting a date in the 420's, see the forthcoming proceedings of a conference held in Oxford in 2004.

6

Periclean Athens

500	475	450	425	400	375	350	325	300

462/1	Ephialtes' reform of Areopagus
451/0	Pericles' citizenship law
447/6	beginning of building work on acropolis
c.444/3	colony at Thurii
c.443	ostracism of Thucydides son of Melesias
438/7	prosecution of Pheidias and of Pericles
437/6	colony at Amphipolis
433/2	winding-up of building work on acropolis

The Completion of the Classical Democracy

Ephialtes' reform, if I am right to represent it as undertaken with the deliberate intention of making Athens more democratic, marks a watershed in Athens' political development (cf. pp. 35–9). The democracy was not welcomed by all Athenians, but it had come to stay. For one more generation, however, political leadership remained in the hands of aristocrats: leaders of a new kind did not emerge until the 430's and 420's (cf. pp. 119–22).

Ath. Pol. 26. ii–iv chronicles three changes of the 450's. In 457/6 the archonship, previously restricted to the two highest of Solon's four property classes, was extended to the third class, putting it on a level with other offices. At first the practice of allotment from an elected shortlist, either reintroduced after what Solon had instituted was abandoned under the tyranny, or else introduced for the first time, in 487/6, was retained; some time later allotment was adopted for the selection of the shortlist as well as for the second stage, a tenth post was created, 'secretary to the *thesmothetai*', and one of the ten was filled from each of the ten tribes (*Ath. Pol.* 8. i, 55. i). The archons were becoming less important as the generals became more important: this will have reinforced the tendency to view them as routine rather than leading officials. 453/2 saw the revival of an institution of the sixth-century tyrants which had been abolished on their overthrow: travelling justices, to decide minor lawsuits (where the sum at issue was not more than 10 dr.: *Ath. Pol.* 53. ii) locally. In their fifth-century manifestation they were called *dikastai kata demous*, 'deme justices', and there were thirty of them, perhaps one for each of the thirty *trittyes* of Attica. Ephialtes' reform, the archons' loss of direct jurisdiction, and the development of the Delian League will all have added to the business of the courts in Athens; many low-level disputes were local, and this will have been a sensible way of relieving the pressure.

In 451/0 we have a law attributed to Pericles, limiting Athenian citizenship to men with an Athenian mother as well as an Athenian father (previously only the father had to be Athenian). According to *Ath. Pol.* 26. iv the change was made 'on account of the large number of citizens'; but if, as is likely, legitimate birth was required for citizenship, this law would tend to restrict citizens' choice of wives more than the number of citizen sons whom they fathered. Earlier, mixed marriages had probably been few but distinguished (one product of such a marriage was Pericles' opponent Cimon – and the law was not retrospective: he did not lose his citizenship). The development of the Delian League and of Athens as a major city was giving more Athenians the opportunity to travel abroad and more foreigners an incentive to visit Athens. Probably mixed marriages were becoming more frequent and were causing anxiety in some circles, and the democrats, proud of the benefits associated with Athenian citizenship, wanted to ensure that those who enjoyed them were genuine Athenians. The law was annulled or ignored towards the end of the Peloponnesian War, when plague and fighting had seriously reduced the citizen body, but in the fourth century it was reaffirmed, and a positive ban on mixed marriages was added.

Ath. Pol. 27 is a rag-bag of material on Pericles. It includes a reform of the Areopagus (probably in fact an allusion to Ephialtes' reform: cf. p. 38); and it ends with his introduction of payment for serving on juries, represented as a political gambit against Cimon, who 'was as rich as a tyrant' and was using his wealth to exercise patronage on a scale which Pericles could not match (cf. Gorgias fr. B 20 DK *ap.* Plut. *Cim.* 10. v). In the form in which the story is told, it is discreditable to Pericles, suggesting that he bought political support with the state's money since he could not afford to do so with his own; but democrats could have respectable grounds for objecting to Cimon's use of his wealth, and could argue that, if institutions which were democratic on paper were to work democratically in practice, the poorer citizens (for jury service there was an age qualification of 30 but no property qualification) had to be compensated for taking time away from their own affairs for public business. This is probably to be dated in the 450's, when the jury-courts were becoming more important: the story should probably not be pressed to yield the conclusion that payment must have been introduced when Cimon was in Athens, between his return from ostracism and his death. It was to be the first of a whole series of payments for the performance of civilian duties, made to enable the poorer citizens to play an active part in public life: by 411 there were payments for holding various offices and serving in the council of five hundred, and at the beginning of the fourth century payment for attending the assembly was added (cf. pp. 162, 262–3). The payments were not lavish: that for jury service was 2 ob. a day at first, increased to 3 ob. in the 420's, about what an unskilled worker could earn. On this as on so many matters we have very little evidence for states other than Athens: almost certainly Athens was the first to make such payments; at the beginning of the fourth century members of the Boeotian federal council received their travelling expenses (*Hell. Oxy.* 19. iv Chambers), and in the late fourth century there was payment for attending the assembly at Iasus (R&O 99).

In 445/4 Athens received a gift of grain from another Egyptian ruler, Psammetichus (perhaps hoping for further support against Persia). Before this was distributed among the citizens the registers were checked, and it is alleged that nearly 5,000 men – perhaps about 10 per cent of the total – were found to be wrongly registered and were deleted (Philoch. *FGrH* 328 F 119 ~ Fornara 86, Plut. *Per.* 37. iv). This probably has no connection with Pericles' citizenship law beyond the belief that those who were to enjoy the benefits of citizenship should be truly Athenian; it is hard to believe that so large a number should have been deprived of citizenship without there being more trace of the upheaval, but we have no basis on which to arrive at an alternative figure.

The Government of the Democracy

At this point it will be convenient to survey the Athenian democracy as it functioned in the second half of the fifth century.

Like every Greek *polis*, Athens was a community of *politai*, citizens – adult males of Athenian descent, on their mother's side as well as their father's after the enactment of Pericles' law (cf. p. 55). The citizens could own land within the city's territory (as non-citizens normally could not) and take part in the government of the city, and they had to pay taxes and fight for the city (though for rowing the navy's ships Athens relied on paid volunteers, not all of them citizens, rather than conscription of the poorer citizens). Citizens' wives and daughters played no part in public life, except in religious matters, but they were important as transmitters of property (a woman with no brother would commonly be married to a relative, to keep property within the family) and of citizenship. Citizens' sons became citizens at the age of 18. From 18 to 20 they were *epheboi*, 'on the verge of adulthood': they formed a separate category in the army, and they had some opportunities for military training, which were to be developed into a regular programme in the 330's (cf. p. 341). There were perhaps as many as 60,000 adult male citizens (some of them living in settlements outside Attica) in 431. Free men who were not of Athenian descent had no automatic right to become citizens, though they might be rewarded with citizenship for exceptional services to the Athenians. Any who stayed for more than a short period were known as metics (*metoikoi*, 'migrants'): they had to pay taxes and fight in the army; we can only guess at their numbers, but there may have been as many as 10,000–15,000 adult males in 431.

It is even harder to estimate the numbers of slaves, most of whom were non-Greek. Some were owned by the state (and some of these had administrative duties which required literacy); most were owned by individuals, and employed in the household, on the land or in workshops; the largest concentration, employed in the worst conditions, was to be found in the silver mines. The statistic with the strongest claim to be taken seriously is Thucydides' statement that more than 20,000 deserted when the Spartans established a fort in Attica in 413 (VII. 27. v: cf. pp. 140–1). In 431 there may have been in the region of 100,000 slaves (of both sexes), and probably only the poorest citizens and metics would not own any. The total population of Attica may have been in the region of 300,000–400,000. The adult male citizens were dependent on the women, children, metics and slaves to the extent that they could not have devoted so much time to public life if there had not been others to work for them while they were working for the city; but most ordinary citizens, for much of the time, had non-citizens working alongside rather than instead of them, and the Athenian citizens were not parasitic on the non-citizens as the Spartan citizens were parasitic on the helots.

Draco in the late seventh century and Solon in the early sixth had been specially appointed legislators; but after that, until the end of the fifth century legislation and decision-making generally were by decree (*psephisma*) of the citizens' assembly (*ekklesia*). As in most Greek states, the assembly's business was prepared by a smaller body, in Athens the council (*boule*) of five hundred. Athens interpreted the general principle in such a way as to limit the assembly's freedom as little as possible: the assembly could not vote on a matter unless it had been the subject of a prior resolution by the council (*probouleuma*), and put to it by the council's standing committee, the *prytaneis* (*Ath. Pol.* 45. iv). Occasionally an ad hoc board of *syngrapheis* was used to draft a decree (e.g. *IG* i³ 78 = M&L 73 ~ Fornara 140). An Athenian *probouleuma* did not have to incorporate a specific recommendation, though it often did so; whether it did or not, any citizen in the assembly was then free to speak, and to propose an alternative motion or an amendment to an existing motion; and the final decision was made by a simple majority (voting was usually by show of hands, with the votes assessed but not precisely counted). There were no organised political parties, and not even a Pericles could be sure that every vote would go as he wanted (there is an element of wishful thinking in Thucydides' representation of Periclean democracy as 'rule by the first man': II. 65. ix). Normally the council could prevent a debate by refusing to refer a matter to the assembly (Hdt. IX. 5 reports an instance from 479); but in one amendment to a decree a man requires the council to put to the assembly what he is going to draft (M&L 73 = *IG* i^3 78 ~ Fornara 140. 59–61).

By the fourth century the assembly was holding four regular meetings in each of the ten prytanies of the year, the periods for which one tribe's fifty representatives in the council provided the standing committee of *prytaneis* (there had perhaps been an increase from one to four in the time of Pericles); and the council met every day except major occasions in the religious calendar. Perhaps until the time of Ephialtes (cf. pp. 37–8), the archons presided; in the second half of the fifth century the *prytaneis* presided, one of their number each day acting as chairman. For some kinds of business in the assembly a quorum was required: in 411, when the citizen body had been reduced by plague and war casualties and many of the survivors were away from Athens, it could be alleged that attendance never reached 5,000 (Thuc. VIII. 72. i); but before 431 attendance probably exceeded 6,000.

There were various safeguards against rash decisions: the council's prior deliberation and publication of the assembly's agenda; the possibility of attacking a motion and its author in a lawcourt, in a *graphe paranomon* (cf. p. 37). Sometimes a major decision was spread over two days, with debate on the first and voting on the second – but no guarantee that the same body of men would be present on both days (cf. p. 83). Sometimes a matter was protected by a clause requiring a vote of immunity, so that one meeting had to vote permission for a discussion before a second could hold that discussion (cf. M&L 58 = *IG* i^3 52 ~ Fornara 119. *B*. 15–19). But in a crisis the safeguards might be suspended or overridden (cf. pp. 161, 167).

In making decisions all the citizens, or as many of them as wished and conveniently could, were involved together; in carrying out decisions the citizens could not be involved together, but the fifth-century democracy involved the citizens in turn, as far as possible, rather than relying on professional administrators or experts of any kind. Administration was simpler and required less expertise than in the modern world – there was no need to regulate broadcasting, because there was no broadcasting; there was no need to regulate education, because education was not regarded as the state's concern – but funds still had to be raised and spent for such purposes as roads, water supply, public buildings, and the army and navy. And the state could not straightforwardly run a deficit (though it could borrow money from its temple treasuries: cf. pp. 91–3): it could not spend money unless it had the money, and we hear, for instance, of occasions when the lawcourts were suspended because there was no money to pay the jurors' stipends (e.g. Dem. XXXIX. *Boeotus i*. 17, XLV. *Stephanus i*. 4, cf. XXIV. *Timocrates* 99).

The fifth-century democracy divided the work that had to be done among a large number of officials, commonly boards of ten, one member appointed each year from each of the ten tribes, and not eligible for reappointment to the same position. The 2 per cent tax on imports and exports (cf. Andoc. I. *Myst.* 134) will serve as an example. There were no officials who collected the tax: interested groups of individuals submitted bids; the contract was made with the group which offered to raise the highest sum, in the presence of the council by the board of *poletai* ('sellers'); the record was kept for the council by a public slave. When the payment fell due it was made to another board, the *apodektai* ('receivers'), again in the presence of the council, and the record of the contract was cancelled (*Ath. Pol.* 47. ii–48. ii). The collectors were bound to pay the sum stipulated in the contract: if they had collected more, they retained the surplus as their profit, but if they had collected less, they had to make good the shortfall. If they failed to pay on time, they were pursued by another board on behalf of the council, the *praktores* ('exacters'). In the fifth century, the money collected was paid into a central treasury, whose location is unknown; expenditure from that had to be authorised, as an individual or as a recurring item, by the assembly, and the payments were made by another board (apparently, owing to fear of peculation, appointed not each year but each prytany), the *kolakretai* ('ham-collectors'). In the fourth century the central treasury was replaced by separate spending authorities (cf. p. 263).

Separate from the state's central treasury were the temple treasuries, with their own treasurers, the most important being the treasury of Athena, on the acropolis; but religion was integrated with the rest of the state's life, the appointments were state appointments, and in time of need the state could borrow from the temple treasuries (cf. pp. 91–3). Also separate, until *c.*411 (cf. p. 94), was the treasury of the Delian League, moved to Athens in 454/3, whose treasurers were the *hellenotamiai* (cf. pp. 17–18, 45).

This fragmentation, and the fact that each year nearly every official was new to his job, did not make for efficiency; but efficiency was not the main objective. The jobs were simple, without great opportunities for doing good or harm, and the record-keeping was assisted by a small number of slave clerks; the understanding was that the average citizen should be able and should be willing to play a part, and that the jobs should be shared equitably among those who were willing. The scope for inefficiency was mitigated by the fact that many of the officials, while new to the current year's job, had done other jobs in previous years; and that the whole administrative process was overseen by the council – itself appointed by lot for one year, from the demes in proportion to their size, and (to provide a large enough pool of candidates) with men allowed to serve twice in their lives (at any rate from the fourth century onwards: we have no evidence for the fifth). The administrative system in turn informed the decision-making of the assembly: the council which prepared the business knew what was happening across the whole range of Athens' public life; and many of the men who attended the assembly were holding some office at the time or had done so recently (*Ath. Pol.* 24. iii claims that fifth-century Athens had about 700 internal officials and [probably a different number] external).

Justice had been dispensed in early Athens by the nine archons, and by the former archons who made up the council of the Areopagus. Prosecution was nearly always left to an individual's initiative; but at the beginning of the sixth century Solon had created a distinction between *graphai* (literally 'writings'), public prosecutions on charges on which any citizen could prosecute, and *dikai* (the general term for 'lawsuits'), where only the injured party or his or her family could prosecute; and he had also provided for appeals against the archons' verdicts (*Ath. Pol.* 9. i). By the second half of the fifth century the system of appeals had developed into one by which the archon held a preliminary enquiry and the case was then tried in a court over which he presided, and the judicial competence of the Areopagus had been reduced (cf. pp. 36–7); while in 453/2 the lesser *dikai* were entrusted to the travelling deme justices (cf. p. 55). There were special procedures for special cases (for cases retained by the Areopagus, for *eisangeliai* on charges of major offences against the state, and for procedures for checking officials, cf. pp. 36–7; for the summary treatment of 'common criminals' see *Ath. Pol.* 52. i); but the great majority of cases were *dikai* and *graphai* tried in a *dikasterion* ('lawcourt') under the presidency of an archon or other official. The archon presided but did not give expert guidance; there were no professional advocates, but litigants were expected to present their own cases (though they could employ speech-writers, and could also call on supporting speakers); the juries were large (never smaller than 201; for major *graphai* 1,001 or more). No trial was allowed longer than one day.

In the modern world states' administrative apparatuses are powerful, and it is thought important to keep the lawcourts independent of the administration so that they can ensure that even the state obeys the law. In Athens, and in the Greek world generally, the administrative apparatus was weak, and it was thought natural that the executive power of the administrative offices should be reinforced by judicial power. Many officials therefore presided over courts trying charges related to their field of administration; and the council also acquired judicial competence in administrative matters, though it had to refer a case to a *dikasterion* if it thought a heavier penalty was needed than a 500-dr. fine.

The courts were thus amateur bodies representative of the *polis*, pronouncing the will of the people without expert legal guidance; but the currently fashionable view of a trial as a contest in which the courts decided on the rival claims to the people's favour of the opposing litigants as citizens rather than on the formal charges made and the cases presented in support of them is misleadingly one-sided. More disturbing from our perspective is the fact that the Athenians did not distinguish as clearly as we should wish between illegal conduct and politically unwise or unsuccessful conduct by public figures: it was too easily assumed that an opposing politician or an unsuccessful commander was wilfully failing to act in the best interests of Athens, and that – since no Athenian would do that of his own free choice – he must have been bribed to do so. Charges like 'deceiving the people' (e.g. Hdt. VI. 136. ii) made it all too easy to blur the line between illegality and political misjudgment, and active politicians and military commanders were frequently brought before the courts.

The principal officials of early Athens had been the nine archons, but by the middle of the fifth century they had become routine officials (cf. pp. 38, 54–5), and, at a time when Athens was militarily powerful, the ten generals (*strategoi*) were not only the commanders of the army and navy but the state's most important officials. Unlike the civilian officials, they were appointed not by allotment but by election, and they could be re-elected indefinitely – so that in this period the citizens elected the men who became their political leaders. When the ten generals were instituted as a regular office, by Cleisthenes, one was appointed from each tribe; by the second half of the fourth century the tribal basis had been abandoned (*Ath. Pol.* 22. ii, 61. i); but at any rate from 441/0 (Androtion *FGrH* 324 F 38 ~ Fornara 110) until the middle of the fourth century it appears that, while one general per tribe remained the norm, at least one exception was allowed (so that there could be two generals from one tribe and none from one of the others). It used to be thought that this was introduced to allow for the predominant position of Pericles, to provide one general who would rank above the others and to give a fair chance to other members of Pericles' tribe. However, it has been made clear that (apart from Alcibiades in 407/6: cf. p. 149) one general did not rank above the others, and it now seems more likely that the intention was to provide for cases in which one tribe did not have a strong candidate. Often, when we know of two generals from one tribe, neither looks like an also-ran who might have been elected only in a second round of voting; so probably in such cases a man from another tribe either offered himself to or was approached by a tribe which lacked a strong candidate of its own, to act as its candidate.

But generals who were elected and who could be re-elected were an exception in a system which was calculated not to create a gulf between the authorities and the ordinary citizens, but which (as in Arist. *Pol.* III. 1277 B 13–16, VI. 1317 B 2–3) assumed that the good citizen should rule and be ruled in turn. In practice some did avoid public life, while those who liked doing so could hold a variety of different offices over the years; but for the system to work a fair number had to be willing to hold office sometimes. Jury service is represented or misrepresented in Aristophanes' *Wasps* as appealing to old men who had time on their hands and found the stipend attractive. For the assembly there was doubtless a spectrum from those who attended regularly to those who attended rarely if ever. At any one time only a small number of men were active politicians who frequently proposed decrees (in the time of Pericles these would include generals and other office-holders, but texts of decrees identify proposers by name without any indication of office), but there would be a large number of men who made a proposal once or twice in their life, perhaps when serving in the council. It was easier to take part in public life for those who lived, or had access to hospitality, in or near the city than for those who lived at a distance (the remotest parts of Attica were about 30 miles = 50 km. from the city); but attending the assembly could be combined with other business in the city, and distance will have been more of a disincentive to regular political activity than to attending the assembly on important occasions. The council, at least, with its membership based on the demes, should not have been dominated by a city clique (though it will inevitably have been easier for those living in or near the city to attend regularly). Similarly, the provision of stipends mitigated but did not eliminate the fact that the rich could devote their time to public service more easily than the poor, but that will have had more effect on the holding of time-consuming offices (and members of the lowest property class were still not eligible to hold offices: cf. p. 260) than on (not yet paid in the fifth century) attendance at the assembly. The *demokratia* of the second half of the fifth century was not totally egalitarian, but it did indeed place considerable power in the hands of the people, or as many of them as chose to exercise it – and Athens' empire meant that there were far more decisions to be made by council and assembly, more administrative jobs to be done and positions to be held, and more cases coming before the lawcourts than would have been the case in an ordinary city.

I end this survey with a paragraph on ostracism, introduced by Cleisthenes and first used in the 480's. Once a year the assembly decided whether to hold an ostracism; if it chose to do so, there was no list of candidates but each voter wrote or had written for him on a potsherd (*ostrakon*) the name of his preferred victim, and if at least 6,000 votes were cast in all the man with the largest number had to go into exile, without loss of property, for ten years. Surviving *ostraka* show that large numbers of men were voted against: some no doubt attracted a few votes because of a private grudge, but those who attracted a large number were voted against as public figures. Ostracism was used in effect to choose between rival political leaders, of whom the winner stayed in Athens while the loser was removed: thus at the end of the 470's Themistocles was ostracised and Cimon was not, at the end of the 460's Cimon was ostracised and Ephialtes was not (cf. pp. 34–5). The outcome of an ostracism might be unpredictable, and after 415, when neither Nicias nor Alcibiades was ostracised but Hyperbolus was, ostracism was not used again (cf. pp. 156–7).

Public Buildings

The inscribed accounts of the relevant boards of overseers (*epistatai*) enable us to date a major programme of work on the acropolis (see ill. 5): the Parthenon, the temple of Athena Parthenos ('Virgin'), was built towards the southern edge of the plateau between 447/6 and 433/2 (on the site of a building begun perhaps after Marathon and not resumed after the Persian Wars: a temple built in the sixth century was nearer the centre of the acropolis) (*IG* i^3 436–51: e.g. M&L 59 ~ Fornara 120). Attributed to the architects Callicrates and Ictinus, the Parthenon is a masterpiece of Doric architecture, which in such respects as the positioning of the columns departs slightly from actual regularity in order to enhance the appearance of regularity; the sculptures included a frieze running round the top of the cella wall, depicting a procession whose significance continues to be disputed (most often, though not always, since J. Stuart in 1789 seen as a representation of the Panathenaic procession – but, if so, what kind of representation?). In recent decades the Parthenon has become controversial

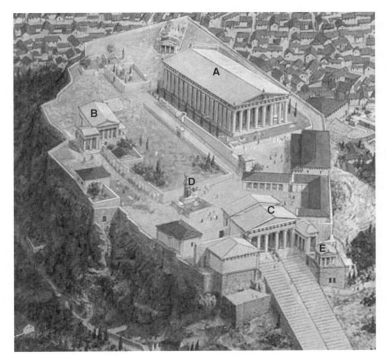

Ill. 5 Reconstruction of the Athenian acropolis: watercolour drawing by Peter Connolly. A = the Parthenon, B = the Erechtheum, C = the Propylaea, D = the statue of Athena Promachos, E = the Temple of Athena Nike. Peter Connolly/AKG Images

in another way: many of its sculptures were among those acquired from the Ottoman empire, which was not interested in caring for its Greek remains, in and after 1801 by Lord Elgin and bought for the British Museum in 1816; these have been particularly emphasised in arguments as to whether objects removed from their original location, legitimately by the standards of the time but illegitimately by the standards which would be applied to comparable objects found nowadays, ought to be returned. The eastern chamber of the temple housed a gold and ivory statue of Athena, by the sculptor Pheidias, who is said to have been a friend of Pericles and the master-mind behind the whole programme: this was made between 447/6 and 438/7 (*IG* i³ 453–60: e.g. M&L 54 ~ Fornara 114). In 437/6 work began under Mnesicles on the new Propylaea, the entrance building at the west end of the acropolis, on an axis exactly parallel to that of the Parthenon (but one did not then have an uninterrupted view of the Parthenon from the Propylaea as one does now) (*IG* i³ 462–6: e.g. M&L 60 ~ Fornara 118. B): this was left unfinished on the approach of the Peloponnesian War (cf. p. 83).

On a bastion at the south-west corner, outside the Propylaea (the symmetry of whose design was modified to allow for it), was built a small temple of Athena

Nike ('Victory': at the time of writing, dismantled with a view to re-restoration). For this we have two inscriptions, on the front and back of the same *stele* (M&L 44, 71 = *IG* i³ 35, 36 ~ Fornara 93, 139): the first, with no date surviving but with older-style lettering, instructs Callicrates to draw up plans and provides for the appointment of a priestess (not from a particular family but from all Athenian women – one of the very few cases in which we can see a connection between fifth-century Athenian religion and the democracy); the second, dated 424/3, arranges for the payment of the priestess's salary. There is argument about the dating of the first decree and the dating of different stages in the building work; but the temple could have been planned in the 440's, to celebrate victory over the Persians from Marathon onwards, even if it was not actually built and the priestess did not take office until later.

War against the Persians had in fact come to an end, whether its ending was marked by a formal treaty or not (cf. pp. 47–8), and resources were now available for a programme which would celebrate victory over the Persians and the greatness of Athens, so that according to Thucydides one would imagine from the remains of the Athens he knew that it was even more powerful than it actually was (I. 10. ii) – but it is not likely that in 479 there had been an undertaking to leave in ruins as a war memorial temples which the Persians had destroyed (cf. p. 15). But on Delos, no longer the centre of the Delian League, work on a new temple of Apollo was broken off about the middle of the century.

Plutarch devotes a substantial section of his *Pericles* (12–14) to this building programme. Pericles' opponents complained that he had taken over the funds of the Greeks from Delos and that money contributed for fighting against the Persians was being spent on adorning Athens like a wanton woman. He replied that Athens was giving the allies the security they were paying for, the work provided not only everlasting glory but also immediate employment for those citizens who could not fight [in fact Athens at this time will have been a flourishing city which did not need to create employment, and many of those employed in this way were not Athenian citizens]; and he offered to pay for the work himself if the assembly was not satisfied. The assembly gave him its enthusiastic backing – fortunately, since the cost must have been far beyond the means of the richest individual, though the figure of 2,000 tal. given for the Propylaea is more probably the total cost of the work on the acropolis in this period (Harp. π 101 = *Suda* π 2579 προπύλαια ταῦτα ~ Fornara 118. A). The League could have helped indirectly to pay for the work, merely by covering the military expenses which Athens would otherwise have had to fund itself; but it may indeed have contributed directly: the campaigning expenses which had to be funded from the tribute will now have been less, but the tribute was not reduced; it is possible that a papyrus fragment attests the transfer of an accumulated surplus from League funds to Athenian funds (cf. p. 50), and it is possible that in the 440's and 430's unspent surpluses were transferred year by year. From the Athenian point of view, it was important that these were public buildings, funded not by rich individuals (cf. p. 33) but (from whatever sources) by the state, under the supervision of publicly appointed *epistatai* (cf. the statue of

Athena Promachos, 'Fighting in Front', set up towards the west end of the acropolis before 450: *IG* i³ 435).

There was a good deal of other building, elsewhere in Athens and in the rest of Attica, about this time: in the mid twentieth century much of it was attributed to a single architect and assigned to the 440's and 430's (including the temple of Hephaestus, formerly misidentified as the Theseum, on the west side of the agora, and the temple of Poseidon at Sunium), but it is now thought that the similarities are not so great as to require a single architect, and that the work was begun earlier and continued later (cf. pp. 122–3). Two other items, attributed explicitly to Pericles, are worth mentioning: the middle wall, built between the two original long walls linking Athens to the Piraeus, and close to the more northerly (Plut. *Per.* 13. vii–viii); and the odeum, south-east of the acropolis, next to the theatre of Dionysus, said to have been 'many-seated and many-columned' (not a very practicable combination) and to have been an imitation of the Persian King's tent (Plut. *Per.* 13. ix–x) – one manifestation of the fact that, although the Persians were the ultimate enemy, the Athenians and other Greeks were willing to adopt Persian fashions. The harbour town of Piraeus is said to have been laid out on a grid plan by Hippodamus of Miletus (Arist. *Pol.* II. 1267 B 22–3), who worked also at the Athenian colony of Thurii in Italy (cf. pp. 68–9).

Pericles and Others

Pericles was undoubtedly one of the leading figures in Athens from the 450's to his death in 429. We have noted above that he cannot within the Athenian framework have been as powerful as Thucydides wanted his readers to think, and some scholars have been reluctant to believe that the policies pursued by Athens in this period were to a serious extent Pericles' policies; but our sources associate him with enough items in both internal and external affairs to justify the more usual assumption that, although Pericles can never have been sure that a particular vote in the assembly would go as he wanted, the assembly's votes did go as he wanted more often than not.

After the death of Cimon, leadership of the opposition to Pericles is said to have passed to one of Cimon's relatives, Thucydides son of Melesias (for a possible reconstruction of the relationship see fig. 2). According to Plutarch, Thucydides was more a man of the agora and a politician, was responsible for a polarisation of the Athenians into democrats and oligarchs, and made his upper-class supporters sit together in the assembly to form a more effective block. He pressed Pericles particularly on the building programme (and threats against Athenian offenders in some imperial decrees may suggest that he attacked other aspects of the empire); but the assembly backed Pericles, and when an ostracism was held it was Thucydides who was expelled (Plut. *Per.* 11–14). Plutarch has tried to reconcile his differing sources by claiming that at first Pericles was one competing politician among several, but after Thucydides' ostracism he was

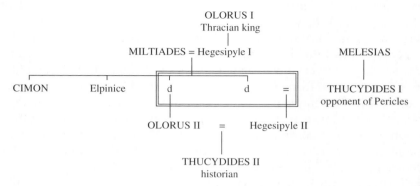

Fig. 2 Thucydides the opponent of Pericles and Thucydides the historian (relationships inside the box are conjectural)

unchallenged leader and was general every year for fifteen years (*Per.* 16. iii): it would be dangerous to count back from his death and insist that Thucydides must have been ostracised in 444/3, but it must have happened about that time. Although Pericles was not himself ostracised, it is possible that an associate of his was: Damon, said to have been his teacher (e.g. Plut. *Per.* 4. i–iv; in *Ath. Pol.* 27. iv and *Per.* 9. ii Damonides is probably an error for Damon son of Damonides). Another man perhaps ostracised about this time was a celebrated athlete, whose political stance if any is not known, Callias son of Didymias ([Andoc.] IV. *Alcibiades* 32). Comedians other than Aristophanes mocked Pericles for his elongated head (a collection of quotations in Plut. *Per.* 3. iii–vii); Aristophanes' description of him as 'the Olympian' (*Ach.* 530–1) may refer to his manner and/or to his predominant position in Athens; Eupolis long after his death referred to him as an exceptional orator (fr. 94 Kock = 98 Edmonds = 102 Kassel & Austin, from his *Demes*).

   After the removal of Thucydides, Pericles did not in fact have everything his own way. Plutarch, misled by Aristophanes' *Peace* (cf. pp. 84–5), links with the outbreak of the Peloponnesian War a series of attacks which seem rather to belong to the early 400's (*Per.* 31. ii–32). Pheidias, on completing his statue of Athena in 438/7, was accused of embezzlement and fled from Athens; he obtained a new commission, to produce a statue of Zeus at Olympia, but ended his life in trouble there in 432/1 (cf. Philoch. *FGrH* 121 ~ Fornara 116. A – but the archons' names have been corrupted in that text and Plutarch badly garbles the story). Pericles' mistress, Aspasia of Miletus, was prosecuted by Hermippus (or, since he was a comic poet, perhaps simply attacked in a comedy) for impiety: since she bore Pericles a son who held office in 410/09, the liaison began not later than 441, and we might expect an attack when it was comparatively new. (According to schol. Ar. *Ach.* 67 ~ Fornara 111, a decree 'concerning not comedying' was in force from 440/39 to 437/6, but we do not know precisely what it forbade.) Diopithes, who seems to have been a religious zealot, was the author of a decree making it an offence 'not to believe in divine things or to teach about things up in the air', apparently aimed at views like those caricatured in Aristophanes' *Clouds*, and said to have been aimed at another Milesian friend of Pericles, the philosopher Anaxagoras. The evidence for Anaxagoras' career is very muddled, but it is possible that he was prosecuted for impiety, possible that that happened in 437/6, and even possible that the prosecutor was Cleon (on whom see pp. 119–21; but an alternative attribution was to Thucydides: for both see Diog. Laert. II. 12).

Finally, Plutarch mentions a prosecution of Pericles himself. A decree proposed by Dracontides required him to submit his accounts to the *prytaneis* and to undergo an archaic, religious form of trial, for which Hagnon substituted an ordinary trial in a *dikasterion*. The charge appears to have been financial; we may guess that it was connected with the charge against Pheidias, and, since we hear no more about it, that Pericles was acquitted. If these attacks are to be dated to the early 430's, they cannot be linked with Thucydides, who will have been out of Athens. In any case, attacks on Pericles' intellectual friends are more likely to have come from the democratic end of the spectrum: Cleon may have been the prosecutor of Anaxagoras, and Hermippus in one of his comedies referred to Pericles' being attacked by Cleon (Plut. *Per.* 33. viii). In Aristophanes' *Knights* (128–49 with schol.) Cleon the 'leather-seller' is preceded by two other 'sellers': it looks as if Cleon and men like him were already making their presence felt in the 430's.

However, Thucydides the historian says nothing anywhere about opposition to Pericles, except in connection with his strategy for the Peloponnesian War (cf. p. 113), but presents him as an unchallenged leader.

External Affairs

The one episode after the Thirty Years' Peace which Thucydides mentions in his survey of the growth of Athenian power is the war against Samos, in 440–439 (I. 115. ii–117). Samos and Miletus were both laying claim to Priene, on the Asiatic mainland north of Miletus, and when Samos gained the upper hand Miletus with the support of some dissident Samians invoked Athens. Athens (according to Plut. *Per.* 24. i, 25. i, after unsuccessfully calling on the Samians to go to arbitration) intervened in Samos, taking hostages, installing a garrison and setting up a democracy; but fugitive Samians obtained the support of Pissuthnes the satrap of Sardis and regained control; Byzantium revolted against Athens in support of Samos. Athens sent sixty ships under Pericles, and then a further forty from Athens and twenty-five from Chios and Lesbos (it appears that by now Samos, Lesbos and Chios were the only members of the Delian League still contributing ships: cf. *Ath. Pol.* 24. ii), and they won a battle, landed on the island and began to besiege the city. On learning that the Persians' Phoenician fleet was to come to support Samos, Pericles went with part of his force to deal with that, and in his absence the Samians won a battle and gained

control of the sea. He returned and recovered control; he received further reinforcements; and after a nine-month siege the Samians were defeated in another
sea-battle and surrendered. They had to demolish part of their walls, to surrender their ships, to give hostages and to refund Athens' expenditure on the
war (what their obligation was after that is not certain, but they were not
assessed for tribute in the usual way). Literary texts point to a figure of 1,200
tal. (Isoc. XV. *Antid.* 111, Diod. Sic. XII. 28. iii, Nep. XIII. *Timoth.* 1. ii). An
inscription recording payments from the treasury of Athena for the war has
items totalling 1,400 tal. or slightly more (M&L 55 = *IG* i³ 363 ~ Fornara 113);
in 434/3 a decree will note that a sum of 3,000 tal. due to the treasury of Athena
has been paid; and it is perhaps best to assume that for this war the Athenians
began the practice of borrowing from the temple treasuries, and that in 434/3
this and other loans were repaid (cf. pp. 91–3). Probably, as at the beginning
of the episode, Athens also installed a democracy (cf. p. 143; what we have of
the inscribed settlement, M&L 56 = *IG* i³ 48 ~ Fornara 115, is too fragmentary
to decide that question, but the text seems to have been more moderate in its
language than texts of a few years earlier).

Thucydides does not mention it here, but in his account of the debate at
Athens over Corcyra in 433 (cf. p. 83) he has the Corinthians claim that in the
Peloponnesian League they had voted successfully against a proposal to support
Samos (I. 40. v): for the matter to have gone that far, Sparta must have been
in favour of supporting Samos, although that would have been a breach of the
Thirty Years' Peace. Pissuthnes did support Samos, and that will have been a
breach of the Peace of Callias if there was one (cf. p. 48). This was a major
episode: Athens had to use very large forces; it came nearer than at any other
time to being defeated by a rebellious ally (cf. Thuc. VIII. 76. iv); the Peloponnesians might have become involved and the Persians did (enabling or
requiring Athens to show that it would still act vigorously against the Persians
if the need arose).

Scattered pieces of evidence indicate that, although the Athenians were
excluded from mainland Greece proper by the Thirty Years' Peace, they
remained interested in expanding where they could. Thucydides does not
mention them in his account of the Pentecontaetia, though it would have
strengthened his case that the Peloponnesian War arose from Athens' power and
Sparta's fear of it (cf. pp. 81–2) if he had done so.

In the west, which was a potential source of grain as well as more generally
an opportunity for expansion, Athens' decree concerning an alliance with
Egesta in Sicily is to be dated not 458/7 but 418/7 (cf. pp. 45, 132). In Italy
there were various attempts at refounding Sybaris, a city which had been
destroyed by its neighbour Croton in 510. On the last of those occasions the
Sybarites appealed to Sparta and to Athens for support and Athens responded;
in this refoundation there was trouble between the original Sybarites and the
newcomers, from which the newcomers emerged victorious; they then made a
fresh start, with the new name Thurii, and sent for more settlers from Greece.
The new Thurii had a democratic constitution, with ten tribes (one named

after Athens, the other after different Greek peoples); its laws are attributed to Charondas (but he was a sixth-century legislator: perhaps some of his laws were adopted in Thurii) and the philosopher Protagoras; the men in charge of the foundation were Lampon (an associate of Pericles and a religious specialist) and Xenocritus (Diod. Sic. XII. 9–11[–18]). Diodorus makes this (after another western item in ch. 8) his main episode for the year 446/5, and includes more on Thurii in his brief entries for the next two years (XII. 22, 23). The orator Lysias is said to have been one of those who joined in the colony, in 444/3 or 443/2 ([Plut.] *X Orat.* 835 C–D; Dion. Hal. 453. *Lys.* 1), and Thucydides son of Melesias may have gone to Thurii when he was ostracised *c.*444/3 (cf. Anon *Life of Thucydides* 7); another famous Greek who is said to have joined the colony is Herodotus (Arist. *Rh.* III. 1409 A 28): it is commonly supposed that the last refoundation of Sybaris was in 446/5 and the new foundation of Thurii in 444/3, though neither date is secure. Settlers came from many places, though Peloponnesians were limited to individuals and places opposed to Sparta. As his main item for 434/3 Diodorus reports conflict within Thurii over who should be regarded as the founder of the city; Delphi was consulted and ascribed the foundation to Apollo – essentially a victory for those who did not want to be beholden to Athens (XII. 35. i–iii); in 415–413 supporters of Athens had the upperhand (e.g. Thuc. VI. 104. ii, VII. 57. xi), but Thurii supported Sparta afterwards (e.g. VIII. 35. i).

It was perhaps about the same time that the Athenians were involved further north, in a refoundation of Neapolis (Strabo 246. V. iv. 7, Lycoph. 732–7 with schol.). In 433/2 Athens was to renew alliances with Rhegium, on the toe of Italy, and Leontini, in Sicily (cf. pp. 83–4): the lettering would support a date in the mid 440's for the original alliance with Rhegium, slightly earlier for Leontini.

In the north-west of Greece (on the mainland but outside the area in which Sparta was interested), at a date which is uncertain but could be in the early 430's, an Athenian force under Phormio assisted in a refoundation of Amphilochian Argos, in opposition to Corinth's colony Ambracia (Thuc. II. 68. ii–viii: cf. p. 102).

In the Aegean world, after the failure of earlier attempts (cf. pp. 19–20), in 437/6 the Athenians at last succeeded in establishing a colony at Amphipolis, in an area important for timber and for silver, where the Strymon could be crossed inland from Eïon; again the settlers were a mixture of Athenians and non-Athenians (Thuc. IV. 102. iii, Diod. Sic. XII. 32. iii, schol. Aeschin. II. *Embassy* 31 ~ Fornara 62). Hagnon was in charge of the foundation; and, unusually, he appears to have been venerated there as a hero during his lifetime (Thuc. V. 11. i with Hornblower's commentary). Amphipolis was to be lost by the Athenians in 424/3, and it was a cause of great annoyance that they never recovered it (cf. pp. 111–12, 114, 299–300, 313–14).

Pericles himself is said to have led an expedition to the Black Sea, founding a colony on the south coast at Sinope (Plut. *Per.* 20. i–ii, cf. the casualty list *IG* i³ 1180); the colony at nearby Amisus (Plut. *Luc.* 19. vii, Strabo 547. XII. iii. 14) may belong to the same occasion, as may a colony at Astacus in the Propontis, reported by Diodorus from his chronological source under 434/3 (XII. 34. v [name emended], cf. Strabo 563. XII. iv. 2). It may also have been in the 430's that Athens first made an alliance with the Spartocid kings of the Cimmerian Bosporus (the Crimea): a new dynasty was founded by Spartocus I c.438/7, and Athens made an alliance with his son Satyrus I, who succeeded him c.433/2 (R&O 64. 20–4).

NOTE ON FURTHER READING

On Pericles' citizenship law see Patterson, *Pericles' Citizenship Law of 451–50 BC*; A. L. Boegehold, 'Perikles' Citizenship Law of 451/0 BC', in Boegehold and Scafuro (eds.), *Athenian Identity and Civic Ideology*, 57–66. On the working of the democracy in general, Stockton, *The Classical Athenian Democracy*, is concerned with the fifth century and earlier; Sinclair, *Democracy and Participation in Athens*, spans the late fifth century and the fourth; Hansen, *The Athenian Democracy in the Age of Demosthenes*, concentrates on the fourth century but contains much that is applicable to the fifth. See also Rhodes, 'Political Activity in Classical Athens', *JHS* cvi 1986, 132–44, reprinted in Rhodes (ed.), *Athenian Democracy*, ch. 7 (a detailed study); 'Who Ran Democratic Athens?', in *Polis and Politics . . . M. H. Hansen*, 465–77, reprinted in Robinson (ed.), *Ancient Greek Democracy*, 201–11 (a broad-brush treatment).

On the modified system for appointing generals, K. J. Dover, 'δέκατος αὐτός', *JHS* lxxx 1960, 61–77 = his *The Greeks and their Legacy*, 159–80, established that one general was not superior to the other nine; on why and how the system was modified see L. G. Mitchell, 'A New Look at the Election of Generals at Athens', *Klio* lxxxii 2000, 344–60. For ostracism see the note at the end of chapter 4.

On all buildings in Athens Travlos, *Pictorial Dictionary of Ancient Athens*, is invaluable. The most up-to-date books on the acropolis are Hurwit, *The Athenian Acropolis*, and *The Acropolis in the Age of Pericles*; the multi-volume publication of the agora excavations includes as vol. xiv Thompson and Wycherley, *The Agora of Athens*. On the temple of Athena Nike see Mark, *The Sanctuary of Athena Nike in Athens*; I. M. Shear, 'The Western Approach to the Athenian Akropolis', *JHS* cxix 1999, 86–127 at 120–5. On Pericles' odeum see M. Miller, *Athens and Persia in the Fifth Century BC*, ch. 9. For a general reconsideration of the dates of fifth-century buildings in Attica see M. M. Miles, 'A Reconstruction of the Temple of Nemesis at Rhamnous', *Hesp.* lviii 1989, 131–249 at 221–35.

Against the view that all Athens' policies were Pericles' policies see, e.g., Gomme, *Historical Commentary on Thucydides*, i. 306–7. On opposition to Pericles see, for the 440's, H. T. Wade-Gery, 'Thucydides Son of Melesias', *JHS* lii 1932, 205–27 = his *Essays in Greek History*, 239–70; A. Andrewes, 'The Opposition to Perikles', *JHS* xcviii 1978, 1–8; for the 430's, F. J. Frost, 'Pericles, Thucydides the Son of Melesias, and Athenian Politics before the War', *Hist.* xiii 1964, 385–99, and 'Pericles and Dracontides', *JHS* lxxxiv 1964, 69–72; R. W. Wallace, 'Private Lives and Public Enemies', in Boegehold and Scafuro (eds.), *Athenian Identity and Civic Ideology*, 127–55. On attempts to restrain comedians see A. H. Sommerstein, 'Comedy and the Unspeakable', in *Law, Rhetoric and Comedy in Classical Athens . . . D. M. MacDowell*, ch. 13.

7

The Greeks in the West: The Rise of Syracuse

500	475	450	425	400	375	350	325	300

480	battle of Himera
478/7	death of Gelon
467	death of Hieron
466	end of Syracusan tyranny
c.446/5	last refoundation of Sybaris
c.444/3	refoundation of Sybaris as Thurii

Introduction

In Sicily Thucydides (VI. 2–5) distinguished among the native peoples between Elymans, in the far west of the island (in particular, at Egesta), allegedly refugees from Troy; Sicans, whom he believed to be the original inhabitants; and Sicels, whom he believed to have arrived from Italy and to have pushed the Sicans into the western part of the island. These lived mostly in the interior, and by the fifth century the different native peoples were still perceived as different; they had to some extent been hellenised, more so in the east than in the west, and the Elymans not until the fifth century; otherwise they are not archaeologically distinguishable. The term Siceliots was used of the Greek settlers who had founded cities at various sites around the coast, except in the far west, between c.735 and c.625. There were also Phoenician settlements in the far west: Carthage claimed Sicily in its treaty of c.509 with Rome (Polyb. III.

22–3); but if the Carthaginians thought of expansion when they accepted an invitation to intervene in a dispute among the Greeks in 480, their defeat prevented it (cf. below), and after that they did not attempt it until the end of the fifth century (cf. p. 275). Similarly, in Italy the various native peoples could be referred to collectively as Itals (most important were the Etruscans, from whom Rome made itself independent c.509), in contrast to the Italiots, Greeks who had occupied sites from the Bay of Naples southwards from somewhat before 750 onwards. The native Italians were not hellenised as the native Sicilians were.

From the original foundation of Greek colonies to the late sixth century we have references to episodes and rulers in different places but cannot put together a connected account. That continues to be the case in the fifth century for Italy, but for Sicily we become better informed with a series of tyrants in Gela, beginning c.505, whose growing power culminated in their acquiring Syracuse c.485, and who became friends or enemies of other tyrants. Events down to 480 are dealt with by Herodotus, in connection with the war which prevented Gelon of Syracuse from helping the Greeks of Greece against the Persians. From 480 we have Diodorus, who may have used Ephorus for the western Greeks as for the rest of his fifth- and fourth-century Greek history (though some have thought that for western matters he used the Sicilian Timaeus as well or instead: cf. pp. 273–4), and who on Sicily has a fair amount of information; and, since many of Pindar's odes were written for Sicilian tyrants, we have them and a substantial body of material in ancient commentaries on them. Diodorus' narrative dates are no more secure for the west than for Greece, but he and Aristotle's *Politics* (V. 1315 B 34–8) have regnal years for the Syracusan tyrants, and some firm dates are given by victor lists and the commentaries on Pindar (where there is no other dating evidence, I give Diodorus' dates in brackets).

After previous tyrants had made Gela, a Rhodian/Cretan colony on the south coast, the most powerful city in the eastern part of Sicily, Gelon, the first ruler from what appears to have been one of the leading families of Gela, acquired the best site, the Corinthian colony of Syracuse on the east coast, c.485. He made that his principal city, transporting people from other cities to build it up and leaving his brother Hieron in charge of Gela. He formed marriage alliances with another family of tyrants, based in Acragas (west of Gela on the south coast: it had been settled from Gela): he himself married Demarete, daughter of the tyrant Theron, and Theron married a daughter of Gelon's brother Polyzelus. Opposed to this southern alliance was a northern alliance based on Rhegium, a Euboean colony on the toe of Italy (now controlling another Euboean colony, originally called Zancle but whose name he had changed to Messene, on the Sicilian side of the strait), and Himera (on the north coast of Sicily, founded from Zancle). Anaxilas of Rhegium married a daughter of Terillus of Himera, and after Theron captured Himera and expelled Terillus, and Terillus and Anaxilas successfully appealed to Carthage for support, a major war was fought in 480. The result was a victory at Himera for the southern alliance, and for Gelon in particular; Anaxilas was brought into the Syracusan

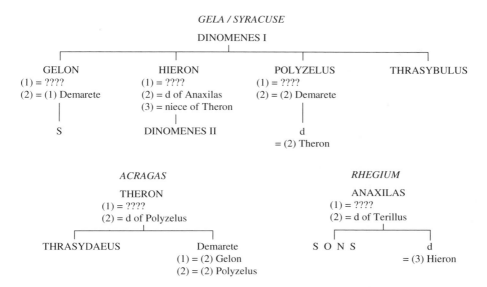

GELA / SYRACUSE

DINOMENES I

GELON	HIERON	POLYZELUS	THRASYBULUS
(1) = ????	(1) = ????	(1) = ????	
(2) = (1) Demarete	(2) = d of Anaxilas	(2) = (2) Demarete	
	(3) = niece of Theron		
S	DINOMENES II	d	
		= (2) Theron	

ACRAGAS

THERON
(1) = ????
(2) = d of Polyzelus

THRASYDAEUS	Demarete
	(1) = (2) Gelon
	(2) = (2) Polyzelus

RHEGIUM

ANAXILAS
(1) = ????
(2) = d of Terillus

S O N S	d
	= (3) Hieron

Fig. 3 Tyrants of Gela/Syracuse, Acragas, Rhegium

orbit, and Hieron married his daughter. The tyrants were active exponents of the aristocratic virtues: they competed successfully in the great games; they attracted poets to their courts, in particular to celebrate their victories; they built impressive temples to the gods. They could be referred to as monarchs in poetry for local audiences, but in inscriptions at the major Greek sanctuaries, with the exception of Polyzelus (below), they identified themselves simply as (e.g.) Gelon son of Dinomenes, the Syracusan (M&L 28 ~ Fornara 54).

One earlier episode is worth mentioning here for its relevance to fifth-century history. In 510 the legendarily rich Sybaris, under the instep of Italy, was destroyed by its neighbour Croton (both were Achaean colonies). Dorieus, half-brother of the Spartan king Cleomenes, who avoided Sparta after Cleomenes became king, fought on the side of Croton, and then went to north-western Sicily, intending to found a colony there, but was defeated and killed by a combination of the Phoenicians and Egesta.

Hieron and Theron

Gelon died in 478/7: according to Diodorus (XI. 38) he insisted that he should be buried in accordance with a law forbidding elaborate funerals, but the people gave him a worthy tomb and a hero's cult: his victory over the Carthaginians was an impressive achievement, and compensated for the unpopularity which his earlier population movements had caused. Presumably Gelon's son was

Ill. 6 Polyzelus' bronze charioteer at Delphi. Erich Lessing/AKG Images

too young to succeed: Hieron moved from Gela to rule in Syracuse; the next brother, Polyzelus, took over the widowed Demarete, and also succeeded Hieron in Gela. (It was Polyzelus who, after a chariot-race victory probably in 478 or 474, dedicated the monument at Delphi from which the bronze charioteer survives – cf. ill. 6; whereas Gelon and Hieron dedicated simply as individuals, the original version of Polyzelus' epigram described him as 'lord of Gela', but that was later replaced by a different text [*SIG*³ 35. D; recent discussions summarised *SEG* xl 427].)

Before long, Polyzelus was seen by Hieron as a rival to be eliminated. An opportunity was provided when men trying to refound Sybaris, besieged by Croton, appealed for help to Hieron. Hieron sent Polyzelus with a force of mercenaries, hoping that he would be killed either by Croton or by the mercenaries. We have differing accounts of what then happened. According to Diodorus, Polyzelus refused to go and fled to Acragas; war between Acragas and Syracuse seemed likely, but was avoided when envoys from Himera protested to Hieron against the rule of Theron's son Thrasydaeus, but Hieron betrayed the envoys to Theron, who then arranged a reconciliation between Hieron and Polyzelus. According to Timaeus, Polyzelus did go to Sybaris but was successful and was not killed, and he fled to Acragas later when accused of plotting revolution; Theron marched out against Syracuse, and war was prevented by the mediation of the poet Simonides (Diod. Sic. XI. 48. iii–viii, 49. iii [476/5]; Timaeus *FGrH* 566 F 93. b *ap.* schol. Pind. *Ol.* ii. 15 [29]).

While Theron built up his power in the west of the island (Paus. V. 25. v reports a victory over Motya, and coins of Motya and Egesta show the influence of Acragas), Hieron took an interest in Italy. He prevented Anaxilas of Rhegium from making war on neighbouring Locri (Pind. *Pyth.* ii. 18–20 with schol. [36–8]). Anaxilas had fortified the straits against Etruscan raiders (Strabo 256–7. VI. i. 5); and Hieron responded to an appeal from Cumae for support against the Etruscans, who were perhaps in alliance with the Carthaginians, and won a great victory (Diod. Sic. XI. 51 [474/3]; Pind. *Pyth.* i. 71–5 with schol. 71 [137]; dedication of bronze helmets at Olympia, in the name of 'Hieron son of Dinomenes and the Syracusans', M&L 29 ~ Fornara 64). Presumably after that, Syracuse established a colony on the island of Pithecusae (Strabo 248. V. iv. 9). In Sicily, Hieron indulged in further population movement: the inhabitants of Naxos and Catana were transported south to Leontini; and in 476 Catana had its territory enlarged and was refounded with new settlers as Aetna – to be a kingdom for Hieron's son Dinomenes, at first under the guardianship of Chromius, a brother-in-law of Gelon (Diod. Sic. XI. 49. i–ii; schol. Pind. *Nem.* i. *inscr.*; Strabo 268. VI. ii. 3). When Dinomenes was proclaimed as king, in 470, Pindar wrote *Pythian* i for the occasion, and Aeschylus wrote the tragedy (not now extant) *Women of Aetna* (among other poets who visited Hieron's court are Simonides [cf. above] and Bacchylides, and we hear of two Syracusan poets, Epicharmus and Phormus).

But by the end of the 470's the tyrants were on their way out. In Acragas the popular Theron died *c.*472. Thrasydaeus, who had already incurred unpopularity in Himera, moved to Acragas and made himself unpopular there; according to Diodorus he planned to attack Syracuse, but Hieron made the first move, and attacked Acragas and defeated it (perhaps 470). Thrasydaeus fled to Megara in Greece, where he was condemned to death; Acragas, and presumably Himera, acquired constitutional government (Diodorus says 'democracy') and treaties with Hieron (XI. 53 [472/1]). Anaxilas of Rhegium died in the 470's, leaving his sons under a regent called Micythus, who founded a colony at Pyxus, on the west coast of Italy (XI. 59. iv [471/0]). Later Hieron encouraged the sons to take over: according to Herodotus, Micythus was expelled; Diodorus has a story that he behaved so unselfishly that they asked him to continue, but he insisted on resigning, and spent the rest of his life in Tegea, in Greece, in high repute (Hdt. VII. 170. iii–iv; Diod. Sic. XI. 52, 66. i–iii [476/5, 467/6]).

Hieron himself, after several years of illness (cf. Pind. *Pyth.* ii, cf. *Pyth.* i. 46 sqq. with schol. 46 [89]), died in 467, at Aetna, where he was honoured as founding hero. Our sources now say nothing of Polyzelus. Thrasybulus, the last brother, took over: Hieron had been oppressive (Arist. *Pol.* V. 1313 B 11–16 refers to his spies), but Thrasybulus was much worse; the whole city united against him (at first, ostensibly in support of Gelon's son: cf. Arist. *Pol.* V. 1312 B 9–16); there was a civil war, in which he relied on Aetna and his mercenaries, while the Syracusans gained help from many cities, Sicel as well as Greek. Thrasybulus was defeated at sea and on land, and, within a year of his succession (466), he had resigned the tyranny and retired to Locri (Diod. Sic. XI. 66. iv, 67–8 [467/6, 466/5]).

Finally, Rhegium and Messene expelled the sons of Anaxilas (Diod. Sic. XI. 76. v [461/0]).

Sicily after the Tyrants

After the departure of Thrasybulus the Syracusans established 'democracy', instituted a cult of Zeus Eleutherios ('of Freedom') and liberated other cities. Diodorus claims that this was a time of peace and prosperity (XI. 68. v–vi, 72. i–ii). For 'democracy' in Syracuse cf. Arist. *Pol.* V. 1316 A 29–33; and Syracuse was certainly democratic by 415 (cf. pp. 133–4). Temples in Himera, Syracuse (Athena) and Gela (Temple C = Athena), begun after the victory of 480, had probably been completed by the end of the Dinomenid tyranny. In Acragas work on Sicily's largest temple, the temple of Olympian Zeus, begun before 500, was perhaps interrupted for a while and then resumed; less ambitious temples were built later, beginning with Hera Lakinia in the 450's. In the major cities the coin types had not been changed by the tyrants, and were not changed on the overthrow of the tyrants (the 10-drachma silver coins of Syracuse – cf. ill. 7 – formerly identified with the gold coins mentioned by Diodorus after the victory at Himera [XI. 26. iii], are now dated after the tyranny: a suggestion that they were actually named not after Demarete but after the goddess Demeter could still be correct with this dating); but many of the smaller cities adopted new types after the return of their original populations. Rhegium changed from the most recent designs (a mule-car on the obverse and a hare on the reverse) to an earlier obverse used by Anaxilas (a lion's head) and a new reverse (perhaps the legendary founder, Jocastus); while Messene, after a period of uncertainty which saw the issuing of gold coins, and some coins using the old name Zancle, continued with Anaxilas' later designs, but changed its spelling to the Doric Messana.

III. 7   Syracuse: 'Demareteum' (c.460; 10 dr.). Ashmolean Museum, Oxford

In terms of population, however, there was considerable upheaval: those who had been transported by the tyrants from one city to another wanted to return to their original homes and recover their property there; while the tyrants' mercenaries found themselves generally unwelcome, but were eventually allowed to settle in Messana (which may be the occasion for the change to the Doric spelling). Camarina, which had been destroyed by Gelon, was refounded by Gela; Catana was reoccupied by its original population (cf. below), and Aetna migrated to the inland Sicel site of Inessa (Diod. Sic. XI. 72. iii–73 [463/2], 76 [461/0], cf. Thuc. VI. 5. iii, Arist. *Pol.* V. 1303 A 38–B 2, *FGrH* 577 F 1).

Some years later, Diodorus reports that the enrolment of citizens and distribution of land was leading to strife and upheaval, particularly in Syracuse. There, when a man called Tyndarides tried to make himself tyrant, he and his supporters were lynched; after further attempts at tyranny the Syracusans instituted 'petalism' (voting with olive leaves), a device similar to the Athenians' ostracism for removing citizens perceived as dangerous; after a few petalisms the leading citizens thought it safer to keep out of politics, and there was a risk of a populist revolution, until petalism was abolished (XI. 86. iii–87 [454/3]). It appears that the popular leaders of this period may have been the first to cultivate a sophisticated rhetorical style (Diod. Sic. XI. 87. v, cf. Cic. *Brut.* 12). In Acragas the philosopher Empedocles is said to have been influential: reliable details are hard to come by, but he may have reconstituted the council of one thousand to make it more democratic; it is said that he refused an offer of kingship, but eventually he was forced to leave the city and fled to the Peloponnese (Diog. Laert. VIII. 63, 66, 71, cf. Plut. *Adv. Col.* 1126 B).

These disturbances provided the opportunity for the rise of the only Sicel leader who is named by our Greek sources, Ducetius. He first appears joining

the recently liberated Syracuse in attacking Aetna–Catana, to allow the original population to return (Diod. Sic. XI. 76. iii [461/0]: cf. above); he founded
a city at Menaenum, west of Leontini, and captured Morgantina, further inland
(XI. 78. v [459/8]); he united all the Sicel cities except Hybla, in the south,
under his leadership, and moved Menae (= Menaenum?) to a new site, refounding it as Palice (XI. 88. vi–90. ii [453/2]). Next he captured Aetna–Inessa and
killed its ruler, perhaps still Hieron's son Dinomenes. He invaded the territory
of Acragas, capturing the fort of Motyum and defeating the Acragantine and
Syracusan forces sent against him. After a winter during which they condemned
their general, the Syracusans sent a fresh expedition; Ducetius was defeated in
a major battle, and most of his allies deserted him; and Acragas recaptured
Motyum. Ducetius then fled to Syracuse as a suppliant, and the assembly,
deciding that the rights of suppliants must be respected, sent him to Corinth,
in Greece, with a maintenance grant (XI. 91–2 [451/0]). But that decision was
made without consultation of Acragas: Acragas declared war on Syracuse, and
Ducetius took advantage of that to return to Sicily, with an oracle for the foundation of a colony at Kale Akte, on the north coast. Syracuse defeated Acragas
(XII. 8 [446/5]); Ducetius built up Kale Akte, and might have used that as a
base for renewed expansion, but he died (XII. 29. i [440/39]).

   The defeat of Acragas left Syracuse without a rival as the most powerful
Greek city in Sicily (XII. 26. ii–iv [442/1]). It gradually gained control of Sicel
cities in the interior, ending perhaps by capturing and destroying Palice (XII.
29. ii–iv [440/39]: *Trinakie* in the manuscripts at this point, *Pikenous* at the corresponding point in an epitome): Diodorus claims that it came to control all
the Sicel cities, but Thucydides suggests that some of the cities either soon
defected or were never conquered (Thuc. III. 103. i, IV. 25. ix, VI. 88. iv).
Diodorus' last report on Sicily before the Peloponnesian War is that Syracuse
built 100 triremes, strengthened its other forces and levied more tribute from
the Sicels (XII. 30. i [439/8]) – but he goes on to mention, several years too
early, Athens' intervention in the war between Corinth and Corcyra (cf. p. 82),
and there is no sign of that large navy when Athens sends an expedition to Sicily
in 427 (cf. pp. 103–4), so he may here be anticipating a later development.

   The cities in the west of the island had gone their own way, and their temples
show stylistic influence from Athens rather than from the other Siceliot cities.
Selinus, on the south coast (colonised from Megara Hyblaea, itself destroyed
by Gelon), was busy building temples from the mid sixth century to the mid
fifth: the temple of Hera and temple G are dated to the early fifth century, and
temples A and O to the mid fifth century. At Elyman Egesta, to the north, a
temple of which fragments survive was built about the 450's, and the temple
which survives substantially complete towards the end of the century. The
inscription concerning Egesta's alliance with Athens is to be dated not 458/7
but 418/7 (cf. pp. 45, 132); under 454/3 Diodorus records a war between Egesta
and 'Lilybaeum' – but Lilybaeum did not yet exist, and both Halicyae and
Selinus have been conjectured (XI. 86. ii); Athens made an alliance with
Halicyae, perhaps in the late 430's (cf. pp. 79, 132).

Italy

In the earlier part of this period the Greeks in Italy are mentioned largely for the tyranny of Anaxilas in Rhegium, and for Hieron's victory over the Etruscans in 474 (cf. p. 75). On the coast south of the bay of Naples Posidonia (Paestum, founded from Sybaris) was a prosperous city which built several temples between the mid sixth century and the mid fifth: the so-called temple of Poseidon, in fact more probably Zeus, has stylistic affinities with temples in Himera and Syracuse and was perhaps built after 474.

Under the instep of Italy Sybaris had been destroyed by Croton in 510 (cf. p. 73), but coins show that the site continued to be occupied as a dependency of Croton. There were various attempts at refounding an independent Sybaris: first in the 470's, when Hieron may have sent Polyzelus to support the Sybarites (cf. p. 75); a second time in 453/2, under a man called Thessalus, issuing coins based on those of Sybaris' colonies Laus and Posidonia (Diod. Sic. XI. 90. iii–iv, cf. XII. 10. ii, Hdt. VI. 21. i). Perhaps in 446/5 (on the chronology and the Athenian dimension cf. pp. 68–9) another attempt was made, after an appeal to Sparta and Athens had elicited support from Athens: the coins show that at this stage the city still used the name Sybaris. But the original Sybarites tried to monopolise the best land and the major offices, and this led to fighting in which the newcomers were victorious. They then brought in further settlers from Athens and elsewhere, and, perhaps in 444/3, made a fresh start with the new name Thurii (Diod. Sic. XII. 9–11[–18], cf. Arist. *Pol.* V. 1303 A 31–3, Strabo 263. VI. i. 13). Some of the original Sybarites settled at Sybaris-on-the-Traes, to the south-east, where they issued coins continuing the designs of Posidonia used in 453/2, but after a while they succumbed to the neighbouring Bruttii (Diod. Sic. XII. 22. i [445/4]).

There are signs of Athens' growing interest in the west in the mid fifth century (cf. pp. 68–9). In the 440's it responded to the invitations to the last foundation of Sybaris and to its refoundation as Thurii; perhaps about the same time it took part in a refoundation of Neapolis. In 433/2 Athens was to renew alliances with Rhegium and Leontini: the lettering would support a date in the mid 440's for the original alliance with Rhegium, slightly earlier for Leontini; and it was perhaps in the late 430's that Athens made an alliance with Halicyae near Egesta. But Thurii did not remain within the Athenian orbit: Diodorus reports conflict among the settlers over who should be regarded as the founder of the city; Delphi was consulted and ascribed the foundation to Apollo – essentially a victory for the opponents of Athens (XII. 35. i–iii [434/3]).

There is a wider Italiot context for the foundation of Thurii, whose details are regrettably uncertain. It is claimed that disciples of the philosopher Pythagoras (who migrated from Samos to Croton in the late sixth century, but ended his life at Metapontium) were for a time influential, and made Croton the most powerful of the Italiot cities; that there was later a period of disturbances in which the meeting-houses (*synedria*) of the Pythagoreans were burned; the

Achaeans were brought in as mediators; and that, some time before 417, Croton, 'Sybaris' and Caulonia joined in a league of Zeus Homarios modelled on the Achaean League (Polyb. II. 39. i–vi, cf. Iambl. *V. P.* 249, 255). Thurii is more likely than any of the communities of Sybarites to be the 'Sybaris' which joined in a league that included Croton. The Sabellian tribes were at this time expanding from the interior of southern Italy and putting pressure on the Greeks, and the new Thurii may have been welcome as a contributor to resisting that pressure: there are stories of Thurii's fighting under the Spartan exile Cleandridas against the Lucanians (Polyaenus, *Strat.* II. 10).

Thurii came into conflict with Sparta's colony Taras over a settlement at Siris to which they both laid claim, and Thurii's forces were again commanded by Cleandridas: Taras was finally successful, and moved the settlement to a new site with the new name Heraclea (Diod. Sic. XII. 23. ii [444/3], 36. iv [433/2], Strabo 264. VI. i. 14); it dedicated spear-butts at Olympia to commemorate its victory (M&L 57 ~ Fornara 112).

NOTE ON FURTHER READING

Freeman, *History of Sicily*, is a detailed account based on the literary sources (the earlier part of the fifth century, vol. ii; the period of the Peloponnesian War, vol. iii; from the end of the fifth century to the beginning of the third, reconstructed by A. J. Evans, vol. iv). For a shorter but more up-to-date account see Finley, *Ancient Sicily*.

On the titles of the tyrants in poetry and in inscriptions see S. E. Harrell, 'King or Private Citizen: Fifth-Century Sicilian Tyrants at Olympia and Delphi', *Mnem.*[4] lv 2002, 439–64. On the dates of temples see Mertens, *Der Tempel von Segesta*, 186–205. On the Syracusan 'Demareteum' see R. T. Williams, 'The Demareteion Reconsidered', *NC*[7] xii 1972, 1–11 (not Demarete but Demeter); C. M. Kraay, 'The Demareteion Reconsidered: A Reply', *NC*[7] xii 1972, 13–24 (10-dr. silver coins *c.*465); N. K. Rutter, 'The Myth of the "Damareteion"', *Chiron* xii 1993, 171–88 (hellenistic invention).

For doubts about Syracuse's alleged new ships of 439/8 see Cawkwell, *Thucydides and the Peloponnesian War*, 79, 86.

On Sybaris and Thurii, emphasising the Italian rather than the Athenian background, see N. K. Rutter, 'Diodorus and the Foundation of Thurii', *Hist.* xxii 1973, 155–76.

8
The Peloponnesian War: Origins

500	475	450	425	400	375	350	325	300

435 battle of Leucimme
433 battle of Sybota
432 battle at Potidaea and beginning of siege
432 Sparta and Peloponnesian League decide on war
431 beginning of Peloponnesian War

Thucydides' Explanation

After devoting the opening chapters of his history to arguing that the Peloponnesian War, fought between Sparta and Athens from 431 to 404, was greater than any previous war, Thucydides writes:

> The Athenians and Peloponnesians began it after breaking the Thirty Years' Treaty which they had made after the capture of Euboea. As to why they broke the treaty, I have first written down the grievances (*aitiai*) and disputes (*diaphorai*), so that no one should ever have to enquire from what origin so great a war broke out among the Greeks. The truest reason (*prophasis*), but most concealed in word, I believe to be that the Athenians became powerful, filled the Spartans with fear, and forced them to go to war. But the following were the publicly mentioned grievances on each side, as a result of which they broke the treaty and embarked on the war. (I. 23. iv–vi)

He then gives a narrative of two episodes, concerning Corcyra and Potidaea, which served as grievances (I. 24–66); and of an assembly in Sparta at which Corinth and others urged the Spartans to act, other grievances, concerning Aegina and Megara, were mentioned, an Athenian delegation warned Sparta not to go to war lightly, and the Spartans did decide that Athens was in the wrong and they should go to war. Thucydides ends that section by repeating that Sparta was moved more by fear of Athens' growing power than by the allies' complaints (I. 67–88); and he then, to justify this view, gives his account of the growth of Athens' power during the Pentecontaetia, the (nearly) fifty years since the Persian Wars (I. 89–118. ii). After that he resumes his narrative, with a congress of the Peloponnesian League, which approves Sparta's decision to go to war; with an exchange of propaganda, in which Sparta begins with particular grievances but ends by demanding that Athens should restore their freedom to the Greeks; and with a speech by Pericles in Athens claiming that Athens was well prepared, and that if it were to give way on the grievances Sparta would come back with others (I. 118. iii–146).

Despite Thucydides' hopes, subsequent generations have not accepted his account as definitive, but have been provoked to ask a variety of questions: in particular, what were his intentions in operating with two kinds of explanation? why, among the four grievances, did he single out two for detailed treatment and say so little about the others? what messages did he mean to convey about the responsibility of Athens, Sparta and Corinth for the war, and should we agree with him? It will be best to look in more detail at what he reports, and then to return to the broader questions.

The Grievances and Disputes

Corcyra (I. 24–55) was a colony of Corinth on an island off the north-west coast of Greece, and Epidamnus, on the mainland further north, was a joint colony of Corcyra and Corinth. When the democrats of Epidamnus expelled the oligarchs, and the oligarchs joined with the neighbouring Taulantians in attacking Epidamnus, the democrats appealed to Corcyra, but Corcyra (which, though comparatively democratic, had stronger links with the oligarchs) refused to help; and the democrats then appealed to Corinth. Fifth-century Corinth liked to maintain close and friendly links with its colonies, but had not succeeded with Corcyra, so it was glad to respond. Corinth sent fresh settlers to Epidamnus; Corcyra besieged the city; after Corcyra defeated the Corinthians in a naval battle off Leucimme, at the south end of Corcyra, Epidamnus capitulated to Corcyra. If we count back in Thucydides from the beginning of the Peloponnesian War, we obtain dates of 435 for Leucimme and the surrender of Epidamnus, and, supported by inscriptions, of 433 for what followed (but Diodorus narrates this affair under 439/8 and 436/5).

Each side devoted 434 to further preparations; in the spring of 433 a deputation from each went to Athens, and Thucydides gives a debate. The Corcyraeans claim that, as they were not listed as allies of either side in the Thirty Years' Peace, they are entitled to join either side now; and that Athens, Corinth and Corcyra have the three best navies in Greece, and since war between Athens and the Peloponnesians is brewing it will be to Athens' advantage to add Corcyra's navy to its own. The Corinthians reply that Corcyra's previous neutrality is a sign not of virtue but of wickedness, that they should be free to deal with Corcyra as they had supported leaving Athens free to deal with Samos (cf. p. 68 – but the cases were not parallel, since Samos was recognised in the Thirty Years' Peace as a member of the Athenian bloc), and that the coming war is 'still uncertain'. The Athenians devoted two days to the debate: on the first they listened to the speeches, and were inclined to favour Corinth, but on the second day they decided to make a purely defensive alliance with Corcyra. (Thucydides was probably present, and must have known more than he tells us: which Athenians changed their minds? and why? and what was Pericles' position? Probably Pericles wanted to support Corcyra, as Plutarch claims [*Per.* 29. i], but Thucydides says nothing that would detract from his view of the Athenians' unanimously following Pericles' lead.) In making a purely defensive alliance the Athenians were hoping to keep their hands clean even if they were drawn into fighting against Corinth; and when they intervened in the battle (below) they insisted that they were not breaking the Thirty Years' Peace.

Athens originally sent just ten ships, under three generals one of whom was Cimon's son Lacedaemonius (the same generals are named in the first half of M&L 61 = *IG* i³ 364 ~ Fornara 126, as drawing money for their expedition from the treasury of Athena): Plutarch regards his appointment as a move by Pericles to humiliate him, but more probably, if he had inherited his father's opposition to Pericles (which is not certain), the appointment results from the strength of Pericles' opponents in the assembly. In a battle at Sybota, between the south end of Corcyra and the mainland, the Corinthians were getting the upper hand and the Athenians had to intervene to prevent them from landing on the island. By then Athens had decided to send a further twenty ships (on the generals there is a disagreement between I. 51. iv and the second half of the inscription, and Thucydides is probably to be convicted of an error), and on their arrival the Corinthians withdrew.

Thucydides comments on the Athenians' decision to support Corcyra that they really were expecting a war with the Peloponnesians (I. 44. ii). Probably in 434/3, so at the same time as or slightly before the alliance with Corcyra, by the decrees of Callias the Athenians put their finances in good order, paying outstanding debts to the sacred treasuries, combining a number of small treasuries in a treasury of the Other Gods, winding up the building programme on the acropolis (as a result of which the Propylaea was left unfinished), and resolving to spend further surpluses on the dockyards and walls (M&L 58 = *IG* i³ 52 ~ Fornara 119: cf. pp. 91–2). In 433/2 they renewed permanent alliances which they had made earlier with Rhegium and Leontini (M&L 63–4 = *IG* i³ 53–4 ~ Fornara 124–5, where the original preambles have been replaced with preambles naming that year's archon). It does indeed appear that as early as

433 the Athenians were envisaging a major war to which the west would be relevant.

The second grievance reported by Thucydides concerns Potidaea (I. 56–66), on the western prong of Chalcidice, a tribute-paying member of the Delian League but a colony of Corinth. He writes as if the Athenians decided to put pressure on Potidaea because of its Corinthian connections, but he goes on to show that they were also worried about the influence in the region of king Perdiccas of Macedon (whose attitude to Athens fluctuated but was currently hostile), and Potidaea's tribute record suggests that the pressure had begun some years earlier. Athens ordered Potidaea to demolish part of its city wall, send hostages and stop receiving the annual magistrates from Corinth whom (remarkably) it was still receiving. Potidaea protested to Athens, in vain, and appealed to Sparta, which promised to invade Attica if Athens attacked Potidaea (but did not do so until the war proper began in 431). In 432 (but Diodorus' date is 435/4), after paying their tribute in the spring, Potidaea and its neighbours revolted, many coming together in nearby Olynthus; Athens sent two expeditions, which went first to Macedon and then to Potidaea. This time it was Corinth which tried to keep its hands clean, sending not an official force but a body of volunteers and mercenaries (cf. 'privately' in I. 66). There was a battle, in which the Athenians were victorious; they settled down to an expensive siege, which lasted until Potidaea capitulated in 430/29 (cf. p. 111).

Next Thucydides reports a Spartan assembly (I. 67–88), at which Corinth and other members of the Peloponnesian League urged Sparta to take action. Here two other grievances were mentioned. Aegina, in the Saronic Gulf, complained that Athens was not allowing it the autonomy promised in 'the treaty' (I. 67. ii, cf. 139. i, 140. iii). Thucydides gives no indication of the basis for the claim, not even whether 'the treaty' was the Thirty Years' Peace or a separate treaty between Athens and Aegina (IG i^3 38 is too small a fragment to be helpful; in 432 Aegina paid less than half of the 30 talents tribute which it had paid at least until 440); but in 431 Athens was to expel the inhabitants of Aegina, alleging that they were 'not least responsible for the war' (II. 27. i: cf. p. 108).

The Megarians, on the Isthmus of Corinth, complained that they were being excluded from the harbours of the Athenian empire and 'the Attic agora' because of a dispute over sacred land in the frontier region near Eleusis and the harbouring of runaway slaves (I. 67. iv, cf. 139. i–ii, 140. iii–iv, 144. ii). Plutarch (*Per.* 29. vii–31. i) shows that this was one of a series of measures, the sequence of which was probably: by a decree of Pericles Athens sent a herald with a moderate statement of Athens' case; then came the exclusion decree; after the Megarians killed a herald called Anthemocritus, a decree of Charinus (which must be dated 431: cf. p. 106) committed Athens to implacable enmity and invasions of the Megarid twice a year. Pericles refused to weaken over Megara (when he insisted that the text of the exclusion decree could not be taken down, an opponent suggested that it should be turned to face the wall). On both occasions when Aristophanes alludes to the causes of the war, he focuses on Megara, with stories (different, and probably both invented: the chorus responds to the second, 'I never heard that before') of Pericles' involvement for disreputable personal reasons (*Acharn.* 514–38, *Peace* 605–18; cf. Cratinus, fr. 38. 44–8 Kassel & Austin) – which were taken seriously by later writers. Thucydides, though he tells us little, indicates that this was the grievance particularly stressed by the Spartans.

Despite an ingenious attempt by de Ste. Croix to argue otherwise, the exclusion decree must be seen as an attempt to prevent Megara from trading with Athens and the empire: the Athenians realised that their control of the sea could be exploited to their own and their friends' advantage and their enemies' disadvantage (cf. pp. 176–7), and Aristophanes in *Acharnians* (535, cf. 719–835) represents the Megarians as starving because of the decree. Megara since the Thirty Years' Peace had been a member of the Peloponnesian League: was Athens breaking the peace? There were no international lawyers, and no standing body which could decide hard cases; the history of the late fifth century shows that a treaty was broken if people chose to regard it as broken, or not if they chose not. The likelihood is that when the peace was made economic sanctions had not been envisaged and so were not explicitly forbidden, and therefore Athens was not breaking the letter of the peace; but it may well have seemed that Athens was overreacting to a small provocation. (Megara had supported Corinth in 435 and 433, but we do not know how long this feud had been going on, and both the first decree and the second may have been earlier than the Corcyraean episode.)

Sparta and Athens

In Thucydides' account of the Spartan assembly a Corinthian speech stresses the Athenians' ambition and contrasts their energy with Sparta's slowness. An Athenian deputation is given permission to speak, refuses to respond to the grievances, emphasises Athens' strength and urges Sparta to think twice before going to war; the empire is justified as the natural exercise of power (I. 72 with 73–81: on this speech cf. pp. 178–9). Of the Spartans, king Archidamus recommends a gradual approach but the ephor Sthenelaidas in a laconic speech insists that Athens is in the wrong so war is necessary – and he gained a very public vote of approval by calling on the Spartans not merely to shout but to stand in different places to declare their opinions.

The Delphic oracle was consulted and gave Sparta its support (I. 118. iii). During the war the Athenians neither stayed away from Delphi nor were debarred from visiting it, but access to and the status of Delphi was the first matter to be mentioned in the truce between Athens and Sparta in 423 and in the Peace of Nicias in 421 (Thuc. IV. 118. i–iii, V. 18. ii).

To commit the Peloponnesian League to war, Sparta had to obtain a majority vote from the members. A congress was held (I. 119–125. i), to which Thucydides assigns a second Corinthian speech, and the members did vote for war.

By now it was fairly late in 432. For the winter of 432/1 Thucydides reports an exchange of propaganda (I. 125. ii–146). The Spartans called on the Athenians to expel those tainted by the curse on the Alcmaeonid family (resulting from the killing of Cylon's supporters when he tried to make himself tyrant, in the seventh century), an attempt to undermine the position of Pericles, whose mother was an Alcmaeonid. Athens responded with Spartan curses, resulting from the death of Pausanias in the 460's (cf. p. 27), perhaps aimed at Pericles' *xenos* Archidamus. Sparta then called for an end to the on-going grievances (the siege of Potidaea, the status of Aegina, and particularly the sanctions against Megara); and finally (in effect invoking Thucydides' 'truest reason') announced that Sparta wanted peace, and there could be peace if Athens would leave the Greeks autonomous (for this theme cf. Thucydides' comment on support for Sparta at the outbreak of the war, II. 8. iv). Thucydides ends book I with the first of the speeches attributed to Pericles: Sparta is refusing Athens' offer to go to arbitration; the grievances are mere pretexts, and if Athens gave way on them Sparta would come back with others; Athens is better prepared than the Peloponnesians, but must not throw away its advantages by fighting in Attica or trying to enlarge the empire; it should reply firmly. As G. W. Hunt put it, in the context of a British warning to Russia in the 1870's,

> We don't want to fight, but by jingo! if we do,
> We've got the ships, we've got the men, we've got the money too.

Athens did reply firmly.

In the spring of 431 the Thebans (allies of Sparta) made a sudden attack on Plataea (geographically in Boeotia, on the route from Thebes to the Peloponnese, but an ally of Athens for nearly a hundred years): the attack misfired and, perhaps in breach of an agreement, the Plataeans killed their captives (Thuc. II. 2–6). This attack allowed the Athenians to claim that the Peloponnesians were in breach of the peace. And so the war began.

Whose Fault?

Formally it was the Peloponnesians who judged that Athens had broken the peace, and who declared war, and in spite of their initial confidence the Spartans were later to feel guilty about this (Thuc. VII. 18. ii); but Thucydides has referred to the grievances of each side against the other (I. 23. vi, 146). Some scholars have thought that he originally concentrated on the grievances and only later came to see the importance of his truest reason, and that book I as we have it has been rewritten in the light of that change; but the book's organisation, though complex, is coherent, and the truest reason is so widespread in book I that it is hard to imagine an earlier version which lacked it. More probably Thucydides was from the beginning operating with two levels of explanation. He was a historian proud of his ability to do better than others, as he made clear in ch. 20, towards the end of the opening section of book I; and in his account of the causes of the war he both emphasised the 'truest reason', which was 'most concealed in word', and gave his own version of the 'publicly mentioned grievances'.

His choice of words for cause, 'grievances and disputes' contrasted with 'reason' (*prophasis*: a person's or a state's reason for acting), need not trouble us: the words are appropriate in their context, but he himself calls the grievances a reason in I. 118. i and 146. What is more important is that the grievances were publicly mentioned while the reason was concealed, and that the reason was truest. The reason is certainly not concealed in book I, from the expectation of war when Athens agrees to support Corcyra to Sparta's final demand. Presumably, when the war had started, other people focused on one or more of the grievances – Aristophanes perhaps reflected public opinion in Athens in blaming Megara and Pericles' obstinacy, the Corinthians perhaps blamed the volunteers who had gone to fight for Potidaea – and Thucydides is showing that he knows better. There are various possible explanations for his giving detailed accounts of two grievances but not of the other two. If Aristophanes is true to Athenian public opinion, Thucydides is perhaps reacting against that; and if the suggestion that Pericles had disreputable personal reasons for not giving way over Megara was widespread, it would not suit Thucydides the admirer of Pericles to dwell on that. Thucydides was also a patriotic Athenian: in his detailed accounts Athens makes an alliance with Corcyra which it is entitled to make, and limits its support so that the conflict with Corinth does not escalate; and it is within its rights in coercing Potidaea as a member of the Delian League: the suspicious reader may wonder if Athens' treatment of Aegina and Megara was harder to justify.

His narrative shows Athens technically in the right over the grievances, and willing to go to arbitration when Sparta was not (but it is easy to score points by offering arbitration when it is unlikely that acceptable arbitrators can be found), and shows a slow Sparta pushed towards war by Corinth (Corinth was indeed the strongest member of the Peloponnesian League after Sparta, but would arguably have seemed less prominent if Thucydides had devoted equal space to all grievances). He traces the growth of Athenian power from the beginning of the Delian League, innocent in intention and accepted by Sparta (but after the Thirty Years' Peace, which tried to establish a balance between Athens and Sparta, he mentions only Athens' war against Samos, whereas to justify his view of the truest reason he should – and could: cf. pp. 68–70 – have done more to show why that treaty did not establish a sustainable balance). Although he formulates his truest reason to state that fear of Athenian power forced Sparta to go to war, the verdict which he has implied to most modern readers is that the Peloponnesians were in the wrong in making war on Athens.

We should not make too much of the Corinthian pressure: it suited Thucydides to contrast Athens' energy with Sparta's slowness, and the Corinthians could actually have made that contrast. However, the view fashionable in the early twentieth century that Athens was in competition with Corinth for control of trade with the west was based on an anachronistic view of trade and the state's interest in it. The willingness of Sparta, or at any rate some Spartans, to support Samos in 440, and the attitude of Sthenelaidas in 432, warn us not to see too much reluctance in Sparta: nearly all those who begin a war like to believe, and to convince others, that they are in the right, and it was the grievances which enabled Sparta to do that. As for Athens . . . my judgment would be that at any rate the Athenians did not try very hard to avoid war. When they could have stayed out of the conflict between Corinth and Corcyra (cf. Thuc. I. 40. iv), allowing them to weaken each other (cf. 44. ii), they chose to make an alliance which could easily and in fact did lead to their fighting against the Corinthians, and at the same time they started preparing for a major war. Potidaea might have been put under pressure in 432 even if there had not been a Corinthian interest there, but what Athens did was bound to annoy Corinth; we know too little about how far back the grievances of Aegina and Megara reached (but the First Peloponnesian War had demonstrated the advantage to Athens of having Megara on its side: cf. pp. 41–5). The Athenian speech in Sparta was not calculated to turn away wrath; the offer of arbitration implies confidence that Athens was in the right and/or that the offer would not be taken up; the message of Pericles' speech was that appeasement would not work, Athens was better prepared than the Peloponnesians, so if the war must come let it come.

I believe that the Athenians, and Pericles in particular, realised that Sparta could not tolerate their continuing and growing power but sooner or later they would have to fight for it; they were certainly not prepared to avoid war by giving up their ambitions; they adopted a high-risk strategy in the hope – which was fulfilled – that the inevitable war would come in circumstances in which they were better prepared than their enemies and could claim to be in the right. Thucydides' judgment about the truest reason is to be accepted, but I should go further than he did on Athens' willingness to provoke war. It was indeed to be a war about the power of Athens.

NOTE ON FURTHER READING

See in general de Ste. Croix, *The Origins of the Peloponnesian War*; Kagan, *The Outbreak of the Peloponnesian War*; also Cawkwell, *Thucydides and the Peloponnesian War*, ch. 2; Lazenby, *The Peloponnesian War*, ch. 2; Pelling, *Literary Texts and the Greek Historian*, chs. 5, 8. The view that a difference can be detected between Thucydides' early and his later view of the causes was supported by A. Andrewes, 'Thucydides and the Causes of the War', *CQ*[2] ix 1959, 223–39; rejected by D. Whitehead, 'Thucydides: Fact-Grubber or Philosopher', *G&R*[2] xxvii 1980, 158–65, Rhodes, 'Thucydides on the Causes of the Peloponnesian War', *Hermes* cxv 1987, 154–65.

On the words *aitia* ('grievance') and *prophasis* ('reason') see particularly de Ste. Croix, *The Origins of the Peloponnesian War*, ch. 2; L. Pearson, '*Prophasis*: A Clarification', *TAPA* ciii 1972, 381–94 = his *Selected Papers*, 120–33.

On the Athenian Decrees proposed by Callias (M&L 58 = *IG* i³ 52 ~ Fornara 119), it has been shown that dating the two decrees to the same day depended on over-bold restoration; but they may still belong to the same year, and, though later dates have been proposed (see, e.g., Samons, *Empire of the Owl*, 113–38), I still believe that the year is 434/3, i.e. before the series of loans to the state recorded in M&L 72 = *IG* i³ 369 (cf. pp. 91–2). J. R. Grant, 'A Note on the Tone of Greek Diplomacy', *CQ*² xv 1965, 261–6, argued that the Athenian speech at Sparta in 432 was not as provocative as modern readers are inclined to think.

On Athens' dispute with Megara, de Ste. Croix, *The Origins of the Peloponnesian War*, ch. 7, advanced an interpretation of the exclusion which has not found acceptance, but I do accept his chronology of the episodes mentioned by Plutarch; for alternative chronologies see C. W. Fornara, 'Plutarch and the Megarian Decree', *YCS* xxiv 1975, 213–28; Cawkwell, *Thucydides and the Peloponnesian War*, 111–14. P. A. Brunt, 'The Megarian Decree', *AJP* lxxii 1951, 269–82 = his *Studies in Greek History and Thought*, ch. 1, stresses that the exclusion decree need not have been very recent when the Megarians complained about it in 432.

The theory of a war to control trade with the west was advanced by Cornford, *Thucydides Mythistoricus*, 1–76, and Grundy, *Thucydides and the History of His Age*, ch. 15; it was answered at the time by G. Dickins, 'The True Cause of the Peloponnesian War', *CQ* v 1911, 238–48; and for a more recent rebuttal see de Ste. Croix, *The Origins of the Peloponnesian War*, ch. 6, esp. 214–20.

9

The Peloponnesian War: Resources and Strategies

500	475	450	425	400	375	350	325	300

434/3 (?)	financial decrees of Callias in Athens
431	outbreak of Peloponnesian War
428	financial anxiety in Athens: *eisphora* of 200 talents
425	Athenian success at Pylos ends Peloponnesian invasions of Attica
425	decree of Thudippus for reassessment of Delian League tribute
421	Peace of Nicias: Athenian decision to repay sums borrowed from sacred treasuries
415–413	Athenian expedition to Sicily
413	Spartan occupation of Decelea in Attica
413	Athens replaces Delian League tribute with harbour tax
412	Sparta first secures Persian support
c.411–406	Athenian treasuries reorganised
404	Peloponnesian War ends with Athens' coming to terms with Sparta

The war of Sparta and its allies against Athens was a war of a land power against a sea power, of states lacking ready money against a state well supplied with ready money; and, since it was a war about the power of Athens, a war which Sparta needed to win, in order to break Athens' power, whereas for Athens avoidance of defeat would count as victory. The Spartan king Archidamus, warning the Spartans not to rush into war, says that the Spartans are inferior in ships, and still more inferior in money, which they neither possess publicly nor readily contribute individually (Thuc. I. 80. iii–iv). Similarly Pericles, in his first speech in Thucydides, says, 'The Peloponnesians are men who farm their own land, and do not have money either individually or publicly; next, they lack experience of lengthy and overseas wars. . . . Most importantly, they will be hindered by the lack of money' (I. 141. iii, 142. i).

Athenian Resources

From his opening chapters (e.g. I. 2. ii, 7) Thucydides shows his awareness of the importance of financial strength, but he rarely gives details. A great exception is his summary of a speech of Pericles at the beginning of the war (II. 13), saying that 'their strength lay in the receipt of money from the allies, and most successes in war were won by judgment and a ready supply of money' (§ii). The Athenians had:

(§iii)   about 600 talents a year in tribute from the allies, apart from other revenue [the tribute lists suggest about 400 talents, and perhaps Thucydides' figure, like his 460 talents at the League's foundation (cf. p. 17), is derived from an optimistic assessment list; Xen. *An.* VII. i. 27 gives Athens' total revenue as not less than 1,000 talents, which is credible];
            in coin on the acropolis, *c.*6,000 talents [in view of §v, this probably refers simply to the treasury of Athena; according to the manuscripts' text, there had earlier been as much as 9,700 talents; in an alternative version they had maintained about 6,000 and currently had 5,700];

(§iv)   uncoined gold and silver in the sacred treasuries, not less than 500 talents;

(§v)   money from the other sanctuaries, 'not a little' [this probably includes the consolidated treasury of the Other Gods, established in 434/3: cf. p. 83];
            for use in desperate straits, the gold on Pheidias' gold and ivory statue of Athena, 40 talents [equivalent to 560 talents of silver; not in fact used until 296/5 (*FGrH* 257a F 4. 1–16)];

(§§vi–viii) for the catalogue of soldiers and ships see p. 95.

Athens seems never to have built up a surplus in the state treasury, but it had built up surpluses in the sacred treasuries, and was willing to use these to finance the war. The first of Callias' financial decrees, probably in 434/3, noted that 3,000 talents due to the treasury of Athena had been paid, and ordered the payment of sums due to the other gods (M&L 58 = *IG* i³ 52 ~ Fornara 119,

A. 2–13). We can only guess how the debts had arisen, but a possibility is that they were sums taken for the war against Samos in 440–439, which could be repaid once Samos paid its reparations (cf. p. 68). Another inscription (M&L 72 = *IG* i³ 369, extracts Fornara 134; table of annual totals M&L p. 217) gives us a detailed record of sums taken as loans from the sacred treasuries in 426/5–423/2, with a summary for 433/2–427/6, a calculation of interest due and (with a minor error) the total sum due in summer 422 – slightly under 5,600 talents capital and *c*.1,424 talents interest. We cannot deduct 5,600 from 6,000 and conclude that Athens had only 400 talents left: some of the money was taken before the time of Pericles' speech; his 6,000 talents is probably the figure for the treasury of Athena only; and the treasuries are likely to have had some income during these years, which may have exceeded their other expenses. A special reserve of 1,000 talents was set aside in 431 and was not used until 412 (Thuc. II. 24. i, VIII. 15. i). What is certain is that at the beginning of the war there were very large loans – *c*.1,145 talents in 432/1, *c*.1,370 in 431/0, *c*.1,300 in 430/29 – but *c*.600 talents in 429/8 and never more than 262 talents after that: Athens had much less money left in 428 than in 431, but not much less in 422 than in 428. Despite the confidence displayed in Thucydides' reports of Pericles' pronouncements, in the early years of the war the Athenians took money from the reserves at a rate which would soon have led to bankruptcy, but about 429/8 (perhaps not coincidentally, Pericles died in autumn 429: Thuc. II. 65. ii) there was a change in policy.

Large and expensive naval expeditions were sent out in the first two years of the war, but not after that (though a campaign in Sicily, which had to be funded throughout the year, was begun in 427 and reinforced in 425). More money was obtained from the Delian League. Thucydides mentions 'fund-raising ships' in 430/29, 428/7 and 425/4 (II. 69. i, III. 129, IV. 50. i) – perhaps referring to special levies or else to pressure on nominal members who did not pay regularly. Assessments of tribute were normally made every four years, in the years of the Great Panathenaea. If the orthodox arrangement of fragmentary tribute lists from the early years of the war is right, there was no major change in the first war-time assessment in 430, but there was an additional assessment, with significant increases, in 428. Then, certainly, in 426 there was no assessment but a decree of Cleonymus tried to improve the collection of tribute by having individual citizens of allied states made *eklogeis*, 'collectors', with personal responsibility for their state's tribute (M&L 68 = *IG* i³ 68 ~ Fornara 133); and in 425 a decree of Thudippus ordered another assessment (*IG* i³ 71; decree and extracts from list M&L 69 ~ Fornara 136). It explicitly stated that the tribute had become too little, and that no state's assessment was to be reduced unless it could demonstrate inability to pay; the list of assessments appended to the decree has a total almost certainly to be restored as somewhat over 1,460 talents. The list is optimistic, including states which are unlikely to have paid (e.g. Melos: cf. p. 131); but if the Athenians managed to collect 1,200 talents, that will have been three times the pre-war level. The decree orders [a return to] assessments in Panathenaic years, and the assessment of 422 probably made little change. Cleinias' decree for the collection of tribute (M&L 46 = *IG* i³ 34 ~ Fornara 98) is probably to be dated after the assessment decree of 425. The Athenians themselves also had to pay more towards the war: Thuc. III. 19. i reports that in 428/7 they 'paid for the first time an *eisphora* (property tax) of 200 talents'; *eisphora* was already a possibility in 434/3 (M&L 58 = *IG* i³ 52 ~ Fornara 119, B. 15–17), and it is possible but not certain that what happened first in 428/7 was that it was used to raise so large a sum.

The sums taken from the sacred treasuries were regarded as loans, and interest was calculated on them – at a rate equivalent to 6 per cent p.a. to 426 but 1.2 per cent afterwards (cf. the War Loan stocks issued by the British government in 1914–17, originally at rates rising from 4 per cent to 5.3 per cent but reduced to 3.5 per cent in 1932): in summer 422 the total of capital and interest due was *c*.7,024 talents. The orator Andocides claimed in 392/1 (III. *Peace* 8–9) that after the Peace of Nicias, in 421, the Athenians deposited 7,000 talents on the acropolis (which may reflect a decision, perhaps partly rather than fully carried out, to repay the whole outstanding debt), and received tribute of 1,200 talents a year (which may reflect assessment rather than payment). Certainly reduced activity after summer 422 will have allowed a substantial recovery, though we happen to have records of small loans from 418/7 onwards (M&L 77 = *IG* i³ 370, part Fornara 144).

The ambitious Sicilian expedition of 415 (the original force will have cost at least 150 talents per month, throughout the year) was undertaken in the false expectation that Egesta would pay the whole cost (Thuc. VI. 6. ii–iii): in fact Egesta provided only 60 talents in advance and 30 when the Athenians arrived (8. i, 46. i), but the Athenians persisted with the campaign and sent substantial reinforcements later; it is possible that a fragmentary inscription refers to the setting aside of 3,000 talents for Sicily in 416/5 (M&L 78 = *IG* i³ 93 ~ Fornara 146, frs. *d* + *g*). Ironically, the sales of property confiscated from those convicted in connection with the religious scandals of 415 (cf. pp. 157–9) will have made a significant contribution to Athens' funds. But the money was spent in vain, and when the campaign ended in disaster in 413 the Athenians did not have left sufficient ships or skilled men for them or money to pay for fighting (Thuc. VIII. 1. ii). Thucydides writes of their being in financial difficulties earlier in 413, when they had sent reinforcements to Sicily and the Spartans had built a fort at Decelea, thus preventing the Athenians from using their land and their silver mines: at that point they replaced the Delian League's tribute with a 5 per cent harbour tax, which they expected to yield more (VII. 28. iv–29. i).

Despite their failure in Sicily the Athenians resolved to keep going but to try to economise (Thuc. VIII. 1. ii–iii); however, in 412 they had to use the 1,000 talents set aside at the beginning of the war (15. i). Sparta obtained Persian support, and for a surprisingly long time the Athenians hoped that that could be redirected to them; one of the reasons for the establishment of an oligarchic régime in 411 was that an oligarchy would not have to pay civilian stipends and so would be cheaper. We hear of fund-raising expeditions in 411/0 (Xen. *Hell.* I. i. 8). Probably the harbour tax was abandoned and the tribute resumed (the assessment *IG* i³ 100 is perhaps to be dated 410; cf. Xen. *Hell.* I. iii. 9), but from 410 a 10 per cent tax was levied at the Bosporus (Xen. *Hell.* I. i. 22). In 410 an attempt was made to repay debts to the sacred treasuries (*IG* i³ 99); but later inscriptions show the treasuries providing money out of income, presumably because they had no capital left (e.g. M&L 84 = *IG* i³ 375 ~ Fornara 154, 3). Reorganisations were attempted, with the Athenian state treasury and the Delian League's treasury merged in or before 411 (cf. *Ath. Pol.* 30. ii) and the treasuries of Athena and the Other Gods combined in 406. Although Pheidias' statue of Athena survived, some gold statuettes were melted down for coinage, and token, silver-plated bronze coins were issued (Ar. *Ran.* 718–26 with schol. 720 = Fornara 164. B, gold, 407/6; 725, bronze, 406/5). After the battle of Aegospotami in 405 Athens could not afford to build yet more ships to replace those lost then, and so the war came to an end.

Peloponnesian Resources

In the fifth century Athens was not merely the most prosperous Greek city but one whose prosperity took a form which made it exceptionally well supplied with ready money. Sparta was at the other extreme, with citizens who lived off the land which was farmed for them by their helots, and who made contributions in kind to the messes at which they ate; but most of Sparta's allies were agricultural communities (cf. Pericles in Thuc. I. 141. iii, and notice III. 5). Corinth is likely to have been the strongest Peloponnesian state financially, and it claimed to be able and willing to contribute (I. 121. v), but there is no sign that it did so on a large scale. Of the great panhellenic sanctuaries, Olympia was controlled by Elis, a member of the Peloponnesian League, and Delphi expressed its support for the Peloponnesians (I. 118. iii): the Corinthians suggested that money could be borrowed from these (I. 121. iii, cf. Pericles in I. 143. i), but again there is no reason to think that this happened on a large scale. Most of the western Greeks were of Peloponnesian origin, and Sparta hoped for help from them (II. 7. ii), but they sent none until 412 and little then.

Almost our only other evidence is an inscription (*IG* v. i 1 = M&L 67 ~ Fornara 132; augmented by an additional fragment, *SEG* xxxix 370), which records a modest number of modest contributions 'to the Spartans for the war' (the total is equivalent to a little over 13 Athenian talents). Some believe the contributions to be spread over the 420's–410's (in which case it is striking that Ephesus, in Asia Minor, and the island of Melos are among the contributors); others date it *c.*411 (in which case the Melians must be exiles who escaped before Athens' destruction of their city in 416/5, and the Chian exiles will be those of Diod. Sic. XIII. 65. iii–iv).

From the beginning of the war Sparta tried to obtain help from Persia, whose wealth was by Greek standards unlimited; and so too did Athens, which had less need for Persian money itself but needed to prevent Sparta from obtaining it (cf. Thuc. II. 7. i). By 413 Athens' financial superiority had been thrown away in Sicily, and from 412 Sparta did obtain help from Persia (and the Athenians' hopes were never fulfilled). This enabled Sparta at last to confront Athens effectively at sea, and to persist until Athens was exhausted.

Athenian Forces and Strategy

Thuc. II. 9 lists the allies of each side at the beginning of the war. Athens had the Delian League (including all the Aegean islands except Thera, which was paying tribute by 429, and Melos), and Corcyra and other allies in north-western Greece; Sparta had the Peloponnesian League (all the Peloponnese except most of Achaea, which had joined by 429, and Argos), much of central Greece and some places in the north-west.

For human as for financial resources we have details on the Athenian side but not on the Peloponnesian. The Periclean speech of 431 summarised by Thucydides lists (II. 13. vi–viii) a field army of 13,000 hoplites (probably those aged 20–39), and, for garrison duties, 16,000 reserves (perhaps 10,000 'oldest and youngest' Athenians, aged 18–19 and 40–59, and 6,000 metics), 1,000 cavalry and 200 mounted archers (cf. Ar. *Eq.* 225), 1,600 archers, and 300 seaworthy triremes (which would require 60,000 crew members, an unknown proportion of whom would be mercenaries from outside Athens, mostly from the Delian League). Thucydides claims that at the beginning of the war the Athenians set aside not only 1,000 talents but also their hundred best triremes (II. 24. ii). That would have been foolish and is hard to believe; but perhaps there was a decision at the beginning of the war not to send out all the ships simultaneously but to keep at least a hundred in the docks (as far as we know, more than two hundred were not in use at once until 413). In the League, Chios and the cities of Lesbos still had navies, and contributed fifty ships in 430 (II. 56. ii), while Corcyra contributed fifty ships in 431 (II. 25. i); allied soldiers were used on a number of occasions, but not frequently or on a large scale. It is usually assumed that the Athenians had about a 3 : 1 superiority in ships, and far greater skill in the use of them, but a 1 : 3 inferiority in hoplites, and Sparta's hoplites were the best in fifth-century Greece (cf. pp. 128–9).

Hoplite fighting was done by the comfortably off, who could afford the equipment: except in Sparta most hoplites were farmers, who would not be eager to fight at times when their farms needed attention. At the beginning of the war not much importance was attached to soldiers other than hoplites; but fighting on rough terrain demonstrated the advantages of light infantry (NB the defeat of Demosthenes in Aetolia in 426: Thuc. III. 97–8), and there were in fact only two major hoplite battles in Greece during the war, in both of which the Athenians were defeated: at Delium in 424/3 and at Mantinea in 418 (cf. pp. 110, 128–9). Siege warfare was still rudimentary, though we are now at the beginning of a century of development: at Plataea the latest in machinery was used by both attackers and defenders, but it was the blockade which finally led to the city's surrender (II. 75–8, III. 52. i–iii).

The Spartans began the war in the traditional way, invading Attica in the spring, destroying the crops, and hoping that the Athenians would come out of the city to fight and be beaten. Remarkably, Pericles' response was not to go out and fight a hoplite battle (though he did use cavalry to harass the invaders: e.g. Thuc. II. 22. ii). The long walls, built in the 450's–440's (cf. pp. 41–2, 65), made a single fortified area of Athens and Piraeus, and Pericles proposed that the Athenians should abandon the countryside, migrate inside the fortifications and rely on their control of the sea to import what they needed; they should keep control of the empire, but not try to expand it or run unnecessary risks (I. 143. ii–144. i, II. 13. ii, 65. vii). Animals were boarded out on Euboea and other islands (II. 14. i). The city whose power had been built up by the navy would continue to rely on its navy.

That, presented with approval by Thucydides, was a strategy for avoiding defeat, not for gaining victory (though for Athens avoidance of defeat would amount to victory: cf. pp. 90–1). Pericles in his first speech says:

> If they come against our land with foot-soldiers, we shall sail against theirs; and the devastation of part of the Peloponnese will not be on the same level as [but more serious than] that of the whole of Attica, for they will not be able to acquire other land instead without fighting for it, but we have plenty of land in the islands and on the mainland, for control of the sea is a great thing. (Thuc. I. 143. iv–v)

In the first two years of the war (but not afterwards) the Athenians did send large and expensive expeditions against the Peloponnese (cf. pp. 106–8), but they seem to have achieved little, and Thucydides' narration of them is very disjointed and unemphatic. As we have seen, Athens began the war spending money at a rate which it could not afford to continue. The naval strategy and Thucydides' presentation of it is therefore problematic; and various explanations have been attempted. Plutarch writes of relieving the overcrowding inside Athens (*Per.* 34. v–35. i), and there is probably something in that. My own suggestion is that Thucydides' emphasis on the strategy of avoiding defeat and the possibility of a long war (NB I. 141. iii and Archidamus in I. 81. vi) reflects Pericles' public pronouncements; but privately Pericles hoped that, if Athens demonstrated that it was invulnerable to the Peloponnesians' attacks and capable of striking back, they would within a few years realise that in challenging Athens' power they had taken on an impossible task, and admit defeat – and Pericles was wrong.

The biannual attacks on Megara which began in autumn 431 (Thuc. II. 31) were the culmination of the dispute that had begun some years earlier (cf. pp. 84–5). Athens' hoplites were not a match for the combined armies of the Peloponnesians, but they could face that of a single city (and withdraw if the other Peloponnesians combined to oppose them); and they would have won a major strategic advantage if they had gained control of the Megarid. There might have been hopes that the naval expedition of 430 would entice Argos out of its neutrality, but Thucydides does not say so (II. 56 – but Ar. *Eq.* 465–9 suggests that Cleon was involved in an approach to Argos later); Prasiae in the Peloponnese was captured in 430 but not retained; and Argos remained neutral until 420.

Thucydides reports discontent with Pericles' defensive strategy in 431, and Plutarch suggests that Cleon was one of the discontented (Thuc. II. 21. ii–22. i, Plut. *Per.* 33. iv–viii). After Pericles' death, more adventurous strategies were attempted. From the beginning of the war Athens took some interest in northwestern Greece, an area containing several Corinthian colonies, and so an outpost of Peloponnesian power, but accessible by sea. Demosthenes campaigned unsuccessfully in Aetolia in 426 (Boeotia, mentioned III. 95. i, may have been a long-term but was probably not an immediate objective: cf. p. 104); and successfully, with the collaboration of Cleon, at Pylos in 425, which gave Athens a stronghold in Sparta's territory (cf. pp. 104–5) and (which could not have been predicted) Spartan hostages whom Athens used to prevent further invasions of Attica. There was an expedition to Sicily begun in 427, in which ambitious hopes were invested eventually if not from the beginning, but which had to be abandoned in 424 when the Sicilian Greeks reached an agreement; Nicias captured Cythera in 424; there was an unsuccessful attack on Boeotia in 424/3, with which Demosthenes was once more involved.

Sparta's weak point was its large subject population of helots and *perioikoi*, whose loyalty could not be taken for granted. After Athens' capture of Pylos and Cythera, Sparta was greatly afraid that Athens would use these to destabilise the whole of Laconia and Messenia (cf. Thuc. IV. 41. iii, 55, V. 14. iii, 23. iii); but that did not happen on a serious scale, and Thucydides does not make it clear whether this was because the Athenians did not try hard enough to exploit their advantage or because they tried but were unsuccessful.

Although Pericles was right to warn against taking unnecessary risks and trying to enlarge the empire – and Athens' Sicilian hopes were certainly misguided – a long war which ended only with Sparta's failing to defeat Athens would not in fact be satisfactory, as the Peace of Nicias in 421 was to show. Despite Thucydides' lack of sympathy, avenues which offered the chance of positive success without excessive risks for Athens were worth exploring.

Peloponnesian Forces and Strategy

The army which invaded Attica in 431 was a two-thirds levy (Thuc. II. 10. ii); Plutarch gives a figure of 60,000 (*Per.* 33. v, *An Seni* 784 E), but most scholars have thought about 30,000 more likely. At first only allies north of the Isthmus could provide cavalry (Thuc. II. 9. iii); Sparta created a force of 400 cavalry in 424 (Thuc. IV. 55. ii; cf. 44. i for Corinth's lack of cavalry). In 433 Corinth and its allies mustered 150 ships, but the largest Peloponnesian fleet between 431 and 412–411 numbered 100 (I. 46. i, contr. II. 66. i).

To break the power of Athens, the Peloponnesians needed a positive victory. They had no short-term prospect of matching the Athenians at sea (but at first did not realise how far they fell short in skill as well as in numbers: Thuc. II. 85. ii), and could not expect to capture Athens and Piraeus by force. They began the war by invading Attica, to damage the crops and provoke the Athenians to come out and fight (II. 11. vi–viii): most Greeks thought the Athenians would not hold out for long (e.g. IV. 85. ii, V. 14. iii), and indeed in 430 (when a plague added to their troubles: cf. pp. 112–13) they did try to come to terms. But invasions of Attica had to be abandoned when Athens threatened to kill the prisoners taken at Pylos in 425, and many Spartans after that were willing to abandon the war and make peace with Athens.

In 429 naval battles in the Gulf of Corinth ended disastrously, and a plan to attack the Piraeus in the following winter was aborted. But, according to Thucydides, the Corinthians in 432 pointed out that there were other possibilities: to detach Athens' allies and take away its revenues, and *epiteichismos*, to establish a fort from which Attica could be continually attacked (I. 122. i: cf. Athens' occupation of Pylos and Cythera, p. 97). *Epiteichismos* required a situation in which a comparatively small force could hold a strong point after a large force had set it up; and the Peloponnesians achieved that only with their occupation of Decelea in 413, when a large proportion of Athens' manpower had been sent to Sicily.

Some Peloponnesians did try to seize opportunities to detach allies from Athens. Mytilene appealed for Peloponnesian support when it revolted against Athens in 428, Sparta's appeal for an additional invasion of Attica came at a time which was too inconvenient for its allies, and the force which was sent to Mytilene was singularly ineffective. Corinth sent back to Corcyra upper-class prisoners captured in 433, to stir up an anti-Athenian movement, but the resulting conflict led to the victory of the pro-Athenian democrats in an exhausted Corcyra. If north-western Greece was the outpost of Peloponnesian power which the Athenians could reach by sea, the Thracian coast was the part of the Athenian empire which the Peloponnesians could reach by land: the Spartans accepted an opportunity to found a colony at Heraclea, near Thermopylae and the route to the north, in 426, and from 424 until his death in 422 Brasidas with a small force was active in winning cities in the Thracian region for Sparta, though the reality turned out to be less generous to the cities than Brasidas' promises. While Demosthenes was the most adventurous Athenian strategically, Brasidas was the most adventurous Spartan: in the earlier years of the war he was associated with the criticism of the Peloponnesian naval squadron in 429 after its first defeat in the Corinthian Gulf, and with the plan to attack the Piraeus; and he was sent as an adviser to Alcidas in the west after his inept attempt to support Mytilene (NB Thuc. III. 79. iii).

Sparta did not control the Peloponnese as Athens controlled the Delian League: at the end of the 420's there was fighting among the Arcadians (Thuc. IV. 134, cf. V. 29. i, 33. i); Lepreum (close to Messenia), which before the war had come to an arrangement with Elis which involved its paying 1 talent a year to Olympian Zeus, stopped paying by 421 and turned to Sparta for support (V. 31. i–v). Argos, always unfriendly to Sparta, kept to the thirty-year peace treaty of 451 (cf. p. 44) until it expired in 421, but Sparta must have been afraid that it would not. In 421 Sparta was not able to persuade all its allies to agree to the Peace of Nicias.

As we noticed above, it was Persian support which from 412 onwards enabled the Spartans to confront the Athenians at sea, and to persist (and grow in experience) until the Athenians were exhausted. To gain that support Sparta had (at least in the short term: cf. pp. 145, 148–9) to be willing to pay Persia's price, the return to Persia of the Greeks of mainland Asia Minor: that was difficult for a state which claimed that it was fighting to liberate the Greeks; and this, in addition to the fact that the defeat of the Athenians became easier to believe in after their failure in Sicily in 415–413, helps to explain why Sparta did not succeed in gaining that support earlier.

NOTE ON FURTHER READING

On the Peloponnesian War in general see Cawkwell, *Thucydides and the Peloponnesian War*; Kagan's three volumes *The Archidamian War*, *The Peace of Nicias and the Sicilian Expedition*, *The Fall of the Athenian Empire*; Lazenby, *The Peloponnesian War*.

On Athenian finance there is a thorough study in Samons, *Empire of the Owl*; Kallet-Marx, *Money, Expense and Naval Power in Thucydides' History*, and Kallet, *Money and the Corrosion of Power in Thucydides*, show that, although he does not often supply the kind of information we should like, Thucydides was by no means as neglectful of financial considerations as has sometimes been alleged.

For the Spartan inscription *IG* v. i 1 = M&L 67 ~ Fornara 132, since the publication of the new fragment dates before the Athenian capture of Melos have been championed by A. P. Matthaiou and G. A. Pikoulas, 'ἔδον τοῖς Λακεδαιμονίοις ποττὸν πόλεμον', *hόρος* vii 1989, 77–124, Loomis, *The Spartan War Fund* (who includes an English translation of the revised text); a later date (involving the supposition that the Melian contributors are men who escaped from the island before it was captured) has been preferred by B. Bleckmann, 'Sparta und seine Freunde im Dekeleischen Krieg: zu Datierung von *IG* v. i 1', *ZPE* xcvi 1993, 297–308, M. Piérart, 'Chios entre Athènes et Sparte', *BCH* cxix 1995, 252–82.

The need of triremes for a friendly coast was stressed by A. W. Gomme, 'A Forgotten Factor in Greek Naval Strategy', *JHS* liii 1933, 16–24, revised in his *Essays in Greek History and Literature*, ch. 10.

On Athenian strategy in general see A. J. Holladay, 'Athenian Strategy in the Archidamian War', *Hist.* xxvii 1978, 399–427 = his *Athens in the Fifth Century*, ch. 6. The problem of Pericles' strategy and Thucydides' downplaying of the naval campaigns of 431–430 has been discussed by G. Cawkwell, 'Thucydides' Judgment of Periclean Strategy', *YCS* xxiv 1975, 53–70; H. T. Wade-Gery, in the article 'Thucydides' in the *OCD* (in the 3rd ed., p. 1519); H. D. Westlake, 'Seaborne Raids in Periclean Strategy', *CQ* xxxix 1945, 75–84 = his *Essays on the Greek Historians and Greek History*, ch. 5. In *Thucydides and the Peloponnesian War*, ch. 3, Cawkwell argues that Thucydides was lacking in strategic understanding.

On Spartan strategy see P. A. Brunt, 'Spartan Policy and Strategy in the Archidamian War', *Phoen.* xix 1965, 255–80 = his *Studies in Greek History and Thought*, ch. 4; T. Kelly, 'Peloponnesian Naval Strength and Sparta's Plans for Waging War Against Athens', in *Studies in Honor of T. B. Jones*, 245–55, 'Thucydides and Spartan Strategy in the Archidamian War', *AHR* lxxxvii 1982, 25–54.

10

The Peloponnesian War: 431–421

500	475	450	425	400	375	350	325	300

431	outbreak of Peloponnesian War
430–426/5	plague in Athens
428/7	revolt of Mytilene against Athens
427–424	Athenian campaign in Sicily
425	Athenian success at Pylos
424	Athens fails to take control of Megara; defeated by Boeotians at Delium
424–422	campaign of Brasidas in north-east
423–422	one-year truce
421	Peace of Nicias

The war began in the spring of 431, when the Spartan king Archidamus sent to Athens a herald who was rebuffed, and then formally invaded Athens' territory (Thuc. II. 10–12): hence this first phase of the war is known as the Archidamian War. Sparta was fighting to liberate the Greeks, and to protect its own position, by breaking up the Athenian empire; it had persuaded itself that it was in the right (though later it came to have doubts: VII. 18. i–ii), and Thucydides claims (though his narrative does not support this) that it had persuaded most of the Greeks (II. 8. iv, cf. Archidamus in 11. ii). The war between Corinth and Corcyra had petered out; Athens was besieging Potidaea; the friction between

Athens and Megara was worsening; and Athens was to expel the inhabitants of Aegina in the first year of the war. After the unsuccessful Theban attack on Plataea in the early spring, Athens evacuated all except the men capable of fighting, and supplied food and a garrison (II. 6. iv).

Almost every year to 425, the Peloponnesians invaded Attica in the spring: in 429 they began the siege of Plataea instead; in 426 they turned back because of earthquakes; in 425 they returned after fifteen days because of the confrontation at Pylos; and after their success the Athenians threatened to kill their prisoners if there was another invasion (Thuc. IV. 41. i). The longest invasion, in 430, lasted forty days (II. 57. ii). The psychological effect on the Athenians was probably worse than the physical: the Peloponnesians will have done considerable short-term damage to Athenian agriculture (but they will not have damaged every field every year, and perhaps some farmers in remote places risked not migrating into the city), but olives and vines are hard to kill, so there will not have been great long-term damage.

Thucydides was dissatisfied with the use of official years (Athens' year, and those of some other states, started in the summer, so that one campaigning season was spread over two years, but other states had other starting-points), and he used his own system of seasonal years, divided into about eight months of summer and four of winter (cf. II. 1–2. i, V. 20, 25. i–26. i). His narrative rarely digresses outside that framework; but here it will be convenient to look at the main events of the Archidamian War by regions rather than year by year.

The War in the West

Athens and the Peloponnesians (particularly Corinth) both had allies in the north-west of Greece, and this was an area which Athens could reach by sea. In their major naval expedition of 431, a hundred Athenian ships were joined by fifty from Corcyra and others from western allies: after descents on Laconia and Elis (Thuc. II. 25), they continued north to Acarnania, and to the uncommitted island of Cephallenia, which they won over (II. 30). In the following winter a Corinthian expedition reinstated a ruler whom they had expelled from the Acarnanian city of Astacus (II. 33). In 430 the Peloponnesians took the initiative, attacking the island of Zacynthus, allied to Athens, but failing to win it over (II. 66); and on the mainland an attack by Ambracia and its barbarian allies on Athens' ally Amphilochian Argos was also unsuccessful (II. 68). In the winter, in order to control the Gulf of Corinth, Athens sent twenty ships under Phormio, who had been active in the west earlier (cf. p. 69), to Naupactus on the north side of the Gulf, where in the 450's (cf. p. 44) it had settled the Messenians who were allowed to leave the Peloponnese (II. 69. i).

In 429 Ambracia asked the Peloponnesians to join it in a major attack on Acarnania. The Spartan Cnemus brought 1,000 hoplites, and the combined army attacked Stratus, in the south of Acarnania; but when the barbarians in the centre rushed ahead of the others, and were caught in an ambush, the attack collapsed, and Cnemus withdrew (Thuc. II. 80–2). A fleet of forty-seven ships from Corinth and its neighbours was intended to join Cnemus, but to do that it would have to pass Phormio at Naupactus. With more than twice the Athenians' numbers, the Peloponnesians did not expect Phormio even to challenge them; but he did. They formed a circle with their ships facing outwards; the Athenians sailed in line round them, and attacked successfully when the wind rose and the Peloponnesians were thrown into confusion (II. 83–4). The Spartans did not appreciate the Athenians' superiority in skill; Cnemus on leaving Acarnania joined the defeated fleet, and Brasidas and others were sent as advisers. In a second battle the Peloponnesians had seventy-seven ships to the Athenians' twenty; Phormio was forced to move westwards from Naupactus to the narrow mouth of the Gulf, and when the Peloponnesians attacked they got the upper hand; but they immediately thought their victory was secure, and when they pursued the eleven Athenian ships which had escaped towards Naupactus Phormio was able to turn defeat into victory (II. 85–92). By that time Athens had dispatched a further twenty ships, but they went first to take part in a conflict in Crete, and did not arrive in time to be of use (II. 85. iv–vi, 92). In the winter Phormio campaigned in support of the Acarnanians, and then returned to Athens (II. 102–3). No more is heard of him: probably he died. In 427 he was succeeded at Naupactus, at the Acarnanians' request, by his son Asopius, who campaigned unsuccessfully in Acarnania and in the pro-Spartan Leucas, where he was killed (III. 7).

In 427 a bitter civil war began in Corcyra, after Corinth had sent back upper-class prisoners taken in 433 (cf. p. 83) to undermine Corcyra's democracy and alliance with Athens. Nicostratus went with twelve Athenian ships from Naupactus to support the democrats, Alcidas with fifty-three Peloponnesian ships to support the oligarchs; Alcidas won a naval battle, but despite the urging of Brasidas (present with him as an adviser after his inept attempt to support Mytilene: cf. pp. 108–9) he failed to follow it up, and when he learned that another sixty ships were approaching from Athens he withdrew. For seven days the Corcyraean democrats massacred many of their opponents, while the Athenians looked on – and Thucydides attaches to this episode a general comment on the collapse of standards in strife between pro-Athenian democrats and pro-Spartan oligarchs in the Greek cities (III. 70–85; general comment 82–3; 84 is an interpolation).

Also in 427 Athens accepted an invitation to intervene in a war in Sicily. Syracuse was getting the upper hand in a war with Athens' ally (cf. pp. 79, 83) Leontini, and Leontini appealed to Athens, sending a delegation which included the orator Gorgias (whose style of rhetoric is said to have made a great impression on the Athenians: Pl. *Hp. Mai.* 282 B, Diod. Sic. XII. 53. ii–v). Athens sent two generals with twenty ships, 'on the grounds of their kinship, and wanting to prevent the transport of grain to the Peloponnese from there and prospecting whether it would be possible for them to get control of affairs in Sicily' (Thuc. III. 86). We do not know to what extent the Peloponnesians were importing grain from Sicily, but if they did they could spare more time from their own farms for fighting. Whether the Athenians were already thinking of conquest in Sicily in 427 cannot be confirmed, but they were certainly doing so by the end of this campaign in 424.

In 426 the Athenian commanders at Naupactus were Demosthenes and Procles. Prompted by the Acarnanians, they first attacked Leucas; but they were then persuaded by the Messenians at Naupactus to march into Aetolia, to the north-east. Success there might pave the way for an attack on Boeotia from the west (cf. Thuc. III. 95. i), and this year the Athenians were in fact to make direct attacks on Boeotia (cf. p. 109); the circumstances of the campaigns make it hard to believe that they were planned in conjunction with each other, but it is possible that Demosthenes knew the other attacks were intended and did at least hope to reach Boeotia in the same summer. The Aetolians were a primitive people, living in mountainous country unsuitable for hoplites, and the Athenians did not wait for light-armed support (III. 97. ii). A town called Aegitium was abandoned by its inhabitants, and the Athenians took it, but they were attacked with missiles by light-armed men from the surrounding hills, Procles was among those killed, and Demosthenes had difficulty in extracting the army and returning to Naupactus (III. 91. i, 94–8). Probably Demosthenes was deposed: Thucydides writes that he was afraid to return to Athens (III. 98. v). Still at Naupactus in the autumn, he persuaded the Acarnanians to come to defend it when the Aetolians prompted Eurylochus, the Spartan commander at Heraclea (cf. p. 111), to attack it (III. 100–2). Eurylochus was then asked to join Ambracia in a winter attack on Amphilochian Argos, and the Acarnanians invited Demosthenes to command their forces against Eurylochus. Learning from his experience at Aegitium, he ambushed and defeated his opponents to the north of the city; to damage their reputation he allowed the Peloponnesians but not the others to escape; and further north, at Idomene, in an early morning attack he defeated a relieving army from Ambracia (III. 102. v–vii, 105–114. ii). Thucydides comments that Ambracia could have been taken but the Acarnanians were afraid to see it in Athenian hands (III. 113. vi); and the peoples of the region then made a hundred-year treaty (III. 114. ii–iv), so that, although the Athenians had had the better of the fighting here, they ultimately derived no benefit from it.

Surviving oligarchs were still harassing the democrats in Corcyra; and the war in Sicily was proceeding (Thucydides' narrative of it is disjointed and low-key, like his narrative of Athens' naval expeditions of 431 and 430). In winter 426/5 the western allies persuaded Athens to send a further forty ships to Sicily: ahead of them, Pythodorus was sent immediately with a few ships, to succeed Laches, the one still living of the original two commanders, who apparently was deposed (III. 115).

In spring 425 the Spartans sent sixty ships to support Corcyra's oligarchs. Athens dispatched under Sophocles and Eurymedon the forty ships destined for Sicily; but on the way they were to support the democrats in Corcyra; and before that Demosthenes (who had returned to Athens and was probably a general-elect for 425/4) had permission to use the squadron as it sailed round the Peloponnese (Thuc. IV. 2. ii–iv).

For what follows Thucydides seems to exaggerate the element of chance (though there was such an element) and to minimise the element of planning. On the west coast of Messenia there is a bay at Pylos (cf. map 3 and ill. 8), with the island of Sphacteria leaving a narrow opening to the north and a wider opening to the south (the modern town of Pylos is on the mainland by the southern opening). A storm provided the opportunity for the Athenians to pause by the northern opening, and build fortifications on the mainland. When the ships continued northwards, Demosthenes and some men stayed behind. The Spartans recalled their invading army from Attica, marched to Pylos, and summoned their ships from Corcyra; Demosthenes recalled the Athenian ships, which had gone only as far as Zacynthus. The Spartan ships arrived first, entered the bay, and landed some men on Sphacteria; then the Athenian ships arrived, and defeated the Spartans, so that the men on Sphacteria were trapped. There was a truce for negotiations, which Cleon wrecked in the Athenian assembly. When he taunted Nicias, the general who had been appointed to go to Pylos, Nicias invited Cleon to go in his place, and Cleon found himself committed to doing so. He promised to bring back the Spartans from Sphacteria, or to kill them there, in twenty days; he took light-armed troops; a fire on the island destroyed much of the brushwood which protected the Spartans; the Athenians landed on the island, and, after some fighting, 292 of the original 420 men, 120 of them being Spartiate citizens, surrendered. They were taken back to Athens – within Cleon's twenty days. Sparta sued unsuccessfully for peace. The Athenians garrisoned Pylos with Messenians from Naupactus, who spoke the Messenian dialect and could go about the country undetected. The Athenians now had a valuable stronghold in Spartan territory; but Thucydides disapproved of this success (it was achieved by Cleon, whom he disliked, and Demosthenes, of whom his approval is muted, and it involved the rejection of Spartan peace offers, which he probably thought should have been accepted [IV. 3–6, 8–23, 26–41]).

Sophocles and Eurymedon continued to Corcyra, where the surviving democrats were captured and treacherously killed (IV. 46–8). But Corcyra was exhausted, and we hear no more of it until its involvement in Athens' Sicilian expedition of 415–413. Sophocles and Eurymedon reached Sicily in the autumn. But in 424 a truce between Camarina, on the Athenian side, and Gela was followed by a congress at Gela of the Sicilian Greeks. Thucydides gives a speech to Hermocrates of Syracuse, warning of the Athenians' ambition, and urging the Sicilians to make peace and not to invoke outside intervention (an argument convenient for Syracuse, which could dominate Sicily if its opponents did not obtain outside help). A treaty was made, and the Athenian generals had to accept it; but they returned to a confident and ambitious Athens (Ar. Eq. 173–4, 1300–15, attributes to Hyperbolus ambitions extending to Carthage),

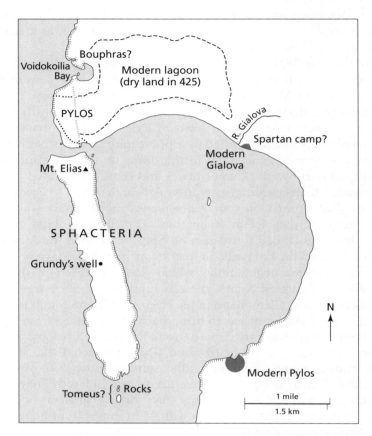

Map 3 The bay of Pylos (after P. J. Rhodes, *Thucydides: History IV. 1–V. 24* [Warminster: Aris and Phillips, 1998])

and were accused of having been bribed to withdraw: Eurymedon was fined and the other two were exiled (IV. 58–65). Leontini, which had asked for Athens' help in 427, was with the support of its upper class taken over by Syracuse, but afterwards some of them with the help of the expelled democrats established strongholds and tried to reassert its independence. In 422 Athens sent Phaeax and two other envoys with a couple of ships, but they met with a mixed reception and returned to Athens (V. 4–5).

Greece and the Aegean

The Peloponnesians invaded Attica in the spring of most years to 425 (cf. p. 102). Athens attacked Megara with a full levy twice a year, beginning in the autumn of 431 (Thuc. II. 31) – which means that the decree of Charinus, ordering these attacks (cf. p. 84), must be dated to the summer of 431. Also in 431

Ill. 8 The bay of Pylos: aerial photograph. Centre for the Study of Ancient Documents, Oxford

the Athenians sent out a large naval expedition, a hundred of their own ships and more than fifty from their western allies, which made raids on the west coast of the Peloponnese and continued further north (II. 17. iv, 23. ii, 25, 30: cf. p. 102); they sent another thirty ships up the Gulf of Euboea (II. 26); they expelled the inhabitants of Aegina, many of whom were settled by the Spartans at Thyrea, on the east coast of the Peloponnese (II. 27). In 430 an expedition of a hundred Athenian ships and fifty from Chios and Lesbos went to the Argolid: an attempt to capture Epidaurus was unsuccessful, other places were raided; Prasiae, south of Thyrea, was captured and sacked, but not retained as a hostile stronghold (II. 56). The naval activity of these years is problematic (cf. p. 96): it used large and expensive forces but does not seem to have achieved significant results.

Confident of their naval superiority, the Athenians were not guarding the Piraeus against an attack by sea. In winter 429/8 the Spartan Brasidas responded to a Megarian suggestion that the Peloponnesians should attack the Piraeus. The Peloponnesians caused panic in Athens, after which the Athenians did take more precautions, but they lost their nerve and did not in fact attack the Piraeus but merely raided Salamis (II. 93–4).

The cities of Lesbos were still relatively independent, ship-providing members of the Delian League. Mytilene was attempting a union of the cities other than Methymna. It had contemplated revolting against Athens before the war, but had not been supported by Sparta; in 428 it did plan revolt, and was hurried into it when opponents informed Athens. Athens sent forty ships; Mytilenaean representatives at the Olympic festival appealed for Peloponnesian support. Sparta's first plan was for an additional invasion of Attica, to distract the Athenians, but August was a busy time for Peloponnesian farmers and the invasion did not take place; and the Athenians manned a hundred ships with which they raided the region of the Isthmus, and sent further forces to block-ade Mytilene (III. 2–18). Eventually, in 427, the Spartans sent Alcidas with forty ships, and, ahead of him, Salaethus to say that help was coming. But Alcidas travelled slowly, taking and killing prisoners rather than winning sup-porters. Salaethus, despairing of his coming, armed the ordinary people of Mytilene for a final burst of resistance, but they refused to fight (apparently because they were starving rather than because they were pro-Athenian: III. 27. iii, cf. p. 182) and Mytilene surrendered. The Athenian commander, Paches, sent Salaethus and those most responsible to Athens. The original decision, on the proposal of Cleon, was to kill all the men and enslave all the women and children, and a ship was sent to take the news to Mytilene; but the next day the decision was reconsidered. Thucydides gives us speeches by Cleon and Diodotus, and Diodotus' proposal to kill only those who had been sent to Athens (still more than a thousand) was carried. A second ship taking the com-paratively good news travelled quickly enough to prevent the killing of all the men. Mytilene lost its ships, its walls and its mainland possessions, and own-ership of its land was given to Athenian cleruchs – but an inscription (*IG* i³ 66) suggests that if Thucydides is right there was a relaxation not long afterwards.

Paches recovered Colophon, on the Asiatic mainland near Ephesus, where since 430 a party backed by the Persians had gained control (III. 34); Alcidas scuttled back to Greece, pursued by storms (III. 25–50). Some Mytilenaean exiles established themselves on the mainland opposite, and made raids from there (III. 52).

In 429 the Peloponnesians, instead of invading Attica, had begun a siege of Plataea (Thuc. II. 71–8): perhaps they were worried about the plague in Athens (cf. pp. 112–13), perhaps they were under pressure from Thebes. No further help for Plataea came from Athens (though those who escaped to Athens were given citizenship); for the winter of 428/7 Thucydides gives a dramatic account of the escape of half of the men (III. 20–4). In the summer of 427 the remainder surrendered: after they and the Thebans had stated their cases the men (about 225 including a few Athenians) were killed and the few women were enslaved (III. 52–68). The fate of Plataea did not have a serious effect on the course of the war, but it was near to Athens and a long-standing ally, and enabled Thucydides to make various points about the war, so he gave it a detailed treatment.

In 426 an Athenian force under Nicias attacked Melos, by now the only Aegean island not in Athenian hands, but failed to win it over. If the inscription recording financial contributions to Sparta (cf. p. 94) belongs to the 420's–410's, Melos afterwards became a supporter of Sparta. He then sailed to the Gulf of Euboea, and at Tanagra in south-eastern Boeotia joined a large army which had marched out from Athens. They won a battle but then returned home (III. 91). This was the summer in which Demosthenes was hoping to reach Boeotia through Aetolia, but a fully coordinated plan is hard to believe in: cf. p. 104.

The main sanctuaries of the Greek mainland were hostile to Athens, and the Athenians may after the plague (cf. pp. 112–13) have felt that the gods were hostile. In winter 426/5 they 'purified' Delos, more drastically than Pisistratus had done in the sixth century, by removing all bodies buried on the island and forbidding births and deaths there, and they established or re-established a major quadrennial festival (Thuc. III. 104). Work on the temple of Apollo, abandoned in the middle of the century (cf. p. 64), was resumed. In 422 they went further and expelled the living Delians, but they allowed them to return in 421 (V. I, 32. i, cf. VIII. 108. iv).

In 425 Nicias sailed into the Saronic Gulf with an Athenian fleet: he landed and won a battle at Solygea, in Corinthian territory, and (as Demosthenes had installed a garrison at Pylos) installed a garrison at Methana in the Argolid (IV. 42–5). An Athenian alliance with Halieis is perhaps to be dated shortly afterwards (*IG* i^3 75: 424/3?), and Cleon seems to have gone on a deputation to Argos (Ar. *Eq.* 465–7: cf. pp. 96–7). Chios had been anti-Spartan in 427 (III. 32. iii); in winter 425/4 it had started building a new wall, but, remembering Mytilene, was obedient when Athens objected (IV. 51). The inscription recording contributions to Sparta includes 'the Chian exiles who are friends of the Spartans': possibly it was when Chios assured Athens of its loyalty that these men were sent into exile. In 424 Nicias again commanded an Athenian fleet, capturing the island of Cythera, and making raids on Laconia, including the area where the Aeginetans were settled: the settlement was destroyed, and the surviving Aeginetans were taken to Athens as prisoners (IV. 53–7). With Pylos and Cythera in their hands the Athenians should have been in a position to intervene effectively in Laconia and Messenia, but, for whatever reason, they never achieved as much as they hoped and the Spartans feared (cf. p. 97).

Athens' regular attacks on Megara had continued. In summer 424, when exiled oligarchs seized Pegae, the port on the Gulf of Corinth, Megara's democratic leaders, preferring Athens to their own oligarchs, plotted to betray the city to Athens, but the plot was revealed. An Athenian force under Hippocrates and Demosthenes was let into the long walls linking Megara to Nisaea, and captured Nisaea; but the city of Megara remained closed, the Spartan Brasidas, preparing for his expedition to the north (cf. p. 111), frightened the Athenians away, and the oligarchic exiles returned and took control of Megara (IV. 66–74). In the winter the Megarians recaptured and destroyed the long walls, but Athens retained Nisaea (IV. 109. i).

In the winter of 424/3 another plot misfired. Pro-Athenian democrats in Boeotia had made contact with Athens, and there was a plan by which simultaneously Siphae, on the Gulf of Corinth, was to be betrayed to Demosthenes, who would arrive by sea from Naupactus, there was to be a rising at Chaeronea, in the north-west, and an Athenian army was to march out to the sanctuary of Delian Apollo (Delium), in the south-east. It is not clear whether there was enough support for Athens across Boeotia to make this worthwhile; but, in any case, the plot leaked out, and the intended synchronism broke down, so that the Boeotians did not have to deal with all the threats at the same time. Boeotian forces occupied Siphae and Chaeronea; Demosthenes went to Siphae but withdrew. After that Hippocrates with in theory a full levy of citizen and metic hoplites (but perhaps not a fully effective levy, since 7,000 is a rather low figure) marched to Delium and fortified it, and then with most of his force set out for Athens. The Boeotians under Pagondas assembled at Tanagra, with 7,000 hoplites, 1,000 cavalry and a large number of light-armed troops. They attacked the Athenians, charging downhill; the Thebans on the right were, unusually, twenty-five deep (eight deep was normal); as tended to happen in hoplite battles (cf. Thuc. V. 71. i, and pp. 128–9, on the battle of Mantinea in 418), the right wing of each phalanx was getting the better of the fighting; but when Pagondas brought in some of the cavalry, whom he had held back out of sight, the Boeotians defeated the Athenians. There followed arguments over the return of the Athenian dead and the status of Delium; eventually the Boeotians recaptured Delium (IV. 76–7, 89–101. iv). An Athenian expedition to Euboea (Philoch. *FGrH* 328 F 130: not in Thucydides) may have been a response to unrest after Delium. In 423 the Thebans destroyed the wall of pro-Athenian Thespiae, west of Thebes (IV. 133. i); in 422 the Athenian fort of Panactum, in the mountains between Attica and Boeotia, was betrayed to the Boeotians (V. 3. v).

The North-East

Macedon was important as the best source of timber for shipbuilding; king Perdiccas continued to shift between Athens and the Peloponnesians in his allegiance. Further east, Athens gained an alliance with the Thracian ruler Sitalces in 431 (Thuc. II. 29, cf. 67, Ar. *Ach.* 134–73). Potidaea, after a long and expensive siege, capitulated in winter 430/29 and was resettled as an Athenian colony (II. 29. vi, 58, 67. i, 70; cf. M&L 66 = *IG* i^3 514 ~ Fornara 129).

The Chalcidians based on Olynthus, and their neighbours the Bottiaeans, continued in revolt against Athens (cf. p. 84); from the early years of the war we know of a few isolated incidents. In 429 the Athenians attacked Spartolus, west of Olynthus: hopes of betrayal did not materialise; they won a hoplite battle but were driven off by their opponents' cavalry and light-armed (II. 79). In the following winter there was a plan for Sitalces to attack Perdiccas and the Chalcidians with Athenian support, but the Athenians, allegedly not believing that he would act, failed to arrive. Sitalces did act: for a month he overran Macedon and the territory towards Chalcidice, but he was then reconciled with Perdiccas and withdrew (II. 95–101). We learn from inscriptions that, in order to keep them loyal (cf. p. 177), Athens made special arrangements for two cities of the Delian League: Methone, on the coast of Macedon, at various points between 430 and 423 (M&L 65 = *IG* i^3 61 ~ Fornara 128); and Aphytis, on the western prong of Chalcidice, perhaps in 428/7 (*IG* i^3 62).

In winter 426/5 we have the first sign of the Spartans' interest in the north, in their acceptance of an invitation from the Trachinians to found a colony at Heraclea, near the pass of Thermopylae (Thuc. III. 92–3: NB 92. iv). After the Athenians' successes at Pylos and Cythera, many Spartans began to lose heart for the war; but at some point the Chalcidians and Brasidas asked for support, and in the summer of 424 we find the adventurous Brasidas preparing a force of liberated helots and 1,000 Peloponnesian mercenaries to go to this part of the Athenian empire which was accessible by land (IV. 70. i, 74. i, 79. ii). He set out after supporting the oligarchs of Megara (cf. p. 110). Travelling via Heraclea and Thessaly he reached Macedon, where Perdiccas hoped to use him against one of his own rivals, Arrhabaeus, but Perdiccas and Brasidas quarrelled, and Perdiccas then reduced his support for Brasidas (IV. 78–83).

Brasidas next went to Acanthus, on the east coast of Chalcidice, where the citizens were divided. Thucydides gives him a speech, and says he made similar speeches elsewhere ('he was not a bad speaker for a Spartan': IV. 84. ii): he insists that he has come as a liberator, not to substitute one master for another or to support one party against another – but he will devastate their crops if they refuse to cooperate. The Acanthians found his speech attractive (but IV. 108. v describes one of his claims as enticing but untrue), and were afraid for their grapes, not yet harvested: by a secret ballot they decided to go over to him (IV. 84–8). Other successes followed, the greatest at the Athenian colony of Amphipolis in winter 424/3: the historian Thucydides, serving as an Athenian general, travelled from Thasos in time to keep Eïon, on the coast, in Athenian hands but not Amphipolis; and for that he was exiled, possibly at the instance of Cleon (Marcellinus, *Life of Thuc.* 46). The cities were inclined to write off Athens, and more of them joined Brasidas. The Athenians sent out garrison forces, and Brasidas appealed to Sparta for reinforcements but without success (IV. 102–16).

In the spring of 423 those who were anxious for peace negotiated a year's truce between Sparta and Athens, which they hoped would lead to a lasting settlement. Scione, on the western prong of Chalcidice, went over to Brasidas after the truce was made but before the news of it arrived: he refused to give it up, and nearby Mende joined him too. Cleon carried a decree for Scione's recapture, and although the truce held elsewhere it did not hold in the north-east (IV. 117–23). While Brasidas again fought for Perdiccas and quarrelled with him, an Athenian force under Nicias and Nicostratus arrived, recovered Mende and started to besiege Scione. By now Sparta had dispatched reinforcements to Brasidas, but the currently pro-Athenian Perdiccas arranged to prevent the main body from travelling through Thessaly, though some men reached Brasidas and some of them were appointed as governors of cities (IV. 124–32).

Early in 422 Brasidas made an unsuccessful attack on Potidaea. The truce was prolonged until August (Thuc. V. 1: cf. p. 113). When it finally lapsed, Cleon had himself sent to the north-east with a substantial force. He recovered Torone, on the middle prong of Chalcidice (a creditable achievement), and went to Eïon. Brasidas was based in Amphipolis. When the Athenian army grew impatient, Cleon took it out to reconnoitre. Brasidas saw the Athenians, and when they turned back towards Eïon he attacked and defeated them; Brasidas and Cleon were both killed. Thucydides exaggerates the heroism of Brasidas and the cowardice of Cleon, but it does seem that the Athenians were caught in a trap which they ought to have avoided. Amphipolis adopted Brasidas in place of the Athenian Hagnon as its founding hero, and Athens was never to recover it; the surviving Athenians sailed home (V. 2–3, 6–11). At the end of the summer the Spartans again sent reinforcements to the north-east, but the Thessalians obstructed them, and on hearing of Brasidas' death they turned back (V. 12–13).

The Progress of the War

At first the Athenians spent their money irresponsibly, and Pericles may have been more optimistic than Thucydides was prepared to admit. Athens survived the Peloponnesian invasions, and suppressed the revolt of Mytilene; the Peloponnesians survived the Athenian attacks, but learned how far they were inferior to the Athenians in skill at sea. The Athenians were doing somewhat better than the Peloponnesians, but there was no prospect of a quick result.

In 430 Athens was struck by a plague, which persisted until 426/5; the crowding of the people inside the fortifications during the summer helped it to spread.

Thucydides gives a vivid account both of the symptoms and of the effect on the Athenians' morale, but the disease has not been, and probably cannot be, conclusively identified. It killed about a third of the hoplites and cavalry, and presumably a similar proportion of the rest of the population (II. 47. iii–54, cf. 57–9, III. 87. i–iii). Whereas in 431 Pericles was criticised for his defensive policy (II. 21. iii–22. i), in 430 he was criticised for leading Athens into the war: he was deposed and fined, and the Athenians attempted to make peace with Sparta. As was to happen so often, peace was not made: the state which had the upper hand thought total victory was within its grasp. Pericles was re-elected and the war continued; he died, weakened by the plague, in autumn 429 (II. 59–65. iv; deposition Diod. Sic. XII. 45. iv, Plut. *Per.* 35. iii–v).

After that the Athenians brought their finances under control and risked more adventurous strategies. Some resulted in failures or empty successes, but the occupation of Pylos in 425 and Cythera in 424 put Athens in a position to exert pressure on Sparta, and in 425 it was Sparta's turn to make peace offers which Athens turned down. But Pylos and Cythera were not effectively exploited, and Athens' run of successes was followed by a run of failures – at Megara in 424, in Boeotia in 424/3, in the north-east from 424 to 422. From 425 there were some Spartans who wanted peace (although that would mean deserting their actual and potential allies), and some Athenians turned towards peace too. Hence the year's truce of spring 423, renewed (as a corrupt sentence in Thucydides almost conceals) until August 422. Cleon and Brasidas were particularly eager to continue the war; and after they were killed Nicias in Athens and king Plistoanax of Sparta (exiled after the Thirty Years' Peace [cf. p. 52] but brought back 427–426) were able to work for peace (Thuc. V. 16. i).

From the beginning both sides had appreciated the potential importance of involving Persia in the war (Thuc. II. 7. i, cf. Archidamus in I. 82. i). In 430 Peloponnesian envoys to Persia were betrayed to the Athenians in Thrace and executed. In spring 425 Aristophanes' *Acharnians* featured an Athenian embassy which had spent years in luxury without obtaining money from Persia (61–125). In winter 425/4 the Athenians captured a Persian envoy bound for Sparta, and had his letters translated: they complained that a series of envoys from Sparta had not brought a clear and consistent message – presumably because Persia was demanding the return of the Asiatic Greeks, to Sparta's great embarrassment. The Athenians sent the envoy back with envoys of their own, but when they learned of the death of King Artaxerxes (in winter 424/3) they abandoned their mission (IV. 50). After that, apart from one sentence (in V. 1), Thucydides has no mention of the Persians until 413/2 (VIII. 5). However, in 392/1 the orator Andocides gave as an example of the Athenians' folly their making an alliance with the King through Andocides' uncle Epilycus, but then abandoning it to support the rebel Amorges (III. *Peace* 29; Amorges appears in Thuc. VIII [cf. p. 143]). An additional fragment of an inscription makes it clear that the Heraclides honoured for helping towards a settlement with the King was Heraclides of Clazomenae, who later became an Athenian citizen, and whose help must have been given before the end of the Peloponnesian War (M&L 70 with 1998 Addenda = *IG* i³ 227 with Addenda ~ Fornara 138 lacking additional fragment: end 424/$\underline{3}$?). It can now hardly be doubted that, although Thucydides mentions the unsuccessful embassy but not the successful, when the bastard Darius II had disposed of rival claimants and established himself as King (by March 423), the Athenians did make a treaty with him. It would have been even harder for them than for the Spartans to hand over the Asiatic Greeks, but in 423 both the Athenians and Darius were insecure, and a non-aggression pact could have satisfied both sides.

Peace discussions between Athens and Sparta were renewed in 422/1. Sparta's anxiety was increased by the fact that its thirty-year peace with Argos was about to expire; and at the end of the winter, to increase pressure on Athens, Sparta announced plans to set up a hostile fort against Attica. What is commonly called the Peace of Nicias was made in the spring, about ten years after the beginning of the war, to last for fifty years, on the basis that prisoners taken and conquests made during the war were to be returned, with a few qualifications: Thebes was to keep Plataea and Athens Nisaea, on the pretext that these had surrendered voluntarily, but it was explicitly stated that Amphipolis was to be returned to Athens; six cities in the north-east were to pay tribute at Aristides' rate but could otherwise be neutral if they wished, but others including Scione could be treated by the Athenians as they liked. If it had been fully implemented this was a peace which should have satisfied Pericles and Thucydides: the Athenian empire had survived the assault on it and Sparta had failed to assert the freedom of the Greeks. But it was not fully implemented. Among Sparta's allies, Boeotia, Corinth, Megara and Elis did not share Sparta's desire to end the war, and all rejected the peace because territorial demands of theirs were not satisfied (cf. pp. 124–5); when Amphipolis refused to be handed back to Athens, the Spartan governor acquiesced. To reassure Athens, Sparta added to the peace a fifty-year alliance, and the Athenians then returned their prisoners from Sphacteria and so gave up their ability to put further pressure on Sparta (V. 14–24). Without full acceptance and implementation on the Peloponnesian side Athens was unwise to accept the peace; and the polarisation of Greece which had been unstable in the 430's was to remain unstable.

NOTE ON FURTHER READING

See in general Cawkwell, *Thucydides and the Peloponnesian War*; Kagan, *The Archidamian War*; Lazenby, *The Peloponnesian War*. For many campaigns there are valuable investigations in Pritchett's series *Studies in Ancient Greek Topography*.

Hanson, *Warfare and Agriculture in Classical Greece*, points out that olives and vines are hard to destroy and that Peloponnesian invasions could not do long-term damage to Athenian agriculture; J. A. Thorne, 'Warfare and Agriculture: The Economic Aspect of Devastation in Classical Greece', *GRBS* xliii 2001, 225–53, stresses in response that appropriation and destruction of the grain harvest would have a serious short-term effect.

On episodes involving the Athenian Demosthenes see Roisman, *The General Demosthenes*. The suggestion that his Aetolian campaign was part of a three-pronged attack on Boeotia was popular in the early twentieth century and was accepted by Kagan, *The Archidamian War*, 199–200, 202; difficulties are noted by Rhodes, *Thucydides: History, III*, 247, 252. On Pylos see also M. H. B. Marshall, 'Cleon and Pericles: Sphacteria', *G&R*[2] xxxi 1984, 19–36; Wilson, *Pylos 425 BC*; and, for different views on the problem of distances, R. A. Bauslaugh, 'The Text of Thucydides iv. 8 6 and the South Channel at Pylos', *JHS* xcix 1979, 1–6, C. Rubincam, 'The Topography of Pylos and Sphakteria and Thucydides' Measurements of Distance', *JHS* cxxi 2001, 77–90.

On the campaign in the north-east which ended with the battle of Amphipolis, further successes of Cleon, suppressed by Thucydides, were suggested by A. B. West and B. D. Meritt, 'Cleon's Amphipolitan Campaign and the Assessment List of 421', *AJA*[2] xxix 1925, 54–69, A. G. Woodhead, 'Thucydides' Portrait of Cleon', *Mnem.*[4] xiii 1960, 289–317 at 304–6, but shown to be unlikely by W. K. Pritchett, 'The Woodheadean Interpretation of Kleon's Amphipolitan Campaign', *Mnem.*[4] xxvi 1973, 373–86, B. Mitchell, 'Kleon's Amphipolitan Campaign', *Hist.* xl 1991, 170–92 at 176–82. On the site of Amphipolis see Lazaridis, *Amphipolis*.

On the plague at Athens see A. J. Holladay and J. F. C. Poole, 'Thucydides and the Plague of Athens', *CQ*[2] xxix 1979, 282–300, with various further studies, all collected in Holladay, *Athens in the Fifth Century*, ch. 9A–F.

The Peace of Epilycus was believed in by H. T. Wade-Gery, 'The Peace of Kallias', *HSCP* Supp. i 1940, 121–56 at 127–32 = his *Essays in Greek History*, 201–32 at 207–11; rejected by D. L. Stockton, 'The Peace of Callias', *Hist.* viii 1959, 61–79 at 74–9; made virtually certain by M. B. Walbank's identification of an additional fragment of M&L 70 = *IG* i[3] 227 ~ Fornara 138, in 'A Correction to *IG* ii[2] 65', *ZPE* xlviii 1982, 261–3, 'Herakleides of Klazomenai: A New Join at the Epigraphical Museum', *ZPE* li 1983, 183–4.

11

The Athens of Cleon

| 500 | 475 | 450 | 425 | 400 | 375 | 350 | 325 | 300 |

429 death of Pericles
425 *Acharnians*, first surviving comedy of Aristophanes
425 Cleon goes to Pylos
422 Cleon killed in battle of Amphipolis

Sources

Thucydides had a narrow view of what should be included in a history of the Peloponnesian War: he makes clear his approval of Pericles and disapproval of Pericles' successors, but except in his extended treatment of the plague (cf. pp. 112–13) he gives only glimpses of the internal affairs of Athens. We therefore have to turn to other literature of the late fifth century.

One fascinating text is the pamphlet of the so-called Old Oligarch, the *Athenian Constitution* preserved with the works of Xenophon but almost certainly not written by him. It is a perverse defence of Athens' democracy: the democracy serves the interests of the 'bad' men, not of the 'good', but is appropriate to Athens, where the lower-class men are important because they row the navy's ships, and it would not easily be overthrown. It begins with the ethos of the democracy, the claim that metics and slaves are scarcely inferior to citizens, Athens' support for democrats in the allied states and the transfer of lawsuits from there to Athens (ch. i). Next come an exposition of the advantages which Athens enjoys as a sea power rather than a land power and comments on comedy and the linking of democracy with lower-class interests (ch. ii). The pamphlet ends with the busy-ness of Athens, support for democrats elsewhere (occasional support for the upper classes has turned out unsuccessfully) and the fact that Athens has few political exiles to form the basis for an attack on the democracy (ch. iii).

When was this written, and in what circumstances? Suggestions have ranged over the second half of the fifth century, or even (to explain some resemblances to Thucydides) a fourth-century writer producing a fifth-century tract as a rhetorical exercise. However, there are strong arguments for locating the pamphlet in the early years of the Peloponnesian War: references to Athens' behaviour when the enemy invades 'now' (ii. 14–16), and to a sea power's corresponding ability to raid the enemy's land (ii. 4), look as if they were written during the Archidamian War, when these things were happening. Since a reference to headlands or islands from which the mainland can be raided (ii. 13) fits Pylos and Cythera in 425–424, but a comment on a land army's inability to travel far from home (ii. 5) was refuted by Brasidas' journey to the northeast in 424, 425/4 is the best guess if we are looking for a precise date.

The sophists, the travelling teachers of the late fifth century, were happy to challenge all conventional wisdom, and the pamphlet should probably be seen as an academic exercise from their circle rather than a manifesto written for would-be revolutionaries. It offers a picture of an Athens where the democracy can be criticised by men of the upper class but is not in serious danger – whereas in 415 religious scandals were thought to be a sign of a plot against the democracy, and in 411 the democracy actually was overthrown (cf. pp. 157–9, 160–5). The claim that the rich suffer from the enemy invasions but the poor do not (ii. 14) is in conflict with Thucydides (II. 65. ii), and is likely to be wrong or at any rate exaggerated, since by no means all of the poor were landless people living in the city.

Of the tragedians (cf. pp. 39–40), Aeschylus died in the middle of the century, but Sophocles was still active and had been joined by Euripides. Sophocles played some part in public life, as a *hellenotamias* in 443/2, a general in 441/0 and later, and one of the older citizens made *probouloi* in 413–411 to serve as an emergency committee to put proposals to the assembly (cf. p. 160). His plays belong, inevitably, to the intellectual climate of the time, as in the exploration of the clashes between state and family, and divine law and human law, in *Antigone*; but there is hardly any passage where we can detect an allusion or response to contemporary events (*Oedipus at Colonus* 616–23 is the most likely instance). Euripides did not have a public career; his plays seem to reflect the thinking of a younger generation, with a more questioning attitude to the gods and their justice, and a greater prominence given to ordinary people (in his *Electra*, Electra has been married to an ordinary peasant, who treats his distinguished wife well). His plays can more easily be located in a particular context: plays of the Archidamian War, such as *Children of Heracles* (430) and *Suppliant Women* (c.422), show both hostility to Sparta and awareness of the horrors of war, with the latter theme becoming more prominent over time; and the refusal of the Thebans to return the bodies of the Argive dead in *Suppliant Women* is likely to have been inspired by the refusal of the Boeotians to return the Athenian dead after the battle of Delium in 424/3 (cf. p. 110). A lost play of Euripides, the *Cresphontes*, contained a passage longing for peace which was quoted in the version of Hermocrates' speech at the congress of Gela by the historian Timaeus (*FGrH* 566 F 22 *ap.* Polyb. XII. 26. v) and was parodied in Aristophanes' *Farmers* of 425–421 (fr. 111 Kassel & Austin). *Suppliant Women* also contains a remarkable passage (399–466) in which a Theban herald attacks and the Athenian king Theseus defends the principle of democracy. Both tragedians give their characters speeches which employ the same kind of argument as speeches in Thucydides: he and the men whose speeches he reported or reconstructed were also products of the intellectual climate of the time.

By the 420's we also have Athenian Old Comedy, which was very much concerned with current personalities, politics, literature and philosophy, but in ways which make historical interpretation difficult and have led to considerable disagreement among scholars. From Aristophanes we know of a play called *Babylonians* (426), in which 'he comedied allotted and elected officials and Cleon', as a result of which he was attacked, and perhaps formally prosecuted, by Cleon (Ar. *Ach.* 377–82 with schol.). We then have a series of surviving plays. In *Acharnians* (425) the hero makes a private peace treaty with Sparta, while the war continues to rage around him. In *Knights* (424) Cleon, Nicias and Demosthenes are slaves of Demos, and Demos is dominated by Cleon; but Cleon the vulgar leather-seller is supplanted by an even more vulgar sausage-seller, who liberates Demos from his thraldom. *Clouds* (423) represents or misrepresents Socrates as a typical sophist, who is interested in celestial phenomena and teaches the rhetorical skill of winning arguments by making the worse cause appear the better. *Wasps* (422) focuses on the Athenians' fondness for litigation, with the young Hate-Cleon trying to cure his father Love-Cleon of his addiction. In *Peace* (421, produced about the time when the Peace of Nicias was ratified, so written before then) the hero rescues Peace from her long imprisonment.

To see Aristophanes as a pacifist, or as an opponent of democracy or of fashionable cleverness, is too simple-minded; but at the other extreme A. W. Gomme was surely wrong to claim that he aimed only to amuse and 'there can be no wrong side in a play'. 'Even comedy knows about justice' (Ar. *Ach.* 500). Longing for peace when one is suffering from war is perfectly natural: Aristophanes was certainly not unpatriotic (Dicaeopolis begins the defence of his treaty with 'I hate the Spartans enormously': *Ach.* 509), but it is possible to see him as suggesting that better policies could have prevented the war and could now end the war (Cleon's rejection of peace is featured in *Eq.* 794–6, cf. 1331–2, 1387–95, written when Athens was doing well). On the causes of the war he tells two different stories, in *Ach.* 514–38 and *Peace* 605–18, each focusing on Megara and the personal involvement of Pericles: the stories are probably invented, but the concentration on Megara and Pericles may well reflect public opinion in Athens, and the starving Megarian of *Ach.* 729–835 supports the view of the decree against Megara as imposing economic sanctions (cf. pp. 84–5, 177). The empire Aristophanes accepted, as all Athenians seem to have accepted it: his only complaints are that flattering speakers from the cities can fool the Athenian *demos* and that the income finds its way into the pockets of men like Cleon rather than those of the ordinary citizens (*Vesp.* 655–712: cf. below).

The Athenian *demos* has a heart of gold, but is capable of being led astray by clever and flattering speakers – a weakness against which Aristophanes claims to protect it (*Ach.* 633–42) and from which the sausage-seller cures it at the end of *Knights* (1316–1408). If Cleon had prosecuted him, Aristophanes will have had a particular reason to dislike Cleon; but there is enough consistency between the plays to suggest that Aristophanes generally disliked upstart demagogues like Cleon and was gentler in his treatment of leaders from an upper-class background, and we can see the same kind of man behind his portrayal of Cleon and that by Thucydides (cf. p. 120). It should not worry us that in the 420's Cleon was the most popular politician and Aristophanes was the most popular comedian: good jokes can be enjoyed by the victims' supporters as well as by their opponents. And surely many Athenians would laugh at Love-Cleon but still turn up to earn their stipend for jury service. It is not always clear how we should take comments on particular events: in *Eq.* 52–7 Demosthenes complains that Cleon had taken over, and taken the credit for, his own achievement at Pylos – but is that how Demosthenes perceived it? or how others perceived it? or a serious or not so serious suggestion of Aristophanes?

Aristophanes is interesting to the historian also for his background depictions: of festivals, for instance in *Ach.* 237–79 and 1000–1234; and various passages allow us to put together a picture of proceedings in the assembly, from the arrival of the citizens (*Ach.* 40–4) and the prayer and curse which began the meeting (*Thesm.* 295–311, 331–51) to the formal closure of the meeting (*Ach.* 172–3). *Clouds* shows us how the sophists could be seen by their opponents, whether or not Aristophanes actually was an opponent, and whether or not Socrates in the 420's actually was that kind of man; from the treatment of Euripides in various plays, and of Aeschylus in *Frogs*, we can see what features of their plays were thought worthy of caricature.

Athens in the 420's

Thucydides in his final assessment of Pericles writes that he,

> since he was strong in both repute and intellect and was conspicuously incorruptible, held the masses on a light rein and led them rather than let them lead him. . . . The result was in theory democracy but in fact rule by the first man. The leaders who followed Pericles were more on a level with one another, and as each strove to become first they tended to abandon affairs to the people to gratify their whims. (II. 65. viii–x)

The Aristotelian *Athenian Constitution* has an over-schematic list of paired aristocratic and democratic leaders, in which Thucydides son of Melesias and Pericles are followed by Nicias and Cleon. After Pericles' death (in 429: cf. p. 113) things became much worse:

> It was then that the people first took a champion who was not of good repute among the better sort, whereas previously it was always men of the better sort who were popular leaders. . . . Cleon, it seems, more than anyone else corrupted the people by his wild impulses, and was the first man who, when on the plat-form, shouted, uttered abuse and made speeches with his clothes hitched up [to make wild gesticulation easier], while everyone else spoke in an orderly manner. (*Ath. Pol.* 28. i, iii)

Thucydides' contrast between the era of Pericles and what followed is at best exaggerated, since Pericles was not an unchallenged leader, and Athens' mechanisms did not allow any man to enjoy as much power as Thucydides attributes to him (cf. pp. 56–62, 65–7). What was different about the era of Cleon?

After the generation of Pericles, nearly all political leaders were men not from the old aristocracy (the most striking exception in the late fifth century is Alcibiades: cf. p. 122). For Aristophanes Cleon is a leather-seller, the latest in a series of 'sellers' (NB *Eq.* 125–43), and the truth behind that appears to be that his father owned a successful tanning business, on the proceeds of which he himself was able to enter public life. He was born probably in the 470's, and may already have challenged Pericles in the 430's (cf. p. 67). As well as coming from a new kind of background, he adopted a new kind of political style. He is not known to have held any office until he took over Nicias' generalship in 425 (cf. p. 105), and he is not known to have performed any liturgies, as rich men commonly did to demonstrate their public-spiritedness and gain supporters (cf. pp. 331–2): his ascendancy was due to his success in making persuasive speeches in the assembly and law-courts. While Pericles' manner seems to have been aloof (Plut. *Per.* 5, 7), Aristophanes represents Cleon as given to making wild promises, and wild accusations against his opponents; this matches Thucydides' description of him as 'most violent' and 'most persuasive' (III. 36. vi, IV. 21. iii) and his account of his denunciation of Nicias and his twenty-day promise over Pylos (IV. 27. iii–v, 28. iv), and *Ath. Pol.*'s account of his manner of speaking. He is the first man in connection with whom we meet the concept of the *demagogos*, 'people-leader' (Thuc. IV. 21. iii, cf. Ar. *Eq.* 191), and probably the term was coined with reference to him and men like him. For Thucydides' complaint that leaders after Pericles gratified the whims of the people, cf., e.g., Ar. *Eq.* 868–911 (and, in the fourth century, Demosthenes' complaints against his opponents, e.g. III. *Ol. iii.* 22, 30–1). Leading politicians had always had to be able to make speeches; but the rise of the demagogues is paralleled by the rise of sophists claiming to teach the art of argument as the key to success in public life (cf. p. 117). If he prosecuted Aristophanes and was responsible for the exile of Thucydides (cf. pp. 111–12, 118), they will both have had personal reasons for disliking him.

In the generations of Cimon and Pericles the same men had dominated the assembly and had held office as generals, and the Athenians' political leaders were thus men who had been elected to office. Now we begin to find a distinction between politicians active in Athens and generals active abroad, and sometimes particular politicians cooperated with particular generals: Demosthenes, with whom Cleon cooperated over Pylos and perhaps on other occasions, is not known to have been active in politics. Politicians who held offices could be called to account in connection with those offices, as Pericles was deposed in 430 (cf. p. 113), but politicians who merely made speeches, proposing courses of action for which the assembly voted, were harder to control. This helps to explain the use of such charges as deceiving the people (often accompanied by a charge of taking bribes, since there was no concept of 'loyal opposition' and it was believed that nobody would want to mislead his fellow citizens unless a foreign enemy had paid him to do so), and the blurring of the line between political misjudgment and illegality.

Nicias, about the same age as Cleon and paired with him in *Ath. Pol.*'s list, came from a similar background: his wealth was derived from the silver mines (Plut. *Nic.* 4. ii), and it is again likely that his father founded the family fortune. But Nicias, although he was not one of the aristocrats, behaved like them and tried to make himself acceptable to them. He was a religious and indeed a scrupulous man (cf. pp. 138, 140). He frequently performed liturgies (cf. p. 156). He may have been general every year from 427/6 until his death in Sicily in 413: he seems to have been a competent commander, but more anxious to avoid failure than eager to achieve success.

Asking which of the two was closer to Pericles is not very profitable. Cleon had more adventurous ideas on how to fight the war, while Pericles would probably have approved of Nicias' peace in 421 and his opposition to the Sicilian expedition in 413. Cleon agreed with Pericles on the need for firm control of the empire (Athens' rule is called a tyranny by Pericles in Thuc. II. 63. ii, by Cleon in III. 37. ii; Pericles is not known to have proposed killing all the men of a rebellious city, but he might have done if he had lived longer), and he sought to dominate the assembly in his way as Pericles had in his. Xenophon has Theramenes say that Nicias and his son, though the son was a victim of the Thirty in 404, 'never did anything populist (*demotikon*)' (*Hell.* II. iii. 39); but while Nicias' brothers were both to be involved in oligarchy at the end of the century, there is no evidence that he himself ever opposed the democracy.

Other politicians whom we encounter in the 420's include Cleonymus, a proposer of decrees including that to improve the collection of tribute in 426 (cf. p. 92): he is represented by Aristophanes as a glutton and a coward, and justified the latter charge by running away after the battle of Delium in 424/3. Thudippus, proposer of the decree for reassessment of the tribute in 425, probably married Cleon's daughter. Hyperbolus, who aspired to take Cleon's place after his death (cf. Ar. *Peace* 679–87), is represented both by Thucydides (VIII. 73. iii) and by Aristophanes (*Nub.* 549–52) as particularly contemptible, we do not know why: he is described as a lamp-maker, and as early as 424 credited with ambitions extending to Carthage (both in *Eq.* 1302–15). Alcibiades (born at the end of the 450's) is not mentioned by Thucydides until V. 43. ii, but we are told there that because of a family connection with Sparta (his grandfather had been Spartan *proxenos* but had renounced the position, probably when Athens turned against Sparta at the end of the 460's: cf. p. 41) he had looked after the Spartan prisoners from Sphacteria, and felt insulted when his Spartan connection was not used in the making of peace in 421. He was an aristocrat; Alcibiades was a name taken from Sparta by his family (Thuc. VIII. 6. iii); when his father Cleinias died at Coronea in 447/6 (cf. p. 51), he was brought up by Pericles, to whom he was related through the Alcmaeonids. He was flamboyant, ambitious and selfish; we happen now to have an inscription showing him as proposer of a decree in 422/1 (*IG* i^3 [Add.] 227 bis, with p. 945 on nos. 91–2).

The plague of the early 420's (cf. pp. 112–13) was devastating in the number of people who died from it and in its effect on the morale of all the Athenians. There was a growing tendency in the second half of the fifth century for educated men to look for natural rather than supernatural explanations of natural phenomena (exemplified almost always in Thucydides' writing, but I. 23. iii is exceptional; for Pericles see Plut. *Per.* 6). Thucydides says that the plague afflicted the pious as badly as the impious (II. 47. iv, 53. iv); but some people were prompted to wonder whether Athens had offended the gods. A sanctuary of Heracles Alexikakos, 'averter of evil', was established in the city (schol. Ar. *Ran.* 501), and in 420/19, when the Peace of Nicias had made Epidaurus accessible, the cult of the healing god Asclepius was brought from there to Athens (cf. below). The 'purification' of Delos (cf. p. 109) in winter 426/5, when the plague finally ended, may well have been another response to the plague (claimed not by Thucydides but by Diod. Sic. XII. 56. vi–vii).

The building programme on the acropolis had been wound up in 434/3 (cf. p. 83), but it now appears that the war had little effect on building elsewhere in Athens and Attica (cf. p. 65). On the acropolis, the temple of Athena Nike outside the Propylaea was perhaps planned in the 440's but built or at any rate completed in the 420's (cf. pp. 63–4); the statue was dedicated in 425 (*IG* ii^2 403). In the agora, the Stoa of Zeus Eleutherios ('of Freedom') and South Stoa I are dated to the 420's, the Hephaesteum was completed then, and some smaller sanctuaries were refurbished. The cult of Asclepius was brought from Epidaurus in 420/19 (cf. above) – by a rich citizen, Telemachus, who had a sanctuary built below the south cliff of the acropolis, west of the theatre of Dionysus, and commemorated his foundation in a monument set up *c.*400 (*IG* ii^2 4960/1/3, cf. 4325). Among buildings elsewhere in Attica, the temple of Nemesis at Rhamnus is also dated to the 420's. For the temple of Athena Nike (and after it the Erechtheum: cf. pp. 159–60, 170) the Ionic order was used, and it has been suggested that the change from Doric to Ionic was a political statement – but the other major buildings of the 420's are still Doric, and there is no evidence earlier than the fourth century for the use of these names for the orders.

One field in which Athens is not unique but participated in a trend to be seen across Greece is that for the first three quarters of the fifth century lavish private burials had been avoided except by a few families, but from *c.* 425 such burials came back into fashion.

In spite of the war, in spite of the plague, Athens was a city which was able to find the money and labour for public buildings, and in which the democracy was not seriously challenged. Leaders like Cleon inserted a frenetic note, which had been absent in the time of Pericles and of which Thucydides and Aristophanes disapproved; until 424 the war brought more successes than failures. Athens was still a confident city.

NOTE ON FURTHER READING

The *Athenian Constitution* of the Old Oligarch is included in the Loeb and other editions of Xenophon's Minor Works; the LACTOR translation has been revised by R. Osborne; there is to be an edition with translation and commentary by J. L. Marr and P. J. Rhodes. The Loeb editor, G. W. Bowersock, dates the pamphlet to the late 440's on account of the examples of Athens' tolerating oligarchies given in iii. 11; among those arguing from ch. ii for a date between 431 and 424 is W. G. Forrest, 'The Date of the Pseudo-Xenophontic Athenaion Politeia', *Klio* lii 1970, 107–16, cf. 'An Athenian Generation Gap', *YCS* xxiv 1975, 37–52 at 43–7; a fourth-century rhetorical work, acquainted with Thucydides, is the suggestion of S. Hornblower, 'The *Old Oligarch* (Pseudo-Xenophon's *Athenaion Politeia*) and Thucydides: A Fourth-Century Date for the *Old Oligarch*?' in *Polis and Politics . . . M. H. Hansen*, 363–84.

Murray, *Aristophanes*, was typical of older studies in its straightforward willingness to see political attitudes and messages in Aristophanes' plays. For extreme opposition to political interpretation see A. W. Gomme, 'Aristophanes and Politics', *CR* lii 1938, 97–109 = his *More Essays in Greek History and Literature*, 70–91; for a return to political interpretation see de Ste. Croix, *The Origins of the Peloponnesian War*, app. 29; for justification of the view that Aristophanes dealt more kindly with upper-class politicians see A. H. Sommerstein, 'How to Avoid Being a *Komodoumenos*', *CQ*[2] xlvi 1996, 327–56. There is a study of Aristophanes in his context by MacDowell, *Aristophanes and Athens*; carefully nuanced interpretations are offered by Pelling, *Literary Texts and the Greek Historian*, chs. 7, 8, 10; in favour of a formal prosecution after *Babylonians* see A. H. Sommerstein, 'Comedy and the Unspeakable', in *Law, Rhetoric and Comedy in Classical Athens . . . D. M. MacDowell*, ch. 13.

Demagogues were presented positively, as structurally necessary in a democracy in which decisions were taken by mass meetings, by M. I. Finley, 'Athenian Demagogues', *P&P* xxi April 1962, 3–24; reprinted in various collections; revised in his *Democracy Ancient and Modern*[2], ch. 2. The change in Athenian politics in the late fifth century is studied by Connor, *The New Politicians of Fifth-Century Athens*.

On burial practices in Athens and in Greece generally see I. Morris, 'Everyman's Grave', in Boegehold and Scafuro (eds.), *Athenian Identity and Civic Ideology*, 67–101.

12

The Peloponnesian War: 421–413

500	475	450	425	400	375	350	325	300

421	Peace of Nicias
420	Athenian alliance with Argos and other Peloponnesian states
418	Spartan victory in battle of Mantinea
416	Athenian capture of Melos
415–413	Athenian expedition to Sicily
413	Spartan occupation of Decelea in Attica

The Unstable Peace

In 421 the Peloponnesian War appeared to be over. Athens and Sparta had made a fifty-year peace and alliance by which Sparta had given up its hope of breaking the Athenian empire. But a peace which resulted from Sparta's failure rather than Athens' success might in any case not have been long-lasting; and, as we have seen (cf. p. 114), the terms of the peace were not fully implemented and several of Sparta's allies refused to swear to it. Thucydides, it seems, hoped that the peace would last, but he came to see that it had not lasted, and to regard the whole conflict from 431 to 404 as a single war: in V. 25–6 he gives us his 'second preface', linking what followed to the Archidamian War.

The Peloponnese was now seriously divided, and Corinth set about building up an alliance of states which had not accepted the peace. Corinth was not to regain cities in the north-west to which it laid claim (V. 30. ii: Acarnania may not have been a party to the peace). It was joined by Mantinea, which had recently subdued some of its neighbours and had fought inconclusively against Tegea (V. 29. i, cf. 33, IV. 134), Elis, which resented Sparta's support of Lepreum against it (V. 31. i–v, 34. i: cf. pp. 98–9), and the Chalcidians based on Olynthus, not wishing to become tributary to Athens once more (Olynthus was one of the cities made tributary but allowed to be neutral, V. 18. v; in general the Thraceward cities not in Athenian hands did not accept the peace, V. 21. i–ii), in making a defensive alliance with Argos, whose thirty-year peace with Sparta was now expiring (V. 27–31). The allies seem to have had no common purpose beyond unwillingness to be aligned with Sparta. Megara, which was not to regain Nisaea, and Boeotia, which was to lose Panactum (V. 17. ii, 18. vii), refused to join, claiming to find oligarchic Sparta a more congenial partner than democratic Athens (V. 31. vi: contrast the attraction of Athens' democracy for Mantinea and Argos, V. 29. i, 44. i); Mantinea's enemy Tegea also was approached but refused (V. 32. iii–iv). The Boeotians made their own, separate 'ten-day' truce with Athens (V. 26. ii, 32. v), perhaps one that could be ended at ten days' notice, and at some point the Chalcidians did likewise (VI. 7. iv). Corinth tried to get the same terms, but was unsuccessful and had to remain in a state of 'treatyless ceasefire' (V. 32. v–vii).

Because of Sparta's failure to enforce the peace in the north-east and on all its allies (in particular, the Boeotians still held Panactum), Athens, while withdrawing the Messenians of Naupactus from Pylos (and finding a home in Cephallenia for the helots who had deserted to them), retained the site and other places which it was supposed to give up (V. 35. ii–viii). Sparta meanwhile intervened in Arcadia to liberate the communities taken over by Mantinea, sent a garrison of liberated helots to Lepreum, and for a time subjected to partial disfranchisement the prisoners returned from Athens (V. 33–4). In the north-east Athens captured Scione and killed all the men; there should have been hardly any women and children left in the city to be enslaved (V. 32. i). In the following winter, however, Olynthus captured Mecyberna, nearby on the coast, although there was an Athenian garrison in it (V. 39. i).

In the winter of 421/0 matters started to become more complicated. When Sparta's new official year began (probably after the autumnal equinox), two of the new ephors, Cleobulus and Xenares, were men opposed to the peace with Athens. After a conference in Sparta had achieved nothing, they suggested to the Boeotian and Corinthian representatives that Boeotia should join the alliance which Corinth and others had made with Argos, and swing that alliance into alignment with Sparta; some Argives also were eager to bring Boeotia into the alliance, but their aim was to create a bloc which would be a match for Sparta. Megara was to be brought in too. But the plan broke down through an excess of secrecy. The senior federal officials of Boeotia, the Boeotarchs, first proposed a defensive alliance of Boeotia, Corinth, Megara and the north-eastern cities opposed to Athens; but they failed to explain to the Boeotian councils the pro-Spartan purpose behind joining the Argive alliance, and the councils rejected the plan out of fear that it would alienate Sparta (V. 36–8).

The Spartans wanted the Boeotians to give them Panactum so that in accordance with the Peace of Nicias they could return that to Athens and themselves recover Pylos. Early in 420 the Boeotians made it a condition of this transfer that Sparta should grant them an alliance – and they demolished the fort before handing over the site (V. 36. ii, 39. ii–iii, 42. i). Argos, having heard no more from Boeotia, and supposing that Sparta's dealings with Boeotia had Athens' consent, began to fear that it would be isolated, and so itself entered into negotiations with Sparta, obtaining a draft of a fifty-year peace with limited rights to fight over the territory disputed between them. But Sparta had not had Athens' consent, its alliance with Boeotia was therefore a breach of its alliance with Athens, and the Athenians were angered by the destruction of Panactum, and afraid that if Argos joined Sparta they would be isolated (V. 42, 43. iii).

This provided an opportunity for those Athenians who were opposed to the Peace of Nicias, in particular Alcibiades. He invited Argos, Elis and Mantinea to send envoys to Athens; at the same time, to prevent a breach, Sparta sent envoys, one of whom was Endius, from the family linked to Alcibiades' family. The story which Thucydides then tells is difficult to believe, but it is hard to imagine a convincing scenario of which it might be a distortion. The Spartans appeared first before the council in Athens, and said that they were *autokratores* ('had full powers', but the expression is often used in circumstances where it is not clear how full the powers are) to settle the disputes. Alcibiades spoke to them privately and promised that if they did not admit to the assembly that they were *autokratores* he would help them to obtain the result they wanted. However, in the assembly, when the Spartans did deny that they were *autokratores*, Alcibiades denounced them. An earthquake led to the adjournment of the assembly. When the assembly resumed, Nicias had himself and others sent on a deputation to Sparta, but they achieved nothing, and at Alcibiades' prompting Athens made a hundred-year defensive alliance with Argos, Elis and Mantinea. However, as relations between Athens and Sparta worsened, Corinth's alienation from Sparta was fading: it was not represented in Athens, and afterwards refused an invitation to join the new alliance (V. 43–8, 50. v, cf. *IG* i³ 83).

Now Sparta had an alliance with Boeotia as well as with Athens, Athens had an alliance with Argos and other Peloponnesians as well as with Sparta, and Athens might be able to challenge Sparta on land in the Peloponnese as it could not in the Archidamian War. However, although the next few years were to see serious conflict between Sparta and Athens, it did not suit either to say that the Peace of Nicias and their alliance were at an end.

Renewed Fighting

420 was an Olympic year, and at the beginning of the Olympic truce Sparta continued its support for Lepreum by sending an army there. Elis responded

by excluding Sparta and Lepreum from the festival. Afraid that Sparta might use force, it was joined by the other members of the alliance in setting up a garrison. Sparta did not break the peace, but harboured a grudge for twenty years (V. 49–50. iv: cf. p. 205). In the winter the Spartan colony at Heraclea, near Thermopylae, was defeated by the neighbouring peoples and its governor was killed; in summer 419, to prevent it from falling into Athenian hands, the Boeotians took it over, to Sparta's annoyance (V. 51–52. i; the Boeotians invited by Heraclea according to Diod. Sic. XII. 77. iv); it was apparently under Spartan control again by 413/2 (cf. VIII. 3. i).

In 419 the Argive alliance tried to put pressure on Corinth. First Alcibiades succeeded in taking an allied army through the Peloponnese to Patrae, in Achaea, and encouraged it to build long walls down to the Gulf of Corinth, but he was prevented by Corinth and Sicyon from establishing a fort at Rhium, at the mouth of the Gulf (V. 52. ii). Argos began a war against Epidaurus, with two expeditions, the second supported by Alcibiades; two Spartan expeditions were halted by unfavourable auspices; in a conference at Mantinea summoned by Athens, Corinth was not won over (V. 53–5). In the winter Sparta sent a garrison to Epidaurus by sea; Argos protested that the Athenians ought to have prevented that; and the Athenians solemnly recorded that Sparta was in breach of the Peace of Nicias, and reinstated in Pylos the helots from Cephallenia (V. 56).

In 418 the Spartans decided that a major effort was needed, and under king Agis assembled an allied army (including Corinthians and Boeotians) at Phlius for an attack on Argos (see map 4). The Argives went out on the main road to Nemea to confront the attackers, but Agis divided his forces: he took a route through the hills via Orneae to the Argive plain, a contingent including the Corinthians took a route bypassing Nemea, and another contingent including the Boeotians was to take the main road. When Agis reached the plain, he was between the city of Argos and the Argive army; the Argive army, which had turned back and had brushed past the Corinthian contingent, was between Agis and the Boeotian contingent. On each side the ordinary soldiers thought they were in a winning position but their commanders did not; which side was in the winning position depends on how far away the Boeotians were, and Thucydides suggests that they were near enough for the advantage to lie with the Spartans. Two leading Argives sympathetic to Sparta approached Agis, who accepted their offer of a four-month truce. The armies dispersed without fighting, but the commanders on each side were in trouble, being thought to have thrown away a good opportunity: Agis was given a suspended sentence, and a board of advisers to prevent future errors (V. 57–60, 63).

An Athenian contingent reached Argos afterwards. Alcibiades was present, but as an envoy, not a general: it is unclear whether the Athenians could not arrive earlier or this year men less enthusiastic for the alliance were more influential (more Athenians were to arrive after the battle of Mantinea: cf. pp. 128–9). The allies attacked and won over Orchomenus, in northern Arcadia; when they chose Tegea rather than Lepreum as their next objective, the Eleans, who had been present at Argos, returned home (V. 61–2).

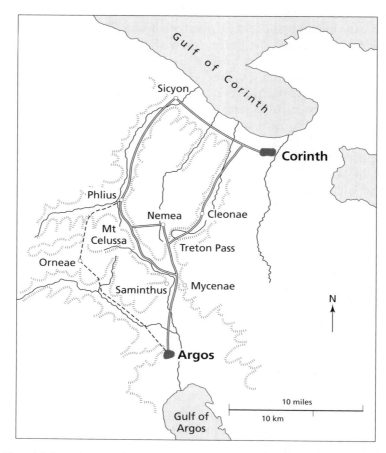

Map 4 The vicinity of Argos (after B. W. Henderson, *The Great War Between Athens and Sparta* [London: Macmillan, 1927], p. 308)

When sympathisers in Tegea appealed urgently for help, the Spartans under Agis hurried there and summoned their allies (cf. map 5). The Argive alliance occupied the hills to the east of Mantinea. First Agis went within shouting distance of the enemy but withdrew. Then, to provoke the enemy into coming down to the plain, he diverted a stream so that it would flood Mantinean territory. Finally he marched north, and was caught unexpectedly by the enemy marching against him (the surprise is easier to understand if there was a wood in the narrow part of the hour-glass-shaped plain, blocking the view; but the wood is not mentioned until Paus. VIII. 11. i, v, of the second century AD). Hoplite phalanxes always tended to sidle to the right (cf. p. 251), and on this occasion each was too far to the right for an effective encounter. Agis ordered his left wing to move to the left, and his right centre to move into the gap; the left wing did move but the right centre did not, and he went into battle with a gap in his line. Now, if ever, the Spartan army ought to have been defeated, but it was not:

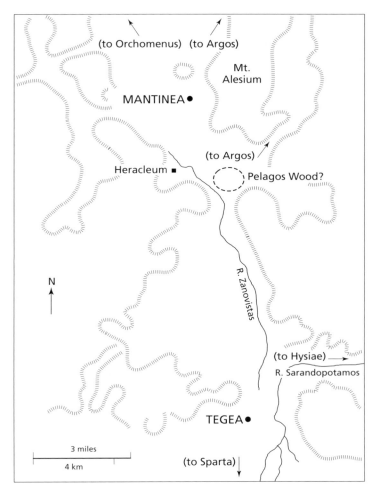

(to Orchomenus) (to Argos)

Mt. Alesium

MANTINEA•

(to Argos)

Heracleum ■

Pelagos Wood?

R. Zanovistas

N

(to Hysiae)

R. Sarandopotamos

TEGEA•

3 miles

4 km

(to Sparta)

Map 5   The vicinity of Mantinea (after J. F. Lazenby, *The Peloponnesian War* [London: Routledge, 2004], p. 119, map 7)

Spartan skill and discipline were still too much for an opposing army of allies who had little experience of fighting together. Agis, in the centre, defeated the Argives and then rescued his left wing; the Athenians, on the left of the opposing army, were able to withdraw but both their generals were killed. Spartan reinforcements and allies, on their way to Mantinea, were not needed (V. 64–75. iii). This battle of Mantinea was the largest hoplite battle in the Peloponnesian War, with perhaps 11,000 on the Spartan side and 10,000 on the other (for Spartiate numbers cf. p. 216): whereas a defeat for Sparta would have been disastrous, this victory enabled the Spartans to reassert their leadership in the Peloponnese, and for the Athenians and Argives it would have been better not to have tried than to have tried and failed so clearly.

Epidaurus took advantage of the engagement at Mantinea to attack Argos; but after the battle the defeated allies, joined by Elis and reinforcements from Athens, struck back and began a blockade of Epidaurus (V. 75. iv–vi).

Defeat improved the prospects of those Argives who sympathised with Sparta: in the winter, despite the presence of Alcibiades arguing on the other side, a draft was produced and a final version agreed of a fifty-year treaty of the Spartans and their allies with the Argives and their allies, which apparently envisaged a leadership of the Peloponnese shared between Sparta and Argos (it was not to last long enough to be put to the test). They won over Perdiccas of Macedon and renewed Sparta's alliance with the Chalcidians of Olynthus; the Athenians in obedience to Argos withdrew from Epidaurus; Mantinea came to terms with Sparta (a thirty-year treaty: Xen. *Hell.* V. ii. 2) and gave up its claim to the neighbouring communities. Sparta established a narrower oligarchy in Sicyon (the first attested instance of such constitutional interference by Sparta; to be followed by interference in Achaea the following summer, V. 82. i), and a pro-Spartan oligarchy came to power in Argos (V. 76–81).

But Argos was not to remain pro-Spartan and oligarchic for long. In the summer of 417 the democrats overthrew the oligarchs at the time of the Spartan Gymnopaediae: the Spartans postponed the festival and set out to support the oligarchs, but turned back on learning that they were too late. Envoys from both sides went to Sparta, and the Spartans decided to intervene but did not act; the Argives with Athenian help (attributed by Plut. *Alc.* 15. iv–v to Alcibiades) started building long walls down to the sea. In the winter Sparta and its allies (except Corinth: we do not know why) attacked Argos: they hoped for treachery, but in vain; they demolished the new walls; and on their way back they captured Hysiae, south-west of Argos, and killed all the free inhabitants. Argos then raided Phlius, which had taken in most of the oligarchic exiles (V. 82. ii–83. iii).

Argos' alliance with Athens was finally renewed in spring 416 (*IG* i³ 86). Alcibiades went to Argos and deported three hundred Spartan sympathisers (V. 84. i); the Argives attacked Phlius again but were caught in an ambush (V. 115. i). In winter 416/5 an intended Spartan attack on Argos was halted by unfavourable auspices, and in Argos more Spartan sympathisers were arrested (V. 116. i). Later Sparta and its allies (again without Corinth) did attack Argos and established exiled oligarchs and a garrison in Orneae, north-west of the city; but afterwards Argos and Athens attacked Orneae, the men escaped and the town was destroyed (VI. 7. i–ii). Alcibiades had been supporting the anti-Spartan democrats, but in summer 415 his friends in Argos were suspected of plotting against the democracy, and to reassure the democrats Athens handed over for execution the men deported the previous year (VI. 61. iii). In 414 the Spartans set out to attack Argos but were halted by an earthquake, after which Argos raided the disputed territory of Thyrea (VI. 95. i). A later invasion by Sparta and its allies did take place; ships came from Athens to support Argos and joined in a raid on the east coast of Laconia, and then Argos raided Phlius again (VI. 105).

In 419/8 Athens had reinstalled dissident helots in Pylos (cf. p. 127). In 416 they made a successful raid on the surrounding territory. The Spartans did not themselves put an end to the Peace of Nicias, but they invited their allies to raid Athens, and Corinth, not a party to the peace, did so (V. 115. ii–iii). Athens' joining Argos in the raid of 414 was the clearest breach yet of the peace: since 421 Athens and Sparta had fought against each other, but this was the first time one party had invaded the other's territory; the Spartans were now confident that they were in the right. Now they offered to go to arbitration and Athens refused (VII. 18. iii: contrast 432/1, pp. 86, 88).

We have glimpses of continuing activity in the north-east. In 417 Dium, on the eastern prong of Chalcidice, defected from Athens (V. 82. i). In 418/7 Perdiccas had made an alliance with Sparta and oligarchic Argos; in 417/6 he refused to support a planned Athenian campaign against the Chalcidians and Amphipolis, and Athens blockaded Macedon (V. 83. iv); in 416/5 Athens sent cavalry, including exiled Macedonians, by sea to harry Perdiccas, and the Chalcidians refused a Spartan request to support him (VI. 7. iii–iv); but by late summer 414 Perdiccas was once more on the Athenian side, joining in an attack on Amphipolis which failed to capture the city but set up a blockade (VII. 9). A fragmentary inscription recording an alliance between Athens and Perdiccas (*IG* i^3 89) is perhaps to be attributed to this last change of alignment. Perdiccas died *c.*413: his successor Archelaus, under whom Macedon became greater than under any of his predecessors (II. 100. ii), was to be consistently pro-Athenian, but, in dealing with a weaker Athens, on his own terms; Athens acquired oars from Macedon *c.*411–410 (Andoc. II. *Return* 11), and new ships commissioned by Alcibiades in 407/6 were apparently built in Macedon (M&L 91 = *IG* i^3 117 ~ Fornara 161).

Melos, in the southern Aegean, was the only island not in Athenian hands. At the beginning of the war it was neutral; in 426 it withstood an Athenian attack; in 425 it was included in the tribute assessment (for 15 talents, M&L 69 = *IG* i^2 71 ~ Fornara 136. i. 65: Melos was one of the larger and more prosperous of the island states), but that does not prove that Athens was in a position to exact payment; if the earlier date for an inscription is correct, Melos contributed money to Sparta in the 420's (cf. pp. 94, 109). Although Thucydides gives a detailed account of the episode, he does not explain why Athens attacked Melos in 416, but Athens must have had respectable grounds for sending a force which included allied ships and hoplites (V. 84). On landing the Athenians first sent envoys, who were allowed to speak not to the assembly but to the officials. Thucydides gives us a dialogue, which must be largely his own reconstruction, since he was in exile from Athens and most of the Melians were to be killed. As in earlier speeches, the Athenians talk the language of power politics, claiming that they have come for their own advantage and it will be better for the Melians if they submit; the Melians appeal to justice, the gods and the Spartans, and refuse to submit. The Athenians set up a blockade and withdrew most of their forces (V. 84–114). The defenders had some successes, but in the winter, when the Athenians sent another force, Melos was betrayed to them: they killed the men and enslaved the women and children (but some escaped: Xen. *Hell.* II. ii. 9), and sent Athenian settlers (V. 115. iv, 116. ii–iv). Later sources give some of the blame to Alcibiades ([Andoc.] IV. *Alcibiades* 22, Plut. *Alc.* 16. v–vi), but he is not mentioned in Thucydides' account.

This particular exercise of power seems not to have given the Athenians a bad conscience (cf. Ar. *Av.* 186, of 414; but Euripides' *Trojan Women*, of 415, may have pricked some consciences), but it became notorious (e.g. Isoc. XII. *Panath.* 63). Thucydides creates a dramatic contrast by placing this detailed account of the sledgehammer's cracking the nut before his detailed account of the Athenians' ambitious but disastrous expedition to Sicily. We should at least remember that almost immediately before Melos he reports the Spartans' killing of the inhabitants of Hysiae – in a single sentence (VI. 83. ii: cf. p. 130).

Sicily

Athens had been interested in the west since the middle of the century, and before the outbreak of the war had expected the west to become involved (cf. pp. 68–9, 83–4). Sparta had hoped for support from the west, but in vain (cf. p. 94). Athens sent forces to support Leontini against Syracuse in 427, and by the time the Sicilians agreed to manage without outside intervention, in 424, if not earlier, had begun to hope for conquests (cf. pp. 103–4, 105–6). There was a further attempt at involvement in 422, soon abandoned (cf. p. 106). Thucydides' allegation that most Athenians knew nothing about Sicily and its inhabitants (VI. 1. i) cannot be true.

The origin of Athens' next intervention lay in the west of the island. Egesta, towards the north, which in 418/7 renewed an alliance made with Athens in 427/6 (Thuc. VI. 6. ii; M&L 37 = *IG* i³ 11 ~ Fornara 81, which contains the oath and above which the decree of renewal could have been inscribed: cf. p. 45; there was added to that *stele* an alliance with nearby Halicyae, *IG* i³ 12), was at war with Selinus, on the south coast. Dorian Selinus gained the support of Syracuse; Egesta (after first appealing to Carthage, according to Diod. Sic. XII. 82. vii) appealed to Athens, claiming to be able to pay the full costs, and Athens sent men to investigate (Thuc. VI. 6). In Thucydides' account the Athenians were altogether too naïve, going from house to house and not realising that they were seeing the same precious objects in each (VI. 46. iii–v): but, in whatever way, they were deceived about Egesta's wealth. He reports for the spring of 415 a decision to send sixty ships under three generals, Alcibiades, Nicias and Lamachus, to support Egesta against Selinus, to help refound Leontini, and 'to settle other matters in Sicily to Athens' advantage' (VI. 8. i–ii); elsewhere he refers directly to hopes of conquering Sicily (VI. 1. i, 6. i), and he attributes to Alcibiades, as Aristophanes in 424 had attributed to Hyperbolus, hopes of Carthage too (VI. 15. ii, 90. ii, cf. 34. ii; for Hyperbolus cf. pp. 121–2). A fragmentary inscription combines with a reference to sixty ships a vote on whether to send one general – who would presumably have been Alcibiades – or a plurality (M&L 78 = *IG* i³ 93 ~ Fornara 146, fr. *b*). Nicias had opposed the expedition: the inclusion of him with Alcibiades among the commanders reflects not a desire of 'the Athenians' that each should counter the excesses of the other but the support in the assembly for him and his opinion.

Four days later, at an assembly to consider detailed arrangements for the expedition, Nicias reopened the question. Thucydides gives him a speech in which he (perhaps too presciently) highlights the difficulties, that Athens has enough enemies nearer home and cannot afford to reach out for more power, that Sicily will be hard to retain even if it is conquered (cf. p. 140), that Athens cannot afford to squander its recently rebuilt resources, and that Alcibiades is more interested in his own advancement than that of Athens. Alcibiades replies that his personal ambitions are good for Athens as well as himself, that the Greek Sicilians though numerous are a mixed rabble, and the opponents of Syracuse will support Athens, that having set out on the path of empire Athens cannot ration its imperialism. When the Athenians were not inclined to give up, Nicias made a second speech, stressing the strength of the cities Athens was going to attack, and the need for land forces of various kinds including cavalry and light-armed, and doubting Egesta's promised funds. When asked how large a force was needed, he said at least a hundred triremes and five thousand hoplites; and in their passion for the venture (VI. 24. iii) the Athenians agreed. Nicias' opposition had resulted in a much larger expedition, of which much more could be expected, than had originally been intended (VI. 8. iii–26). Despite the promise of money from Egesta, the inscription cited above can be restored with a reference to 'three thousand', possibly the setting aside of 3,000 talents for the campaign (M&L 78 = *IG* i³ 93 ~ Fornara 146, frs. *d*+*g*).

Before the expedition was ready to sail, panic was caused by the mutilation in a single night of most of the herms in Athens (cf. pp. 157–9). This may have been an unsuccessful attempt by opponents of the expedition to create unfavourable omens; investigation uncovered stories of mock celebrations of the Eleusinian Mysteries in which Alcibiades was involved. It was agreed that he should sail with the expedition but be recalled to stand trial (VI. 27–9).

The expedition departed in the middle of the summer: the total force, including those who joined at Corcyra, was larger than any Athens had sent out since 430: 134 triremes (100 Athenian) and two smaller warships, 5,100 hoplites (1,500 Athenian; allies supplying soldiers included Argos and, technically as mercenaries, Mantinea), various light-armed, thirty cavalry and a great variety of camp-followers (VI. 30–32. ii, 42–44. i). These would have to be paid not for a short campaign but all the year round.

While the Athenians had been divided over whether to go to Sicily, Thucydides claims that the Syracusans were divided over whether to expect them (but this is hard to believe, since they had been to Sicily before and there can have been no secret about their preparations). We are given a speech by Hermocrates, warning that the Athenians will come, suggesting an alliance with Carthage (allegedly afraid of an Athenian attack) and an appeal to Sparta and

Corinth, and proposing to sail across to the south-east of Italy and challenge the Athenians there (which would probably have had disastrous results); a speech by Athenagoras, refusing to believe that the Athenians will come, accusing young men of using the bogey of Athens as an excuse for bringing in an oligarchy and himself defending the principle of democracy; after which an unnamed general tries to calm the situation and promises suitable precautions (VI. 32. iii–42). Serious preparations were begun when the Syracusans learned that the Athenians had reached Rhegium (VI. 45).

The Athenians crossed from Corcyra, making their way along the Italian coast and finding that they were not very welcome, until they reached Rhegium, on the toe of Italy. They were allowed to camp outside the city but not go inside; Rhegium declared itself neutral, but if the Italian Greeks adopted a common policy it would go along with that (VI. 44. ii–iv). Ships sent ahead brought back the news that Egesta was not, after all, rich, and the generals reconsidered their strategy. Nicias wanted to sail to Selinus and make a show of force, then unless Egesta could after all provide funding return home (which he would presumably have justified by claiming that the Athenians had been deceived). Alcibiades wanted the Athenians to base themselves on Messana and to gain friends in Sicily until they could attack Syracuse and Selinus. Lamachus wanted to make an immediate attack on Syracuse (which might have succeeded if Syracuse was as ill prepared as Thucydides suggests, but would have been disastrous if it failed). To resolve the deadlock, Lamachus backed Alcibiades, and his plan was chosen (VI. 46–50. i).

Messana was unwelcoming, Naxos slightly less so. Catana was hesitant but allowed the generals to address the assembly; while they were doing so, the Athenian soldiers managed to enter the city, the supporters of Syracuse fled, and Catana made an alliance with Athens and became their base in Sicily (VI. 50–2). The *Salaminia*, one of Athens' state ships, arrived to take back Alcibiades and others for trial in connection with the religious scandals. They went quietly but escaped during the journey: Alcibiades made his way (perhaps via Argos: Isoc. XVI. *Chariot* 9, Plut. *Alc.* 23. i) to Sparta (VI. 53, 60–1, 88. ix). His colleagues now had to pursue his strategy without him.

Late in 415 the Athenian forces, provoked by detachments of Syracusan cavalry, were growing impatient for action. The generals sent a deceitful messenger to entice the Syracusans to march north and attack the Athenians at Catana on a particular day; and then, while the Syracusans were on their way, themselves sailed south by night, entered the great harbour and landed on the west side near the Olympieum (see map 6 and ill. 9). They were able to prepare a stockade before the Syracusans came back to confront them; they won a battle; but the Syracusan cavalry prevented them from following up their victory and they returned to Catana (VI. 63–71). A promising plan had achieved nothing: Nicias was criticised (Plut. *Nic.* 16), and Thucydides himself was perhaps critical (VII. 42. iii). A hoped-for revolution in Messana failed to occur, since Alcibiades on his departure had warned the supporters of Syracuse; and the Athenians spent the winter at Naxos, sending home for money and cavalry (VI. 74).

In Syracuse, which currently had a democratic constitution with a board of fifteen generals, Hermocrates tried to restore morale and argued for fewer and more powerful generals: he was made one of a board of three (to take office at the new year, perhaps in the spring), and Syracuse appealed for help to Corinth and Sparta (VI. 72–3). Both sides tried to gain support in Sicily (Thucydides gives us opposing speeches at Camarina from Hermocrates and an Athenian called Euphemus). The Syracusans, to make the attackers' job harder, built a new wall which probably ran northwards from the north shore of the great harbour to the sea; the Athenians appealed to Carthage (not now a further target for conquest) and Etruria, where some cities were offering support (VI. 75–88. vi). Corinth as the mother city of Syracuse was eager to support it, and joined in the approach to Sparta. By now Alcibiades was in Sparta. Thucydides gives him a speech to the Spartan assembly, claiming that Athens' democracy is 'agreed folly', setting out an extreme version of Athens' ambitions and suggesting that there is a serious danger of their being achieved, and urging Sparta to send soldiers and, even more, a Spartan to take command, and to fortify Decelea in the north of Attica. The Spartans were persuaded. On the other side, the Athenians sent 250 cavalry and thirty mounted archers, and 300 talents (VI. 88. vii–93). How much difference did Alcibiades make? According to Thucydides, before his intervention the authorities were inclined to tell Syracuse not to surrender, but not to send help (VI. 88. x). In the event, Sparta sent Gylippus as commander (perhaps a *mothax*, a Spartan of inferior origin brought up with the Spartiates [Ael. *V.H.* XII. 43]; cf. Lysander, p. 149) and, we later discover, two Spartan ships (VI. 104. i), and, in 413, 600 liberated helots (VII. 19. iii), which it might have done in any case in response to the appeal from Syracuse and Corinth. It was not to invade Attica and fortify Decelea until 413 (cf. pp. 140–1). Probably Alcibiades was not as important as Thucydides suggests; but the sending of Gylippus was nevertheless to prove crucial.

In 414 the Athenians began a major attack on Syracuse. They sailed south and disembarked their soldiers at Leon, north-west of the city. These soldiers made their way to Euryelus, at the west end of the plateau of Epipolae outside the city, before the defenders were ready to guard the approaches, and when a force did arrive they defeated it. They established a fort at Labdalum, on the north edge of the plateau; reinforcements reached them, from Sicily and from Athens; and, nearer to the city and towards the south edge of the plateau, they built what Thucydides called 'the circle', which was to be the base for their siege (VI. 96–8). They needed to match the whole length of the Syracusan wall built in the winter, from the great harbour to the sea to the north; and Hermocrates persuaded the Syracusans that it would be best to build an east–west wall across the line of the Athenian wall, south of the circle, to prevent its completion. The Athenians waited until the Syracusans grew careless, then attacked and captured the cross-wall. The Syracusans built a second cross-wall, further south. The Athenians captured that too, though Lamachus was killed in the pursuit of some fleeing Syracusans. While most of the Athenians were still on the low ground, the Syracusans attacked the circle: Nicias, suffering from a kidney disease, was there and saved the circle. At this point the Athenian fleet, which

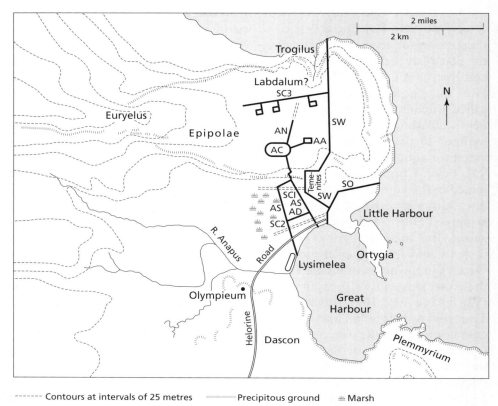

Map 6 Syracuse (after K. J. Dover, *Thucydides Book VII/Thucydides Book VII* [Oxford: Oxford University Press, 1965], p. viii)

had been waiting at Thapsus, sailed into the great harbour and joined the army (VI. 99–102).

The Athenians appeared to be in a winning position, and gained further allies. They now built two walls from the circle to the harbour, to protect them against attacks either from the city or from outside. The Syracusans considered surrendering and made overtures to Nicias; and they deposed their generals and elected others (VI. 103). Gylippus, on his way with four Peloponnesian ships, to be followed by a further thirteen, heard of this and despaired of Sicily, but still hoped to make sure of Italy; Nicias heard of Gylippus' coming but did not take his small force seriously (VI. 105). In particular, Nicias failed to cut off Syracuse entirely by completing the wall to the north of the circle.

Ill. 9 Syracuse: aerial photograph. Science Photo Library, London

Gylippus sailed to Himera, on the north coast, and from there advanced on Syracuse, picking up allies as he went. The Corinthian Gongylus with one advance ship from the following squadron reached Syracuse in time to prevent its capitulation; the Syracusans marched out to meet Gylippus, and he arrived via Euryelus and the northern part of Epipolae. Nicias did not respond to an immediate challenge, when he might still have succeeded, and Gylippus entered the city (VII. 1–3. iii).

Nicias still did not have the northern wall completed while there was time. The Syracusans captured the Athenian fort at Labdalum, and started building a third cross-wall, north of the circle. Nicias, in a futile diversion, built forts on Plemmyrium, the headland south of the harbour entrance, and sent ships to try to intercept those coming to join Gylippus. In fighting on Epipolae Gylippus was defeated in a first battle but returned and was victorious in a second, and the cross-wall was continued beyond the line of the Athenian wall, so that Syracuse could not now be cut off; and the Peloponnesian ships arrived and entered the harbour (VII. 3. iv–7. i). Gylippus set out to raise more forces in Sicily, and asked for more from Corinth and Sparta. Nicias sent a letter to Athens, asking either to be recalled or to be sent reinforcements as substantial as the forces already with him, and to be relieved of his own command. The Athenians did not relieve Nicias, but they appointed two men with him as immediate colleagues, and Eurymedon, who had been in Sicily in 425–424, and Demosthenes, the most energetic commander of the 420's, to take reinforcements, Eurymedon during the winter and Demosthenes the main force in the spring (VII. 7. ii–17).

In Syracuse in 413 Hermocrates returned to influence, if not to office (VII. 31. iii); and the Syracusans made simultaneous attacks by land and sea: they were defeated at sea, but their land forces captured the Athenian forts on Plemmyrium and gave them control of the entrance to the harbour (VII. 21–5). Wanting to achieve more before the Athenian reinforcements arrived, they strengthened their ships for an old-fashioned ramming battle, and again attacked by land, against the Athenian wall, and by sea: this time they were unsuccessful on land but at sea on a third day of fighting they caught the Athenians unprepared and defeated them (VII. 36–41).

Demosthenes engaged in raiding around the Peloponnese on his way (cf. p. 140); Eurymedon returned and joined him; and they arrived at Syracuse together: Athens' total reinforcements amounted to 82 ships, 5,000 hoplites and many light-armed. Demosthenes wanted to strike immediately while the shock of his arrival was greatest, and decided on a night attack, going up to Epipolae by Euryelus and proceeding along the Syracusan cross-wall from the west. This started well but, with too many men recently arrived and not knowing the terrain, ended in confusion and slaughter (VII. 42–6). Demosthenes then wanted to withdraw; but Nicias still had hopes (with some justification, Thucydides suggests) of a Syracusan surrender, and would not even move to Thapsus or Catana. When he at last relented, there was an eclipse of the moon (on 27 August), and he let the seers persuade him to wait another month (VII. 47–50).

The Athenians were defeated in another naval battle, in which Eurymedon was killed; and in yet another, with every available man on every available ship. After that they still had sixty ships, more than the enemy, but the men refused to fight again (VII. 51–72). If they had moved at once, the Athenians could have extricated themselves by land while the Syracusans were celebrating, but Hermocrates sent men posing as traitors to Nicias to persuade the Athenians to wait until the Syracusans were ready for them (VII. 73–4). Finally the Athenians set out in a westerly direction, until they came to the head of a valley, where the Syracusans blocked their advance. After forcing their way through, they turned south-eastwards towards the sea. They became separated; Demosthenes with the rearguard was trapped in an olive grove on the sixth day of the retreat, and eventually surrendered; two days later Nicias surrendered after discipline had broken down at the crossing of a river (VII. 75–85).

Thucydides states that Gylippus wanted to take Nicias and Demosthenes back to Sparta, but they were executed; otherwise the survivors were imprisoned in the quarries outside Syracuse, some sold into slavery after ten weeks but the Athenians and their western Greek allies kept for eight months (VII. 86–7). Diodorus (XIII. 19. iv–33. i) and Plutarch (*Nic.* 28) give different versions of a debate the truth behind which is probably that what was actually done was proposed by the demagogue Diocles (cf. pp. 274–6), while Hermocrates and Gylippus argued for milder treatment.

Thucydides calls this the greatest success for the victors and greatest disaster for the defeated in Greek history (VII. 87. v–vi), and the superlative is justified. The Athenians had started with great ambitions, had spent large sums of money and had sent large numbers of ships and men; but few of the men and none of the ships returned home, the money was spent in vain, and the psychological effect, on them and on the whole Greek world, was enormous. (The one comparable shock was to be the defeat of the Spartan army at Leuctra in 371: cf. pp. 216, 251). The impression given by books VI–VII is that the attack on Syracuse could have succeeded (and if Syracuse was conquered the rest of Sicily would probably have followed: cf. Alcibiades in VI. 91. iii), and indeed very nearly did succeed; but the chance of victory was thrown away when Nicias failed to prevent Gylippus' entry, and his subsequent mistakes, and his refusal to withdraw when he was likely to be blamed for withdrawal, made a bad situation worse. II. 65. xi has a different emphasis: the expedition

> involved not so much an error of judgment about the people against whom it was sent as the failure by those who sent out the expedition to make the right decisions in support of the men who had gone. Instead, through the accusations made against individuals in the struggle for political supremacy, they made the expeditionary force less effective.

The allusion is presumably to the trial of those accused of involvement in the religious scandals (cf. pp. 157–9), in particular the recall of Alcibiades and his consequent exile; and we may also fault the refusal to relieve Nicias in 414/3;

but otherwise the detailed narrative does not suggest that the Athenians at home did not support the expedition adequately. We are more likely to think that the venture was 'an error of judgment about the people against whom it was sent': controlling a large and populous island at a distance from Athens would be much harder than controlling the islands and coastal cities of the Aegean; and, although in the short term Athens could have conquered Sicily, it is hard to believe that it could have retained Sicily for long against opposition (cf. Nicias in VI. 11. i, Euphemus in VI. 86. iii).

The hard-headed Thucydides has puzzled his readers by making no comment on Demosthenes but remarking that Nicias was particularly undeserving of his fate because of his devotion to virtue (VII. 86. iv–v). Although Thucydides did not believe in piety, he did believe in moral standards as well as in hard-headedness, and the morality of a Nicias who was by conventional standards a good man but who took decisions as a result of which more Athenians suffered and died than need have done was perhaps more easily praised by Thucydides than by some of Nicias' critics in our time. Gylippus' achievement seems not to have been appreciated by the Spartans, and he is mentioned only in one later episode (cf. p. 152).

Meanwhile

For 415–413 Thucydides concentrates almost entirely on the Sicilian expedition, and gives us only fragments of information on other matters. In 415, at the time of the religious scandals in Athens, Boeotian troops were active near the Athenian frontier and a Spartan force went as far as the Isthmus to co-operate with them (Thuc. VI. 61. ii, Andoc. I. *Myst.* 45). In 414 in Thespiae (where Thebes had intervened in 423: cf. p. 110) a democratic rising was put down with Theban help, and some democrats fled to Athens (VI. 95. ii).

In spring 413 the Athenian Conon (the first appearance of a man who was to be important later), who was at Naupactus with eighteen ships, reported to Demosthenes and Eurymedon that he was being challenged by twenty-five Corinthian ships (so that troop-carriers could take Peloponnesian reinforcements to Sicily) and could not fight against them without more: they let him have ten ships from their force (VII. 19, 31. iv–v). Later in the year he had been succeeded by another commander and the Athenians had thirty-three ships; the Corinthians manned a few more, and fought a close battle which for them was as good as a victory (VII. 34): the Athenians no longer had the overwhelming naval superiority which they had enjoyed in the 420's (cf. p. 103).

But the most important development in Greece in 413 was that the Spartans, believing themselves to be in the right after the raid of 414 (cf. p. 130), and thinking it safe since so much of Athens' manpower was committed to Sicily, sent a Peloponnesian force to invade Attica under king Agis, and built a fort at Decelea, in the hills east of north from Athens: Alcibiades is said to have been urging this since 415/4 (cf. p. 135), and the location at any rate may have

been his suggestion. Agis was to remain there with a garrison until the end of
the war, and this, by denying the Athenians the use of the countryside and the
silver mines, was to do the Athenians much more psychological and economic
damage than the short invasions of the early years of the war (VII. 19. iii, 27–8,
Hell. Oxy. 20. iii–v Chambers). The Athenians still did not abandon Attica
entirely: a fort was built at Sunium in 413/2 (VIII. 4), and another at nearby
Thoricus in 409 (Xen. *Hell.* I. ii. 1). While the Peloponnesians were invading
Attica, the Athenians sent out thirty ships, together with those bound for Syracuse under Demosthenes, to attack Spartan territory: they collected hoplites
from Argos, raided the east coast of Laconia, then opposite Cythera (which they
still retained, as they did Pylos) they set up a fort on the mainland (VII. 20,
26).

NOTE ON FURTHER READING

See in general Cawkwell, *Thucydides and the Peloponnesian War*; Kagan, *The Peace of Nicias
and the Sicilian Expedition*; Lazenby, *The Peloponnesian War*. For many campaigns there
are valuable investigations in Pritchett's series *Studies in Ancient Greek Topography*.

On the diplomatic problems following the Peace of Nicias see particularly H. D.
Westlake, 'Thucydides and the Uneasy Peace – A Study in Political Incompetence', *CQ²*
xxi 1971, 315–25 = his *Studies in Thucydides and Greek History*, ch. 7; R. Seager, 'After
the Peace of Nicias', *CQ²* xxvi 1976, 249–69. The view of 'ten-day' truces adopted here
is that of A. Andrewes in Gomme et al., *Historical Commentary on Thucydides*, iv. 11: the
alternative view that they had to be renewed every ten days is championed by M. Arnush,
'Ten-Day Armistices in Thucydides', *GRBS* xxxiii 1992, 329–53; D. Whitehead, 'The
Ten-Day Truce (Thucydides, 5. 26. 2, etc.)', in Frézouls and Jacquemin (eds.), *Les Relations internationales . . . 1993*, 189–210.

On the battle of Mantinea see A. W. Gomme, 'Thucydides and the Battle of Manti-
neia', in his *Essays in Greek History and Literature*, 132–55; and, on the problem of
Spartan numbers, Gomme et al., *Historical Commentary on Thucydides*, iv. 110–17 (by
Andrewes, believing in an error in Thuc. V. 68. iii, but starting from the material of
Gomme, who did not believe in an error).

Athens' Sicilian expedition is treated by Freeman, *History of Sicily*, vol. iii, ch. 8. On
the Syracusan leader Hermocrates see H. D. Westlake, 'Hermocrates the Syracusan',
BRL xli 1958/9, 239–68 = his *Essays on the Greek Historians and Greek History*, 174–202.
For a suggestion that Thuc. VI–VII consciously exposed the Athenians' inadequacies see
B. Jordan, 'The Sicilian Expedition was a Potemkin Fleet', *CQ²* 1 2000, 63–79.

13

The Peloponnesian War: 413–404

```
  500      475      450      425      400      375      350      325      300
```

412 Sparta first secures Persian support
411 oligarchic revolution in Athens
410 Athenian victory at Cyzicus
406 Spartan victory at Notium
406 Athenian victory, but failure to recover bodies, at Arginusae
405 Spartan victory at Aegospotami
404 Peloponnesian War ends with Athens' coming to terms with Sparta

Thucydides, VIII

Despite the great blow of their failure in Sicily, the Athenians resolved to fight on. They built more ships and made other preparations, and took economy measures including the abandonment of the fort opposite Cythera (VIII. 1, 4). Nevertheless, their new weakness significantly changed the situation. Sparta was now more hopeful of defeating Athens and becoming the undisputed leader of Greece (VIII. 2); and called on its allies to join in building a hundred ships, including twenty-five each from Sparta and Boeotia and (fewer than we might expect) fifteen from Corinth (VIII. 3. ii). Whatever we think of the popularity of the Delian League with its member states (cf. pp. 178–85), Athens will now have looked much less able to compel loyalty than in the past. Various members of the League made contact with the Spartans: first the Euboeans and then the Lesbians with Agis at Decelea, who decided Lesbos was the more important; then the oligarchic leaders of Chios, and Erythrae, with the authorities in Sparta (VIII. 5. i–iv).

Approaches to Sparta were also made by Tissaphernes and Pharnabazus, the Persian satraps of Sardis and Dascylium: they were under pressure from Darius to collect tribute from the Asiatic Greeks, and Tissaphernes was given a superior position in the region (VIII. 5. iv–6. i). According to Andocides, after making the treaty with the King with which his uncle Epilycus was involved (cf. pp. 113–14), the Athenians foolishly broke it and supported the rebel Amorges (III. *Peace* 29). Amorges was a bastard son of Pissuthnes, a satrap of Sardis who had revolted perhaps at the end of the 420's and had been replaced by Tissaphernes (Ctesias *FGrH* 688 F 15 § 53 [52]); he himself was in revolt with Athenian support in Thuc. VIII (cf. 28. ii, 54. iii), and Tissaphernes had orders to take him dead or alive. When his revolt began is not certain; an Athenian general was present at Ephesus in spring 414 (M&L 77 = *IG* i³ 370. 78–9), and it is possible that an Athenian called Melesandrus was involved with Amorges in 414/3 (*IG* i³ 371. 3, *TAM* i 44. *a*. 45, 55). Though some have doubted it, it does seem credible that the Athenians had decided for some reason to back Amorges and this provoked the Persians into supporting Sparta.

The Spartans were torn between a Hellespont strategy (which was ultimately to win the war for them) and an Aegean strategy (for which they would have the support of Chios' navy). They were inclined to the Aegean by Alcibiades (who had friends in Miletus: VIII. 17. ii) and his Spartan family friend (cf. p. 126) Endius, currently ephor – Alcibiades perhaps exercised more influence on Spartan policy now than earlier – and a meeting in Corinth in spring 412 adopted Chios–Lesbos–the Hellespont as an order of priority. While the Isthmian games were celebrated, in mid-summer, the Athenians discovered what was intended. When the Peloponnesians set out from Cenchreae, Corinth's port on the Saronic Gulf, with just twenty-one ships, an Athenian squadron chased them back to land, but Alcibiades, after he had put pressure on Endius, went at last with the Spartan Chalcideus and five ships to Chios. Other cities joined in revolt against Athens; Athens used its emergency reserve of 1,000 talents (cf. pp. 92–3), and replied by blockading the Peloponnese and sending ships to Samos, which was to be Athens' main base in the Aegean until the end of the war (VIII. 6. ii–17. iii). If the Athenians had imposed a democracy on Samos in 439 (cf. p. 68), they must later have tolerated a return to oligarchy; but a democratic rising in 412 had their approval (VIII. 21, cf. *IG* i³ 96).

At this point Thucydides quotes the first of three treaties between the Spartans and the Persians: it is made with 'the King and Tissaphernes' and claims that 'whatever land and cities the King possesses and the King's fathers possessed shall belong to the King'; the war is to be prosecuted jointly (VIII. 17. iv–18). Revolt against Athens continued to spread. Both sides reinforced their Aegean fleets, and Hermocrates brought Sparta twenty ships from Syracuse and two from Selinus (a few more from the west were to follow). Astyochus as navarch (Sparta's principal naval commander) was reluctant to take risks against the Athenians; the Athenians were fairly successful at striking back, particularly in the islands (but they never recovered Chios, though it was divided between anti-Athenian and pro-Athenian factions). After the Athenians had won a battle off Miletus and the Peloponnesians had gained reinforcements, the Athenian general Phrynichus refused to risk another battle against slightly superior numbers: Thucydides praises his caution, but some other Athenians thought and some modern scholars have agreed that a little more boldness would have been worthwhile. His withdrawal enabled the Spartans to capture Iasus, in Caria, and hand over it and Amorges to Tissaphernes (VIII. 19–28).

In winter 412/1 campaigning continued, Tissaphernes reduced his rate of pay for the Peloponnesian fleet (VIII. 29–36. i), and we are given a second treaty between the Spartans and the Persians: this states not what the King is to possess but that neither Sparta nor the King shall attack or levy tribute from what the other possesses; the King is to pay for forces in his territory at his invitation, which could provide an excuse for withholding payment (VIII. 36. ii–37). On Chios the Athenians were building a fort, and, when the city asked Astyochus for help and he refused, Pedaritus, the Spartan commander there, complained to Sparta. A squadron of ships from Sparta brought Lichas (winner of the chariot race at Olympia and an influential man) and ten other inspectors/advisers to Astyochus, with permission to go north to the Hellespont and to replace Astyochus with their own commander Antisthenes. Astyochus was retained in office, but Lichas objected to the extent of the Persian claims – as far as central Greece – which, though probably not intended, would be allowed by the wording of the two treaties. The Spartans won over Rhodes, but the Athenians, though too late to prevent that, were becoming more confident than Phrynichus had been earlier, while the Spartans were afraid to face them in a straightforward naval battle; and Pedaritus was killed in fighting against the Athenian fort on Chios (VIII. 38–45, 55, cf. 60. ii–iii).

By now Alcibiades had fallen out with the Spartans. In Sparta, he had allegedly formed a liaison with the wife of the absent Agis (cf. p. 205); his influence was presumably reduced when Endius' year as ephor ended in autumn 412; and it is alleged that Astyochus was sent orders to kill him. At some point he moved from Miletus to Tissaphernes' court at Sardis, urging Tissaphernes to limit his support for Sparta and suggesting that a balance or even an Athenian victory would be better for him than a Spartan victory (cf. Sparta's inland ambitions in the 390's: pp. 207–9). The two lovers of intrigue doubtless enjoyed manoeuvring around each other. Wanting to return to Athens, Alcibiades made contact with leading men in the fleet at Samos, suggesting that if Athens overthrew its democracy and recalled him he could obtain Persian support for Athens. We shall follow the oligarchic movement at pp. 160–5. Alcibiades was distrusted by Phrynichus, who, not realising how far he had already lost the confidence of the Spartans, tried to betray him to them. The Athenians negotiated through Alcibiades with Tissaphernes, but gave up when confronted with a demand not only for mainland Asia Minor but also for the offshore islands and a Persian presence in the Aegean (45–56). It seems unlikely that Tissaphernes, under orders from the King, seriously considered changing sides; we cannot be sure what Alcibiades believed; but the Athenians were to continue to hope that Persia could be won over until 407 (cf. pp. 148–9).

That round of negotiations had broken down in time for a new treaty to be made between Sparta and the Persians in spring 411. This has a more elaborate preamble, so may have been ratified at a higher level, than its predecessors, and it involves a larger number of Persians, including Pharnabazus. In response to Lichas it limits the King's claims to mainland Asia Minor, but makes it clear that there they are total (in the mention of 'territory' but not 'cities' the Spartans may have seen a loophole, but the Persians surely did not); if Tissaphernes continues to pay for the Peloponnesian fleet after the arrival of the Persians' fleet, that payment is to be treated as a loan (VIII. 57–8).

The war started to move northwards. The Spartan Dercylidas went to the Hellespont by land from Miletus, and Abydus and Lampsacus went over to him. The Athenian Strombichides went by sea from Chios, was able to recover Lampsacus but not Abydus, and established a fort opposite Abydus at Sestos (VIII. 61–2). Neither side was eager to fight unless it could be sure of winning. Among the Peloponnesians there were increasing complaints about Astyochus and about Tissaphernes, while Pharnabazus was eager to attract them into his area. Clearchus took forty Peloponnesian ships and won over Byzantium; the Athenians sent ships to Sestos (VIII. 78–80). When the Milesians captured a fort established in their territory by Tissaphernes, they were rebuked by Lichas, who said that they 'must submit to moderate slavery and cultivate Tissaphernes until they got a good settlement of the war': that raises doubts about his commitment to the third treaty. Mindarus arrived as Spartan navarch to succeed Astyochus: Astyochus, Hermocrates and an envoy of Tissaphernes all went with their various complaints to Sparta. Tissaphernes himself set off for Aspendus, on the south coast of Asia Minor, allegedly in order to bring 147 Phoenician ships, but he never brought them (it is possible that they were needed against a revolt in Egypt and were no longer available to him). Meanwhile Alcibiades had joined the (once more democratic) Athenian fleet at Samos, where he had been made general. He prevented the fleet from abandoning the Aegean to sail back and restore the democracy at Athens; he followed Tissaphernes as far as Phaselis, and claimed the credit for the ships' not coming to support the Peloponnesians (VIII. 81–8, 99, 108. i–ii).

In the autumn Mindarus accepted Pharnabazus' invitation and went north with his full force, managing to reach Abydus (which was to be Sparta's main base in the region) while the Athenians under Thrasybulus and Thrasyllus were preoccupied with recovering Eresus on Lesbos. After they had followed him, a major battle was at last fought, off Cynossema, with seventy-six Athenian ships against eighty-six Peloponnesian: the Athenians' centre was driven to the shore, but the Peloponnesians relaxed too soon and the Athenians' wings closed in and defeated them. This victory did a good deal to restore Athenian morale (VIII. 99–107).

In Greece, early in 411 the Boeotians with help from Eretria had captured the border territory of Oropus from Athens (VIII. 60. i–ii). The oligarchic régime of the Four Hundred tried to make peace with Sparta, but was not prepared to concede all that Sparta demanded – and in any case the democrats at Samos would not have accepted an agreement made by the oligarchs in Athens (VIII. 70. ii–71, 86. ix, 90, 92. iv, *Ath. Pol.* 32. iii). In the autumn a Peloponnesian fleet bound for Euboea caused panic in Athens and was pursued into the Euripus; the Peloponnesians won a battle, and all Euboea except Oreus in the north went over to them: Euboea was economically important to the Athenians, and this was a disaster for them. However, the Peloponnesians then failed to sail back and attack Athens, which was in disarray as the Four Hundred were deposed (VIII. 91–6).

Thucydides' text ends with the expulsion of Persian garrisons from Antandrus and Cnidus, and the return of an anxious Tissaphernes from Aspendus to Ephesus (VIII. 108. iii–109).

After Thucydides: Sources

Thucydides' text breaks off in the autumn of 411, and all that we have must be all that was ever made public, since a number of fourth-century historians started their works at that point.

One of those works is the *Hellenica* (411–362) of Xenophon, an Athenian who spent much of his life, in the first half of the fourth century, in exile as a dependant of the Spartans. He was not a historian of the calibre of Thucydides. In the earlier part of his work, covering the end of the Peloponnesian War, where he marks a new year pseudo-Thucydidean indications of time have been added by an interpolator (e.g. I. i. 37–ii. 1); but in this narrative we have one new year too few between 411 and the end of the war: no attempt to identify the 'empty year' has solved all the problems, but in this book I have assumed that the empty year is 410/09, after the battle of Cyzicus, so that the return of Thrasyllus to the Aegean (I. ii. 1) belongs to 409, not 410.

Our other continuous narrative for this period is that of Diodorus Siculus (415/4–405/4 in book XIII). As for the rest of the fifth century and the first half of the fourth, his principal source was Ephorus (and he has forced into an annalistic framework material which was not organised annalistically by Ephorus: cf. p. 15); papyrus fragments have made it clear that for the late fifth century and the early fourth Ephorus used another continuation of Thucydides, which has become known as the *Hellenica Oxyrhynchia* from Oxyrhynchus in Egypt, where the first fragment was found (chs. 1–3 Chambers deal with 409, 4–8 with 409–406,[1] 9–25 with the mid 390's). The fragments point to a detailed and fairly sober narrative, following Thucydides' organisation by summers and

---

[1] NB Chambers modifies Bartoletti's arrangement of the Florence fragments, so that chs. 3, 4, 5 Bartoletti become chs. 7, 8, 6 Chambers.

winters and numbered years (NB 12. i; in 5. v a résumé of earlier events on Chios refers to Thucydides). Theopompus of Chios (*FGrH* 115) wrote *Hellenica* in continuation of Thucydides (411–394: Diod. Sic. XIII. 42. v), but what we know of him does not match the style of these fragments. Cratippus of Athens (*FGrH* 64) is alleged to have edited Thucydides' text (Dion. Hal. *Thuc.* 16): if the fragments are to be attributed to a writer whose name is known, he is the least unlikely candidate, but we know so little about him that, if he was the author, we are not much wiser. Whereas to 411 Ephorus had based his account on Thucydides, from 411 this account and Xenophon's are independent of each other: neither is to be preferred invariably and automatically; but, even where we have only Diodorus' version of the alternative, there are several places where that seems preferable to Xenophon's account. One fault presumably to be blamed on Diodorus himself is a confusion of names: in book XIII he never uses the name Tissaphernes but calls both satraps Pharnabazus; similarly, in XIII. 64–97 he uses the name Thrasybulus for both Thrasybulus and Thrasyllus, and in XIII. 69. v he mentions Thrasybulus where he apparently should have mentioned Conon.

Plutarch, as always, used a variety of sources. Two of his lives cover the end of the war, *Alcibiades* and *Lysander*.

After Thucydides: The End of the War

After Cynossema Mindarus summoned the Peloponnesian force from Euboea, but that was wrecked off Mount Athos with few survivors. He was joined by Dorieus, who had been guarding against a pro-Athenian revolution in Rhodes; and the Athenians were joined by Alcibiades. The Peloponnesians won a first battle (unless this is a careless reference to the battle in the Euripus: Xen. *Hell.* I. i. 1); Alcibiades arrived in time to help the Athenians to victory in a second (Xen. *Hell.* I. i. 2–7, Diod. Sic. XIII. 41. i–ii, 45–47. ii, Plut. *Alc.* 27. i–ii).

In winter 411/0 the Athenians dispersed. Thrasyllus went to Athens to fetch reinforcements; Alcibiades went in state to visit Tissaphernes, was imprisoned but managed to escape (Xen. *Hell.* I. i. 8–10, Plut. *Alc.* 27. vi, 28. i). In spring 410 he rejoined Thrasybulus in the Hellespont, and from Athens there came not Thrasyllus but Theramenes, one of the leading figures of the intermediate régime currently in power (cf. pp. 164–5). Thrasyllus, it seems, was more of a committed democrat than the others, and did not cooperate easily with them. Mindarus and Pharnabazus captured Cyzicus. The battle of Cyzicus is one of the episodes for which Diodorus has what seems to be the better account: Athens had eighty-six ships to the Peloponnesians' sixty (Xen.); the Athenians landed their soldiers at a distance and divided their fleet; Alcibiades with part of the fleet enticed Mindarus away from the harbour, and then the others came up and cut him off; Mindarus fled to Pharnabazus on the mainland, his ships were destroyed or captured, and on land he was defeated and killed. The Athenians took control of the Propontis, and set up a toll post at Chrysopolis, opposite Byzantium (Diod. Sic. XIII. 47. iii–viii, 49–51, 64. ii; Xen. *Hell.* I. i. 11–22, Plut. *Alc.* 28. ii–ix). Xenophon and Plutarch quote the message sent to Sparta, in eleven words of Greek: 'Ships gone; Mindarus dead; men starving; don't know what to do' (Xen. *Hell.* I. i. 23, Plut. *Alc.* 28. x). In breach of its treaty with Persia, Sparta sent envoys including Endius to Athens to offer peace, on the basis of the status quo except that forts (i.e. Pylos and Decelea) were to be returned; but in Athens, once more democratic, the demagogue Cleophon had the offer rejected (Diod. Sic. XIII. 52–3, Philoch. *FGrH* 328 F 139). It is understandable that the Athenians did not think this a good enough offer, but at this point it might have been to their advantage to accept it.

In the west, the democrats in Corcyra, helped by the Athenian Conon from Naupactus, got the upper hand in another bout of civil disturbance (Diod. Sic. XIII. 48). Elsewhere Athens was less successful: in 410 or 409, when Sparta attacked Pylos by land and sea Athens sent Anytus to defend it, but he was turned back by storms, and his acquittal when he was put on trial became notorious as an instance of bribery (Diod. Sic. XIII. 64. v–vii, cf. Xen. *Hell.* I. ii. 18, *Ath. Pol.* 27. v). In 409 Megara recaptured Nisaea, after which the Athenians won a hoplite battle but did not recover the site (*Hell. Oxy.* 4, Diod. Sic. XIII. 65. i–ii).

In the Hellespont Pharnabazus supported the defeated Spartans and enabled them to build new ships (Xen. *Hell.* I. i. 24–6). Athens' forces dispersed; they were short of hoplites and cavalry, and achieved little (Xen. *Hell.* I. i. 35–6, Diod. Sic. XIII. 64. i). When Thrasyllus left Athens, in 409, he went not to the Hellespont but to Samos and Ionia: his campaign started well but in an attack on Ephesus he was defeated by Tissaphernes and the Peloponnesians' Sicilian contingent (Xen. *Hell.* I. ii. 1–13, *Hell. Oxy.* 1–3, Diod. Sic. XIII. 64. i). In the autumn he joined the other Athenians at Sestos, but at first there was tension between his contingent and the others; in the winter they fortified Lampsacus and made raids on Pharnabazus' territory (Xen. *Hell.* I. ii. 13–17, Diod. Sic. XIII. 64. iv, Plut. *Alc.* 29. iii–v). In 408 the Athenians concentrated on the Bosporus, and made generous settlements with the cities as they were recovered: first Calchedon came to terms with Theramenes; after Alcibiades had collected allies from Thrace and the Chersonese he captured Selymbria; late in the year Byzantium was betrayed to the Athenians when the Spartan governor Clearchus became unpopular for giving food only to his garrison (Xen. *Hell.* I. iii, *Hell. Oxy.* 6, Diod. Sic. XIII. 66–7, Plut. *Alc.* 29. vi–31. viii; treaty with Selymbria M&L 87 = *IG* i³ 118 ~ Fornara 162). Athens now controlled the whole Bosporus–Hellespont region, and must have seemed to be in a strong position. A fragment of Androtion tells us of another Spartan peace offer, again involving Endius, which resulted in a return of prisoners but no more (*FGrH* 324 F 44 ~ Fornara 157).

Both sides at this point made further approaches to Persia. After the fall of Calchedon Pharnabazus agreed to escort Athenian and other envoys to the King, and they spent the winter at Gordium in Phrygia. But in spring 407 they met a Spartan delegation, returning with the news that the King had granted all that they wanted, and had appointed his younger son Cyrus (aged 16: Plut. *Artax.* 2. iv) as *karanos* to take charge of the campaign (Xen. *Hell.* I. iii. 8–14, iv. 1–7). It has been argued that what the King granted included a 'Treaty of Boeotius', conceding that the Asiatic Greeks were to pay tribute to Persia but otherwise to be autonomous (cf. the terms discussed in the 390's, p. 192, and the terms offered to some north-eastern cities in the Peace of Nicias, p. 114). After the war Sparta did not immediately hand over the Asiatic Greeks to Persia; Tissaphernes when he returned to Sardis demanded them; they appealed to Sparta for support against him and Sparta responded. It is easier to believe that this new treaty existed and Tissaphernes was regarding it as obsolete after Sparta's support for Cyrus' revolt than that an ungrateful Sparta was wilfully breaking the treaty of spring 411. The Athenians still did not despair of Persian help: in 407 they approached Cyrus through Tissaphernes, without success (Xen. *Hell.* I. v. 8–9); and we have a frustrating decree for Evagoras of Salamis, in Cyprus, which cannot be dated, in which the Athenians appear to regard the Persian King as an ally (*IG* i^3 113: 411–407?). By now Spartan navarchs were appointed for a year, beginning in the spring. Lysander (from a distinguished family which had fallen on hard times, and, like Gylippus, brought up as a *mothax*: Plut. *Lys.* 2, Ael. *V.H.* XII. 43) was appointed for 407/6 and established a good relationship with Cyrus, and they refitted the Spartan fleet at Ephesus (Xen. *Hell.* I. v. 1–10, Diod. Sic. XIII. 70, Plut. *Lys.* 3–4).

In 407 Thrasybulus, who since Cyzicus had been active off the Thracian coast with a detachment from Athens' fleet, recovered Thasos and other cities (Xen. *Hell.* I. iv. 9, Diod. Sic. XIII. 72. i–ii); Neapolis on the mainland opposite Thasos had remained loyal and Athens was duly grateful (M&L 89 = *IG* i^3 101 ~ Fornara 156). The main fleet returned to Athens under Thrasyllus. Alcibiades, still an exile after the scandals of 415 (he had been accepted by the fleet but not yet by the democratic régime in Athens: cf. pp. 164–5), was cautious; but the Athenians welcomed him back and cleared him of the old charges. On his proposal they ratified treaties he had made in the field (M&L 87–8 = *IG* i^3 118–19 ~ Fornara 162–3), and they made him supreme commander, the only occasion when one Athenian general was superior to his colleagues. He raised fresh forces, and in the autumn, after winning a battle on Andros but not recovering the city, proceeded eventually to Samos (Xen. *Hell.* I. iv. 8–23, Diod. Sic. XIII. 68–9, Plut. *Alc.* 32–35. iv).

He later moved to Notium, on the mainland north of Lysander's position at Ephesus; and early in 406 he left the fleet (going to different destinations according to different sources, but possibly to Phocaea, which Thrasybulus was besieging), entrusting it not to another general but to Antiochus, a helmsman who was a friend of his, with orders not to risk a battle before he returned. But Antiochus did risk a battle. It appears that he and Lysander were each trying a version of the tactics which had worked at Cyzicus, and Lysander was the more successful. Leaving the main fleet in reserve, Antiochus took ten ships and with two of these tried to tempt a small squadron of Lysander's ships; but Lysander sank Antiochus' ship and killed him; the other Athenians panicked;

and when Lysander brought out his whole fleet the main Athenian fleet was unprepared and was defeated. Alcibiades on his return offered a second battle, which Lysander refused; he then withdrew the Athenian fleet to Samos (*Hell. Oxy.* 8, Diod. Sic. XIII. 71; Xen. *Hell.* I. v. 11–15, Plut. *Alc.* 35. v–viii, *Lys.* 5. i–ii). Without waiting to be prosecuted, he withdrew to Thrace. The Athenian generals elected for 406/5 did not include him but did include Conon and Thrasyllus, and Conon went from Andros to Samos to take over the Athenian fleet (Xen. *Hell.* I. v. 16–20, Diod. Sic. XIII. 74, Plut. *Alc.* 36. i–v, *Lys.* 5. iii–iv). About this time Athens appears to have made an alliance with Carthage, now fighting against Athens' enemies in Sicily (M&L 92 = *IG* i³ 123 ~ Fornara 165); but it had no practical effect.

Lysander was succeeded by Callicratidas (allegedly another *mothax*: Ael. *V.H.* XII. 43) as Spartan navarch for 406/5, and this led to considerable friction. Lysander returned the unspent balance of Cyrus' money, and his friends did not cooperate with Callicratidas; Callicratidas was unhappy at fighting with Persian help against fellow Greeks, disliked paying court to Cyrus, and moved from Ephesus to Miletus, less convenient for communication with Sardis (Xen. *Hell.* I. vi. 1–11, Plut. *Lys.* 5. v–6. viii, cf. Diod. Sic. XIII. 76. ii). He then went north to Lesbos and captured Methymna, releasing his non-slave captives other than the Athenians. Conon arrived too late to save Methymna, and Callicratidas trapped and blockaded him in the harbour of Mytilene (Xen. *Hell.* I. vi. 12–23, Diod. Sic. XIII. 76. iii–79. vii). The Athenians made a special effort to send out another fleet: gold dedications were melted down for coinage (Ar. *Ran.* 718–26 with schol. 720 = Fornara 164. B), slaves were liberated to row (Xen. *Hell.* I. vi. 24, Ar. *Ran.* 693–4 with schol. 694 = Hellanicus *FGrH* 323a F 25 ~ Fornara 144. A; *IG* i³ 1032, a list of ships' crews including *therapontes*, l. 227, may belong here), and all eight available generals went with the ships via Samos to Lesbos. At the beginning of the Athenian year 406/5 more than 150 ships confronted Callicratidas. He left fifty ships blockading Conon and with 120 attacked the Athenians near the Arginusae Islands, off the mainland opposite Lesbos. The Peloponnesians were more experienced than the newly recruited Athenians, and were now prepared to try skilled manoeuvres; but the Athenians were overwhelmingly victorious, losing twenty-five ships to more than seventy Peloponnesian, and Callicratidas was killed. The weather was bad, and the Athenians were unable either to pick up survivors and their dead (for the consequences of that cf. p. 167: six generals including Thrasyllus were executed and two escaped into exile) or to go to relieve Conon, but the blockading squadron withdrew to Chios (Xen. *Hell.* I. vi. 24–38, II. i. 1–5, Diod. Sic. XIII. 97–100. vi). *Ath. Pol.* 34. i has another Spartan peace offer now, but this appears to be the post-Cyzicus offer misplaced.

Sparta's allies and Cyrus asked for Lysander to be appointed as navarch again for 405/4. That was not allowed, so Aracus was made figurehead navarch with Lysander as his secretary. He returned to Ephesus, and revived the Spartan fleet with more Persian money, while Cyrus departed to his father's deathbed and a succession dispute (cf. p. 205) (Xen. *Hell.* II. i. 6–14, Diod. Sic. XIII. 100.

vii–viii, 104. iii–iv, Plut. *Lys.* 7. ii–9. ii). He moved to Miletus, apparently unchallenged by the Athenians at Samos, supported an oligarchic revolution (Diod. Sic. XIII. 104. v–vi, Plut. *Lys.* 8, 19. iii), and continued south to Caria and Rhodes; Diodorus and Plutarch have him crossing the Aegean to Aegina and Attica, and meeting Agis; finally, in the autumn he went to the Hellespont, pursued by the Athenians, and captured Lampsacus (Xen. *Hell.* II. i. 15–19, Diod. Sic. XIII. 104. vii–105. i, Plut. *Lys.* 9. iii–iv).

The Athenians went first to Sestos; then, short of supplies and hoping for a quick battle, to the open beach of Aegospotami opposite Lampsacus; but Lysander did not give them their quick battle. Alcibiades came to the Athenians – to offer his help and that of the Thracians and/or to urge a move to the greater safety of Sestos (both may be true but the first is the more important) – but the Athenians were not prepared to trust him again (Xen. *Hell.* II. i. 20–6, Sestos; Diod. Sic. XIII. 105. ii–iv, help; Plut. *Alc.* 36. vi–37. iii, *Lys.* 9. v–11. i, both). In the more probable account of the battle Philocles, one of the Athenian generals and commanding on the day in question, put out with thirty ships to tempt Lysander, while holding the remainder in reserve; but Lysander was ready for him and put out with his whole fleet; and the rest of the Athenians were not ready. Lysander destroyed or captured nearly all the Athenian ships (though some more escaped than the nine or ten, from a total of 180, of our main sources), and all the Athenian prisoners, perhaps 3,000–4,000, were killed. Conon, who got away with a few ships, went to Evagoras of Salamis (Diod. Sic. XIII. 106. i–vii; a different account Xen. *Hell.* II. i. 27–32, Plut. *Alc.* 37. iv–v, *Lys.* 11. ii–13; for Conon cf. pp. 192, 207–8).

Lysander recaptured Byzantium and Calchedon, closing the route from the Black Sea, and proceeded slowly through the Aegean to Athens (only Samos did not surrender: he returned to capture it in 404; for Athens' gratitude see M&L 94 = *IG* i³ 127 ~ Fornara 166 + R&O 2, complete dossier *IG* ii² 1), sending back to swell the starving crowds all the Athenians whom he captured. Pausanias, the other Spartan king, brought an army from the Peloponnese to join Agis in blockading Athens by land, and Lysander's fleet completed the blockade (Xen. *Hell.* II. ii. 1–9, iii. 6–9, Diod. Sic. XIII. 106. vii–107. iii, Plut. *Lys.* 13. iii–14. iv). Cleophon refused to surrender, but the Athenians' resources were exhausted, and it is hard to see what they could have done; he was removed on a trumped-up charge (cf. p. 168), and Theramenes spent three months talking to Lysander. Eventually, in spring 404, Theramenes headed an Athenian delegation to Sparta: some of Sparta's allies would have liked Athens to be totally destroyed, but that did not suit Sparta; the terms agreed were that Athens should demolish the long walls and the Piraeus walls, lose all but twelve ships and all its overseas possessions, take back its exiles (mostly oligarchs from 411–410), and become a subordinate ally of Sparta (Andoc. III. *Peace* 11–12, Xen. *Hell.* II. ii. 10–23, Diod. Sic. XIII. 107. iv–v, cf. XIV. 3. ii, vi, Plut. *Lys.* 14. iv–x). 'They proceeded to tear down the walls to the accompaniment of pipe-girls with great enthusiasm, thinking that day was the beginning of freedom for Greece' (Xen. *Hell.* II. ii. 23).

Lysander received extravagant honours: the 'navarchs dedication' at Delphi, placed at the beginning of the Sacred Way, immediately before the Athenian monument for Marathon, was a large group of statues in the foreground of which was Lysander crowned by Poseidon (M&L 95, Paus. X. 9. vii–xi, cf. Plut. *Lys.* 18. i); in Samos games named after him and other honours make him one of the first Greeks seriously to challenge the boundary between men and gods (Duris *FGrH* 76 FF 26, 71, *IG* XII. vi 334). Agis replied to Lysander with a dedication in which he claimed to be king of land and sea (Plut. *De Tranq. Anim.* 467 E–F). Gylippus, who defeated the Athenians in Sicily, makes a less glorious appearance: he was entrusted by Lysander with taking captured money back to Sparta, and was found to have helped himself to some of it (Diod. Sic. XIII. 106. viii–x, Plut. *Lys.* 16–17. i).

Athens Defeated

Sparta had set out in 431 to break the Athenian empire and liberate the Greeks, and in 404 the Athenian empire was broken. The Archidamian War, from 431 to 421, had confirmed the superiority of the Athenians at sea and their invulnerability as long as they maintained that superiority; the attempt to destabilise Sparta from Pylos and Cythera had achieved little, but the Peace of Nicias, with its return to the prewar situation, would have looked a sufficient success for Athens if it had been fully implemented. It was not fully implemented. In the years which followed, Athens' resources and ambitions recovered; but the new alliance which faced Sparta on land in the Peloponnese was defeated at Mantinea in 418, and Athens squandered its resources in the misguided attempt to conquer Sicily in 415–413. Athens' raiding Spartan territory in 414 was followed by Sparta's establishing a fort at Decelea in 413; and when Athens backed the rebel Amorges, Sparta in 412–411 agreed to abandon the Asiatic Greeks in exchange for Persian support.

Both sides were hampered by internal disagreements: in Sparta between those who were happy to pay Persia's price and those who were not, in Athens between oligarchs and democrats. After 413 Athens' ability to continue building more ships and finding men to row them was greater than might have been expected (cf. Thuc. II. 65. xii), and from late 411 to early 407 it must still have seemed possible that Athens would win the war; but with Cyrus' more wholehearted support Sparta could keep going until Athens was exhausted – and it was that exhaustion rather than the political disagreements blamed by Thucydides which finally lost Athens the war.

The Athenian empire was indeed broken; and shortly after the war we find Sparta paying dues to a Delian sanctuary freed from Athenian control (*I. Délos* 87 = R&O 3). However, the war did not solve the problems of power within Greece. The members of the Delian League found themselves not liberated or (in the case of mainland Asia Minor) handed back to Persia but taken over by Sparta; and, as Thucydides has the Athenians predict in 432 (I. 76. i, 77. vi), the Spartans soon became no less unpopular than the Athenians. They became unpopular with their allies in mainland Greece too, who saw their wishes ignored in the final settlement and derived little benefit from being on the winning side in the war. Within ten years of the end of the war, several of them made an anti-Spartan alliance in which Athens joined; in 386, after fitfully fighting for the Asiatic Greeks against Persia, Sparta finally abandoned them to Persia; in 378 Athens founded a new league to resist Spartan imperialism.

In Athens the combined effects of plague and war had reduced the population to about half its prewar level. The democracy had lost the war, and with the navy limited to twelve ships the lower-class oarsmen were not in the immediate future going to be important; but the oligarchy set up with Spartan support in 404 was to prove so unpleasant that the restored democracy of 403 proved exceptionally stable, and in other respects recovery seems to have been faster than we might have expected. Victory in the war brought unprecedented quantities of foreign wealth into Sparta (though wealth had not previously been as totally absent as the Spartans later liked to imagine). More seriously, at least since the earthquake of c. 464 (cf. pp. 28–9) Sparta's citizen population had been declining, and casualties in the war will have assisted the decline; there was a growing division within the citizen body between the very rich families and the others, and it is not clear how far the decline is due to an absolute shortage of men of citizen ancestry and how far it reflects the downgrading of men unable to pay their mess dues. In any case, an increasingly ambitious Sparta was based on a decreasing number of citizens; and when Sparta's hoplite army was defeated by Thebes at Leuctra in 371 the bubble burst.

The rest of Greece was therefore to lose the stability which the polarisation around Sparta and Athens had maintained for much of the fifth century. Argos, Sparta's traditional rival in the Peloponnese, and Corinth, the leading member after Sparta of the Peloponnesian League, both suffered from internal divisions and were unable to step into the gap. Instead the centre of gravity moved northwards. Thebes as the strongest city in Boeotia tried to become the dominant power on the Greek mainland; Jason of Pherae in Thessaly, in the 370's, and Philip of Macedon, in the middle of the fourth century, developed ambitions, finally fulfilled by Philip, to control Greece. It suited Persia to continue as Tissaphernes had begun, to maintain a balance among the Greeks; and when the Greek states were at peace Greek mercenaries were available to fight in the western provinces of the Persian empire. The abandonment of the Asiatic Greeks in 386 was seen as a great betrayal; fourth-century Greeks claimed that Greece had been great when it was united against Persia at the beginning of the fifth century, and Philip of Macedon planned and his son Alexander undertook a war against Persia for which Greek enmity provided a convenient excuse.

NOTE ON FURTHER READING

See in general Cawkwell, *Thucydides and the Peloponnesian War*; Kagan, *The Fall of the Athenian Empire*; Lazenby, *The Peloponnesian War*.

On Sparta's treaties with Persia see Lewis, *Sparta and Persia*, chs. 4–5; and, on one particular problem, Lewis, 'The Phoenician Fleet in 411', *Hist.* vii 1958, 392–7 = his *Selected Papers in Greek and Near Eastern History*, 362–8, D. Lateiner, 'Thucydides and the Phoenician Fleet (Thuc. VIII. 87)', *TAPA* cvi 1976, 267–90. On Tissaphernes see H. D. Westlake, 'Tissaphernes in Thucydides', *CQ*² xxxv 1985, 43–54 = his *Studies in Thucydides and Greek History*, 166–80. Among those who have rejected Lewis's Treaty of Boeotius is C. J. Tuplin, 'The Treaty of Boiotios', *Achaemenid History* ii 1984 [publ. 1987], 133–53.

For the suggestion that Athens' support for Amorges was not a cause (as in Andoc. III. *Peace* 29) but a result of Persia's support for Sparta see H. D. Westlake, 'Athens and Amorges', *Phoen.* xxxi 1977, 319–29 = his *Studies in Thucydides and Greek History*, 103–12. The effect of political divisions on Athenian generals and strategies is discussed by A. Andrewes, 'The Generals in the Hellespont, 411–407', *JHS* lxxiii 1953, 2–9.

For a series of studies of episodes of which Xenophon and Diodorus give markedly different accounts see R. J. Littman, 'The Strategy of the Battle of Cyzicus', *TAPA* xcix 1968, 265–72; C. Ehrhardt, 'Xenophon and Diodorus on Aegospotami', *Phoen.* xxiv 1970, 225–8; A. Andrewes, 'Notion and Kyzikos: The Sources Compared', *JHS* cii 1982, 15–25. For the problem of Xenophon's missing year see A. Andrewes, *CAH*² v. 503–5.

On the population of Athens Hansen, *Three Studies in Athenian Demography*, ch. 3, and Rhodes, *Thucydides: History*, *II*, 271–7, independently arrived at a total of *c.*60,000 adult male citizens before the Peloponnesian War (higher than earlier estimates); and I agree with Hansen, *Demography and Democracy*, that there were *c.*30,000 adult male citizens in the fourth century (rather than *c.*20,000).

14

Athens in the Late Fifth Century

500	475	450	425	400	375	350	325	300

417	Nicias at Delian festival
416 (?)	Alcibiades at Olympic games
415 (?)	ostracism of Hyperbolus
415	mutilation of herms
411	régime of Four Hundred
411/0	intermediate régime of Five Thousand
407	return to Athens of Alcibiades
406	battle of Arginusae and condemnation of generals
404	surrender of Athens to Sparta

Alcibiades, Nicias and Hyperbolus

When Cleon died in 422, Hyperbolus, a demagogue of similar style and with a similarly activist policy for Athens, hoped to gain greater prominence for himself, and he was a member of the council in 421/0 (*IG* i³ 82. 5 with 42, cf. Plato Com. fr. 182 Kassel & Austin). On the less activist side, the truce of 423 is associated with Laches, a general on various occasions until he died at Mantinea in 418 (Thuc. IV. 118. xi), and the peace of 421 was the work of Nicias and Laches; Alcibiades felt insulted because in spite of his family connection with Sparta he was not used in the negotiations (V. 16. i, 43. ii; on the whole of this paragraph cf. p. 121–2).

In the years which followed, Alcibiades set about aligning Athens with Argos and other Peloponnesian states opposed to Sparta – no doubt partly because of the perceived insult, partly because the peace was proving unsatisfactory, partly because that new alliance provided opportunities for the adventurous kind of policy which appealed to him – while Nicias tried to salvage the peace. The allies were defeated at Mantinea in 418, and it is possible that that year Athens did not participate as enthusiastically as it might have done; but Alcibiades continued to work with Argos. He was not one of the generals involved in the capture of Melos in 416/5, but Plutarch makes him a supporter of the decree by which the men were killed and the women and children enslaved (*Alc.* 16. vi), and a speech to which we shall return below alleges that he had a child by one of the women ([Andoc.] IV. *Alcibiades* 22). It is no surprise to find Alcibiades eager and Nicias reluctant to undertake the Sicilian expedition of 415; the appointment of both as commanders reflects the support for both in the assembly.

As well as standing for different policies, Alcibiades the flamboyant aristocrat and Nicias the respectable emulator of the aristocrats were personal rivals. Nicias was a great performer of liturgies, and put a particular effort into leading Athens' delegation to the Delian festival of 417 (Plut. *Nic.* 3. v–4. i); it was probably in 416 that Alcibiades indulged in a more personal form of ostentation by entering no fewer than seven teams in the chariot race at Olympia, of which his best came first, second and fourth (Thuc. VI. 16. ii, cf. 12. ii, Plut. *Alc.* 11).

At some point not later than 415 what was to be Athens' last ostracism was held. According to Plutarch, Hyperbolus proposed an ostracism, hoping that the Athenians would use it to choose between Alcibiades and Nicias, but Alcibiades and Nicias joined forces and persuaded their supporters to vote against Hyperbolus, and it was he who was ostracised; an alternative version gave the role of Nicias to the less prominent Phaeax (Plut. *Nic.* 11, *Alc.* 13, cf. *Arist.* 7. iii–iv). We have surviving *ostraka* against all of those, and various others including Cleophon, to be prominent later (cf. p. 166), and a brother of his. A fragment of Theopompus appears to say that Hyperbolus was ostracised for six years (*FGrH* 115 F 96. b ~ Fornara 145. B), which if we counted from his death in 412/1 (Thuc. VIII. 73. iii) would point to 418 or 417; but Theopompus may actually have said that Hyperbolus was Athens' leading demagogue for six years until his ostracism, which if we counted from Cleon's death in 422/1 would point to 416 or 415, and a fragmentary inscription perhaps shows Hyperbolus still active in Athens at the end of 418/7, after the spring when the ostracism would have been held (*IG* i³ 85). Most scholars now accept that we must choose between 416 and 415.

Preserved with the speeches of Andocides is a speech (IV) *Against Alcibiades*, apparently written in the character of Phaeax for a situation in which he, Nicias and Alcibiades are the prospective victims; but, as far as we know, speeches were not delivered before the votes were cast, and there are passages in the speech which it is hard to think were written at the time. Probably the speech is a later rhetorical exercise; it does not mention the imminent Sicilian expedition, but in other respects the year envisaged is 415. An invitation to the citizens to choose between Alcibiades and Nicias would make sense in any of the possible years; since we know that the Sicilian expedition was hotly debated, and it is possible (though not certain) that the writer of the speech knew when the ostracism had been held, 415 is the likeliest year. Thucydides mentions the ostracism only in connection with Hyperbolus' murder; but he despised Hyperbolus and the ostracism failed to resolve the clash between Alcibiades and Nicias, so his not mentioning it in its place is intelligible.

Hyperbolus would presumably have preferred Alcibiades to be ostracised, as the man whose style and policies made him the greater threat to Hyperbolus' own position. It would be typical of Alcibiades to resort to a device which eliminated Hyperbolus, and which weakened Nicias, who could have been told that unless he cooperated with Alcibiades he might be the victim. Subsequently the assembly continued to be asked each year whether it wanted to hold an ostracism, but regularly decided against. This will be not because Hyperbolus was worthless, but because his banishment showed that ostracism was an unreliable weapon. Prosecution in the lawcourts could be aimed specifically at the intended victim, and that was done all too often over the next century.

The Herms and the Mysteries

In 415, shortly before the Sicilian expedition was due to sail, Athens was rocked by a religious scandal. Most of the herms (busts of the god Hermes on a plinth with a phallus) were damaged in a single night: 'The affair was taken rather seriously; it seemed to be an omen for the expedition and to have been done with a view to conspiracy for revolution and the overthrow of the democracy' (Thuc. VI. 27. iii). An enquiry elicited information not about the mutilation but about mock celebrations of the Eleusinian Mysteries in private houses, in which Alcibiades was said to have participated. Alcibiades wanted to stand trial immediately, but his enemies reckoned that with the expedition about to sail he would too easily secure acquittal, so it was resolved that he should be recalled later (Thuc. VI. 27–9). Information came in and arrests were made; Thucydides comments that no accusations were ignored but good men were considered suspect on the evidence of bad. Eventually one of the arrested men was persuaded to give information about the herms, on which Thucydides remarks that nobody could be sure either at the time or later whether he was telling the truth, but the people were greatly relieved to believe that the matter was settled (VI. 53. ii, 60). The tension was heightened by operations of the Spartan and Boeotian armies near the Athenian frontiers, and there was renewed suspicion that the profanation of the Mysteries and Alcibiades' involvement were part of the same plot. The *Salaminia*, one of the state ships, was sent to Sicily to fetch him and other men accused, but he escaped to the Peloponnese (VI. 53. i, 61: cf. p. 134).

In addition to Thucydides' account we have that of the man who turned informer, Andocides, in the speech (I) *On the Mysteries* which he delivered when his involvement in these matters was used against him in 400 (cf. p. 267); Lysias, VI. *Against Andocides*, from the same trial, is less informative. According to Andocides, a man called Dioclides gave false information, that he had seen the mutilators, about three hundred, of whom he named forty-two including Andocides and several of his relatives. These were all arrested, and one of the innocent relatives persuaded Andocides to tell what he knew in return for a promise of immunity. His story is that the mutilation was the work of a *hetaireia*, an association of upper-class 'companions', to which he belonged; it was proposed at a drinking party and he had opposed it; it was carried out later, when he had been injured in an accident and could not take part; the deed was a *pistis*, an act undertaken as a 'pledge' to cement the loyalty of the participants (Andoc. I. *Myst.* 37–69). He says less about the Mysteries, but he admits that the men accused included his father and other relatives (17–24), and it is possible that he was himself involved.

Those who stood trial were sentenced to death, and those who fled into exile were condemned in their absence. Their property was confiscated and sold, and substantial fragments survive of the 'Attic *stelai*' recording the sale of the confiscated property (*IG* i³ 421–30, extracts M&L 79 ~ Fornara 147. D, cf. Poll. X. 97, Philoch. *FGrH* 328 FF 133–4 ~ Fornara 147. A–C). The *stelai* give fascinating information on the possessions of rich Athenians and the prices which they could fetch when sold in these abnormal circumstances; for the economic exploitation of the Delian League by Athenians it is particularly interesting that Oeonias, known otherwise only as one of the accused men named by Andocides (I. *Myst.* 13), had estates in Euboea which were sold for the enormous sum of $81\frac{1}{3}$ talents (*IG* i³ 422. 375–8: cf. p. 176).

Public mutilation of herms and private mocking of the Mysteries were different kinds of act, though some men were accused and convicted of both. The mutilation, at a time of heightened tension, was presumably intended to shock, and did shock; there had been previous occasions when statues were damaged by drunken young men (Thuc. VI. 28. i), but this does seem to have involved more than drunkenness and high spirits. If the plotters had hoped to overthrow the democracy, we might have expected further moves to take advantage of the initial panic, perhaps seizure of the acropolis or the council-house. There were no such moves, and although plotters can be incompetent there was probably not a plot against the democracy; but fear of such a plot shows that the stability of the 420's (cf. pp. 116–17) was wearing thin. More likely, perhaps, is a last-ditch and again unsuccessful attempt to stop the Sicilian expedition by creating unfavourable omens: the pious Nicias would not have tried to prevent the expedition in this way, but there may have been men who shared his disapproval of the expedition but not his piety. On the other hand, profaning the Mysteries in private was presumably intended not to become public knowledge but to amuse the participants, men who will not have been thoroughgoing atheists but who, while perhaps thinking of themselves as such, will have had enough residual religion to derive amusement and a guilty thrill from daring the gods to punish them for their mockery of religious rites.

It fits the suggestion that there was an attempt to stop the Sicilian expedition, for which Alcibiades was enthusiastic, that, when the mutilation had created the initial panic, men came forward to accuse Alcibiades and others of profanation; and there are some signs that Dioclides' denunciations may have been an attempt to hit back at enemies of Alcibiades. The men named by Andocides as eager for the investigation were leading demagogues, Cleonymus, Pisander and Androcles (I. *Myst.* 27), while Alcibiades was an aristocrat challenging the demagogues at their own game (cf. pp. 155–7), and Andocides and his *hetairoi* seem not to have been enthusiastic democrats. On the other hand, the formal prosecutor of Alcibiades was Thessalus, one of the sons of Cimon (Plut. *Alc.* 19. iii, 22. iv). Thucydides' account prompted him to a digression on the overthrow of the Pisistratid tyranny, and the connection is probably that Alcibiades was perceived both by democrats and by 'respectable' aristocrats as dangerously like a tyrant (and fear of Spartan involvement reminded him of the ending of the tyranny, in which Sparta had been involved). The expedition went ahead, and, ironically, the proceeds from the sales will have made a significant contribution to the funding of it. Alcibiades made his way to Sparta, where Thucydides reports him as saying that in Athens he had to accept and try to moderate the democracy; democracy is agreed folly, but a change of régime in the middle of the war would not be safe (VI. 89. iii–vi).

Euripides' *Trojan Women* was produced in the spring of 415, between the capture of Melos and the sailing of the Sicilian expedition: it focuses on the disasters accompanying the destruction of Troy, and may in part have been prompted by the fate of Melos. Aristophanes' *Birds* was produced in spring 414, when it was still hoped that the Sicilian expedition would succeed: two men who have had enough of Athens set out to found a new city in the sky, Cloud-cuckooland; the new city turns out to possess the familiar faults of Athens' internal and imperial politics; but it is all light-hearted, including a reference to the fate of Melos (*Av.* 186: cf. pp. 131–2), and attempts to see the Sicilian expedition or Alcibiades in the play are unconvincing. A scholium on *Av.* 1297 infers from a passage in a play by Phrynichus produced at the same time that a man called Syracosius carried a decree 'that people should not be comedied by name' (cf. p. 66, on an attempt to restrain comedy in 440/39); while the attacks in *Birds* show that there cannot have been a total ban, the play does not name any of the men known to have been accused of involvement in the religious scandals, and some scholars have thought of a decree protecting them, but more probably there was no decree of Syracosius.

The principal item in Athens' building history in this period is the beginning of the Erechtheum, the complex temple on the northern part of the acropolis (the name is used rarely in ancient texts, but see Paus. I. 26. v). The building accounts for 409/8 (*IG* i³ 474) start with a reference to a decree of the beginning of that year authorising the resumption of work which was already well advanced, and scholars assume that construction began shortly after the Peace of Nicias and was suspended perhaps when resources were concentrated on the Sicilian expedition, perhaps when economy measures were taken after the expedition's failure.

The Four Hundred and the Five Thousand

In 415 the stability of the democracy was wearing thin; in 411 the democracy was overthrown, only to be restored in 410.

The Sicilian expedition of 415–413, debated and approved by the assembly, ended in disaster; and by the time it ended the Spartans were established in their fort at Decelea, in the north of Attica. The Athenians nevertheless decided to fight on, but 'to restrain matters in the city somewhat with a view to economy', and they appointed an emergency committee of ten older citizens as *probouloi*, to make preliminary proposals to the assembly as was traditionally done by the council (Thuc. VIII. 1. iii, cf. *Ath. Pol.* 29. ii). We do not know how their duties were dovetailed with those of the council: in Aristophanes' *Lysistrata* we encounter a *proboulos*, attended by Scythian archers, where we should expect to encounter the *prytaneis*, the tribal contingent serving as the council's standing committee (387–610); he is a pompous official but is not something new and dangerous; he has obtained wood for oars and needs to arrange for payment (421–3). Probably the *probouloi* had to be over 40; we know two of them, the tragedian Sophocles, who was born *c.*496 and had a civic as well as a literary career, and Hagnon, who was born before 470, was a supporter of Pericles and served as general several times between 440/39 and 429/8 (cf. pp. 117; 67, 69). With the need for economy we might be tempted to link the creation of a board of *poristai*, 'providers' of funds, but they are first attested as early as 419, when Athens was not in financial difficulties (Antiph. VI. *Chor.* 49).

By the end of 415 Alcibiades was in Sparta; after prompting Sparta to concentrate its effort in the Aegean rather than the Hellespont, by the end of 412 he had moved to the court of Tissaphernes and had made contact with sympathetic Athenians in the fleet at Samos (Thuc. VIII. 45–9). About the end of December a deputation was sent to Athens headed by Pisander, who in 415 had been a demagogue eager for investigation of the religious scandals (cf. p. 159), claiming that 'if Alcibiades were recalled and they did not keep to the same style of democracy they could have the King as an ally and get the better of the Peloponnesians'. This was opposed at first, especially by the families responsible for the Eleusinian cult, whose Mysteries Alcibiades had mocked, but was finally accepted as Athens' only hope. Pisander encouraged the *hetaireiai* of politically minded upper-class men to work together for the oligarchic movement, obtained the deposition of Phrynichus (who had been working against Alcibiades: cf. p. 144) and another general, and the sending of replacements, and returned to Samos with men authorised to negotiate with Alcibiades and Tissaphernes (VIII. 53–4). The negotiations with Tissaphernes broke down, and about the end of March 411 the Persians made a new treaty with Sparta (cf. p. 145). The champions of oligarchy in the fleet decided to go ahead without Alcibiades; they won over some of the Samians (despite their recent restoration of democracy: cf. p. 143); they sent some men to allied states to set up oligarchies there, and Pisander and others back to Athens (VIII. 63. iii–65. i). Pisander and his colleagues reached Athens about April/May. The oligarchic movement was under way: Androcles (cf. p. 159) and some other democrats had been assassinated; an oligarchic programme was circulating, that civilian stipends should be abolished and political rights limited to not more than five thousand men 'able to serve with their wealth and their bodies', i.e. those of hoplite class and above; the democratic political processes were still functioning but were dominated by the oligarchs (VIII. 65. ii–66).

For what follows we have two accounts: in Thucydides, VIII, interspersed with his narrative of other events, and, since he was in exile, based on what others told him; and in *Ath. Pol.* 29–33, which is partly based on Thucydides, partly derived from a source with access to documents in which the oligarchic revolutionaries tried to make their actions look respectable by democratic criteria of respectability. How we are to reconstruct what happened has given rise to much controversy.

An assembly was held at which *syngrapheis*, a drafting committee (used on other occasions in the fifth century: cf. p. 57), were appointed to draw up proposals. *Ath. Pol.*, which cites the decree, probably has the details right: the ten *probouloi* were to be joined by twenty others; other citizens could submit proposals; and an amendment called on the *syngrapheis* 'to look for the traditional laws which Cleisthenes enacted when he established the democracy' (Thuc. VIII. 67. i, *Ath. Pol.* 29. ii–iii). The word 'oligarchy' was being avoided, as on Pisander's first visit, and the propaganda offered a democracy purged of its recent excesses; the council was to be of four hundred because that was the size of Solon's council. There was much talk now and later of the *patrios politeia*, the 'traditional constitution': this was useful propaganda for the oligarchs, and probably some of them believed it themselves, but to committed democrats the traditional constitution was the democracy under which they lived until 411.

The *syngrapheis* reported to a later assembly, held according to Thucydides at Colonus, about a mile (1.5 km.) outside the city: modern scholars have suspected that, with the Spartans in Attica, poorer men who could not afford arms would be more reluctant to attend than richer, but at that distance the danger cannot have been great, and there must have been a respectable pretext for meeting there. The poorer citizens will in any case have been under-represented, since many of them will have been with the fleet at Samos. Our sources agree that the *syngrapheis* began by suspending all the normal safeguards against improper legislation and insisting that all proposals should be put to the vote. They then diverge. Thucydides attributes the positive proposals emphatically to Pisander, *Ath. Pol.* by implication to the *syngrapheis*, and both may be true if Pisander was one of the *syngrapheis* and claimed to be speaking on behalf of all.

Almost all civilian stipends were abolished, as in the programme already circu-lating. Thucydides, who has already mentioned that programme, then mentions the appointment of the Four Hundred – five men to choose a hundred, who were to choose the remaining three hundred – as a body who were to rule with full power and convene the Five Thousand when they saw fit. *Ath. Pol.* men-tions the entrusting of the state for the duration of the war to not less than five thousand, and the appointment of a hundred men to draw up a register of them; it defers the Four Hundred to a document quoted later. The two accounts should be combined: what was proposed now was a citizen body of five thou-sand, with residual sovereignty, and a powerful council of four hundred; the Four Hundred were probably appointed on the spot by Thucydides' method (Thuc. VIII. 67–68. i, *Ath. Pol.* 29. iv–v).

The Four Hundred did not take over the state immediately. *Ath. Pol.* 30–1 has a second committee of a hundred appointed, to work out the details of the constitution (credible enough, after the basic principles had been decided at Colonus), and two constitutional documents, one 'for the future time' and a second 'for the immediate crisis'. Probably the committee set to work in the days after Colonus, and a split opened between moderates who were seriously interested in a different kind of constitution (the future constitution divides the restricted citizen body into quarters in the manner of the Boeotian constitu-tions: cf. p. 245) and extremists who wanted to seize power for themselves (the immediate constitution includes a mechanism for the appointment of the Four Hundred, which will explain why *Ath. Pol.* has not mentioned them earlier); the extremists insisted that in the present crisis things must be done their way, but to appease the moderates offered the possibility of another kind of constitution later.

When they were ready the Four Hundred occupied the council-house by force, giving the democratic council its pay for the remainder of its year of office (about a month). *Ath. Pol.* dates the dissolution of the old council to 14 Thargelion (xi) (*c.*9 June) and the 'entry' of the Four Hundred to 22 Thargelion (*c.*17 June); Thucydides refers to the Four Hundred's prayers and sacrifices (Thuc. VIII. 69–70. i, *Ath. Pol.* 32. i). Presumably the old council was dismissed and the Four Hundred took over de facto on the 14th, and the new régime was formally inaugurated, and the constitutional documents were perhaps published, on the 22nd.

Four men are named as particularly responsible for the revolution (Thuc. VIII. 68, *Ath. Pol.* 32. ii: the absence of Phrynichus from the papyrus text of *Ath. Pol.* is probably due to a copyist's error): Pisander, who played the leading role in public; Antiphon, the *éminence grise* in the background (scholars argue over whether he is the same man as 'Antiphon the sophist', but probably he is not; Thucydides admired the speech which he made when put on trial after the fall of the Four Hundred); Phrynichus, who particularly distrusted Alcibiades, and joined the oligarchs when they broke with Alcibiades; and Theramenes, son of the *proboulos* Hagnon, who proved to be unhappy both with democracy and with extreme forms of oligarchy. The original argument for a change to oligarchy had been that it would enable Athens to bring back Alcibiades and obtain Persian help in defeating Sparta; but Persian help had not been obtained, the oligarchs had broken with Alcibiades, and they were to attempt to make peace with Sparta. Richer citizens could easily be persuaded that a democracy in which they had to share power with poorer citizens was not in their interests (cf. the Old Oligarch, pp. 116–17); after the failure in Sicily democratic Athens could no longer be represented as successful; when Athens was short of money an oligarchic régime in which the citizens did not have to be paid for public service had the attraction of cheapness; and (though the movement began at Samos) the absence of the fleet and its oarsmen will have tilted the social and political balance in Athens. Probably some men sincerely believed that the democracy had gone too far and a more restrained form of constitution would be better, while others wanted power for themselves and their friends. No doubt different men supported or acquiesced in the oligarchy for different combinations of these reasons. While Thucydides represents the establishment of the oligarchy as due to conspiracy and intimidation, he also suggests that nobody tried very hard to preserve the democracy.

Once they were in power, the Four Hundred ruled by force, killing, exiling or imprisoning some of their opponents (Thuc. VIII. 70, *Ath. Pol.* 32. ii). The register of the Five Thousand was begun but never completed – a speech in defence of a man who was one of the Four Hundred and one of the registrars claims that he tried to enrol as many as nine thousand (Lys. XX. *Polystratus* 13) – and no assemblies of the Five Thousand were held (Thuc. VIII. 92. xi, 93. ii, cf. 89. ii; *Ath. Pol.* 32. iii, 33. ii).

Far from prosecuting the war against Sparta, the Four Hundred tried to make peace. First they approached Agis at Decelea, but he responded by attacking Athens; later with Agis' support they sent a series of embassies to Sparta, the last headed by Antiphon and Phrynichus, but achieved nothing (Thuc. VIII. 70. ii–71, 86. ix, 90. ii, 91. i). *Ath. Pol.* 32. iii claims that Sparta was demanding that Athens should give up its empire: that may well be true, and there was the additional problem that the régime at Athens could not commit the fleet at Samos.

The Four Hundred had sent envoys to Samos to announce the change of régime, with an assurance that all of the Five Thousand would be involved in affairs (Thuc. VIII. 71). However, about the time when the Four Hundred came to power in Athens, the fleet reverted to democracy. In the *polis* of Samos the men won over by the Athenian oligarchs were plotting against their democracy, and had assisted in the murder of Hyperbolus, living there since his ostracism, but with the help of democratically minded Athenians the plot was frustrated. While the Four Hundred's envoys were travelling to Samos, the state ship the *Paralus* was sent with the news from Samos to Athens: there most of the crew were transferred to another ship, but the messenger Chaereas got back to Samos with an exaggerated account of what had happened in Athens. In the fleet Thrasybulus and Thrasyllus emerged as democratic leaders. The Athenians and the Samians swore to be loyal to the democracy and to persevere in the war against Sparta. The fleet behaved as a *polis* in exile, electing new officials including Thrasybulus and Thrasyllus as generals; it recalled Alcibiades, who still claimed that he could obtain Persian support, and made him general too (Thuc. VIII. 73–7, 81–2). The envoys from Athens, hearing the news from Samos, delayed but eventually arrived and were allowed to make a statement, in which they denied any intention of surrendering to Sparta. Alcibiades was now in Samos; Thucydides praises him for arguing against abandoning the Aegean to the Spartans in order to return to Athens and restore the democracy there (cf. VIII. 82. ii), and the envoys were sent back with the message that Alcibiades approved of the Five Thousand and of the abolition of civilian stipends, but not of the Four Hundred (VIII. 77, 86. i–vii).

The return of the envoys stimulated discontent among the ordinary citizens in Athens; the lead was taken by Theramenes (cf. p. 162) and by Aristocrates, a man from an old-established family, who commanded a tribal regiment under the Four Hundred and was a general both before and after the oligarchy. The Four Hundred started to build a wall at Eetionea, on the north-west of the Piraeus, allegedly to defend Athens against an attack by the Athenian fleet from Samos but in reality, Theramenes argued, to let the Peloponnesians in. When it was learned that Peloponnesian ships were on their way to Euboea (cf. p. 146), he suggested they were actually bound for Athens. When Phrynichus returned from the last, unsuccessful, embassy to Sparta, he was assassinated in the agora. As the ships came nearer to Athens, there was a mutiny among the hoplites building the wall, which ended with their demolishing it and claiming that the Five Thousand rather than the Four Hundred should rule. The Four Hundred offered to convene an assembly; but on the day in question the ships, which had been to Megara, were sighted sailing past Salamis. The Athenians rushed down to the Piraeus; when the ships moved on to the Euripus, the Athenians manned ships which followed them and were defeated in a battle; but the Peloponnesians did not seize the opportunity to sail back and attack Athens (Thuc. VIII. 89–96). This was about the beginning of Boedromion (iii) 411/0, late September (*Ath. Pol.* 33. i).

In an ad hoc assembly on the Pnyx, the regular meeting-place, the Athenians voted to depose the Four Hundred and entrust the state to the Five Thousand; and this was followed by a series of further meetings. Thucydides and *Ath. Pol.* express approval of the government of Athens under this intermediate régime, but they do not give details: the abolition of civilian stipends was upheld, and Thucydides writes of 'a reasonable mixture with regard to the few and the many' (Thuc. VIII. 97. i–ii, *Ath. Pol.* 33). Some have suggested that the future constitution of *Ath. Pol.* 30 was now put into effect, but what little evidence we have does not support that. Others, emphasising the shortage of evidence for the restoration of the democracy later (cf. p. 165), have argued that this régime was almost identical with the democracy. More probably this régime combined the democratic principle that power should reside in the assembly rather than in the council (and perhaps reverted to a council of five hundred, but elected rather than allotted) with the oligarchic principle that the citizen body should be limited to those 'able to serve with their wealth and their bodies'. The intermediate régime voted to persevere with the war, recalling Alcibiades and seeking a reconciliation with the fleet at Samos. Some of the extremists escaped to the Spartans at Decelea (Thuc. VIII. 97. iii–98); others including Antiphon stayed in Athens, and were put on trial and condemned (Craterus *FGrH* 342 F 5; [Plut.] *X Orat.* 833 D–834 B ~ Fornara 151; fragments of Antiphon's speech fr. B. 1 in the Loeb *Minor Attic Orators*, i).

The full democracy was restored in 410, probably after the battle of Cyzicus had once more demonstrated the importance of the navy for Athens. Thucydides' narrative ends in the autumn of 411 (cf. p. 146); neither Xenophon nor Diodorus mentions the restoration; *Ath. Pol.* 34. i begins a short and inaccurate passage bridging 410–404 with what is probably an allusion to it. The best evidence for the restoration is a decree quoted by Andocides (I. *Myst.* 96–8) which is dated to the first prytany of 4<u>10</u>/09, goes out of its way to refer to 'the council of five hundred appointed by lot', and reaffirms the law against the overthrow of the constitution; probably the calendar was adjusted so that a new year for the council began at the restoration.

We have seen above that there was a mixture of motives for overthrowing the democracy in 411. The way in which the régime of the Four Hundred developed could not please those who were hoping for more effective prosecution of the war or for a moderation of democracy's recent excesses, and the reversion of the fleet at Samos to democracy produced a fatal split between the Athenians in Athens and those at Samos. Those who were dissatisfied included Theramenes, who had been one of the leaders of the original revolution, and Aristocrates, a member of and a military officer under the Four Hundred. The collapse of that régime after the battle in the Euripus is no cause for surprise. The lack of Thucydides' narrative makes it harder to pronounce on the end of the intermediate régime; but it followed a success, not a failure, and Theramenes and Aristocrates were not put on trial. We shall see some signs of friction, but this was apparently a much less traumatic change.

The Restored Democracy

In terms of personalities, there seems superficially to be a considerable degree of continuity between the intermediate régime and the democracy. The commanders of the Hellespont fleet at Cyzicus, including Alcibiades, and also Theramenes, who had joined it in 410, remained with it until it returned to Athens in 407. However, Alcibiades, who had his rights restored by the intermediate régime in 411, did not have them restored by the democracy until 407, and neither he nor Theramenes or Thrasybulus seems to have been elected general by the democracy: they continued to command the fleet because they were acceptable to the fleet. Aristocrates, however, was elected general for 410/09, and so was Thrasyllus, who had returned from Samos to Athens in 411. On the chronology adopted in this book, Thrasyllus stayed in Athens in 410, began 409 campaigning separately in the Aegean, and was not wholly welcome when he rejoined the main fleet in the autumn (cf. pp. 147–8).

Those who had killed Phrynichus were now honoured (M&L 85 = *IG* i³ 102 ~ Fornara 155, Lys. XIII. *Agoratus* 70–6, Lycurg. *Leocrates* 112–15); and Phrynichus himself was posthumously condemned, either now or earlier, under the intermediate régime. The prosecutor was Critias (Lycurg. *Leocrates* 113), related both to Andocides and to the philosopher Plato, and tenuously to the early sixth-century reformer Solon. The leading demagogue in this period was Cleophon, regularly referred to as a lyre-maker (e.g. Andoc. I. *Myst.* 146, *Ath. Pol.* 28. iii); *ostraka* show that he and a brother attracted votes in 415; their father Cleïppides was a general in 429/8 and a candidate for ostracism in the 440's. He introduced the *diobelia* (*Ath. Pol.* 28. iii), a 2-obol grant whose basis is unclear but which must have been some kind of state support for men unable to maintain themselves while the Spartans were at Decelea. He was strongly opposed to peace with Sparta, and still unwilling to come to terms after Athens' defeat at Aegospotami (cf. pp. 151, 168).

Draco in 621/0 and Solon in 594/3 had been specially commissioned law-givers; but since then laws had been enacted by decrees of the assembly, which were not systematically dated and preserved. By the end of the fifth century it must have been hard to discover what the current law on a particular matter was; and the oligarchic revolution of 411 will have exposed that fact, as men who were distressed at what had happened thought that there must surely be laws to prevent such happenings. We have noticed that in 410/09 the law against overthrow of the constitution was reaffirmed (cf. p. 165); and in the same year, to guard against the formation of claques, members of the council were required to sit in the seats allocated to them (Philoch. *FGrH* 328 F 140). At the same time the restored democracy embarked on a recodification of Athens' laws. We learn from a speech of Lysias for the prosecution of Nicomachus, one of the commissioners appointed for the purpose, that what was envisaged as a short and simple task, 'to write up the laws of Solon', was still unfinished when the democracy was overthrown again in 404; it was resumed in 403 and finally completed in 400/399 (Lys. XXX. *Nicomachus*, esp. 2–5; for the later stages cf. pp. 260–1). Now and later the Athenians tended to refer to all their current laws as 'the statutes of Draco [on homicide: cf. *Ath. Pol.* 7. i] and the laws of Solon', and the task will have taken time because of the difficulty of finding and identifying those more recent enactments which modified the original laws of Draco and Solon and were currently valid. There survive from the first phase of the commissioners' work an inscription of 409/8 giving Draco's homicide law (M&L 86 = *IG* i³ 104 ~ Fornara 15) and an inscription collecting various laws about the council of five hundred (*IG* i³ 105).

After the successes of the Hellespont fleet in 410–408 (cf. pp. 147–8), it returned to Athens in 407. It was Thrasyllus, trusted by the democracy, who brought the main fleet: Alcibiades came by an indirect route and did not arrive until he had been elected general for 407/6. (Thrasybulus, from the Hellespont fleet, was elected general also, but Theramenes, as far as we know, was not.)

Alcibiades was cleared of the religious charges made against him in 415, treaties he had made in the field were ratified (cf. p. 149), and unprecedentedly he was made commander-in-chief, superior to the other generals. Ever since the Spartans had occupied Decelea, the normal procession from Athens to Eleusis for the Mysteries had been replaced by a journey by sea; but this year Alcibiades paid his debt to the Eleusinian goddesses by using a detachment of soldiers to escort the traditional procession (Xen. *Hell.* I. iv. 8–21, Diod. Sic. XIII. 68–69. iii, Plut. *Alc.* 32–4). Either on this occasion or under the intermediate régime a decree for his recall was proposed by Critias (Plut. *Alc.* 33. i).

The run of successes, for Athens and for Alcibiades, ended with the battle of Notium, early in 406 (cf. pp. 149–50). Possibly Alcibiades was formally deposed (Nep. VII. *Alc.* 7. iii, Plut. *Lys.* 5. iii); possibly he was prosecuted by Cleophon (Phot. *Bibl.* 377 A 18–19); certainly he withdrew into exile in Thrace. It was perhaps because of his links with Alcibiades that Critias was exiled at the same time, on the proposal of Cleophon: he went to Thessaly, where he is said to have worked for democracy and to have supported the serfs known as *penestai* against their masters (Xen. *Hell.* II. iii. 15, 36, *Mem.* I. ii. 24, Arist. *Rh.* I. 1375 B 31–4). The generals elected for 406/5 included Conon, who took over Alcibiades' fleet, Aristocrates and Pericles (son by Aspasia of the famous Pericles), all re-elected from the previous year; also Thrasyllus; but not Thrasybulus, another man associated with Alcibiades.

Conon was blockaded in the harbour of Mytilene by the Spartan Callicratidas; and to rescue him Athens made a supreme effort, melting down gold dedications for coinage, liberating slaves who were willing to row, equipping and manning another 110 ships (to which others were added from the allies) and sending with them all eight available generals. The battle of Arginusae was won, but in bad weather, and the Athenians did not pick up corpses or shipwrecked survivors (cf. p. 150). That news, arriving after the news of the victory, led to a great outburst of anger in Athens: two of the eight generals did not return; by an irregular procedure the six who did return were all condemned to death by the assembly. Xenophon has a dramatic account in which this was the result of a campaign orchestrated by Theramenes (he and Thrasybulus had been serving in the fleet as trierarchs, commanders of individual ships, and the generals claimed to have given them the job of picking up); Diodorus has a less sinister and more credible account in which the trierarchs and the generals each tried to save themselves by blaming the other party. The story has gained additional notoriety from the fact that one of the *prytaneis* (the presiding committee comprising one tribal contingent of councillors: cf. p. 58), who tried in vain in an emotional meeting to insist on lawful procedure, was the philosopher Socrates. The formal proposer of the motion to condemn the generals was Callixenus, not otherwise known; the demagogue Cleophon plays no part in the story. Once the generals had been killed, the Athenians' mood changed, and Callixenus and others were arrested and charged with deceiving the people; but in the turmoil at the end of the war they escaped trial (Xen. *Hell.* I. vii, Diod. Sic. XIII. 101–103.ii).

Conon, to rescue whom the battle had been fought, survived, retained command of the fleet, and was re-elected for 405/4. Theramenes, who had not been elected since the restoration of the democracy, was elected now but rejected in the *dokimasia* which men had to undergo before entering office (Lys. XIII. *Agoratus* 10; for the procedure cf. p. 37); there is no mention of Thrasybulus. At Aegospotami in 405 Alcibiades tried to join the Athenians once more, but they would not have him; in the more probable account of the battle, Philocles was the general who attempted to trap Lysander but was trapped by him. He and other generals were captured by Lysander, and he was put to death; but Conon escaped to Evagoras of Salamis in Cyprus, and was to play an important part in the history of the 390's (cf. p. 151, and for Conon's later career pp. 207–8, 210, 226–7).

While Athens was blockaded, during the winter of 405/4 (cf. p. 151), those who for various reasons had been made *atimoi*, deprived of rights, had their rights restored (cf. Andoc. I. *Myst.* 73–9). A first attempt to come to terms with Sparta was unsuccessful; but a member of the council who proposed accepting Sparta's demand for the demolition of the long walls was imprisoned, and Cleophon was opposed to surrender (cf. Aeschin. II. *Embassy* 76). Theramenes had himself sent to talk to Lysander, and spent three months with him at Samos. During his absence a legal 'discovery' enabled the council to add itself to a normal jury and condemn Cleophon on a technical charge of desertion (cf. Lys. XIII. *Agoratus* 7–12, XXX. *Nicomachus* 10–14). Theramenes then headed a formal delegation to Sparta, and brought back terms which were reluctantly accepted. All exiles were recalled (Xen. *Hell.* II. ii. 10–23: cf. p. 151). Lysander returned to Athens, and at his prompting the oligarchic régime of the Thirty was instituted (cf. pp. 257–60).

The democracy had lost the war; while Cleophon tried to prevent a settlement Theramenes obtained one, under which Athens' navy and oarsmen were not going to be significant. Lysander himself was particularly fond of narrow oligarchies: it is no surprise that Athens was to undergo another bout of oligarchy. In the last years of the war Theramenes and Thrasybulus had been suspect, primarily, it seems, because of their links with Alcibiades. Afterwards it could be alleged that oligarchic sympathisers had been disloyal in the last campaigns (Lys. XII. *Eratosthenes* 36) and that the council of 405/4 was full of oligarchs (Lys. XIII. *Agor.* 20), but those charges may be the result of hindsight: until the war was over, the war and personalities seem to have counted for more than forms of constitution. As for Alcibiades, after the defeat of Athens he made his way to the court of Pharnabazus, hoping to be escorted to the Persian King, but at the prompting of the Thirty in Athens and Lysander Pharnabazus had him killed (Diod. Sic. XIV. 11. i–iv, Plut. *Alc.* 37. vi–39, cf. Xen. *Hell.* II. iii. 42).

Not surprisingly, there is more of an atmosphere of crisis in the comedies produced in the later years of the war than earlier. Eupolis' *Demes*, commonly dated 412 though some would put it slightly earlier, does not survive complete, but there are papyrus fragments which allow a reconstruction (see Loeb *Select*

Papyri, iii, no. 40): Myronides (who commanded Athenian armies in the 450's but is not attested subsequently) has recently died, and on arrival in the underworld reports on the parlous state of Athens; Solon, Miltiades, Aristides and Pericles are chosen to investigate and Myronides escorts them back to contemporary Athens; they are met perhaps by a *proboulos* (but this speaker is left unidentified in the latest edition, Eupolis fr. 99 Kassel & Austin), who cannot offer generous hospitality, and they deal with rogues of various kinds. Aristophanes' *Lysistrata* and *Thesmophoriazusae* are probably to be dated to January/February and March/April 411 respectively. In *Lysistrata* the women, to force their husbands to make peace, refuse to have sexual intercourse with them, and seize the acropolis and the treasuries on it; in this play, certainly, a *proboulos* plays the part which would normally be played by the *prytaneis* (cf. pp. 58, 167); Pisander (ll. 489–91) is still perceived as a demagogue. *Thesmophoriazusae*, if the normal dating is correct, is nearer to but still before the oligarchic coup: the women hold an assembly to discuss punishing Euripides for his travesties of them; current politics are largely avoided, but there are allusions to fear of an alliance with the Persians (ll. 336–7, 365–6) and of tyranny (ll. 338–9, 1143–4, cf. 361–2), behind which may lie a suspicion that Alcibiades might return as a Persian-backed tyrant.

Of contemporary tragedies, Euripides' *Iphigenia Among the Taurians* (413), *Helen* (412) and *Ion* (410) tend to be regarded as 'escapist'; *Orestes* (408?) and *Iphigenia at Aulis* (408–406) are more melodramatic. From antiquity onwards readers have tried to see Cleophon and others behind the characters of *Orestes*: the characters are better seen as types than as identifiable individuals, but the play undoubtedly presents a pessimistic view of public processes and private agendas. *Phoenician Women* (*c.*409) focuses on the personal ambition and absolute power of Eteocles, and may have been inspired by the selfish lust for power of men in Athens. Sophocles' *Philoctetes* was produced in 409: reflections of a particular context are always hard to find in his plays, but some modern scholars have been inclined to see in the need to reintegrate Philoctetes into society an allegory for the problem of Alcibiades. Euripides (it is usually believed but has recently been doubted) left Athens for the court of Archelaus of Macedon, and he and Sophocles both died in 406. Aristophanes' *Frogs* (405) is a reaction to their deaths: there are no good tragedians left in Athens, so Dionysus goes to the underworld to bring one back; Sophocles is uninterested, so the play turns into a contest between Aeschylus and Euripides, in which Aeschylus is the winner. Aristophanes had always preferred upper-class leaders to upstarts (cf. p. 119); as we might expect, he is hostile to Cleophon (ll. 678, 1504, 1532–3); he deals gently with Theramenes' wavering between democracy and oligarchy (ll. 534–41, 967–70); more generally, in passages which appear serious he complains that the city is relying on worthless men rather than good (ll. 718–37, 1446–58), and, while approving of the liberation of slaves who rowed at Arginusae, argues that men who have lost their rights [mostly men involved in the oligarchy of 411–410] should have them restored. By now Alcibiades had gone into exile for the second time, and in the contest the first question put to each poet as a test of their value to Athens is, 'What should be done about Alcibiades?' (ll. 1418–23). The state's need to economise had impinged on the poets: *Frogs* 367 (cf. schol.) alludes to a reduction in the fee paid to competing dramatists.

We noted above that work on the Erechtheum was suspended *c.*415–413 but resumed in 409: that was a time when it seemed possible that Athens might yet win the war, and those given employment on the work will have been glad of it; apart from a few details, the temple was finished by the end of the war. Xen. *Hell.* I. vi. 1 reports that in 406/5 the 'old temple of Athena' was destroyed by fire: that was perhaps the *opisthodomos*, reconstructed as a treasury on the site of an older temple between the Parthenon and the Erechtheum (cf. M&L 58 = *IG* i³ 52 ~ Fornara 119, A. 15–18, B. 23–5, and for the fire Dem. XXIV. *Timocrates* 136); an inscription which has been thought to show that the fire spread to the Erechtheum (*IG* ii² 1654) is more probably of about the 370's.

The assembly met on the Pnyx to depose the Four Hundred in 411 (cf. p. 164), but the retaining wall may have collapsed soon afterwards: shortly before the installation of the Thirty it met in the theatre at Munichia (Piraeus) (Lys. XIII. *Agoratus* 32, 55; cf. the ad hoc meeting in 411, Thuc. VIII. 43. i), and the only assembly known to have been convened by the Thirty met in the odeum (Xen. *Hell.* II. iv. 9–10). The Thirty are alleged to have rebuilt the Pnyx, changing its orientation (so that speakers faced inland instead of seawards: Plut. *Them.* 19. vi) and increasing its area by about 40 per cent, but they were not much interested in assemblies, and this is more probably the work of the restored democracy. In the agora a new council-house was built to the west of the old, probably in the last years of the war: the old council-house remained standing, and came to be used as a repository for records and to be known as the Metroum, sanctuary of the Mother of the Gods.

At the end of this chapter it must be stressed that 413–404 was a period of considerable hardship for individual Athenians – largely (cf. pp. 140–1) deprived of the use of the countryside throughout the year (but the smaller population and the absence of many ships for most of the time will have made Athens less crowded than in the early summers of the war), and having to buy imported food. Nevertheless, dramatic and other festivals continued to be celebrated, and building work proceeded and provided employment for some of the men.

NOTE ON FURTHER READING

On Alcibiades see Ellis, *Alcibiades*; Rhodes, *'What Alcibiades Did or What Happened to Him'*.

On the ostracism of Hyperbolus, Theopompus *FGrH* 115 F 96 (b) = Fornara 145B was reinterpreted by A. E. Raubitschek, 'Theopompos on Hyperbolos', *Phoen.* ix 1955, 122–6 = his *The School of Hellas*, ch. 40. Ostracism in 416 was argued for by C. Fuqua, 'Possible Implications of the Ostracism of Hyperbolus', *TAPA* xcvi 1965, 165–79; in

415 by Rhodes, 'The Ostracism of Hyperbolus', in *Ritual, Finance, Politics . . . D. Lewis*, 85–98; 417 has been defended by some continental scholars. On Plutarch's treatments of the story see Pelling, *Literary Texts and the Greek Historian*, ch. 3.

On the religious scandals of 415: the fullest study is Furley, *Andokides and the Herms*; on the approaches of Thucydides and Andocides see Pelling, *Literary Texts and the Greek Historian*, ch. 2. On the alleged decree of Syracosius restricting attacks in comedy see A. H. Sommerstein, 'Comedy and the Unspeakable', in *Law, Rhetoric and Comedy in Classical Athens . . . D. M. MacDowell*, ch. 13.

The revolutions of 411 are discussed thoroughly by Hignett, *A History of the Athenian Constitution*, ch. 10 and app. 12. The failure of democrats to resist the oligarchs is stressed by M. C. Taylor, 'Implicating the *Demos*: A Reading of Thucydides on the Rise of the Four Hundred', *JHS* cxxii 2002, 91–108. That what I call the intermediate régime of 411–410 scarcely differed from the democracy was argued by G. E. M. de Ste. Croix, 'The Constitution of the Five Thousand', *Hist.* v 1956, 1–23, and rejected by Rhodes, 'The Five Thousand in the Athenian Revolutions of 411 BC', *JHS* xcii 1972, 115–27; the view that it was an embodiment of the 'future' constitution of *Ath. Pol.* 30, popular in the early twentieth century, has been revived by E. M. Harris, 'The Constitution of the Five Thousand', *HSCP* xciii 1990, 243–80. Antiphon the speech-writer and Antiphon the sophist are considered to be the same man by Gagarin, *Antiphon the Athenian*, to be different men by Pendrick, *Antiphon, of Athens*.

On the revision of the laws begun in 410/09 when the democracy had been restored see Rhodes, 'The Athenian Code of Laws, 410–399 BC', *JHS* cxi 1991, 87–100.

On the differing treatments by Xenophon and Diodorus of the sequel to Arginusae see A. Andrewes, 'The Arginousai Trial', *Phoen.* xxviii 1974, 112–22.

On Eupolis see Storey, *Eupolis, Poet of Old Comedy*: at 112–14 he suggests a date of 417 or perhaps 416 for *Demes*.

Attribution of the rebuilding of the Pnyx to the restored democracy in and after 403 (rather than to the Thirty, as in Plut. *Them.* 19. vi) is due to R. A. Moysey, 'The Thirty and the Pnyx', *AJA*[2] lxxxv 1981, 31–7.

15

The Athenian Empire: Retrospect

500	475	450	425	400	375	350	325	300

478/7 foundation of Delian League
454/3 treasury moved to Athens
c.449 Peace of Callias between Athens and Persia (?)
446/5 Thirty Years' Peace between Athens and Peloponnesians recognises two power blocs
431 Sparta begins Peloponnesian War professing intention of liberating the Greeks
404 end of Peloponnesian War and of Delian League

Rise and Fall

As we have seen in earlier chapters, the Delian League was founded in 478/7 to continue the war against the Persians, when the Spartan Pausanias had made himself unpopular with the allies. Athens had the executive power, providing the commanders and the treasurers; but Thucydides emphasises the League's innocent beginning, and those who remembered the Ionian Revolt will have been more afraid that Athens would lose interest than that it would become domineering. However, the League was unlike any earlier alliance in Greece: Athens took a permanent alliance to mean permanent campaigning, and required contributions of ships or tribute in cash from the allies year after year. Even from the beginning, activity was not limited to campaigning against the

Persians (Eïon was justified on that basis but Scyros was not), and Athens found ways of furthering its own interests through the League's activity (e.g. the colonies at Eïon and Scyros). Within ten years Naxos had been forced to remain in the League against its will; within fifteen, Thasos had been coerced when it resisted Athens' desire for its mainland possessions.

In the early years League campaigns were regularly led by the pro-Spartan Cimon, and Sparta acquiesced in the League's development; but from 462/1, while Cimon was ostracised, Athens' democratic leaders were prepared to challenge Sparta's supremacy in mainland Greece, and while fighting against the Persians continued (now in Cyprus and Egypt), allied forces were used also in Greece as Athens built up its power there. However, c.454 that expansion ran out of steam, and the forces in Egypt suffered a major defeat, after which there was a serious possibility that the Persians might strike back. The moving of the treasury from Delos to Athens, which appears to us as a symbol of growing Athenian imperialism, may at the time have seemed a reasonable precaution. In 451 Athens made a five-year truce with the Peloponnesians. Shortly afterwards Cimon died in another campaign in Cyprus; and, after that, regular fighting against Persia came to an end, whether the formality of the Peace of Callias is authentic or is a fourth-century invention.

One result of the moving of the treasury was the inscription of the 'Athenian tribute lists', an annual series beginning in 453 recording the offering to Athena of $\frac{1}{60}$ of the tribute, calculated separately on each state's payment. These tribute lists indicate that in the late 450's and early 440's there were some years in which Athens' demands met with considerable resistance; and, if some decrees assigned to the middle of the century are rightly so assigned, there is evidence for Athens' interfering in individual states (such as Erythrae, where there was a Persian-backed revolt, and Miletus, which had a democracy modelled on that of Athens by the 430's). However, decrees on the collection of the tribute and the sending of offerings to festivals, and on the use of Athenian weights, measures and coinage, are more probably to be dated to the 420's. Almost certainly, when the treasury was moved, councils in which the allies were represented were discontinued. Garrisons, and officials of various kinds, were sent to member states. The language of the League changed, with oaths sworn to the Athenians rather than to the Athenians and the allies, and 'the Athenian alliance' became 'the cities which Athens rules'. It is now reasonable to speak of an Athenian empire.

By the 440's all the allies except Samos, Chios and the cities of Lesbos were paying tribute rather than providing ships: this was probably cheaper as well as easier on their manpower, but lessened their ability to pursue an independent policy (cf. Thuc. I. 98. ii–iii). Work on the temple of Apollo at Delos was abandoned, and in 447 Athens embarked on an ambitious building programme on the acropolis, financed partly from surplus tribute. Even in the 470's Athenian settlements had been planted abroad, and about the middle of the century several allied states received settlements which both provided land for the settlers and served as informal garrisons.

Revolts in mainland Greece were followed by the Thirty Years' Peace of 446/5, by which Athens lost its mainland possessions but its control of the League was recognised; the Greek world was divided between a Spartan bloc based on the mainland and an Athenian bloc based on the Aegean. In 440–439 Athens' intervention in a dispute between Samos and Miletus led to a major war against Samos, which had Persian support, after which Samos was deprived of its ships and had to refund Athens' war expenses.

The Thirty Years' Peace lasted only fifteen years before the outbreak of the Peloponnesian War in 431. Thucydides' 'truest reason' for the war is Athens' power and Sparta's fear of it. I have argued that after the Thirty Years' Peace, while Athens did not encroach on the part of the Greek world in which Sparta was interested, it continued to expand elsewhere, so that the balance of power could not be held; and that in the late 430's Athens pursued a high-risk strategy, which suggests that it was prepared to accept the challenge and tried to ensure that the conflict would break out in circumstances favourable to itself.

According to Thucydides (who perhaps does not tell the whole truth: cf. p. 96), Pericles had a defensive strategy for Athens in the war: to avoid a major battle on land, to rely on sea power for survival, to keep a firm hold on the empire but not to try to enlarge it. Mytilene, on Lesbos, revolted in 428–427 and was firmly dealt with; Chios, in 425/4, when ordered to demolish a new wall, obeyed. The level of tribute was increased, as Athens used up its reserves, but the Athenians also taxed themselves more heavily to pay for the war. It is probably to this period that we should date decrees improving the mechanisms for collecting the tribute (Cleonymus' decree, M&L 68 = IG i^3 68 ~ Fornara 133, is certainly of 426/5; Cleinias' decree, M&L 46 = IG i^3 34 ~ Fornara 98, is best dated c. 425/4), and requiring the allies to use Athenian weights and measures and Athenian silver coins (M&L 45 = IG i^3 1453 ~ Fornara 97): these texts threaten heavy penalties for non-compliance (and seem to envisage opposition in Athens as well as among the allies: cf. p. 181), and assume that there will be Athenian officials present in most allied cities.

After Pericles' death, not all Athenians shared his view that they should not try to enlarge the empire: in more than one part of the Greek world there was fear that Athenian support would lead to Athenian control, including Sicily, where a force which had become large and ambitious had to withdraw in 424. The part of the empire most vulnerable to Spartan intervention was the Thraceward region: the Spartan Brasidas was there from 424 to 422, insisting that he had come not to substitute Spartan rule for Athenian but to liberate the cities; he had considerable success, but there was an iron fist inside his velvet glove (cf. pp. 182–3). Another intervention in Sicily, in 415, in response to the opposition of Nicias made larger and more ambitious than it might otherwise have been, was to prove the turning-point in the war. In 413 the Athenians were totally defeated there, with great loss of men, ships and money, and damage to their morale. Before their defeat they replaced the tribute with a harbour tax, which they hoped would yield more money (but they probably reverted to tribute in 410); after it, various allied states made contact with

Sparta, as for the first time it seemed possible that Athens would be defeated in Greece and the Aegean too.

In the last phase of the war Sparta, in order to obtain Persian help, promised to return the Greeks of mainland Asia Minor to Persia: there are some signs of discontent among the Asiatic Greeks, but certainly not overwhelming repugnance; it is possible that in 408/7 Sparta obtained the lesser commitment that the Asiatic Greeks were to pay tribute to Persia but be independent otherwise. Some allies, notably Samos, remained loyal to Athens or returned to loyalty; others, notably Chios (torn between anti-Athenian and pro-Athenian factions), held out against Athens. There were times when it seemed that the Athenians might yet be victorious, but in 405/4 they were defeated, and their empire came to an end.

Burdens and Benefits

All states which join an alliance lose the total freedom to decide their own policies without any reference to others. How serious that loss is depends on how the policies of the alliance are decided. In the Delian League there were at first meetings in which Athens, though influential as holder of the executive power, probably had one vote like each other member; but the meetings were probably discontinued when the treasury was moved to Athens in 454/3, and states which contributed by paying tribute could not withdraw their forces from a campaign of which they disapproved.

There had not been any previous Greek alliance in which the leader (*hegemon*) had interfered in the internal affairs of the other members. When Thucydides writes that the Athenians 'were leaders of allies who were at first autonomous' (I. 97. i), this is probably a comment prompted by hindsight; no guarantees are likely to have been thought necessary at the League's foundation. Internal interference need not lie behind his remark that Naxos 'was the first allied state to be enslaved contrary to what was established' (I. 98. iv), but it was occurring by the middle of the century (in general, Thuc. III. 82. i, [Xen.] *Ath. Pol.* i. 14, 16, iii. 10–11), with the imposition of democracies in Erythrae in the late 450's (M&L 40 = *IG* i^3 14 ~ Fornara 71), in Samos in 440/39 (Thuc. I. 115. iii) and in Miletus by the mid 430's (*Klio* lii 1970, 163–73). In 411 Athens' oligarchs similarly set up oligarchies in the allied states (Thuc. VIII. 64–65. i, and cf. [Xen.] *Ath. Pol.* i. 14). Other forms of political interference occurred too: major lawsuits were transferred from local courts to Athenian courts, which were likely to favour litigants with a pro-Athenian record, at first in individual cases (e.g. Chalcis in 446/5, M&L 52 = *IG* i^3 40 ~ Fornara 103) and later generally (Antiph. V. *Herodes* 47, cf. Thuc. I. 77. i, [Xen.] *Ath. Pol.* i. 16–18), though much of the interference was not systematic but was in response to particular provocations. Offenders against imperial decrees would be tried in Athens (M&L 45 §12 = *IG* i^3 1453 §10 ~ Fornara 97 §12, M&L 46 = *IG* i^3 34 ~ Fornara 98. 31–43), and Athens claimed the right to exile offenders from the territory of all League members (M&L 40 = *IG* i³ 14 ~ Fornara 71. 31). Supporters of Athens could be awarded the privileged status of Athenian *proxenos* (representative) and benefactor (e.g. *IG* i³ 19; for collaboration with Athens notice Thuc. III. 2. iii).

Economically, the most obvious burden on the allies was (except in the cases where they provided ships) the payment of tribute, for which there were precedents not within the Greek world but in barbarian rule over Asia Minor (Hdt. I. 6. ii, 27. i, Lydia; III. 89–96, VI. 42. ii, Persia). As remarked above, it was probably less burdensome to pay tribute than to provide ships and man them every summer, but on account of the near-eastern precedents it could easily be seen as a sign of subjection. The general level of tribute seems to have remained constant until after the beginning of the Peloponnesian War, when increases were imposed not in a spirit of greater exploitation but to contribute to the cost of fighting the war. Tribute could be remitted when Athens wanted to retain the loyalty of a strategically located member (M&L 65 = *IG* i³ 61 ~ Fornara 128. 5–9, 29–32, *IG* i³ 62. 16–17), and some of the money found its way back to the allies through wages for oarsmen and others employed by Athens. In Athens, the League provided employment for more officials and oarsmen than would otherwise have been needed; surplus tribute seems to have contributed directly to financing the acropolis building programme of the 440's–430's, and the fact that some items could be charged to the tribute will have helped the Athenians to pay for other things out of their own funds; but catalogues of Athenians maintained at the allies' expense are caricatures (*Ath. Pol.* 24. iii, cf. Ar. *Vesp.* 707–11, [Xen.] *Ath. Pol.* i. 15–17, iii. 4).

The other main aspect of the economic burden for the allies and gain for the Athenians concerns Athenians' acquisition of allies' land. Athens had been interested in founding settlements in important locations from the beginning of the League and before; from about the middle of the century a number of allies whose conduct had provoked Athens had to give up some of their land for an Athenian cleruchy (*klerouchoi*, 'allotment-holders', were men who occupied land abroad but remained citizens of Athens; the previous owners may then have had to lease back the land or work as hired labourers on it) (e.g. Plut. *Per.* 11. v–vi, Diod. Sic. XI. 88. iii). Those settlements will have benefited poorer citizens (cf. M&L 49 = *IG* i³ 46 ~ Fornara 100. 43–6), but there were opportunities for the rich also: normally non-citizens of a state could not own land in that state unless given exemption from that rule as a privilege, but it seems to have become possible for Athenians to acquire land in allied states, to such an extent that Oeonias, one of the men involved in the religious scandals of 415, had land in three parts of Euboea which when confiscated was sold for as much as 81⅓ talents (*IG* i³ 422. 375–8).

Athens' control of the Aegean and ability to prevent piracy will to some extent have benefited everybody (except would-be pirates), and insistence on the use of Athenian weights, measures and coinage (M&L 45 = *IG* i³ 1453 ~ Fornara 97) will have been beneficial economically but may have been perceived by some of the allies as an affront to their pride (cf. contemporary debates about the

European Union and its currency, the Euro). However, the chief beneficiary will have been Athens, which became the focal point of the Aegean's trade: it could itself import whatever it wanted, and it could use its power to help friends and harm enemies (Thuc. I. 120. ii, II. 38. ii, III. 86. iv, [Xen.] *Ath. Pol.* ii. 6–7, 11–12): economic sanctions were imposed on Megara in the 430's (cf. p. 85), while in the 420's Methone on the coast of Macedon was given permission, which other states must have lacked, to import grain from the Black Sea, in a decree which reveals the existence of Athenian *Hellespontophylakes*, 'guardians of the Hellespont' (M&L 65 = *IG* i³ 61 ~ Fornara 128. 34–41, cf. *IG* i³ 62. 0–5 for Aphytis). Economic benefits of another kind for Athens are highlighted by [Xen.] *Ath. Pol.* i. 17: when traders came with their goods, when men came from the allied states to bring their tribute or to put a request to the assembly or to be tried in the lawcourts, the Athenian state profited from increased tax revenue and there were various opportunities for individual Athenians to make money from the visitors.

Some scholars have claimed that, whereas in the archaic period the Greek cities of Asia Minor and the offshore islands were prosperous and intellectually active, when they were incorporated in the Delian League it was Athens that was prosperous and intellectually active while the eastern Greeks were in decline. Literary evidence does not suggest impoverishment (e.g. Thuc. VIII. 24. iv, 40. ii, on Chios), and recent work has cast doubt on the extent of the material decline. For all the incompleteness of our archaeological knowledge, it appears to be true that the eastern Greeks did not build monumental temples in the fifth century as some of them had in the sixth, but that appears equally true of most other Greeks, both inside the Delian League and outside. In terms of building temples and celebrating the festivals centred on them, in the fifth century the rest of the Greek world chose not to compete with Athens – but that is a sign of Athens' cultural predominance in the Greek world rather than of its economic exploitation of the empire.

Religion

That leads us to the use of religion to reinforce Athens' position in the League. When the League was founded, it suited Athens to represent it as an Ionian league (cf. pp. 18–19). For that purpose Delos, a small island but home of an Ionian sanctuary and cult of Apollo, was appropriate as the focal point of the League, and a new temple was begun and other buildings were erected while it served that function. In the middle of the century, when the treasury was moved to Athens, work on the temple was suspended; in the 420's there was renewed Athenian interest in Delos, but now in a Delos wholly under Athenian control (cf. p. 109).

From the middle of the century the allies were involved in the cults and festivals of Athens. The tribute was brought to Athens before and displayed at the Great Dionysia, which thus became an imperial festival (schol. Ar. *Ach.* 504,

Isoc. VIII. *Peace* 82; cf. M&L 46 = *IG* i³ 34 ~ Fornara 98. 18–22, M&L 68 = *IG* i³ 68 ~ Fornara 133. 10–15). At first only those who were Ionian in the narrow sense, who could be expected to regard Athens as their mother city, had to send offerings to the Panathenaea (e.g. Erythrae, M&L 40 = *IG* i³ 14 ~ Fornara 71. 2–8), but in 425/4 offerings of a cow and a suit of armour were required from all the allies (instituted M&L 69 = *IG* i³ 71 ~ Fornara 136. 55–8; cf. M&L 46 = *IG* i³ 34 ~ Fornara 98. 41–3). Perhaps in the 430's, the allies were required but the other Greeks were merely invited to send offerings to the Eleusinian Mysteries (M&L 73 = *IG* i³ 78 ~ Fornara 140. 14–21; 24–6 with 30–6). In allied cities *horoi* (markers) invoking Athena, and Ion and his sons (e.g. *IG* i³ 1481–99), may attest the imposition of Athenian cults or alternatively the confiscation of land which was then added to the possessions of Athenian deities.

The League did not only help to pay for the work on the acropolis, but there was League symbolism in the work. If the temple of Athena Nike was planned in the 440s (cf. pp. 63–4), it was surely inspired by the consciousness of victory over the Persians (scenes on the frieze perhaps included the battle of Marathon), whether or not that victory had been sealed by a Peace of Callias. Among the statues set up on the acropolis was one of Athena Lemnia by Pheidias, celebrating the sending of cleruchs to Lemnos *c.*450 (Paus. I. 28. ii, Lucian *Imagines* 4, cf. 6).

In Samos a sculpture group showed the introduction of Heracles to Olympus, and featured not Samian Hera but Athena with Heracles and Zeus (Strabo 637. XIV. i. 14): this was perhaps set up by supporters of Athens in Samos after the war of 440–439. Ephesus, on the other hand, was prepared to rival Athens: a group of Amazons, carved by several leading sculptors including Pheidias (Plin. *H.N.* XXXIV. 53), advertised the Artemisium there as being no less venerable and distinguished than Athens' sanctuaries.

These developments should not be seen as surprising or as a sinister manipulation of religion. Religion was 'embedded' in Greek society as Christianity used to be but no longer is embedded in the society of the European states and their overseas colonies, and as other religions are still embedded in some present-day societies; and it will have been thought natural that Athens' dealings with the allies, like other aspects of Athenian life, should have a religious dimension.

Attitudes to the Empire

Thucydides' speakers frequently claim that it was natural that the Athenians should exercise such power as they could, and that those who were subjected to Athenian power should dislike it. The Athenian envoys to Sparta in 432 are represented as saying that Athens' empire is based on the three considerations of fear, honour and advantage; Athens acquired its leadership at the allies' invitation, but as it became unpopular had to tighten its control; one cannot object when states protect their own interests; Athens had done nothing surprising or contrary to human nature, but deserved gratitude for behaving with more justice than its power would allow (I. 75–6; cf. Pericles in II. 64. v). However, it was first suggested by G. Grote in the nineteenth century, and argued strongly by G. E. M. de Ste. Croix in the middle of the twentieth, that the truth may be different, that, because democratic Athens supported democracies in the empire, the empire may have been disliked by upper-class oligarchs but liked by lower-class democrats.

De Ste. Croix, who held a minimal view of the authenticity of Thucydides' speeches, believed that the speeches reflect Thucydides' own view that the Athenians exercised their power unashamedly and the allies hated it, but that Thucydides' narrative shows his view to be mistaken. I believe that, although there is an element of invention in the speeches, the arguments in them are those that the speakers actually did use or could genuinely have been expected to use. Thucydides does at any rate allow speakers to contradict one another, so that in the debate on Mytilene Cleon claims that everybody joined in opposition to Athens but Diodotus alleges that the upper-class leaders in the cities are anti-Athenian while the lower classes are pro-Athenian (III. 39. vi; 47. ii, iv): we can never be confident that a statement made by a Thucydidean speaker is believed by Thucydides to be true.

There are certainly many passages where speakers express what de Ste. Croix regarded as Thucydides' own view: the empire is described as a tyranny not only by the Corinthians (I. 122. iii, 124. iii) and by Cleon and Euphemus (III. 37. ii, VI. 85. i) but also by Pericles (II. 63. ii). Pericles proposed in 432/1 that Athens should leave the allies autonomous if they had been autonomous at the time of the Thirty Years' Peace and if Sparta left its *perioikoi* autonomous (I. 144. ii), and his strategy for Athens in the Peloponnesian War included keeping a firm control of the empire: the honour could not be had without the effort, and even if it was unjust to acquire the empire it would be dangerous to let it go (II. 63). In the debate on Mytilene, Diodotus no less than Cleon talks the language of power politics and Athens' advantage (III. 37–48), though Thucydides in his introduction remarks that after the original decision the Athenians 'had a sudden change of mind and reckoned that it was a savage policy and a big decision to destroy a whole city rather than those who were guilty' (III. 36. iv). In 415/4 Euphemus addresses Camarina in the same way: the Athenians have indeed gone to Sicily to protect their own interests, but it suits their interests that Syracuse should be weak and its enemies strong (VI. 82–7). The fullest exposition of this attitude is to be found in the Melian Dialogue (V. 85–111), where the Athenians do not deign to justify their attack, but

> we know and you know that considerations of justice weigh in men's arguments when they are equal in coercive strength, while those who are superior do what they can and the weak acquiesce. . . . We are here for the advantage of our empire. (V. 89, 91)

It is unlikely that Thucydides could have obtained a detailed account of what was said on that occasion, and he has certainly written up this episode for dramatic effect (cf. p. 132), but the message is the same as in the speeches, and we cannot obtain a milder picture by jettisoning the dialogue but retaining the speeches.

This view of Athenian power is not a private fantasy of Thucydides. For Aristophanes also Athens is a tyrant (cf. below); for the Old Oligarch the Athenian *demos* treats the empire in ways conducive to its own interests ([Xen.] *Ath. Pol.* i. 14–18); and it is clear from fragments from the sophists and representation of their arguments by Aristophanes and Plato that the exercise of power, by states and by individuals, was indeed discussed in terms of that kind in the late fifth century. However, it may well be that Thucydides distorts by including so many and such emphatic expressions of this view. He represents his hero Pericles as claiming that Athens' empire was something to be proud of (II. 36. ii–iii, 63. i, 64. iii); as an Athenian and an admirer of Pericles he surely shared in that pride; but also, although he was not a religious man, he believed in morality and lawful conduct (cf. II. 53 on the effects of the plague, III. 82–3 on stasis) – and what was Athens' empire but the successful exercise of lawlessness on the largest scale? I suspect that he returns to the question so often because he could not satisfactorily resolve it.

Some modern liberals, disappointed in Thucydides, have hoped to find in Aristophanes a renunciation of cynical imperialism, but he probably offers little to comfort them. In his lost *Babylonians* of 426 the Babylonians seem to have been slaves, branded and working a treadmill, but the context is unclear, and it is by no means certain (as was once maintained) that this was a depiction of Athens' cruelty towards the allies. The reason for Cleon's attack on the play (cf. p. 118) was that in the presence of foreigners (i.e. at the Dionysia) Aristophanes slandered Athens; specifically, he slandered 'allotted and elected officials, and Cleon' (Ar. *Ach.* 501–2, 630–1, schol. 378); and behind that probably lies the claim made in *Acharnians* that Aristophanes benefits the Athenians 'by preventing them from being deceived too much by the words of foreigners, from delighting in being flattered, from being gaping citizens; for previously envoys would come from the cities to cheat you', and thus by showing up what democracy, in Athens and generally, is really like (*Ach.* 633–42). Similarly, in *Knights*,

> Demos, you have a fine empire, since all people fear you like a man who is a tyrant [that Athens is a tyrant is taken for granted]; but you are easily led astray, you delight in being flattered and cheated, you gape at whoever is currently speaking, you have a mind but it's never at home. (*Eq.* 1110–20)

In *Wasps* Hate-Cleon tries to show his father Love-Cleon how he is imposed on by the demagogues, by reckoning up the income from the allies and showing how little of it is spent on jurors' pay, i.e. how little benefit accrues to the ordinary citizens (*Vesp.* 655–85, 698–712): the only objection to the extraction of money from the allies is that those who grow rich on it are the politicians.

Beyond that there is *Birds*, where the new city in the clouds turns out to have all the familiar faults of Athens (cf. p. 159); among the uninvited guests who arrive are an *episkopos*, one of the 'inspectors' sent by Athens to the allied states, who begins by asking, 'Where are the *proxenoi*?', the 'representatives' who can be expected to be pro-Athenian (*Av.* 1021–53); and a decree-seller, whose three sample decrees are parodies of a judicial settlement between Athens and an ally, a requirement to use Athenian measures, weights and coins (cf. p. 174), and sanctions against allies who refuse to welcome Athenian officials (*Av.* 1035–57). There are perhaps a few crumbs of comfort for liberals here, but to my mind the emphasis is on Athenian busybodyness rather than oppressiveness.

Another comedian, Eupolis, seems to have focused on the allied cities in his *Cities* (*Poleis*: perhaps to be dated to the end of the 420's): recent work suggests that they were depicted unsympathetically as women bringing tribute to Athens.

There are a few pointers in inscriptions to opposition – Cleinias' tribute decree threatens penalties for any Athenian or ally who commits an offence in connection with the tribute (M&L 46 = *IG* i³ 34 ~ Fornara 98. 31–41); an undertaking to enforce the decree on weights, measures and coinage is added to the councillors' oath (M&L 45 §12 = *IG* i³ 1453 §10 ~ Fornara 97 §12) – but opposition of what kind? Thucydides son of Melesias objected not to the League or to the collection of tribute but to the spending of the tribute on buildings in Athens rather than on war against Persia (Plut. *Per.* 12. i–iv, 14. i). Cleon in the 420's seems to have been obsessed with his enemies (cf. p. 120), and this could be reflected in decrees of that time. The oligarchs in 411 wanted not to abandon the empire but to replace democracy with oligarchy among the allies as well as in Athens (Thuc. VIII. 64–65. i, cf. 91. iii); but Thucydides says that Phrynichus, just as he believed that Alcibiades was committed neither to oligarchy nor to democracy but to the furtherance of his own career, believed that the allies wanted neither slavery combined with oligarchy nor slavery combined with democracy but freedom irrespective of constitution (VIII. 48. iv–v), and Thucydides himself endorses that belief (VIII. 64. v).

As for the Athenians' treatment of opposition, as far as we know they had not gone to the extent of killing all the men in a city before Cleon proposed to do that in Mytilene in 427, and on that occasion a (slightly) less severe decision was taken ultimately; they did kill all the men in Scione in 421 and in Melos in 416/5; but this severity was not peculiar to Athens: the Peloponnesians killed all the men in Plataea in 427, and in Hysiae in 416. However, in Thucydides' Mytilene debate Diodotus argues that rebels who expect the ultimate punishment have no reason not to resist to the end (Thuc. III. 46. i), and on occasions the Athenians realised that it was important to treat a state generously in order to retain its loyalty. From the 420's we have a series of decrees making special provisions for Methone, on the coast of volatile Macedon (M&L 65 = *IG* i³ 61 ~ Fornara 128), and similar provisions were made for Aphytis, in Chalcidice near to the hostile Olynthus (*IG* i³ 62). In 408 on recovering Calchedon and Byzantium they levied tribute at the previous rate but did not take reprisals (Xen. *Hell.* I. iii. 8–9, Diod. Sic. XIII. 66. iii, 67. v–vii);

Alcibiades' treaty with Selymbria included the return of hostages, freedom for Selymbria to choose its own constitution, possibly the cancellation of debts to Athens, and the renunciation of Athenian and allied claims to property in the city (M&L 87 = *IG* i³ 118 ~ Fornara 162. 8–26).

The Athenians normally encouraged, and when provoked sometimes installed, democracies in the allied states (cf. p. 175; [Xen.] *Ath. Pol.* iii. 11 notes that occasions when they supported oligarchies turned out badly). Meanwhile Sparta, though not itself a typical oligarchy, encouraged oligarchies among its allies (cf. Thuc. I. 19, V. 81. ii). Thus, as the Greek world became polarised between Athens and Sparta, there was a tendency for democrats to look to Athens for support and oligarchs to Sparta (Thuc. III. 82. i). It is this that led Grote and de Ste. Croix to believe that the Athenian empire was not universally hated by those subjected to it, as the Thucydidean analysis of power politics requires, but while hated by upper-class oligarchs was in fact popular with lower-class democrats: the burden of paying the tribute will have fallen largely on the rich upper class, while political support and opportunities for employment, for instance in the Athenian navy, will have benefited the poor lower class.

The facts suggest that both the Thucydidean view and the alternative are too one-sided. From Naxos in the League's first ten years to Potidaea and Olynthus in 433/2 we can draw up a long list of revolts before the outbreak of the Peloponnesian War; in most cases we do not know what led to the revolt or how widely it was supported. Mytilene, which revolted in 428, was one of the few ship-providing allies which had not been subjected to Athenian interference; it had considered revolting before the war but had not then been encouraged by Sparta (Thuc. III. 2. i). It was oligarchic, so its revolt was the work of the oligarchs. After the city had been under siege during the winter, supplies of food ran short and there was no sign of the promised help from Sparta; the ordinary people were given weapons for a final effort but refused to fight, accusing the men in power of hoarding food for themselves, and forcing them to come to terms with Athens (III. 27–28. i): the impression given by the narrative is that the people could endure no more, not that they were pro-Athenian.

When the Spartan Brasidas went to the Thraceward region in 424, he went first to Acanthus, which was divided between those who had encouraged his expedition and the *demos*; 'nevertheless the mass (*plethos*) through fear for the [grape] harvest, which was still outside, was persuaded by Brasidas' to give him a hearing (IV. 84. ii). Brasidas made a speech which he was to repeat in other cities, and which included a claim which Thucydides describes as enticing but untrue (IV. 108. v): he had indeed come as a liberator, not to substitute Spartan rule for Athenian or to support one party against another in the city, and had bound the Spartan authorities by an oath [which suggests that they might not have been so generous otherwise], but if Acanthus did not accept his liberation he would impose it by force (IV. 85–7). After debate, by a secret ballot, the Acanthians decided to go over to him, 'because what Brasidas said was attractive and through fear for their harvest . . . and making him give pledges to keep the oaths sworn by the Spartan authorities' (IV. 88). Athens had sent additional garrisons to the region (IV. 82). Most cities, like Acanthus, hesitated but did in the end go over to Brasidas; Argilus and Scione (IV. 103. iv, 120. i), and perhaps some others about which Thucydides says little, joined him spontaneously. Amphipolis, where the primary division was between Athenians and non-Athenians, was won over by generous terms (IV. 105–6); Torone was betrayed by a few men (IV. 110–113. i). In spite of his promises, Spartan governors were in due course sent to the cities (IV. 132. iii). In Mende a few men had outmanoeuvred the majority, and Athens treated it generously on recovering it (IV. 123. ii, 130. iv–vii); but Scione, threatened with destruction, held out until 421, when it was captured and destroyed (IV. 122. vi, V. 32. i), and Amphipolis, which should have been returned to Athens under the Peace of Nicias, refused to comply (V. 18. v, 21. i–ii). Those who revolted 'thought they were in no danger, being as greatly deceived about Athenian power as it was afterwards shown to be . . . and they became bold and thought that no retaliatory force would reach them' (IV. 108. iv–v).

This does not point to a simple conclusion: where there was a division, the lower classes were more likely to support Athens than the upper; but Brasidas was popular because he offered freedom rather than pro-Spartan oligarchy, and he was feared because if his offer was not accepted he would enforce it, while the rebels thought they could safely go over to him because the Athenians would not be able to recover them.

There was large-scale allied involvement in Athens' Sicilian expedition of 415–413. Thucydides gives a catalogue for the summer of 413, when all those who were going to take part had arrived, listing both tribute-paying (they provided soldiers: cf. VI. 25. ii) and ship-providing members of the League, as well as allies of other kinds and mercenaries (VII. 57). Most of these remained loyal to the end, not accepting the Syracusans' invitation to desert when they were caught in their retreat (VII. 82. i), but Thucydides suggests that the chief concern of the League members during the campaign was 'for their immediate safety, of which there was no hope unless they won, and as a bonus that if they helped to subdue someone else their subjection might become easier' (VI. 69. iii).

After the failure of that attempt to enlarge the empire, it did begin to seem possible that Athens might be unable to hold on to the empire it had, and the last phase of the war began with approaches to Sparta by the cities of Euboea and Lesbos, and by Chios and Erythrae (VIII. 5. i–v). Others joined in the revolt, and Athens recovered some but not others. Chios resisted repeated Athenian attempts to regain it. In Samos, on the other hand, a democracy came to power and was staunchly loyal to Athens (VIII. 21, cf. *IG* i^3 96); after Aegospotami the democrats killed some of their opponents and, alone of the allies, refused to submit to Lysander until he besieged the city (Xen. *Hell.* II. ii. 7, iii. 6–7, cf. Diod. Sic. XIV. 3. iv–v, Plut. *Lys.* 14. ii); in 405/4 Athens showed its gratitude by conferring citizenship on all the Samians (*IG* ii^2 1: M&L 94 = *IG* i^3 94 ~ Fornara 138 + R&O 2 ~ Harding 5). The situation was complicated by Sparta's promising in 412/1 that the Greeks of mainland Asia Minor would not be liberated but would be returned to the Persians. Persian rule was by now only a distant memory, and the prospect does not seem to have caused widespread alarm. However, in 411 Miletus captured a fort built by Tissaphernes, and was angry when told by the Spartan Lichas that it and the others in the King's territory 'must submit to moderate slavery and cultivate Tissaphernes until they got a good settlement of the war' (VIII. 84. v); and later that year Persian garrisons were expelled by Antandrus and Cnidus (VIII. 108. iv–109. i).

Other considerations need to be borne in mind, as well as liking or loathing for Athens and the League. Athens and Sparta were both much larger and more powerful than most Greek cities, and, whatever a city's sympathies, if a Spartan force arrived on its doorstep it might well seem prudent to join the Spartans, and later if an Athenian force arrived it might seem prudent to return to its old allegiance and plead that it had had no choice. Beyond any immediate threat to itself, a city might well judge that its interests would best be served by being on the winning side (cf. Paus. VI. 3. xv–xvi), and notice Thucydides' remark, quoted above, that the Thraceward cities misjudged Athens' strength. Other considerations likely to be important in some cases are a city's proximity to the Persians and liking or disliking of them, and proximity to a more powerful Greek city against which Athens might be seen as a protector. Whatever the attitudes of the ordinary members of the lower classes, one group of men likely to have been enthusiastic for Athens will have been those democratic political leaders who were in a position of power in their cities with Athenian support, and who without it might well lose that position: all too often in Greece political leaders of various hues would rather be in power with external support than out of power in an independent city (see Thuc. III. 82. i, and cf., for instance, Megara in 424, IV. 66. iii).

Class loyalty did count for something in the Greek world, and there are passages where Thucydides notes that because of a city's constitution it was perceived as a congenial or uncongenial ally by another city (V. 29. ii, 31. vi, 44. i). But *polis* loyalty counted for something too, and Athens had infringed the independence of its allies as no Greek city had done before: Thucydides states that at the beginning of the Peloponnesian War people's sympathies were with the Spartans because they proclaimed that they were going to free Greece (II. 8. iv–v); Brasidas insisted that he would be a liberator, and Phrynichus thought that what the allies wanted was freedom irrespective of constitution (cf. pp. 181, 182–3); Xenophon writes that the day when the demolition of Athens' long walls was begun was hailed as the beginning of freedom for Greece (Xen. *Hell.* II. ii. 13). In more than one area in the Greek world Thucydides notes fears that Athenian support would turn into Athenian domination (north-west Greece, III. 114. ii–iv with 113. vi; Sicily, IV. 60–1 in Hermocrates' speech at Gela; cf. Boeotia, IV. 92. v–vi in Pagondas' speech before Delium). Certainly the richer citizens in the allied states are more likely to have been opposed to Athens and the League, and the poorer more likely to have been in favour, and

probably there were some places at some times when that was the more important consideration; many may have been comparatively happy to stay in the
League while it seemed secure, but eager to abandon the ship when it began
to sink; but the desire for local independence was genuine and important,
and although Thucydides over-simplifies he may not have been fundamentally
wrong.

After 404

At the end of the Peloponnesian War Athens lost all its overseas possessions, not
only the League proper but also the islands in the northern Aegean which it had
acquired early in the fifth century, Lemnos and Imbros. What Sparta was committed to in respect of the Asiatic Greeks depends on whether we accept a Treaty
of Boeotius in 408/7 (cf. pp. 149, 191); as we shall see, what actually happened
was that immediately Sparta took over the Athenian empire, including the cities
on the Asiatic mainland; and when Tissaphernes claimed the Asiatic Greeks for
Persia they appealed to Sparta for support and were granted it; then for some
years Sparta vacillated between fighting in Asia Minor and trying to negotiate a
compromise. Thucydides has the Athenians in 432 predicting that if Sparta were
to rule in Athens' place it would be even more unpopular than Athens (I. 77. vi,
cf. 76. i), and this was borne out. In 395 Athens joined several of Sparta's former
allies in the Corinthian War against Sparta; and Xenophon gives the Thebans a
speech appealing for Athenian support in which they take it for granted that
Athens would like to recover its empire, and say, 'When you ruled over the largest
number, you had the largest number of enemies' (Xen. *Hell.* III. v. 8–15). In
387/6 Sparta did by the Peace of Antalcidas finally surrender the Asiatic Greeks
to Persia in return for Persia's backing terms which Sparta wanted in Greece
(and the fifth-century Peace of Callias between Athens and Persia was perhaps
invented then to demonstrate how much more glorious the past had been: cf.
pp. 47–8); elsewhere in the Greek world Sparta's conduct was increasingly interfering, to such an extent that in 378 Athens founded a new league with the aim
of resisting Spartan imperialism.

Orators and others in Athens could offer a conventional defence of or attack
on the fifth-century empire to suit their current purposes. Lysias' *Funeral Speech*
of *c*.390, generalising from the Corinthian War to claim that Athens has always
fought on the side of freedom and justice, insists that in the fifth century 'the
Athenians made Greece free and their own fatherland the greatest'; for seventy
years they kept the allies free from stasis, obliging them to live in equality [i.e.
democracy], and made them as well as Athens strong, keeping the Persians at
bay (Lys. II. *Epitaph.* 54–7). In Plato's *Gorgias* (*c*.390–385?) it is the creators
of Athens' power, Themistocles, Cimon and Pericles, who are responsible for
Athens' troubles rather than Alcibiades (Plat. *Grg.* 518 E–519 B). Isocrates in
his *Panegyric* of *c*.380, arguing for a Greek war under Athenian leadership
against Persia, claims in response to objections that Athens was milder than any

other ruler, dealing with the cities not as a master but as an ally, supporting the people and opposing oligarchies (Isoc. IV. *Paneg.* 100–6, cf. 80–1). By contrast, in *On the Peace*, *c.*355 at the end of the Social War, he rejects imperialism as a failure, and writes of 'the licentiousness of our fathers, who . . . made themselves hated amongst the Greeks and drove into exile the best men in the other cities' (Isoc. VIII. *Peace* 79). Later still, in his *Panathenaic* of *c.*342–339, in the course of a contrast between Athens and Sparta, he sets the Peace of Callias against the Peace of Antalcidas (Isoc. XII. *Panath.* 106), and, while admitting the unpopularity of the transfer of lawsuits, the collection of tribute and the severe treatment of rebel cities, claims that Sparta's behaviour has in every respect been worse (§§56–73). Demosthenes in his *Third Philippic* of 341 contrasts with the Greeks' leaving Philip of Macedon free to do whatever he likes the assertion that, when Athens, Sparta or Thebes tried to be overbearing, the other Greeks did not let them get away with it but rallied in support of those who were wronged (Dem. IX. *Phil. iii.* 22–5).

The clearest indication of what was remembered and resented is the series of promises made in the prospectus of the Second Athenian League (378/7) that Athens would not do various things which it had done in the Delian League: the allies are to be free and autonomous, living under whatever constitution they wish, not receiving a garrison or governor, not paying tribute; and no houses or land in allied territory are to be owned by Athenians, either publicly or individually (*IG* ii² 43 = R&O 22 ~ Harding 35. 19–46). As we shall see in chapter 18, at the beginning the Second League was popular (Sparta in the present was a greater cause of worry than an Athens which seemed to have learned from the past), and on the whole kept its promises; but, as Athens had not disbanded the Delian League when it ceased wanting to fight against Persia, it did not disband the Second League when, within ten years of its foundation, far from wanting to resist Sparta it made an ally of Sparta, and the League failed to find a new purpose and its promises were increasingly broken.

What are we to make of the Delian League? There had never before in the Greek world been an organisation which embraced so many Greek states and subjected them to such an extent to the will of the leader (cf. Thuc. II. 64. iii: various passages in Thucydides contrast the alternatives for Athens of ruling others and being ruled by others). This was, however, accomplished within what Greeks could regard as an acceptable framework: the members were not incorporated in the Athenian state, as Rome was to incorporate its subjects (to be made part of a greater Athens, even with citizenship, would have been far more shocking to Greeks than what was done in the Delian League), but remained technically independent *poleis*, with their own laws, their own political machinery, their own cults and festivals, and so on. Nevertheless, most of them not only did lose the freedom to decide their own foreign policy but also were subjected to various kinds of internal interference (the form of constitution, the transfer of lawsuits to Athens, the payment of tribute as well as the sending of offerings to Athenian festivals, the loss of land for settlements of Athenian citizens), though much of this interference was not systematic throughout the

League but took the form of ad hoc reactions to particular provocations. On the other hand, there were economic benefits for everybody in belonging to an organisation which kept the Aegean free from pirates, whose use of common standards facilitated trade, and which provided employment for many men who were not self-sufficient landowners. Where Athens had encouraged or demanded democracy many individuals enjoyed political rights which they might otherwise not have enjoyed; and the polarisation of the Greek world between Athenian-backed democracies and Spartan-backed oligarchies made for stability, as we shall see when we look at the less stable world of the fourth century.

Whether a state would be better off inside the League or outside depends on what alternative is set up for comparison: a world in which the League existed but a particular state tried to go it alone, a world in which the League as we know it did not exist but some other kind of organisation did, or a world in which there was no significant entity larger than the individual *poleis* and each *polis* had to do the best that it could for itself. As the Athenians themselves were to find when facing Philip of Macedon (cf. chapter 22), local pride and material interest might point in different directions, and how that dilemma was to be resolved would depend on one's own priorities; the same dilemma has faced the states of Europe confronted by the European Union.

For Athens itself there can be no doubt that its position at the head of the League made available to it resources which would have been beyond the reach even of this exceptionally large Greek *polis* on its own, and it is hard to believe that fifth-century Athens could have risen to such heights of achievement in drama and in the visual arts without these resources and without the confidence which came with the success of the League. It was the state which built up the empire which was 'an education for Greece' (Thuc. II. 41. i).

NOTE ON FURTHER READING

For general books on the Delian League see the note at the end of chapter 2.

On the extent to which the empire was exploited economically by Athens see Meiggs, *The Athenian Empire*, chs. 13–14; M. I. Finley, 'The Fifth-Century Athenian Empire: A Balance Sheet', in Garnsey and Whittaker (eds.), *Imperialism in the Ancient World*, 103–26. On the previous owners of land given to Athenian cleruchs see R. Zelnick-Abramovitz, 'Settlers and Dispossessed in the Athenian Empire', *Mnem.*[4] lvii 2004, 325–45. That we should see the cultural predominance of Athens, not only in the empire but throughout the Greek world, rather than the impoverishment of the other members, is argued by R. Osborne, 'Archaeology and the Athenian Empire', *TAPA* cxxix 1999, 319–32. On the transfer of lawsuits from allied cities to Athens see G. E. M. de Ste. Croix, 'Notes on Jurisdiction in the Athenian Empire', *CQ*[2] xi 1961, 94–112, 268–80; Meiggs, *The Athenian Empire*, ch. 12.

The suggestion of Grote, *History of Greece*, vi. 9–10, 182–4 (12-vol. edition) = v. 149–51, 319–21 (10-vol. edition) that, in contrast to the view of Thucydides, the empire was not unpopular with all its subjects but popular with lower-class democrats and unpopular only with upper-class oligarchs, was argued vigorously by G. E. M. de Ste. Croix, 'The Character of the Athenian Empire', *Hist.* iii 1954–5, 1–41. Among the responses which he elicited, see particularly D. W. Bradeen, 'The Popularity of the Athenian Empire', *Hist.* ix 1960, 257–69; J. de Romilly, 'Thucydides and the Cities of the Athenian Empire', *BICS* xiii 1966, 1–12. Fifth- and fourth-century judgments on the empire are reviewed by Meiggs, *The Athenian Empire*, chs. 21, 22.

The view of Aristophanes' *Babylonians* as a sympathetic portrayal of Athens' oppressed subjects was developed by G. Norwood, 'Aristophanes' *Babylonians*', *CP* xxv 1930, and criticised by W. G. Forrest, 'Aristophanes and the Athenian Empire', in *The Ancient Historian and His Materials . . . C. E. Stevens*, ch. 2. On Eupolis see Storey, *Eupolis: Poet of Old Comedy*, and on his *Cities* see I. Storey, 'The Politics of Angry Eupolis', *AHB* viii 1994, 107–20 at 109–11.

16

Introduction to the Fourth Century: The Common Peace

500	475	450	425	400	375	350	325	300

392   first Spartan attempt at a common peace treaty
387/6 Peace of Antalcidas
375   renewal of peace
371   peace treaties before and after battle of Leuctra
367   Thebes wins support of Persians but Greeks reject peace treaty
365   Thebes makes treaty with Corinth and other cities
362   treaty after battle of Mantinea
346   Peace of Philocrates between Athens and Philip II of Macedon
338/7 common peace treaty and creation of League of Corinth after battle of Chaeronea

The fourth century can be divided into four sections, the first three of which are included in this book. (1) To about 360 Sparta, Athens and Thebes attempted in turn to dominate the Greek world, with Persia in the background as a power to be invoked by the currently predominant Greek city to reinforce its predominance. (2) From 359 to 336 Philip II of Macedon achieved a leading position in the Greek world, which he clothed in familiar Greek diplomatic forms, and at the end of his reign he took advantage of the Greeks' hankering after unity through another war against Persia, to plan such a war. (3) Philip was assassinated after he had sent out his advance forces; his successor Alexander III (336–323) undertook the campaign and conquered the Persian empire, but his increasing adoption of oriental practices alienated the more conservative Macedonians and Greeks. (4) Alexander died young, without leaving a viable heir; after his death his leading generals competed for supremacy, originally on behalf of a possible heir but later for themselves; and the first phase in this competition reached its climax when in 306–304 the leading contenders each took the title king and it became clear that the Graeco-Macedonian world was to centre on a plurality of large kingdoms.

For the second and third sections Macedon provides a unifying thread, but the first is more complex. In this chapter an outline narrative of the period 404–336 will be given, linked to a series of 'common peace' treaties; in chapters 17–19 the years 404–359 will be explored in more detail, from the angles of Sparta, Athens and Thebes in turn, and in chapter 20 the internal affairs of Athens in the same period will be studied. This will involve some repetition, but will allow the most important themes and events to appear in different contexts.

Sources (cf. pp. 146–7, on 411–404)

Xenophon's *Hellenica* (probably resumed after a pause) covers the régime of the Thirty and the restoration of democracy in Athens in II. iii. 11–iv, and then continues to 362 in books III–VII. He spent most of that period as an exile from Athens, living in the Peloponnese as a dependant of the Spartans: not every sentence is favourable to Sparta (NB V. iv. 1: Sparta was deservedly punished for its occupation of Thebes in 382), but the general tendency of his account is, and in particular favourable to king Agesilaus; and, more seriously for those who want to use it as a historical source, it shows little interest in areas and episodes in which Sparta was not involved and/or which Xenophon found uncongenial. Nothing is said of the foundation of the Second Athenian League; the only mention of the new Arcadian capital Megalopolis is in a list of supporters of Thebes in 362 (VII. v. 5); and the Theban leaders Pelopidas and Epaminondas are similarly neglected. The *Hellenica* like Thucydides' history contains speeches, but it does not contain a declaration of policy on the speeches. A defender has argued that the substance of the speeches is usually authentic; at worst the speeches represent what a contemporary thought plausible that particular men should have said on particular occasions. Xenophon also wrote a separate work on *Agesilaus*, and his *Anabasis* gives an account of Cyrus' campaign against his brother Artaxerxes II (book I) and the return of Cyrus' mercenary army, in which Xenophon himself became one of the leaders, to the Greek world.

Diodorus continued to use Ephorus, and Ephorus for the period which it covered – to 386? – continued to use the *Hellenica Oxyrhynchia*. Diodorus' account is not consistent in its sympathies, but (presumably reflecting changes in Ephorus' sources) is particularly hostile to Sparta and Agesilaus in the opening chapters of book XV (1–22, covering 386/5–381/0) yet becomes favourable to Sparta and Agesilaus after that. Narrative dates, as always, are Diodorus' own; accounts of battles tend to be conventional, and Leuctra is badly garbled (cf. pp. 251–2); he is capable of striking errors, e.g. killing Chabrias in 375 (XV. 36. iv), when he still had a long career ahead of him; but he gives a far more balanced account of the period than Xenophon. As for the last years of the Peloponnesian War, when there is a direct disagreement between the two, we cannot assume automatically that one is the superior source and must therefore be right.

From Plutarch we have lives of the Spartans *Lysander* and *Agesilaus*, and of the Theban *Pelopidas*; he wrote an *Epaminondas* which has not survived (the formerly widespread view that Paus. IX. 13–15. vi is a résumé of it is fragile). From the beginning of the period we have Andocides' speeches (I) *On the Mysteries* and (III) *On the Peace*, and speeches written by or attributed to Lysias. Isocrates, who lived from *c.*436 to 338, wrote lawcourt speeches for clients in the 390's, but is best known as a teacher of rhetoric and a writer of pamphlets in the form of speeches. He was a reflecter of current ideas rather than an original thinker; one theme to be found in several of his speeches is that the Greeks were at their best when they were united in fighting against Persia rather than quarrelling among themselves, so they ought to unite in fighting against Persia once more (an idea given added momentum by the return of the Asiatic Greeks to Persia under the Peace of Antalcidas in 386). From one decade to the next Isocrates looked to a different state or man to lead the Greeks in that war.

As in the fifth century, Athens was the state most given to inscribing public documents on stone: we have a particularly rich collection of texts, with which Diodorus' account harmonises well, on the foundation of the Second Athenian League (cf. pp. 229–33).

The Origins of the Common Peace

When the Peloponnesian War ended, Sparta was committed to the unqualified return of the Asiatic Greeks to Persia if the treaty of 411 was still in force, to their becoming tributary to Persia but otherwise autonomous if the sending of Cyrus had been preceded by a Treaty of Boeotius in 408/7 (cf. pp. 149, 185). In fact it took over the cities in Asia Minor along with the other cities of the Athenian empire; and when Cyrus revolted against Artaxerxes, in 402, he was supported by nearly all of the Asiatic Greeks and by Sparta. When Artaxerxes reinstated Tissaphernes as satrap of Sardis, he demanded the submission of the Asiatic Greeks, they appealed to Sparta, and Sparta agreed to support them: it is more likely that there was a treaty of 408/7 which Tissaphernes regarded as obsolete after the Greeks' support for Cyrus than that Sparta was wilfully breaking the treaty of 411. The first Spartan forces were sent to Asia Minor in autumn 400.

Sparta's intervention was originally on a small scale, with men other than kings as commanders, and the fighting was punctuated by truces. In 398

Spartan envoys went to the Persian court (Ctesias *FGrH* 688 F 30 §74 [63]). After some truces which the Spartan Dercylidas made with one enemy in order to concentrate on another (cf. p. 207), in 397 he accepted a truce offered by Tissaphernes to explore the possibility of a treaty by which the Asiatic Greeks would be autonomous and Sparta would withdraw its troops and commanders (Xen. *Hell.* III. ii. 12–20, Diod. Sic. XIV. 39. iv–vi). In 396 king Agesilaus went to Asia and took reinforcements: on arrival he accepted a truce to enable Tissaphernes to consult the King about the autonomy of the Asiatic Greeks, but Tissaphernes in fact asked for a large army (Xen. *Hell.* III. iv. 5–6, *Ages.* i. 10–11, Plut. *Ages.* 9. i, Polyaenus *Strat.* II. 1. viii). In 395, after a victory of Age-silaus near Sardis, Tissaphernes was executed and replaced by Tithraustes, who announced the King's terms: that Sparta should withdraw and the Asiatic Greeks should be autonomous but pay 'the ancient tribute'. Agesilaus said he could not agree without authority from Sparta, but let Tithraustes pay him to move into Pharnabazus' satrapy of Dascylium (Xen. *Hell.* III. iv. 25–6, Diod. Sic. XIV. 80. viii, Plut. *Ages.* 10. vi–viii). In 394 there was a meeting between Agesilaus and Pharnabazus but not another proposal for a settlement (Xen. *Hell.* IV. i. 29–40: cf. p. 208).

In Greece Sparta had been alienating its former allies, and showing an inter-est north of the Isthmus of Corinth as well as in the Peloponnese. Timocrates of Rhodes was sent, probably by Pharnabazus in 397, with money to subsidise opponents of Sparta. In 395 a border dispute between Phocis, backed by Sparta, and Locris, backed by Boeotia, led to the outbreak of the Corinthian War against Sparta; Lysander was defeated and killed at Haliartus, and in 394 Agesilaus had to return from Asia to fight for Sparta in Greece. The Athenian Conon, who had escaped to Cyprus at the end of the Peloponnesian War, was by now com-manding ships for Pharnabazus. In 394 they defeated Sparta's fleet at Cnidus, effectively ending Sparta's supremacy in the Aegean, and in 393 they sailed to Greece, taking money to Corinth and to Athens.

Sparta was not doing well either in Asia Minor or in Greece, and in 392 turned to diplomacy. Antalcidas was sent to Tiribazus, the current satrap in Sardis; Conon headed a delegation from Athens; deputations went also from Sparta's other main opponents in the Corinthian War, Boeotia, Corinth and Argos. Antalcidas proposed that Persia's claim to the Asiatic Greeks should be accepted, and all other islands and cities should be autonomous; but this worried Athens (which had recovered the north Aegean islands of Lemnos, Imbros and Scyros, and did not want to lose them again), Boeotia (since Sparta was threatening in the name of autonomy to require the breaking-up of the Boeotian federation), and Corinth and Argos (which were forming a poli-tical union and did not want that to be undone), so no agreement was reached. Tiribazus supported the Spartans and arrested Conon, but the failure of the peace proposals suggested that Sparta would continue fighting against Persia, so Tiribazus was replaced by the anti-Spartan Struthas (Xen. *Hell.* IV. viii. 12–17, cf. Diod. Sic. XIV. 85. iv).

The next stage is omitted both by Xenophon and by Diodorus; but, though not all have accepted it, we should probably use a fragment of Philochorus (*FGrH* 328 F 149 ~ Harding 23) and Andocides' speech (III) *On the Peace* to date to 392/1 a congress at Sparta in which the Spartans tried to gain acceptance for modified terms. Athens was to be allowed the three islands as an exception to the principle of autonomy for all (Andoc. III. *Peace* 12, 14); and the rest of the Boeotian federation could remain if Orchomenus, which had gone over to Lysander in 395, were allowed to secede (§13, cf. §20); but no concession was made to Corinth and Argos (cf. §§24–8, 31–2); and Andocides' speech says nothing about the Asiatic Greeks. Andocides and his fellow-envoys urged the Athenians to accept the peace, but the Athenians were not prepared to abandon the Asiatic Greeks, rejected the peace and exiled their envoys. We do not know whether the Boeotians were prepared to accept the peace as their envoys recommended, but Corinth and Argos rejected it, and no peace was made.

The wars continued, in Asia Minor and in Greece. Most strikingly, in 390 the Athenian Thrasybulus in a one-year campaign went some way towards reviving the Athenian empire, but the next year he was killed and his successors did not build on what he had begun. In a pair of inscriptions, in 38*7*/6 Athens abstained from interfering with Clazomenae as long as it paid Thrasybulus' 5 per cent tax (*IG* ii² 28 = R&O 18 ~ Harding 26), and about the same time it made a decree for a politically divided Erythrae which gave a reply (unfortunately not preserved) 'about not giving up Erythrae to the barbarians' (*SEG* xxvi 1282 = R&O 17 ~ Harding 28). However, in 388/7 Antalcidas as Spartan navarch made an alliance with Tiribazus (who had been reinstated in Sardis), defeated the Athenians and recovered control of the Hellespont. From this position of strength he was able once more to try for a peace treaty, and this time the other Greeks did not feel able to resist.

In 387/*6* Tiribazus proclaimed 'the peace which the King had sent down' (which is commonly referred to either as the King's Peace or as the Peace of Antalcidas): the cities in Asia and Clazomenae and Cyprus were to belong to the King [Cyprus was currently in revolt, and the Greeks had tangled with it; Clazomenae was barely separate from the mainland, and was in an area important for Persia's preparations against Cyprus: cf. pp. 221–2]; Lemnos, Imbros and Scyros were to belong to Athens; all other Greek cities, small and great, were to be autonomous. The Greeks returned home to report the terms; Agesilaus had to threaten invasion to make Thebes accept the disbanding of the Boeotian federation and Corinth and Argos dissolve their union, but the others accepted without demur (Xen. *Hell.* V. i. 29–36, Diod. Sic. XIV. 110. iii–iv, Plut. *Artax.* 21. iv–v).

Persia at last gained the Asiatic Greeks, whom it had long been demanding: this was a price which the Greeks had to pay, but it was widely regarded as a betrayal, and Sparta's finally coming off the fence on this side harmed its reputation. How Persia treated the Asiatic Greeks, and how they reacted, we are not

told; but we shall see that by the 360's it had broken the treaty by taking possession of Samos. That and the other offshore islands will in any case have been
weakened by the fact that their mainland dependencies passed into Persian
hands. A settlement which maintained a balance of weakness among the Greeks
would help to ensure that none was likely to cause trouble for Persia; and while
the Greeks were at peace Greek mercenaries were available to fight for Persia
(but also for rebels against Persia) in the western provinces of the empire.

This was to be a lasting 'common peace' for all the Greeks (Andoc. III. *Peace*
17, cf. 34; the term 'common peace' appears in *IG* iv 556 = R&O 42 ~ Harding
57. 2, probably of 362/1, and is used frequently by Diodorus but never by
Xenophon), and in that respect it differed from earlier treaties which simply
made peace for a specified period between states which had been at war. A settlement on the basis of autonomy for all seems at first sight straightforward and
fair, but the reality was far more complicated. Who were 'all the Greeks' who
accepted it, and to whom was it to apply? Primarily, still, those who had been
involved in the Corinthian War; beyond them, the treaty was probably thought
of as applying generally to Greece proper and the Aegean and its Thracian coast,
but perhaps not to Crete or the north-west of Greece and more certainly not
to the more distant Greek settlements; and probably the terms were heard in
Sardis and subsequently ratified by some of those other Greeks, particularly
those who wanted to make it clear that the provision for autonomy applied to
them. How great a degree of independence was autonomy and what were the
entities entitled to it? Sparta used the treaty to break up the Boeotian federation, but did not break up other federations (such as the Achaean, within
the Peloponnese and certainly within the treaty's geographical scope, and the
Aetolian), in which it was less interested, and it may well not have insisted
on a change in status for the lesser cities in Boeotia which were not members
represented in the federation but were subordinate to one of those members.
It broke up the union of Corinth and Argos, and in 385 it was to split the
century-old *polis* of Mantinea into its component villages. But there was no suggestion that Salamis, which had been a possession of Athens since the sixth
century, was an island which was entitled to autonomy or else needed to be
mentioned as an exception like Lemnos, Imbros and Scyros; or that the cities
of Sparta's *perioikoi* were cities which were entitled to autonomy of a kind which
they had not hitherto possessed.

There was no impartial machinery for deciding hard cases or for enforcing
the treaty: Sparta decided on the interpretation, and with the threat of Persian
backing enforced the treaty, not because the treaty gave Sparta a privileged position but because, although it had not been strong enough to achieve military
victory, it was currently in a superior position and had surrendered the Asiatic
Greeks in return for Persian support in Greece. Agesilaus was an enemy of
Antalcidas, but he saw how the treaty could be exploited to Sparta's advantage,
and in a remark quoted by Plutarch on three occasions he replied to a complaint that the Spartans were medising that it was the Persians who were laconising (Plut. *Ages.* 23. iv, *Artax.* 22. iv, *Spartan Sayings* 213 B). We shall see that

later treaties did try to incorporate a mechanism for enforcement, but each treaty was made at the instance of one state which hoped to use it in its own interests.

Breaches and Renewals of the Peace

Sparta showed that the peace was to be interpreted by it to suit its own interests. In 385 it attacked Mantinea, and ended by splitting it into the separate villages which had coalesced to form a single *polis* perhaps *c.*470 (cf. p. 23); Mantinea appealed to Athens, but Athens 'did not choose to break the common agreement' (Diod. Sic. XV. 5. v); presumably Sparta claimed that the principle of autonomy should be applied to the villages rather than to the single *polis*. In 382 Sparta responded to an appeal to intervene against the Chalcidian federation being built up by Olynthus in the north-east. The appeal came from the threatened cities of Acanthus and Apollonia according to Xenophon, from Amyntas of Macedon according to Diodorus (Xen. *Hell.* V. ii. 11–20, Diod. Sic. XV. 19. ii–iii): both may be true, but Xenophon's version suggests that Sparta was again claiming to enforce the autonomy principle (we do not know whether Olynthus or any of its neighbours had sworn to the peace). Olynthus appealed to Athens and Thebes: Athens is not known to have responded but Thebes did. On their way north in 382 Sparta's forces accepted an invitation to enter Thebes, where they installed a garrison and a pro-Spartan régime: this direct occupation of one of the major cities of Greece was greatly shocking, and is easier to understand if Sparta gave as its excuse the refusal of Thebes to join in enforcing the peace against Olynthus (cf. Xen. *Hell.* V. ii. 34). The war in the north continued to 379, when the federation was dismantled and Olynthus was made a subordinate ally of Sparta; meanwhile in the Peloponnese Sparta insisted on the restoration of exiles in Phlius *c.*384–383, and in 379 after a long siege imposed a garrison and a new constitution. Sparta had apparently reached a new height of power.

It must have been hard for other states to know what kinds of relations Sparta would allow. In 386/5 Athens praised the Thracian king Hebryzelmis, but did not grant him an alliance (*IG* ii^2 31 = Tod 117 ~ Harding 29); in 385 it refused to help Mantinea against Sparta; but in 384 a way forward was found: with Chios (which had been hostile to Athens in the last years of the Peloponnesian War but defected from Sparta after the battle of Cnidus) Athens made a purely defensive alliance, which was stated very emphatically to be on the basis of freedom and autonomy and within the framework of the King's Peace (*IG* ii^2 34–5 = R&O 20 ~ Harding 31).

Theban opponents of Sparta fled to Athens, and a series of setbacks for Sparta began when in winter 379/8 these exiles returned and assassinated the pro-Spartan leaders. A raid on Athenian territory by the Spartan garrison commander in Thespiae, Sphodrias, prompted Athens to action, and in 378/7 the Second Athenian League was founded. We possess an inscribed prospectus setting out the terms on which states were invited to join (*IG* ii^2 43 = R&O 22 ~ Harding 35): the League's aim was that Sparta should allow the Greeks to live in freedom and autonomy, and to support the King's Peace [that clause was deleted in the 360's when Athens had reason to dislike the Persians]; Greeks and barbarians outside the King's domain were invited to join, on the basis of freedom and autonomy, 'on the same terms as Chios, Thebes and the other allies', and subject to various promises, which may be seen both as undertakings that Athens would not treat the new League as it had treated the Delian League and as an attempt to spell out what was to be understood by autonomy. This defensive alliance, which bound its members to support one another against Sparta or any other breaker of the peace, also provided its members with a mechanism for enforcing the peace.

While successfully recruiting members for the new League, the Athenians won their first major naval victories since the Peloponnesian War, defeating the Spartans off Naxos in 376 and off Alyzia in Acarnania in 375; and on the mainland the Thebans drove the Spartans out of Boeotia, began organising a new federation, more dominated by Thebes than the old, and in 375 defeated a Spartan army at Tegyra, near Orchomenus. In 375 the King's Peace was renewed. Xenophon, not mentioning Sparta's plight, says that Athens was exhausted, and worried by the resurgence of Thebes, and so made peace with Sparta (Xen. *Hell.* VI. ii. 1). According to Diodorus, however, the Persians wanted Greek mercenaries for a campaign in Egypt and so urged the Greeks to make a common peace, which they gladly did (Diod. Sic. XV. 38). Diodorus badly confuses this treaty and the next, in summer 371, ascribing both to Persia's initiative and on each occasion having the Thebans excluded because of their claim to swear for the whole of Boeotia. The exclusion of Thebes belongs to the later occasion (and on this occasion Thebes must have made some show of dismantling the new federation), but a fragment of Philochorus (*FGrH* 328 F 151 ~ Harding 44) confirms for this occasion the involvement of Persia, and mentions Athens' celebration with a cult and statue of Eirene (Peace); Diodorus' clause that the cities were to be 'autonomous and ungarrisoned' is probably authentic.

The new peace was broken almost immediately. Conflict between Athens and Sparta continued in the west, culminating in victory for Athens and the democrats in Corcyra in 372. On the mainland Thebes resumed the development of a Boeotian federation under its control; in 373/2 it angered Athens by destroying Plataea (which had been destroyed in 427, cf. p. 109, but refounded after the Peace of Antalcidas) and interfering in Thespiae; then it began to threaten Phocis, and Sparta sent an army to help in the defence. In summer 371 the Athenians, increasingly uncomfortable with their Theban allies, sent envoys to Sparta to discuss peace and invited the Thebans to send envoys too. Xenophon gives us speeches by three of the Athenian envoys: Callias, full of his own importance; Autocles, criticising Sparta's conduct; and the leading politician Callistratus, arguing that Athens and Sparta ought to be on the same side. Peace was agreed on condition that governors should be withdrawn and forces demobilised, and the cities should be autonomous. The Thebans were originally included, as Thebans; afterwards they returned and asked to be recorded as Boeotians. Sources other than Xenophon report a heated altercation between Agesilaus and the Theban Epaminondas, in which Epaminondas argued that if the Boeotian cities were to be autonomous the cities of Sparta's *perioikoi* should be too; Xenophon agrees that it was Agesilaus who finally excluded Thebes from the treaty. Diodorus both ascribes the initiative to Persia and has the Thebans excluded, as in 375: this time he is right about the exclusion of the Thebans but it does not seem likely that the Persians were involved (Xen. *Hell.* VI. iii, Diod. Sic. XV. 50. iv–v [cf. 38. iii: Callistratus and Epaminondas, 375], Plut. *Ages.* 27. v–28. iv, Nep. XV. *Epam.* 6. iv, cf. Paus. IX. 13. ii). This time the treaty included what may be called an optional sanctions clause: if any state broke the peace, the others might if they wished support those who were wronged, but were not obliged to do so (Xen. *Hell.* VI. iii. 18).

The Spartan king Cleombrotus, commander of the army sent to Phocis, asked what he should do, and was told to attack Thebes if it would not leave the Boeotian cities autonomous. The result was the battle of Leuctra, in which Sparta was overwhelmingly defeated. After that, Athens took the initiative in convening a conference of 'the cities which wished to participate in the peace which the King had sent down' (which means that this was a renewal of the King's Peace, not that the King was involved on this occasion). The participants swore to 'the treaty which the King sent down and the decrees of the Athenians and their allies': it is not credible that all the participants, including Sparta, were now enrolled in the Second Athenian League, and the best explanation is that autonomy was to be defined for the peace as it was in the League. This time there was a compulsory sanctions clause: if any state broke the peace, the others were obliged to support those who were wronged. Thebes was certainly not a participant; Elis refused to swear, because its claim to recover dependent territories lost *c.*400 was not allowed (Xen. *Hell.* VI. v. 1–3).

The Athenians were later to claim that the Greeks, and Amyntas III of Macedon (who died in 370/69), and the Persian King had all recognised their right to Amphipolis and the Chersonese (Dem. XIX. *Embassy* 253, Aeschin. II. *Embassy* 32, [Dem.] VII. *Halonnesus* 29, Dem. IX. *Phil. iii.* 16). Since they began fighting for Amphipolis and the Chersonese in 368, and this is the one conference convened by Athens, this is probably the occasion to which they are alluding; but it is likely that the claim is doubly disingenuous. Peace treaties could be made on the basis of the status quo, as in the Peace of Philocrates between Athens and Philip in 346, or on the basis of a return to an earlier situation, as in the Thirty Years' Peace in 446/5 or the Peace of Nicias in 421, or, in a gambit which was often to be employed in the fourth century, on the basis of *echein ta heauton*, that states should possess what belonged to them (a formula which usually covered a claim to some territory which they did not at the time possess). Probably the peace of autumn 371 was made on the basis of *echein ta heauton*, and the participants agreed to that, but the Athenians' claim that

Amphipolis and the Chersonese belonged to them was not spelled out in the peace: 'possessing what belongs to them' was included in the promises made in the prospectus of the Second Athenian League, which underlay this peace (*IG* ii² 43 = R&O 22 ~ Harding 35. 11–12), and Isoc. VIII. *Peace* 16 indicates that at least one common peace was made on that basis. That the Persian King accepted the Athenians' claim was probably a further instance of 'spin': he was not in fact involved on this occasion, but, since the participants swore once more to 'the treaty which the King sent down', his agreement could be postulated.

Leuctra revealed suddenly that Sparta was not as strong as everybody had assumed, and the next few years were to see a number of revolutions in Peloponnesian cities, where Sparta was no longer able to underwrite pro-Spartan oligarchies. Most important was the re-creation by Mantinea in 370 of the single *polis* dismantled in 385, and after that Mantinea's joining with the other Arcadians in a new federal state, which built a new major city at Megalo-polis, in the south-west near Laconia and Messenia. Arcadia joined with Argos and Elis an in anti-Spartan alliance, and failed to gain the support of Athens but did gain that of Thebes. In the winter of 370/69 the allies invaded Laconia and liberated Messenia – which Sparta was never prepared to accept. In this new world, despite the declared objectives of the Second Athenian League, it was now in Athens' interests to support Sparta rather than Thebes, and Athens made an alliance with Sparta in 369 (Xen. *Hell.* VII. i. 1–14, Diod. Sic. XV. 67. i).

In the next few years there was a good deal of fighting in the Peloponnese (and Thebes built up a league of its own in central Greece, and intervened in Thessaly, but this did not involve Sparta or interest Xenophon), while the Athenians started campaigning, without much success, for the territories which they claimed in the north. Ariobarzanes, the satrap of Dascylium, was still a be-liever in Persian support for a Spartan-backed common peace. In winter 369/8 he sent Philiscus of Abydus, who convened a peace conference at Delphi: agreement could not be reached, more probably because of Sparta's claim to Messenia (Xenophon), which was currently the live issue, than because of Thebes' claim to Boeotia (Diodorus), so Philiscus' money was spent on mer-cenaries to fight for Sparta (Xen. *Hell.* VII. i. 27, Diod. Sic. XV. 70. ii), and Ariobarzanes, he and others were made Athenian citizens (Dem. XXIII. *Aristocrates* 141–2, 202).

In 367 the Thebans tried to obtain a common peace to their advantage. According to Xenophon Sparta was the first to send an envoy to the King; envoys then went also from Thebes and its Peloponnesian allies, and from Athens. The Theban representative was Pelopidas, and he dominated the con-ference and obtained a draft which included rulings on a number of current issues: Messenia was to be independent, the region to the south of Olympia now known as Triphylia was to belong to Elis and not to Arcadia, the Athen-ian navy was to be beached (perhaps that was the only anti-Athenian clause and there was not a clause stating that Amphipolis and the Chersonese were to be independent); there was to be a compulsory sanctions clause. One of Athens' envoys was persuaded to acquiesce, for which he was prosecuted by his colleague (and it was probably on this occasion that the Athenians deleted the clause in favour of the King's Peace from the prospectus of their league: cf. p. 196); the Spartan Antalcidas committed suicide. Back in Greece, in 367/6, the Thebans convened a conference at which they hoped to gain acceptance of the terms, but too many states had grounds for dissatisfaction: the Arcadians walked out of the conference, and when the Thebans sent envoys calling on the cities to swear to the peace they all refused (Xen. *Hell.* VII. i. 33–40, cf. Diod. Sic. XV. 81. iii, 90. ii, Plut. *Pel.* 30). One result of Thebes' gaining the support of Persia was that, in the Satraps' Revolt in the western provinces of the Persian empire, Athens and Sparta both supported the rebels: in 366–365 the Athenians besieged Samos and captured it from the Persians, but then did not liberate it but turned it into an Athenian cleruchy.

Theban policies in the Peloponnese were proving unsuccessful: in 366 an attempted annexation of Achaea by Thebes and Argos misfired, and the Achaeans became allies of Sparta; and the Arcadians, alienated by Thebes' proposal to award Triphylia to Elis, did not end their alliance with Thebes but made a new alliance with Athens. The next peace treaty is problematic. Diodorus under the year 366/5 (for which he has no major episode but a few short entries) reports that the King persuaded the Greeks to end their wars and make a common peace (Diod. Sic. XV. 76. iii). Xenophon in a context of 366–365 reports that in Corinth, which was in an unstable condition (about this time a man called Timophanes tried to make himself tyrant but was assassinated), Athens attempted to intervene but was frustrated. The Corinthians then tried to make peace with Thebes for themselves and their allies; Sparta gave permission, but would not itself join the peace and thereby give up the attempt to recover Messenia. Corinth insisted on peace only with Thebes, not alliance; and (perhaps in spring 365) a peace was made, on the basis of *echein ta heauton*, which included several cities in the north-eastern Peloponnese (Xen. *Hell.* VII. iv. 4–11). Isocrates' (VI) *Archidamus* was written for this context, and some have used it to support Diodorus; the best solution is that the participants claimed to be renewing the King's Peace once more but the participants were a limited range of states. This treaty involving Peloponnesian allies of Sparta but not Sparta itself marked the end of the Peloponnesian League.

In Thessaly Thebes had been supporting a federation of cities against a dynasty of tyrants in the city of Pherae, and Thebes' intervention ended successfully (but with the death of Pelopidas) in 364, when the tyrants had their power limited to that one city and were made allies of Thebes. Athens had been supporting Pherae, and Theban hostility to Athens continued: in 366 Thebes managed to gain possession of the disputed territory of Oropus; Diodorus reports a plan, instigated by Epaminondas, to build a hundred triremes and win over Athens' Aegean allies, and a Theban naval campaign in 364 stirred up trouble in Ceos. In 362 and 361 Alexander of Pherae, now constrained on land, turned to attack Athens by sea.

In the Peloponnese friction over Triphylia led to the outbreak in 365 of a war between Elis and Arcadia, with other Peloponnesians and Athens supporting Arcadia but Sparta supporting Elis. In 364 with Arcadian support the people living near Olympia, the Pisatans, celebrated the Olympic festival, and in fighting in the sanctuary the Eleans won a battle but could not dislodge the Pisatans. However, in 363 a rift opened up in Arcadia, with a Mantinean faction unhappy to spend sacred funds from Olympia on mercenaries, and sympathetic to Sparta, while a Tegean faction was happy to spend the money and remained friendly with Thebes. In winter 363/2 the Mantinean faction was powerful enough to make peace between Arcadia and Elis, but the disagreement developed into open war, with Mantinea allied to Sparta, Elis, Achaea and Athens, and Tegea and Megalopolis to the other Peloponnesians and Thebes. In 362 Epaminondas took an army to the Peloponnese, and after he and the Spartans under Agesilaus had marched and counter-marched between Arcadia and Laconia there was a battle at Mantinea, in which Epaminondas was killed when his army was getting the upper hand. Xenophon ends his *Hellenica* by remarking that the battle which might have resolved the power struggle in Greece resulted in fact in even more indecisiveness and confusion than before (Xen. *Hell.* VII. v. 26–7).

The Greeks then made 'a common peace and alliance', i.e. a peace with a compulsory sanctions clause; because it was stipulated that Messenia was to be autonomous, Sparta stood out; but presumably the Theban-dominated Boeotia was allowed to participate as 'Boeotia' (Diod. Sic. XV. 89. i–ii, Polyb. IV. 33. viii–ix, Plut. *Ages.* 35. iii–iv). This is probably the context to which we should assign an inscription in which the Greeks who have made a common peace reply to 'the man who has come from the satraps' that if the King does not make trouble for them they will not make trouble for him (*IG* iv 556 = R&O 42 ~ Harding 57): i.e. they refuse to help the rebels in the Satraps' Revolt (though the Athenian Chabrias went to Egypt as a freelance mercenary commander), but Sparta, not participating in the peace, sent Agesilaus to Egypt (he died on the return journey, after about thirty years as one of Sparta's most active kings).

Philip II of Macedon

The Greek world was transformed by the reign of Philip (359–336). Previously Macedon had been an unstable kingdom on the edge of the Greek world; in the 360's Athens had tangled with it through its attempt to recover Amphipolis, and Thebes through its intervention in Thessaly. When Philip came to the throne he quickly strengthened the kingdom, and began to seize opportunities to expand it eastwards towards the Hellespont and southwards towards Greece. At an early stage he annoyed Athens, by seizing Amphipolis in 357, in circumstances which led the Athenians to allege that he had cheated them: Athens declared war, but was prevented from acting against him by the

Social War of 356–355 against members of a League which had lost its purpose since Leuctra and was unstable after Thebes' activity in the late 360's.

In Greece Thebes, though it had lost Pelopidas and Epaminondas, was still the strongest and most ambitious single power; and it attempted to use the Amphictyony of mostly central Greek states which controlled Delphi as an instrument of its power. In 363 Thebes was granted precedence in the consultation of the oracle, and some leading men of the *polis* of Delphi were expelled by the Amphictyony and welcomed in Athens. Thebes also used the Amphictyony to impose fines on states hostile to it: Sparta for sacrilege committed during the occupation of Thebes in 382, and Phocis for cultivating the sacred plain of Cirrha, by the Gulf of Corinth below Delphi. In 356 the Phocians seized Delphi, thus provoking the Third Sacred War, in which Phocis was supported by Sparta and Athens and opposed by the Amphictyony and Thebes. Philip took advantage of this to become involved on the side of the Amphictyony, while his expansion towards the Hellespont led to further conflict with Athens.

Athens turned to less ambitious policies after losing several of its League members in the Social War, but was prepared to oppose Philip when he directly threatened Athenian interests, and in the early 340's tried to build up a southern Greek alliance to resist his expansion southwards. Philip encouraged uncertainty as to whether he would continue to support the Amphictyony; at the beginning of 346 the Athenians' plans were frustrated when the Phocians, hoping Philip would change sides, refused to cooperate with them, and so they tried to make peace with Philip. They wanted a common peace treaty, which would embrace all their allies including the Phocians; Philip insisted on peace between himself and his allies and 'Athens and its allies' (meaning the League), and, when it was too late for anybody to help the Phocians, made it clear that he was still on the side of the Amphictyony. The Phocians surrendered, Philip was given their place in the Amphictyony, and Athens again felt cheated (Diod. Sic. XVI. 59–60, Just. *Epit.* VIII. 4. i–5. v, cf. speeches of Demosthenes and Aeschines: pp. 309–13).

In Athens Aeschines wanted to accept the peace and make the best of it; Demosthenes, claiming that Philip had designs on Athens and all of Greece, wanted to renew the conflict. Philip offered to renegotiate the peace, and to enlarge it into a common peace, which he now thought he could turn to his advantage, but Athens wrecked the negotiations by making demands which Philip could not have been expected to accept. Athens declared war on Philip in 340; a Fourth Sacred War began later that year, and Philip entered it in 339; by then Athens and Thebes were united against him, and he defeated them at Chaeronea in 338. After that he combined several strands in fourth-century institutions: a common peace treaty, based on territorial adjustments which would help to maintain a balance of weakness; a league of allies, the so-called League of Corinth, with Philip as its *hegemon*, 'leader', and with a representative council (thus providing mechanisms not only for enforcing the treaty when it was broken but also for deciding what should count as breaches of it); and in the council not equality of representation as in the Peloponnesian and

Athenian Leagues but proportional representation as in the Boeotian federation dissolved in 386 and in the Arcadian federation of the 360's. Sparta, on account of Messenia, refused once more to take part; Athens joined (and so what remained of the Second Athenian League was disbanded); Thebes (more severely treated, as a former ally which had turned against Philip) had a pro-Macedonian government and a garrison installed (Diod. Sic. XVI. 89, Just. *Epit.* IX. 5. i–iv, cf. *IG* ii^2 236 = R&O 76 ~ Harding 99. A). Mainland Greece, except Sparta, was now subject to Philip. He did install some garrisons (in Thebes, Ambracia and Corinth, the so-called 'fetters of Greece'), but in general his supremacy did not take the form of outright conquest and direct intervention: like the leading Greek cities before him he clothed his supremacy in garb which left the cities theoretically autonomous members of an alliance, but the mechanisms he created made it clear that his allies would be expected to decide as he wanted.

Since before the Peace of Antalcidas there had been talk of the desirability of uniting the Greeks once more in a war against Persia, and the abandonment of the Asiatic Greeks under that treaty was a further wrong to be avenged. From 346 (in his V. *Philip*) Isocrates had looked to Philip to lead the Greeks in that war: I argue in this book that gaining supremacy in Greece was an objective in its own right for Philip, not just a necessary preliminary to that war, but towards the end of his reign he was contemplating war against Persia, and the Greeks' desire for revenge provided a convenient excuse. The League of Corinth formally decided to fight that war and appointed Philip as commander; he sent out advance forces in 336; when he was assassinated that summer, his son Alexander succeeded to his position in Macedon and in the League, and successfully undertook the war.

NOTE ON FURTHER READING

On the common peace treaties in general see Ryder, *Koine Eirene*. Problems in the interpretation of the terms are explored by Rhodes, 'Making and Breaking Treaties in the Greek World', in de Souza and France (eds.), *War and Peace in Ancient and Medieval History*, forthcoming.

On the question whether Andoc. III. *Peace* and Philoch. *FGrH* 328 F 149 = Harding 23 refer to 392/1 or to 387/6 see E. Badian, 'The King's Peace', in *Georgica . . . G. Cawkwell*, 25–48 at 26–34 (387/6); A. G. Keen, 'A "Confused" Passage of Philochoros (F 149A) and the Peace of 392/1 BC', *Hist.* xliv 1995, 1–10, 'Philochoros F 149A&B: A Further Note', *Hist.* xlvii 1998, 375–8 (392/1). More drastically, it is argued that Andoc. III is not an authentic speech but a later rhetorical exercise by E. M. Harris, 'The Authenticity of Andokides' *De Pace*: A Subversive Essay', in *Polis and Politics . . . M. H. Hansen*, 479–505.

On the peace of 387/6 and its aftermath see R. Seager, 'The King's Peace and the Balance of Power in Greece, 386–382 BC', *Ath.*^{2} lii 1974, 36–63; Badian, 'The King's Peace' (cf. above).

The interpretation which I give of 'the decrees of the Athenians and their allies' in the peace of autumn 371 is due to M. Sordi and is accepted by Ryder, *Koine Eirene*, 132–3: against it see Lewis, *Selected Papers in Greek and Near Eastern History*, ch. 5.

The view that the peace of 365 was in theory a renewal of the King's Peace but the participants were a limited range of states is due to M. Zahrnt, 'Xenophon, Isokrates und die κοινὴ εἰρήνη', *RM*² cxliii 2000, 295–325 at 314–21.

17

Sparta's Imperialism and Collapse

500	475	450	425	400	375	350	325	300

402–400 (?)	Spartan war against Elis
400	Sparta begins fighting in Asia Minor
395	Corinthian War begins in Greece
392	first Spartan attempt at a common peace treaty
387/6	Peace of Antalcidas
382	Spartan occupation of Thebes
382–379	Spartan war against Olynthus
371	Sparta defeated by Thebes in battle of Leuctra
370/69	Messenia liberated from Sparta
362	stalemate battle of Mantinea

To the Peace of Antalcidas: Lysander, Pausanias, Agesilaus

After the defeat of Athens in the Peloponnesian War, the member states of the Delian League were not liberated but taken over by Sparta: tribute was collected (Diod. Sic. XIV. 10. ii, claiming over 1,000 talents a year, cf. Isoc. XII. *Panath.* 67–9, Polyb. VI. 49. x), and oligarchic constitutions were imposed. Sparta in general favoured oligarchies, but the rule of small cliques is associated particularly with Lysander: he was behind decarchies, rule by boards of ten, in many cities, and the Thirty in Athens (Nep. VI. *Lys.* 1. v, Plut. *Lys.* 13. v–ix, but ephors' orders Diod. Sic. XIV. 13. i; for Athens see below). In Byzantium the Spartan commander Clearchus made himself tyrant, but the Spartans drove him out (Diod. Sic. XIV. 12). Coins issued by a number of east Greek cities, with Heracles strangling two snakes, and ΣΥΝ (for *symmachikon*, 'alliance'), on the obverse and the city's normal design on the reverse, are best attributed to supporters of Lysander *c.*405–400. Lysander himself, as the man who had won the war for Sparta, received extravagant honours (cf. p. 152).

For a while there was a reaction against Lysander. In 403, when the Thirty in Athens withdrew to Eleusis, he supported them, but king Pausanias won the backing of a majority of the ephors, and arranged a reconciliation between the men in the city and the returning democrats (cf. p. 259). For that Pausanias was brought to trial before the *gerousia* and the ephors, and was narrowly acquitted, with king Agis voting against him but all the ephors for him (Paus. III. 5. ii). Around the Aegean Lysander's decarchies were replaced by *patrioi politeiai*, 'traditional constitutions', on the orders of the ephors. Diodorus has a story that, after setting up oligarchies elsewhere, for Sparta itself Lysander plotted to replace the hereditary kings with elected kings. He tried to buy the support of oracles, was denounced by the oracle of Ammon (in north Africa) and was tried but acquitted; a speech advocating the plan was discovered among his papers after his death – a detail which, even if invented, must have seemed plausible, though we tend to think of the Spartans as particularly uninterested in written texts (Diod. Sic. XIV. 13, cf. Plut. *Lys.* 19. vii, 20, 24–5, 30. iii–v). However, when Lysander's friend Cyrus prepared to revolt against Artaxerxes II, in 402, he employed Clearchus, who became the principal commander of his mercenaries, and Sparta sent a substantial contribution and a commander, Chirisophus (Xen. *Anab.* I. iv. 2–3 less clear than *Hell.* III. i. 1, Diod. Sic. XIV. 19. ii–v).

Sparta still resented its exclusion from the Olympic games by Elis in 420 (cf. pp. 126–7), and Elis was among the states which defied Sparta by harbouring democratic exiles from Athens in 404–403. Probably in 402–400, after demanding the autonomy of the *perioikoi* living to the south and east of Elis proper, Agis fought a three-year war. In the second year he called on Sparta's allies, and Boeotia and Corinth refused; in the third year Elis capitulated, and was required to leave the *perioikoi* autonomous (the southern cities united in a Triphylian federation: cf. *SEG* xxxv 389, xl 392 = R&O 15. *A, B*), but not to give up the superintendence of Olympia, 'since the Spartans thought the rival claimants were rustics and not competent to superintend'; also to give up its triremes, and to leave its harbours of Phea and Cyllene, to which Sparta wanted access, unfortified (Xen. *Hell.* II. ii. 21–31; Diod. Sic. XIV. 17. iv–xii, 34. i, has two campaigns and Pausanias as commander). Sparta then expelled the Messenians who had been living in Naupactus since the 450's and in Cephallenia since 421 (Diod. Sic. XIV. 34. ii–vi, cf. pp. 44, 125).

About 400, after his victory in Elis, Agis died. He had a son, Leotychidas, but Lysander successfully supported rumours that Leotychidas' father was Alcibiades (cf. p. 144) and obtained the throne for Agis' half-brother Agesilaus (Xen. *Hell.* III. iii. 1–4, Plut. *Alc.* 23. vii–ix, *Ages.* 3, *Lys.* 22. vi–xiii). Lysander hoped to rule through a grateful Agesilaus, but Agesilaus proved to be one of Sparta's strongest kings; he also stressed his attachment to traditional Spartan

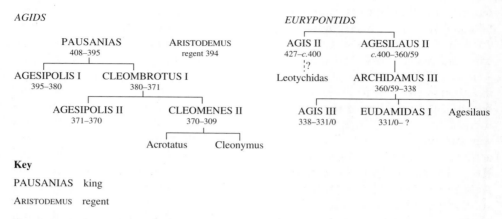

Key

PAUSANIAS   king

ARISTODEMUS   regent

Fig. 4   Fourth-century Spartan kings and a regent

virtues, refusing a statue when other leading Spartans were setting up ostentatious monuments, and refusing divine honours in Thasos (Xen. *Ages.* xi. 7, Plut. *Spartan Sayings* 210 C–D). Soon after his accession a revolt was planned by Cinadon, a *hypomeion* ('inferior', perhaps a man of Spartiate ancestry who had been downgraded for inability to provide his mess contributions) who hoped to unite all the unprivileged classes against the *homoioi* ('equals', a term perhaps introduced when full Spartiates needed to be distinguished from 'inferiors'). He was dealt with firmly, and in a typically Spartan way (sent out of the city with a detachment of men who had orders to arrest him); but the episode, though not necessarily the tip of an already large iceberg, reminds us that Sparta was becoming more fragile (Xen. *Hell.* III. iii. 4–11, Arist. *Pol.* V. 1306 B 34–6, Polyaenus *Strat.* II. 14. i).

Sparta's citizen numbers were suffering an irreversible decline, owing in particular to the earthquake of *c.*464 (cf. pp. 28–9) and losses during the Peloponnesian War, but also to a social structure which was not conducive to the frequent fathering of children. Ancient texts allege that there was a moral decline, attributable especially to the influx of foreign wealth at the end of the Peloponnesian War, and claim that previously coinage in precious metals had been totally banned but after the war it was conceded that coinage could be held by the state but not by individuals (Xen. *Lac. Pol.* vii. 6, Plut. *Lys.* 17, Posidonius *FGrH* 87 F 48. c ~ Fornara 167). The truth appears to be that, although Sparta did not issue coins, possession had not previously been banned, but the ban on private possession was a response to the suddenly increased quantity after the war, enforced at first but not for long. Plutarch's life of the third-century *Agis* claims that originally Spartans had not been able to dispose of their *kleros*, their 'allotment' of land, and this was first allowed by the *rhetra* (literally 'saying': used of Spartan laws) of an ephor called Epitadeus (Plut. *Agis* 5. iii–iv), a change which scholars have tended to date to this period; but more probably Spartans were never forbidden to dispose of their land, and the original ban and the *rhetra* were invented by third-century reformers, perhaps under the influence of Plato. However, it remains true that in the fourth century a small number of families, and often women where there were no male heirs, got possession of an increasing proportion of the land (cf. Arist. *Pol.* II. 1270 A 15–29), and Sparta's shortage of citizens was due to the downgrading of potential citizens as well as to a shortage of citizen births (cf. Arist. *Pol.* II. 1271 B 26–37). There were some attempts to stimulate the birth rate within the existing social framework (e.g. wife-sharing; privileges for fathers of many sons); sons of 'inferiors' and some others could be brought up with the 'equals' as *mothakes* (cf. pp. 135, 149, 150); but this was not enough, and the Spartan army relied increasingly on *perioikoi* and liberated helots (cf. below, esp. pp. 216–17).

When Tissaphernes returned to Sardis, he claimed the Greek cities of Asia Minor; they appealed to Sparta and Sparta agreed to support them. In autumn 400 Sparta sent not a citizen army but an army of liberated helots and allies (including Athenians), commanded by a man called Thibron: the term harmost (*harmostes*, 'arranger') is used, especially by Xenophon, of such commanders of non-citizen forces, whether employed for campaigning or for garrison duties. This force was joined by the survivors of Cyrus' mercenary force; it penetrated further inland than the Athenians had done (for the likelihood that Sparta would do this cf. Alcibiades in Thuc. VIII. 48. iii), but, although Thibron appears less incompetent in Diodorus' account than in Xenophon's, he did not make much progress in liberating the Asiatic Greeks (Xen. *Hell.* III. i. 3–7, Diod. Sic. XIV. 35. vi–37. iv).

In spring 399 Thibron was recalled, and fined and exiled for letting his troops ravage the land of the Greeks he had gone to help. His successor was Dercylidas (the first of a series of men linked with Lysander), described as deceitful and unSpartan, and as liking to be away from home (Ephorus *FGrH* 70 F 71, cf. Xen. *Hell.* III. i. 8; *Hell.* IV. iii. 2). He made a truce with Tissaphernes in order to concentrate on Pharnabazus, the satrap of Dascylium; he had considerable success, and made a truce with Pharnabazus before wintering in Bithynia (Xen. *Hell.* III. i. 8–ii. 5, Diod. Sic. XIV. 38. vi–vii). In 398 three inspectors, headed by another man connected with Lysander, reappointed Dercylidas: he renewed his truce with Pharnabazus and went to the Chersonese to fortify that against Thracian attacks; and he besieged and captured Atarneus, on the Asiatic coast opposite Mytilene (Xen. *Hell.* III. ii. 6–11, Diod. Sic. XIV. 38. vi–vii). In 397 he was probably inspected and appointed again; in response to another appeal from the Asiatic Greeks, Sparta ordered him to move south into Caria to put pressure on Tissaphernes, and Pharax, again connected with Lysander, was sent with ships to support him. Pharnabazus joined Tissaphernes; but when a battle was about to be fought near Ephesus, Tissaphernes offered a truce to discuss a deal by which the Spartans would withdraw and the Asiatic Greeks would be autonomous (Xen. *Hell.* II. iii. 12–20, Diod. Sic. XIV. 39. iv–vi; for the truce cf. p. 192). However, in 398 Pharnabazus had gone to the King and had obtained permission to raise a fleet to be commanded by the Athenian Conon (who since the end of the Peloponnesian War had been with

Evagoras in Cyprus: cf. p. 151); in 397/6 Conon with a first contingent of ships was besieged in Caunus, north-east of Rhodes, by Pharax but was relieved by Pharnabazus, after which Rhodes defected to him from the Spartans (Diod. Sic. XIV. 39. i, 79. iv–vii, Philoch. *FGrH* 328 F 144 ~ Harding 12. B).

The war continued, and in 396 Sparta sent reinforcements, and Agesilaus as commander. He still did not have Spartiate soldiers, but he had a board of thirty Spartiate assistants including Lysander; of Sparta's allies, Boeotia, Corinth and Athens all refused to serve. Seeing himself as a successor to Agamemnon in the Trojan War, Agesilaus went to Aulis to sacrifice before crossing the Aegean, but the Boeotians interfered, an act for which he never forgave them. On arrival at Ephesus he accepted Tissaphernes' offer of a truce to discuss terms, but Tissaphernes asked the King for an army (cf. p. 192). Lysander hoped to control Agesilaus, but Agesilaus got him out of the way to the Hellespont, where he won over Spithridates, a subordinate of Pharnabazus. Agesilaus campaigned against Tissaphernes, was hampered at first by a lack of cavalry but proceeded to raise a force (Xen. *Hell.* III. iv. 1–15, Diod. Sic. XIV. 79. i–iii, Plut. *Ages.* 6–9). In 395 Agesilaus' thirty Spartiates were replaced by a new board. He defeated the Persians in a battle near Sardis of which we have very different accounts from Xenophon and the other tradition: either in the absence of Tissaphernes he won a straightforward cavalry battle (Xenophon) or he ambushed a force which Tissaphernes was commanding. He was unable to take the city; but Tissaphernes was executed and replaced by Tithraustes, the King's grand vizier (the decision will have been taken before the battle). Tithraustes announced the King's terms: that Sparta should withdraw and the Asiatic Greeks should be autonomous but pay 'the ancient tribute' (cf. p. 192). Agesilaus said he could not agree without authority from Sparta, but let Tithraustes pay him to move against Pharnabazus (Xen. *Hell.* III. iv. 16–29, *Hell. Oxy.* 14–17, Diod. Sic. XIV. 80, Plut. *Ages.* 10). He then engaged in campaigning and diplomacy. Agesilaus hoped with Spithridates' help to win over the king of Paphlagonia (east of Pharnabazus' satrapy), but his plans were wrecked when his subordinate Herippidas won a victory but took all the booty for Sparta. After ravaging Pharnabazus' estates Agesilaus had a meeting at which he urged Pharnabazus to defect from the King, and Pharnabazus replied that if he were made subordinate to another commander he would defect, but if he were made commander himself he would fight for the King. Agesilaus then moved south, intending in spring 394 to advance into the interior (Xen. *Hell.* IV. i, *Hell. Oxy.* 24–5, Plut. *Ages.* 11–15. i).

What were the two sides trying to achieve? For Persia, which suggested the compromises, the terms always included the withdrawal of Spartan forces; and if the Asiatic Greeks paid tribute a formal concession of autonomy would not make much difference to the ways in which Persian power was actually exercised. Agesilaus' attempt to sacrifice at Aulis was a strong gesture, and there are passages suggesting that he had extensive ambitions for conquest (Xen. *Hell.* IV. i. 41, *Ages.* i. 8, 36, *Hell. Oxy.* 25. iv, Diod. Sic. XIV. 80. v, Plut. *Ages.* 15. i–iii), yet at first he like Dercylidas before him was prepared to consider the compromise. He had to satisfy the authorities in Sparta, who may well have been divided in their attitudes to adventures in Asia, and indeed he had Spartiate advisers with him; probably his own ambitions increased as he campaigned successfully, but it is not clear how far he hoped to go, or what kind of demarcation he wanted to establish or could have established between a reduced Persian empire and the territories detached from it.

Agesilaus' high point came after his meeting with Tithraustes, when the Spartans gave him authority at sea as well as on land, and he gave the naval command to his inexperienced brother-in-law Pisander (Xen. *Hell.* III. iv. 27–9). But Conon had been building up the fleet he commanded for Pharnabazus (*Hell. Oxy.* 12. ii, Diod. Sic. XIV. 79. viii). In 395 he supported a democratic revolution in Rhodes (*Hell. Oxy.* 18, Androtion *FGrH* 324 F 46; cf. Athenian honours for a Rhodian in 394/3, *IG* ii² 19), obtained funding from Tithraustes and dealt with a mutiny of Cypriots in his fleet (*Hell. Oxy.* 22–3); then he visited the King and obtained full support from him (Diod. Sic. XIV. 81. iv–vi). In August 394 (dated by an eclipse) Conon and Pharnabazus defeated and killed Pisander in a major battle off Cnidus (Xen. *Hell.* IV. iii. 10–12, Diod. Sic. XIV. 83. iv–vii, Philoch. *FGrH* 328 F 145 ~ Harding 12. B). This ended Sparta's control of the Aegean: Conon and Pharnabazus won over mainland and island cities, expelling Spartan garrisons and promising autonomy (Xen. *Hell.* IV. viii. 1–6, Diod. Sic. XIV. 84. iii–iv). Although the victory was technically a Persian one, Athens honoured both Conon and Evagoras, and fragments of the decree for Evagoras show him represented as fighting as a Greek for the freedom and autonomy of the Greeks (R&O 11). By then Agesilaus had had to return to Greece.

In 404 Sparta had dealt with Athens as it wanted, not as its allies had wanted (cf. p. 151); it seemed to have monopolised the profits of victory, and it had not liberated but had taken over the Delian League. Boeotia and several Peloponnesian states harboured Athenian democrats in 404–403, and Boeotia and Corinth refused to join Pausanias' expedition (cf. p. 259); the war of revenge on Elis harmed Sparta's reputation, and Boeotia and Corinth abstained from that conflict; Athens began to show signs of independence from 397 (cf. pp. 226–7); and in 396 Boeotia, Corinth and Athens abstained from Agesilaus' expedition and the Boeotians interfered with his sacrifices. Sparta's ambitions at this time were widespread: the first Spartan mentioned in connection with Dionysius of Syracuse was a freelance, but later Dionysius was given official support (cf. pp. 276, 280). Another area of interest was northern Greece: Sparta expelled the Messenians from Naupactus (cf. p. 44), put down a revolt in its colony at Heraclea and installed a garrison at Pharsalus, in Thessaly (Diod. Sic. XIV. 38. iv–v, 82. vi; cf. below). Timocrates brought money from Pharnabazus to encourage Sparta's enemies (cf. p. 192).

In 395 the Boeotians engineered a dispute between Locris (probably eastern Locris, towards Thermopylae) and Phocis; Phocis appealed to Sparta and Boeotia was joined by Athens in backing Locris; and so began what is called the Corinthian War since after the first two years the war was centred on Corinth

(Xen. *Hell*. III. v. 3–16, *Hell. Oxy*. 20–1, Diod. Sic. XIV. 81. i–ii, cf. Athenian alliances, *IG* ii² 14, 15 = R&O 6, Tod 102 ~ Harding 14. A, 16). Sparta sent Lysander to Boeotia via Phocis and Pausanias via the Megarid: Lysander won over Orchomenus, in north-western Boeotia, but fought a battle at Haliartus before Pausanias (perhaps reluctant to cooperate) had joined him, and was defeated and killed. Pausanias withdrew under a truce, for which he was condemned in absence: he retired to Tegea (where he wrote a book on Sparta's legendary reformer, Lycurgus) and was succeeded by his son Agesipolis I (Xen. *Hell*. III. v. 67, 17–25, Diod. Sic. XIV. 81. ii–iii, Plut. *Lys*. 28–30. i). Sparta's enemies were joined by Corinth and Argos, the Euboeans and states in northern Greece; in Thessaly they enabled Larisa to take Pharsalus from the Spartans, and Heraclea was returned to the neighbouring Trachinians (Diod. Sic. XIV. 82: Heraclea perhaps after Agesilaus' march in 394).

Sparta therefore recalled Agesilaus, who left Asia but hoped to return. In July 394 Aristodemus, regent for Agesipolis, defeated the alliance at the River Nemea, west of Corinth: Dercylidas, travelling east to Abydus, where after Cnidus he assembled a number of expelled harmosts, met Agesilaus and gave him the news (Xen. *Hell*. IV. ii. 9–23, iii. 1–3, Diod. Sic. XIV. 82. x–83. ii). Agesilaus travelled through Thrace and Thessaly to Boeotia; in August, on hearing the news of Cnidus, for the sake of morale he announced that Pisander was dead but victorious; he then gained a far from decisive victory at Coronea and after it abandoned Greece north of the Isthmus (Xen. *Hell*. IV. iii. 3–iv. 1, *Ages*. ii. 1–13, Diod. Sic. XIV. 83. iv–v, 84. i–ii, Plut. *Ages*. 17–19. iv).

In 393 Conon and Pharnabazus sailed to Greece. They raided Laconia and occupied Cythera, and took money to Corinth, which spent it on ships to fight against Sparta in the Gulf of Corinth, and to Athens, where it helped to pay for the rebuilding of the walls which was already under way (Xen. *Hell*. IV. viii. 7–11, Diod. Sic. XIV. 84. iv–v, Philoch. *FGrH* 328 F 146 ~ Harding 12. B). Conon also established a force of light-armed mercenaries, based in Corinth but commanded by Athenians: at first Iphicrates, later Chabrias (Androtion *FGrH* 324 F 48 = Philoch. *FGrH* 328 F 150 ~ Harding 22. A). Corinth became the base of the anti-Spartan alliance and Sicyon the Spartans' base. In spring 392 the enemies of Sparta in Corinth engineered a massacre of their opponents, and shortly after that, to strengthen the position of the anti-Spartan party, some kind of political union was made between Corinth and Argos, perhaps *isopoliteia*, 'equal citizenship', by which citizens of each had the rights of citizens in the other. Some survivors of the massacre left Corinth but returned under an amnesty, and enabled a Spartan force to capture Corinth's long walls and the harbour town of Lechaeum (Xen. *Hell*. IV. i. 1–13, Diod. Sic. XIV. 86. i–iii).

Things were not going well for the Spartans, either in Greece or in the Aegean, so in 392 they tried to win by diplomacy what they could not win by fighting, and Antalcidas obtained the first draft of a common peace treaty by which the Asiatic Greeks would be returned to Persia and all other cities and islands would be autonomous. When this was rejected by their opponents, the Spartans offered modified terms at a conference in 392/1, with concessions to

Athens and Boeotia but not to Corinth and Argos, but Athens as well as Corinth and Argos still objected, and no peace was made (cf. pp. 192–3).

Fighting continued in the north-eastern Peloponnese, particularly over Corinth's long walls and Lechaeum. In 390, when Argos on the strength of its union with Corinth was about to hold the Isthmian games, Agesilaus enabled the Corinthian exiles to hold the games, but afterwards the Argives returned and held the games again. Iphicrates and his mercenary force, backed up by Callias with Athenian hoplites, caught a division of the Spartan army outside Lechaeum and annihilated it. It was perhaps after this that Iphicrates tried to get control of Corinth but failed and was dismissed, and then the union between Corinth and Argos may have been intensified (Xen. *Hell.* IV. iv. 14–v. 9, viii. 34, Diod. Sic. XIV. 86. iv–vi, 91. ii–92. ii). North of the Gulf of Corinth, in 389–388 Agesilaus enabled the Achaeans to retain Calydon, which they had acquired some time before (Xen. *Hell.* IV. vi–viii. 1, Plut. *Ages.* 22. ix–xi). In 388 or 387 Agesipolis attacked Argos, and when Argos tried to prevent him by changing its calendar to bring on the festival of the Carnea he gained permission from Olympia and Delphi to ignore that, and also refused to be put off by an earthquake (Xen. *Hell.* IV. vii. 2–7, Arist. *Rh.* II. 1398 B 33–1399 A 1; cf. Diod. Sic. XIV. 97. v [Agesilaus]). From Aegina the Spartans made trouble for Athens, and in 387 raided the Piraeus (Xen. *Hell.* V. i. 1–24).

The war was not over in the east. In 391 Sparta sent the earlier unsuccessful Thibron to fight against Struthas, the current satrap of Sardis, but he was defeated and killed (Xen. *Hell.* IV. viii. 17–19, Diod. Sic. XIV. 99. i–iii). He was succeeded by the more successful Diphridas (who managed to capture and obtain a ransom for Struthas' daughter and son-in-law), and Ecdicus was sent to Rhodes (where there was renewed conflict between oligarchs and democrats). In 390 Teleutias succeeded Ecdicus, and on his way out captured an Athenian squadron sailing to support Evagoras of Salamis (Xen. *Hell.* IV. viii. 20–4, Diod. Sic. XIV. 97. i–iv). The Athenian Thrasybulus was sent to help the Rhodian democrats, but went first to the Hellespont and had a highly successful campaign as he made his way from there to Rhodes; but in 389, when fundraising took him to Aspendus, on the south coast of Asia Minor, he was killed (Xen. *Hell.* IV. viii. 25–31, Diod. Sic. XIV. 94, 99. iv–v). Sparta sent Anaxibius to the Hellespont; Athens sent Iphicrates with those of the mercenaries who had left Corinth with him; and Anaxibius was defeated and killed (Xen. *Hell.* IV. viii. 31–9). While Struthas was satrap of Sardis, *c.*391–388, Miletus and Myus referred a territorial dispute to him and he referred it to a jury from the other cities of the Ionian *koinon* (*Milet* I. ii 9 = R&O 16 ~ Harding 24).

Antalcidas was made Spartan navarch for 388/7: he went to Ephesus and sent Nicolochus to the Hellespont; with Tiribazus, reinstated as satrap of Sardis, he went to talk to the King. When he returned, in 387, Nicolochus was being blockaded in Abydus by the Athenians; by pretending to head for the Bosporus, Antalcidas ended the blockade; he then captured a relief squadron and regained control of the Hellespont for Sparta (Xen. *Hell.* V. i. 6–7, 25–8, cf. *IG* ii² 29 = R&O 19). The anti-Spartan Pharnabazus had been removed from Dascylium to marry the King's daughter (Xen. *Hell.* V. i. 28); and from its position of comparative strength Sparta was able to obtain and impose on the Greeks the King's Peace: Persia received the Asiatic Greeks; elsewhere, apart from Athens' three north Aegean islands, there were no exceptions to the principle of autonomy for all, and Agesilaus by threatening to invade insisted on the dismantling of the Boeotian federation and of the union of Corinth and Argos. The anti-Persian Agesilaus could see the advantage for Sparta, and declared that the Persians were laconising (cf. p. 194). Corinth rejoined the Peloponnesian League, and some opponents of Sparta were exiled and went to Athens (Xen. *Hell.* V. i. 36, iii. 27, Dem. XX. *Leptines* 54). There may subsequently have been approaches to Sparta by Evagoras of Salamis (Theopompus *FGrH* 115 F 103. x) and the Persian rebel Glos (Diod. Sic. XV. 9. iii–v, 18. i–ii, 19. i), but it is unlikely that they obtained anything.

From the Peace of Antalcidas to Leuctra: Agesilaus, Agesipolis, Cleombrotus

After the Peloponnesian War Sparta had taken revenge on Elis; after the Peace of Antalcidas it took revenge on Mantinea, as an ally which had not been sufficiently loyal. Because of his father's connections with Mantinea, Agesilaus had the command given to Agesipolis, though Agesipolis' father had connections with the Mantinean democrats. In 385 Mantinea refused to demolish its walls, and appealed to Athens, which was cowed by the Peace of Antalcidas and would not help; Agesipolis invaded, and summoned a contingent from Thebes. When he diverted a river to undermine the wall, Mantinea capitulated: the *polis* was split into the separate villages which had united perhaps *c.*470, and these became oligarchic and pro-Spartan; the democratic leaders were allowed to leave, and some went to Athens (Xen. *Hell.* V. ii. 1–7, Diod. Sic. XV. 5. iii–v, 12; Thebans Plut. *Pel.* 4. v–viii, Paus. IX. 13. i; exiles to Athens *IG* ii² 33. 7–8). Probably Sparta announced its intention of dismantling the *polis* from the beginning, and was abusing the autonomy principle by applying it to the villages.

Appeals came to Sparta to act against the expanding Chalcidian federation of Olynthus: from Acanthus and Apollonia according to Xenophon, from Amyntas of Macedon according to Diodorus. If cities threatened with absorption did appeal, Sparta in responding may have invoked the autonomy principle once more. Olynthus was in touch with Athens and 'Boeotia': there is no secure evidence for Athenian support, but there is some for Theban (Xen. *Hell.* V. ii. 15, 27, 34, *FGrH* 153 F 1). Sparta's campaign was approved by the Peloponnesian League, but for the first time League members were allowed to contribute cash instead of soldiers, as the members of the Delian League had been allowed to pay tribute instead of contributing ships (Xen. *Hell.* V. ii. 11–22, Diod. Sic. XV. 19. iii; *Hell.* VI. ii. 16 reports that nearly all paid cash for Sparta's expedition to Corcyra in 373). The contributions would be spent on the mercenaries who were increasingly being used by all states: by the time of the battle of Mantinea, in 362, the presence of mercenaries even in a Spartan army fighting in the Peloponnese did not call for comment (Xen. *Hell.* VII. v. 10).

Agesilaus did not go to Olynthus, but the commanders sent in 382 were men connected with him. Thebes refused to join the campaign, but Leontiades, leader of the pro-Spartan party, invited Phoebidas to enter the city as he was marching north with part of Sparta's advance force; he did, and occupied the acropolis, the Cadmea. The anti-Spartan leader Ismenias was arrested, and (despite Sparta's current alignment) condemned as a mediser for accepting Timocrates' money in the 390's; many of his supporters fled to Athens. The ephors and other Spartans were angry at Phoebidas' unauthorised action; Agesilaus, who may have been privy to the plan, talked them round (he had hated the Thebans since the incident at Aulis in 396), though according to most of the sources Phoebidas was still fined (Xen. *Hell.* V. ii. 23–36, Diod. Sic. XV. 20, Plut. *Ages.* 23. vi–24. i, *Pel.* 5–6). Pro-Spartan régimes were set up in the other Boeotian cities too (Xen. *Hell.* V. iv. 46).

Phoebidas' brother Eudamidas continued north with his part of the force, and the main army from the Peloponnesian League followed under Teleutias. In 381 Teleutias was killed and Agesipolis went with reinforcements (not another League army, but it included volunteers from the *perioikoi*, and there were thirty Spartiate advisers). He captured Torone in 380 but was taken ill and died; the throne passed to his brother Cleombrotus; his command was taken over by Polybiadas, who in 379 starved Olynthus into submission. It was mildly treated, and made a subordinate ally of Sparta; its Chalcidian federation was presumably dismantled or at least reduced, but Olynthus and whatever remained continued to use the title 'the Olynthians' (Xen. *Hell.* V. ii. 24, 37–iii. 9, 18–20, 26, Diod. Sic. XV. 22. ii, 23. ii–iii; title coins and *IG* ii^2 43 = R&O 22 ~ Harding 35. 101–2). Perhaps during this northern war, Sparta became involved in Thessaly again and in Histiaea in Euboea (cf. pp. 250–1).

Agesilaus meanwhile had been dealing with Phlius, in the north-eastern Peloponnese. Sparta had not insisted on the return of pro-Spartan exiles in 391 (Xen. *Hell.* IV. iv. 5), but did insist *c.*384–383 (*Hell.* V. ii. 8–10); in 381 Phlius supported Agesipolis' expedition to Olynthus, but was grudging in its treatment of the returned exiles, who included friends of Agesilaus. In spite of doubts among the Spartans, Agesilaus campaigned enthusiastically against Phlius, besieging it for twenty months until it surrendered in 379. It tried to surrender to the authorities in Sparta, but Agesilaus arranged for the decision to be referred to himself: the offenders were executed, a new constitution was introduced and he installed a garrison (*Hell.* V. iii. 10–17, 21–5).

At this point both Xenophon and Diodorus remark on the extent of Sparta's power: Olynthus and Phlius had been subdued, Thebes was occupied, Corinth and Argos had been weakened, and the Persian King in the east and Dionysius of Syracuse in the west were friendly (Xen. *Hell.* V. iii. 27, Diod. Sic. XV. 23. iii–iv). From now onwards, however, Sparta was going to encounter problems; and the friction between the two royal houses, which can already be detected in the reign of Agesipolis, was to increase in the reign of Cleombrotus. Agesilaus favoured hard-line policies, and tended to have links with oligarchs in other cities; he may still have hankered after a war against Persia; in Greece his main enemy was Thebes. The Agid kings were more willing to conform to treaty obligations and the wishes of Sparta's allies, and tended to have links with democratic leaders; and Cleombrotus preferred fighting against the traditional enemy, Athens; the ephors when mentioned were on their side.

Sparta's troubles began in winter 379/8, when Theban exiles returned and assassinated the ruling clique (cf. pp. 229, 248). The Spartan garrison commander withdrew under a truce, for which he was executed. While it was still winter, Sparta sent an army, under Cleombrotus since Agesilaus pleaded that (in his mid sixties) he was too old. Cleombrotus entered Boeotia, but did very little apart from leaving Sphodrias with a garrison in Thespiae. Athens had given Thebes some help; while Spartan envoys were in Athens to complain, Sphodrias raided the Thriasian plain, in the west of Attica, allegedly intending to go on to the Piraeus. Athens protested, and Sphodrias was put on trial. Cleombrotus backed him from the beginning; at first he was opposed by Agesilaus and 'those in the middle' (probably those uncommitted, rather than a 'middle party'); but Agesilaus' son was the lover of Sphodrias' son, and Agesilaus was won over. Sphodrias was acquitted, and Athens came out openly against Sparta (Xen. *Hell.* V. iv. 1–34, Diod. Sic. XV. 25–7, 29. v–vii, Plut. *Ages.* 24. iv–26. i, *Pel.* 14–15. i; for the foundation of the Second Athenian League see pp. 229–30). According to Diodorus, Sphodrias acted on the orders of Cleombrotus, and that seems likely enough, since in the years that followed Cleombrotus was happier fighting against Athens than against Thebes; but, according to Xenophon and Plutarch, Sphodrias was bribed by the Thebans, who wanted to create an incident that would commit Athens to their side.

In summer 378 Agesilaus invaded Boeotia. He was perhaps a better commander than Cleombrotus (Xenophon), but he also had more enthusiasm for fighting against Thebes (Plut. *Ages.*). But he too made little headway: he left Phoebidas as harmost in Thespiae, and Phoebidas was killed in a cavalry battle. In 377 he invaded again: there was skirmishing near Thebes, with Athenians on the Theban side and Olynthians on the Spartan. Because of the invasions, Thebes had to import corn from Thessaly: the ships were intercepted by the Spartan harmost at Oreus, in the north of Euboea (where Sparta had earlier expelled a supporter of Jason of Pherae: Diod. Sic. XV. 30. iii–iv), but the Thebans managed to detach Oreus from Sparta (Xen. *Hell.* V. iv. 35–57, Diod. Sic. XV. 31. iii–34. ii, Plut. *Ages.* 26, *Pel.* 15). On his return journey Agesilaus burst a blood vessel (cf. Plut. *Ages.* 27. i–iii), as a result of which he was out of action for several years. In 376 Cleombrotus tried to invade, but the Thebans and Athenians held the mountain passes against him. Since the allies were eager for a naval campaign against Athens, Pollis was sent out with sixty ships, and prevented the corn ships from continuing to Athens beyond the south of Euboea; but an Athenian fleet under Chabrias convoyed the ships, and then besieged Naxos and defeated Pollis (Xen. *Hell.* V. iv. 58–61, Diod. Sic. XV. 34. iii–35. ii).

After the Athenian League's campaign of 377 but in connection with Agesilaus' campaign of 378, Diodorus reports a change in Sparta's military organisation: fear of the League was making Sparta more anxious to conciliate its allies, so to spread the burden fairly the army was organised in ten divisions on a regional basis, Sparta providing one and the Peloponnesian League, allies in northern Greece and 'Olynthus and the Thraceward region' providing the others; as in the war against Olynthus, cash equivalents of soldiers were allowed. Different scholars have guessed at different contexts. Agesilaus is not normally associated with consideration for the allies, but that may not have been the motive for a system in which members of the Peloponnesian League were on the same level as Olynthus; and, whatever the date, this is best seen as a sequel to the defeat of Olynthus.

There were further setbacks for Sparta in 375. In Boeotia two of the six *morai* of the Spartan army, guarding Orchomenus, were defeated at Tegyra by the Theban cavalry and 'sacred band' (the professional nucleus of their hoplite force: cf. p. 249) under Pelopidas (Plut. *Pel.* 16–19, cf. *Ages.* 27. iv, Diod. Sic. XV. 37. i–ii; omitted by Xenophon). Prompted by Thebes, Athens began a war in the west to distract Sparta: Timotheus won the support of Cephallenia, Acarnania and Corcyra, and when Sparta sent a fleet under Nicolochus Timotheus defeated him off Alyzia, opposite Leucas (Xen. *Hell.* V. iv. 626, Diod. Sic. XV. 36. v–vi, cf. *IG* ii² 96 = R&O 24 ~ Harding 41). In Thessaly Jason, tyrant of Pherae, was building up his power (cf. pp. 250–1): Polydamas of Pharsalus appealed to Sparta, and Xenophon gives him a speech claiming that, if Sparta sent a large army, the cities would desert Jason, but, if it thought liberated helots and a harmost would be enough, it need not bother – and Sparta could not support on a large scale so advised Pharsalus to submit (Xen. *Hell.* VI. i. 2–19). Another appeal came from Phocis, under attack by a Thebes which now dominated Boeotia: here Sparta did respond on a large scale, sending Cleombrotus with four *morai*, and the Thebans withdrew (Xen. *Hell.* VI. i. 1, ii. 1).

In 375/4, at Persia's prompting, the King's Peace was renewed: probably the first moves were made early in 375 and the year's events only increased Sparta's willingness to make peace (cf. p. 196). But the peace was broken almost at once. Late in 375 Timotheus, on his way back to Athens, restored exiles in Zacynthus, and Sparta protested. In 374 Sparta sent expeditions to Zacynthus and to Corcyra; in 373 it sent a further sixty ships under Mnasippus to Corcyra, and he ravaged the countryside and blockaded the city, but kept his own mercenaries short of pay and provisions. Timotheus delayed in coming from Athens, because of difficulties in raising men and money. He was dismissed; Ctesicles went over land in winter 373/2 and enabled the Corcyraeans to defeat and kill Mnasippus; Iphicrates arrived by sea in 372, in time to defeat a Syracusan squadron sent to support Sparta (Xen. *Hell.* VI. ii. 2–39, Diod. Sic. XV. 45–46. iii, 47. i–vii). On land Thebes was becoming increasingly strong, to the discomfiture of Athens (cf. pp. 235, 249–50); in 372/1 it again moved against Phocis and Sparta again sent Cleombrotus (Xen. *Hell.* VI. iii. 1, iv. 2).

Athens' worries about Thebes led to the conference in Sparta in summer 371 (perhaps mid July), where the common peace was renewed and Agesilaus, making his first appearance in the record since his illness, excluded the Thebans when they claimed to swear for Boeotia (cf. pp. 196–7). The terms included the withdrawal of forces, so Cleombrotus asked what he should do. One Spartan, Prothous, wanted to recall him and invite contributions to rebuilding the temple of Apollo at Delphi, recently destroyed by fire and/or earthquake (cf. p. 254), but this was dismissed as nonsense (by Agesilaus, according to Plutarch) and he was told to attack Thebes if it would not respect the autonomy of the Boeotian cities. Cleombrotus avoided the route guarded by the Thebans, and reached Leuctra in the territory of Thespiae, but Sparta's weakness was exposed when he was outgeneralled, defeated and killed, by an army using novel tactics which he could not cope with; despite his best attempts, Cleombrotus died implementing Agesilaus' policy (for the battle, perhaps mid August, cf. pp. 251–2). The surviving officers made a truce to withdraw, and returned to Sparta with the reserve force brought by Agesilaus' son Archidamus (Xen. *Hell.* VI. iv. 3–26, Plut. *Pel.* 20–3, *Ages.* 28. vii–viii, Paus. IX. 13. iii–xii; Diod. Sic. XV. 51–6 is badly muddled). Athens organised a peace treaty, from which Thebes was excluded (cf. pp. 197–8). Cleombrotus' throne passed first to his elder son Agesipolis II, who died in 370; then to his younger son Cleomenes II, who reigned until 309 but about whom hardly anything is recorded.

After Leuctra: Sparta in Decline

The defeat of a Spartan army in a major battle was a great shock. After this Sparta was on the defensive; within the next ten years it was to lose Messenia, lose the Peloponnesian League, and see Agesilaus serving as a mercenary commander in Egypt.

Sparta's shortage of citizen manpower (cf. pp. 206–7) was now all too evident. Stories about the distribution of *kleroi* in the archaic period assume 9,000 citizens (e.g. Plut. *Lyc.* 8. v–vi); for the early fifth century Herodotus estimates 8,000 adult males, of whom 5,000 fought at Plataea (Hdt. VII. 234. ii; IX. 10. i, 28. ii). But the earthquake of *c*.464 caused heavy losses (cf. pp. 28–9), and the Peloponnesian War will have hampered recovery. *Perioikoi* seem to have formed half of 'the Lacedaemonians' at Plataea, 40 per cent in the Peloponnesian War (cf. the prisoners from Sphacteria, Thuc. IV. 38. v with 40). Thucydides' details of the Spartan army at Mantinea in 418, a five-sixths levy (Thuc. V. 68 with 64. iii), allow us to estimate 2,100–2,500 adult Spartiates if the text is right, 3,600–4,300 if there were not six *lochoi* but six *morai* each of two *lochoi* in the main army. Heavy casualties continued after the Peloponnesian War: for instance, about 250 out of perhaps *c*.600 Lacedaemonians were killed at Lechaeum in 390 (Xen. *Hell.* IV. v. 17). At Leuctra Cleombrotus had a two-thirds levy of men up to 55, which included 700 Spartiates, of whom 400 were killed (Xen. *Hell.* VI. iv. 15 with 17): in the main army Spartiates may now have been only 10 per cent, and in all there were perhaps *c*.1,300 adult Spartiates before the battle and *c*.900 after. Aristotle remarked that the land would support 1,500 cavalry and 30,000 hoplites, but in fact there were not even 1,000 (Arist. *Pol.* II. 1270 A 29–31). The decline continued: Plutarch claims that in the 240's there were not more than 700, of whom perhaps 100 'possessed land and an allotment', but probably his 100 were the very rich, there were 700 'equals' and the 'inferiors' were his 'destitute and disfranchised mass' (Plut. *Agis* 5. vi).

The Spartiates were better trained than other Greek hoplites, but as army numbers were maintained by increasing the proportion of non-Spartiates the Spartiates' skill will not have counted for much. Leuctra showed suddenly that Sparta had been 'punching above its weight' and was no longer to be feared; its conduct since the Peloponnesian War had won it enemies rather than friends; a determined revolt by the lower orders could not have been suppressed, but, fortunately for the Spartiates, the lower orders did not immediately lose the habit of obedience. Other Greeks adjusted to the new reality more easily: Sparta's allies in northern Greece transferred their allegiance to Thebes; we should transpose to this context what Diodorus says of the aftermath of the peace of 375, that the cities fell into confusion, especially in the Peloponnese, and there were moves towards democracy and the exile of pro-Spartan oligarchs (Diod. Sic. XV. 40). He reports separately under 370/69 a particularly violent episode in Argos, the *skytalismos*, 'clubbing': the people were first incited against the rich but then turned against the demagogues who had incited them (Diod. Sic. XV. 57. iii–58, cf. Plut. *Praec. Ger. Reip.* 814 B). Neither Corinth nor Argos was capable of filling the gap created by Sparta's weakness.

But the most serious threat to Sparta came from Arcadia. In 370 the Mantineans voted to recreate and fortify their single city, dismantled in 385. Agesilaus unsuccessfully tried to dissuade them, but was not prepared to break the peace by attacking; they were supported by other Arcadians and Elis. They then supported a party in Tegea which wanted an Arcadian federation. Oligarchic anti-federalists fled to Sparta; in the skirmishing which followed Sparta under Agesilaus did support the anti-federalists, while Elis and Argos supported the federalists, who emerged successful when Agesilaus withdrew (Xen. *Hell.* VI. v. 3–21, Diod. Sic. XV. 59, 62. i–ii, Plut. *Ages.* 30. vii). The federation was based on an assembly of ten thousand (perhaps all who satisfied a low property qualification), a council and a body of *damiorgoi* (in an inscription, fifty appointed in proportion from participating communities). 'Lepreum', i.e. Triphylia, the southern part of the territory liberated from Elis *c*.400, at first supported Sparta but was induced to join (Xen. *Hell.* VII. iv. 33–4, *IG* V. ii 1 = R&O 32 ~ Harding 51). Xenophon mentions a professional nucleus for the army, the *eparitoi* (cf. the Theban sacred band: p. 249); Diodorus' five thousand *epilektoi*, 'chosen', may be the same body but given too high a figure (Xen. *Hell.* VII. iv. 33, cf. 22, v. 3; Diod. Sic. XV. 62. ii, 67. ii). The man who emerged as leader of the federation was Lycomedes of Mantinea (e.g. Diod. Sic. XV. 62. ii: in 'Lycomedes of Tegea' in 59. i either the man's name or the city is wrong).

Arcadia and its allies appealed first to Athens, which was not now interested in opposing Sparta, and then to Thebes (Diod. Sic. XV. 62. iii, cf. Xen. *Hell.* VI. v. 19). In winter 370/69 the Arcadians attacked Heraea and forced it to join the federation (Xen. *Hell.* VI. v. 22, cf. *IG* V. ii 1). When the Thebans and their central Greek allies arrived, under Epaminondas and Pelopidas, they invaded Laconia: some of the *perioikoi* supported them, but when Sparta offered freedom to loyal helots over 6,000 responded; Sparta itself escaped but the port of Gytheum was attacked. Then – omitted by Xenophon – the invaders moved west into Messenia, which Sparta had possessed since the eighth/seventh centuries, and liberated that: a *polis* of Messene was founded on Mount Ithome, and some other independent *poleis* came into existence. Wintry conditions and shortage of supplies led to the break-up of the expedition; Sparta and its allies had persuaded Athens to send a force under Iphicrates, but he was singularly ineffective in trying to prevent the Thebans from returning home (Xen. *Hell.* VI. v. 22–52, Diod. Sic. XV. 62–67. i, Plut. *Ages.* 31–33. iv, *Pel.* 24, Paus. IX. 14. iv–vii; on Iphicrates cf. p. 236). Sparta was never willing to accept the loss of Messenia; and the loss was a blow to Sparta's economic base as well as to its pride. The Arcadians dedicated a statue group at Delphi, at the beginning of the Sacred Way, directly opposite Sparta's navarchs dedication.

Another important development omitted by Xenophon is the creation from a number of small communities of the new 'great city' of Megalopolis, in the south-west of Arcadia near Laconia and Messenia. This was part of Arcadia's assertion of itself against Sparta: eventually, if not immediately, Megalopolis incorporated some communities which had previously been under Spartan control. Different texts point to different dates for the foundation, but the decision, building and formal inauguration will have taken some time; the ascription of credit to Thebes suggests that the process was not completed until after 370/69, but there are Megalopolitan *damiorgoi* in *IG* V. ii 1 = R&O 32 ~ Harding 51, probably of 369–367 (Parian Marble *FGrH* 239 A 73, 370/69 or 369/8; Diod. Sic. XV. 72. iv, 368/7; Paus. VIII. 27. i–viii, cf. IX. 14. vi, 15. vi, 371/0 but Theban involvement).

In 369 envoys from Sparta and the Peloponnesian League went to Athens to make a firm alliance (Xen. *Hell.* VII. i. 1–14, Diod. Sic. XV. 67. i: cf. p. 236). This year (probably) saw the first of a series of campaigns in the north-east Peloponnese: Epaminondas came south with the Thebans once more; Dionysius of Syracuse sent light cavalry to support Sparta (Xen. *Hell.* VII. i. 15–25, Diod. Sic. XV. 68–70. i). Phlius, where friends of Sparta had been in control since Agesilaus' intervention in 381–379, resisted attacks this year and again later (Xen. *Hell.* VII. ii). In 369/8 Philiscus came to Greece from Ariobarzanes; a conference at Delphi failed to agree on a new treaty, since Sparta would not abandon its claim to Messenia, so his money was spent on mercenaries for Sparta (cf. p. 198). In 368 another force from Syracuse arrived and, though Athens would have liked to use it against Thebes in Thessaly, this was again used by Sparta. In southern Arcadia Agesilaus' son Archidamus won the 'tearless victory' in a battle in which no Spartans were killed (but hardly more than ten thousand of the enemy, as claimed by Diodorus) against a combination of Arcadia, Messene and Argos (Xen. *Hell.* VII. i. 28–32, Diod. Sic. XV. 72. iii, Plut. *Ages.* 33. v–vi).

In 367 the states were preoccupied with the talks in Susa from which Thebes brought a draft treaty through which it hoped to add the weakening of Athens to the weakening of Sparta, thus ending the link between Sparta and Persia (cf. pp. 198–9), and there was no major campaign in the Peloponnese. In 366 Epaminondas with Argive support attacked hitherto neutral Achaea, originally bringing it into a subordinate alliance but not interfering internally. When the Arcadians objected that the oligarchic régimes were likely to go over to Sparta, Thebes sent harmosts, exiled the oligarchs and set up democracies. But this policy backfired: the oligarchs returned and regained control, and did then align Achaea with Sparta (Xen. *Hell.* VII. i. 41–3, Diod. Sic. XV. 75, ii). In Sicyon, between Achaea and Corinth, a leader called Euphron had originally supported Sparta, but in 368 (Diodorus: better than Xenophon's later context) with support from Arcadia and Argos he had set up an anti-Spartan democracy and then 'made himself tyrant' and liberated a body of serfs. In 366 the Arcadians under Aeneas of Stymphalus (probably the Aeneas Tacticus whose manual *On Withstanding a Siege* survives) occupied the city of Sicyon and restored the oligarchic exiles; Euphron fled to the harbour and handed that over to Sparta. Later a Theban harmost was installed on the acropolis; Euphron returned with mercenaries from Athens and with the support of the democrats got possession of the city but not the acropolis. He went to Thebes to try to buy a settlement, but was followed there and assassinated by his opponents; despite the label 'tyrant' his supporters secured a public funeral for him (Xen. *Hell.* VII. i. 44–6, iii, Diod. Sic. XV. 70. iii).

A breach between Arcadia and Thebes began with the inclusion in the draft treaty of a clause returning to Elis the territory which it claimed, and Lycomedes and the other Arcadians walked out of the conference in Thebes (cf. p. 199). In 366, without breaking off the Theban alliance, Lycomedes persuaded the Arcadians to make a new alliance with Athens, which was thus allied both to Arcadia and to Sparta. He was killed on his way home, but the alliance held, and Athens sent cavalry with instructions to defend Arcadia but not to attack Sparta (Xen. *Hell.* VII. iv. 2–3, 6).

Corinth was in an unstable state. The Athenians when making their alliance with Arcadia decided to ensure that Corinth 'should be kept safe for the Athenian people', but the Corinthians expelled Athenian forces from their territory and refused admission to an Athenian fleet under Chares, and then hired mercenaries to fight against their neighbours (Xen. *Hell.* VII. iv. 4–6). It was perhaps at this point that Timophanes tried to make himself tyrant, and was assassinated by opponents including his own brother, Timoleon (Plut. *Tim.* 4–5, cf. 7. i; contr. Diod. Sic. XVI. 65, 340's; for the later career of Timoleon see pp. 289–92). In 365, feeling isolated, Corinth made an approach to Thebes for a peace treaty, and at the same time consulted Sparta: Sparta was willing to let its allies make peace, though it lamented that they would not fight for it now when it had fought for them in the past, and that Thebes was allowing Persia's claim to Asia Minor but not Sparta's much older claim to Messenia; and Sparta would not itself participate in a treaty which guaranteed the independence of Messenia. Corinth refused the Thebans' request for an alliance as well as a peace treaty. The upshot was probably a treaty which was represented as another renewal of the King's Peace but which covered only Thebes and its allies, and the cities of the north-east Peloponnese; and it marked the end of the Peloponnesian League (cf. p. 199). Isocrates' pamphlet (VI) expressing Sparta's reaction was written in the name of *Archidamus*: Agesilaus, who might have tried harder not to let the League go, was out of Sparta assisting in the Satraps' Revolt (cf. p. 223), and the other king, Cleomenes, was a nonentity.

War between Elis and Arcadia followed Thebes' proposal to restore territory to Elis, when in 365 Elis captured Lasion (one of the more northerly of the communities which it lost *c*.400, which must have joined the Arcadian federation). The Arcadians fought back vigorously, getting possession of Olympia and at one point entering the city of Elis and fighting in the agora there; Elis was supported by Achaea. In 364 the Arcadians invaded Elis again. Sparta, like Achaea, was now allied to Elis, and a force under Archidamus occupied Cromnus, south of Megalopolis, but the Arcadians, supported by Messene, Argos and Thebes, captured almost all of the Spartan garrison. The Arcadians had encouraged those living around Olympia to form a Pisatan state (cf. *SIG*³ 171, and the adventurously restored *SEG* xxix 405; gold coins Kraay, *Archaic and Classical Greek Coins*, no. 333 = *CAH*² plates v–vi no. 260), and with support from Arcadia, Argos and Athens the Pisatans celebrated that year's Olympic festival; Elis and Achaea tried to dislodge them, fighting in the sanctuary but without success (Xen. *Hell.* VII. iv. 12–32, Diod. Sic. XV. 77. i–iv, 78. ii–iii, 82. i). One result of this episode was that the Arcadians started using sacred funds from Olympia to pay their *eparitoi*; but upper-class leaders in Mantinea headed a faction which disapproved of this, and despite the opposition of the federal officials (probably the *damiorgoi*) obtained a majority vote in the Arcadian assembly; the officials appealed to Thebes for support but the assembly countermanded the appeal. In winter 363/2 the Mantinean faction remained dominant, and negotiated peace between Arcadia and Elis. During the peace celebrations in Tegea a Theban harmost was persuaded to arrest members of that faction; Mantinea persuaded him to release them, and protested to Thebes, but in 362 Epaminondas came south with an army from Thebes and its allies. The Mantinean faction, with Elis and Achaea, appealed to Sparta and Athens (Xen. *Hell.* VII. iv. 33–v. 3; Diod. Sic. XV. 82. i–iv makes the Mantineans those who favoured using the sacred funds).

Epaminondas went to Tegea, and was joined by Argos and Messene, and Tegea's Arcadian supporters. While Agesilaus (back from the Satraps' Revolt, now aged 80 or over) was marching north, Epaminondas headed south to attack Sparta. Agesilaus was warned and returned in time; Epaminondas reached the outskirts of the city but was driven back. He then returned to Arcadia; Agesilaus followed him; and in a battle outside Mantinea the Theban army was getting the upper hand when Epaminondas was killed. The result was a stalemate, with both sides claiming victory and (as Xenophon lamented) the power struggle unresolved (Xen. *Hell.* VII. v. 4–27, Diod. Sic. XV. 82. v–88, Plut. *Ages.* 34. iii–35, Polyb. IX. 8). Afterwards another common peace treaty was made, with Sparta again excluded on account of Messenia (cf. p. 200).

In 361 some of the men who had been drafted into Megalopolis tried to return to their old homes, with the support of the Mantinean faction and its allies; but the Megalopolitans appealed to Thebes, Thebes sent an army under Pammenes, and he forced the dissidents to return (Diod. Sic. XV. 94. i–iii). After that the division in Arcadia persisted, with each side claiming to be 'the Arcadians'; it was the Mantinean faction which joined with Achaea, Elis and Phlius in making an alliance with Athens in 362/1 (*IG* ii² 112 = R&O 41 ~ Harding 56).

APPENDIX: PERSIA AND ITS REBELS

Artaxerxes II (Mnemon) succeeded Darius II in 405/4, and reigned until 359/8; but he was challenged by his younger brother Cyrus (born in 423, just after Darius' accession, whereas Artaxerxes may have been born as early as 453). Cyrus collected forces in 402, including a body of ten thousand Greek mercenaries; in 401 he marched east, but in a battle at Cunaxa, by the Euphrates upstream from Babylon, he was defeated and killed, though his Greeks were undefeated (Xen. *An.* I, Diod. Sic. XIV. 19–24). Tissaphernes, whom Cyrus had supplanted in Sardis in 407 (cf. p. 148–9), fought on Artaxerxes' side, and after the battle he treacherously killed the Greek commanders (Xen. *An.* II. iii, v, Diod. Sic. XIV. 26). He returned to Sardis in 400 (Xen. *Hell.* III. i. 2, Diod. Sic. XIV. 35. ii), while the Greeks made their way through Armenia to the Black Sea (Xen. *An.* II–VII, Diod. Sic. XIV. 25–31).

In Egypt a revolt against Persia began under Amyrtaeus *c.*404/3; despite several attempts the Persians were not to recover Egypt until 343/2, and then only for a short time. Tamos, an Egyptian who had served in Ionia under both Tissaphernes and Cyrus, on Tissaphernes' return fled to Egypt but was put to death (Diod. Sic. XIV. 35. iii–v). In 396 the Spartans tried to make an alliance with Egypt, and were granted supplies but not an alliance (Diod. Sic. XIV. 79. iv).

Cyprus was another problem area. The city of Salamis had long been ruled by kings of a Greek dynasty, as vassals of Persia; a Tyrian had seized power by the 430's, and *c.*415 he was killed and succeeded by another Phoenician; Evagoras, of the old ruling family, expelled him in 411 and set about increasing the power of Salamis within Cyprus (Diod. Sic. XIV. 98. i, Isoc. IX. *Evagoras* 18–20, 26–32, Theopompus *FGrH* 115 F 103. ii). There was also contact between him and Athens, as a result of which he was made an Athenian citizen some time between 411 and 407 (*IG* i³ 113, cf. Isoc. IX. *Evagoras* 54, [Dem.] XII. *Letter of Philip* 10). Conon took refuge with him after Aegospotami (Xen. *Hell.* II. i. 29, Diod. Sic. XIII. 106. vi), and it was with his support that Conon was appointed to command a fleet for Pharnabazus in 398 (Isoc. IX. *Evagoras* 55–6, cf.

Diod. Sic. XIV. 39. i–ii). After the battle of Cnidus, in 394, Athens honoured Evagoras as well as Conon, describing him as a Greek fighting on behalf of the Greeks (R&O 11).

Diodorus mentions a ten-year war (cf. Isoc. IX. *Evagoras* 64) between Evagoras and the King, beginning it under 391/0 when the Cypriot cities not yet in Evagoras' power appealed to the King (Diod. Sic. XIV. 98. i–iv) but ending it under 386/5 and 385/4 (Diod. Sic. XV. 2–4, 8–11): an astronomical diary allows us to conclude that the war began in 391, the fighting recorded in Diodorus XV was in 386 and 385, but Evagoras did not capitulate until 381. In 391 the King gave the command against Evagoras to Autophradates and to 'Hecatomnos the dynast of Caria' (Diod. Sic. XIV. 98. iii–iv, where Autophradates' name has probably been lost at the beginning of §iv, Theopompus *FGrH* 115 F 103. iv): Hecatomnos' family is attested at the beginning of the fifth century (Hdt. V. 118. ii), and it is most likely that *c.*392/1 Caria had been detached from the satrapy of Sardis and, in a departure from the fifth-century policy of appointing Persian satraps (though vassal rulers had been tolerated in some areas, e.g. Cyprus), had been given to the head of this leading family. About 390 there was an embarrassing episode when Athens, currently on the Persians' side, sent ships to Evagoras, and these were captured by Sparta, currently opposed to Persia (Xen. *Hell.* IV. viii. 24); *c.*388 a second Athenian force, under Chabrias, did reach Evagoras (Xen. *Hell.* V. i. 10–12).

The Peace of Antalcidas, in 387/6, allowed Persia to concentrate on its rebels. The treaty stated that Cyprus was to belong to the King (Xen. *Hell.* V. i. 31); but it did not mention Egypt, so Chabrias moved there (Dem. XX. *Leptines* 76). Evagoras made an alliance with Acoris in Egypt, and Hecatomnos supported him; and he captured Tyre and other places in Phoenicia. Against him Artaxerxes sent Tiribazus, now satrap of Sardis, and Orontes, previously satrap of Armenia, with Glos, son of Tamos and son-in-law of Tiribazus, commanding the ships. Evagoras was defeated in a naval battle off Citium, and the Persians began to besiege Salamis (Diod. Sic. XV. 2–4, Isoc. IX. *Evagoras* 62, Theopompus *FGrH* 115 F 103. vi). When it seemed unlikely that he could hold out, Evagoras approached Tiribazus, whose terms were that his power should be limited to Salamis, he should pay tribute, and he should be obedient 'as a slave to his master'. Evagoras refused to accept the last clause, and made contact with Orontes, who denounced Tiribazus for disloyalty and had him sent to Artaxerxes as a prisoner, and made a treaty by which Evagoras was to obey 'as a king to a king' (Diod. Sic. XV. 8–9. ii, Theopompus *FGrH* 115 F 103. ix). Eventually Tiribazus vindicated himself and Orontes was in trouble (Diod. Sic. XV. 10–11). Evagoras survived until he was assassinated in 374/3 (Diod. Sic. XV. 47. viii), and the dynasty lasted until 310.

In Egypt Acoris and Chabrias fought successfully against Persia for three years, probably 385–383 (Isoc. IV. *Paneg.* 140). When Tiribazus was arrested Glos defected to Egypt and made an alliance with Acoris; he may have approached Sparta but it is unlikely that he obtained an alliance; before long he was murdered (Diod. Sic. XV. 9. iii–v, 18. i). Once Evagoras had been dealt with, Persia concentrated on Egypt. The command was given to Pharnabazus (one of three commanders in 385–383; transferred from Dascylium, where he was succeeded by his son Ariobarzanes). In 380/79 he protested to Athens against Chabrias' fighting for the Egyptians, and the Athenians recalled him and sent Iphicrates to fight for the Persians (Diod. Sic. XV. 29. i–iv). Substantial preparations were made over several years; the need for Greek mercenaries underlay Persia's interest in renewing the King's Peace in 375 (Diod. Sic. XV. 38. i: cf. p. 196); and the invasion finally took place in 374. Large forces were mustered at Ace, in Palestine, and sailed to Egypt. With one contingent they gained a foothold in the Nile delta, but when

Iphicrates wanted to advance inland and attack Memphis, Pharnabazus insisted on waiting for the rest of his force. The Egyptians fought back, and when the Nile flooded the Persians had to withdraw. Iphicrates returned to Athens in time to take over Timotheus' command in 373/2 (Diod. Sic. XV. 41–3: cf. pp. 234, 269), while Timotheus took over Iphicrates' position ([Dem.] XLIX. *Timotheus* 25–8, 59–60). Pharnabazus was replaced by Datames, satrap in the east of Asia Minor (perhaps originally Cilicia, to which he had added Cappadocia), but he seems not to have acted against Egypt (Nep. XIV. *Dat.* 3. v).

Instead Datames became involved in what is seen as the beginning of the Satraps' Revolt. Our only continuous account is by Diodorus, all under the year 362/1 (XV. 90–3), but our other, scattered, evidence shows that his account is badly confused. About 370/69 Datames returned to Cappadocia, dealt with a rebel but then rebelled himself, and got in touch with Ariobarzanes at Dascylium; but Autophradates was sent from Sardis, besieged him and induced him to return to apparent loyalty (Nep. XIV. *Dat.* 4–8). Ariobarzanes became vulnerable, as a supporter of Persia's pro-Spartan policy left behind when in 367 Artaxerxes was won over by Thebes (cf. p. 198), and because the satrapy was claimed by his half-brother Artabazus. In 366 Ariobarzanes was in revolt, and Athens sent Timotheus to support him yet not to break the King's Peace. Persia at some point had broken the peace by occupying Samos, and from autumn 366 to autumn 365 Timotheus besieged it, capturing it for Athens (Isoc. XV. *Antid.* 111, Dem. XV. *Lib. Rhod.* 9). Ariobarzanes was besieged by Autophradates in Assus or Adramyttium, and Timotheus and the Spartan Agesilaus went to relieve him, whereupon Autophradates and Mausolus (who had succeeded his father Hecatomnos: cf. p. 323) withdrew, and even gave Agesilaus money (Xen. *Ages.* ii. 26, Polyaenus *Strat.* VII. 26, Nep. XIII. *Timoth.* 1. iii, Isoc. XV. *Antid.* 112). Autophradates and Mausolus came out on the side of the rebels, and so did Orontes (restored to favour and given a command in Mysia, in northwestern Asia Minor), who became the leader of the revolt; and the rebels made an alliance with Tachos, the current ruler in Egypt. In 362/1 the rebels approached the Greeks: the participants in the latest common peace refused to back them (*IG* iv 556 = R&O 42 ~ Harding 57: cf. p. 200), though the Athenian Chabrias went back as a freelance to command the fleet (Nep. XII *Chab.* 2. i, iii); but Sparta was not a participant and sent Agesilaus officially, with thirty Spartiate advisers, to command the Greek mercenaries – so that at last he found himself fighting against Persia once more (Xen. *Ages.* ii. 28–30, Plut. *Ages.* 36–37. i).

But the revolt then collapsed, with treachery all round. In 361, while Tachos advanced into Syria against Agesilaus' advice, in Egypt his nephew Nectanebo was proclaimed king: Chabrias wanted to support Tachos, Agesilaus after consulting Sparta backed Nectanebo, and Tachos, deserted, surrendered to the Persians. Agesilaus supported Nectanebo against another claimant, and in winter 360/59 died in Cyrene on his way home, to be succeeded by his son Archidamus III (Plut. *Ages.* 37. ii–40, cf. Xen. *Ages.* ii. 29–31, Nep. XVII. *Ages.* 8). He had been a strong king, and an exponent of active policies for Sparta, but he had not been successful, partly because of Sparta's inherent weakness and partly because he was not interested in making Sparta popular.

Meanwhile Rheomithres, used by the satraps to communicate with Tachos, had gone over to the King. In 360 Orontes took an army to Syria, heading for Mesopotamia, and Datames, once more on the rebels' side, crossed the Euphrates (Polyaenus *Strat.* VII. 21. iii), but Orontes then changed sides – after which he disappears from history. Autophradates, who had captured Artabazus, the claimant to Dascylium, released him and made peace, and Artabazus took possession of Dascylium (Dem. XXIII. *Aristocrates*

154–8). Ariobarzanes was betrayed by his son Mithridates (Xen. *Cyr.* VIII. viii. 4, Arist. *Pol.* V. 1312 A 16). Datames returned to Cappadocia: in 359 he beat off an attack by Artabazus, but in winter 359/8 he was murdered by Mithridates (Nep. XIV. *Dat.* 9–11). Artaxerxes himself died, at an advanced age, in 359/8, and, since his other sons had already been eliminated by plots, was succeeded by Artaxerxes III (Ochus) (Plut. *Artax.* 26–30). He began his reign by ordering the disbanding of the satraps' mercenary armies, but the main danger had passed.

NOTE ON FURTHER READING

For general studies of Sparta see the note at the end of chapter 3. Books devoted to Sparta in this period include Cartledge, *Agesilaos and the Crisis of Sparta*; David, *Sparta Between Empire and Revolution*; Hamilton, *Sparta's Bitter Victories* (on the Corinthian War), and his *Agesilaus and the Failure of Spartan Hegemony*.

On the ΣΥΝ coinage the view which now seems likely to be correct (earlier interpretations had attributed the coins to one side or the other in the 390's) is that of S. Karwiese, 'Lysander as Herakliskos Drakonopnigon,' *NC* cxl = ^{7}xx 1980, 1–27. On Spartan imperialism after the Peloponnesian War see H. W. Parke, 'The Development of the Second Spartan Empire', *JHS* 1 1930, 37–79. On Sparta's dealings with Persia see Lewis, *Sparta and Persia*, ch. 6. On Agesilaus and his opponents see R. E. Smith, 'The Opposition to Agesilaus' Foreign Policy, 394–371 BC', *Hist.* ii 1953–4, 274–88; G. L. Cawkwell, 'Agesilaus and Sparta', *CQ*² xxvi 1976, 62–84. On the Locrians whose quarrel with the Phocians led to the outbreak of the Corinthian War see J. Buckler, 'The Incident at Mount Parnassus, 395 BC', in Tuplin (ed.), *Xenophon and His World . . . 1999*, 397–411 ch. 8. 2.

On Sparta's social problems see Hodkinson, *Property and Wealth in Classical Sparta*, and his earlier article, 'Warfare, Wealth and the Crisis of Spartiate Society', in Rich and Shipley (eds.), *War and Society in the Greek World*, 146–76. For the suggestion that the '*rhetra* of Epitadeus' is a fiction influenced by Plato see E. Schütrumpf, 'The Rhetra of Epitadeus; A Platonist's Fiction', *GRBS* xxviii 1987, 441–57. On the size of the citizen population see Gomme et al., *Historical Commentary on Thucydides*, iv. 110–17 (by Andrewes, believing in an error in Thuc. V. 68. iii, but starting from the material of Gomme, who did not believe in an error); de Ste. Croix, *The Origins of the Peloponnesian War*, app. 16.

On the chronology of the 360's I follow J. Roy, 'Arcadia and Boeotia in Peloponnesian Affairs, 370–362 BC', *Hist.* xx 1971, 569–99, in preference to the lower chronology of J. Wiseman, 'Epaminondas and the Theban Invasions', *Klio* li 1969, 177–99. On Megalopolis and Arcadia see S. Hornblower, 'When was Megalopolis Founded?', *BSA* lxxxv 1990, 71–7 (foundation begun 371/0, as in Pausanias, but took some time); Nielsen, *Arkadia and Its Poleis*, 229–69 (Triphylia), 414–55 (Megalopolis).

The chronology of Persia's war against Evagoras was settled by R. J. van der Spek, 'The Chronology of the Wars of Artaxerxes II in the Babylonian Astronomical Diaries', *Achaemenid History* xi 1998, 239–54 at 240–51.

On Glos see T. T. B. Ryder, 'Spartan Relations with Persia After the King's Peace: A Strange Story in Diodorus 15. 9', *CQ*² xiii 1963, 105–9 (believing a deal with Sparta was made); G. L. Cawkwell, 'Agesilaus and Sparta' (above), 70–1 (not believing); S. Ruzicka, 'Glos, Son of Tamos, and the End of the Cyprian War', *Hist.* xlviii 1999, 23–43.

On the Satraps' Revolt see M. J. Osborne, 'Orontes', *Hist.* xxii 1973, 515–51, and his *Naturalization in Athens*, ii. 61–80; Hornblower, *Mausolus*, 170–82; Weiskopf, *The So-Called 'Great Satraps' Revolt'*; J. D. Bing, 'The Iconography of Revolt and Restoration in Cilicia', *Hist.* xlvii 1998, 41–76.

18

The Second Athenian League

| 500 | 475 | 450 | 425 | 400 | 375 | 350 | 325 | 300 |

395	Athens joins enemies of Sparta in Corinthian War
390	campaign of Thrasybulus in the Aegean
387/6	Peace of Antalcidas
378	foundation of Second Athenian League
371	battle of Leuctra ends need for Athens to oppose Sparta
356–355	Social War
338/7	formation of League of Corinth ends Second Athenian League

Athens' Recovery after the Peloponnesian War

By the treaty which ended the Peloponnesian War Athens lost all its overseas possessions, had its navy limited to twelve ships, and became a subordinate ally of Sparta, bound to follow Sparta's lead in foreign policy (cf. p. 151). Accordingly it contributed to Sparta's war against Elis *c.*401 (Xen. *Hell.* III. ii. 25) and to Thibron's expedition to Asia Minor in 400 (Xen. *Hell.* III. i. 4: sending oligarchic cavalrymen Athens was glad to be rid of). But it is not long before we find moves towards an independent policy. Arms and officers were sent to the Persian fleet being assembled under Conon's command, and in 397 envoys were sent to the Persian King, but were caught by the Spartans and executed (*Hell. Oxy.* 10. i ~ Harding 11. A). In 396 Athens refused to contribute to Agesilaus' expedition (Paus. III. 9. ii–iii). Demaenetus with the secret backing of the council and of democratic leaders set out with a trireme to join Conon: when he was discovered and reported to the Spartans, the council panicked and pretended to know nothing, but he got away (*Hell. Oxy.* 9 [~ Harding 11. a], 11).

In 395 Athens was drawn into the Corinthian War fairly readily (and Thrasybulus, opposed to war in 396, was ready for war now: *Hell. Oxy.* 9. ii, contr. Xen. *Hell.* III. v. 16). Xenophon's Theban speech in Athens accepts that Athens wants to recover its empire; Sparta is unpopular in the Peloponnese and has deceived those whom it liberated from Athens; Athens could now become more powerful than ever (Xen. *Hell.* III. v. 8–15). Athens had started rebuilding the Piraeus walls by 395/4, before Cnidus (*IG* ii² 1656–7 = R&O 9); work on them and the long walls was helped by the money which Conon brought in 393 (Xen. *Hell.* IV. viii. 9–10, Diod. Sic. XIV. 85. ii–iii), and the mercenary force at Corinth was commanded by Athenians, first Iphicrates and, after he unsuccessfully tried to seize Corinth for Athens, Chabrias (Androtion *FGrH* 324 F 48 = Philoch. *FGrH* 328 F 150 ~ Harding 22. A; Xen. *Hell.* IV. viii. 34, Diod. Sic. XIV. 92. ii). Cnidus and its aftermath, though in fact a victory of Athens' traditional enemy, Persia, were treated as a Greek and an Athenian success (cf. p. 209), so extravagantly that Conon became the first living Athenian to be honoured with a statue in the agora (Dem. XX. *Leptines* 68–70); Athens also honoured Evagoras of Salamis, likewise associated with Cnidus (R&O 11), Dionysius of Syracuse, whom Conon hoped to detach from Sparta (*IG* ii² 18 = R&O 10 ~ Harding 20, Lys. XIX. *Property of Aristophanes* 19–20; cf. p. 282) and others, and Conon was honoured in Erythrae (*IK Erythrai und Klazomenai* 6 = R&O 8 ~ Harding 12. D).

By 392 Athens had begun to rebuild its navy, and had regained the north Aegean islands of Lemnos, Imbros and Scyros, protecting the route from the Hellespont to Athens, which it had possessed for most of the fifth century (cf. Xen. *Hell.* IV. viii. 15, Andoc. III. *Peace* 12). It had also regained Delos (independent shortly after the war, *I. Délos* 87 = R&O 3; administered by Athenian and probably Andrian amphictyons 393/2–389/8, *I. Délos* 97). The first peace proposals in 392 would have deprived it of all overseas possessions once more; the second in 392/1 made an exception of the northern islands but not of Delos; Andocides' speech on that occasion suggests that some Athenians were hankering after more (Andoc. III. *Peace* 15). In any case the Athenians were not yet ready to agree to a treaty which would abandon the Asiatic Greeks (cf. p. 193). Sparta returned to the Aegean in 391, and Athens' support for Evagoras when Persia had begun to regard him as a rebel caused embarrassment on all sides; but in 390 Thrasybulus had a remarkable campaign. He was sent to support the democrats in Rhodes; but he went first to the Hellespont, where he mediated between two Thracian rulers and made both allies of Athens; he restored the democracy in Byzantium, made an alliance with Calchedon and imposed a 10 per cent tax on trade passing through the Bosporus (cf. Dem. XX. *Leptines* 60); he defeated a Spartan harmost on Lesbos; there are traces of his activity in various other places in the islands and on the mainland; he imposed a general 5 per cent tax, and claimed the right to exile men from the territory of Athens and its allies (*IG* ii^2 24/28 = R&O –/18 ~ Harding 25/26). He finally reached Rhodes, but early the next year he was killed on a fund-raising expedition to Aspendus, on the south coast of Asia Minor (Xen. *Hell.* IV. viii. 25–30, Diod. Sic. XIV. 94, 99. iv–v). By then he had been ordered back to Athens, and his colleague Ergocles was charged with embezzlement (Lys. XXVIII. *Ergocles*, XXIX. *Philocrates*). His successor Agyrrhius did little, but Iphicrates, sent to the Hellespont, defeated and killed the Spartan Anaxibius at Abydus (Xen. *Hell.* IV. viii. 31–9).

In 387 Iphicrates and Diotimus blockaded the Spartan Nicolochus in Abydus, but Antalcidas rescued him by a trick, captured a further Athenian squadron coming from Thrace, and so regained control of the Hellespont (Xen. *Hell.* V. i. 6–7, 25–8). Athenian recriminations are revealed by a decree honouring Phanocritus of Parium: the original proposal, which was presumably bland, does not survive, but an amendment makes it clear that Phanocritus had given information about the enemy ships which the generals had disbelieved (*IG* ii^2 29 = R&O 19). The Athenians did not lose hope: inscriptions show Athens giving reassurances to Erythrae 'about not giving up Erythrae to the barbarians', and deciding not to send a garrison and governor to Clazomenae as long as it paid Thrasybulus' 5 per cent tax (*SEG* xxvi 1282/*IG* ii^2 28 = R&O 17/18 ~ Harding 28/26). But when Antalcidas again offered a common peace treaty the Athenians and the other Greeks had to accept it: the Asiatic Greeks were surrendered to Persia; Athens' three northern islands were the only exceptions to the autonomy rule, so it lost Delos once more; and Sparta proceeded to interpret the autonomy rule in its own interests. Athens had, nevertheless, made a very rapid and convincing recovery from its defeat in the Peloponnesian War.

The Foundation of the Second Athenian League

The abandonment of the Asiatic Greeks, to which Sparta had committed itself in 412–411, had at last taken place, and was seen as a great betrayal. In Aristophanes, as early as *Peace* (421), we can find the idea that while the Greeks quarrel among themselves they are exposing themselves to the possibility of an attack by Persia (*Peace* 105–8, 406–8, *Lys.* 1128–35). Gorgias in his *Olympic Speech*, best dated 408, and his *Funeral Speech*, of unknown date, had claimed that the Greeks ought to fight against the barbarians, not against one another (82 A 1. iv–v DK). Lysias' (XXXIII) *Olympic Speech* is dated 388 by Diodorus (XIV. 109. iii) but more probably belongs to 384: it appears to be complaining of the situation after the King's Peace, when some Greeks were subject to Persia and others to the tyranny of Dionysius of Syracuse, and calling on Sparta to lead the Greeks in reasserting their freedom. Isocrates in his (IV) *Panegyric*, c.380, contrasted the glories of the alleged fifth-century Peace of Callias (cf. pp. 47–8) with the humiliation of the Peace of Antalcidas (§§117–20) and, while nominally pleading for Athens and Sparta to be reconciled and to cooperate against Persia (§§16–17), went on to defend Athens' fifth-century empire (§§100–6) and to claim that Athens should lead the Greeks against Persia once more (cf. his later summary, XV. *Antid.* 57–62; another condemnation of the Peace XII. *Panath.* 106).

But in the years after 386 the peace and Sparta's interpretation of it were facts to be lived with. In 386/5 the Thracian Hebryzelmis was praised but not granted an alliance (*IG* ii² 31 = Tod 117 ~ Harding 29). In 385 Athens was afraid to help Mantinea against Sparta, though it did take in refugees afterwards (Diod. Sic. XV. 5. v, *IG* ii² 33. 7–8). In 382 there was talk of an alliance with Olynthus when that was threatened by Sparta (Xen. *Hell.* V. ii. 15), but none seems to have been made; refugees were taken in once more, from Thebes when that was occupied by Sparta (Xen. *Hell.* V. ii. 31, Plut. *Pel.* 6. iii–v). But Chios, Mytilene and Byzantium maintained their connection with Athens (Isoc. XIV. *Plataic* 26–7), and in 384/3 Athens found a solution appropriate to the new circumstances: a defensive alliance with Chios was made, on the basis of freedom and autonomy and within the framework of the King's Peace (*IG* ii² 34–5 = R&O 20 ~ Harding 31).

In 379/8 the Theban exiles set out from Athens to overthrow the pro-Spartan régime (Xen. *Hell.* V. iv. 2, Diod. Sic. XV. 25. i, Plut. *Pel.* 7–12), and they received military support from Athens – apparently unofficial according to Xenophon, official according to Diodorus and others; perhaps forces were sent officially to the border and on their own initiative entered Boeotia (Xen. *Hell.* V. iv. 9; Diod. Sic. XV. 25. iv–26, cf. Din. I. *Demosthenes* 38–9, Aristid. I. *Panathenaic* 294). When Cleombrotus took a Spartan army he had to go via Plataea since Chabrias was blocking the route through Attica (Xen. *Hell.* V. i. 14). When Sparta protested, Athens panicked and condemned the generals who had gone to Boeotia (Xen. *Hell.* V. iv. 19, cf. 22, Plut. *Pel.* 14. i; omitted by Diod. Sic.). It was while Spartan envoys were in Athens that Sphodrias invaded Attica from Thespiae; Athens protested but the Spartans acquitted him; and Athens then came out openly in opposition to Sparta (cf. p. 214).

Xenophon reports that the Athenians put gates on the Piraeus, and proceeded to build ships and support the Boeotians enthusiastically, but he does not directly mention the Second Athenian League. Diodorus has an account (XV. 28–9) which dovetails well with an important series of inscriptions. After Cleombrotus' winter expedition (27. iii) the Boeotians united in an alliance [perhaps the first move towards the revival of the federation], and Athens sent envoys to the states under Sparta's control, inviting them to assert their common freedom. This met with considerable success, first with Chios and Byzantium, then with Rhodes, Mytilene and others. Excited at the good will of the allies, Athens established a council (*synedrion*) of allies, to meet in Athens, each member having one vote, the members to be autonomous and Athens to be the leader (*hegemon*). Sparta tried to discourage cities from joining, and prepared for a hard war (28). After a digression on Persia's current attempt to recover Egypt (29. i–iv), Diodorus continues with the episode of Sphodrias, whom he calls Sphodriades, and which he is probably wrong to place here rather than before the creation of the League; the Athenians voted that Sparta was in breach of the peace and decided to go to war; they admitted Thebes to the *synedrion* on the same terms as the other members; and they voted to give up existing cleruchies and forbade Athenians to farm land outside Attica (29. v–viii).

In the epigraphic record the first stage is the alliance of 384/3 with Chios, which was used as a model for the League. Next Byzantium is made an ally of Athens and the other allies, on the same terms as Chios (*IG* ii² 41 = Tod 121 ~ Harding 34). A later stage is represented by a decree for Methymna, on Lesbos, which is already an ally of Athens and now has its alliance extended to the other allies; the *synedrion* now exists and is involved in the oath-taking, and Methymna is to be added to an already existing list of allies (*IG* ii² 42 = R&O 23 ~ Harding 37; for adding to the list cf. below). A very fragmentary inscription contains an amendment to a decree concerning Thebes, and mentions men from Chios and Mytilene (*IG* ii² 40; trans. of a speculative reconstruction Harding 33).

We also have an inscription of spring 378/7 which embodies a prospectus for the League, setting out not its organisation (the existence of the *synedrion* is taken for granted) but its aim and the terms on which states are invited to join, followed by a list of members (*IG* ii² 43 = R&O 22 ~ Harding 35: see ill. 10). The aim of the League is, 'So that the Spartans shall allow the Greeks to be free and autonomous, and to live at peace occupying their own territory in security, [[and so that the peace and friendship sworn by the Greeks and the King in accordance with the agreements may be in force and endure]]' (ll. 9–15; for the later erasure of the bracketed clause see p. 236). An invitation is extended to Greeks and barbarians outside the King's domain to join, subject to various promises: they are to be free and autonomous, with whatever constitution they wish, not subjected to a governor or garrison or to the payment of tribute, on the same terms as Chios, Thebes and the other allies (ll. 15–25). All property publicly or privately owned by Athenians in allied territory will be renounced; all *stelai* (inscribed stones) at Athens unfavourable to any allies will be demolished; from 378/7 it will be illegal for Athenians publicly or privately to own property in allied territory, and charges in connection with this are to be laid before the *synedrion* (ll. 25–46). The alliance is to be a defensive alliance (ll. 46–51). After a clause providing for the publication of the decree with a list of members (ll. 63–72), the decree ends with the appointment of envoys to go to Thebes [possibly to persuade the Thebans to join as Thebans, not as Boeotians] (ll. 73–7).

The promises are promises that Athens will not treat this League as it had treated the Delian League, and they also serve to spell out what freedom and autonomy are to mean in practical terms. The model is now not just Chios but Chios and Thebes, which suggests that these specific promises may have been added at the point when Thebes joined. The promise about Athenian-owned property is separate from the original list, and also appears at a later point in

III. 10 The prospectus of the Second Athenian League, inv. no. EM10397. Epigraphical Museum, Athens

Diodorus' account, so it should be seen as an addition to the original scheme: it applies only to states which join the League as free and autonomous allies, and therefore not to Lemnos, Imbros and Scyros (which had been recognised as Athenian possessions in the King's Peace). It is not in fact likely that there was much Athenian-owned property elsewhere at this date, or that there were many *stelai* unfavourable to potential allies: these clauses indicate that the decks will be completely cleared, not that there is much clearing to be done.

The list of members was inscribed in instalments by different hands. It begins below the original decree; below that part of the list there survives the beginning of another decree; the list continues on the left-hand side of the *stele*.

Inscribed in the same hand as the original decree, presumably at the same time, are Chios, Mytilene, Methymna, Rhodes, Byzantium and, heading a second column, Thebes (i. 79–83, ii. 79): these were still the only members in the spring of 377. (The decree for Methymna, mentioned above, provided for Methymna to be added to an already existing list: perhaps Methymna joined after the general decree had been enacted but before it was inscribed.) The remaining batches of names will be considered below when we look at the development of the League. Diodorus claims that seventy members joined (XV. 30. ii); Aeschines claims that seventy-five were lost in the Social War of the 350's (Aeschin. II. *Embassy* 70); there were fifty-three or slightly more in the inscribed list. Despite the League's declared purpose, most of the members were states not seriously threatened by Sparta in the 370's.

The structure of this League was different from that of the Delian League (cf. p. 18). Probably (until 454/3, when the council was abandoned) the Delian League had a council in which Athens had one vote along with each of the allies. This League had a *synedrion* permanently in Athens, of which Athens was almost certainly not a member, with its own presidential apparatus (a Theban president in R&O 29). For League matters, the *synedrion* and the Athenian council both acted as probouleutic bodies, and the Athenian assembly took the final decision, but presumably could not commit the allies to a decision they had said they would not accept. Thus Athens' two decrees of 368 for Dionysius of Syracuse (*IG* ii² 103/105 + 223 = R&O 33/34 ~ Harding –/52: cf. p. 236) show the council sending a recommendation directly to the assembly on an Athenian matter but asking the opinion of the *synedrion* 'about the building of the temple [at Delphi] and the peace', which must cover the question of admitting Dionysius to the League; and the *synedrion* must have refused to have Dionysius as a member, since the second decree makes a bilateral alliance between Dionysius and Athens. In a decree of 362/1 (*IG* i² 112 = R&O 41 ~ Harding 56) the *synedrion* took the initiative in accepting an alliance with Peloponnesian states, it passed its recommendation to the council and the council passed it to the assembly. We shall see that, at different stages in the negotiation of the Peace of Philocrates between Athens and Philip in 346, the *synedrion* put forward recommendations; but by then it was a weak body, and it also said it would accept whatever Athens decided (cf. pp. 241, 310). At the end of 373/2 the *synedrion* imposed a settlement after a civil war in Paros, and Athens required Paros to send offerings to festivals as a colony (R&O 29).

We do not hear of any trials of the kinds provided for – by the *synedrion* if Athenians were accused of owning property in allied territory, by Athens and the allies [perhaps in these cases the *synedrion* would have been invited to confirm an Athenian verdict] if anybody [apparently any Athenian] was accused of trying to overturn the arrangements for the League. The first procedure envisages a common fund of the allies, to benefit from confiscations. On the other hand, the promise not to collect tribute, repeated in decrees for some individual allies, makes it hard to believe that there were regular financial levies from the beginning; presumably the assumption was that allied states would provide and pay for their own forces. There may have been some voluntary fund-raising: in 375 there is a complaint that the Thebans were not providing money for a naval campaign which they had instigated (Xen. *Hell.* VI. ii. 1, cf. V. iv. 62). There were financial problems in 373 (cf. below), and it may have been at that point that the decision was taken to collect money after all, but to call the payments not *phoros*, 'tribute', but *syntaxeis*, 'contributions' ([Dem.] XLIX. *Timotheus* 49, Theopompus *FGrH* 115 F 98 ~ Harding 36). Evidence for sums collected is scanty and late: totals of 45 talents in the late 350's, 60 talents *c.*347 (Dem. XVIII. *Crown* 234, Aeschin. II. *Embassy* 71) and 5 talents each from Eretria and Oreus in the late 340's (Aeschin. III. *Ctesiphon* 94, 100). The *synedrion* seems to have approved both assessments and expenditure (*IG* ii² 233 = R&O 72 ~ Harding 97. 27–8; *IG* ii² 123 = R&O 52 ~ Harding 69. 9–11). 'The men elected by the people to exact from the islanders the money that they owe' (*IG* ii² 111 = R&O 39 ~ Harding 55. 12–14) were perhaps men appointed to collect arrears of *syntaxeis*. It does not look as if there was ever a likelihood that the *syntaxeis* would become a means of Athenian oppression.

The Development of the League: To Leuctra

The second batch in the League's list of members (ii. 80–4) comprises the cities of Euboea other than Histiaea/Oreus, and nearby Icus: these are the first additions mentioned by Diodorus (XV. 30. i), and we have a decree for the admission of Chalcis, still in 378/<u>7</u> (*IG* ii² 44 = Tod 124 ~ Harding 38). In the summer of 377 Chabrias attacked Histiaea but did not capture it (cf. p. 251; force could be used against states reluctant to join), and then recruited members elsewhere in the Aegean, including Peparethus and Sciathus (Diod. Sic. XV. 30. ii–v; on the *stele* i. 85–9, including Peparethus and Sciathus). 376 was the year in which a Spartan blockade threatened Athens' corn supply but Chabrias with an Athenian fleet escorted the corn ships and then besieged Naxos and defeated the Spartans (Xen. *Hell.* V. iv. 60–1, Diod. Sic. XV. 34. iii–35. ii): perhaps all the remaining members on the front of the *stele* joined this year. His victory was the first major Athenian naval success since the Peloponnesian War, and he was honoured with a statue in the agora (Aeschin. III. *Ctesiphon* 243, Arist. *Rh.* III. 1411 B 6–7, Nep. XII. *Chab.* 1. iii); a surviving statue base (*Hesp.* xxx 1961, 74–91) records honours awarded by various bodies resulting from his campaigns of 376 and 375.

Probably the first entry on the left-hand side of the *stele* is ll. 131–4, level with the beginning of the list on the front, and some distance below the other entries: 'The People of Zacynthus in Nellus'. This must be connected in some way with Timotheus' campaign of 375, possibly the beginning rather than the end. At the top of the left-hand side (ll. 97–8) the best restoration is: 'The People of Pyrrha', on Lesbos, known to be a member but not listed elsewhere. Next come Abdera and other places in the north-east (ll. 99–105: Olynthus is included, as 'The Chalcidians from Thrace'). These will result from a campaign of Chabrias in 375, when he defended Abdera against a Thracian attack, installed a garrison (breaking one of the League's promises, however virtuously), and, despite an error in Diodorus' text, was not murdered (Diod. Sic. XV. 36. i–iv). Prompted by the Thebans, Conon's son Timotheus campaigned in the west: of his gains Xenophon mentions Corcyra, Diodorus mentions Cephallenia, Acarnania and king Alcetas of the Molossi; he defeated the Spartans off Alyzia, after which the King's Peace was renewed, and he was recalled to Athens but restored exiles in Zacynthus on his way home (Xen. *Hell.* V. iv. 62–6, Diod. Sic. XV. 36. v–vi). Acarnania, one city of Cephallenia, and Alcetas and his son Neoptolemus appear on the *stele* (ll. 106–10; we do not know what name has been erased in l. 111, but the frequent guess that it was Jason of Pherae is insecure: cf. p. 251), but not Corcyra or the other cities of Cephallenia; separate inscriptions provide for the admission of Corcyra, Acarnania and Cephallenia (*IG* ii² 96 = R&O 24 ~ Harding 41, dated 375̲/4) and record the admission of Corcyra (*IG* ii² 97 = Tod 127 ~ Harding 42) and arrangements with Cephallenia including reference to a garrison (*Agora* xvi 46). The most likely explanation is that proceedings were interrupted by the renewal of the King's Peace and the recall of Timotheus to Athens, then further delayed by the renewed fighting in the west, and not completed until the end of that fighting in 372 (cf. below). Timotheus like Chabrias was honoured with a statue in the agora (Aeschin. III. *Ctesiphon* 243, Nep XIII. *Timoth.* 2. iii). He and Conon were honoured in other places too, and texts referring to him and the year 375/4 have been read on the base of the 'dancing girls' column north-east of the temple of Apollo at Delphi (cf. *SEG* xxxiii 440).

Other names on the *stele* (ll. 112–30) are from the Aegean; certainly none is later than 373 and probably none is later than 375. This batch begins with Andros: Delos was presumably made independent of Athens under the Peace of Antalcidas (cf. pp. 227–8), but Athenian amphictyons are attested there again from 377/6, and they are joined by Andrians from 374/3 (*I. Délos* 98 = R&O 28). There was room on the *stele* for further names but, for whatever reason, although the League continued to grow (cf. Xen. *Hell.* VI. ii. 11–13, Diod. Sic. XV. 47. ii–iii, on Timotheus' activity in the Aegean in 373), further names were not added to the list.

When Timotheus, on his way back to Athens, restored exiles in Zacynthus, Sparta protested. In 374 Sparta sent expeditions to Zacynthus and to Corcyra; in 373 it sent a further sixty ships under Mnasippus to Corcyra, and he ravaged the countryside and blockaded the city. Timotheus delayed in coming from Athens, because of difficulties in raising men and money in the Aegean, and it was perhaps in response to these difficulties that the levying of *syntaxeis* was introduced (cf. p. 233). He was deposed and put on trial (cf. [Dem.] XLIX. *Timotheus* 6–24, naming Callistratus and Iphicrates as prosecutors and saying that Alcetas and Jason spoke in his defence; Diodorus wrongly has him reinstated). Ctesicles went over land in winter 373/2 and enabled the Corcyraeans to defeat and kill Mnasippus; Iphicrates arrived by sea in 372, pausing in Cephallenia when he knew that Mnasippus was dead; he arrived in time to defeat a Syracusan squadron sent to support Sparta, and then hired out his sailors to work on the land in Corcyra and himself and his soldiers to fight for the Acarnanians. In 371 he collected money in Cephallenia and was preparing to attack Laconia when he was overtaken by the next peace treaty (Xen. *Hell.* VI. ii. 2–39, Diod. Sic. XV. 45–46. iii, 47. i–vii). Before the campaign of 373/2 Diodorus has a chapter on Iphicrates' military innovations, crediting him in particular with converting hoplites into peltasts by giving them the light Thracian shield, the *pelte*, lengthening their swords and spears and devising the Iphicratid boot (cf. the Wellington boot of the nineteenth century AD) (Diod. Sic. XV. 44, cf. Nep. XI. *Iph.* 1. iii–iv): apart from the boot, there is no other indication that hoplite equipment was changed in these ways, and if there is any truth behind the report it may refer to an experiment with the mercenaries whom Iphicrates had been commanding in Egypt.

Thebes was becoming an increasingly embarrassing member of the League. It provided ships for Timotheus in 373 ([Dem.] XLIX. *Timotheus* 14–16), and a president for the *synedrion* on the last day of 373/2 (R&O 29); but it destroyed Plataea, refounded after the Peace of Antalcidas, in 373/2 and put increasing pressure on Thespiae (cf. pp. 249–50). The peace of summer 371 resulted from an approach by Athens to Sparta when Callistratus argued that Athens and Sparta ought to be on the same side, and Thebes was excluded from the treaty (cf. pp. 196–7). That was followed by Thebes' defeat of Sparta at Leuctra, a battle in which Athens was not involved.

The Development of the League: From Leuctra to the Social War

The Thebans announced their victory at Leuctra to their Athenian allies, but the herald was received with a stony silence (Xen. *Hell.* VI. iv. 19–20). The peace treaty of autumn 371 was organised by Athens: it included Sparta and excluded Thebes; it was based on 'the decrees of the Athenians and their allies' [i.e. freedom and autonomy were to be understood as in the League]; its territorial basis was probably *echein ta heauton*, that states should possess what belonged to them, which Athens was to exploit in the years that followed (cf. pp. 197–8). The aim of the League, 'So that the Spartans shall allow the Greeks to be free and autonomous, and to live at peace occupying their own territory in security', had been accomplished by Thebes' defeat of Sparta – Sparta would not after this be a threat to the freedom and autonomy of the Greeks – but, as Athens did not disband the Delian League when it gave up regular warfare against Persia in the middle of the fifth century (cf. pp. 47–50), it did not now disband the Second League. However, it was increasingly to pursue policies which the League's members could not join in supporting.

Thebes must now have ceased to be a member of the League, as did the other central Greek members, which adhered to Thebes rather than to Athens. It was now in Athens' interests to support not Thebes but Sparta, so in 370 Athens rejected the appeal from Arcadia and its allies (Diod. Sic. XV. 62. iii;

later denounced as a bad decision by Dem. XVI. *Megalopolitans* 12, 19), and in winter 370/69 sent Iphicrates to attack the Thebans on their homeward journey – which he did ineffectively: some Athenians were slower than others to recognise the new reality (Xen. *Hell.* VI. v. 49–52: cf. pp. 269–70). In 369 a firm alliance was made between Athens and Sparta, but anachronistic fear led to the decision that the command should alternate between the two every five days, not be given to Athens at sea and Sparta on land (Xen. *Hell.* VII. i. 1–14, Diod. Sic. XV. 67. i: cf. p. 270). When the Thebans returned to the Peloponnese, Chabrias was effective in fighting against them (Diod. Sic. XV. 69). We learn from an inscription that in 369/8 envoys went to Athens from Mytilene, anxious about the new policy: the leading politician Callistratus was responsible for the reply, that when Sparta broke the treaties and threatened the Greeks Athens called on the Greeks to join in resisting, but . . . [and frustratingly the rest of the text is lost] (*IG* ii² 107 = R&O 31 ~ Harding 53. 35 sqq.). Now that Athens and Sparta were on the same side, Athens made an alliance with Dionysius of Syracuse, but it appears that the *synedrion* refused to have him as a member of the League (*IG* ii² 103/105 + 223 = R&O 33/34 ~ Harding –/52: cf. p. 232).

To add to the allies' discomfiture, Athens began to exploit the *echein ta heauton* clause in the peace to attempt to recover former possessions in the north-east: Amphipolis, which it had lost to the Spartans in 424/3 and should have recovered under the Peace of Nicias in 421 but did not (cf. pp. 111–12, 114), was a matter of pride as well as economic advantage; the Chersonese, on the European side of the Hellespont, through which the corn ships sailed from the Black Sea to Athens, was an area in which Athens had been interested since the sixth century. In the hinterland was the Odrysian kingdom of Thrace, with which Athens was always anxious to maintain a good relationship: Hebryzelmis was succeeded by Cotys in 383/2; at some date he was made an Athenian citizen, and *c.*386 Iphicrates married his sister (Dem. XXIII. *Aristocrates* 118, 129).

In 368 Iphicrates was sent against Amphipolis: he at first supported one claimant to the Macedonian throne, Ptolemy, against his rival Pausanias, but later fell out with Ptolemy (Aeschin. II. *Embassy* 26–9, Dem. XXIII. *Aristocrates* 149). Thebes too became interested in Macedon through its involvement in Thessaly, and in 368, when Thebes was attacking Alexander of Pherae, Athens sent a force under Autocles to support him (Diod. Sic. XV. 71. v). So in 367, when Pelopidas gained the King's support for peace terms advantageous to Thebes, those terms were to include the disbanding of the Athenian navy (cf. pp. 198–9). Too many states were provoked, and Thebes did not get its treaty, but it was probably at this point that the Athenians erased the reference to the King's Peace in the prospectus of the League (cf. p. 230: it did not occur to them to erase the hostile reference to Sparta immediately before), and Athens like Sparta gave its support to the satraps in revolt against the King. Ariobarzanes and Philiscus, the agent he sent to Greece in 369/8 (cf. p. 198), were made Athenian citizens (Dem. XXIII. *Aristocrates* 141, cf. 202), and in 366 Timotheus was sent to support Ariobarzanes yet not break the King's Peace.

From autumn 366 to autumn 365 he besieged Samos and captured it from the Persians (Isoc. XV. *Antid.* 111, Dem. XV. *Lib. Rhod.* 9), after which Athens shocked the Greek world by not liberating Samos but turning it into an Athenian cleruchy (Diod. Sic. XVIII. 18. ix, Strabo 638. XIV. i. 18, Arist. *Rh.* II. 1384 B 32–5; reinforced in 362/1, schol. Aeschin. I. *Timarchus* 53). He was joined by the Spartan Agesilaus in relieving Ariobarzanes when he was besieged in Adramyttium or Assus (Xen. *Ages.* ii. 26, Polyaenus *Strat.* VII. 26). In 365/4 he replaced Iphicrates on the Amphipolis front (Dem. XXIII. *Aristocrates* 149, schol. Aeschin. II. *Embassy* 31), after which Iphicrates first fought for Cotys against Athens, then retired to fortresses of his own (Dem. XXIII. *Aristocrates* 130–2). Timotheus captured various cities including Potidaea, which by invitation became another Athenian cleruchy (Diod. Sic. XV. 81. vi, Din. I. *Demosthenes* 14; cleruchy 362/1 *IG* ii² 114 = Tod 146 ~ Harding 58).

The continuation of this war need not be followed in detail: it included some successes (Timotheus captured Sestos and Crithote, in the Chersonese: Nep. XIII. *Timoth.* 1. iii, Isoc. XV. *Antid.* 108, 112) but also some failures (in 360/59, after being defeated near Amphipolis, Timotheus burned his fleet rather than let it fall into enemy hands [schol. Aeschin. II. *Embassy* 31, Polyaenus *Strat.* III. 10. viii]). Shortage of money remained a problem: Timotheus issued bronze coins, some of which have been found at Olynthus ([Arist.] *Oec.* II. 1350 A 23–30, cf. *CAH*² pls. v–vi no. 227). Several commanders were insufficiently successful and were prosecuted; Amphipolis continued to elude Athens.

Nearer home Oropus, disputed between Athens and Boeotia (cf. p. 146), was made independent in 404 (cf. Lys. XXXI. *Philon* 9) but not long afterwards absorbed into Boeotia again (Diod. Sic. XIV. 17. i–iii); it was presumably made independent again under the Peace of Antalcidas; but by 373/2 it had placed itself in Athens' hands (Isoc. XIV. *Plataic* 20). In 366 Themison, tyrant of Eretria, seized it, claiming to support a body of exiles. Athens recalled Chares from the Peloponnese and tried to recapture it; it was entrusted to the Thebans pending arbitration, and they were allowed to keep it (Xen. *Hell.* VII. iv. 1, Diod. Sic. XV. 76. i, schol. Aeschin. III. *Ctesiphon* 85 = Agatharchides *FGrH* 86 F 8). Chares returned to the Peloponnese and was involved in an unsuccessful attempt 'to keep Corinth safe for the Athenian people'. As affairs in the Peloponnese became more complicated, in 366 Athens became an ally of Arcadia and in 364 it supported the Arcadians in their war against Elis (cf. p. 220).

In 364 the Thebans stepped up their hostility to Athens. Epaminondas had urged them to build dockyards and a hundred triremes (it is not clear whether all of these were built); he tried to win over Rhodes, Chios and Byzantium (we have a decree in which Cnidus makes Epaminondas its *proxenos*, *SEG* xliv 901, and one in which the Boeotians appoint a Byzantine *proxenos*, *SEG* xxxiv 355, but neither is precisely dated); in a naval campaign he drove away an Athenian fleet under Laches (Diod. Sic. XV. 78. iv–79. i). Revolts in Ceos in 363/2, dealt with by Chabrias (*IG* ii² 111 = R&O 39 ~ Harding 55), may have been encouraged by Thebes' challenge to Athens, but there seems to have been a local reason, in that the Ceans preferred to function as a single entity while Athens preferred to deal with the cities separately. Whatever Thebes' naval campaign may have achieved, it was not repeated; but in 362 and 361 Alexander of Pherae in Thessaly, after being subjected to Thebes, turned against his Athenian allies, attacking some of the Aegean islands and defeating an Athenian fleet under Leosthenes, and even raiding the Piraeus (Diod. Sic. XV. 95. i–iii, Polyaenus *Strat.* VI. 2, [Dem.] L. *Polycles* 4). In response to that, in 361/0 the Athenians broke off their alliance with Alexander and made an alliance with the federation of Thessalians opposed to him (*IG* ii² 116 = R&O 44 ~ Harding 59).

In the course of the 360's Athens had done a great deal to alarm its allies. The founder of an anti-Spartan League had become an ally of Sparta. Already in the 370's garrisons, however justifiable, and levies of money called *syntaxeis* had appeared, and Paros had been treated as a colony and required to send offerings to Athenian festivals (R&O 29). Cleruchies in Samos and Potidaea, and attempts at conquest in the north, did not impinge directly on the states which were members of the League, but they were worryingly reminiscent of the fifth century, and the members must have wondered how far the League's promises would protect them. In Ceos revolts were firmly put down, and some major lawsuits had been made transferable to Athens (*IG* ii² 111 = R&O 39 ~ Harding 55). Chares in 361/0 supported the oligarchs in civil strife in Corcyra, and gained Athens a bad reputation (Diod. Sic. XV. 95. iii, Aen. Tact. xi. 13–15). Athens' alliance with Peloponnesian states in 362/1 was recommended by the *synedrion* (*IG* ii² 112 = R&O 41 ~ Harding 56. 18–19), but there is no sign that for the alliance with the Thessalians it was consulted or given the chance to swear, though the alliance included the League (*IG* ii² 116 = R&O 44 ~ Harding 59).

The situation in the north was transformed by two deaths. In 360/59 the Thracian Cotys was murdered, and his son Cersebleptes was challenged by two rivals, Berisades and Amadocus. We learn, mostly from Demosthenes, of a series of Athenian attempts to reach a satisfactory settlement with them. After earlier agreements, which he regarded as shameful, in winter 357/6 Chares secured 'most excellent and just' terms: Thrace was divided between Berisades in the west, Amadocus in the centre and Cersebleptes in the east, but for some purposes was regarded as a single entity, and some Greek cities were regarded both as dependent on the Thracian rulers and as allies owing *syntaxeis* to Athens (Dem. XXIII. *Aristocrates* 163–73, cf. *IG* ii² 126 = R&O 47 ~ Harding 64).

In 359 Perdiccas of Macedon was killed in a war against the Illyrians and succeeded by his brother Philip. One of the rival claimants, Argaeus, was backed by Athens. Philip tried to keep his enemies divided, and withdrew from Amphipolis, suggesting that he would allow Athens to acquire it (for references to secret talks or promises cf. p. 299). The Athenian force failed to support Argaeus, and he was defeated (Diod. Sic. XVI. 2. vi–3. vi). But in 357 Philip captured Amphipolis and retained it for himself, leaving the Athenians to claim that he had cheated them, as a result of which they declared war on him (Diod.

Sic. XVI. 8. ii–iii, Isoc. V. *Philip* 2, Aeschin. II. *Embassy* 70, III. *Ctesiphon* 54);
at the beginning of the year 35<u>6</u>/5 they made an alliance with Philip's barbarian neighbours (*IG* ii² 127 = R&O 53 ~ Harding 70). We shall look at Philip
and the Athenians' dealings with him in chapter 22; but other concerns prevented them from prosecuting the war against him for Amphipolis.

In 357 the Athenians had an important success. Since Leuctra the cities of
Euboea had been allied with Thebes, not Athens, but now Athens took advantage of disagreement between pro-Theban and pro-Athenian parties to regain
Euboea for Athens – within thirty days according to Aeschines (Diod. Sic. XVI.
7. ii, Aeschin. III. *Ctesiphon* 85). An inscription of 357/6 preserves the end of
the treaty with Carystus and mentions the other cities (*IG* ii² 124 = R&O 48 ~
Harding 65), and ends with eight names of generals who swore to it: the first
name is erased but decipherable as Chabrias; of the second there survives only
the beginning, Cha[–]. Editors have usually supposed the second name to be
Chares, and have been puzzled as to why Chabrias should have been erased;
but we obtain an easier timetable and an explanation if we suppose that Chares
was not included, because he was away making the final agreement with the
Thracian rulers, and that Chabrias' name was inscribed twice in error and
therefore erased once.

But that success was followed by failure in the Social War, Athens' war with
the allies. Different texts point to different dates and durations; Diodorus narrates it in two sections, under 358/7 and 356/5, and probably his sections actually belong to the campaigning seasons of 356 and 355. He states that Rhodes,
Chios, Cos and Byzantium rose against Athens (we have no other evidence that
Cos was a member of the League, but it is not unlikely). In the background
was Mausolus of Caria, for whom the Greek world provided the easier option
for expansion after the collapse of the Satraps' Revolt (Dem. XV. *Lib. Rhod.* 3;
Erythrae's honours for Mausolus, *IK. Erythrai und Klazomenai* 8 = R&O 56,
may have been awarded at this time). An Athenian fleet under Chares blockaded Chios, but was decisively beaten at sea, and Chabrias (not a general,
despite Diodorus, so the date must be 35<u>6</u>/5) was killed (Diod. Sic. XVI. 7.
iii–iv; Chabrias Nep. XII. *Chab.* 4. i, cf. Dem. XX. *Leptines* 82). In 355 the
rebels took the offensive, raiding Lemnos, Imbros and other islands and besieging Samos. Athens sent Timotheus, Iphicrates and Menestheus with sixty ships
to join the sixty under Chares (making the largest Athenian fleet known in the
period 404–323). They headed for Byzantium and the rebels followed; at
Embata, between Chios and the mainland, the others refused to fight owing to
bad weather, and Chares had to withdraw or fought and was defeated. He
denounced his colleagues, who were deposed and recalled for trial (cf. p. 271),
and himself retired into the service of Artabazus the satrap of Dascylium, now
in revolt against Persia, but was recalled when the Persians protested. There was
a fear that Persia might in response support the rebels, so the war ended, with
Athens accepting defeat and several east Greek members leaving the League;
those to the south passed into the orbit of Mausolus (Diod. Sic. XVI. 21–22.

ii, Polyaenus *Strat.* III. 9. xxix; loss of members Isoc. VIII. *Peace* 16, Dem. XV. *Lib. Rhod.* 26; for Artabazus and Mausolus cf. pp. 323–5).

Before and during the war we find further garrisons in allied territory. It was probably in 357/6 (to fit what is known of his career) that Arcesine on Amorgus honoured Androtion, who had been governor for at least two years and had lent money without interest for purposes including the payment of a garrison (*IG* XII. vii 5 = R&O 51 ~ Harding 68): we do not know why Athens had subjected Arcesine to a governor and a garrison, but on my dating of the war and the inscription this will have been before the war. An Athenian decree of summer 357/<u>6</u>, during the war on all chronologies and arising out of the war, provides for one of the generals to take care of Andros, and for its garrison to be paid 'out of the *syntaxeis* in accordance with the resolutions of the allies' (*IG* ii² 123 = R&O 52 ~ Harding 69).

Defeats at sea and the secession of major allies suggest that Athens was weaker now than at any time since the Peloponnesian War. Isocrates' pamphlet (VIII) *On the Peace* belongs to this context: *c.*380 in his (IV) *Panegyric* he had foreshadowed the foundation of the League (cf. pp. 228–9), but now he wrote it off as a failure. True peace was needed, not a mere breathing space (§§16–26); Athenian imperialism with its *syntaxeis* and *synedroi* had not worked (§29); Athens should stop aiming to rule at sea, which was neither just nor possible nor expedient (§§64–94, 114–15) – but if Athens did so the Greeks would admire it so much that they would concede all that it wanted (§§22–3, 136–40). Xenophon's *Ways and Means* (*Poroi*), written about the same time, likewise claims that Athens needs peace, and that a policy of peace rather than war is more likely to make friends for Athens (§v). These works reflect the current mood in Athens: since Leuctra Athenian foreign policy had lost its way, and under a new generation of politicians ambitious foreign adventures were renounced and the priority was given to financial recovery (cf. pp. 332–3, 336).

The Last Years of the League

After the Social War the history of the League is bound up with that of Athens' dealings with Philip of Macedon: for the context cf. chapter 22. The Chalcidians of Olynthus seem to have left the League in the 360's as a result of Athens' revived ambitions in the north-east: an Athenian decree of 363/2 refers to 'the war against the Chalcidians and against Amphipolis' (*IG* ii² 110 = R&O 38. 8–9). In 357 Athens and Philip competed for their allegiance, and Philip was the winner (cf. R&O 50 ~ Harding 67), promising to capture Potidaea for them: he did that in 356, sending the Athenians home (Diod. Sic. XVI. 8. iii–v). By 352/1, however, Olynthus was encircled by Philip and worried, and it then made peace with Athens and rejoined the League (Dem. XXIII. *Aristocrates* 107–9, cf. *IG* ii² 211 = Tod 166. 1–3). After Philip had absorbed western and central Thrace, Cersebleptes in the east had come under threat; in 353/2, when Chares had captured Sestos, Cersebleptes ceded the Chersonese (except Cardia, on the isthmus) to Athens, and Athens sent cleruchs (Diod. Sic. XVI. 34. iii–iv, cf. references to Athenian *archontes* in Dem. XXIII. *Aristocrates* 159–61).

In 349/8 Philip moved against Olynthus, and there was renewed trouble in Euboea. Demosthenes, who by this time wanted to strike against Philip as near as possible to the heart of Macedon, considered Olynthus the more important, but most Athenians attached a higher priority to Euboea: in the event, Euboea passed out of the Athenian orbit and Philip captured Olynthus. Refugees from Olynthus went to Athens (*IG* ii² 211 = Tod 166, as normally restored) and to Lemnos (*IG* XII. vii 4 ~ Harding 81).

Athens still had friends, inside and outside the League: there are records of crowns dedicated in Athens by various cities between 354/3 and 345/4 (*IG* ii² 1437. 10–18, 1438. 15–16, 1441. 5–18, 1443. 89–122). We happen to know that Mytilene was ruled by an anti-Athenian oligarchy in the late 350's (Dem. XIII. *Organisation* 8, XV. *Lib. Rhod.* 19) and then by a tyrant ([Dem.] XL. *Boeotus. ii.* 37); but in 347/6 the tyranny was overthrown, perhaps with help from Athens, and Mytilene rejoined the League (*IG* ii² 213 = Tod 168 ~ Harding 83).

When Athens made peace with Philip in 346, nominally to end the war over Amphipolis, the League was involved. Athens chose a representative of the allies (from Tenedos) to serve on the first embassy to Philip (Aeschin. II. *Embassy* 20). The *synedrion* wanted to wait until the results of Athens' attempts to build up an alliance against Philip were known, but it would then accept whatever Athens decided; Athens followed Demosthenes in putting proposals to Philip's representatives as soon as they arrived (Aeschin. II. *Embassy* 60–2). The *synedrion* then wanted a peace which any Greek state could join within three months, but Demosthenes, after establishing that Philip would not accept that, gained approval for a more limited peace. That more limited peace was between Philip and his allies and Athens and its allies ([Dem.] VII. *Halonnesus* 31, cf. Dem. XIX. *Embassy* 278). Some Athenians hoped to interpret that to cover every state with which Athens had an alliance, including Phocis and Halus, with which Philip had not been prepared to make peace. Officially, however, 'Athens and its allies' meant the League: Cersebleptes tried but was not allowed to join the League in time to be included in the peace, and then the *synedrion* swore to the peace on behalf of the allies (Aeschin. II. *Embassy* 82–90, III. *Ctesiphon* 73–4). Later, when Philip offered to renegotiate the peace, the Athenians ensured the failure of the negotiations by making demands which Philip could not accept, applying the principle of possessing what belongs to a state to Amphipolis and also to the island of Halonnesus, which Philip offered to give to them but they said he must 'give back', since it belonged to them by right ([Dem.] VII. *Halonnesus*: Amphipolis §§24–9).

At the end of the 340's the cities of Euboea returned once more to the Athenian side. Callias of Chalcis, who hoped to form a Euboean league, fell out with Philip and turned to Athens. In 342 Philip enabled unpopular leaders to take control of Eretria and Oreus, but in 341 Athens overthrew them, and Callias was able to include these cities in his league with a special affiliation to the

Athenian League, by which they paid *syntaxeis* only to the Euboean League (Philoch. *FGrH* 328 FF 159/160 ~ Harding 91/92, Charax *FGrH* 103 F 19 ~ Harding 91, Dem. IX. *Phil. iii.* 57–62, Aeschin. III. *Ctesiphon* 89–105 with schol. 85, 103, Diod. Sic. XVI. 74. i). That was an unusually generous arrangement, and Aeschines complains that Demosthenes deprived Athens of the *syntaxeis*, but the Athenians had been generous on previous occasions when they were anxious to keep cities loyal (cf. Methone in the 420's, p. 177; Calchedon and its neighbours in 408, p. 148). Elsewhere Aenus, on the coast of Thrace, deserted Athens for Philip *c.*341 ([Dem.] LVIII. *Theocrines* 37–8); but an Athenian decree of 340/<u>39</u> praises Tenedos, which has lent money to Athens and is therefore not to be subjected to any exactions or assessed by the *synedrion* for *syntaxeis* until the loan has been repaid (*IG* ii^2 233 = R&O 72 ~ Harding 97).

In 339 Philip's entry into the Fourth Sacred War led to an alliance between Athens and Thebes once more; but in 338 he defeated them at Chaeronea, and his victory put an end to the League (cf. Paus. I. 25. iii), with Athens and all the other mainland Greeks except Sparta enrolled in the League of Corinth under Philip's leadership.

Isocrates' last major work, (XII) *Panathenaic*, was written *c.*342–339, and aimed to show that it was Athens rather than Sparta that had benefited the Greeks (§§24, 96, 112). In §§53–69, 88–94, he contrasts Athens' conduct in the Delian League favourably with Sparta's conduct after the Peloponnesian War; he scarcely mentions the Second League, except to say that when Sparta's supremacy was ended two or three Athenian generals copied the Spartans' bad habits (§§100–1).

NOTE ON FURTHER READING

For general studies of Athenian policy in the fourth century see E. Badian, 'The Ghost of Empire: Reflections on Athenian Foreign Policy in the Fourth Century BC', in Eder (ed.), *Die athenische Demokratie im 4. Jahrhundert v. Chr.*, 79–106; P. Harding, 'Athenian Foreign Policy in the Fourth Century', *Klio* lxxvii 1995, 105–25.

For the beginning of the fourth century see R. Seager, 'Thrasybulus, Conon and Athenian Imperialism, 396–386 BC', *JHS* lxxxvii 1967, 95–115; G. L. Cawkwell, 'The Imperialism of Thrasybulus', *CQ*^{2} xxvi 1976, 270–7.

On the Second Athenian League Marshall, *The Second Athenian Confederacy*, is still useful; see also Larsen, *Representative Government*; Cargill, *The Second Athenian League* (believing that after the closing of the inscribed list there were no further members and that Athens kept its promises to the members).

On the League's foundation I follow D. G. Rice, 'Xenophon, Diodorus and the Year 379/378 BC', *YCS* xxiv 1975, 95–130 (foundation after Sphodrias' raid), against G. L. Cawkwell, 'The Foundation of the Second Athenian Confederacy', *CQ*^{2} xxiii 1973, 47–60 (foundation before Sphodrias' raid, as in Diod. Sic. XV. 28–9). For a recent attempt to settle the chronology of the later 370's see C. M. Fauber, 'Deconstructing 375–371 BC: Towards An Unified Chronology', *Ath.*^{2} lxxvii 1999, 481–506. On the chronology of Androtion's career, Athens' recovery of Euboea and the Social War I follow G. L. Cawkwell, 'Notes on the Social War', *C&M* xxiii 1962, 34–49: among other views, earlier dates had been proposed, for Androtion's year in the council with effects for Euboea and the Social War, by E. Schweigert, 'Greek Inscriptions, 4. A Decree Concerning Elaious', *Hesp.* viii 1939, 12–17; D. M. Lewis, 'Notes on Attic Inscriptions, xiii. Androtion and the Temple Treasures', *BSA* xlix 1954, 39–49.

19

Thebes and Northern Greece

500	475	450	425	400	375	350	325	300

395 Corinthian War begins in Greece
387/6 Peace of Antalcidas
382 Spartan occupation of Thebes
379/8 liberation of Thebes
371 Sparta defeated by Thebes in battle of Leuctra
367 Thebes wins support of Persians but Greeks reject peace treaty
364 Thebes defeats Pherae in battle of Cynoscephalae; Pelopidas killed
362 stalemate battle of Mantinea; death of Epaminondas

The Boeotian Federation to the Peace of Antalcidas and the Spartan Occupation

By 519 there was a Boeotian federal state, and Plataea gained an alliance with Athens when it resisted pressure to join the federation (Hdt. VI. 108; date Thuc. III. 68. v). In 480–479 the principal officials of the federation, the boeotarchs, are attested (Hdt. IX. 15. i, Paus. X. 20. iii), but the Thebans later blamed their going over to the Persians on a ruling clique of a few men, contrasted with what they called 'an oligarchy based on legal equality' (*dynasteia*: Thuc. III. 62. iii). Boeotia came under the control of Athens *c.*457 but broke away in 447/6 (cf. pp. 44, 51–2); and there was then reconstituted a federation which lasted until the Peace of Antalcidas in 387/6.

Thebes (2 units on its own account + 2 on account of Plataea and its dependencies)	4
Orchomenus and Hyettus	2
Thespiae with Eutresis and Thisbae	2
Tanagra	1
Haliartus, Lebadea, Coronea	1
Acraephnium, Copae, Chaeronea	1

Fig. 5 The electoral units of the Boeotian federation in the late fifth and early fourth centuries

Its organisation in the 390's is set out by *Hell. Oxy.* 19. ii–iv ~ Harding 15: it differed from Athens and its demes in that Boeotian cities had a greater degree of separate existence and independence than Athenian demes (they could, for instance, issue their own coins as Athenian demes could not). There were eleven electoral units (see fig. 5 and map 7). However, in 424 Chaeronea had been dependent on Orchomenus (Thuc. IV. 76. iii), and we may guess that before the destruction of Plataea in 427 (cf. p. 109) Thebes had two out of a total of nine units. There were also lesser cities, dependent on one or another of the greater (e.g. Mycalessus, dependent on Tanagra), which were not directly represented in the federation. Each unit provided one boeotarch (in the last two units the cities were represented in turn) and sixty members of the federal council; and the army and every aspect of the federation were based on these units. There was a property qualification for citizenship; in the individual cities the citizens were divided into four councils, which took it in turn to act as the probouleutic body; and we learn from Thucydides (V. 38. ii) that the federal council was divided into quarters in the same way. The boeotarchs were powerful officials; in the cities it is not clear whether there were assemblies or only meetings of the four councils; there is no sign of a federal assembly.

In the Peloponnesian War the Boeotians had been allies of Sparta. The Thebans, in addition to securing the destruction of Plataea, had incorporated dependent communities by synoecism (*Hell. Oxy.* 20. iii), and had interfered in Thespiae, where there were Athenian sympathisers (Thuc. IV. 133. i, VI. 95. ii). In 412/1 they had taken over Oropus, on the borders of Attica (Thuc. VIII. 60. i); in 404 it was made independent (cf. Lys. XXXI. *Philon* 9), but they recovered it in 402/1 and eventually incorporated it in Thebes (Diod. Sic. XIV. 17. i–iii). During Sparta's occupation of Decelea, in the last years of the Peloponnesian War (cf. pp. 140–1), they had seized the opportunity to acquire deserting slaves and movable property from the Attic countryside (*Hell. Oxy.* 20. iv–v). At the end of the war they were among the allies of Sparta who would have liked to see Athens totally destroyed (Xen. *Hell.* II. ii. 19).

But it did not suit Sparta to destroy Athens, and the Boeotians like others were soon alienated: Thebes was one of the cities which defied Sparta by harbouring democratic refugees from Athens (*Hell. Oxy.* 20. i, Diod. Sic. XIV. 6), and the Boeotians joined Corinth in refusing to contribute to Pausanias' campaign against Athens and Agis' second campaign against Elis (Xen. *Hell.* II. iv.

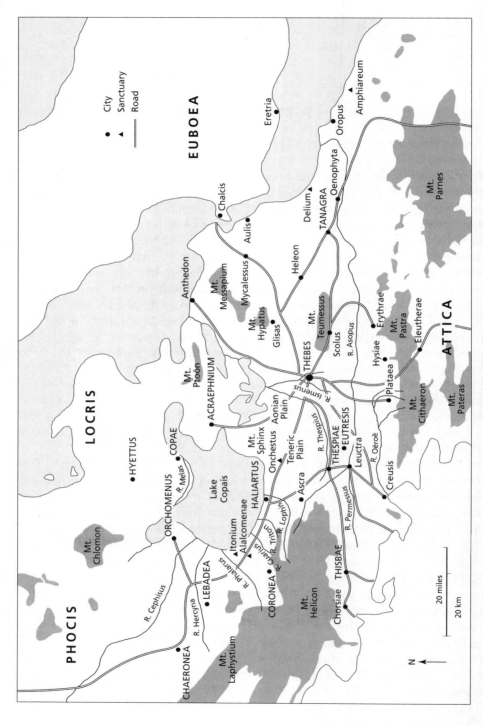

Map 7 Boeotia (block capitals denote cities formally represented in the pre-386 federation)

30, III. ii. 25: cf. pp. 205, 259). The *Hellenica Oxyrhynchia* contrasts a pro-Spartan party led by Leontiades and others with an opposing party, 'accused of atticising but not in fact pro-Athenian', led by Ismenias and others. The pro-Spartan party had been dominant during the war, but after it the other party grew in power, in Thebes and in the rest of Boeotia (20. i–ii). The climax came when Agesilaus set out for Asia Minor in 396, and the Boeotians not only refused to contribute soldiers but also interfered with his sacrifice at Aulis (Xen. *Hell.* III. iv. 3–4, Plut. *Ages.* 6. vi–xi: cf. p. 208).

Boeotia was one of the places visited by Timocrates with money from Pharnabazus (*Hell. Oxy.* 10. ii, 21. i, Xen. *Hell.* III. v. 1: cf. p. 192), and in 395 the Boeotians supported Locris against Phocis and brought about the Corinthian War (cf. pp. 209–10). Lysander, before he was defeated and killed at Haliartus, won over Orchomenus to the Spartan side; Agesilaus, recalled from Asia Minor to fight in Greece, travelled by land round the north of the Aegean: he was successful enough at Coronea to continue to the Peloponnese, but Sparta then abandoned Greece north of the Isthmus.

Lysander's success at Orchomenus suggested that Boeotia, which under Thebes was hostile to Sparta, might be broken up; and so, when Sparta turned to diplomacy in 392, the terms proposed were that all islands and cities should be autonomous: this was intended to mean that the federation should be broken up, and the Thebans objected (Xen. *Hell.* IV. viii. 14–15). In 392/1 Sparta was prepared to allow the rest of the federation to survive if Orchomenus could secede (Andoc. III. *Peace* 13, 20): Andocides suggests that the Boeotians accepted this, but probably, as in the case of Athens, the Boeotian representatives in Sparta accepted but they still had to gain the approval of the council. In the Peace of Antalcidas in 387/6 there was no concession to Boeotia: Thebes wanted to swear for the whole of Boeotia, but Agesilaus did not allow it, and when he threatened to invade the Thebans did accept the treaty and Sparta's interpretation of it (Xen. *Hell.* V. i. 31–3). We are not told how far the Spartans went in applying the principle of autonomy to Boeotia, but may guess that they were not interested in those lesser cities which were subordinate to one of the greater, and left their status unchanged. However, an independent Plataea was refounded, and families which had been granted Athenian citizenship returned (Paus. IX. 1. iv); and presumably Oropus was made independent too.

Thebes was sufficiently cowed to assist in the Spartan attack on Mantinea in 385 (Plut. *Pel.* 4. v–viii, Paus. IX. 13. i). Ismenias and Leontiades remained at the head of their opposing parties (both polemarchs in Xen. *Hell.* V. ii. 25), and Ismenias remained influential enough for Thebes to be in touch with Olynthus, and to refuse to join in Sparta's campaign of 382. Leontiades invited Phoebidas, as he was marching north with part of Sparta's advance force, to occupy Thebes, and he did so. Agesilaus was certainly responsible for Sparta's acceptance of what had been done, and may have approved the plan in advance. A Spartan garrison was installed on Thebes' acropolis, the Cadmea, and pro-Spartan régimes were installed in the other cities; Ismenias was condemned as a mediser for accepting Timocrates' money in the 390's, and three hundred of his supporters fled to Athens, where Leontiades' party managed to have one of them murdered (cf. p. 213).

The Revival of Thebes and the Federation; Jason of Pherae

Although in general Xenophon says little about Thebes, he regarded Sparta's occupation of the Cadmea as wicked, and gives a detailed account of the liberation. Phillidas, secretary to the ruling board of polemarchs, met Melon, one of the exiles, in Athens, and Melon enlisted a few collaborators, among them Pelopidas. In winter 379/8, when the polemarchs were holding a symposium to celebrate the end of the year, Melon and his associates were brought in, and each took a place beside one of the polemarchs and killed him; Leontiades was killed in his own house. The Spartan garrison commander called for help from Plataea and Thespiae, but help came for the other side from Athens, and he made a truce and left Thebes (cf. pp. 214, 229). To hamper Sparta's attempts to reassert control, early in 378 the Thebans constructed a ditch and stockade, running west–east for a considerable distance about 3 miles = 5 km. south of the city (Xen. *Hell.* V. iv. 38–41, 48–9).

We have looked above at those attempts, at Sphodrias' raid on Athenian territory (more probably incited by Cleombrotus, as stated by Diodorus, than by the Thebans, as claimed by Xenophon and Plutarch), and at Athens' institution of its Second League, with Thebes as a founder member. When the Athenians issued a prospectus for the League, early in 377, negotiations with Thebes were still continuing (*IG* ii² 43 = R&O 22 ~ Harding 35. 73–7): perhaps the Thebans were trying to join the League in the name of Boeotia, and Athens was resisting.

When the Boeotian federation was revived, it had an archon as its titular head and seven boeotarchs; and we now find not a federal council with proportional representation of the greater cities but a federal assembly. (At city level Thebes, at least, seems to have had a council as well as an assembly: Xen. *Hell.* VII. iii. 5–12, Diod. Sic. XVII. 9. i.) Some have supposed that the seven boeotarchs represent the old electoral units without Orchomenus and Thespiae, but that is hard to reconcile with there already being seven in 371 (Paus. IX. 13. vi–vii). All known boeotarchs of the revived federation were Thebans: probably the units were not used, the boeotarchs could in theory come from any city, but an assembly meeting in Thebes and dominated by Thebans usually if not always elected Thebans. On account of its being governed by an assembly rather than a council, the revived federation has often been considered democratic, but there is little evidence to support this. The pro-Spartan régimes in Thebes and the other cities are referred to as a tyranny (Xen. *Hell.* IV. iv. 2, Thebes) or a *dynasteia* (§46, the other cities); but as the Thebans showed in the 420's the opposite of such a régime need not be democracy (cf. Thuc. II. 62. iii–iv). There is no reason to think that the property qualification for citizenship in the cities and the federation was abandoned; the combination of a limited citizen body with a citizen assembly is reminiscent of Athens' intermediate régime of 411–410 (cf. pp. 164–5); the main effect of the change from council to assembly will have been to strengthen the position of Thebes within the federation.

How soon the federation was set up and how quickly cities were incorporated in it is uncertain. Plutarch has boeotarchs in 378, immediately after the liberation (*Pel.* 13. i, 14. ii); but according to Isocrates (XIV. *Plataic* 29) the Thebans at first assured the Spartans that they would not disturb 'any of the previous agreements', presumably the Peace of Antalcidas and Sparta's application of it to Boeotia. Xenophon has Thebes campaigning against Thespiae and other cities early in 377 (*Hell.* V. iv. 42–4). When Pelopidas died in 364, that is said to have been his thirteenth year as boeotarch (Plut. *Pel.* 34. vii). Despite the claim that he served every year (Diod. Sic. XV. 81. iv), we know that he was not boeotarch in 371; but it may be that that was his only year out of office, and in that case Plutarch will be wrong to write of boeotarchs in 378, and the federation (however extensive) and the office will have been revived in 377.

In the fourth century fighting was increasingly done by mercenaries, who were more professional than citizen soldiers but less likely to remain loyal. Thebes now tried to combine the advantages of citizens and mercenaries by creating a body of three hundred citizen hoplites, allegedly all homosexual couples, maintained on the Cadmea, known as the *hieros lochos* (commonly referred to in English as the sacred band). This was created by Gorgidas and at first regularly commanded by Pelopidas, and it proved highly successful until it was annihilated at Chaeronea in 338 (Plut. *Pel.* 18–19, Polyaenus *Strat.* II. 5. i). In 375 Pelopidas took the sacred band and a few cavalry to attack the still pro-Spartan Orchomenus while its Spartan garrison was away; on learning that the Spartans were returning he withdrew, but the two forces met at Tegyra: the Spartans with two of their army's six *morai* outnumbered the Thebans and were overconfident, but the Thebans defeated them (Plut. *Pel.* 16–17, Diod. Sic. XV. 37. i–ii; omitted by Xen. *Hell.*).

The Thebans then moved to attack Phocis, and Sparta sent Cleombrotus with the rest of the Spartan army to defend it (Xen. *Hell.* VI. i. 1, cf. ii. 1); but things were going badly for Sparta, and Athens was beginning to feel uncomfortable with an increasingly powerful Thebes as an ally, so Persia's proposal of a renewal of the King's Peace was accepted (cf. p. 196). Diodorus' claim that, after an argument between the Theban Epaminondas and the Athenian Callistratus, Thebes was excluded because it demanded to swear for Boeotia (XV. 38. iii) is a contamination from the peace of summer 371. On this occasion Thebes was included: presumably as Thebes, and presumably it made a show of dismantling the Boeotian federation which it had been reviving.

The show did not last long. The refounded Plataea, like the earlier city, inclined to Athens rather than to Thebes, and in 373/2 the Thebans destroyed it and its inhabitants again fled to Athens (Diod. Sic. XV. 46. iv–vi, Paus. IX. 1. v–viii). This prompted Isocrates' (XIV) *Plataic*, in which we read that Thespiae and Tanagra have been 'made subordinate to Thebes', presumably

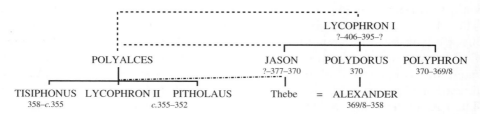

Fig. 6 Tyrants of Pherae (Polyalces was either a brother or a son of Lycophron I; Tisiphonus, Lycophron II and Pitholaus were probably sons of Polyalces, adopted by Jason when he inherited Polyalces' wife)

forced into the federation (§§8–9); pressure on Thespiae continued, and it is possible that by 371 the city had been destroyed and its citizens dispersed in scattered settlements (cf. Xen. *Hell.* VI. iii. 1, 5, Diod. Sic. XV. 46. vi, 51. iii; Thespians at Leuctra but allowed to withdraw, Paus. IX. 13. viii). However awkwardly, Thebes remained a member of Athens' League, providing ships for Timotheus in 373 and a chairman for the *synedrion* on the last day of 373/2̲ (cf. p. 235).

By now Thebes had as an ally Jason, the ruler of Pherae in south-eastern Thessaly (perhaps named after that famous legendary Thessalian, Jason the Argonaut). Thessaly, a fertile region in north-eastern Greece, continued for a long time to be dominated by land-owning aristocrats, and was traditionally organised in four regional units known as tetrads; there were large settlements in the east in the archaic period, but the development of cities as important entities began in the fifth century, in particular Larisa, Pharsalus and Pherae. In the last years of the Peloponnesian War Lycophron had become tyrant of Pherae, 'wanting to rule the whole of Thessaly'; he was opposed particularly by Larisa, where the Aleuadae family was dominant, but won a major battle at the time of an eclipse, in September 404 (Xen. *Hell.* II. iii. 4). The Aleuadae were supported by king Archelaus of Macedon (cf. Thrasymachus, 85 B 2 DK, Arist. *Pol.* V. 1311 B 17–20; also [Herodes], *Peri Politeias*). If, whoever wrote it, *Peri Politeias* is well informed, Sparta too may have tried to establish a link with Larisa; but at some point Sparta had an alliance with Lycophron (Xen. *Hell.* VI. iv. 24), and in the early 390's put down a revolt in Heraclea and installed a garrison in Pharsalus (Diod. Sic. XIV. 38. iv–v, 82. vi). In 395 Medius of Larisa was at war against Lycophron, gained the support of the Corinthian War coalition and conquered Pharsalus; since Agesilaus was able to pass through Thessaly to Boeotia in 394, it may have been afterwards that the coalition took Heraclea and returned it to the neighbouring Trachinians (Diod. Sic. XIV. 82. v–vii).

We next hear of Thessaly in the 370's, when Jason had succeeded his father Lycophron in Pherae. He had helped a man called Neogenes to become tyrant of Histiaea, at the north end of Euboea. Neogenes was unpopular, and the

Spartans expelled him; Histiaea therefore resisted incorporation in the Athenian League in 377, when the other cities of Euboea joined (Diod. Sic. XV. 30, cf. p. 233; it joined in 375). In Pharsalus, perhaps during the Olynthian war, a pro-Spartan tyrant called Polydamas had come to power, and seems to have ruled well. Xenophon reports an appeal by him in 375 for support against Jason: with Polydamas' support Jason could easily become *tagos* of all Thessaly (an old military office which he was resuscitating for his own purposes); the Boeotians and others were Jason's allies, and the Athenians would like to be but he thought he could become more powerful at sea (which renders the restoration of his name in an erasure in the list of League members unlikely); if the Spartans sent a substantial Spartan army, the cities would desert Jason, but it would be pointless to send merely liberated helots commanded by a private citizen. Sparta could not send the help asked for, and Jason did become *tagos* and proceeded to raise large forces from the cities of Thessaly (Xen. *Hell.* VI. i. 2–19; cf. pp. 215, 234). By 373 Jason was friendly with Athens, if not a member of the League: he went there in 373/2 to speak for Timotheus at his trial ([Dem.] XLIX. *Timotheus* 10), and the Athenian force sent to Corcyra during the winter probably travelled through Thessaly as well as Molossis (Xen. *Hell.* VI. ii. 10). Jason's expansion took him into Perrhaebia, the mountainous region between Thessaly and Macedon, where he dictated terms to king Amyntas (Diod. Sic. XV. 57. ii, 60. ii, cf. Isoc. V. *Philip* 20, Arr. *Anab.* VII. 9. iv).

In 372/1 as in 375 the Thebans moved against Phocis. In July 371 the Athenians invited the Thebans to join them at a peace conference in Sparta; the Thebans were represented by Epaminondas (making his first certain appearance in history, though there are stories pushing his career back many years earlier). He did originally agree to a treaty in which the Thebans were to participate as Thebans; when he returned and asked to have 'Thebans' changed to 'Boeotians', that led to an argument with Agesilaus and the exclusion of the Boeotians (cf. pp. 196–7, 216, 235). Sparta had sent king Cleombrotus to defend Phocis; since the treaty required the withdrawal of forces, he asked what he should do, and was ordered to attack Thebes if it would not leave the Boeotian cities autonomous. He avoided the Theban army and reached Leuctra, south of Thespiae; but there in August Epaminondas defeated him in one of the most pivotal battles in Greek history (cf. p. 216).

Exactly how the Thebans defeated the Spartans it is hard to make out from the sources. It is at any rate clear that, whereas the nature of hoplite equipment encouraged phalanxes to shift to the right, and the right wing was regularly the strong wing (cf. p. 128), the Thebans concentrated their attack on the left, with an unusually deep formation (this time fifty men: they had used deep formations before) and the sacred band at the front on the wing; and, after an initial cavalry skirmish in which the Spartans were driven back, the Theban cavalry were used to guard the held-back right wing of their phalanx. The Spartans were unable to cope with this reversal of normal tactics (Xen. *Hell.* VI. iv. 10–15, Plut. *Pel.* 23, Paus. IX. 13. iii–xii, Diod. Sic. XV. 55–6).

The Thebans announced their victory to allies not involved in the battle, Athens and Jason. Athens gave the messenger an icy reception; Jason hurried south with land and sea forces, but a strong Thebes would have been a threat to him, so instead of helping Thebes to defeat the reserve forces sent from Sparta he negotiated for the Spartans' withdrawal (Xen. *Hell.* VI. iv. 19–26: Diod. Sic. XV. 54. v–vii has Jason arriving and arranging a truce, after which Sparta's reinforcements join Cleombrotus and the battle is fought). Jason returned home, making a show of force in Phocis and Locris, and capturing Heraclea (Xen. *Hell.* VI. iv. 27, Diod. Sic. XV. 57. ii). He 'persuaded the Thessalians to lay claim to the leadership of Greece' (Diod. Sic. XV. 60. i–ii, cf. Xen. *Hell.* VI. iv. 28); there may even have been a suggestion that he would undertake the war against Persia after which Isocrates and others had been hankering (Xen. *Hell.* VI. i. 12, cf. pp. 228–9). He planned to attend and preside over the Pythian games at Delphi in 370, perhaps hoping to reinvigorate the Amphictyony rather than, as Xenophon suggests, to plunder the sacred treasures; but before the festival he was assassinated at a cavalry review, leaving contemporaries and us to wonder what he would have achieved if he had lived. Certainly he had united Thessaly and was making it a force to be reckoned with – but strong leaders can inspire fear, and his killers were honoured in the Greek cities (Xen. *Hell.* VI. iv. 29–32, Diod. Sic. XV. 60. v).

After Leuctra

Thebes/Boeotia did not participate in the common peace organised by Athens in autumn 371 (cf. pp. 197–8); and, whether it resigned or was expelled or no formal step was taken, Thebes ceased to belong to the Second Athenian League. Instead it built up its own alliances in central Greece: Diodorus mentions Phocis, Locris and Aetolia (XV. 57. i), and Xenophon gives a list of allies who joined in the invasion of Laconia in 370/69, beginning with 'Phocians, made subject, and Euboeans from all the cities' (*Hell.* VI. v. 23, cf. Diod. Sic. XV. 62. iv): the Euboeans too must have left the Athenian League. There are signs that Thebes organised its allies in a league, with a *synedrion*: a speech in Xenophon's *Hellenica* refers to a 'common resolution of the allies' (VII. iii. 11), and Byzantium's contributions to Thebes in the Third Sacred War were brought by its *synedroi* (*IG* vii 2418 = R&O 57 ~ Harding 74. 11, 24). Within Boeotia, the Thespians took refuge in a stronghold called Ceressus, but that was captured by Epaminondas, and references in the orators suggest that the survivors were expelled from Boeotia (Paus. IX. 14. ii–iv, cf., e.g., Isoc. VI. *Archidamus* 27). When Diodorus says that the Thebans intended to enslave Orchomenus but were dissuaded by Epaminondas and included it among their allies (XV. 57. i), this probably means that it was forced to join the Boeotian federation. In 364 aristocratic refugees from Thebes joined the knights of Orchomenus in a plot; but this was betrayed to the boeotarchs, and, in the absence of Epaminondas and Pelopidas and to the disapproval of at least Epaminondas, the city was captured, the men were killed and the women and children were enslaved (Diod. Sic. XV. 79. iii–vi, cf. Paus. IX. 15. iii).

We have seen that in winter 370/69 the new Arcadian federation and its allies, when their appeal to Athens was rejected, gained the support of Thebes and its central Greek allies for the attack on Sparta which resulted in the liberation of Messenia, and the Thebans gained some of the credit for the foundation of Megalopolis, in south-western Arcadia (cf. p. 218). Pelopidas and Epaminondas were among the boeotarchs and commanders of this expedition: on their return they were prosecuted because they had not been in Thebes to leave office at the end of the year, but they were acquitted (Nep. XV. *Epam.* 7–8, Plut. *Pel.* 24–5, *Sayings of Kings and Commanders* 194 A–C). It was probably in summer 369 that Epaminondas went south again, and took part in the fighting in the north-eastern Peloponnese (cf. p. 218). On his return he was again prosecuted: this time he was accused of taking bribes to spare Sparta, and was deposed and not re-elected boeotarch for 368 (Diod. Sic. XV. 72. i–ii).

In Thessaly Jason on his death in 370 had been succeeded by his brothers Polydorus and Polyphron, of whom the latter soon killed the former. Polyphron, who 'made the *tageia* like a tyranny' and intervened in both Pharsalus and Larisa, was in 369/8 killed and succeeded by Polydorus' son Alexander, who became 'a harsh *tagos* to the Thessalians, and a harsh enemy to the Thebans [immediately] and the Athenians [later]' (Xen. *Hell.* VI. iv. 33–5, cf. Diod. Sic. XV. 60. v, 61. ii). The Aleuadae of Larisa appealed first, in 369, to Alexander II of Macedon, who responded by taking over Larisa and Crannon for himself (Diod. Sic. XV. 61. iii–v). They then appealed to Thebes, and an army was sent under Pelopidas (who had been a friend of Jason: Plut. *Pel.* 28. v–x): he took over Larisa, fought and negotiated inconclusively with Alexander of Pherae, mediated between Alexander of Macedon and his rival Ptolemy, and imposed on this Alexander an alliance under which he sent hostages to Thebes. It was perhaps now that the Thessalians opposed to Pherae were organised in a *koinon* (Diod. Sic. XV. 67. iii–iv, Plut. *Pel.* 26, but Aeschin. II. *Embassy* 26–9 shows that Philip must be one of the hostages taken from Ptolemy in 368; on Macedon cf. p. 297).

Alexander of Macedon was assassinated, and was succeeded by Ptolemy (cf. p. 297). In 368 Pelopidas and Ismenias went as envoys: first to Macedon with mercenaries, where Ptolemy tried to outbid them for the mercenaries but came to terms and sent further hostages; then to Alexander of Pherae, who arrested them. While Thebes sent an army, Alexander made an alliance with Athens, which sent ships and men to support him, and would have liked to send the soldiers sent to the Peloponnese by Dionysius I of Syracuse. The Thebans were abandoned by their Thessalian allies and withdrew, pursued by Alexander; Epaminondas, serving this year as a private soldier, was elected commander and extricated the army (Diod. Sic. XV. 71–72. ii, Plut. *Pel.* 27–29. i, Paus. IX. 15. i–ii, cf. Xen. *Hell.* VII. i. 28). In 367 Epaminondas returned as boeotarch commanding an army: Alexander released Pelopidas and Ismenias, and offered peace and alliance; Epaminondas agreed only to a thirty-day truce, but took no further action when it expired (Diod. Sic. XV. 75. ii, Plut. *Pel.* 29, Paus. IX. 15. i–ii). On the Athenian side, Isocrates considered Alexander a possible leader of a Greek crusade against the Persians (Speusippus, *Letter to Philip* 13).

In 366 Epaminondas returned to the Peloponnese, attacking Achaea and making it an ally; he did not interfere in the cities' internal affairs; afterwards at the Arcadians' prompting the Thebans set up anti-Spartan democracies, but the oligarchs recovered control and made alliances with Sparta (cf. p. 219: this is Epaminondas' first appearance in Xen. *Hell.*).

In 369/8 Philiscus, sent to Greece by Ariobarzanes, after failing to arrange a common peace spent his money on mercenaries for Sparta (cf. pp. 198, 218); but in 367, when Sparta sent a delegation to the King, Pelopidas, returned from Thessaly, headed a rival delegation from Thebes and its allies, and won over the King to an anti-Spartan stance (this is his only appearance in Xen. *Hell.*). In particular, having defeated Sparta and having been opposed by Athens in the north, the Thebans now wanted to challenge Athens, and one of the proposals was that the Athenian navy should be beached. Other proposals annoyed other Greeks; in winter 367/6 the Arcadians walked out of the conference held in Thebes, and Corinth took the lead in refusing to swear to the treaty. Corinth and its neighbours did make peace with Thebes, but refused to make an alliance, in 365 (cf. pp. 198–9, 219–20, 236).

The challenge to Athens continued. Oropus, presumably made independent of Thebes under the Peace of Antalcidas, was in Athens' hands by 373/2. When Themison of Eretria seized it on behalf of a body of exiles in 366, it was entrusted to Thebes, and in the ensuing arbitration Epaminondas successfully defended Thebes' right to it (cf. p. 237). Diodorus records a speech of Epaminondas, persuading the Thebans to build a hundred triremes and enlist the support of Rhodes, Chios and Byzantium: it is not clear whether the hundred ships were built, but in a naval campaign in 364 he drove away an Athenian fleet. There are undatable decrees in which Cnidus appointed him *proxenos* and the Boeotians appointed a Byzantine *proxenos*; also one in which the Boeotians appointed a Carthaginian *proxenos* – but that need have nothing to do with the naval policy (cf. pp. 237–8; the inscriptions are *SEG* xliv 901, *SEG* xxxiv 355, *IG* vii 2407 = R&O 43 ~ Harding 48).

Thebes' northern interests extended to Delphi. The temple of Apollo there had been destroyed by fire and/or earthquake in 373/2 (Parian Marble *FGrH* 239 A 71); in 371 one Spartan proposed that Cleombrotus should attend to that rather than to the Boeotians (Xen. *Hell.* VI. iv. 2), and in 368 that was one of the matters raised with the Athenians by Dionysius I of Syracuse (*IG* ii² 103 = R&O 33. 8–10); the Amphictyony of mostly central Greek peoples responsible for Delphi began collecting funds for the rebuilding in 367/6 (e.g. *C. Delphes* ii 4 = R&O 45 ~ Harding 60). The Thebans built a treasury at the south-west corner of the site to commemorate their victory at Leuctra; and near Sparta's navarchs monument (cf. p. 152) dedications were set up in the 360's by the Arcadians and the Argives (Paus. X. 11. v, 9. v–vi ['Tegeans'], 10. v). In 363/2 after a period of stasis some aristocrats of the *polis* of Delphi were expelled, and took refuge in Athens (*IG* ii² 109 = *SIG*³ 175, an Athenian decree explicitly denying the legality of their expulsion); and it was perhaps in 360/59 that Thebes was granted *promanteia*, precedence in the consultation of the oracle (*SIG*³ 176). In the 350's fines imposed by the Amphictyony on enemies of Thebes were to provoke the Third Sacred War (cf. pp. 302–4).

Alexander of Pherae had a run of successes in Thessaly, so in 364 his opponents appealed to Thebes again, and in July, though an eclipse of the sun was seized on by doubters, Pelopidas went with volunteer cavalry and mercenaries. At Cynoscephalae, west of Pherae, he was victorious but was killed, and the Thebans then sent a major army which won a second battle. The Thessalians gave Pelopidas a lavish funeral, and dedicated a statue of him at Delphi; Alexander was allowed to survive, but as a subordinate ally of Thebes and with his power restricted to Pherae (Diod. Sic. XV. 80, Plut. *Pel.* 31–35. iv; statue *SEG* xxii 460 ~ Harding 49). In 362 and 361 Alexander turned to attacking the Athenians by sea, and in 361/0 they broke off their alliance with him and made one with the *koinon* (cf. p. 238).

Relations between the Arcadians and Thebes had been worsening, and before he was killed in 366 Lycomedes of Mantinea had made an alliance between Arcadia and Athens (cf. p. 219). In 363 a split opened in Arcadia between a Mantinean faction which was unhappy about using temple funds from Olympia to pay Arcadia's professional citizen soldiers, the *eparitoi*, and was inclining towards Sparta, and a Tegean faction which was happy with the use of the sacred funds and remained loyal to Thebes. In 362 Epaminondas went to the Peloponnese with an army from Thebes and its allies, including Thessalians both from the *koinon* and from Pherae, but not including the Phocians, who claimed to have only a defensive alliance with Thebes (Xen. *Hell.* VII. v. 4); Mantinea was supported by Sparta and its allies including Athens. After both sides had marched and counter-marched from Arcadia to Laconia and back, a battle was fought outside Mantinea: when Epaminondas seemed likely to repeat the success of Leuctra, he was killed, and the result was a stalemate. Thebes continued to support the Tegean faction, sending Pammenes in 361 to force back citizens of Megalopolis who were trying to return to their original homes (cf. pp. 220–1).

This was not the end of Thebes' supremacy – it remained the most ambitious and powerful city in Greece until, by the end of the Third Sacred War, it was exhausted despite being on the winning side – but Pelopidas and Epaminondas were both dead, and much of Thebes' success had been due to them. While Xenophon minimised the importance of both, Diodorus gave them their due (obituaries of Pelopidas XV. 81. i–iv, of Epaminondas XV. 88, cf. 39. ii–iii). Earlier both were praised by Polybius (Pelopidas for opposing Alexander, VIII. 35. vi–viii; Epaminondas at Mantinea, IX. 8; Thebes' short-lived success due to them, not to the constitution, VI. 43. v–vii); and Nepos and Plutarch wrote lives of both (but Plutarch's *Epaminondas* has not survived). They are praised, by writers for whom 'democracy' need mean nothing more specific than constitutional government as opposed to tyranny, as champions of freedom and democracy, and Paus. IX. 15. vi quotes the inscription on a statue base of Epaminondas, ending, '. . . and the whole of Greece is autonomous in freedom'. It can at least be said that they are not associated with the worst episodes, the reversal of Epaminondas' original decision on Achaea and the treatment of Orchomenus; but in general they stood for a powerful Thebes. The new federation was dominated by Thebes as the old had not been; and the Thebans were willing to use force against opponents both inside and outside Boeotia, and to exploit the principles of the common peace as the Spartans and Athenians had done before them. Pelopidas and Epaminondas were not, of course, without opponents in Thebes: our sources mention Meneclidas, who is accused of jealousy but may have had genuine disagreements with them on policy (Nep. XV. *Epam.* 5. ii–vi, Plut. *Pel.* 25).

The greatest legacy of this Theban supremacy was a weakened and isolated Sparta. Improvements on traditional hoplite tactics were to be developed further by Philip of Macedon; Thessaly had been made a field for Greek and Macedonian intervention, and Thessaly and Delphi were to bring Philip into Greece.

NOTE ON FURTHER READING

On Thebes and Boeotia in general, see, before 371, Buck, *Boiotia and the Boiotian League*; after, Buckler, *The Theban Hegemony*. On the cities of Boeotia see M. H. Hansen, 'An Inventory of Boeotian *Poleis* in the Archaic and Classical Periods', in Hansen (ed.), *Introduction to an Inventory of Poleis*, 73–116.

On the organisation of the Boeotian federation before the Peace of Antalcidas see also Bruce, *Historical Commentary on the Hellenica Oxyrhynchia*, 102–18, 157–64; Larsen, *Greek Federal States*, 26–40. On Pelopidas and Epaminondas see G. L. Cawkwell, 'Epaminondas and Thebes', CQ^2 xxii 1972, 254–78. On the Leuctra campaign see J. M. Buckler, 'Plutarch on Leuctra', *SO* lv 1980, 75–93; Lazenby, *The Spartan Army*, ch. 9; C. J. Tuplin, 'The Leuctra Campaign; Some Outstanding Problems', *Klio* lxix 1987, 72–107. That after Leuctra Thebes organised its allies in a league is argued by D. M. Lewis, 'The Synedrion of the Boeotian Alliance', in Schachter (ed.), *Essays in the Topography, History and Culture of Boiotia*, 71–3; that it did not is argued by Buckler, *The Theban Hegemony*, 222–33, and 'The Phantom *Synedrion* of the Boiotian Confederacy, 378–335 B.C.', in *Polis and Politics . . . M. H. Hansen*, 431–46.

On Thessaly see Westlake, *Thessaly in the Fourth Century BC*; Sprawski, *Jason of Pherae*. There is a text of [Herodes], *Peri Politeias*, in Meyer, *Theopomps Hellenika*, 202–8.

20

Athens After the Peloponnesian War

500	475	450	425	400	375	350	325	300

410–399	revision of laws
404–403	régime of Thirty
400/399	trials of Andocides and Socrates
c.380's–370's	institution of *proedroi*
367–363	change in appointment of principal secretary
361	exile of Callistratus

The Thirty and the Restoration of the Democracy

Xenophon, who may have served in the cavalry under the Thirty (e.g. *Hell.* III. iv. 2–7; for his horses cf. *An.* III. iii. 19), gives a detailed account in *Hell.* II. iii. 11–iv; Diodorus and Justin follow Ephorus (who was not here using *Hell. Oxy.*) in giving accounts favourable to Theramenes, who played an important part in making peace with Sparta and bringing the régime into existence but then fell out with the extremists; *Ath. Pol.* 34–8 has a version in which the order of events is changed to minimise Theramenes' responsibility for the Thirty's misdeeds, and has an additional board of Ten invented to portray Rhinon in a good light (cf. pp. 259–60), but 39–40 contains valuable information on the reconciliation; Lysias' speeches (XII) *Against Eratosthenes* and (XIII) *Against Agoratus* are important. The term Thirty Tyrants, often found in modern books, is apparently due to Ephorus: fourth-century Athenians referred to them as 'the oligarchy' or 'the Thirty'.

Probably Athens' peace treaty with Sparta in 404 did not prescribe a change of constitution (Xen. *Hell.* II. ii. 20, Diod. Sic. XIII. 107. iv, Andoc. III. *Peace* 11–12, contr. *Ath. Pol.* 34. iii, Diod. Sic. XIV. 3. ii, vi, Just. *Epit.* V. 8. v); but it may have contained some reference to tradition which could be exploited to imply the 'traditional constitution' (cf. p. 161), and, since the democracy had lost the war and for the foreseeable future the navy was to be unimportant, the change is not surprising. The treaty did require the restoration of exiles, mostly oligarchs from 411–410, among them Critias (cf. pp. 166–7). The council of 405/4 is said to have had an oligarchic bias (Lys. XIII. *Agoratus* 20); a man called Agoratus was used to give evidence against prominent democrats (Lys. XIII. *Agoratus*); in the upper-class *hetaireiai* five 'ephors' (using a Spartan word) were appointed, and with 'phylarchs' as tribal agents they intimidated citizens before meetings of the assembly (Lys. XII. *Eratosthenes* 43–7).

Early in the summer, with that champion of narrow oligarchies Lysander present, an assembly was held at which Dracontides proposed the appointment of a board of thirty, to revise the constitution and in the meantime to act as a provisional government. Theramenes spoke (not against, as his apologists alleged); Lysander remarked that, by not demolishing the walls soon enough, the Athenians were in breach of the treaty, and they must accept the change; opponents walked out; and the motion was carried. According to Lysias the Thirty were to be ten nominated by Theramenes, ten nominated by the 'ephors' and ten chosen from those present (a show of representing all shades of opinion); we have a list of the Thirty, including Critias, Dracontides and Theramenes, which as far as it can be checked is compatible with the suggestion that they comprised three from each tribe (Xen. *Hell.* II. iii. 2 [list], 11, Diod. Sic. XIV. 3. v–4. i, *Ath. Pol.* 34. iii, Lys. XII. *Eratosthenes* 71–6).

Xenophon agrees with the sources most favourable to Theramenes that the new régime began mildly, but there is no sign of mildness in Lys. XII. *Eratosthenes*, where it is claimed that Theramenes was as bad as the other oligarchs. Officials and a council of five hundred were appointed; the Thirty did not draw up a new constitution, but they annulled the laws which had weakened the council of the Areopagus (cf. pp. 35–9), and they removed from the laws qualifying clauses (e.g. those invalidating a will drawn up under improper pressure), according to *Ath. Pol.* because these provided opportunities for jurors to exercise discretion. They condemned democrats denounced by Agoratus, but also 'sycophants' accused of making a living through prosecutions and threats of prosecution (Xen. *Hell.* II. iii. 11–12, Diod. Sic. XIV. 4. ii, *Ath. Pol.* 35. i–iii, Lys. XIII. *Agoratus* 34–5).

If Xenophon has the right order of events, the degeneration began with the request (opposed by Theramenes) for a Spartan garrison. A reign of terror began; when Theramenes protested, Critias and others drew up a list of three thousand men who were to retain some rights; after a further protest those not on the list were disarmed. When Theramenes objected to a plan to kill rich metics for their money (for the plan cf. Lys. XII. *Eratosthenes*, esp. 5–8), he was denounced at a meeting of the council by Critias. Theramenes replied, Critias did not trust the council to condemn him but removed him from the three thousand and then, in the name of the Thirty, condemned him (Xen. *Hell.* II. iii. 13–56, cf. Diod. Sic. XIV. 4. iii–5. iv). Theramenes was a controversial figure at the time and has remained so ever since: a man of principle or a trimmer who finally guessed wrongly? It is at any rate possible that he was genuinely unhappy both with full democracy and with extreme oligarchy, and that, when memories of 411 were still fresh and he was the man who had made the treaty which had ended the war, he thought that in 404 he would be able to get the kind of régime that he wanted, but the extremists were too ruthless for him.

Those not on the list of the three thousand were excluded from the city, and many went into exile, given refuge in defiance of Sparta's orders by Megara, Argos and Thebes. The democrats' fight back began during the winter of 404/3, when Thrasybulus (for whose earlier career cf. pp. 165–7) with about seventy supporters set out from Thebes and occupied Phyle, on the slopes of Mount Parnes in north-western Attica. Gradually more men joined him; an attempted blockade was frustrated by a snowstorm; when his force had grown to seven hundred he made an attack on the oligarchs' camp and defeated them (Xen. *Hell.* II. iv. 1–7, Diod. Sic. XIV. 5. v–6, 32–33. i). The Thirty grew worried, and prepared two possibilities for a safe retreat by sentencing to death all the men of Eleusis and Salamis (Xen. *Hell.* II. iv. 8–10, Diod. Sic. XIV. 32. iv, Lys. XII. *Eratosthenes* 52, XIII. *Agoratus* 44). A few nights after his victory Thrasybulus took advantage of the demolished walls to move to the Piraeus, and occupied Munichia, the hill on the side towards Phalerum. After the restoration there was to be a distinction between the 'men of Phyle', who had joined Thrasybulus when that was still a risky thing to do, and the 'men of Piraeus' (e.g. the opening lines of R&O 4; Harding 3 translates a different reconstruction). The oligarchs attacked, but they were beaten off, and Critias was among those killed (allegedly his funeral monument depicted Oligarchy setting fire to Democracy and had an inscription referring to the *hybris* of the accursed *demos*: schol. Aeschin. I *Tim.* 39 [82 Dilts] = Critias 88 A 13 DK).

The three thousand, or a body claiming to represent them, deposed the Thirty, most of whom withdrew to Eleusis, and to replace them elected a new board of Ten. There may have been hopes among the democrats that the Ten would be more tractable, but if so the hopes were not fulfilled. There was further skirmishing; the democrats' numbers continued to grow, and they prepared to besiege the city. Both the city and the oligarchs at Eleusis appealed to Sparta, and Lysander arranged for money to be lent for hiring mercenaries, while he went by land to Eleusis and his brother Libys went by sea. Later, however, king Pausanias gained the support of three of the ephors, and took an army of Spartans and allies to Athens (but the Boeotians and Corinth refused). After making a show of force, he arranged for both sides to send envoys to Sparta, and Sparta sent commissioners to help him make a settlement (Xen. *Hell.* II. iv. 10–38, Diod. Sic. XIV. 33. ii–vi, cf. Lys. XII. *Eratosthenes* 58–61). *Ath. Pol.* 38 distinguishes between the original Ten, who proved hostile to the democrats, and a second Ten, including Rhinon, who worked for reconciliation:

Rhinon managed to continue his career under the democracy, and this is presumably a device to separate him from the original anti-democratic stance of the Ten.

The settlement of summer 403 was that the democracy was to be restored in Athens but, for those unhappy with that arrangement, Eleusis was to be available as a semi-independent state; there was to be an amnesty for all except the Thirty, the Ten and those officials most closely associated with them, and even for them if they successfully submitted to *euthynai* (Eratosthenes, attacked by Lysias [XII] for killing Lysias' brother Polemarchus, was one who attempted this: we do not know the outcome). To ease the settlement Archinus foreclosed on the period during which withdrawal to Eleusis was allowed, and he introduced the procedure of *paragraphe*, under which a defendant could plead for a prosecution in breach of the amnesty to be disallowed (Isoc. XVIII. *Callimachus* 2–3). Thrasybulus wanted to be generous in rewarding citizens and non-citizens who had fought on his side, but Archinus resisted that too, and eventually, in 401/0, limited rewards were decreed, probably including citizenship for non-citizens who had been at Phyle (*IG* ii² 10 = R&O 4 ~ Harding 3). In that year the oligarchs at Eleusis hired mercenaries to attack Athens, but those in the city marched out against them and Eleusis was once more fully incorporated in the Athenian state (Xen. *Hell*. II. iv. 38–43, *Ath. Pol*. 39–40).

We know from a fragment of a speech by Lysias (XXXIV. *Traditional Constitution*) that a man called Phormisius proposed that citizenship should be restricted to landowners; but the full democracy was restored, and indeed with the number of citizens halved by the plague and the war the exclusion of the *thetes* from offices was no longer enforced (*Ath. Pol*. 7. iv–8. i). However, Pericles' citizenship law (cf. p. 55), allowed to lapse during the war, was reaffirmed and strengthened (*Ath. Pol*. 42. i, Dem. LVII. *Eubulides* 30, [Dem.] LIX. *Neaera* 16). The state officially made a fresh start: oaths were sworn, the laws were to be applied to acts committed in and after 403/2, and Athens officially adopted the Ionian alphabet (the alphabet which we regard as the standard Greek alphabet) in place of its local alphabet (Theopompus *FGrH* 115 FF 154–5), thus formalising what was in fact a long process already under way. We shall see that the understanding of democracy was to change after the middle of the fourth century, but after 411–410 and 404–403 nobody active in politics would admit to being an opponent of democracy.

Laws and Decrees

On the first restoration of the democracy, in 410, the Athenians had begun to compile their first coherent code of laws since the time of Solon. What was perhaps envisaged as a short and simple task turned out not to be, and was still unfinished when the Thirty came to power (cf. p. 166). They began a legal reform of their own (cf. p. 258). In 403 the democratic compilation was resumed, and the code and the religious calendar associated with it were completed in 400/399 (see particularly Lys. XXX. *Nicomachus*, accusing one of the commissioners of malpractice in connection with the compilation; Andoc. I. *Myst.* 81–9).

In the sixth and fifth centuries laws were made by decree of the assembly, and the same enactment could be termed law (*nomos*) or decree (*psephisma*, 'thing voted') according to how one thought of it. The procedures used between 403 and 399 involved boards of *nomothetai*, 'law-enacters' (Andoc. I. *Myst.* 83–4); the Athenians decided to make a distinction between (superior) laws and (inferior) decrees (Andoc. I. *Myst.* 87, 89), and set up a procedure for enacting further laws, by *nomothetai* after the assembly had set the machinery in motion, after 399. The word *nomos* embraces law and custom. Herodotus had observed that different peoples have different *nomoi* and each consider their own the best (III. 38); many of the sophists of the late fifth century had contrasted *nomos*, as human convention, which could have been decided otherwise, with *physis*, nature, which is unalterably as it is, and some had represented laws as a device used by some members of society to constrain others, as regulations which one might disobey if it was to one's advantage and one could get away with it (for variations on that theme see *P. Oxy.* xi 1364 = Antiphon the Sophist 87 B 44 DK, Hippias of Elis in Pl. *Prt.* 337 D 1–3, Thrasymachus in Pl. *Resp.* I and Callicles in Pl. *Grg.*). That way lay the jungle, and the distinction between laws and decrees, in Athenian practice and in Aristotle's philosophy (e.g. *Eth. Nic.* V. 1137 B 11–29, *Pol.* IV. 1292 A 4–37), was in part an attempt to rescue law for the respectable side of the fence. It may also have been an attempt to make future attacks on the democracy more difficult.

The theory was that permanent decisions applicable to all should be embodied in laws, decisions for particular occasions or particular individuals in decrees (cf. also the orators, e.g. Dem. XXIII. *Aristocrates* 86–7, 218). In practice, I suspect, the code of 399 was taken as a starting-point, so that it required a law to modify the code of laws, but other matters – including all questions of foreign affairs, even treaties intended to last for ever – could still be decided by decrees. One area which was regulated by law was finance: there are decrees which add to the burden of the assembly's expense account (on which cf. p. 263) and call on the *nomothetai* to increase the allocation to that account (e.g. *IG* ii^2 222. 41–52). Our corpus of inscribed laws from fourth-century Athens is gradually growing, but we still have far more decrees than laws. The evidence for fourth-century law-making is problematic, but it seems likely that at first the procedure was so restrictive that it was rarely used; later it was made easier and was used more frequently. Procedures for detecting and eliminating contradictions suggest that the Athenians aimed to have a coherent code with no contradictions, but by the third quarter of the century that aim was no longer achieved, and in 330 conflicting laws on the proclamation of crowns could be cited (Aeschin. III. *Ctesiphon* 32–48, Dem. XVIII. *Crown* 120–1; cf. p. 342).

The procedure for the enactment of decrees by the assembly after *probouleusis* by the council remained as it had been in the fifth century (cf. pp. 57–8); but the use of ad hoc boards of *syngrapheis* to draft some decrees was discredited by the *syngrapheis* who ushered in the oligarchy of 411, and instead in the fourth century the assembly sometimes instructed the council to produce a *probouleuma* for the next meeting (e.g. *IG* ii^2 125 = R&O 69 ~ Harding 66). The language of inscribed decrees becomes more informative, and by the second half of the century a distinction had become established between formulae mentioning the council, used when the assembly enacted what had been recommended to it by the council ('Resolved by the council and people', etc.: e.g. *IG* ii^2 110 = R&O 38), and formulae not mentioning the council, used when the assembly enacted something not recommended by the council, either because it rejected or rewrote the council's recommendation or because the council's *probouleuma* was open and made no recommendation ('Resolved by the people', etc.: e.g. *IG* ii^2 337 = R&O 91 ~ Harding 111, where an open *probouleuma* is followed by the assembly's decree). Fourth-century decrees are divided fairly evenly between the two categories, which suggests that council and assembly were both taking their decision-making duties seriously (but from the middle of the third century the assembly tended to rubber-stamp the council's recommendations).

Institutional Changes

The last change in the constitution chronicled by the *Athenaion Politeia* was the restoration of democracy in 403, 'from which the constitution has continued to that in force today, continually increasing the power of the masses' (41. ii). Certainly there was no single point at which a major change in the constitution occurred, until the failure of a rising against Macedon led to the introduction of an oligarchic régime in 321; but there were a number of single changes at different points. It is hard to maintain that Athens became ever more democratic. Some scholars have argued that, on the contrary, the democracy of the fourth century was less extreme than that of the fifth; I argue that changes made in the early fourth century were in the spirit of the fifth-century democracy, but some changes made later (cf. pp. 328–36, 339–40) were not.

Soon after the restoration payment was introduced by Agyrrhius for the one civic duty for which it had not been provided before, attendance at the assembly: originally 1 obol but raised to 2 and then to 3 by the time of Aristophanes' *Ecclesiazusae*, in the late 390's (*Ath. Pol.* 41. iii, Ar. *Eccl.* 183–8, 289–92, etc.). Payment was not for all who attended, but for a limited number or perhaps for those who arrived by a specified time: the aim may have been to encourage punctual attendance as much as a large attendance, but after the recent bouts of oligarchy it was no doubt considered important to strengthen the democracy's assembly. Payment for holding many routine offices is not positively attested in the fourth century, and some have argued that many of the old stipends were abolished, but more probably the silence is accidental. Most of the payments which are attested had been increased by the time of the *Athenaion Politeia* (62. ii), but jurors' pay remained the 3 obols fixed by Cleon (cf. pp.

55–6; also 118–19). The assembly needed six thousand or more men to attend on the same day (which will have become harder to achieve from the reduced number of citizens at the end of the Peloponnesian War: cf. p. 260), as the courts did not, and it appears that 3 obols were still sufficient to attract the numbers of jurors that were needed.

More will be said about financial matters later (cf. pp. 328–35), but one important change belongs to the early fourth century. In the fifth century there was a single state treasury, into which revenue was paid and from which expenditure was made on the authorisation of the assembly; *c*.411 that was amalgamated with the treasury of the Delian League (cf. pp. 59, 94). In the fourth century there was a *merismos* (allocation) of funds to different spending authorities – the assembly, the council, etc. – which were free to use their funds as long as they presented satisfactory accounts at the end of the year (*Ath. Pol.* 48. i–ii; first attested in *IG* ii² 29 = R&O 19, of 386). This devolved budgeting suggests that the Athenians were thinking about what they could afford to spend in different areas; but the combination of devolved budgeting and insufficient funds produces inflexibility, since if all the money has been allocated it is impossible to provide more in one area without taking away from another.

During the first half of the century two changes were made in the organisation of government. In the second half of the fifth century meetings of the council and assembly had been presided over by the *prytaneis*, the fifty members of the council from one tribe who served as standing committee for a tenth of the year (cf. p. 58). That was still the case probably at the time of Aristophanes' *Ecclesiazusae* (*prytaneis* 86–7, no mention of *proedroi*), and possibly until *c*.384/3 (possible date of law in [Dem.] LIX. *Neaera* 89). Not later than 379/8 that duty had been transferred to a new board of *proedroi*, 'presidents', one member of the council from each tribe except the current prytany, picked by lot each day (*Ath. Pol.* 44. ii–iii; first attested *CSCA* v 1972, 164–9 no. 2).

Until at least 368/7 inscriptions show that the principal secretary of the Athenian state, responsible for publishing decrees and laws, was a member of the council, elected for one prytany from a tribe other than the current prytany; by 363/2 the secretary was appointed by lot for a whole year and from the whole citizen body, but before long each tribe in the regular order was in turn providing the secretary (*Ath. Pol.* 54. iii; decrees of 368/7 *IG* ii² 104 = Tod 134 contr. *IG* ii² 105 + 523, 106, 107 = R&O 34, –, 31 ~ Harding 52, –, 53; decrees of 363/2 *IG* ii² 109, 110, 111 = R&O –, 38, 39 ~ Harding –, –, 55). For the old-style secretary the standard title was 'secretary of the council'; for the new either that could be used or 'secretary by the prytany' (a strange title for the new secretary, which has to be interpreted as meaning 'prytany by prytany' throughout the year), and in the hellenistic period this second title became standard. *Ath. Pol.* 54. iv mentions a secretary 'in charge of the laws'; but laws like decrees were published by the principal secretary, and inscriptions attest a parallel secretary 'in charge of the decrees' (e.g. *IG* ii² 223 *C* = *Agora* xv 34. 3, 1700. 216 = 43. 230); neither is found before the middle of the century. *Ath. Pol.* 54. v mentions an elected secretary who read out documents at meetings of the council and assembly: this was important when papers could not be distributed, and was considered a skilled job.

Proedroi whose identity was not known before the day of the meeting could not be bribed (cf. below, on jurors); but there is no indication that the *prytaneis* were accused of taking bribes or were considered dangerously powerful, and the creation of the *proedroi* was probably a further embodiment of the fifth-century principle of distributing work as widely as possible. Efficiency was not a high priority in democratic Athens (cf. p. 59); but expecting each tribal contingent of councillors to contain at least one man capable of serving as the principal secretary for just one prytany in his life, while it tells us something about expectations of literacy among politically active Athenians, was perhaps an excessive defiance of efficiency. The change to a secretary who, though still not eligible for reappointment, served for a whole year and was appointed from the citizen body at large, is one of a number of moves in the direction of efficiency which we see from the middle of the fourth century. There was a growing body of secretaries, serving the courts and various officials, and men attracted by this work could hold different secretarial posts in different years.

One judicial change we have noticed above: the introduction of *paragraphe* as a procedure to have a prosecution dismissed if, whatever its other merits, it was in breach of the amnesty of 403; later it was extended to allow other grounds for dismissal. There was a major change in the trial of private suits, those in which only the injured party could prosecute. In the fifth century the smaller cases had been decided locally by the thirty *dikastai kata demous*, the larger by a jury in the same way as public suits (cf. p. 55). But in the last years of the Peloponnesian War the *dikastai kata demous* stopped travelling to the demes, and the events of 404–403 made thirty an inauspicious number, so in the fourth century there were forty of them, and they continued to work in the city. For the larger private suits, for sums over 10 drachmae, a new procedure was created. Each citizen (probably only of hoplite status or above) spent his last year on the military registers, when he was aged 59, as a public arbitrator (*diaitetes*): the larger private suits went first to one of these, and then to a jury only if one of the parties appealed. This will have reduced the money spent on juries, at a time when Athens was short of money but had accepted the extra burden of paying for attendance at the assembly: the use of all men, or all but the poorest men, in a year-group as arbitrators was a substitute consonant with the fifth-century understanding of democracy (*Ath. Pol.* 53).

Another feature compatible with democratic principles was the increasingly elaborate way of assigning jurors to courts. Six thousand men over 30 years old were enrolled each year. In the late fifth century each magistrate had a panel of jurors assigned to him for the whole year, so that it will have been known in advance which jurors would decide which case. Bribery will have been easy, and there was a notorious instance in 410 or 409 (cf. p. 148). In the early fourth century the six thousand were divided into ten sections for the year, so that jurors would still have the same colleagues during the year, but sections were allotted to courts day by day (Ar. *Eccl.* 681–8, *Plut.* 277–8, 972). By the second half of the century the ten sections were still used, with approximately equal numbers in each tribe; each juror had a ticket (*pinakion*), bearing his name, demotic and section letter; and at the beginning of each day when the courts were to meet there were elaborate allotment procedures (some involving the placing of jurors' tickets in allotment-machines) to assign jurors and magistrates to courts. This will have made it impossible to predict which jurors would serve, with which colleagues, in which courts, for which magistrates; indeed, the development acquired a momentum of its own, and generated more levels of arbitrariness than were needed to achieve the desired result (*Ath. Pol.* 63–6; many bronze *pinakia* survive).

Fourth-century judicial procedures may have seen an increasing use of written documents. We cannot date changes, and in any case practices may have become increasingly frequent before they were made compulsory; but by the 350's it was a requirement that prosecutors should submit a written document when initiating their cases, and in court witnesses no longer gave their evidence orally but simply acknowledged the correctness of a document prepared in advance. Certainly when a private suit went to a court on appeal against an arbitrator's decision (*Ath. Pol.* 53. ii), and apparently when a public suit went to a court from the magistrate's preliminary hearing (a lid referring to an *anakrisis*), documents were placed in a sealed jar and only those documents could be used in the court.

Originally different bodies and officials had kept their own records; but late in the fifth century a new council-house was built beside the old, and the old came to be used as a central record office; the rebuilding and enlargement of the Pnyx, where the assembly met, is probably the work of the restored democracy (cf. p. 170).

Politics and Politicians

The split between political and military leaders which had begun in the generation of Cleon (cf. pp. 119–21) continued in the fourth century, and military leaders are often found taking employment abroad when not commanding for Athens. Civilian leaders are often referred to as *politeuomenoi*, 'politicians', or *rhetores*, 'speakers' (the latter already by Aristophanes, e.g. *Ach.* 38). This development presented problems for a *demos* which liked to control its leaders: officials were appointed for one year and were subject to various checks, and military officials, who could be reappointed, were appointed by election; but men who were simply habitual speakers in the assembly and lawcourts held no office through which they could be called to account, and if things turned out badly could claim that the decisions had been taken not by themselves but by the assembly or a jury.

Already in the early fifth century it had been possible to prosecute a leading man for deceiving the people, by promising a success which did not materialise

(Miltiades in 489: Hdt. VI. 136). By 415 there existed the *graphe paranomon*, which could be used against a decree and its proposer (cf. pp. 37, 58), and the fourth century added the *graphe nomon me epitedeion theinai* against a law and its proposer ('prosecution for enacting an inexpedient law', *Ath. Pol.* 59. ii; in fact either illegality or inexpediency could be alleged in either suit). The code of laws completed in 399 included a consolidated law on *eisangelia*, the procedure used for major offences against the state (cf. pp. 36–7), and one possible charge there was 'being a *rhetor* and taking bribes to speak contrary to the best interests of Athens' (Hyp. IV. *Euxenippus* 7–9, where Hyperides stresses that this is aimed at *rhetores* and not at ordinary citizens). When there was no concept of 'loyal opposition', and the understanding of gift-giving and bribery was such that giving bribes in the interests of one's own state was acceptable (cf. p. 52, on Pericles), it is not surprising that accusations of bribe-taking were frequently made and are hard for us to evaluate.

Aeschines invoked against Timarchus in 346/5 a *dokimasia* of *rhetores*, which we should perhaps see as an equivalent for non-office-holders of the *dokimasia* which men appointed to offices had to undergo (Aeschin. I. *Timarchus* 28–32; cf. the questions asked at the *dokimasia* of archons, *Ath. Pol.* 55. iii). This may have been instituted at the beginning of the century. There was no list of approved *rhetores*, to which politicians were added after passing a *dokimasia*, but if a man thought a *rhetor* unworthy he could institute a *dokimasia* against him; Aeschines' prosecution of Timarchus is the only known instance of this. Ostracism remained theoretically available, but was not used after 415 (*Ath. Pol.* 43. vi; cf. pp. 156–7). For the next century prosecutions of leading political and military figures were frequent, sometimes on charges directly connected with their public careers, sometimes on other charges but still with their public careers in the background. The Athenians did not distinguish clearly between political or military misjudgment or misfortune and illegal conduct, and charges such as speaking contrary to the best interests of Athens encouraged the blurring of that distinction.

As in the fifth century, there was nothing resembling the party politics and party organisation of modern states (though Athens came nearer to that in the time of Philip of Macedon than at other times: cf. p. 337). Politicians were perceived primarily as individuals, though particular men might be known for championing particular policies, such as friendship with Thebes, and might have particular associates and particular opponents. I believe that in the earlier part of the fourth century most men had similar hopes for Athens most of the time, but at crucial turning-points some men turned more promptly than others. (Most of what follows is focused on foreign affairs: for more details and references see chapters 16–19.)

Men prominent in the early years of the restored democracy included Thrasybulus, the leader of the returning democrats; Agyrrhius, the introducer of assembly pay and a councillor and secretary in 403/2; and Anytus, one of the men of Phyle. Archinus, a man of Phyle but careful to avoid democratic triumphalism (cf. p. 260), is not heard of afterwards.

There are two important trials known to us which were held in 400/399. Andocides had been involved in the religious scandals of 415 and had had oligarchic sympathies (cf. p. 158); he returned under the amnesty of 403 and held various religious offices; but he allegedly fell foul of the aristocratic Callias on personal grounds and of Agyrrhius by beating him to a tax-collecting contract. He could not now be prosecuted directly for what he had done in 415, but in autumn 400 his opponents claimed, probably wrongly, that his case was not covered by the amnesty: we have his defence (Andoc. I. *Myst.*) and part of a speech for the prosecution (Lys. VI. *Andocides*). His formal prosecutors were men with oligarchic connections, including Meletus (Andoc. I. *Myst.* 92–5); his supporting speakers were men of democratic respectability, including Anytus and perhaps Thrasybulus (Andoc. I. *Myst.* 150: 'Thrasyllus' MSS); he was acquitted.

In spring 399 the philosopher Socrates was prosecuted, accused of impiety in that he was religiously unorthodox himself and corrupted the young by teaching them his unorthodoxy (Xen. *Ap.* 10, Diog. Laert. II. 40). As formulated, that did not break the amnesty, but those whom Socrates was alleged to have corrupted included men involved in oligarchy, such as Alcibiades and Critias, and Socrates had himself remained in Athens under the Thirty, though he had not obeyed them (Pl. *Ap.* 32 C 4–D 8, cf. Xen. *Mem.* I. ii. 31–8), so the prosecution had a political dimension. Whether Socrates had ever held the views on heavenly bodies and on rhetoric as a skill to be used in bad causes as well as in good which are attributed to him in Aristophanes' *Clouds* remains uncertain, but some Athenians had come to be worried by such views. The formal prosecutor was Meletus, perhaps the prosecutor of Andocides (though the name is not rare), but associated with him was Anytus, one of Andocides' defenders. Notoriously, Socrates was convicted, and, since he did not propose a serious alternative penalty, condemned to death.

The author of the *Hellenica Oxyrhynchia* liked identifying groups of politicians and attributing political stances to them (cf. p. 247, on Thebes). For 396, when Demaenetus, allegedly with the secret backing of the council, was caught taking a trireme to join the Persian fleet commanded by Conon, he reports that the council denied responsibility. The distinguished and elegant = the respectable and property-owning were content with the status quo and did not want to quarrel with Sparta; a group centred on Thrasybulus, Aesimus and Anytus thought it would be dangerous to fall foul of Sparta, while a group including Epicrates, a man of Piraeus, and Cephalus, a defender of Andocides, had been eager for war even before they took Timocrates' money; and the many and democratic had been anti-Spartan but through fear acquiesced in the disowning of Demaenetus (*Hell. Oxy.* 9–10. ii: there is not much support for this division between rich and poor, but see Ar. *Eccl.* 197–8).

To make sense of Athenian politics it is worthwhile to see how far particular men are associated with particular policies, or are regularly found to be cooperating with or opposed to other men. In what follows I shall comment from this angle on Athens' involvement in the affairs of the wider Greek world in the first half of the fourth century (cf. above, esp. chapter 18).

In 395 Thrasybulus was no longer unwilling to quarrel with Sparta: he proposed the alliance with Boeotia, and commanded the Athenian force sent there (Xen. *Hell.* III. v. 16; Plut. *Lys.* 29. i, Paus. III. 5. iv). After the victory at Cnidus in 394 Conon became the first living man to be honoured with a statue in the agora. The comedian Plato represented Epicrates and Phormisius (the man who had proposed limiting citizenship to landowners) as receiving rich bribes from the Persian King (frs. 119–23 Kock/Edmonds = 127–31 Kassel & Austin), and Plut. *Pel.* 30. xii and Ath. VI. 251 A–B have a story of Epicrates' responding successfully in the assembly: interpreting fragments of a lost comedy is dangerous, but it is possible that this is not simply a comedian's fantasy and they did serve on an embassy to Persia.

Thrasybulus perhaps went through a period of unpopularity (cf. Ar. *Eccl.* 202–3, 356). When Sparta turned to diplomacy, the Athenian envoys who proposed accepting the revised terms of 392/1 included Andocides and Epicrates: the assembly, unwilling to abandon the Asiatic Greeks, rejected the terms and condemned them in absence; the prosecutor was Agyrrhius' nephew Callistratus, who was to become a leading figure in the 370's and 360's (Philoch. *FGrH* 328 F 149 ~ Harding 23). Aggressive policies followed. Iphicrates, the first commander of the mercenary force established at Corinth with Persian money, tried but failed to get control of the city; ships were sent to support Evagoras against the Persians in Cyprus; and in 390 Thrasybulus had his highly successful Aegean campaign, reminiscent of the fifth-century empire and extending to the Asiatic territory claimed by the Persians. He died in 389, and was given a lavish tomb in Athens (Paus. I. 29. iii), but there were accusations of embezzlement and suggestions that he might have become tyrant of Byzantium (cf. Lys. XXVIII. *Ergocles* 5, Ar. *Plut.* 550), and two men who had been with him were put on trial (Lys. XXVIII. *Ergocles*, XXIX. *Philocrates*). Agyrrhius succeeded him in the Aegean: he was not very successful, but the Athenians continued to take an active line in general. Iphicrates fought against Sparta in the Hellespont. Chabrias, a leading military commander from now until the mid 350's, went to support Evagoras against Persia *c.* 388, and the decrees for Erythrae and Clazomenae shortly before the King's Peace show that Athens did not want to abandon the Asiatic Greeks to the barbarians and had not changed its policy. Iphicrates was to establish a particular connection with Thrace, marrying the sister (probably) of the future king Cotys not later than 387/6 (Dem. XXIII. *Aristocrates* 129, Anaxandridas fr. 41 Kock/Edmonds = 42 Kassel & Austin).

In 387 Sparta tricked the Athenians and regained control of the Hellespont, and after that Athens did have to agree to the King's Peace and the abandonment of the Asiatic Greeks. Cephalus was the author of the amendment expressing indignation about the trick (*IG* ii² 29 = R&O 19). When Athens found a way forward in the new world after the Peace, he and Aesimus were two of the envoys sent to Chios to receive its oath to the alliance (*IG* ii² 34–5 = R&O 20 ~ Harding 31. 39–43). One man disappears from view for some time: Agyrrhius was found guilty of embezzling public money and, unable to repay, spent several years in prison (Dem. XXIV. *Timocrates* 135).

We learn from one of Lysias' speeches (XXVI. *Evandrus*) of an odd episode in 382. The man originally appointed archon for 382/1, Leodamas, on the oligarchic side in 404–403 (Arist. *Rh.* II. 1400 A 32–6), was successfully challenged in his *dokimasia* by a Thrasybulus (of the deme Collytus, whereas the more famous Thrasybulus was of Stiria; he was a man of Phyle, he was one of the generals tricked in 387, he had been Amphictyon of Delos, one of the men appointed by Athens to administer the sanctuary of Apollo there, and he appears in Aeschin. III. *Ctesiphon* 138–9 in a list of Theban sympathisers). The man appointed as substitute was Evandrus, more implicated in the oligarchy than Leodamas. He was challenged by a friend of Leodamas (Lysias' speech was written for this challenger) and defended by Thrasybulus – and his appointment was upheld. Twenty years after the event involvement with the Thirty could still be cited against a man, but it was clearly not the most important consideration.

Among those who supported the liberation of Thebes in 379/8 were Cephalus and a nephew of Thrasybulus of Collytus (Din. I. *Demosthenes* 38–9); and Thrasybulus served with the men involved in the organisation of the Second Athenian League on the embassy to Thebes of *IG* ii² 43 = R&O 22 ~ Harding 35. 72–7. Agyrrhius had emerged from gaol in time to be the proposer of the grain-tax law of 374/3 (*SEG* xlviii 96 = R&O 26); and his nephew Callistratus became one of the major figures of the 370's–360's. Diodorus includes in his account of the League's foundation the appointment as generals of Timotheus, Chabrias and Callistratus (XV. 29. viii), but he may be wrong to include Callistratus among the generals. Callistratus was active in politics in Athens – it was he who was responsible for at any rate the name of the *syntaxeis* collected after a while from the League members (Theopompus *FGrH* 115 F 98 = Harding 36) – while Timotheus and Chabrias in the early years commanded Athens' forces. Timotheus was Conon's son, here beginning his career, while Chabrias was the general most closely linked with Callistratus; both were honoured with statues, Chabrias for his victory off Naxos in 376, Timotheus for Alyzia in 375. Iphicrates was for many years an enemy of Timotheus ([Dem.] XLIX. *Timotheus* 66): he was sent to fight for Persia against the Egyptians when Chabrias was recalled from fighting for the Egyptians; in 373, when Timotheus was in trouble for not going promptly enough to Corcyra, Iphicrates, back from Egypt, joined Callistratus in prosecuting him ([Dem.] XLIX. *Timotheus* 9) – and Timotheus took over Iphicrates' position on the Persian side against the Egyptians. In 372 Iphicrates took Callistratus ('though not a friend') and Chabrias as fellow generals to Corcyra.

In summer 371 the Athenians were becoming worried about Thebes, and invited the Thebans to a peace conference in Sparta. Xenophon names eight Athenian delegates, who seem to have had a range of views, and gives speeches to three: the aristocrat Callias, full of his own importance; Autocles, hostile to Sparta as his family consistently was; and Callistratus, arguing successfully for reconciliation between Athens and Sparta (Xen. *Hell.* VI. iii). The only previous evidence for Callistratus' hostility to Thebes is that Diodorus has Thebes excluded from the peace of 375 after argument between him and Epaminondas (XV. 38. iii), but that is not to be relied on: it is better to see the Athenians in general as pro-Theban before 371 and anti-Theban after, and Callistratus as one of the first to make the change.

After Leuctra Callistratus had Iphicrates sent to oppose the Thebans' return from the Peloponnese in 370/69 ([Dem.] LIX. *Neaera* 27), and Iphicrates' lack of success suggests that he was unhappy with that task; Chabrias did better against the Thebans in 368. An Athenian commander in the Peloponnese in 366, Timomachus, was a son-in-law of Callistratus ([Dem.] L. *Polycles* 48). Callistratus himself was the proposer of the frustrating decree of 369/8 which explained to Mytilene Athens' change of alignment: the justification of opposition to Sparta in the 370's survives but the justification of Athens' new policy does not (*IG* ii^2 107 = R&O 31 ~ Harding 53. 35 sqq.). Not all Athenians accepted the change: in the alliance of 369 with Sparta Cephiosodotus, still afraid of Sparta, insisted on an alternation of command every five days rather than Spartan command on land and Athenian at sea (Xen. *Hell.* VII. i. 12–14). Unfortunately we know nothing about the Athenian delegates to the peace conference in Persia in 367: one, Timagoras, accepted rich gifts from the King, supported Pelopidas and was prepared to accept his proposed terms; the other, Leon, objected and on their return had Timagoras condemned.

In 366 we have the first attested appearance of a man who was to serve often as general during the next forty years, Chares. He was transferred from the Peloponnese for the unsuccessful attempt to recover Oropus for Athens; we do not know how they were connected with him or Oropus, but Callistratus and Chabrias were prosecuted and acquitted in connection with Oropus. The prosecutor was Leodamas, who had opposed Chabrias' honours in 376; Callistratus' defence is said to have inspired the young Demosthenes; Plato is said to have spoken for Chabrias (Arist. *Rh.* I. 1364 A 19–23, Plut. *Dem.* 5. i–iv, Diog. Laert. III. 23–4). Chares then failed in an attempt on Corinth; and in 361/0 he gained a bad reputation for supporting oligarchs in Corcyra. The politician to whom Chares seems to have been closest is Aristophon, active from the democratic restoration until he died at the age of about a hundred in the 330's but prominent from the late 360's onwards; he was allegedly prosecuted in seventy-five *graphai paranomon* but never convicted (Aeschin. III. *Ctesiphon* 194). At this time, after Chabrias had suppressed the original revolt in Ceos, he was sent back to deal with the further trouble and proposed the surviving decree. In connection with some aspect of this affair he was prosecuted by Hyperides (on whom cf. p. 337) and narrowly acquitted (*IG* ii^2 111 = R&O 39 ~ Harding 55; schol. Aeschin. I. *Timarchus* 64 [145 Dilts]; Hyp. IV. *Euxenippus* 28). He proposed a decree dispatching forces to the north in 36<u>2</u>/1 ([Dem.] L. *Polycles* 4–6), and prosecuted Leosthenes when he was defeated by Alexander of Pherae in 361 ([Dem.] LI. *Trierarchic Crown* 8–9).

At some time in the 360's Timotheus and Iphicrates were reconciled, and Timotheus' daughter married Iphicrates' son Menestheus ([Dem.] XLIX.

Timotheus 66). Both Timotheus and Iphicrates were involved in Athens' wars in the Aegean and the north, though never together. Many generals found themselves prosecuted for their failures in these wars, including Timotheus ([Dem.] XXXVI. *Phormio* 53).

Callistratus and Chabrias remained active to 362, but in 361 there was major trouble, of which we know only the outcome: Callistratus was prosecuted, probably on a charge of not speaking in Athens' best interests, and in his absence was condemned to death; he appears in exile to have helped the Macedonians to increase their tax revenues ([Arist.] *Oec.* II. 1350 A 16–23); later he risked returning to Athens but was put to death (Hyp. IV. *Euxenippus* 1–2, Lycurg. *Leocrates* 93). Chabrias left Athens in 361 to fight once more for the Egyptians against Persia.

Familiar names persist to the Social War of 356–355. In Athens' attempts to reach a satisfactory agreement with the successors of Cotys in Thrace, Chabrias, back from Egypt, in 358 accepted what Demosthenes called the worst terms yet (but seems not to have suffered for it); Chares in 357/6 achieved the final settlement, of which Demosthenes approved (Dem. XXIII. *Aristocrates* 163–73). In that year Chabrias and Iphicrates were among the generals who swore to the alliance with Carystus after Athens' success in Euboea (*IG* ii² 124 = R&O 48 ~ Harding 65. 19–23: on the list of generals who swore cf. p. 239). In the Social War, in 356/5 Chares was the general defeated off Chios, and Chabrias, not now a general, was killed. In 355 Timotheus, Iphicrates and Menestheus because of the weather refused to join Chares in fighting at Embata, where he was defeated. Chares then joined the Persian rebel Artabazus. Aristophon prosecuted the others; Timotheus was fined and went into exile, Iphicrates and Menestheus were acquitted, and Timotheus and Iphicrates both died soon after (Diod. Sic. XVI. 21, Nep. XI. *Iph.* 3. iii, XIII. *Tim.* 3, Isoc. XV. *Antid.* 129, Din. I. *Demosthenes* 13–14 = III. *Philocles* 17).

In general, there seems to be more long-term consistency in men's personal friendships and hostilities (though the reconciliation of Timotheus and Iphicrates warns us not to rely too much on that contention) than in their political stances (though some men remained friends of Thebes when that was no longer fashionable). The major turning-points in Athenian foreign policy are the abandonment of subordination to Sparta in the 390's and the realisation that Sparta was less of a threat than Thebes from 371 onwards, and here we see some men making the change sooner than others, though most Athenians did in the end make the change. On internal matters there is no evidence that in the early fourth century there were serious disagreements or that particular men stood for distinctive policies.

NOTE ON FURTHER READING

On the régime of the Thirty see Hignett, *History of the Athenian Constitution*, ch. 11 and apps. 13–14; Krentz, *The Thirty at Athens*.

On the working of the constitution in the fourth century see in general Sinclair, *Democracy and Participation in Athens*; Hansen, *The Athenian Democracy in the Age of Demosthenes*.

On laws and decrees see M. H. Hansen, '*Nomos* and *Psephisma* in Fourth-Century Athens', *GRBS* xix 1978, 315–30, 'Did the Athenian *Ecclesia* Legislate After 403/2?', *GRBS* xx 1979, 27–53 = his *The Athenian Ecclesia*, 161–76(–177), 179–205(–206). On the enactment of laws in the fourth century see the different views of D. M. MacDowell, 'Law-Making at Athens in the Fourth Century BC', *JHS* xcv 1975, 62–74; Rhodes, '*Nomothesia* in Fourth-Century Athens', *CQ*² xxxv 1985; M. H. Hansen, 'Athenian *Nomothesia* in the Fourth Century BC and Demosthenes' Speech Against Leptines', *C&M* xxxii 1971–80, 87–104, 'Athenian *Nomothesia*', *GRBS* xxvi 1985, 345–71.

For the suggestion that the purpose of assembly pay was to secure a punctual attendance rather than a large attendance see P. Gauthier, 'Sur l'institution du *misthos* de l'assemblée d'Athènes', in Piérart (ed.), *Aristote et Athènes*, 231–50. On the widespread continuation of payment for office-holding see M. H. Hansen, '*Misthos* for Magistrates in Classical Athens', *SO* liv 1979, 5–22, 'Perquisites for Magistrates in Fourth-Century Athens', *C&M* xxxii 1971–80, 105–25 (disbelieving); Gabrielsen, *Remuneration of State Officials in Fourth-Century BC Athens* (believing). On the *merismos* of revenue to different spending authorities see Rhodes, *The Athenian Boule*, 99–101. On the institution of the *proedroi* see *The Athenian Boule*, 25–7 with (1985 reissue) 306. On the secretaries see *The Athenian Boule*, 134–41; A. S. Henry, 'The Athenian State Secretariat and Provisions for Publishing and Erecting Decrees', *Hesp.* lxxi 2002, 91–118.

Among a great many studies of the trial of Socrates, see Guthrie, *A History of Greek Philosophy*, iii. 380–5; also Stone, *The Trial of Socrates* (regarding Socrates as an authoritarian élitist who deserved his fate). On politicians of the early fourth century see R. Sealey, 'Callistratos of Aphidna and His Contemporaries', *Hist.* v 1956, 178–203 = his *Essays in Greek Politics*, 133–63; Rhodes, 'On Labelling Fourth-Century ⟨Athenian⟩ Politicians', *LCM* iii 1978, 207–11. On politics and society see Strauss, *Athens After the Peloponnesian War*.

21
The Western Greeks from Dionysius I to Timoleon

500	475	450	425	400	375	350	325	300

410 (?)	first Carthaginian forces sent to Sicily
406/5	Dionysius appointed general in Syracuse
405	end of first Carthaginian war
c.397–392	second Carthaginian war
386	Dionysius I's capture of Rhegium
383/2–374 (?)	third Carthaginian war
368	Dionysius I begins fourth Carthaginian war
368/7	Dionysius I dies, succeeded by Dionysius II
357	exiled Dion returns to Sicily
354	Dion murdered
c.346	exiled Dionysius II returns to Syracuse
344	Timoleon arrives in Sicily
337	final victories of Syracuse under Timoleon; death of Timoleon

Sources

The west throughout this period is covered by Diodorus, but the unevenness of his treatment suggests that he did not follow the same source throughout, and there has been a good deal of inconclusive argument as to which sections derive from which sources. On western as on other matters, there are some short insertions into the narrative from a chronological source (cf. p. 15). In XIII. 34–XIV (412/1–387/6) his account is detailed and hostile to Dionysius: several times he cites Timaeus of Tauromenium (*FGrH* 566), who lived from the mid fourth century to the mid third; but he also cites Ephorus, whom he was following on Greece and the Aegean (the two contrasted XIII. 54. v, etc.), so perhaps he was using both – and probably behind both lay the favourable account of Dionysius' early supporter Philistus (*FGrH* 556). Book XV (386/5–361/0) is much briefer on Sicily, uncommitted on Dionysius and hostile to demagogues: it may be based on Ephorus without Timaeus, or else on the fourth-century Theopompus of Chios (*FGrH* 115), whose *Philippic History* included three books on the two Dionysii (cf. XVI. 71. iii). Within book XVI (360/59–336/5) there seems to be a mixture of sources, with Theopompus and Timaeus the principal but not the only candidates.

For Dionysius II and the liberators there are eulogising biographies of *Dion* and *Timoleon* by both Nepos and Plutarch: for *Dion* it appears that Heraclides' supporter Athanis (*FGrH* 562) underlies the hostile, later part of Nepos' life and Dion's supporter Timonides of Leucas underlies Plutarch's; both lives of *Timoleon* depend on Timaeus, directly and/or through a hellenistic biography.

We have independent fourth-century material in the Platonic *Letters* iii, vii, viii, which, whether or not they are by Plato, appear to be well informed, and in passages of Aristotle's *Politics*. The western Greeks were not given to inscribing public documents on stone, but there are relevant inscriptions from mainland Greece; and there are some interesting coins.

The Origins of the Syracusan Tyranny

Hermocrates of Syracuse led the resistance to Athens' Sicilian expedition of 415–413 (on which cf. pp. 132–40); he was deposed when the resistance seemed likely to fail, but was in favour though apparently not in office by the time the Athenians were defeated (Thuc. VI. 103. iv; VII. 21. iii, 73). What turned the tide was the arrival of forces from the Peloponnese led by the Spartan Gylippus. After the Athenians' defeat, the truth behind the accounts of Diodorus and Plutarch is probably that Hermocrates and Gylippus argued for more generous treatment of the captives, and the harsh treatment decided on was urged by Diocles (Diod. Sic. XIII. 19. iv–33. i, Plut. *Nic.* 28).

In 412 Hermocrates and others were sent with just twenty ships from Syracuse and two from Selinus to support the Spartans in the Aegean (a few more western ships followed), and he became critical of the Persian Tissaphernes and of Sparta's navarch Astyochus (Thuc. VIII. 26. i, 29. i, 45. iii, 84–5). In his absence there was a democratic revolution in Syracuse. Aristotle says the *demos* changed from *politeia* (his word for a compromise between democracy and oligarchy) to democracy (*Pol.* V. 1304 A 27–9); Diodorus has an account which confuses the Diocles of the late fifth century with an archaic lawgiver (XIII.

33. ii–iii, 34. iv–35), and all we can be sure of is an increase in the number of generals and allotment for civilian appointments. Either in 411 or in 410 Hermocrates and his colleagues were exiled and three men were sent to take over. Hermocrates joined the entourage of the Persian Pharnabazus (Thuc. VIII. 85. iii contr. Xen. *Hell.* I. i. 27–31, cf. Diod. Sic. XIII. 63. i–ii).

While Syracuse became involved in a war with the cities to the north (cf. Diod. Sic. XIII. 56. ii), Egesta gave way in its dispute with Selinus, but Selinus took more than the land originally at issue, and so, perhaps in 410, Egesta appealed to Carthage. There were Carthaginian traders and settlements in Sicily, and Greek traders in Carthage; but Carthage had not tried to interfere in Sicily since its defeat in 480, and had not responded to an appeal from Egesta in 416/5 (Diod. Sic. XII. 82. vii) or taken advantage of the Athenian expedition. Some Athenians may have hoped to conquer Carthage after Sicily, but after their arrival they asked for Carthaginian support, and an inscription reveals contact in 406 (*IG* i³ 123 = M&L 92 ~ Fornara 165). At this time the leading position in Carthage, given the title *basileus*, 'king', by our Greek sources (not the *shophet*, 'judge', as often claimed, but the *milk*, war-leader), was hereditary in the Magonid family; Hannibal, grandson of the Hamilcar who was defeated and killed at Himera in 480, now welcomed an opportunity to avenge that defeat. The council (*gerousia* in our sources) was divided, but made Hannibal *strategos*, while first unsuccessfully trying to arrange for arbitration by Syracuse. That year Carthage sent 5,000 Libyans and 800 Campanian mercenaries to Egesta, and they took advantage of Selinus' carelessness to win a victory. As Hannibal prepared for a major expedition, Egesta looked to him and Selinus to Syracuse (Diod. Sic. XIII. 43–4).

At the beginning of 409 Syracuse sent five more ships to the Aegean (Xen. *Hell.* I. ii. 8); but Hannibal went to Sicily with a large force (Ephorus said 200,000 infantry and 4,000 cavalry, Timaeus half that number) but a limited objective. He landed near the Carthaginian settlement of Motya, at the west end of the island. He first attacked Selinus, and captured it and killed many of the inhabitants, while forces from Acragas and Gela waited to be joined by Syracuse in going to the rescue. When the Syracusans reached Acragas they sent envoys who negotiated a settlement: survivors could remain in Selinus but pay *phoros* to Carthage (Diod. Sic. XIII. 54–59. iv). Hannibal then crossed the island to Himera, being joined by many Sicans and Sicels, while Diocles pursued him with the Greek forces from Acragas, and the ships sent to the Aegean returned. A false rumour of an attack on Syracuse led Diocles to start evacuating Himera and hurry back, and enabled Hannibal to capture a weakened city. He killed the inhabitants and destroyed the city, disbanded his forces but left some to support his allies, and returned home. The campaign had lasted three months, and the opposition had failed disastrously (Diod. Sic. XIII. 59. iv–62; three months interpolation in Xen. *Hell.* I. i. 37).

It is perhaps after this that coins from Panormus continue to copy Syracusan designs but bear the legend *ZIZ*, perhaps the Punic name of Panormus

(Kraay, *Archaic and Classical Greek Coins*, pp. 227–8 no. 866), and it is perhaps in connection with this first invasion that the Carthaginians began issuing Greek-type coins with their own designs (Kraay p. 234 no. 872).

If the dates given above are correct, 408 was a quiet year. Hermocrates was still with Pharnabazus, waiting to be sent along with others to the Persian court (Xen. *Hell.* I. iii. 13, iv. 1); but early in 407 he arrived in Messana with money from Pharnabazus. He hired mercenaries and collected some fugitives from Himera; after failing to gain reinstatement in Syracuse, he went to Selinus and began building that up again. As he raided the area of the Carthaginian settlements he gained more adherents and a good reputation. Collecting the bones of the Syracusans left unburied when Diocles had abandoned Himera, he took them to Syracuse and waited outside for a response: the Syracusans, afraid of a tyranny, exiled Diocles and accepted the bones, but did not accept him. Later he returned on the invitation of some friends and forced his way into the agora, but he and most of his supporters were killed and the remainder were exiled; allegedly one supporter was Dionysius, mistakenly left for dead (Diod. Sic. XIII. 63, 75. ii–ix).

Hermocrates had shown that the Carthaginian settlements were vulnerable to attack, but Hannibal's easy success at Himera may have aroused Carthaginian ambitions. Diodorus next mentions a Syracusan embassy to Carthage (XIII. 79. viii), perhaps prompted by news of the preparations. The elderly Hannibal had a relative, Himilco, appointed as colleague, and collected forces from around the western Mediterranean; this time the army was given as 300,000 by Ephorus, as 120,000 by Timaeus. In spring 406 an advance squadron of Carthaginian ships was defeated by the Syracusans off the west end of the island, but their main force reached Sicily without trouble and made for Acragas, an obvious target east of Selinus on the south coast and at the height of its prosperity (its agricultural produce was sold to Carthage: Diod. Sic. XIII. 81. iv–v). When Acragas rejected an offer of alliance or neutrality the Carthaginians besieged it; Acragas hired a mercenary force under the Spartan freelance Dexippus, and also the Campanians whom Hannibal had used in 409 but then dismissed. The Carthaginians' desecration of tombs outside the city led (it was said) to a plague and the death of Hannibal. Supporting forces came to Acragas from Syracuse and elsewhere under Daphnaeus, and between Gela and Acragas they won a battle, but the victory was not followed up either by them or by the generals of Acragas, who were consequently stoned by their fellow citizens. Daphnaeus began a blockade of the Carthaginian camp, but as winter approached his men grew careless, a supply squadron from Syracuse was captured by the Carthaginians, and it was now Acragas that was short of food. The Campanians switched to the Carthaginian side, the Italian Greeks among Acragas' defenders returned home, and in December the people of Acragas decided to abandon the city (going to Gela at first, eventually settled by the Syracusans at Leontini). After a siege of seven or eight months, the Carthaginians occupied Acragas, another striking achievement (Diod. Sic. XIII. 80–91. i, cf. interpolation in Xen. *Hell.* I. v. 21).

The Greek Sicilians were desperate, converging on Syracuse and some sending their families to Italy. At an assembly in Syracuse the young Dionysius, a secretary (Dem. XX. *Leptines* 161) and a man who had fought well, proposed that the generals should be lynched; when the officials imposed a fine, the rich Philistus offered to pay that and any subsequent fine. Dionysius urged the appointment of better men as generals, and a new board was appointed including himself. He proceeded to avoid his colleagues, claiming that they were in league with the enemy, and endeared himself to the ordinary citizens but not to the upper class; and he persuaded the assembly to recall exiles, many of whom had (like himself) been supporters of Hermocrates. For Diodorus, he was from the beginning planning to make himself tyrant, but he could well have begun as a sincere objector to the disastrous failure to resist Carthage (Diod. Sic. XIII. 91. ii–92).

In 405 Gela, the Carthaginians' next obvious target, appealed to Syracuse for help. Dionysius took a force there. He exploited a conflict between the rich and 'the people' to secure the condemnation of the rich, and he used their wealth to pay Dexippus' mercenaries. He promised to double the pay of his own soldiers and return to Gela with a larger force. Arriving in Syracuse, he protested at the holding of a festival while the soldiers went unpaid, and persuaded the assembly to appoint him *strategos autokrator* and double the soldiers' pay. (The Platonic *Letter* viii. 353 A 6–B 4, 354 D 5–6, has Dionysius and his future father-in-law Hipparinus appointed, but that may be a falsification in the interest of Hipparinus' son Dion. Hipparinus is a backer of Dionysius in Arist. *Pol.* V. 1306 A 1–2.) Next we have one of the favourite gambits of the would-be tyrant. He ordered the army to assemble at Leontini, claimed to have been attacked on the way, and persuaded the people there to vote him a bodyguard (Arist. *Pol.* III. 1286 B 39–40 suggests there was an argument over the size of the bodyguard). He then armed a rabble of men as mercenaries and filled the military offices with his supporters (but he distrusted Dexippus and sent him back to Greece). He took up residence in the dockyard at Syracuse, and contracted a double marriage with Hermocrates' family: he married Hermocrates' daughter and his sister married Hermocrates' brother-in-law. An assembly was held to condemn Daphnaeus and Demarchus, the latter one of the generals who had supplanted Hermocrates in 410 (Diod. Sic. XIII. 93–96. iv, cf. interpolation in Xen. *Hell.* II. ii. 24; in Arist. *Pol.* V. 1305 A 26–6, 1310 B 30–1, cf. 1313 B 26–8, Dionysius is a demagogue who attacks Daphnaeus and the rich). Dionysius was a man of humble origins who used demagogic methods and attacked the rich in order to provide for his supporters. However, there were also rich men among his supporters, and the primary reason for his rise to power was most probably indignation at the inadequacy of the resistance to the Carthaginians – and resistance to the Carthaginians was still needed.

In the summer the Carthaginians destroyed Acragas and advanced on Gela. The women and children refused evacuation to Syracuse, and joined in a valiant defence; Dionysius brought a large army and navy. When he attempted a three-pronged attack there was a failure of coordination, with both wings defeated

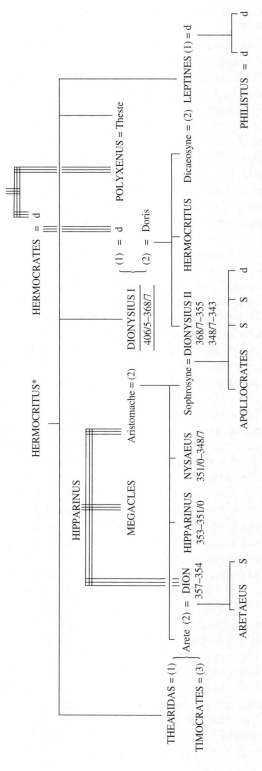

Fig. 7 The family of Dionysius I. (The manuscripts of our source texts call Dionysius I's father Hermocrates, but almost certainly the correct name is Hermocritus, given to one of his sons)

while Dionysius and his mercenaries in the centre were delayed in passing through the city – after which he decided to evacuate Gela, and also Camarina, the next city along the coast. Not surprisingly, it was now Dionysius' turn to be accused of collusion with the enemy. His Italian allies deserted him; the Syracusan cavalry, unable to get at him on the journey, beat him back to Syracuse, where they raped his wife and drove her to suicide. Dionysius hurried in pursuit, burned the city gate which had been closed against him, fought a battle in the agora and killed and exiled opponents. The surviving cavalry fled to Aetna (the inland site at Inessa: cf. p. 77); the people of Gela and Camarina, distrusting Dionysius, joined the fugitives from Acragas in Leontini (Diod. Sic. XIII. 108. ii–113, cf. interpolation in Xen. *Hell.* II. ii. 24; suicide Plut. *Dion* 3. ii).

At this point there is a lacuna in Diodorus. The text resumes with the Carthaginians suffering from a plague (perhaps on account of the marshy land outside Syracuse: cf. Thuc. VII. 47. ii) and offering terms which Dionysius accepted. Carthage was to possess its original settlements and the Elymans and Sicans of the west; Selinus, Acragas, Himera, Gela and Camarina could continue as cities, but unfortified and tributary to Carthage; Leontini, Messana and the Sicels were to be autonomous, as was Syracuse (but a stipulation that Syracuse was to be ruled by Dionysius is implausible); captured men and ships were to be returned. The Carthaginians departed, taking the plague with them (Diod. Sic. XIII. 114. i–ii). Having gained a greater interest in Sicily, the Carthaginians were to retain it until driven out by the Romans in the third century. They never captured Syracuse but sometimes overran the rest of the island; each of the following wars was to end with a distinction between a western part of Sicily which they controlled and an eastern part which they did not.

The Rule of Dionysius I

The next Carthaginian war was started by the Greeks. Before that Dionysius had consolidated his position. He fortified the peninsula of Ortygia (see map 6) and reserved that for his friends and mercenaries, and he reassigned land to supporters among citizens and non-citizens, including liberated slaves, possibly the serf class of *Kyllyrioi* (Diod. Sic. XIV. 7. i–v; *Kyllyrioi* Hdt. VII. 155. ii). His position was such that he could be called *basileus*, 'king', in an Athenian speech of 400 (Lys. VI. *Andocides* 6–7); in three Athenian decrees he is given the title *archon* of Sicily (*IG* ii² 18 = R&O 10 ~ Harding 20, of 394/3; 103, 105 + 523 = 33, 34 ~ –, 52, of 368). In the fifth century Gelon and Hieron had dedicated at Delphi and Olympia as individuals, but Polyzelus as 'lord of Gela' (cf. p. 74). Dionysius began a war against the Sicels, but a mutiny led to his hurrying back to Syracuse. The rebels blockaded him, and obtained ships from Messana and Rhegium. Dionysius was now in serious difficulties, but while opening negotiations for his withdrawal he invited the Campanian mercenaries to come from western Sicily, and in the end he defeated the rebels (Diod. Sic. XIV. 7. v–9). A Corinthian, Nicoteles, was acting as champion of the citizens; but a Spartan agent perhaps called Aristas arrived, nominally to support them but in fact to support Dionysius and try to earn his gratitude. Dionysius disarmed the citizens, built further walls, eventually one enclosing the whole of Epipolae (see map 6), and strengthened his forces (Diod. Sic. XIV. 10 [Aristus], cf. 70. iii [Aretes], 18).

Perhaps in 402, Dionysius began a war against the Greek cities north of Syracuse. First he captured Aetna, the refuge of his dissident cavalry. He attacked Leontini, occupied by fugitives from the cities of the south coast, but did not have the machines for a siege. He turned inland to the Sicels, helping a tyrant to seize power in Enna but then deposing him, attacking but making a treaty with Herbita (its ruler Archonides afterwards founded the city of Halaesa on the north coast). On the east coast, Naxos and Catana were both betrayed to Dionysius: he enslaved the citizens, sacked the cities, and gave the land to the Sicels in the case of Naxos, to the Campanian mercenaries in the case of Catana. When Dionysius returned to Leontini, the people there agreed to migrate to Syracuse (Diod. Sic. XIV. 14–16. iv). Like Gelon and Hieron, Dionysius seems to have been anxious that there should be no east coast city which could rival Syracuse. Under 400/399, from his chronographic source, Diodorus notes that Dionysius founded a colony at Adranum, below Mount Etna (Diod. Sic. XIV. 37. v). However, Rhegium, incited by Syracusan exiles, was becoming worried and decided to attack Dionysius before it was too late. It sent out a large force which was joined by one from Messana; but Messana's generals had not consulted the assembly, their soldiers mutinied, the campaign collapsed and the two cities made peace with Dionysius (Diod. Sic. XIV. 40).

Dionysius next began preparations for a war with Carthage – presumably more to regain lost ground than to keep the Sicilian Greeks submissive, as Diodorus alleges. Perhaps building on developments in machinery which had reached Carthage from Phoenicia, he is credited with technical innovations: quadriremes and quinqueremes, and catapults, which are not found in mainland Greece until later (cf. pp. 316, 341). If this is correct, and it is not impossible, the larger ships will have had more than one man to an oar rather than more than three banks of oars, and the catapults will have been arrow-firing mechanical bows. He built up a large citizen and mercenary army, with particular encouragement from Sparta. For the payment of his mercenaries he issued gold and 10-drachma silver coins (Kraay pp. 231–3 nos. 815–16, 818–19). To assure himself of support, he adopted a more conciliatory attitude. He won over Messana with a gift of land. He offered land and a marriage alliance to Rhegium but was rebuffed; but Rhegium's rival Locri provided Dionysius with a wife called Doris, and at the same time he married Aristomache, the daughter of his Syracusan supporter Hipparinus. When he held an assembly to urge war against Carthage, Diodorus says the citizens hated the Carthaginians and blamed them for their subjection to him, and they hoped that the war would result in better treatment for them and would provide an opportunity to reclaim their freedom (Diod. Sic. XIV. 41–43. iv, 44–5).

In an exceptional occurrence, perhaps in 397, the Greeks in Syracuse and the other cities drove out the Carthaginian traders, and Dionysius sent an ultimatum demanding the liberation of the cities. He took a large army and navy (said to be 80,000 infantry, over 3,000 cavalry, nearly 200 warships); Eryx in the north-west of the island submitted to him, but Motya demolished the causeway linking it to the mainland and prepared to resist. Dionysius built a mole, and campaigned in the vicinity while the work proceeded. Meanwhile Carthage sent ten ships to raid the harbour of Syracuse, and Himilco took a hundred ships to Motya but did not fight a battle. The siege of Motya was a contest of machines and ingenuity; Dionysius finally captured the city with much slaughter. At the end of the summer he returned to Syracuse, leaving a garrison in Motya, Egesta and Entella under siege, and his brother Leptines as navarch with 120 ships (Diod. Sic. XIV. 46. i–v, 47, 53. v).

In 396 Dionysius had smaller forces, perhaps owing to shortage of funds, but he returned to the west, where Egesta held out against his siege and burned the attackers' camp. The Carthaginians appointed Himilco *basileus* (it is not clear what his position had been since Hannibal's death: perhaps he was already *basileus* and was now made *strategos autokrator*). Himilco went to Panormus, on the north coast, with large forces (300,000 infantry, 4,000 cavalry, 400 warships according to Ephorus, 100,000 plus 30,000 raised in Sicily according to Timaeus). He recovered Motya and the other western cities (founding Lilybaeum, to the south, to replace Motya: Diod. Sic. XXII. 10. iv, cf. XIII. 54. iv), and as Dionysius withdrew, destroying the crops, Himilco proceeded along the north coast to Messana: when its army had gone out against his army, his ships sailed in and captured the city, which he destroyed (Diod. Sic. XIV. 54. ii–57, 58. iii–iv).

Dionysius prepared to resist in Syracuse and Leontini. Himilco encouraged the Sicels in Naxos to found Tauromenium, to the north; and an eruption of Etna forced him to take an inland route to Catana while his fleet under Mago sailed directly there. Dionysius sent Leptines to fight against Mago before Himilco could join him, but Leptines was defeated, Dionysius retired to defend Syracuse, and his abandoned allies left him (Diod. Sic. XIV. 58. i–ii, 59–61). In the winter of 396/5 he sent his brother-in-law Polyxenus with a further appeal to the Greeks of Italy and to the Spartans and other Greeks. Himilco sailed into the great harbour of Syracuse, landed and overran the countryside, allegedly raiding temples of Demeter and Core and desecrating tombs (Diod. Sic. XIV. 62–63. iii).

In 395 Polyxenus brought thirty ships from Sparta and elsewhere, with the Spartan 'Pharacidas' (perhaps the Pharax who had been active in the Aegean: cf. pp. 207–8). While Dionysius and Leptines were away to fetch supplies, the Syracusans won a naval battle: this led to a Syracusan challenge to Dionysius, but Pharacidas and the mercenaries remained loyal to him. Then the Carthaginians were again hit by a plague. Dionysius was victorious in a combined land and sea attack, after which Himilco gave him a bribe of 300 talents, it is alleged, and sailed away at night. Of the remainder of his force the Sicels escaped, the Iberians were enrolled as mercenaries by Dionysius, the rest were captured and sold. Himilco's shameful return prompted a serious revolt in Libya and led him to commit suicide (Diod. Sic. XIV. 63. iv–77).

Dionysius' mercenaries were unpaid and disaffected: in the last attack on the Carthaginians he had contrived the death of some (Diod. Sic. XIV. 72. ii–iii); after the war he settled the others in Leontini and hired a fresh force. In Messana he settled Locrians and others, including fugitive Messenians (cf. pp. 28–9, 44, 125), but he moved the Messenians elsewhere when Sparta protested against their being placed in the city named after Messenia. In 395–394 he campaigned successfully against the Sicels (Diod. Sic. XIV. 78). In 394, with Locri allied to Dionysius and Messana resettled by him, Rhegium felt threatened. It therefore welcomed opponents of Dionysius and settled some at Mylae, on the north coast, and then (under Heloris, a former supporter of Dionysius now in exile) attacked Messana; but Messana defeated the Rhegians and captured Mylae. In the winter Dionysius made an unsuccessful attack on Tauromenium, in which he was nearly killed; after which Messana and Acragas defected from him (Diod. Sic. XIV. 87–8).

In the same winter, 394/3, Athens honoured Dionysius and tried to detach him from Sparta. Conon's plan for a marriage alliance between Dionysius and Evagoras of Salamis came to nothing, but it was claimed that Dionysius had been dissuaded from sending ships to support Sparta (*IG* ii^2 18 = R&O 10 ~ Harding 20, Lys. XIX. *Property of Aristophanes* 19–20; cf. p. 227).

Mago, it seems, had been left by Himilco in Sicily, and he began a Carthaginian recovery, with mild treatment of subjects and encouragement of Dionysius' opponents. In 393 he attacked Messana but was defeated by Dionysius at Abacaene. Dionysius next made a surprise attack on Rhegium, burning the gates but failing to get in, and then made a year's truce (Diod. Sic. 90. ii–vii). In 392 Mago was sent reinforcements from Carthage, and he won over most of the Sicels' cities but not the strong city of Agyrium. Dionysius went there, cut Mago's supply lines and waited to starve him, but was unsuccessful since the Syracusan army grew impatient and returned home. Carthage offered and Dionysius accepted terms similar to those of 405 (cf. p. 279), except that the Sicels were made subject to him: the Carthaginians were thus accepting that they had failed to conquer the east of the island. Dionysius replaced the Sicels in Tauromenium with some of his mercenaries (Diod. Sic. XIV. 95–96. i; from the chronological source XVI. 7. i has under 358/7 another foundation of Tauromenium, with survivors from the old Naxos, by Andromachus, father of the historian Timaeus).

In southern Italy a league comprising Croton and neighbouring cities, with institutions copied from Achaea, had been formed some time before 417 (cf. pp. 79–80). About 393, under pressure from the Lucanians on one side and Dionysius on the other, other cities of south-west Italy including Rhegium joined them in an enlarged Italiot League (Diod. Sic. XIV. 91. i). Peace with

Carthage enabled Dionysius to deal with Rhegium, and that was now to involve dealing with the League. In 390 he made Locri his base for a war against Rhegium and Croton, but an attempt to intercept ships sailing from Croton to Rhegium failed when Dionysius was caught in a storm. He made an alliance with the Lucanians, who in 389 defeated Thurii: some surviving Thurians fled to passing ships, which turned out to be a Syracusan squadron under Leptines. However, instead of completing the Lucanian victory Leptines arranged a settlement between the Lucanians and the League, to which Dionysius reacted by replacing him with his brother Thearidas (Diod. Sic. XIV. 100–102. iii).

In 388 Thearidas captured a Rhegian squadron in the Lipari Islands, while Dionysius began a siege of Caulonia; the resistance was coordinated by Croton, with the exiled Syracusan Heloris in command. At the River Eleporus, north of Caulonia, Dionysius first defeated and killed Heloris with an advance party and then defeated the main army, but he released his prisoners and left the cities of the League independent. Rhegium, threatened with a siege, submitted, and had to pay an indemnity, surrender its ships and give hostages. Caulonia and Hipponium were destroyed, their citizens transported to Syracuse and their land given to Locri (Diod. Sic. XIV. 103–106. iii, 107. ii–iv). Dionysius was not yet finished with Rhegium. In 387 after provoking a breach of the settlement he began a siege. He suffered a nearly fatal wound, but in 386, after almost a year, starvation led to Rhegium's unconditional surrender; its general Phyton was humiliated and killed, and its citizens were ransomed or sold as slaves (Diod. Sic. XIV. 107. v–108, 111–12). It is said that Dionysius intended, but did not manage, to build a wall across the toe of Italy to strengthen his position there (Strabo 261. VI. i. 10).

With Dionysius at the height of his power, we pass from the detailed narrative of Diodorus XIV to the scraps of book XV.

Since Lysias' speech urging Dionysius' exclusion from the Olympic games (XXXIII. *Olympic*, where 5 calls him 'the tyrant of Sicily') fits better into a context after the Peace of Antalcidas, it was probably in 384 rather than 388 that Dionysius sent his brother Thearidas with chariots and his poems to compete there: not only did Lysias denounce Dionysius, but his poems were laughed at, his chariots were involved in accidents and the homeward-bound ship was driven into Taras by a storm (Diod. Sic. XIV. 109. i–vi, 388/7; XV. 7. ii–iii, 386/5). In Syracuse Dionysius was trying to build up a court circle, but had to face home truths about his poetry from the dithyrambist Philoxenus and about his tyranny from Plato. Dionysius' brother-in-law Dion had introduced Plato to Dionysius, and after the encounter Plato had to be got out of Syracuse, though the story that Dionysius had him sold as a slave is likely to be a fiction (Diod. Sic. XV. 6–7. i, Plut. *Dion* 4–5. vii).

Dionysius had trouble with men who initially had supported him. Of early supporters, Hipparinus had died; Polyxenus is not heard of after being sent to support Sparta in 387 (below); Heloris, previously described as Dionysius' adopted father (Diod. Sic. XIV. 8. v), was in exile by the late 390's, serving Dionysius's enemies Rhegium and the Italiot League. Of Dionysius' brothers,

Leptines was dismissed after reconciling Thurii and the Lucanians, but Thearidas seems not to have suffered for his involvement in the fiasco at Olympia. Diodorus reports that Leptines and Dionysius' early backer Philistus were exiled and welcomed in Thurii but later returned; Leptines on his return married one of Dionysius' daughters, and fought and died at Cronium (XV. 7. iii–iv; Cronium p. 285). According to Plutarch Philistus was exiled for showing his ambition by marrying a daughter of Leptines: he went to the Adriatic and (this at least seems to be correct) did not return until after Dionysius I's death (Plut. *Dion* 11. iv–vii).

Abroad, after conquering the toe of Italy, Dionysius extended his interests further. While he had not sent help to Sparta in 393, he did send Polyxenus with ships to join Antalcidas in the Hellespont in 387 (Xen. *Hell.* V. i. 26: cf. above). Diodorus (XV. 13, 385/4; 14, 384/3) begins by mentioning the Ionic Gulf, Epirus and a plan to sack Delphi (presumably an unfounded rumour: cf. Jason of Pherae, p. 252). Dionysius made an alliance with the Illyrians and helped them to restore Alcetas, an exile in Syracuse, as king of Molossis, despite Spartan intervention on the other side (for Alcetas in the 370's cf. p. 234). He had already founded a colony at a site probably to be read as Issa = Vis, one of the islands off the Dalmatian coast. (The manuscripts of Diodorus seem to refer to Lissus = Lesh, on the mainland 35 miles = 55 km. north of Epidamnus, but that seems not to have been settled this early; however, *SIG*³ 141, recording the sending of settlers from Issa to Black Corcyra = Korčula, is now known to be of the late fourth or early third century, and so does not prove that Issa was settled by Dionysius.) From this base Dionysius did something which is lost in a lacuna in Diodorus' text, and he helped the Parians when they colonised nearby Pharos = Hvar, and again later when the Illyrians supported the natives against the settlers. A fragment of Theopompus (*FGrH* 115 F 128c) seems to credit Dionysius with a presumably short-lived colony at Adria, at the mouth of the Po; but Ancona, on the Italian mainland about the same latitude as Issa, is said to have been founded by opponents of Dionysius (Strabo 241. V. iv. 2). On the other side of Italy Dionysius raided the Etruscan temple of Agylla = Caere (cf. Strabo 226. V. ii. 8: the Etruscans were friends of Carthage; and it is alleged that the Gauls after their sack of Rome in 386 offered him an alliance [Just. *Epit.* XX. 5. iv]).

In Syracuse Dionysius devoted himself to public works, as ambitious tyrants often did: he is credited with grandiose temples and gymnasia, but also docks and walls (Diod. Sic. XV. 13. v); and he spent the proceeds from Agylla on mercenaries, with a view to another war against Carthage (Diod. Sic. XV. 14. iv). Diodorus, while implying that that war was a lengthy one, narrates the whole of it under 383/2 (XV. 15–17); some scholars prolong it to 374 because a Spartan force sent to Corcyra then pretended to be heading for Sicily (Diod. Sic. XV. 46. ii), which is possible but not certain. Dionysius provoked the war by winning over the cities subject to Carthage. Carthage made an alliance with the Italiot League, and its restoration of Hipponium, which Dionysius had destroyed in 388 (Diod. Sic. XV. 24. i, from the chronological source), is presumably an episode in this war. So too, probably, are a naval attack by Dionysius on Thurii, frustrated by the wind (Ael. *V.H.* XII. 61), and his capture of Croton (Livy XXIV. 3. viii, Dion. Hal. *Ant. Rom.* XX. 7. iii). It is possible also that during this war he lost Locri and had to recover it (cf. Just. *Epit.* XXI. 2, Pl. *Leg.* I. 638 B 1–2). The war ended with two major battles. First, at Cabala Dionysius was victorious and Mago was killed. Then the Carthaginians offered terms and Dionysius demanded withdrawal from Sicily and repayment of his costs, so they made a truce. However, Mago's son (Himilco if Polyaenus *Strat.* V. 10. v belongs here) revived the army and returned (cf. Polyaenus *Strat.* VI. 16. i). Then at Cronium, near Panormus, the Carthaginians were victorious and the reinstated Leptines was killed. Carthage now proposed terms which Dionysius accepted: Carthage was to have Selinus and the territory of Acragas as far as the River Halycus, and Dionysius had to pay 1,000 talents. (These cities had been in the Carthaginian sphere before, but had perhaps gone over to Dionysius. It is disputed whether the river is correctly called Halycus or Lycus, but it appears in any case to be the Platani, between Selinus and Acragas with Heraclea Minoa at its mouth: Heraclea will have been a possession of Acragas now ceded to Carthage.)

Dionysius was sufficiently recovered to send help to Sparta in 372, and again in 369 and 368 (cf. pp. 215, 218: in 372 his ships, with dedications for Delphi and Olympia, were captured by the Athenian Iphicrates). After Leuctra Athens was on the same side as Sparta, and in 368 Dionysius was made an ally of Athens but was not accepted by Athens' allies as a member of the League (cf. pp. 232, 236).

As for Carthage, Diodorus mentions a plague and a revolt of the Libyans and Sardinia in connection with the restoration of Hipponium (XV. 24. ii–iii, 379/8), and a plague and a revolt of the Libyans as providing the opportunity for Dionysius' last Carthaginian war, in 368 (XV. 73. i). Presumably these references are to the same plague and revolt, which will have begun not many years before 368. In 368 Dionysius manufactured a border dispute and invaded western Sicily; he won over Selinus and Entella, and captured Eryx but failed to take Lilybaeum. On hearing of a fire in the Carthaginian docks he sent most of his ships back to Syracuse, but the Carthaginians sent a fleet under Hanno (Polyaenus *Strat.* V. 9), which unexpectedly attacked the ships in the harbour below Eryx and captured them. A truce was made for the winter (Diod. Sic. XV. 73. i–iv) – and during that winter Dionysius died (cf. below), and his successor Dionysius II made peace with Carthage (Diod. Sic. XV. 73. v, XVI. 5. i–ii).

Himilco seems not to have succeeded Mago as Carthaginian *basileus*: Hanno, the commander in 368, was a rich man and strongly anti-Greek but not a Magonid. He secured the condemnation of his rival Suniatus [Eshmuniaton], who was in touch with Dionysius; and some time later he tried to seize autocratic power, eventually with the support of a slave class and the Libyans, but was suppressed (Arist. *Pol.* V. 1307 A 2–5, Just. *Epit.* XX. 5. xi, XXI. 4). After that Carthage settled into the constitution which Aristotle compared with the

Spartan and the 'Cretan'. The council (*gerousia*) was divided into pentarchies which chose the Hundred and Four; there were still *basileis*, from a range of families, who commanded the armies subject to the control of the Hundred and Four; there were institutions which could be compared with the Spartan messes; and there was an assembly, which had the opportunity to exercise power when the officials and council disagreed (*Pol.* II. 1272 B 24–1273 B 26).

Having become an ally of Athens in 368, Dionysius I sent his tragedy *The Ransom of Hector* for performance at the Lenaea early in 367, and it was awarded the first prize. Diodorus has a story of his dying through excessive celebration of that success, and in this way rather than by beating the Carthaginians fulfilling an oracle that he would die when he had defeated his betters (XV. 74. i–iv). *IG* ii² 105 + 223 = R&O 34 ~ Harding 52 should not, as it once was, be dated to the later part of 368/7, and there is no reason why Dionysius should not have died shortly after the Lenaea and why the story should not be based on that much truth: if he 'became tyrant' in 406/<u>5</u>, the sources will be correct in giving him thirty-eight years in power.

It is hard to make a fair assessment of Dionysius' rule, since we hear of little apart from warfare, and have a detailed but hostile account for the first half of his reign but a perfunctory account for the second. He rose to power through dissatisfaction with the unsuccessful resistance to Carthage, but was not himself a great deal more successful, which provoked opposition to him. Carthage tended to deal more cruelly than Greeks with defeated enemies, and Greeks forced to choose between Carthage and Dionysius tended to prefer Dionysius; Syracuse itself was never taken by the Carthaginians, and a division of Sicily between Carthage in the west and Syracuse in the east became established. Outside the Carthaginian sphere, at his most powerful Dionysius controlled much of Sicily, the toe of Italy and some places further afield. In Sicily some old cities died, some new ones came into existence, movements of population and Carthaginian attacks were so frequent that there was little stability except in Syracuse. Dionysius portrayed himself as a just ruler, and gave his daughters the names of virtues; intellectuals were welcome at his court as long as they did not speak too freely; the constitutional mechanisms of the *polis* seem not to have been entirely abolished, but his son Dionysius II succeeded to his position without difficulty. In some ways Dionysius I foreshadows the hellenistic kings, but it is unlikely that he used the title *basileus*, and the story of his wearing the Persian diadem (Livy XXIV. 5. iii–iv) was perhaps invented as a precedent for Hieron in the third century.

Dionysius II and the Liberators

Dionysius II, whose mother was Doris of Locri, was Dionysius I's eldest son. Whereas Dion and Timoleon caught the Greeks' imagination, we know little about him. It was alleged that Dion had tried to induce the elder Dionysius to leave the tyranny to his sons by Dion's sister Aristomache (Nep. X. *Dion* 2. iv–v,

Plut. *Dion* 6. ii–iii). Diodorus suggests that the younger Dionysius had had little education and was not a dynamic man (Diod. Sic. XVI. 5).

Dion tried to attend to his education, bringing back Plato for the purpose, and Dion's opponents secured the recall of Philistus to act as a counterpoise. Dion was accused of instructing the Carthaginians to negotiate only through him, and was got out of the city to Greece; Plato failed to achieve a reconciliation, and at the end of a war about which we know nothing he returned to Athens (Pl. *Ep.* vii. 328 B–330 C, 337 E–338 A, cf. *Ep.* iii. 316 C–317 A, Plut. *Dion* 9–17, Diod. Sic. XVI. 6. ii–iv). Later Dionysius induced Plato to visit again (he was in Syracuse when there was an eclipse of the moon, on 12 May 361: Plut. *Dion* 19. vi), but he failed to achieve a recall of Dion; instead relations worsened, Dion's property was confiscated and his niece and wife Arete given another husband. A mutiny among mercenaries whose pay had been reduced was blamed on Heraclides, an associate of Dion, who escaped from Syracuse; and in 360 Plato left (Pl. *Ep.* vii. 338 A–341 A, 345 C–350 B, cf. *Ep.* iii. 317 A, 318 C, Plut. *Dion* 18–21; Diod. Sic. omits this visit, and XVI. 6. iv has Heraclides leaving with Dion). Plato met Dion at the Olympic festival that summer, and Dion began to plan his return to Syracuse (Pl. *Ep.* vii. 350 B–E).

It took time for Dion to gather supporters: his links with Plato will have made him suspect to some, others will have thought he merely wanted to take Dionysius' place. Even Plato saw in him ambition and desire for revenge as well as idealism (*Ep.* vii. 350 B–351 C); Aristotle, who is silent on the Platonic connection, mentions Dion's contempt for Dionysius as a drunkard, and categorises Dion as ambitious not for his own advantage but for glory, and as a man within the family who overthrew a tyrant (*Pol.* V. 1312 A 4–6, 21–39, B 16–17). In 357 (after an eclipse of the moon on 9 August: Plut. *Dion* 24. i) he set out from Zacynthus with a few fellow exiles, a small mercenary force and a supply of arms for the Sicilians (the success of so small a force was remarked on already in 355: Dem. XX. *Leptines* 162). Dionysius was away in Italy, and Philistus was watching the short sea crossing, so Dion crossed the open sea to Heraclea Minoa, where the Carthaginian governor was a friend. As in Diodorus' account, Heraclides should be seen as a partner, to follow with reinforcements; Plutarch projects back their later quarrel and makes him a rival liberator (Diod. Sic. XVI. 6. v, 9. ii–iv, cf. 10. v, 11. iii, Plut. *Dion* 22–26. i, 32. iii–iv).

Dion advanced on Syracuse, picking up support from Greek cities, Sicans and Sicels, and some Italiots. He was welcomed by the Syracusans despite the attempts of Timocrates (the man who had taken over his wife) to keep them under control, and made a triumphal entry into the outer city. The assembly offered to make him and his brother Megacles *strategoi autokratores*, but they insisted on a board of twenty, half from the city and half returned exiles. Timocrates fled, leaving Ortygia with a garrison but no commander. Dionysius had heard the news, and returned seven days after Dion's entry. He opened negotiations and tried to import food; on one occasion he attacked the outer city but was beaten back. In reporting the negotiations, Diodorus concentrates on Dion's attempts to outwit Dionysius, while Plutarch shows Dionysius trying to drive a wedge between Dion and the citizens. Philistus returned, bringing cavalry from Rhegium (which Dionysius II had refounded: Strabo 258. VI. i. 6); he tried to recover Leontini for Dionysius, but the Syracusans helped the Leontinians to defeat him (Diod. Sic. XVI. 9. v–13, 16. i, Plut. *Dion* 26. ii–32. ii).

Perhaps in 356 Heraclides arrived with his forces. He was elected navarch, but Dion insisted on his being a subordinate, not an independent commander, and in a battle he defeated Philistus, who committed suicide or was killed. Dionysius resumed negotiations, and when unsuccessful departed to Locri, leaving his son Apollocrates with the garrison in Ortygia. A rift opened between Dion, who had perhaps been too tolerant of Dionysius' overtures and was certainly no democrat, and Heraclides, who was blamed for letting Dionysius escape and who became a supporter of extreme measures including redistribution of land. A new board of twenty-five generals was appointed, including Heraclides but not Dion. Dion joined the mercenaries, whose pay was in arrears, and withdrew to Leontini, pursued by the Syracusans but defeating them (Diod. Sic. XVI. 16. ii–17, Plut. *Dion* 32. ii–40). It was perhaps at this point that three *prostatai* of the city were elected: Heraclides, Athanis (who was to continue Philistus' history) and an Achaean (Theopompus *FGrH* 115 F 194).

The garrison in Ortygia was starving, but in 355 Dionysius sent a man called Nypsius with supplies. After his arrival the citizens won a battle, but later he overran the outer city; and in response the Syracusans recalled Dion and the mercenaries, who regained the outer city. Dion was proposed as *strategos autokrator* by Heraclides, but the poorer citizens objected; Dion retained Heraclides as navarch, but insisted on annulling the redistribution of land. Heraclides led an expedition to Messana and disparaged Dion; a Spartan agent called Pharax complicated matters before joining Dionysius; another Spartan agent, Gaesylus, arranged an uneasy reconciliation between Dion and Heraclides. By now the garrison was again starving, Apollocrates negotiated for its withdrawal, and the whole of Syracuse came under the control of Dion; the citizens voted to honour him as a hero (Diod. Sic. XVI. 18–20, Plut. *Dion* 41–52: hero, benefactor and saviour Diod. 20. vi, saviour and god Plut. 46. i). Perhaps now, Dion and Heraclides were listed together in the record of *thearodokoi* to look after messengers from the sanctuary at Epidaurus (*IG* IV². i 95. 39–40).

Dion was still in touch with Plato (cf. Pl. *Ep.* iv). In Syracuse he refused to demolish the citadel or Dionysius I's tomb, or to discharge his mercenaries; he apparently hoped to set up some kind of oligarchy, and summoned advisers from Corinth. Heraclides objected, and we read that Dion procured his assassination but when he was safely dead gave him a grand funeral. In 354, however, the Athenian Callippus, who had come to Syracuse with Dion (said to be a Platonist, but Plat. *Ep.* vii. 333 E denies this), had Dion murdered (Plut. *Dion* 53–7, cf. *Tim.* 1. ii, Diod. Sic. XVI. 31. vii). It is hard to be sure what kind of régime Dion had envisaged for Syracuse: he had no doubt learned something from Plato, but he probably objected specifically to Dionysius II rather than to autocratic rule as such. The Platonic *Letters* vii, defending Plato's involvement in Syracuse, and viii, advising what to do next, belong to the context shortly after Dion's death.

Syracuse then suffered under a series of rulers. Callippus lasted thirteen months: in 353, while he was attacking Catana, Hipparinus (half-brother of Dionysius II and nephew of Dion) set out from Leontini, where Dion's supporters had fled, and captured Syracuse (Plut. *Dion* 58. i–iv, cf. Diod. Sic. XVI. 36. v). Callippus, driven from Sicily, captured Rhegium from a garrison installed by Dionysius, but was murdered there (Plut. *Dion* 58. v–vii, cf. Diod. Sic. XVI. 45. ix). In 351, when Hipparinus was killed, he was succeeded by his brother Nysaeus; both are said to have been drunkards (Theopompus *FGrH* 115 FF 186–8, Ael. *V.H.* II. 41). Dionysius since 356 had been based in Locri: about 346 he was expelled from there and his wife and daughters were tortured and killed. He returned to Syracuse, captured it from Nysaeus and, embittered by his exile, ruled savagely (Plut. *Tim.* 1. i–v, Just. *Epit.* XXI. 3. ix–x). Dion's supporters then appealed to Hicetas, a friend of Dion (Plut. *Dion* 58. viii) now ruling in Leontini (and recorded as Leontini's Epidaurian *thearodokos* in *IG* iv². 1 95. 66–8): 'not better than any of those who were admittedly tyrants, but they had no one else to turn to' (Plut. *Tim.* 1. vi).

Hicetas encouraged the Syracusans to appeal to their mother city, Corinth, but also opened negotiations with Carthage. Corinth saw this as an opportunity to deal with the embarrassment of Timoleon, who *c.*365 (but Diodorus makes the episode recent) had been involved in the killing of his own brother Timophanes when he tried to make himself tyrant (cf. p. 219): if Timoleon wanted to oppose tyranny, let him do it in Sicily. Early in 344 Timoleon was sent with a small force (but a dedication, *SEG* xi 126*a* = R&O 74, points to more support from Corinth and its colonies, eventually if not at first, than our literary sources reveal). Hicetas, once he was certain of Carthaginian support, told the Corinthians not to bother to send help, but Timoleon went nevertheless (Diod. Sic. XVI. 65, 66. i–v, Plut. *Tim.* 2–8).

Hicetas attacked Syracuse, feigning retreat and defeating Dionysius' forces when they pursued him. Meanwhile the Carthaginians sent a large force under Hanno (if this is Hanno the great, his downfall came soon afterwards, and Mago's withdrawal from Syracuse in 343 may be connected with it), which captured Entella. Hicetas had some Carthaginian ships sent to intercept Timoleon at Rhegium, but he slipped away and reached Tauromenium, where he was welcomed by Andromachus. (Andromachus, whose son was Timaeus, is never described as a tyrant, and was not overthrown by Timoleon – whether because he was virtuous or because he was the first to welcome Timoleon.) At Adranum, to the south of Mount Etna, Hicetas and Timoleon were invited to support opposing parties, and Timoleon, despite his inferior numbers, was successful in a surprise attack (Diod. Sic. XVI. 66. v–68. x, Plut. *Tim.* 9–12).

On the liberation of Syracuse Diodorus and Plutarch diverge irreconcilably. In Diodorus' account, spread over three years (XVI. 68. xi, 69. iii–vi, 70. i–iii), Timoleon marched on Syracuse immediately after his success at Adranum

[345/4]. He occupied the outskirts while Hicetas was in the middle city and Dionysius in Ortygia, and the Carthaginian fleet arrived in the great harbour. He received reinforcements from 'Marcus' of Catana and from Corinth; the Carthaginians withdrew, leaving Hicetas isolated and Timoleon able to take over the whole of the outer city [344/3]. Finally Dionysius surrendered, and was dispatched to retirement in Corinth [343/2: cf. the papyrus chronicle, *P. Oxy.* i 12 = *FGrH* 255, iv]. In Plutarch's account (*Tim.* 13–21) the success at Adranum won Timoleon allies, in particular Mamercus of Catana. Within fifty days of Timoleon's arrival in Sicily (16. ii) Dionysius surrendered to him, and Timoleon sent men to take over Ortygia and dispatched Dionysius to Corinth. Hicetas besieged Ortygia but failed to procure the assassination of Timoleon; the Carthaginians under Mago sailed into the great harbour. Hicetas and Mago attacked Catana, from which Timoleon was supplying Ortygia, but returned to Syracuse when the garrison captured part of the outer city. Despite Hanno's attempt to prevent it, reinforcements from Corinth reached Timoleon, and he then marched on Syracuse. His soldiers and those of Hicetas began to fraternise; Mago departed; Timoleon made a three-pronged attack and was victorious with no losses, and so gained control of all Syracuse.

Certainty is impossible, but most scholars have preferred Plutarch's order of events. If that is right, what will have happened quickly is that Timoleon, perhaps representing himself to Dionysius as an ally, persuaded him to hand over Ortygia and retire to Catana; in 343 the Carthaginians arrived in the harbour but inexplicably departed, Hicetas was defeated but was allowed to withdraw with his surviving forces, and finally Dionysius was shown that he had no future in Sicily and sent to Corinth.

Unlike Dion, Timoleon did demolish the tyrants' buildings in Ortygia. He gave Syracuse a new constitution, reported by Diodorus in two phases: in the first, 'democracy', with a new code of laws, emphasising equality in private relations, and the *amphipolos* of Olympian Zeus as the chief annual official; in the second, connected with an invitation to men to settle in Syracuse, a revision of the 'laws of Diocles' (cf. pp. 274–5) bearing on public affairs, guided by a Corinthian called Cephalus (Diod. Sic. XVI. 70. iv–vi [343/2], 82. vi–vii [339/8], cf. Plut. *Tim.* 22. i–iii, 23, 24. iii). The two phases may be authentic; the Dionysii had not abolished all political institutions, but after the ending of the tyranny and the departure of its supporters a comprehensive reform was necessary, and while some matters had to be decided quickly others will have taken time. Under Corinthian influence, 'democracy' is not likely to be more specific than constitutional government; a powerful council is likely, but it is not clear whether the *synedrion* of six hundred involved in the later rise of Agathocles (Diod. Sic. XIX. 5. vi with 4. iii, 6. iv: cf. p. 292) is that council degenerated or a later creation; there are various references to decisions of an assembly (Diod. Sic. XVI. 90. i, XIX. 3. iv, 5. v, Plut. *Tim.* 38. iv, 39. v). However, Timoleon himself retained a powerful position, probably as *strategos autokrator*, and Plutarch quotes a resolution of 'Timoleon and the Syracusans'

(*Tim.* 22. viii); after he finally resigned, there was perhaps an annual board of generals (cf. Diod. Sic. XIX. 3. i, iii).

Settlers (Diod. Sic. XVI. 82. iii, v, 83, cf. XIX. 2. viii, Plut. *Tim.* 22. iv–24. i) must have been badly needed, as in the upheavals since the return of Dion many people had been killed and many more must have fled from what had previously been Sicily's greatest city. Attracting settlers will have taken time, since at first people must have hesitated to believe that Timoleon's régime would be better than previous régimes; but in the end they came, more from Sicily and southern Italy than from Greece and the Aegean, and the archaeological evidence points to an impressive revival not only in Syracuse but throughout Greek Sicily. Coins of Corinth and its colonies found their way to Sicily in large quantities, presumably in payment for Sicilian agricultural produce, and Syracuse and briefly Leontini issued coins of Corinthian type (Kraay p. 236 nos. 820, 854).

Meanwhile, in the rest of Sicily there were still tyrants and Carthaginians, and Timoleon set out to deal with both. In 342 he failed to capture Leontini, to which Hicetas had returned, but he liberated Engyum and Apollonia, sending Apollonia's tyrant Leptines to join Dionysius in Corinth. In Timoleon's absence Hicetas attacked Syracuse and was defeated, but it seems unlikely that, as Plutarch claims, he was persuaded to resign his tyranny. Timoleon raided the rest of the island, to liberate Entella and other cities, and to obtain booty to help pay for the mercenaries (Diod. Sic. XVI. 72. ii–73. ii, Plut. *Tim.* 24. i–ii, iv). Mago had committed suicide after abandoning Syracuse in 343 (Plut. *Tim.* 22. viii); but perhaps in 341 (Diodorus has nothing on Sicily between 342/1 and 340/39) the Carthaginians sent a fresh expedition, and Timoleon was able to include in his army troops from Leontini. He invaded the west of the island, and his great inferiority in numbers (12,000 [Diodorus] or 7,000 [Plutarch] against 70,000 infantry and 10,000 cavalry from Carthage) was increased when a body of mercenaries deserted. However, at the River Crimisus (probably the Belice, which enters the sea near Selinus) he was helped by a hailstorm which blew on to his men's backs and into the enemy's faces to defeat the Carthaginians and capture their camp; the surviving Carthaginians withdrew to Lilybaeum. Timoleon did not follow up the victory, but it was celebrated as a great success, with dedications in Syracuse and Corinth (Diod. Sic. XVI. 73. iii, 77. iv–81. ii, Plut. *Tim.* 25–30. iii: Plutarch 29. v–vi quotes a dedication by 'the Corinthians and Timoleon the general', but the surviving inscription from Corinth, *SEG* xi 126*a* = R&O 74, is a dedication by Syracuse and various Corinthian colonies).

In 340 we find Hicetas and Mamercus of Catana in alliance with the Carthaginians, commanded by Gescon (Hanno's son, recalled from exile) and for the first time using Greek mercenaries, and they had successes both in the west and in the north-east of Sicily (Diod. Sic. XVI. 81. iii–iv, Plut. *Tim.* 30. iv–x). In 339, however, Timoleon won victories over Hicetas and over Mamercus and the Carthaginians, after which the Carthaginians made peace.

Their sphere was once more to be bounded by the River (Ha)lycus (cf. p. 285); the Greek cities were to be free, and Carthage was not to support tyrants (Diod. Sic. XVI. 81. iii–iv, 82. iii, Plut. *Tim.* 31, 34. i–ii). Timoleon was then free to deal with the remaining tyrants. Hicetas was captured and executed, perhaps after a trial; the tyrants of Centuripa and Agyrium were overthrown and publicly executed; liberated cities were brought into alliance with Syracuse. Mamercus went to Italy to gain the support of the Lucanians, but his supporters turned back and surrendered Catana to Timoleon; Mamercus took refuge with Hippo in Messana, but in 337 Hippo was captured in an attempted escape and tortured to death. After that Mamercus surrendered and was put to death in Syracuse (Diod. Sic. XVI. 82. iv, Plut. *Tim.* 32–3, Polyaenus *Strat.* V. 12. ii). The population of Leontini was transported to Syracuse, but that of Camarina was reinforced (Diod. Sic. XVI. 82. vii).

The tyrants had been disposed of, and Timoleon was going blind, so he resigned 'after serving as general for eight years'. Soon afterwards he died; he was honoured before his death and buried gloriously after it (Diod. Sic. XVI. 90. i, Plut. *Tim.* 37. iv–39). His propaganda attributed his success to the favour of the gods and the good fortune which that brought; Polybius belittled his achievement, and criticised Timaeus for his extravagant praise of it (XII. 23. iv–vii). The truth appears to be that Timoleon genuinely did disapprove of despotic rule, but was prepared to hold a quasi-tyrannical position and to beat the tyrants at their own tricks in order to achieve their overthrow. He was an able commander, good at improvising, and picked good subordinates. He did not drive the Carthaginians back from the position they had obtained at the beginning of the century, but he limited them to that, and he brought the rest of Sicily a generation of peace and prosperity, at a time when Philip of Macedon was making himself master of Greece (cf. chapter 22). But he could not satisfy everybody: we hear nothing of Sicily in the time of Alexander the Great, but in 317 Agathocles made himself tyrant in Syracuse, offering a cancellation of debts and redistribution of land.

On the Italian Greeks we have little information except where they are caught up in Sicilian history. Sparta's colony Taras was one of the most flourishing cities, becoming the leader of the Italiot League, and transferring the League's sanctuary from Croton to Heraclea in 374. An influential figure in the second quarter of the century was Archytas, a philosopher-politician who was general seven times in wars against the Messapians, and who helped to arrange for Plato's final departure from Syracuse in 360 (Pl. *Ep.* vii. 338 C, 350 A–B, Plut. *Dion* 20, Diog. Laert. VIII. 79–82). Rhegium seems to have become independent after it was captured from Dionysius II by Callippus at the end of the 350's, and Locri expelled Dionysius *c.*346 (cf. p. 289). In 346 Taras was at war with the Lucanians. Phalaecus, the last Phocian general in the Third Sacred War, set out with his mercenaries to find employment in this war, but they mutinied; Sparta sent king Archidamus with a force to support Taras, but he was killed in battle in 338 (Diod. Sic. XVI. 61. iv–63. ii, 88. iii–iv: cf. pp. 344–5). Perhaps from 334 to 331 Alexander of Molossis went to fight for Taras (the first of a series of Epirote interventions in Italy which eventually were to bring Rome into the Balkan peninsula; he is said to have made a treaty with Rome): he overran much of southern Italy, but his successes alarmed Taras, which turned against him, and he died in a battle against the Italians (Livy VIII. 3. vi, 24, Strabo 256. VI. i. 5, 280 VI. iii. 4, Just. *Epit.* XII. 2. i–xv). The other Greek city which became particularly important was Neapolis, which seems to have enjoyed a good relationship with its Italian neighbours, and which may have made a treaty with Rome in 326 (Livy VIII. 26. vi).

NOTE ON FURTHER READING

Freeman, *History of Sicily*, vol. iv, was edited after Freeman's death by A. J. Evans. For a shorter but more up-to-date account see Finley, *Ancient Sicily*.

On the sources of our sources, for Diod. Sic. XIII–XV see D. M. Lewis, *CAH*[2] vi, 121–3, with citation of earlier discussions; for book XV Caven, *Dionysius I*, 187–8, despairingly suggests that an original, fuller text has been ousted by an epitome. For book XVI and the lives of *Timoleon* by Nepos and Plutarch see Talbert, *Timoleon and the Revival of Greek Sicily*, ch. 2. On the Platonic *Letters* see Brunt, *Studies in Greek History and Thought*, ch. 10, esp. 312–30, 339–42 (arguing that vii is reliable, whether by Plato or not, iii is a rhetorical exercise derived from vii, viii must be a later exercise since it is unaware of the suicide of Dion's son).

On Dionysius I see Caven, *Dionysius I*. Dionysius' ambitions and achievements in the Adriatic are minimised by A. G. Woodhead, 'The "Adriatic Empire" of Dionysius I of Syracuse', *Klio* lii 1970, 503–12.

On Dion see H. D. Westlake, 'Dion: A Study in Liberation', *DUJ*[2] vii 1945–6, 37–44 = his *Essays on the Greek Historians and Greek History*, ch. 15; 'Friends and Successors of Dion', *Hist.* xxxii 1983, 161–72; Berve, *Dion* (in German). On Dion's heroic honours see A. B. Bosworth, 'Heroic Honours in Syracuse', in Heckel and Tritle (eds.), *Crossroads of History: The Age of Alexander*, ch. 1.

On Timoleon see H. D. Westlake, 'Timoleon and the Reconstruction of Syracuse', *CHJ* vii 1941–3, 73–100 = his *Essays*, ch. 17; 'The Purpose of Timoleon's Mission', *AJP* lxx 1949, 65–75 = his *Essays*, ch. 16; *Timoleon and His Relations with Tyrants*; Talbert, *Timoleon and the Revival of Greek Sicily*.

On the Carthaginians in Sicily see C. R. Whittaker, 'Carthaginian Imperialism in the Fifth and Fourth Centuries', in Garnsey and Whittaker (eds.), *Imperialism in the Ancient World*, ch. 3.

22
Philip II of Macedon

500	475	450	425	400	375	350	325	300

359	accession of Philip
357	capture of Amphipolis
356–346	Third Sacred War
346	Peace of Philocrates between Philip and Athens
340	Athenian declaration of war against Philip
340–338	Fourth Sacred War
338	Philip's victory over Athens, Thebes and others in battle of Chaeronea
336	assassination of Philip

Sources

Xenophon's *Hellenica* ends in 362. Diodorus covers the reign of Philip in book XVI: Ephorus wrote as far as the siege of Perinthus in 340/39 but without completing his history, and his son Demophilus filled a gap by writing book XXX, on the Third Sacred War. A possible source for Diodorus where they were not available is the rhetorical and anecdotal Athenian Diyllus (*FGrH* 73: cf. Diod. Sic. XVI. 14. iii–v, 76. v–vi). The result in Diodorus is an account which is generally favourable to Philip, and more detailed before 346 than after. Our other narrative account is in Latin, in the epitome of the *Philippic History* of Pompeius Trogus (first century BC) by Justin (variously dated between *c*.200 and *c*.400 AD), VII–IX, which is hostile to Philip.

There is plentiful but difficult material in the Athenian orators, particularly Demosthenes and Aeschines, who were much involved in the history of the period and anxious to justify the positions which they had adopted at different times. Demosthenes was born probably in 384/3, the son of a rich manufacturer of knives and beds. His father died when Demosthenes was seven, leaving him under guardians who misappropriated his inheritance. It is alleged that he originally studied oratory so that he could prosecute his guardians, and he won his cases in 363 but had difficulty in recovering the property. From 355 he made speeches in the assembly (he is the only Athenian orator from whom assembly speeches survive: as with lawcourt speeches, the relationship between the texts transmitted and the speeches originally delivered is controversial; cf. p. 315) and in public prosecutions, but for some time he was consistently on the losing side. He regarded Philip as a major threat from c.351 onwards, but between 348 and 346 favoured a peace which he expected to prove that his fears were justified. He was therefore behind the Peace of Philocrates made with Philip in 346 but did not expect it to last; from 344 he looked for renewed conflict, and gained support inside and outside Athens, but the conflict led to Philip's victory at Chaeronea in 338. He led the rejoicing when Philip was killed in 336, and supported the revolt of Thebes in 335, but for much of Alexander's reign he was out of the limelight. He was involved in the scandal surrounding Alexander's fleeing treasurer, Harpalus, in 324–323; he was behind the rising against Macedon in the Lamian War after Alexander's death; in 322 when Athens was defeated he was demanded by Macedon but committed suicide. His speeches and his policies have elicited strong reactions. In trying to evaluate them we need to distinguish different questions: whether Philip was indeed a threat to Athens and to all of Greece, and, if so, whether Demosthenes' was the right policy for opposing him.

Aeschines, one of Demosthenes' opponents, was an older man, born probably c.390, and not from a rich background. His father was on the democratic side and lost property in 404–403, and afterwards worked as a schoolmaster; his mother was perhaps a priestess in a secret cult. He learned the art of speaking as an actor, and by serving among the state secretaries he gained familiarity with the working of Athens' institutions and with the archives. Politically, he was a supporter of Eubulus, opposed to Demosthenes' plans for resistance to Philip. Until 346 opposition to Demosthenes' plans did not entail opposition to any plans for resistance, but when the plans which Aeschines was supporting at the beginning of 346 collapsed he felt peace had to be made with Philip, and then and afterwards he wanted to trust Philip and make the best of the peace. In 343 he was narrowly acquitted when Demosthenes prosecuted him for his role in 346 (Dem. XIX. *Embassy* and Aeschin. II. *Embassy* belong to this trial); in 330 he was overwhelmingly defeated when he revived the prosecution, started but abandoned in 336, of a man who had proposed honours for Demosthenes (Aeschin. III. *Ctesiphon*, Dem. XVIII. *Crown*); and he then left Athens.

Isocrates was old but still writing. Speech-pamphlets from this period include VIII. *Peace*, c.355, and VII. *Areopagitic*, c.354, on the external and internal politics of Athens respectively; XV. *Antidosis*, *c.*353, and XII. *Panathenaic*, 342–339, defences of his career and the policies he had urged; V. *Philip*, 346, and two *Letters to Philip*, urging Philip to lead the Greeks in a patriotic war against Persia (cf. p. 191). Hyperides was a supporter of Demosthenes against Macedon from the late 340s onwards, but prosecuted him in the affair of Harpalus. Lycurgus is best known as a financier, but his one preserved speech is *Against Leocrates*, a man accused of deserting Athens at the time of Chaeronea. From the Corinthian Dinarchus we have three prosecution speeches for the Harpalus affair. Demades was a man willing to collaborate with Macedon in the 330's and 320's, but the speech *On the Twelve Years* defending his policies is a student's exercise.

From Plutarch for the reign of Philip we have lives of two Athenians, *Demosthenes* and *Phocion*. We have inscriptions from Athens and elsewhere, including part of the foundation document of Philip's League of Corinth.

Macedon before Philip

Lower Macedonia was the plain surrounding the Thermaic Gulf (which stretched farther inland than it does now: Pella was not far from the coast), with communications in four directions: south via Tempe and Thessaly to central and southern Greece, east through coastal Thrace to the Hellespont (these were the two most attractive options for a king looking to expand), west across the mountains to Illyria and the Adriatic, north by the Axius (present-day Vardar/Axios) valley to the Danube basin. Surrounding the plain were the hilly regions of Upper Macedonia, peopled by tribes with their own rulers, which the kings of Macedon hoped to control.

In terms of ancient perceptions, the Macedonians were fringe Greeks, who could be regarded as Greek or barbarian according to one's convenience. Their language was probably a dialect of Greek; their kings claimed to be descended from Heracles, and were accepted as Greek for the purpose of competing in the Olympic games from the beginning of the fifth century (cf. Hdt. V. 22, VIII. 137. i, Thuc. II. 99. iii, V. 80. ii). In terms of present-day boundaries, Lower and the southern part of Upper Macedonia are in Greece, but the northern part of Upper Macedonia is in the Republic of Macedonia which was part of the former Yugoslavia.

Macedon in the classical period had a kingship limited by tacit understanding rather than by explicit rules (Thuc. I. 13. i was perhaps thinking of Macedon; cf. Arr. *Anab.* IV. 11. vi): the succession was within the Temenid family, but not necessarily from father to son, and the new king had to be acceptable to the people embodied in the army; capital trials also were decided by the people (Curt. VI. viii. 25). The ruler of Macedon was commonly referred to as king, but probably did not use *basileus* as a formal title; the oath sworn by the members of his League of Corinth in 338/7 refers to his *basileia* (*IG* ii² 236

= R&O 76 ~ Harding 99. *a.* 11–12), but *basileus* first appears as a title in Alexander's letter to Chios in 334 (Tod 192 = R&O 84. *A* ~ Harding 107. 1). Until the fourth century the army effectively comprised the cavalry force of the king and his 'companions' (*hetairoi*), and the infantry was a disorganised mob (Thuc. IV. 124. i).

If Amyntas I made token submission to the Persians after Darius' Scythian expedition of *c.*514 (Hdt. V. 17–21), that had little effect; Macedon was (re)conquered in 492 (Hdt. VI. 44. i), and in 480–479 Alexander I was nominally on the Persian side but was on good terms with the Greeks and was used as a go-between. Before and during the Peloponnesian War Perdiccas I manoeuvred successfully between Athens and Sparta until his death *c.*413. His successor Archelaus was pro-Athenian, at a time when Athens needed his support more than he needed Athens'; Thucydides describes him as a strong king who constructed roads and buildings, strengthened the cavalry and infantry, and achieved more than the eight kings before him (II. 100. ii). It is probably he who moved the capital from Aegeae (now discovered at Vergina and excavated: cf. p. 321) to Pella; he attracted a cultural court circle; and at the end of his reign he was strong enough to interfere in Thessaly (cf. p. 250). But his death in 399 was followed by a period of dynastic trouble, until Amyntas III, from another branch of the family, became king *c.*393. At least once he was driven out by the Illyrians and some of his territory was taken by Olynthus (Diod. Sic. XIV. 92. iii–iv, XV. 19. ii, perhaps records the same episode twice), but he returned and remained king until his death in 370/69.

Then followed another period of instability, with a succession of kings who were all sons of Amyntas III apart from Ptolemy of Alorus, who was husband of Amyntas' daughter and technically regent for Perdiccas (Aeschin. II. *Embassy* 29). Athens became involved with Macedon through its attempt to recover former possessions in the north, in particular Amphipolis, and Thebes became involved through its interest in Thessaly (cf. pp. 236–7, 253). Perdiccas III was killed in 359 in an attack on the Illyrians. He had a son, Amyntas, but he was very young; only Justin claims that Philip was appointed regent for him, and since one charge never made against Philip by Demosthenes is that he was not rightfully king, we should accept that Philip was made king on Perdiccas' death (Diod. Sic. XVI. 2. i–iv, Just. *Epit.* VII. 5. viii–x); after returning from Thebes (cf. p. 253) he had held some regional command (Ath. XI. 506 E–F). Amyntas lived through Philip's reign, and at some point married Philip's daughter Cynanne, but was one of those put to death after Philip's assassination.

Philip in the 350s

The Illyrians, to the west, and the Paeonians, to the north, were both threatening, and there were also other claimants to the throne. Perdiccas' son Amyntas

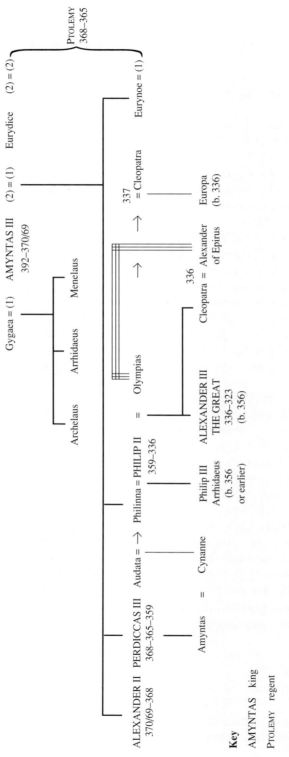

Fig. 8 Amyntas III of Macedon and his descendants (This stemma does not include all the wives and children of Philip II)

was left alive throughout Philip's reign, to be put to death by Alexander (cf. p. 349); it was perhaps now that Archelaus, eldest son of Amyntas III by his first wife, was put to death and his brothers were exiled (cf. Just. VIII. 3. x); but the two claimants of whom we hear most were apparently from other branches of the Temenid family: Pausanias, backed by Thracians (probably by Berisades, in western Thrace), and Argaeus, backed by Athens (Diod. Sic. XVI. 2. v–vi).

Diodorus (XVI. 3. i–ii) credits Philip immediately with an army reform which must have taken some time, in particular organising an effective infantry phalanx for the first time (whether or not he was the first to give this body the name *pezetairoi*, 'foot companions': cf. p. 360). These men were more lightly armed than Greek hoplites, but equipped with the *sarissa*, a spear which at 18 ft. = 5.5 m. was twice as long as Greek hoplites' spears, so that, when Macedonian infantry fought Greek hoplites, the Greeks would be impaled on the Macedonians' spears before the Macedonians came within reach of the Greeks'. He used his cavalry in wedge-shaped units, echoing the diamond used by Jason of Pherae (Arr. *Tact.* 16. vi, cf. iii). Demosthenes commented several times on the variety of his forces and his ability to use them all the year round, without having to disclose his plans in advance through the public procedures of a *polis* (Dem. I. *Ol. i.* 4, IX. *Phil. iii.* 49–50, XVIII. *Crown* 235). The military development was accompanied by economic and social development. Arrian gives Alexander a speech in which he claims that Philip transformed the Macedonians from primitive pastoralists into city-dwelling agriculturalists (*Anab.* VII. 9. ii): how much had already been done before Philip and how much was left for him to do is disputed, but it must be under Philip that the plain of Philippi was drained (Theophr. *Caus. Pl.* V. 14. v–vi). His conquests enabled him to found cities (cf. Just. *Epit.* VIII. 5. vii); and by making grants of estates he recruited Thessalians and other Greeks to the ranks of his cavalry companions (Theopompus *FGrH* 115 F 224).

To give himself time, by bribes and promises Philip made peace with the Paeonians (and presumably with the Illyrians too; this is probably when he married the Illyrian Audata: e.g. list in Ath. XIII. 557 B–E), and detached the Thracians from Pausanias (Diod. Sic. XVI. 3. iv, cf. Just. *Epit.* VII. 6. i–v). To detach the Athenians from Argaeus, he withdrew a garrison installed in Amphipolis by Perdiccas; Argaeus, accompanied by an Athenian general to Methone, advanced on Aegeae but was unwelcome there and was defeated by Philip; then, says Diodorus, Philip made peace with Athens on the basis that he abandoned all claims to Amphipolis (Diod. Sic. XVI. 3. iii, v–vi, 4. i). When, in 357, he captured Amphipolis (below), the Athenians claimed to have been cheated, and referred to a secret (Dem. XXIII. *Aristocrates* 116, II. *Olynth. ii.* 6, [Dem.] VII. *Halonnesus* 27, Theopompus *FGrH* 115 F 30): there cannot have been a secret treaty, since only the assembly could commit Athens to a treaty, but there could have been secret negotiations, and Philip was to prove very good at dropping hints which were accepted as promises by others but not intended as promises by him.

In 358 the army was sufficiently revived for Philip to fight successfully first against the Paeonians and then against the Illyrians (Diod. Sic. XVI. 4. ii–vii, crediting him with 10,000 infantry and 600 cavalry). In 35<u>8</u>/7 he seems to have made his first contact with the Thessalian *koinon*, marrying Philinna of Larissa, who bore him the mentally handicapped Philip Arrhidaeus (garbled in Just. *Epit.* VII. 6. viii); and in 357 he made an alliance with Molossis, marrying Olympias, the niece of king Arybbas, who bore him Alexander in 356 and a daughter, Cleopatra (Just. *Epit.* VII. 6. x–xii). Then, late in 357, he captured Amphipolis (by force: a consequence of the developments in machinery which were tipping the balance in favour of the attackers): the Athenians, trusting his hints, had rejected Amphipolis' plea for help (Dem. I. *Olynth. i.* 8, Theopompus *FGrH* 115 F 42), but Philip kept Amphipolis for himself (Diod. Sic. XVI. 8. ii, cf. Tod 150 = R&O 49 ~ Harding 63). The Athenians indignantly declared war (Isoc. V. *Philip* 2, Aeschin. II. *Embassy* 70, III. *Ctesiphon* 54), but were distracted by the stasis in Euboea in 357 and the outbreak of the Social War in 356 (cf. pp. 239–40).

Olynthus, which the Athenians had spurned when they thought Philip would be cooperative, abandoned an earlier alliance with the Illyrians (*Staatsverträge* 307) and made an alliance with him, by which he promised to capture Potidaea for Olynthus. In 356 he did that, letting the Athenian cleruchs leave but selling the Potidaeans into slavery; he also took Pydna (which the Athenians had perhaps contemplated giving him in exchange for Amphipolis) for himself (Diod. Sic. XVI. 8. iii–v, Tod 158 = R&O 50 ~ Harding 67). In western Thrace Datus had been refounded as Crenides by Thasos in 360/59, about the time of Cotys' death, and in 356 Philip responded to its appeal for help against the Thracians and refounded it again as Philippi. With Amphipolis and Philippi he controlled the gold and silver mines of the Mount Pangaeum region, and this provided him with a secure financial base (Diod. Sic. XVI. 3. viii, 8. vi–vii, Steph. Byz. *s.v.* Philippoi). At first Philippi continued coining under its new name (Kraay, *Archaic and Classical Greek Coins*, p. 145 nos. 509, 510); and Philip's own coinage, in silver and after 348 in gold, was to supplant Athens' coinage as the most desirable currency in the Greek world (Kraay pp. 146–7 nos. 511–13).

In the summer of 356 Athens made an alliance with Philip's barbarian enemies, western Thrace, Paeonia and Illyria, but it was still preoccupied with the Social War, and in 355 Philip was able to frighten the barbarians into submission (Diod. Sic. XVI. 22. iii, *IG* ii² 127 = R&O 53 ~ Harding 70). It was perhaps in 355 too that Philip responded to another invitation from the Thessalian *koinon*: in 35<u>8</u>/7 Alexander of Pherae was murdered by his wife Thebe and her brothers (cf. p. 250, fig. 6); one of these, Tisiphonus, took over the city, and after an initial period of good rule became as despotic as Alexander. We should regard as indecisive an episode recorded by Diodorus in which Philip intervened and defeated Pherae (XVI. 14. i–ii). Methone, on the coast of Macedon, remained hostile to Philip, but it was besieged and captured in the first half of 354, in a campaign during which an arrow blinded Philip in one eye (Diod. Sic. XVI. 31. vi, 34. v–vi, Just. *Epit.* VII. 6. xiii–xiv).

Thus by the mid 350's Philip had made substantial advances both eastwards and southwards. His further southward progress is bound up with the Third Sacred War, which we shall consider below, but it will be convenient to pursue his Thracian activity here. In 353 Chares, recalled to Athens' service after supporting the Persian rebel Artabazus (cf. pp. 239–40), was based at Neapolis, on the Thracian coast: he failed to obstruct a naval squadron of Philip's, returning from an attack on Abdera and Maronea; he perhaps now defeated a mercenary force commanded for Philip by Adaeus; and he reported a meeting of Philip, the Theban Pammenes and Apollonides, agent of the east Thracian Cersebleptes (Polyaenus *Strat.* IV. 2. xxii, Theopompus *FGrH* 115 F 249, Dem. XXIII. *Aristocrates* 183). Chares also captured Sestos, in the Chersonese, for Athens. Perhaps as a result of that, Cersebleptes decided against an alliance with Philip, and in 353/2 allowed Athens to send cleruchs to the Chersonese (Diod. Sic. XVI. 34. iii–iv, *IG* ii² 1613. 297–8, cf. Dem. XXIII. *Aristocrates* 181).

In 352 after his successes in Thessaly Philip advanced to Thermopylae, but the Athenians blocked his passage there (cf. p. 305). He promptly returned to Thrace, and late in 352 at the invitation of Byzantium, Perinthus and the central Thracian Amadocus was engaged in a siege of Heraion Teichos, a fortress of Cersebleptes near the Propontis. Athens voted a relief expedition of forty ships, but delayed when the news came that Philip was ill, and finally sent ten ships in the autumn of 351. How much Philip finally achieved now is uncertain: Cersebleptes was left in his kingdom, but on sufferance, and perhaps now had to send his son as a hostage to Macedon (Theopompus *FGrH* 115 F 101, schol. Aeschin. II. *Embassy* 81 [178 Dilts], Dem. III. *Olynth. iii.* 4–5). On his way to or from Thrace Philip made a demonstration against Olynthus, which had welcomed him as an ally earlier but was now feeling threatened by him: Olynthus made peace with Athens, and there was talk of an alliance (Dem. XXIII. *Aristocrates* 108, III. *Olynth. iii.* 7). In the Aegean, Philip's ships attacked Lemnos and Imbros, and the southern tip of Euboea, and even raided Marathon and captured a sacred trireme (Dem. IV. *Phil. i.* 34).

Philip was a long way from making war on Athens, but by advancing to Thermopylae and the Hellespont he could be perceived as threatening Athens (cf. Dem. XIX. *Embassy* 180), and he had harmed Athens' interests and pride in various ways. We should probably date to 352/1 the first speech in which Demosthenes treats Philip as a major threat to Athens, his (IV) *First Philippic*. The message of the speech is that Athens has lost allies and northern settlements by waiting for Philip to strike and reacting apathetically; Athens should seize the initiative by maintaining a permanent raiding force in the north, with a nucleus of citizens (a sign of the extent to which fourth-century wars were being fought by mercenaries), living largely off booty (since the Social War Eubulus had been trying to prevent unprofitable military expenditure: cf. pp. 332–3). The Athenians did not follow this advice – probably rightly. Philip was certainly conscious of Athens, as a city whose interests had several times clashed with his, but it is doubtful if at this stage he was specifically targeting Athens. In any case, Demosthenes was recommending this policy too late: it might have achieved something in the early years of Philip's reign, but by now he was too strong in and near Macedon to be vulnerable to attacks on a scale which Athens could afford.

The Third Sacred War to 352

Many scholars have supposed that Diodorus without realising it narrated one year of the war twice, but what I say below is based on the view that that supposition is mistaken. Diodorus' account probably does, however, include some smaller duplications, with an episode included in the main narrative at one point and noted from his chronological source at another.

We have seen that in the 360's Thebes took an interest in Delphi (cf. pp. 254–5). In the early 350's the Amphictyony imposed fines on two enemies of Thebes: on Sparta, for sacrilege committed in the occupation of the Theban Cadmea from 382 to 379; and on Phocis, which had refused to support the Thebans at Mantinea in 362 (cf. p. 255), probably for cultivating the sacred plain of Cirrha, by the Gulf of Corinth below Delphi, which was used for pasturing sacrificial animals. Both refused to pay, and one of the Phocians, Philomelus, urged his people to assert their traditional claim to control Delphi (cf. p. 51). He was elected *strategos autokrator*, and gained a promise of unofficial support from king Archidamus of Sparta (Diod. Sic. XVI. 23–24. ii, cf. 29. ii–iv, Just. *Epit.* VIII. 1. iv–vii).

In 357/6 (Diod. Sic. XV. 14. iii–iv, Paus. X. 2. iii) Philomelus seized Delphi, killing the Thracidae who opposed him but reassuring the other Delphians, defeated a Locrian attack, erased the decree against the Phocians, and insisted that he would not plunder the sanctuary but was merely asserting the Phocians' rights. While the Boeotians prepared to fight against him, he raided Locris; and, being in possession of Delphi, he 'consulted' the oracle by forcing the frightened Pythia on to the tripod, in reaction to which she exclaimed that he could do what he liked (Diod. Sic. XVI. 24. iii–27. ii, Just. *Epit.* VIII. 1. viii–xi). In the winter of 356/5 he sent embassies to the Greek cities, gaining the support of Athens, Sparta and some other Peloponnesian cities, and did not touch the sacred treasures but taxed the rich Delphians to build up a mercenary army (Diod. Sic. XVI. 27. iii–28. ii, Just. *Epit.* VIII. 1. ix–x).

Inscriptions from Delphi show that the men expelled in 363 (cf. pp. 254–5) returned and one of them, Aristoxenus, was archon of Delphi for 356/5. The board of *naopoioi* responsible for rebuilding the temple functioned normally until 357/6. However, there were no sessions in 355 or 354; then 'wartime *naopoioi*' from states on the Phocian side met from spring 353 to spring 351 (they deposited their funds, with which the Phocians did not interfere, with the city of Delphi). After that, meetings were abandoned until after the war (*C.*

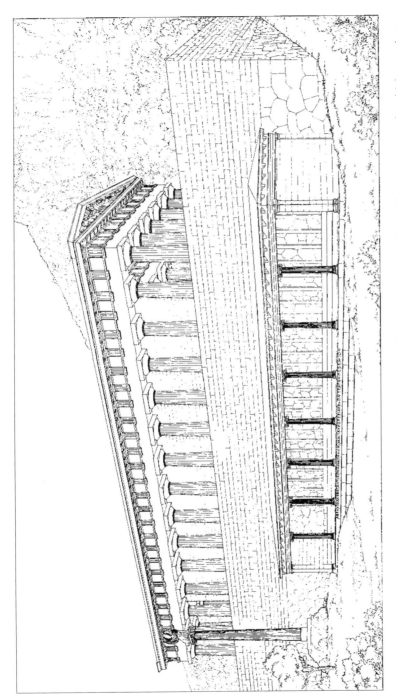

III. 11 Delphi: The temple of Apollo and the stoa of the Athenians (the drawing shows the sixth-century temple which was destroyed in 373/2; the replacement was built on the old plan, and as far as possible used the old columns). From *Guide de Delphes, le Site*. © EFA/Y. Fomine, D. Laroche

Delphes ii 31. 1–70; resumption 345/4, *C. Delphes* ii 34 = R&O 66). The wartime
naopoioi include unspecified Locrians, perhaps from Amphissa (cf. below), and
we have a fragment of an Athenian alliance with unspecified Locrians of about
this time (*IG* ii² 148). Probably in 356/5 the city of Delphi honoured the sons
of Athens' ally Cersebleptes (*SIG*³ 195: archon restored). An inscription from
Thebes records contributions of money to the Boeotians for the war over three
years *c.*354–352: the contributors include Byzantium, which in the Social War
had left the Athenian League, and the Boeotian *proxenos* in the pro-Athenian
Tenedos (*IG* vii 2418 = R&O 57 ~ Harding 74). Xenophon's *Poroi*, of the late
350's, says that all will be supportive if Athens works not by fighting but by
diplomacy to make Delphi 'autonomous as in the past' (v. 8–9).

In 355 Philomelus was attacked by the Locrians but defeated them by the
Phaedriadae cliffs. The Locrians then appealed to the Thebans, who appealed
to the Thessalian *koinon*. The Amphictyony formally declared a sacred war
against the Phocians, and most of the central Greeks joined the Amphictyonic
side (Diod. Sic. XVI. 28. iii–29. i): alignments were much as they had been in
the 360's. In winter 355/4 Philomelus further increased his forces, and possibly
now did use the sacred treasures (Diod. Sic. XVI. 30. i–ii; contr. acquittal 56.
v). His successes continued in 354, with a cavalry victory over the Locrians and
Thebans, and then a victory over the Thessalians at Argolas, in eastern Locris;
but later in the year he was defeated by the Thebans at Neon, near the head of
the Cephisus valley, and committed suicide (Diod. Sic. XVI. 30. iii–31. iv, Just.
Epit. VIII. 1. xii–xiii, cf. Paus. X. 2. iv). This might have ended the war. The
Thebans did not follow up their victory, and were confident enough to send
their general Pammenes to support the Persian rebel Artabazus in 353 (Diod.
Sic. XVI. 34. i–ii). The Phocians considered admitting defeat, but Onomarchus,
the first of three generals from the same family, persuaded them to persevere
and drew on the sacred treasures to strengthen his forces (Diod. Sic. XVI. 31.
v, 32. i–33. ii, Just. *Epit.* VIII. 1. xiv).

In 353 Onomarchus had a series of successes in the territories around Phocis,
among other things gaining the submission of the Locrians of Amphissa; in
Boeotia he took Orchomenus but was unsuccessful in a siege of Chaeronea.
Philip was brought in to support the Thessalian *koinon*, while Onomarchus'
brother Phayllus went to support Lycophron of Pherae (Tisiphonus was dead).
Philip defeated Phayllus, but Onomarchus went to Thessaly and in two battles
gave Philip the most serious defeats in his reign – which perhaps gave the Greeks
the false impression that he was not strong enough to pose a serious threat.
Late that year or early 352 Onomarchus turned to Boeotia, where he won a
battle and took Coronea (Diod. Sic. XVI. 33. iii–iv, 35. i–iii, Just. *Epit.* VIII. 2.
i–ii, Arist. *Eth. Nic.* III. 1116 в 15–23, Ephorus *FGrH* 70 F 94).

In 352 Philip returned to Thessaly and persuaded the Thessalians 'to undertake the war jointly'; it was probably at this point that the *koinon* took the surprising step of appointing him as its archon (cf. Alexander's succession to the
position, p. 349). On the other side Lycophron summoned Onomarchus and
the Phocians, 'offering to organise the affairs of Thessaly together with them';

the Athenians sent Chares by sea to the Gulf of Pagasae. In the major 'battle of the Crocus Field', to the west of the Gulf, Philip's soldiers wore laurel crowns so symbolise their holy cause, the Phocians were defeated, and Onomarchus was among those killed in the stampede to the ships. Phayllus took over the command of the Phocians, and set about reviving their forces; but Lycophron and Pitholaus surrendered Pherae to Philip (they and their mercenaries were allowed to withdraw, and joined the Phocians). Philip went on to capture Pagasae (an earlier capture, after that of Methone, must be either an error by Diodorus or a mistaken restoration in the text of XVI. 31. vi). He then advanced to Thermopylae, but the Athenians reacted promptly, and he did not force the passage. Phayllus moved into Boeotia but was three times defeated (Diod. Sic. XVI. 35. iii–36. i, 37–38. ii, Just. *Epit.* VIII. 2. iii–xii, cf. Dem. XIX. *Embassy* 84, 319).

An episode in the Peloponnese displays the same alignment of the Greek states. While the Greeks were preoccupied with the Sacred War, Sparta tried to exploit the principle of *echein ta heauton* (cf. p. 197) to recover Messenia, and in 353 attacked Megalopolis. Megalopolis appealed to its allies, including (thanks to the treaty after Mantinea) Athens; Athens' sympathies were with Sparta, on the same side in the Sacred War; Demosthenes in (XVI) *For the Megalopolitans* urged Athens to support Megalopolis rather than leave it to Thebes to do so. Athens reaffirmed its support for the independent Messene but did not take part in the war; Thebes and several Peloponnesian states supported Megalopolis; Sparta was supported by the Phocians and, from the summer of 352, the mercenaries from Pherae. In 352 Sparta captured Orneae, west of Argos, and sacked Helisson, west of Mantinea; in 351, with little happening in central Greece, the Thebans sent a larger force and were victorious at Thelphusa, in the west of Arcadia, and elsewhere; in 350 there was a Spartan victory and the war ended with a truce which changed nothing (Diod. Sic. XVI. 34. iii, 39).

Olynthus and Euboea

Two crises blew up in 349/8, both of concern to Athens. We have seen that in the late 350's Olynthus was feeling threatened by Philip and was moving towards Athens. Olynthus took in Philip's surviving step-brothers as refugees (Just. *Epit.* VIII. 3. x); this provided Philip with the excuse for an attack, and he began in the summer of 349 by taking some of the smaller cities of Chalcidice. Olynthus made an alliance with Athens, which sent Chares with an expedition in support (Diod. Sic. XVI. 52. ix, Philoch. *FGrH* 328 F 49). It may be true that Philip then had to interfere in Pherae, but hardly that Pitholaus had returned and had to be expelled again (Diod. Sic. XVI. 52. ix, cf. Dem. I. *Ol. i.* 22, II. *Ol. ii.* 11).

Euboea had rejoined Athens in 357 (cf. p. 239), but in enemy hands could provide an invader from the north with a means of by-passing Thermopylae.

Early in 348 Plutarchus of Eretria appealed for Athenian support when challenged by the exiled Clitarchus, and Phocion was sent with a small force; Callias of Chalcis obtained mercenaries from Phocis to support the other side. There was anxiety in Athens: Apollodorus proposed that surplus revenue should be transferred to the stratiotic fund (cf. p. 334) and the council proposed a major expedition. However, Apollodorus' proposal was quashed, and the major expedition was not sent since Phocion reported that he had won a victory although Plutarchus had turned against Athens. Early in the summer Phocion called for reinforcements, expelled Plutarchus from Eretria and returned to Athens. But by midsummer things had gone badly wrong for Athens: Molossus, Phocion's successor, was captured by Plutarchus, Athens had to pay 50 talents to ransom him and others, and all of Euboea except Carystus, in the south, passed out of Athens' sphere of influence (Plut. *Phoc.* 12–14. ii, Dem. XXI. *Midias* 161–4, and various allusions by Demosthenes and Aeschines; schol. Dem. V. *Peace* 5 [21 Dilts], Aeschin. III. *Ctesiphon* 86 [190 Dilts]). There are slight indications that Philip gave some help to the anti-Athenian side (Aeschin. III, *Ctesiphon* 87, Plut. *Phoc.* 12. i).

Meanwhile, in spring 348 Athens sent further help to Olynthus, transferring a force under Charidemus from the Hellespont. Philip took more of the cities of Chalcidice; the Olynthians were defeated in battle and besieged; and when they appealed for a citizen force Athens prepared a substantial expedition, once more under Chares. But during the summer that was delayed by the regular 'etesian' winds, which hampered sailing to the north; at some point the pro-Athenian Apollonides was expelled from Olynthus and fled to Athens, and a decree to grant him citizenship was proposed but was quashed through a *graphe paranomon* (Dem. IX. *Phil. iii.* 56, 66, [Dem.] LIX. *Neaera* 91). In late summer, before Athens' expedition could arrive, Olynthus was betrayed to Philip; the population was enslaved and the city destroyed (Philoch. *FGrH* 328 FF 50–1, 156, Diod. Sic. XVI. 53. ii–iii, 55. i).

For Demosthenes, supporting Olynthus was in line with the policy of the *First Philippic*, to strike at Philip as near to the heart of Macedon as possible, and he was energetic in championing Olynthus. His (I–III) *Olynthiacs i–iii* were probably delivered, in that order, in the second half of 349. In a speech of 346 he describes the Euboean campaign as inglorious and expensive, and claims to have been the only man to have opposed it (V. *Peace* 5). But Athens could not save Olynthus if Philip was determined to take it; Euboea in 348, like Thermopylae in 352, was more obviously relevant to the security of Athens, and it is not surprising that most Athenians thought Euboea more important than Olynthus. The Euboean campaign was a campaign of Eubulus and his supporters: Demosthenes describes Eubulus' friend Midias as an agent of Plutarchus (Dem. XXI. *Midias* 110, 200), and Eubulus' relative Hegesilaus was prosecuted for deceiving the people in connection with it (Dem. XIX. *Embassy* 290 with schol. [513 Dilts]).

In midsummer 348 there were reports that Philip would like peace with Athens (Olynthus had not yet fallen, and this suggestion was probably a device to undermine Athenian support). Philocrates proposed that Athens should receive a deputation from Philip; he was prosecuted in a *graphe paranomon*, was defended by Demosthenes, and, in Demosthenes' first success in a public issue, was acquitted (Aeschin. II. *Embassy* 12–15, III. *Ctesiphon* 62). From this point until peace was made in 346 Demosthenes was in favour of peace, and we have to assume that he was sulking at the Athenians' failure to take notice of his warnings, and wanted a treaty not because he believed in peace but because he believed that Philip's subsequent conduct would show that his warnings had after all been justified. On the other hand, Eubulus and his associates, including Aeschines, were alarmed after the failure in Euboea and the fall of Olynthus, and in winter 348/7 under a decree of Eubulus embassies were sent out to rouse the Greeks against Philip, Aeschines going to Arcadia (Dem. XIX. *Embassy* 9–11, 203–14, Aeschin. II. *Embassy* 79).

The End of the Third Sacred War

Phayllus had succeeded Onomarchus as Phocian general after the battle of the Crocus Field. In 351, while the Thebans were making their main effort in the Peloponnese, he was defeated in one night attack but nevertheless captured the whole of eastern Locris. He died in the winter of 351/0, and was succeeded by Onomarchus' son Phalaecus under the guardianship of Mnaseas. In 350 the Thebans pulled out of the Peloponnese. They first killed Mnaseas in a night attack and then defeated Phalaecus in a cavalry battle; Phalaecus took Chaeronea but was driven out, and the Boeotians then ravaged Phocis. In 349 there were only minor skirmishes (Diod. Sic. XVI. 38. iii–vii, 39. viii, 40. ii, Paus. X. 2. vi–vii). Although Athens and Phocis were on the same side in the Sacred War, the Phocians supported the anti-Athenian side in Euboea. In the Sacred War 348 was a largely successful year for them: after a Boeotian raid on Hyampolis, north of Boeotia, Phalaecus defeated the Boeotians at Coronea and captured several cities, and another Boeotian raiding party was defeated as it returned home (Diod. Sic. XVI. 56. i–ii).

The Phocians had good prospects of victory, but some were feeling uneasy about their use of sacred treasures to pay for mercenaries, and so in winter 348/7 Phalaecus was deposed, a triumvirate was appointed in his place, and an investigation into the use of the sacred treasures was made. Philomelus was absolved, but the treasurer, Philo, and the remaining generals were found guilty (Diod. Sic. XVI. 56. iii–57, cf. Paus. X. 2. vii). In 347 the Phocians continued the war, building on their successes of 348, and the Thebans appealed to Philip, who had played no part in the war since 352. He sent a token force, not displeased at the Thebans' weakness but not wanting to condone the Phocians' sacrilege, according to Diodorus, and the Thebans successfully attacked a fort which the Phocians were building at Abae, near Hyampolis (Diod. Sic. XVI. 58, cf. Dem. XIX. *Embassy* 141).

The Thebans asked Philip to support them again in 346. The Phocians appealed to Sparta and Athens, inviting the Athenians to occupy forts in Locris to the east of Thermopylae, and Athens sent Proxenus with an expedition of fifty ships. But in a counter-revolution about February 346 Phalaecus returned to power, Athenian and Spartan offers of help were rebuffed, and the Phocians refused the truce for the Lesser Eleusinian Mysteries (Diod. Sic. XVI. 59. i–ii, Aeschin. II. *Embassy* 132–5, cf. 37, Dem. XIX. *Embassy* 322): presumably there had been contact between Phalaecus and Philip, and Philip was dropping encouraging hints to Phalaecus.

We shall look in more detail below at the effect of this on Athens. Eubulus and his associates had been trying to organise resistance to Philip by the southern Greeks, but this depended on cooperation with Phocis, and without that cooperation resistance was no longer feasible, so they turned to peace. The terms – peace for 'Athens and its allies', i.e. the Second Athenian League – were agreed and sworn to in Athens in mid to late April. Philip and his allies had to swear, but he was in Thrace fighting against Cersebleptes, and envoys from Athens and almost all of Greece spent June waiting at Pella for him to return. When he did return he was in no hurry to swear, but assembled a large army, and the envoys accompanied him and it south. There was considerable uncertainty about his intentions, and Aeschines hoped that the Phocians might yet be saved. When the Athenian embassy reached home, on 8 July, Philip was at Thermopylae, giving dubious assurances to the Phocians; Demosthenes in his report to the council urged that the Phocians should not be abandoned; but on 11 July, when the assembly met, Philip's position was known and Athens could only advise the Phocians to submit. On 18 July the Phocians capitulated; Phalaecus secured terms by which he and his mercenaries were allowed to withdraw (Dem. XIX. *Embassy* 53–66, Diod. Sic. XVI. 59. iii, Just. *Epit.* VIII. 5. i–iii). In a caricature of the roaming mercenaries' existence, Phalaecus first tried to take them to a war in Italy, but they mutinied (cf. p. 292); he then took them to Crete, where in fighting for Cnossus they were defeated and he was killed by Archidamus and a Spartan force fighting for Lyctus (cf. p. 344). Philip had remained true to the Amphictyony's aim of punishing the sacrilegious Phocians, and by encouraging uncertainty about his intentions he had on behalf of the Amphictyony won a bloodless victory.

In late summer 346 he convened an extraordinary meeting of the Amphictyonic council. The Phocians were expelled from the Amphictyony, required to repay the stolen funds, allegedly more than 10,000 talents altogether, originally at the rate of 30 talents per half-year (they began in autumn 343 [*C. Delphes* ii 36 = R&O 67], and by the last attested payment, probably in 319/8, had paid *c.* 400 talents; cf. below), were disarmed and were made to live in small villages. Nicaea, immediately to the east of Thermopylae, which had been in the hands of the Phocians, was given to the Thessalians (Aeschin. III. *Ctesiphon* 140). Sparta also was expelled from the Amphictyony (Paus. X. 8. ii: it had perhaps voted with the Dorians of central Greece), but Athens (which had one of the two Ionian votes) was not. The Amphictyony was reconstituted, with

Thessaly, of which Philip was archon, taking first place and Philip himself (not Macedon) second. If it had not already happened earlier, two of the smaller peoples who had originally been represented separately were now combined in a single unit, and the unit thus freed was assigned to the *polis* of Delphi. In the autumn Philip presided over the Pythian games (Diod. Sic. XVI. 59. iv–60, Just. *Epit.* VIII. 5. iv–vi). In 34<u>3</u>/2 the Delphian building accounts record the removal of statues of Onomarchus and Philomelus (*C. Delphes* ii 34 = R&O 66. ii. 56–9): either this was a surprisingly delayed *damnatio memoriae* or in their current position the statues were simply in the way of the building works.

What Philip hoped to achieve in 346 will be discussed below. What he did achieve was a recognised position of importance in the Greek world through his membership of the Amphictyony. The Phocians had been justly, though perhaps not as drastically as the Thebans and Thessalians wished, punished for their sacrilege; the Thebans, after ten years of war, much of it fought in Boeotian territory, were weakened and gained little from being on the winning side (cf. Isoc. V. *Philip* 53–5); Athens and Sparta had both been on the losing side, and Greek states or parties within states hostile to them were increasingly likely to look to Philip for support (cf. Isoc. V. *Philip* 74, Dem. V. *Peace* 18, Polyb. IX. 33. ii–xii, XVIII. 14).

The Peace of Philocrates

Demosthenes and Aeschines told their stories in 343, when Demosthenes prosecuted Aeschines, and again in 330, when Aeschines prosecuted Ctesiphon (in this section their four major speeches are cited briefly as A. II, III, D. XIX, XVIII). What actually happened is hard to disentangle, since each had made a major change in policy which he was anxious to conceal: Demosthenes from 348 until peace was made wanted to get peace on whatever terms he could, but once it had been made looked for renewed conflict (once Philip provided a justification: see p. 312 on Dem. V. *Peace*); Aeschines originally, from 348 until in 346 Phalaecus made resistance impossible, wanted to resist, but he was then forced to look for peace, and wanted to make the best of Philip's hints at the time and of the disappointing outcome afterwards (he was still proud of the peace in 346/5, I. *Timarchus* 174; contrast his defensiveness in 343, A. II. 56, 79).

Theoretically Athens had been at war with Philip since his capture of Amphipolis in 357, and the Peace of Philocrates was to end that war. In the summer of 348, to weaken Athens' support for Olynthus, Philip let it be known that he was interested in peace, Philocrates proposed that Athens should receive a deputation from him, and he was successfully defended by Demosthenes (cf. pp. 306–7). No deputation came, but Philocrates and Demosthenes had Aristodemus (an actor with contacts in Macedon and elsewhere) sent to negotiate with Philip over Athenians captured in Olynthus; eventually, perhaps early 346, Aristodemus reported that Philip would like even an alliance (A. II. 15–17).

Eubulus and Aeschines had become worried about Philip: embassies were sent
to southern Greek states in winter 348/7 (cf. above); and again in winter 347/6
to invite representatives to a war congress (A. II. 87–9, III. 64–70, D. XIX. 15,
XVIII. 23–4). About February 346 Phalaecus returned to power in Phocis and
rejected Athenian and Spartan help.

Probably the news of that rejection led the Athenians to seek peace (cf.
A. II. 134). Late in February Philocrates proposed the dispatch of the first
embassy to Philip, including himself, Demosthenes (he was nominated by
Philocrates, but in his speeches he tries to distance himself from Philocrates),
Aeschines and Aristodemus (A. II. 18–20, D. XIX. 12–13). The envoys
hurried (D. XIX. 163); allegedly Demosthenes as the youngest member lost his
nerve when addressing Philip (A. II. 34–5). In mid March they returned, bringing a letter from Philip. Demosthenes was a councillor for this crucial year
347/6. In the council he proposed the standard honours for the envoys; in the
assembly, again speaking last, he disparaged Philip but proposed that the assembly should meet on two successive days (cf. the decision over Corcyra and
Corinth in 433, p. 83) to discuss peace and alliance (A. II. 45–54, 110, D. XIX.
234).

The *synedrion* of Athens' League proposed waiting until the envoys inviting
to a war congress had returned, and then holding assemblies to discuss
peace; but added that it would accept what Athens decided (A. II. 60). Demosthenes' original plan was for assemblies on 8–9 Elaphebolion = 5–6 April,
before the Dionysia (A. III. 67), but Philip's envoys did not arrive in time.
Demosthenes saw to their entertainment at the Dionysia (A. II. 55, 110–11, III.
76, D. XIX. 234, XVIII. 28), and his revised plan was for assemblies on the
first two days available after the festival, 18–19 Elaphebolion = 15–16 April,
with discussion on the first day and the vote on the second (A. II. 61–2, 65,
109).

It now becomes particularly hard to work out what happened, but a possible solution is as follows. On the 18th there were at any rate two proposals
under discussion: one from the League *synedrion*, that there should be a
common peace, which any Greek state might join within three months (A. III.
69–70); and another from Philocrates, that there should be a peace explicitly
excluding Phocis and Halus, a city on the Gulf of Pagasae which was currently
being besieged by Pharsalus with support from Philip (D. XIX. 159). The
synedrion's proposal was supported by Aeschines, who wanted peace but did
not want to abandon Phocis (A. II. 63, III. 71, D. XIX. 14), and also by Demosthenes, who proposed that it should be put to Philip's envoys (D. XIX. 144).
Philip's envoys were not brought in until the 19th. Demosthenes alleges that
on that day he continued to support a common peace but Aeschines had
changed his position and now supported Philocrates. Demosthenes goes on to
claim that the Macedonians said an alliance with Phocis was impossible, and
Aeschines said they had to say that because of Thebes and Thessaly but Athens
should nevertheless trust Philip (D. XIX. 15–16, 144, 321, cf. A. II. 63). To
Demosthenes' allegations Aeschines has various responses: that there was to be

no debate on the 19th, so he could not have supported Philocrates; that Demosthenes himself had prepared a motion identical with that of Philocrates (A. II. 64–8); that when circumstances were against Athens Aeschines did advocate the peace which Demosthenes calls disgraceful (A. II. 79). In 330 Aeschines claims that Demosthenes said the *synedrion*'s proposal was pointless unless the Macedonians accepted, there could not be peace without alliance and Athens could not wait on others; and that after that Demosthenes interrogated Antipater, Philip's chief representative, and gained acceptance for Philocrates' motion (A. III. 71–2).

On the 18th, it seems, the Athenians had discussed unrealistically what kind of peace they would like; on the 19th Demosthenes discovered from Antipater what kind of peace Philip would allow – and then there must have been a renewed debate, considering peace on Philip's terms or no peace. Aeschines, trusting in Philip's hints, wanted peace; Demosthenes, wanting Philip to be committed to something, wanted peace; Eubulus dwelled on the financial consequences of not making peace (D. XIX. 291). Not everybody agreed: Hegesippus, who had proposed the alliance with the Phocians at the beginning of the Sacred War, was opposed on their account (A. III. 118 with schol. [265 Dilts]; D. XIX. 72–4 with schol. 72 [172 Dilts]), and Aristophon insisted on Athens' claim to Amphipolis and thought it had the resources to fight (Theopompus *FGrH* 115 F 166). Philocrates' proposal was carried but in an amended form, not excluding Phocis and Halus but including 'Athens and its allies' (D. XIX. 159). As what followed in the next few days makes clear, that was taken to mean Athens and the League, but there was a loophole which people could try to exploit, since the words might mean Athens and every state allied to Athens, including Phocis.

The peace was not made until both sides had sworn to it. After meeting Athens' first embassy Philip had set out for Thrace, promising not to touch the Chersonese. On 23 or 24 Elaphebolion = 20 or 21 April he captured Hieron Oros, and Cersebleptes 'lost his kingdom' (though he was not finally evicted until 342). The next day in Athens Demosthenes tried to rule out of order, and the assembly considered but rejected, a request from Cersebleptes to be admitted to the League and the peace; and on the proposal of Philocrates the League *synedroi* swore to the peace (A. II. 82–90, III. 73–4, D. XIX. 174, 181). Philip and his allies had to swear too. Athens' second embassy, to receive their oaths, did not hurry; but, despite Demosthenes' indignation (D. XIX. 154–6, XVIII. 25–31), while Philip was in Thrace there was no point in hurrying. They arrived at Pella in late May, and Philip arrived in late June. As he prepared for a major expedition, the envoys from Athens and elsewhere lobbied him. Demosthenes, at odds with his colleagues, refused to tangle with Philip over Phocis and Thebes but arranged the ransom of some Athenian prisoners (A. II. 97–100, 106–12, D. XIX. 166–73). Aeschines claims to have urged Philip to punish only the individuals responsible for the sacrilege at Delphi and not to allow Boeotia to be dominated by Thebes (A. II. 101–5, 113–19); Demosthenes blames Aeschines for excluding Phocis, Halus and Cersebleptes from the peace (D. XIX. 44, 174,

278). Probably Philip did drop hints that he would not punish the innocent and did not want a powerful Thebes; Aeschines wanted to believe and did, Demosthenes did not.

Philip swore at Pella (D. XVIII. 32), but his allies did not swear until the expedition reached Pherae (D. XIX. 158). He was at Thermopylae when the Athenians reached home, on 13 Scirophorion = 8 July. Demosthenes persuaded the council to recommend to the assembly not to abandon Phocis, but in the assembly on 16 Scirophorion = 11 July this *probouleuma* was not read out: presumably it was now known that it was too late to save Phocis. Aeschines reported Philip's hints and urged the Athenians to trust them; a formal letter from Philip was read out; a motion of Philocrates (who seems to have been a sincere supporter of peace with Philip) was carried, extending the treaty with Philip to his descendants, calling on the Phocians to surrender Delphi to the Amphictyony, and promising that Athens would help to enforce that (D. XIX. 31–50, cf. A. II. 119–23). A third embassy was appointed, to report this to Philip; Demosthenes refused to serve, and Aeschines stayed in Athens too. Philip sent a letter asking Athens to send its army against the Phocians, but Demosthenes persuaded the assembly not to do so (D. XIX. 121–4, cf. 51–2, A. II. 94–5, 137–8).

The Phocians capitulated on 23 Scirophorion = 18 July; the third embassy turned back on hearing the news. The Athenians panicked, deciding to strengthen their fortifications, bring their women and children into the city and celebrate the Heraclea inside the city – but Philip made no move against Athens. He dealt with Phocis through the Amphictyonic council; he captured Halus and gave it to Pharsalus (D. XIX. 36–9, Str. 433. IX. v. 8). A fourth embassy went to Philip, and Aeschines claims to have saved some innocent Phocians (D. XIX. 59–60, 86, 125, A. II. 95–6, 139, 142–3).

The hints encouraged by Aeschines had proved vain, and the Athenians were angry. They boycotted the Pythian games (D. XIX. 128); they gave a hostile reception to the request to recognise Philip's admission to the Amphictyony (D. XIX. 111–13); and they remained in touch with Sparta (Dem. V. *Peace* 18). It seems that some men were prepared to go to war against Philip, but Demosthenes in (V) *On the Peace* took the line that war was inevitable but Athens should wait for a suitable occasion; if they fought now they would be technically in the wrong and the Greeks would unite against them; they should not risk that for the sake of 'a shadow at Delphi'. Isocrates, however, now focused on Philip as the man to lead the Greeks in a patriotic war against the Persians (V. *Philip*, of 346; *Letters to Philip*).

What of Philip? Some have thought that his hints were intended seriously, and that he would have preferred to act on them but was prevented by the intransigence of Demosthenes. That is hard to believe – he had no reason to turn against Thebes, and would have lost face badly if he had decided that the Phocians were not wicked after all – but he was fond of keeping his opponents guessing and undermining their opposition, and by doing this now he was able to win the war without a battle. Others have suggested that he was already thinking of a war against the Persians, and wanted a cooperative Athens for the sake of its navy; but despite Isocrates there is no sign that Philip was interested in Persia before 341 (the claim that at some point there was an alliance between Philip and Artaxerxes, in Darius' letter in Arr. *Anab.* II. 14. ii, is almost certainly false). More probably, for a man brought up on the edge of the Greek world, a recognised position in Greece was an important objective in its own right; Demosthenes' opposition was tiresome, but there were Athenians willing to acknowledge him; and Athens was a well-fortified city and could not easily be taken by force.

Philip's Final Victory

In Athens there was a revision of the citizen registers (Aeschin. I. *Timarchus* 77 with schol. [169 Dilts], 86, Androtion *FGrH* 324 F 52, Philoch. *FGrH* 328 F 52, cf. Isae. XII. *Euphiletus*, Dem. LVII. *Eubulides*), and one of the men rejected was to be charged by Demosthenes with attempting to burn Athens' dockyards for Philip (cf. pp. 339–40). Although Phocis was a sore point, Philip's campaign in Thrace while the peace was pending was more obviously unfair and more of a threat to Athens' interests: Euclides was sent to remonstrate, and Philip offered to cut a canal through the isthmus of the Chersonese (Dem. VI. *Phil. ii.* 30, [Dem.] VII. *Halonnesus* 39–40).

Philip strengthened his position at home, with various movements of population (Dem. XIX. *Embassy* 89, Just. *Epit.* VIII. 5. vi–6. ii). Perhaps in 345, he campaigned against the Illyrians and was wounded (Diod. Sic. XVI. 69. vii, Just. *Epit.* VIII. 6. iii, Didymus xii. 64–xiii. 2). In 344 he 'expelled tyrants' from Thessaly (there was trouble involving a man called Simus in Larisa, and he installed a garrison in Pherae), and Demosthenes refers to his instituting a 'decadarchy', the rule of a clique of ten men (Diod. Sic. XVI. 69. viii; Dem. XVIII. *Crown* 48, Arist. *Pol.* V. 1306 A 26–30 with Kraay p. 119 no. 395; [Dem.] VII. *Halonnesus* 32; Dem. VI. *Phil. ii.* 22). In 343/2 Athens tried to win over the Thessalians (schol. Aeschin. III. *Ctesiphon* 83 [181 Dilts]), but did not succeed, and in 342 Philip revived the old organisation of Thessaly in four regional units known as tetrads (Dem. IX. *Phil. iii.* 26, Theopompus *FGrH* 115 FF 208–9).

In the course of 344 various envoys from Philip and his allies went to Athens, complaining of slanders against Philip and support for Sparta, and offering an amendment (*epanorthosis*) of the peace terms. Demosthenes' (VI) *Second Philippic* is a fairly early reply. A little later there coincided with a deputation from Philip one from Persia, and the Athenians together with the Spartans confirmed their friendship with Persia but (unlike Thebes) declined to send troops for the latest attempt on Egypt (Philoch. *FGrH* 328 F 157, Diod. Sic. XVI. 44. i–ii [misdated: cf. p. 325]). At this stage Athens was without a settled policy, but the pendulum swung towards hostility to Philip. Hegesippus persuaded the

Athenians to take a hard line, demanding under the principle of *echein ta heauton* the return of Amphipolis and of forts in Thrace which Philip had captured in 346, and the expansion of the Peace of Philocrates into a common peace. Hegesippus visited Macedon and made himself highly unpopular, and in response to Philip's offer to give (*didonai*) to Athens Halonnesus, an island in the north Aegean which he had cleared of pirates, Hegesippus insisted that it belonged to Athens and Philip could only give it back (*apodidonai*). The matter dragged on to 342, when Philip was willing to submit to arbitration over the Thracian forts (where he had a strong case) and to accept a common peace (which he now thought he could use to his advantage), but only to 'give' Halonnesus and not to give Amphipolis. [Dem.] VII. *Halonnesus* is Hegesippus' unrepentant reaction; and Philip seems to have lost patience. Plato's nephew Speusippus in his *Letter to Philip* of 343/2, trying to outdo Theopompus and Isocrates, suggested that through Heracles Amphipolis (§6) and other places 'belonged' to Philip.

Immediately after the peace Demosthenes planned with Timarchus to prosecute Aeschines for his conduct on the second embassy (Aeschin. II. *Embassy* 96), but Timarchus' private life left him vulnerable and in 346/5 Aeschines prosecuted him (Aeschin. I. *Timarchus*: cf. p. 337). In 343, as attitudes to Philip were hardening, charges were brought to court. Philocrates was prosecuted by Hyperides, and was condemned in absence (Dem. XIX. *Embassy* 116–19, Aeschin. II. *Embassy* 6, Hyp. IV. *Euxenippus* 29–30); Proxenus was perhaps condemned for delay in conveying the second embassy to Philip (Dem. XIX. *Embassy* 280 with schol. [493 Dilts]). Nevertheless, when Demosthenes himself prosecuted Aeschines, Eubulus spoke for the defence, and by a small majority Aeschines was acquitted (Idomeneus *FGrH* 338 F 10 *ap.* Plut. *Dem.* 15. v, [Plut.] *X Orat.* 840 c).

In various parts of Greece there were local conflicts, not stirred up by Athens or Philip but often leading to their being invoked as supporters. In 344 Argos and Messene accepted help from Philip against Sparta, despite a warning from Demosthenes (Dem. VI. *Phil. ii.* 15, 19–26); but in 343/2 they and other Peloponnesian states became allies of Athens (schol. Aeschin. III. *Ctesiphon* 83 [181 Dilts], cf. *IG* ii² 225). In Megara (with which Athens had had frontier problems in the late 350's: *IG* ii² 204 = R&O 58, Androtion *FGrH* 324 F 30, Philoch. *FGrH* 328 F 155) a pro-Athenian party asked Athens for help against an aristocratic, pro-Philip party, and Phocion was sent and rebuilt the long walls linking Megara to the harbour town of Nisaea (Dem. XIX. *Embassy* 87, 204, 294–5, 326, 394, Plut. *Phoc.* 15). In Elis there was a revolution, for which Demosthenes blamed Philip (Dem. XIX. *Embassy* 260, 294, X. *Phil. iv.* 10). In 343/2 Philip intervened in Molossis, ousting king Arybbas in favour of Alexander, Arybbas' nephew and Olympias' brother: Arybbas fled to Athens and was welcomed with a decree making the (unfulfilled) promise to restore him to his realm ([Dem.] VII. *Halonnesus* 32, Theopompus *FGrH* 115 FF 206–7, Just. *Epit.* VIII. 6. iv–viii, Diod. Sic. XVI. 72. i [garbled], *IG* ii² 226 = R&O 70). Demosthenes served on an embassy to Ambracia and Acarnania, and to oblige

Corinth the Athenians campaigned in Acarnania (Dem. IX. *Phil. iii.* 34, 72, [Dem.] XLVIII. *Olympiodorus* 24–6, Aeschin. III. *Ctesiphon* 97–8).

In Euboea, which Athens had lost in 348, Philip's interventions were badly judged. Demosthenes refers to Philip's partisans as tyrants and their opponents as the *demos*: probably 'tyrant' is simply a smear-word, and Philip might have reversed the labels, but the men Philip supported do seem to have been unpopular. In Eretria in 343 he destroyed the harbour town of Porthmus and put Clitarchus and others in power; in 342 further expeditions were needed to keep them in power. In Oreus Philip established Philistides and others (Dem. IX. *Phil. iii.* 57–62). Callias of Chalcis fell out with Philip and, failing to get help from Thebes, gained an alliance with Athens. With his help the Athenians overthrew the régime in Oreus at the end of 342/1 and the régime in Eretria at the beginning of 341/0 (a recently published Eretrian law to protect their democracy probably belongs to this context). Callias then with Demosthenes' support created a Euboean League affiliated to the Athenian, on terms that if the Euboeans paid *syntaxeis* to their own league they did not have to pay to the Athenians also (Aeschin. III. *Ctes.* 89–94, 100–5, schol. 85, 103 [184, 222 Dilts], Philoch. *FGrH* 328 FF 159–60, Diod. Sic. XVI. 74. i).

Open conflict between Philip and Athens was to arise from the Chersonese. In 342 Philip returned to Thrace, finally expelled Amadocus' son Teres from the middle kingdom and Cersebleptes from the eastern ([Dem.] XII. *Philip's Letter* 8–10), and set about founding military colonies. Athens sent further cleruchs to the Chersonese, with a garrison under Diopithes; and Diopithes came into conflict with Cardia, on the isthmus. Cardia had been retained by Cersebleptes when he ceded the Chersonese to Athens (Dem. XXIII. *Aristocrates* 181–3) and had been specified as an ally of Philip in the Peace of Philocrates, but Athens had been disputing the extent of its territory ([Dem.] VII. *Halonnesus* 39–44). Philip, spending the winter of 342/1 in Thrace, protested to Athens, and 'the philippisers among the politicians' wanted to give way (Dem. VIII. *Chersonese, hyp.* 3); but Demosthenes championed Diopithes, claiming that Philip could not want Thrace for its own sake but, although he was not openly at war, his aim was to conquer Athens and all Greece (cf. Diod. Sic. XVI. 71. i–ii). The Demosthenic corpus contains three speeches of 341: VIII. *Chersonese*, IX. *Philippic iii* (in longer and shorter versions), X. *Philippic iv* (repeating some material from VIII). It need not surprise us if at this crucial time Demosthenes revised and recycled material for delivery in Athens and for circulation outside. Thrace was not as undesirable as Demosthenes claims, but, if Philip did not want Thrace for its own sake and needed some further motive for reaching the Hellespont, cutting Athens' corn supply was not the only possibility: Dem. X. *Phil. iv.* 31–4 shows the earliest awareness that Philip might make war on Persia.

Diopithes was left in command: by midsummer he had attacked the Thracian coast and Philip was known to be supporting Cardia. Demosthenes was determined to represent Philip as a threat not just to Athens but to everybody. He won over Byzantium and various others to the Athenian side (Dem. XVIII.

Crown 244, 302, Aeschin. III. *Ctesiphon* 256); Hyperides won back Rhodes and Chios ([Plut.] *X Orat.* 850 A, cf. Dem. IX. *Phil. iii.* 71, Hyp. frs. 5–6 Burtt). Persia too was approached, and Persian money reached Diopithes after his death (Arist. *Rhet.* II. 1386 A 13) and perhaps reached Demosthenes and Hyperides too ([Plut.] *X Orat.* 848 E). In winter 341/0 Demosthenes and Callias of Chalcis toured the Peloponnese to invite representatives to a war congress. Aeschines gives a date and suggests that the congress never met; but, whether or not it did meet then or later, it is clear that an alliance against Philip was growing.

Various acts of hostility were committed against Philip: Callias attacked cities on the Gulf of Pagasae and captured ships bound for Macedon; the people of Peparethus expelled Philip's troops from Halonnesus; the Athenians seized a Macedonian herald and published his dispatches ([Dem.] XII. *Philip's Letter* 5, 12–15, 2). Diopithes was kept in the north-east, and by spring 340 Chares was there too (*IG* ii² 228 = R&O 71 ~ Harding 94). Tenedos lent money to Athens to help pay for action against Philip (*IG* ii² 233 = R&O 72 ~ Harding 97). A mercenary force was stationed on Thasos ([Plut.] *X Orat.* 845 F). At the Dionysia of 340 Demosthenes was for the first time awarded a crown for his services to Athens (Dem. XVIII. *Crown* 83, 223). In summer 340 Philip sent a fleet into the Propontis and, because of the hostility of the Athenian cleruchs, an army to support it. He began a siege of Perinthus, using the most up-to-date machinery. There seems to have been a particularly significant development in military technology under Philip and Alexander: at Perinthus both sides used arrow-firing catapults, and Philip's may have been torsion-powered, but there is still no sign of stone-throwing catapults, though the Phocians are said to have had what may have been non-torsion stone-throwers in 353–352 (Polyaen. II. 38. ii); for the attribution of the first catapults to Dionysius I of Syracuse cf. p. 280. The Persian King ordered his satraps to support Perinthus; and Byzantium sent help, so Philip detached part of his force to besiege that, and probably Selymbria too (Diod. Sic. XVI. 74. ii–76. iv, Just. *Epit.* IX. 1. ii–v, Philoch. *FGrH* 328 FF 53–4).

[Dem.] XII. *Philip's Letter* to Athens, complaining of incidents to the summer of 340, and effectively if not explicitly declaring war (§23), appears to be authentic in substance if not word for word (but [Dem.] XI. *Reply* is a compilation from Demosthenes' speeches). When Philip captured Athenian merchant ships waiting for Chares to escort them from the Black Sea, Athens declared war on Philip, with each side accusing the other of breaking the Peace of Philocrates (Diod. Sic. XVI. 77. ii, Just. *Epit.* IX. 1. v–viii, Philoch. *FGrH* 328 FF 55, 162, schol. Dem. XVIII. *Crown* 76 [140 Dilts]). Chares was unpopular with the cities under siege, but Phocion and Cephisophon were acceptable (Plut. *Phoc.* 14. iii–viii, *IG* ii² 1629. 957–65); help came from Athens' allies, and from Persia (Paus. I. 29. x, Arr. *Anab.* II. 14. v). Philip was making no progress, and in spring 339 decided to withdraw, tricking the Athenians in order to extract his ships from the Black Sea (Frontin. *Str.* I. iv. 13, 13A). He surely did not, as Diodorus claims (XVI. 77. iii), make a treaty, but this was his first setback since he had been stopped at Thermopylae in 352. He went north and raided the lands of a Scythian ruler in the Dobrudja, but as he returned he was attacked and wounded by the Triballians (Just. *Epit.* IX. 1. ix–3. iii).

Philip was brought back into Greece by the Fourth Sacred War. At Delphi Athens had been renewing Persian War dedications, with inscriptions emphasising that Thebes had then fought on the enemy side. At the Amphictyonic council in autumn 340, when the representatives of Thebes' ally Amphissa used that as the starting-point for a denunciation of Athens, Aeschines as Athens' representative responded by pointing out that the Amphissans were themselves at fault for cultivating the sacred plain of Cirrha, and a skirmish on the plain followed. In the winter an extraordinary meeting of the Amphictyonic council was held, and declared a sacred war against Amphissa. Thebes, not wanting to attack Amphissa, stood out of the war; and Demosthenes, now seeing Thebes as the only possible bulwark between Philip and Athens, by sharp practice in the assembly kept Athens out too. Early in 339 an Amphictyonic force, commanded by a Thessalian as was appropriate when Thessaly occupied the leading position in the Amphictyony, attacked Amphissa, and Amphissa submitted; at the spring council the Amphictyony imposed a fine on Amphissa. However, by the time of the autumn council the fine had still not been paid, and Philip, back from the Propontis and the Dobrudja, was invited to command. In their accounts of this affair in their speeches of 330, Aeschines accuses Amphissa of acting for Thebes, while Demosthenes accuses Aeschines of acting for Philip. Very probably Aeschines innocently thought that the best way to avoid trouble for Athens was to make trouble for somebody else, and the affair ran out of control; Philip did not plan or want the war, but when called in he made effective use of it (Aeschin. III. *Ctesiphon* 107–29, Dem. XVIII. *Crown* 143–55).

Philip had a garrison in Nicaea, east of Thermopylae, which he had taken over from the Phocians in 346. By the time he marched south, Thebes had expelled this garrison (Philoch. *FGrH* 328 F 56). Instead of going through Thermopylae to attack Nicaea, he took the high-level north–south route which begins west of Thermopylae; but from Cytinium, instead of continuing south to Amphissa, he turned south-east down the Cephisus valley. The news that he had captured Elatea in that valley caused panic in Athens, vividly described by Demosthenes, and (in spite of Thebes' action at Nicaea) fear that Philip and Thebes would again act as allies and would attack Athens. Demosthenes got himself sent to Thebes; Philip also sent a deputation; but Demosthenes succeeded in securing an alliance with Thebes. The alliance came at a price – Thebes' control of Boeotia was recognised, Thebes was to command solely on land and jointly at sea, Athens was to pay two thirds of the campaign's cost – but if Thebes was to join Athens against Philip the price had to be paid (Dem. XVIII. *Crown* 156–88, 211–17, Aeschin. III. *Ctesiphon* 130–51, Plut. *Dem.* 18, Diod. Sic. XVI. 84. ii–85. iv, Just. *Epit.* IX. 3. iv–vi). Each side appealed to allies for support; many joined Athens and Thebes, and none from the Peloponnese is known to have joined Philip (Dem. XVIII. *Crown* 237).

In the winter Thebes and Athens held a line running west–east from Mount Parnassus to Parapotamii, and Philip failed to break through. In spring 338 Demosthenes was honoured in Athens for the second time. But Philip tricked the Theban Proxenus and the Athenian Chares by pretending to withdraw from Cytinium, and then advanced to take Amphissa and to reach the Gulf of Corinth at Naupactus. With Philip in their rear, his opponents' position was untenable. They moved to Chaeronea, and it was not until early August (7 Metageitnion in the Athenian calendar: Plut. *Cam.* 19. viii) that the final battle was fought there. Philip had 30,000 infantry and 2,000 cavalry, his opponents perhaps about the same numbers. In the Cephisus valley below the city he was facing south-east, on the right himself with his young son Alexander on the left; his opponents were facing north-west, with the Athenians on the left and the Thebans and other Boeotians on the right. Philip with his wing drew back, tiring the Athenians, before he attacked, while Alexander on the left annihilated the Theban sacred band; the Macedonians were victorious. Among the Athenian captives were the general Chares and Demades, who for the next twenty years was to be a leading pro-Macedonian politician; among those who escaped after the battle was Demosthenes (Diod. Sic. XVI. 85. ii–86, Just. *Epit.* IX. 3. ix–xi, Polyaenus *Strat.* IV. 2. ii, vii, Plut. *Dem.* 20. i–ii). The evidence we have does not justify Demosthenes' attempt to blame the Theban generals for the defeat (Dem. LX. *Epitaph.* 22).

After Chaeronea

In Athens the news was greeted with alarm: Hyperides was responsible for emergency measures (Lycurg. *Leocrates* 36–7, [Plut.] *X Orat.* 848 F–849 A, cf. Hyp. fr. 18 Burtt), and so after his return was Demosthenes, perhaps through his friends (Dem. XVIII. *Crown* 248, Aeschin. III. *Ctesiphon* 159, Plut. *Dem.* 21. iii); originally there was a proposal to make Charidemus, an extreme opponent of Macedon, commander in chief, but in the end the position went to the experienced Phocion (cf. p. 340). Philip exulted in his victory, chanting the decree preamble 'Demosthenes son of Demosthenes, of Paeania, proposed', but was reproached by Demades, who afterwards went with Aeschines to negotiate, and obtained lenient terms (Diod. Sic. XVI. 87, Just. *Epit.* IX. 4. i–v, Plut. *Dem.* 20. iii). As in 346, it is hard to think that Philip could have taken Athens by force if he had wanted to do so, and he had reason to be lenient to Athens. By now he was thinking of a Persian war, for which the Athenian navy could be useful – and, while Athens had been an honest enemy, Thebes was an ally which had turned against him.

Philip toured Greece, to have his supremacy acknowledged by all except Sparta, which he deprived of border territories and which could conveniently be left in isolation (Just. *Epit.* IX. 5. iii; Diod. Sic. XVII. 3. iv–v says Arcadia). Otherwise he imposed a general settlement designed to keep his enemies weak. In Boeotia the federation was retained, but Plataea, Thespiae and Orchomenus

were to be refounded (their rebuilding took some time), and Thebes was given
a garrison and a régime dominated by returned pro-Macedonian exiles (Diod.
Sic. XVI. 87. iii, Just. *Epit.* IX. 4. vi–x, cf. Arr. *Anab.* I. 7. xi, Just. *Epit.* XI. 3.
viii). Oropus was probably made independent (*IG* vii 4250–1 = R&O 75, suggesting 338–335). Philip also installed garrisons in Corinth (Plut. *Arat.* 23. iv)
and Ambracia (Diod. Sic. XVII. 3. iii), but Chalcis, another 'fetter of Greece',
may not have been garrisoned until later. For Athens 'deprivation of the islands
and the ending of sea power' (Paus. I. 25. iii) meant the loss of the League, but
not of Lemnos, Imbros, Scyros, Delos and Samos. On what now seems to be
the best dating of the Phocians' repayments to Delphi (cf., e.g., Ellis, *Philip II
and Macedonian Imperialism*, 123 table 2), after beginning in 34<u>3</u>/2 to make
semestrial payments of 30 talents, they changed in 341/0 to annual payments
of 30 talents, made no payment in 338/7, and changed to annual payments of
10 talents in 336/5 or 335/4. Nonpayment in 338/7 may be linked to the
Chaeronea campaign, in which (some of) the Phocians were restored to their
cities by Thebes and Athens and fought on their side (Paus. X. 3. iii–iv), but
the other changes cannot be linked to known events.

   To consolidate his arrangements, Philip convened a meeting in Corinth in
winter 338/7, at which he imposed on the Greeks a common peace treaty and
organised them in what modern scholars call the League of Corinth (Diod. Sic.
XVI. 89, Just. *Epit.* IX. 5. i–iv). An inscription gives us part of the oath sworn
by the members, and part of the list of members, with numerals against the
names (*IG* ii² 236 = R&O 76 ~ Harding 99. A). The undertakings include: not
to overthrow the kingdom of Philip or his descendants, or the constitution
which each participant had when it joined; not to break the agreement or allow
anyone else to do so; if anyone did break it, to respond to the injured party's
call and to fight against the offender as decided by the *synedrion* and called
on by the *hegemon* ('leader'). Another text provides the qualification that the
constitutional guarantee did not apply when the existing constitution was a
'tyranny', and mentions guarantees against execution and exile, land reform,
liberation of slaves and the like ([Dem.] XVII. *Treaty with Alexander* 7; 15–16).

   Enforcement of a common peace had always been problematic, though the
later treaties had tried to make some provision; now the obligations were drawn
up stringently, and enforcement was guaranteed by combining the common
peace with a league of allies, which had a *synedrion* and a *hegemon*. The guarantee of constitutional stability may be compared with the guarantee of constitutional freedom in the Second Athenian League (cf. p. 230); the numerals
in the list suggest not one vote for each state but proportional voting and military contributions as in the Boeotian federation prior to 386. But Philip was in
control: it was inconceivable that anyone but he would be *hegemon* (and Alexander succeeded to this position as of right in 336: cf. p. 349); in the *hegemon*'s
absence a board of 'those appointed to the common protection' (cf. the title of
the Comité de Salut Public in France in 1793) deputised for him (e.g. [Dem.]
XVII. *Treaty with Alexander* 15); and the members swore allegiance to the
kingdom of Macedon in perpetuity. Certainly when the League was revived in

302, and perhaps in the League as originally organised, decisions were binding on member states, and they could not call their representatives to account (*IG* IV². i 68 = *Staatsverträge* 446. iii. 18–21).

Earlier in the century Sparta, Athens and Thebes in turn had used the common peace as a means of advancing their partisan interests; now Philip used the common peace and the League to dress up in familiar diplomatic garb his control of Greece. For the lesser cities, membership of a league controlled by Philip (distant, and with other things to think of) was probably preferable to membership of a league controlled by Sparta, Athens or Thebes, and preserving what autonomy they could between or under the shadow of one of their powerful neighbours had always been the best they could hope for. For the major cities, by contrast, freedom meant freedom both to give orders to lesser cities and not to take orders from any superior, and they had now lost that freedom. (The ideal of freedom combined with rule over others is found in many texts from Hdt. I. 210. ii onwards; Lycurg. *Leocrates* 42 disingenuously represents Athens as a champion of freedom for the Greeks but a ruler over barbarians, and §50 makes Chaeronea the end of freedom for all the Greeks.)

The kind of position Philip finally attained in Greece is presumably the kind of position he wanted to attain, both in 338/7 and earlier: he wanted a recognised position as the leader of the Greeks; he wanted the Greeks to cooperate in his further plans; but except when they ungratefully turned against him, as Thebes did, he wanted to get his way without direct interference in their affairs, and he was happy to control them through the League of Corinth rather than by direct conquest. Demosthenes was right to see him as a threat to Athens, and to the position in the Greek world to which Athens had aspired for the past century and a half, but he was not right to see him as a threat to the freedom of all the Greeks.

Probably a foundation meeting of the League was followed by a second meeting which decided on a war of revenge against Persia (coincidentally, being weakened by dynastic troubles: cf. p. 326) and appointed Philip to command (Diod. Sic. XVI. 89, Just. *Epit.* IX. 5. v–vii), and which outlawed any Greeks who might fight for the Persians (Arr. *Anab.* I. 16. vi). The theme of Greek revenge was convenient; but when the Persians had invaded Greece in 480 Macedon was on the Persian side, and in the last years of Philip's reign and the first years of Alexander's some Greeks looked to Persia for support against Philip. In due course the Aegean islands were to be added to the League, but the Greeks of mainland Asia Minor probably were not (cf. p. 367). To confirm the incorporation of the islands in the League, we have an inscription which shows Argos arbitrating between Melos and Cimolus 'in accordance with the resolution of the council of the Greeks' (*IG* XII. iii 1259 = R&O 82).

While prosecutions raged in Athens (cf. p. 338), Philip returned to Macedon and ended his reign with dynastic trouble (cf. fig. 8). There had been many women in Philip's life: it is not profitable to distinguish between wives and mistresses, but, since Philip Arrhidaeus had been judged unsuitable and Alexander had been recognised as heir (cf. p. 300), Alexander's mother, Olympias of Molossis, will have had an entrenched position. But in 337, in love (according to the sources) and/or under pressure from the Macedonian nobility, Philip took a Macedonian wife, Cleopatra, and her uncle Attalus prayed for a 'legitimate' heir. Probably this marriage produced only a daughter, but it could have produced a son, who if Philip lived long enough could have supplanted Alexander. Alexander and Olympias fled to Molossis, but a reconciliation with Alexander was arranged (Plut. *Alex.* 9. v–xiv, cf. Just. *Epit.* IX. 5. ix, 7. ii–vi, XI. 11. iii–v). Plutarch has a story that Pixodarus, satrap of Caria, offered his daughter in marriage to Philip Arrhidaeus, Alexander angrily claimed her for himself, and Alexander was not exiled but several of his friends were (Plut. *Alex.* 10. i–iv; cf. Arr. *Anab.* III. 6. v, confirming the exile of several friends). In spring 336 Philip sent out his advance forces to Asia Minor, commanded by Parmenio, his best general, an Amyntas, probably of Lyncestis in Upper Macedonia, and Attalus, the uncle of his new wife (Diod. Sic. XVI. 91. ii–v, XVII. 2. iv, Just. *Epit.* V. 9. viii).

Alexander of Molossis was angered by Philip's breach with his sister Olympias, and to placate him Philip offered him in marriage the Cleopatra who was his daughter by Olympias. The marriage was celebrated at Aegeae in summer 336; but at the celebration Philip was stabbed to death. The killer, a member of his bodyguard called Pausanias, was caught and killed by friends of Alexander before he could tell his story; Antipater presented Alexander to the soldiers as the new king. Pausanias had a personal motive, which Aristotle believed: he had been sexually humiliated by Attalus, and Philip would not allow him revenge. The official investigation blamed the princely family of Lyncestis (though Alexander of Lyncestis himself was spared because he was quick to acknowledge Alexander) and Philip's nephew Amyntas. Philip's new wife Cleopatra and her daughter, and Cleopatra's uncle Attalus, who was in Asia Minor with Philip's advance forces, might pose a threat to Alexander, so they were put to death. There were rumours that Olympias and/or Alexander were behind the murder, not wanting to be supplanted by Cleopatra and a son she might bear. It is likely enough that Pausanias acted from more than personal motives, but the truth is irrecoverable (Diod. Sic. XVI. 91. iv–94, XVII. 2. iii–vi, 5. i–ii, Just. *Epit.* IX. 6, 7. i, viii–xiv, Plut. *Alex.* 10. v–vii, *De Alex. Fort.* i. 327 C, cf. Arist. *Pol.* V. 1311 B 1–3, Arr. *Anab.* I. 25. i–ii; Amyntas Arr. *FGrH* 156 F 9. 22 cf. Polyaenus *Strat.* VIII. 60).

Among the finds at Aegeae (Vergina) are lavish tombs under a great tumulus, with grave-goods pointing to the second half of the fourth century. It has been suggested that tomb II was the tomb of Philip and one of his wives, that one of the ivories in the tomb is a portrait of Philip, and that the bones found there are the bones of Philip, reflecting his loss of an eye in the siege of Methone (and an over-developed right side and under-developed left side for which there is no other evidence): cf. ill. 12. This has been accepted by many scholars though not by all, and may be judged likely; those who do not accept it consider this tomb to be that of Philip Arrhidaeus and his wife Eurydice.

Ill. 12   Reconstruction of Philip's skull, from tomb II at Vergina. Manchester Museum, University of Manchester

Theopompus wrote that Europe had never produced a man like Philip (*FGrH* 115 F 27). Diodorus described him as the man who from the lowest of beginnings had created the greatest of kingdoms, achieving this not so much by fighting as by talking to people (XVI. 95. ii–iii, but more emphasis on military achievement in 1. iii–vi). For Justin he was a man given to deceit, for whom no means of prevailing were shameful (*Epit.* IX. 8). Arrian gives Alexander a speech in which he says that Philip transformed the Macedonians from primitive pastoralists into city-dwelling agriculturalists (cf. p. 299) and made Macedon powerful in Greece (Arr. *Anab.* VII. 9. ii–v). Philip did not begin with a totally primitive Macedon, but at his accession it was weak and threatened by its Greek and barbarian neighbours, and in twenty-three years he made it prosperous and the ruler of the mainland from the Peloponnese to the Hellespont. But at the moment of his assassination it must have seemed entirely possible that the throne would be contested and that what Philip had gained would be lost. In Athens, Demosthenes led the rejoicing, while Phocion deplored it (Aeschin. III. *Ctesiphon* 77–8, Diod. Sic. XVII. 3. ii, Plut. *Dem.* 22, *Phoc.* 16. viii).

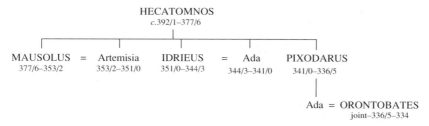

HECATOMNOS
c.392/1–377/6

| MAUSOLUS | = | Artemisia | IDRIEUS | = | Ada | PIXODARUS |
| 377/6–353/2 | | 353/2–351/0 | 351/0–344/3 | | 344/3–341/0 | 341/0–336/5 |

Ada = ORONTOBATES
joint–336/5–334

Fig. 9 Satraps of Caria

APPENDIX: PERSIA AND THE GREEKS IN THE REIGN OF ARTAXERXES III

Artaxerxes II (Mnemon) died in 359/8, and was succeeded by his son Artaxerxes III (Ochus), who ruled until 338. The Satraps' Revolt of the 360's had collapsed, but the new king took the precaution of ordering the satraps to disband their mercenary armies (cf. p. 224).

Prominent between Persia and the Greeks in the reign of Artaxerxes III was Caria, which c.392/1 had been detached from the satrapy of Sardis and entrusted to the local aristocrat Hecatomnos (cf. p. 222). He died in 377/6, and power then passed to his various sons and daughters in succession, the daughters marrying the sons and retaining power when their husbands died. The Carians were not Greek, but their history had been bound up with that of the Asiatic Greeks for a long time, and they were considerably hellenised. Hecatomnos gained control of Miletus, and issued coins of Milesian type, which continued into the early years of Mausolus (Kraay p. 275 no. 998). Miletus must then have been lost, since we hear of Mausolus' failing to capture it (Polyaenus *Strat.* VI. 8); but later Miletus set up statues of Idrieus and Ada at Delphi (Tod 161. *B = Fouilles de Delphes*, III. iv 176). Early in his term of office, which coincided with the beginnings of the Second Athenian League, Mausolus moved his capital from inland Mylasa to coastal Halicarnassus, and strengthened that by incorporating neighbouring communities (Vitr. *De Arch.* II. viii. 10–11, Strabo 611. XIII. i. 59). His tomb there, the Mausoleum, a building which combined Greek and near-eastern *motifs*, was one of the wonders of the ancient world (Plin. *H.N.* XXXVI. 30–1, ill. 13).

In the 360's Mausolus dabbled in the Satraps' Revolt, but not sufficiently to make his position untenable (cf. p. 223); after that he decided that the Greek world offered the better prospects for expansion. He was behind the League members which revolted against Athens in the Social War of 356–355 (Diod. Sic. XV. 7. iii, Dem. XV. *Liberty of Rhodians* 3: cf. pp. 239–40), and after the war Rhodes, where an oligarchy replaced a democracy, Cos and Chios came under his control (Dem. XV, *hyp.*, V. *Peace* 25). Between 353/2 and 351/0 (§27) exiled Rhodian democrats appealed to Athens for support which Demosthenes wanted to grant (XV. *Liberty of Rhodians*), but the Athenians did not act there, though they did in 352/1 reinforce their cleruchy in Samos (Philoch. *FGrH* 328 F 154). The islands of the south-east Aegean were still in Carian hands in 346; and when in 341 Hyperides made them allies of Athens once more this does not mean that they had broken away from Caria. In 341 Ada was ousted by the last brother, Pixodarus. Presumably under pressure from the centre, he married his daughter, another Ada, to a Persian, Orontobates, who was made joint satrap of Caria

Ill. 13 Reconstruction of the Mausoleum at Halicarnassus. © Museum of Ancient Art, University of Aarhus, Denmark

and retained the satrapy when Pixodarus died in 336/5. The elder Ada submitted to Alexander and was reinstated by him – but made him her heir, and after her death he appointed an ordinary satrap (Diod. Sic. XVI. 74. ii, XVII. 24. ii, Arr. *Anab.* I. 23. vii–viii, VII. 23. i, Strabo 656–7. XIV. ii. 17).

Inscriptions shed interesting light on the rule of the Hecatomnids. We have a series of decrees in Greek from Mylasa (dated by Persian Kings and Mausolus as satrap), and a decree from Iasus (dated by local officials), dealing with the punishment of men disloyal to Mausolus (*IK Mylasa* 1–3 = R&O 54, *SIG*[3] 169 = *IK Iasos* 1). We have decrees of Erythrae, opposite Chios, honouring 'Mausolus son of Hecatomnos, of Mylasa' and Artemisia, and 'Idrieus son of Hecatomnos, of Mylasa', as if they were citizens of a Greek city (*IK Erythrai und Klazomenai* 8 = R&O 56, *SEG* xxxi 969 ~ Harding 28. B). Also we have a decree of Mausolus and Artemisia themselves, identified simply by name, and referring in the text to 'as much territory as Mausolus rules', which by either an ignorant or a creative adaptation of a Greek institution confers the status of *proxenos* on the whole Cretan city of Cnossus (*Labraunda* III. ii 40 = R&O 55). We have a decree of Xanthus, in Lycia (to the east of Caria), of 337, whose dating formula names Pixodarus as 'satrap of Lycia' and officials whom he had appointed: this is a trilingual inscription, in Greek, Lycian (these two texts are fairly close) and Aramaic, the administrative language of the Persian empire (this text seems to be aimed more at the Persians, inter alia dating by Artaxerxes IV and styling Pixodarus 'satrap of Caria and Lycia') (*Fouilles de*

Xanthos, vi; Greek text R&O 78). Technically the Hecatomnids were satraps, and at some point they acquired Lycia in addition to Caria. In the Aegean world, however, their subordination to Persia was played down, they behaved like independent rulers, and Erythrae at least treated them as distinguished citizens of a city: they may be seen as forerunners of the hellenistic kings.

By the end of the Satraps' Revolt Artabazus had taken over the satrapy of Dascylium, but by 355 he was in revolt. After the Social War the Athenian Chares joined him with a mercenary army, and in 354 they won a famous victory over a Persian commander called Tithraustes; but Persia complained to Athens, Demosthenes was with the majority in opposing conflict with Persia, and Chares was recalled. Instead in 353 Thebes sent Pammenes to support Artabazus, and they won two victories but Artabazus then fell out with Pammenes (Diod. Sic. XVI. 22. i–ii, 34. i–ii, schol. Dem. III. *Ol. iii.* 31, IV. *Phil. i.* 19 [146, 84b Dilts], *FGrH* 105 F 4, Polyaenus *Strat.* VII. 33. ii, Dem. XIV. *Symmories* 2–13). We then hear no more of Artabazus until the late 340's, when he was a refugee in Macedon (cf. below).

Artaxerxes campaigned twice against Egypt, unsuccessfully in the late 350's and successfully in the late 340's; but Diodorus records the successful campaign under 351/0–350/49 and nothing under the 340's (traces of the unsuccessful campaign XVI. 40. iii, iv–v, 44. i, 48. i–ii; cf. Dem. XV. *Liberty of Rhodians* 5, 11–12, Isoc. V. *Philip* 101). If Persia's subsidy to Thebes (Diod. Sic. XVI. 40. i–ii) belongs to this war, Thebes like Athens must have recanted its support for Artabazus.

By the mid 340's Egypt's revolt had spread to Phoenicia and Cyprus (Diod. Sic. XVI. 41, 42. iii–iv, cf. 40. v). In 344 Artaxerxes, preparing to campaign in person, sent an appeal for support to the Greek cities: Athens and Sparta merely confirmed their friendship, but Thebes, Argos and the Asiatic Greeks provided a total of 10,000 men (Diod. Sic. XVI. 40. vi, 44. i–iv: cf. p. 313) – while there were 4,000 Greeks with Mentor and 20,000 with Nectanebo (42. ii, 47. vi). The recovery of Cyprus was entrusted to Idrieus of Caria (though in 346 Isocrates had thought he might join the rebels: V. *Philip.* 102–3), accompanied by the Athenian Phocion as a mercenary commander: Salamis in Cyprus endured a siege for a while, but finally submitted (Diod. Sic. XVI. 42. vi–ix, 44. i–iii). In 343 the Phoenicians, with Greek mercenaries from Egypt under Mentor of Rhodes, repelled Persia's advance forces. The revolt there collapsed when Tennes of Sidon betrayed the city to the Persians; the city was destroyed but Tennes was put to death (Diod. Sic. XVI. 43, 44. iv–45. i). A story of the Egyptian Nectanebo's dream about his neglect of the temple of the war-god Onuris is dated 5/6 July 343; Speusippus' *Letter to Philip*, probably of 343/2, complains of a shortage of papyrus because of the reconquest (§14; date from §7); so the recovery of Egypt should be dated winter 343/2. Artaxerxes was joined by his Greek mercenaries, and Mentor with his force defected to him. Nectanebo held Pelusium, at the eastern mouth of the Nile delta, but failed to make trusting use of his mercenary commanders; after a defeat which need not have been fatal he withdrew to Memphis, at the apex of the delta. The Persians' forces mastered Egypt (thanks particularly to Mentor and the grand vizier Bagoas), and Nectanebo fled to Ethiopia (Diod. Sic. XVI. 46. iv–51). At some point in the next few years (perhaps 338–336) Egypt rebelled again, under Khababash, but was conquered by Persia again (cf. the hieroglyphic 'satrap *stele*' of 312/1: see note on further reading at the end of the chapter).

After this success Mentor was able to intercede for his brother Memnon and his brother-in-law Artabazus, who were now exiles in Macedon. Mentor was given a command on the coast of Asia Minor, where he dealt with Hermias of Atarneus (said by Demosthenes to be in league with Philip) and other trouble-makers (Diod. Sic. XVI. 50. vii, 52, cf. Theopompus *FGrH* 115 F 291, Dem. X. *Phil. iv.* 32); on his death he was succeeded by Memnon, who was to be important in the resistance to Alexander in 335–334. Bagoas remained with Artaxerxes, and in Diodorus' account came to fancy himself as a king-maker. In November 338 he poisoned the king, killed his older sons and put the youngest, Arses, on the throne as Artaxerxes IV, hoping to rule through him. Arses proved intractable, so in June 336 Bagoas killed him and his children, extinguishing the direct royal line, and installing as Darius III Codoman, descended from a son of Darius II. After that he tried to kill Darius too, but Darius switched the cups and it was Bagoas who died (Diod. Sic. XVI. 50. viii, VII. 5. iii–6. iii, Just. *Epit.* X. 3, cf. Trogus *Prologue* X, Arr. *Anab.* II. 14. v). Darius had a good record, and was not an unworthy successor; but his succession certainly resulted from a period of major upheaval, in which members of the royal family may have played a greater part and Bagoas a lesser than in Diodorus' story.

NOTE ON FURTHER READING

On Macedon before Philip II see Hammond and Griffith, *History of Macedonia*, vol. ii, chs. 1–4 (by Hammond: accepting the Argive origins claimed by the royal family, as other scholars do not, and taking a more formal view than other scholars of the working of the kingdom); Borza, *In the Shadow of Olympus*.

On the reign of Philip see Cawkwell, *Philip of Macedon* (preceded by various articles, which are cited there: some of these are reprinted in Perlman's collection, noted below); Ellis, *Philip II and Macedonian Imperialism*; Hammond and Griffith, *History of Macedonia*, vol. ii, chs. 5–21 (ch. 20 by Hammond, otherwise by Griffith). Hatzopoulos and Loukopoulos (eds.), *Philip of Macedon*, contains chapters by experts as well as good pictures.

The point that Athens could not make a secret treaty with Philip about Amphipolis was made by G. E. M. de Ste. Croix, 'The Alleged Secret Pact Between Athens and Philip II Concerning Amphipolis and Pydna', CQ^2 xiii 1963, 110–19 (reprinted in Perlman, ch. 3). On the Third Sacred War see Buckler, *Philip II and the Sacred War*; the once-popular view that Diodorus had reduplicated a whole year of the war was rebutted by N. G. L. Hammond, 'Diodorus' Narrative of the Sacred War', *JHS* lvii 1937, 44–78 = his *Studies in Greek History*, ch. 15 (but he was perhaps wrong not to allow minor doublets).

Among many treatments of Athens' responses to Philip see Harris, *Aeschines and Athenian Politics*; Sealey, *Demosthenes and His Time*. Perlman (ed.), *Philip and Athens*, reprints a number of important articles. On Euboea in the 340's see P. A. Brunt, 'Euboea in the Time of Philip II', CQ^2 xix 1969, 245–65; J. M. Carter, 'Athens, Euboea and Olynthus', *Hist.* xx 1971, 418–29. The view championed by Ellis, that in 346 Philip would have preferred to cooperate with Athens against Thebes but was frustrated by Demosthenes, was first advanced by M. M. Markle, 'The Strategy of Philip in 346 BC', CQ^2 xxiv 1974, 253–68. For Speusippus' letter see Natoli, *The Letter of Speusippus to Philip II*.

The Eretrian law to protect the democracy is published by D. Knoepfler, 'Loi d'Érétrie contre la tyrannie et l'oligarchie', *BCH* cxxv 2001, 195–238 and cxxvi 2002, 149–204.

On military technology see especially Marsden, *Greek and Roman Artillery*, i. *Historical Development*.

On the origins of the Fourth Sacred War see P. D. Londey, 'The Outbreak of the 4th Sacred War', *Chiron* xx 1990, 239–60 (not planned by Philip). On the battle of Chaeronea see N. G. L. Hammond, 'The Two Battles of Chaeronea (338 BC and 86 BC)', *Klio* xxxi 1938, 186–218, of which the part on 338 is reprinted in his *Studies in Greek History*, ch. 16; W. K. Pritchett, 'Observations on Chaironeia', *AJA*[2] lxii 1958, 307–11. On Philip's territorial settlements after the battle see C. Roebuck, 'The Settlements of Philip II with the Greek States in 338 BC', *CP* xliii 1948, 73–102 = his *Economy and Society in the Early Greek World*, 131–50 (and reprinted in Perlman [ed.], *Philip and Athens*, ch. 12 – but by a printer's error there the first half of the article was originally omitted).

On the murder of Philip, Alexander was suspected by E. Badian, 'The Death of Philip II', *Phoen.* xvii 1963, 244–50; Olympias by R. Develin, 'The Murder of Philip II', *Antichthon* xv 1981, 86–99; the official verdict was accepted by N. G. L. Hammond, 'The End of Philip', in Hatzopoulos and Loukopoulos (eds.), *Philip of Macedon*, 166–75; Olympias and Alexander are exonerated by E. Carney, 'The Politics of Polygamy: Olympias, Alexander and the Murder of Philip II', *Hist.* xli 1992, 169–89.

For tomb II at Vergina as that of Philip and one of his wives see N. G. L. Hammond, 'The Evidence for the Identity of the Royal Tombs at Vergina', in Adams and Borza (eds.), *Philip II, Alexander the Great and the Macedonian Heritage*, 111–27 = his *Collected Studies*, ii. 271–87, and for the reconstruction of the skull as Philip's skull A. J. N. W. Prag et al., 'The Skull from Tomb II at Vergina: King Philip II of Macedon', *JHS* civ 1984, 60–78; in favour of Philip Arrhidaeus and Eurydice see Borza, *In the Shadow of Olympus*, 256–66.

On the Hecatomnids of Caria see Hornblower, *Mausolus*. For the story of Nectanebo's dream see L. Koenen, 'The Dream of Nektanebos', *BASP* xxii 1985, 171–94; for Speusippus' letter see Natoli, *The Letter of Speusippus to Philip II*. The 'satrap *stele*' is translated by Bevan, *A History of Egypt under the Ptolemaic Dynasty*, 28–32; and the episode of Khababash is discussed by Briant, *From Cyrus to Alexander*, 717–18 with 1017–18, S. Burstein, 'Prelude to Alexander: The Reign of Khababash', *AHB* xiv 2000, 149–54. On Hermias of Atarneus see P. Green, 'Hermias of Atarneus and His Friendship with Aristotle', in Heckel and Tritle (eds.), *Crossroads of History: The Age of Alexander*, ch. 2. Against Diodorus' account of Bagoas and the Achaemenid royal family see Briant, *From Cyrus to Alexander*, 769–80 with 1033–4; also E. Badian, 'Darius III', *HSCP* c 2000, 241–68.

23

Demosthenic Athens

500	475	450	425	400	375	350	325	300

357	Periander's law for trierarchic *symmoriai*
356/5	Leptines' law on exemptions from festival liturgies
late 350's (?)	institution of theoric fund
346	Peace of Philocrates with Philip
343	Aeschines acquitted in *Embassy* trial
336	Ctesiphon's proposal to honour Demosthenes
336	law threatening Areopagus
c.336–324	Lycurgus and friends *epi tei dioikesei*
c.335/4	reorganisation of *ephebeia*
331–330	Spartan-led rising against Macedon
330	Ctesiphon acquitted in *Crown* trial
324	Harpalus in Athens
323–322	Athens leads Lamian War against Macedon

Finance

Athens like other ancient states lived from hand to mouth. There was no notion of 'controlling the economy' in a modern sense (though in the fourth century the *merismos*, on which cf. p. 263, shows that the Athenians were trying to work out what they could afford): taxes were imposed to raise funds for necessary expenditure. Without the kind of credit system with which we are familiar, not even the state could spend money which it did not have; shortage of funds was said to bias the courts against rich men whose property might be confiscated if they were condemned (e.g. Ar. *Eq.* 1357–61, Lys. XXVII. *Epicrates* 1, XXX. *Nicomachus* 22, but we do not find this allegation in the Demosthenic period), and in crises lack of money to pay jurors led to a suspension of the courts (e.g. in 348: Dem. XXXIX. *Boeotus i.* 17). When there was surplus money, it had traditionally found its way into the temple treasuries, from which the state might later borrow (cf. pp. 91–3); the treasuries of Athena and of the Other Gods, amalgamated in 406, were separated in 385 and recombined (as 'the treasury of Athena') *c.*346. We have noticed already that, whereas in the fifth century Athens had a central state treasury, in the fourth it made an allocation to separate spending authorities (cf. p. 263). It is not until the middle of the fourth century that we find any conscious attempt to build up surplus funds.

In the fifth century the Delian League had added to the number of salaried posts, but the tribute had reduced the range of purposes for which the Athenians had to spend their own money; in the fourth century the *syntaxeis* of the Second League did not raise large sums and the sums they did raise did not enrich Athens. The silver mines had been abandoned in the final phase of the Peloponnesian War, and were not very productive in the first half of the century. In the years immediately after the Peloponnesian War, the collectors of the 2 per cent import tax in 402/1 paid 30 talents and made a profit of 3 talents; the collectors in 401/0 paid 36 talents and made a small profit (Andoc. I. *Myst.* 133–4). At the beginning of the Peloponnesian War Athens' total annual revenue, including about 400 talents tribute, had been about 1,000 talents. In 341 Demosthenes claimed that 'not long ago' (the 350's?) Athens' annual revenue was only 130 talents but now was 400 talents (X. *Phil. iv.* 37–8); [Plut.] *X Orat.* 842 F credits Lycurgus (who was influential *c.*336–324; cf. p. 334) with increasing the revenue to 1,200 talents whereas once it was only 60 talents (but in the light of Andocides, above, the 60 talents is hard to believe for any date; the 1,200 talents is perhaps credible if seen as the equivalent of 600 a century earlier). As for expenditure, I believe that the posts that remained in the fourth century were still salaried, and the burden of assembly pay was added; by the 330's–320's payments (except to jurors) were at about double the rate of the beginning of the century (cf. pp. 262–3), and then the assembly will have cost about 45 talents a year, the council 26 talents, the courts perhaps 150 talents. Money will have been needed for festivals (and estimates of grants paid from the theoric fund, on which see pp. 333–4, to enable citizens to attend festivals have ranged from *c.*15 to *c.*100 talents a year), and for roads and buildings. But Athens' greatest expenditure, in the first half of the century beyond Athens' means and without producing commensurate results, was on wars and on ships and other equipment for wars. Demosthenes in a speech of *c.*353/2 remarks that the revenue from taxes is not sufficient for the state's regular expenditure, so recourse is needed to 'additional payments' (XXIV. *Timocrates* 96–7): this probably includes fines and confiscations, and also *eisphorai* and *epidoseis*.

Most Athenian taxes were indirect taxes, such as the 2 per cent import tax, where the amount paid by individuals depended on their consumption (and metics and visitors paid like citizens – but there were some additional burdens on foreigners, such as the poll tax called *metoikion* levied on metics: Harp. μετοίκιον [μ 27 Keaney]); a recently discovered inscription has revealed a tax in kind levied on the grain grown on Lemnos, Imbros and Scyros (*SEG* xlviii 96 = R&O 26); but Athens devised particular means of raising larger sums from the richer inhabitants.

One of these is the property tax known as *eisphora* ('paying in'), which was available in 434/3 and was levied at any rate from 428/7 (cf. p. 93): modern books often refer to it as the 'war tax', since military needs were usually the reason for its being levied. *Eisphora* was levied ad hoc in the years and at the rate (usually 1 per cent or 2 per cent) decided by the assembly, on the property of all residents rich enough to qualify (it is not clear how many these were but probably rather more than the number liable for the liturgies to be discussed below). We are given 6,000 and 5,750 talents for the total declared valuation (*timema*) of all inhabitants or all liable in 378/7 and 354/3 (Polyb. II. 62. vii, Dem. XIV. *Symmories* 19); the 'sixth part' paid by metics (Dem. XXII. *Androtion* 61, *IG* ii^2 244. 20) perhaps indicates that a metic paid $\frac{1}{6}$ more than a citizen with the same valuation. In this area as in many, Athens suffered from weak enforcement procedures. In 378/7 those liable were organised in a hundred contribution groups, *symmoriai* (Clidemus *FGrH* 323 F 8, Philoch. *FGrH* 328 F 41). By 364/3 the liturgy (cf. below) of *proeisphora* had been created, by which the richest three members of each *symmoria* were required to advance the whole sum due from the *symmoria*, and were left to reimburse themselves from the other members (Dem. XXI. *Midias* 153 with 157, XVIII. *Crown* 103 with 171; first attested Isae. VI. *Philoctemon* 60). In the 350's Androtion served on a commission to collect arrears of *eisphora* from 378/7 to (perhaps) the introduction of *proeisphora*: from a total of somewhat over 300 talents, 14 talents were outstanding, and the commission collected 7 talents (Dem. XXII. *Androtion* 44).

Sometimes an appeal was made for *epidoseis*, voluntary gifts. At Artemisium in 480 Clinias provided his trireme and crew at his own expense (Hdt. VIII. 17), and we hear of a man who provided two triremes in the Peloponnesian War (Xen. *Hell.* II. iii. 40). Our earliest occurrence of the word is in 394, when cash contributions were invited, and lists were published of those who paid and those who promised but did not pay (Isae. V. *Dicaeogenes* 37–8). References to *epidoseis* become frequent from the middle of the century (Dem. XXI. *Midias* 160–1 calls an appeal in 357 the first); a decree of the 240's invites *epidoseis* of not more than 200 dr. and not less than 50 dr. and is followed by a list of contributors (*IG* ii^2 791, revised *Agora* xvi 213). We shall notice a particular category of *epidoseis* below, in connection with Lycurgus' building programme.

The rich were also expected to contribute to the state's expenses through the institution of liturgies. *Leitourgia*, in Athens and elsewhere in classical Greece, denoted 'work for the people' in the sense that a man was given a public task to perform directly at his own expense, without the intervention of officials or contractors to collect the money and spend it. Those at Athens fall into two classes: festival liturgies, commonly involving responsibility for a sequence of plays or a team of performers at a festival; and the trierarchy, where the state provided a warship, its basic equipment and the crew's wages, and the trierarch had to take charge of the ship and cover the other running costs for the year.

The maximum that could be required of a man was one festival liturgy in two years (Dem. XX. *Leptines* 8) or one trierarchy in three (Isae. VII. *Apollodorus* 38). Probably the rule was that liturgies should be assigned to the richest men who could not claim exemption; if a man thought that somebody richer than himself had been passed over, he could challenge him in an *antidosis* ('giving in exchange') either to take over the liturgy or, if the man challenged did not accept that he was richer, to exchange property with him (Lys. IV. *Wound* 1 cites an exchange; [Dem.] XLII. *Phaenippus* in connection with a challenge reports the making of an inventory and the sealing of buildings). But, while some men tried to avoid liturgies, others were proud to demonstrate their public spiritedness by performing more, and spending more on them, than was positively required: one man claims to have performed eleven festival liturgies between 411/0 and 403/2, and to have spent $3\frac{1}{2}$ talents on them when he could have spent only 1 talent; in the same period he spent 6 talents on seven years of trierarchy (Lys. XXI. *Taking Bribes* 1–5). Lavish performance of liturgies was a way in which a public figure could acquire a favourable image: many festival liturgies were performed in a competitive context (e.g. competitions between tribal teams); there could be prizes for trierarchs too (e.g. *IG* ii^2 1629 = R&O 100 ~ Harding 121. 190–204; Dem. LI. *Trierarchic Crown*); and it was natural to want one's own team or ship to be better than others. Thus through the institution of liturgies Athens channelled the competitive instincts of the upper class in the direction of public service.

At state level there were at least 97 festival liturgies in an ordinary year, 118 in the years of the Great Panathenaea, and there were some deme liturgies too; metics shared in some festival liturgies and had some liturgies of their own. Ant. VI. *Chorister* gives a good impression of what was involved. The trierarchy was limited to citizens, and the burden was unpredictable: in any one year many or few ships might be needed, for a long or a short period, and they might or might not encounter the hazards of battle and bad weather. The trierarchy had originally involved personal as well as financial responsibility for a ship, but in the fourth century it was possible to pay a contractor (Dem. XXI. *Midias* 80, 155). The minimum level of property which made a man liable for liturgies was about

3–4 talents; as farmers will still insist today, some kinds of wealth in terms of property do not generate large quantities of ready money, and a liturgy could be a heavy burden for a man who barely qualified, especially if he had to pay an *eisphora* in the same year.

In the fourth century it became increasingly difficult to find enough men to perform liturgies: Athens' citizen population after the Peloponnesian War was about half what it had been before (cf. p. 260), and proportionately there were perhaps more very rich men but fewer moderately rich. The first concession was the appointment of two men as joint trierarchs for a single ship (Lys. XXXII. *Diogiton* 24–6, Dem. XXI. *Midias* 154). In 357 a law of Periander organised the 1,200 richest citizens in twenty trierarchic *symmoriai* (modelled on the *symmoriai* for *eisphora*, above), after which there were still particular trierarchs for particular ships, but some at least of the costs were shared equally by all the 1,200, who thus had to pay small sums regularly rather than large sums occasionally ([Dem.] XLVII. *Evergus and Mnesibulus* 21 with Dem. XIV. *Symmories* 16–17). A particular problem with festival liturgies was that exemptions had been awarded to many individuals and office-holders: Leptines proposed to deal with these by banning almost all exemptions; in 355/4 Demosthenes in an unsuccessful attack on that law protested that the lack of rewards would discourage benefactors and that it would be better to use a system of *symmoriai* here too (Dem. XX. *Leptines*). In 354/3 Demosthenes attacked the system of trierarchic *symmoriai*, again unsuccessfully, claiming that there were so many exemptions that a list of 2,000 would be needed to obtain 1,200 actual contributors, and that contributions in proportion to wealth would be better than equal contributions (Dem. XIV. *Symmories*). In 340, when Athens declared war on Philip and Demosthenes was in a dominant position, he did introduce proportional contributions: references to 'the three hundred' (those liable for *proeisphora*) may mean that under the new system they bore the whole burden, or simply that they bore the lion's share (Dem. XVIII. *Crown* 102–9, Aeschin. III. *Ctesiphon* 222, Din. I. *Demosthenes* 42, Hyp. fr. 43. i Burtt). It is possible but not certain that this was modified by Aeschines (Aeschin. III. *Ctesiphon* 222, Dem. XVIII. *Crown* 312 but contr. 107). Overall, the effect of the various changes was to spread the burden of liturgies somewhat more fairly among the richer Athenians.

Until the 350's Athens was spending heavily on military activity (after Leuctra trying, without much success, to recover fifth-century possessions: cf. pp. 236–7), and was perpetually short of money. After the Social War we see a considerable financial recovery, associated with Eubulus in the 350's and 340's and with Lycurgus in the 330's and 320's. Xenophon, back in Athens, wrote his *Ways and Means (Poroi)* in the late 350's and this seems to reflect the thinking of Eubulus (Eubulus is said to have proposed Xenophon's recall: Diog. Laert. II. 59). Athens should be revived as a trading centre, with inducements for non-citizens such as the right (for those judged suitable) to own land and houses, and quick settlement of disputes (ii. 1–iii. 5) – privileges were granted more frequently to favoured foreigners, and special 'monthly' commercial suits had been created by 343/2 ([Dem.] VII. *Halonnesus* 12). (Remarkably) sub-scriptions should be invited to a capital fund, and spent on such objects as hotels (or perhaps brothels) and a state-owned merchant fleet (iii. 6–14) – state-owned hotels and merchant ships were too much for Athens, but Lycurgus did raise substantial loans ([Plut.] *X Orat.* 841 D, 852 B). More should be made of the silver mines, and the capital fund could provide state-owned slaves to work them (iv) – inscriptions show that mining activity revived, and reached a peak in the 340's. All this needs peace, and a board of *eirenophylakes*, 'guardians of the peace' (v) – after the Social War Athens did try to avoid fighting except where its interests were directly threatened; in 346 Eubulus stressed the finan-cial consequences of not making peace with Philip (cf. p. 311), and even Demosthenes in his *First Philippic* tried to work out what the campaigning he wanted would cost (IV. *Phil. i.* 21–2).

An important contribution to this recovery was made by what seems at first sight to be an extension of the old-style democracy, the creation of the theoric (festival) fund to pay grants to citizens covering the cost of theatre tickets at the major festivals: Demades called this 'the glue of the democracy' (Plut. *Quaest. Plat.* 1011 B). Some texts attribute this to Pericles (e.g. Plut. *Per.* 9. i), others to Agyrrhius (e.g. Harp. θεωρικά [θ 19 Keaney]); but they introduced other state payments (Pericles jury pay, Agyrrhius assembly pay), and it is noticeable that Aristophanes never mentions that citizens were paid to go to his plays, so it is better to follow the texts which link the fund with Eubulus and Diophantus (Hesychius [δ 2351 Latte], *Suda* [δ 1491 Adler] δραχμὴ χαλαζῶσα, schol. Aeschin. III. *Ctesiphon* 24 [65 Dilts]), and to date it to the second half of the 350's.)

Like all funds, this received an annual allocation; and it benefited from the provision that it should also receive any surplus revenue, which previously had gone to the stratiotic (army) fund (cf. [Dem.] LIX. *Neaera* 4–5). This allowed it to accumulate a substantial surplus, to be spent for purposes which its con-trollers approved, so that Aeschines could claim that 'because of your trust in Eubulus, those elected to control the theoric fund, before Hegemon's law was passed, [controlled various financial offices, were responsible for various build-ing projects,] and had virtually the whole financial administration (*dioikesis*) of the city' (III. *Ctesiphon* 25). By the time of the *Ath. Pol.* the fund was controlled by a board of ten men; but an inscription of 343/2 is best interpreted as in-dicating that at that date the fund had a single treasurer (*IG* ii^2 223. *C.* 5–6, where the man named, Cephisophon, was a man of some prominence). Lycur-gus later was subject to a law which limited tenure of his office for four years ([Plut.] *X Orat.* 841 B–C: 'five' years by inclusive counting), and it is an attrac-tive possibility that that was Hegemon's law, aimed at weakening the theoric treasurer by limiting tenure and substituting a board for a single man. After-wards the theoric board and the stratiotic treasurer joined with the council in supervising the old-style financial officials (*Ath. Pol.* 47. ii), and perhaps pre-viously it was just the theoric treasurer who had this power. The theoric offi-cials were elected, (presumably) by analogy with the treasurer of the stratiotic fund, who was elected as all military officials were elected. In the time of Eubulus the single treasurer directly controlled the one fund in which there was spare money, and was in a strong position in combining with the annually changing council to supervise the other officials, so that he was better placed than any one else to understand Athens' financial position.

In 349/8, when Demosthenes wanted energetic support for Olynthus, he and Apollodorus attacked the rule directing surpluses to the theoric fund (Dem. I. *Ol. i.* 19–20, III. *Ol. iii.* 10–13, [Dem.] LIX. *Neaera* 4–5; cf. Dem.'s attack on the fund in XIII. *Organisation* 1–2, 10, probably of the late 350's). In 346 Eubulus mentioned 'making the theoric monies stratiotic' among the consequences which would follow from not making peace with Philip (Dem. XIX. *Embassy* 291). After the Peace of Philocrates Demosthenes gained increasing support, and a favourable reference to the fund in 341 (X. *Phil. iv.* 35–45) suggests that by then he and his friends were in control. In 339/8, when Philip had entered the Fourth Sacred War, on the proposal of Demosthenes work on the ship-sheds and the storehouse for hanging tackle (paid for from the fund: recently excavated, and cf. *IG* ii^2 1668) was halted, and 'they decreed that all the [surplus?] monies should be stratiotic' (Philoch. *FGrH* 382 F 56a). That decision was perhaps reversed after Chaeronea, but in 337/6 Demosthenes himself was the theoric treasurer (Aeschin. III. *Ctesiphon* 24). It seems likely that a position which had been acceptable when in the hands of Eubulus was perceived by Demosthenes' opponents as undemocratic when in the hands of Demosthenes, and that we should place Hegemon's law here as a reaction by Demosthenes' opponents.

Whatever the political implications, the financial achievements of the theoric treasurer were undoubted, and those achievements were continued by Lycurgus. For three quadrennia, perhaps *c.*336–324, first Lycurgus himself and then (because tenure was limited) friends of his held a position connected with financial administration ([Plut.] *X Orat.* 841B–C, cf. decree *ap.* 851 F–852 E, Diod. Sic. XVI. 88. i). Probably there was created for him the office well attested in the hellenistic period, *epi tei dioikesei* ('in charge of the financial administration'), and the Xenocles honoured for his work in that position (*Agora* xvi 77) was one of the friends who held office after him.

Lycurgus 'found sources of revenue, built the theatre, the odeum, the dockyards, constructed triremes and harbours' (Hyp. fr. 23 Burtt); the decree posthumously honouring him alleges cash distributions totalling 18,900 talents (hard to believe), the raising of capital and the making of loans from it, the provision of sacred treasures and of ships and military equipment (*X Orat.* 851 F–852 E). We shall look at some aspects of his achievement below. The decree claims that he underwent accounting many times and was never convicted; when he died, about 325/4, the office passed to an opponent, Menesaechmus (Dion. Hal. 660. *Din.* 11), who alleged that Lycurgus was a state debtor and had his sons arrested, but Demosthenes and Hyperides secured their release (*X Orat.* 842 E, Dem. *Letter iii*, Hyp. fr. 23 Burtt).

Athens went into the hellenistic period with the official (from 287 a board) *epi tei dioikesei* and the stratiotic treasurer as its principal financial officials; the allocation of funds to separate authorities seems to have been changed to the maintenance of separate accounts within a central treasury.

Institutional Changes

The new financial posts provided scope for administrators with expertise, as the old-style administrative posts did not; and we have seen that changes in the secretaryship in the 360's provided some scope for expertise there (cf. p. 263). The same may be said of a change in the appointment of the ten generals. They were elected and could be re-elected; originally one had to come from each tribe, but from at any rate 441/0 some exceptions were allowed, probably to cater for cases in which a tribe had no strong candidate (cf. p. 61). That system was probably still operating in 357/6, when we know eight of the generals and they come from seven tribes, but by the 330's–320's they were elected irrespective of tribe (*Ath. Pol.* 61. i): it had come to seem more important to have competent generals than to maintain tribal representation. Another change in the generalship was made too. Originally all the generals had been given particular duties ad hoc; there is no sign that things were different in 357/6 (*IG* ii^2 124 = R&O 48 ~ Harding 65. 19–23; *IG* ii^2 123 = R&O 52 ~ Harding 69. 13–15); but a 'general for the defence of the territory' seems now to be attested in 356/5 (*SEG* xlvii 159. 2–4, where the crucial words are restored; certain in 352/1, *IG* ii^2 204 = R&O 58. 19–20), and by the time of the *Ath. Pol.* there were regular postings for five of the ten, 'for the hoplites' in expeditions outside Attica, 'for the territory', two 'for the Piraeus' and the military buildings and equipment there, and one 'for the *symmoriai*', in charge of the trierarchic system (61. i). In the hellenistic period the link with the tribes was so far forgotten that the number of generals remained ten when the number of tribes was increased, and eventually there were regular duties for all ten.

Piecemeal changes in the machinery of justice continued. We do not know whether it was a matter of regulation or simply of practice, but it is striking that we know of no *eisangeliai*, charges of major offences against the state, tried by the assembly after 362/1. A jury-court contained fewer men, paid at a lower rate, and the use of juries rather than the assembly may have been an economy measure introduced after the Social War.

In the 340's a new kind of lawsuit was introduced, the 'monthly' suit, probably available every month and accelerated by by-passing the Forty and the arbitrators and going straight to a court. Probably the first of these were the 'commercial' suits, in existence by 343/2, concerning trade to and from Athens where there was a written contract, and open to citizens, metics and foreigners on an equal basis (*Ath. Pol.* 52. ii–iii, 59. v, [Dem.] VII. *Halonnesus* 12, Dem.

XXXII. *Zenothemis* 1); these accelerated suits for traders are foreshadowed in Xen. *Poroi* ii. 3.

There were also important changes in the powers and activities of the Areopagus, which we shall examine below in connection with politics and politicians.

Policies, Politics, Politicians

Some men already prominent before the Social War remained active after, notably Aristophon and Chares, but the stage was largely occupied by a new generation (evidence supporting many statements undocumented here is cited in chapter 22, above). Eubulus, who had been one of the nine archons in 370/69, and Diophantus were both important in the late 350's and the 340's, and were responsible for the development of the theoric fund (cf. p. 333). They were not military men, but can be associated with the policy of concentrating on serious threats which Athens pursued after the Social War. In 352 Diophantus proposed the thanksgiving sacrifice when Philip was halted at Thermopylae (Dem. XIX. *Embassy* 86 with schol. [199 Dilts]). Men involved in the Euboean war of 348 had links with Eubulus: Phocion, who was primarily a general but saw himself as a general-cum-politician in the older manner (Plut. *Phoc.* 7. v–vi), when he did engage in politics was on the side of Eubulus and Aeschines; Hegesilaus was related to Eubulus (Dem. XIX. *Embassy* 290); Midias was to be defended against Demosthenes by Eubulus (Dem. XXI. *Midias* 205–7). After the fall of Olynthus Eubulus proposed the decree under which envoys were sent to mobilise southern Greek opposition to Philip (Dem. XIX. *Embassy* 304); but Phalaecus' rejection of Athenian help in 346 forced a change of policy, and Eubulus was in favour of the Peace of Philocrates (Dem. XIX. *Embassy* 291, XVIII. *Crown* 21). Aeschines had at one time supported Aristophon but switched his support to Eubulus (Dem. XIX. *Embassy* 290–1, XVIII. *Crown* 162), and he served on one of Eubulus' embassies in 348/7 (Aeschin. II. *Embassy* 79, Dem. XIX. *Embassy* 303–6).

Demosthenes began speaking in major prosecutions and on public issues in 355, but until 348 was consistently on the losing side. The prosecutions of Androtion (XXII), Leptines' law (XX), Timocrates (XXIV) and Aristocrates (XXIII) all seem to have failed. XIV. *Symmories* did not secure a reform of the trierarchic system; XVI. *Megalopolitans* did not persuade Athens to support Megalopolis against Sparta; XIII. *Organisation* did not undermine the theoric fund; IV. *Philippic i* did not result in a campaign against Philip in the north; XV. *Liberty of Rhodians* did not secure support for the Rhodian democrats against a Carian-backed oligarchy; I–III. *Olynthiacs i–iii* did not persuade Athens to support Olynthus as strongly as Demosthenes wanted, and Demosthenes was alone in opposing the Euboean war (V. *Peace* 5). But in 348, when Eubulus was becoming alarmed about Philip, Demosthenes, disgruntled at the Athenians' failure to act on his warnings, defended Philocrates when the latter was prosecuted for proposing to follow up Philip's offer of negotiations, and was successful.

In 346 Aeschines and Eubulus were in favour of the Peace of Philocrates, because Phalaecus had made it necessary, and because they trusted Philip's hints; Demosthenes was in favour, in the expectation that Philip's subsequent conduct would justify his warnings; two men mentioned as opposing the peace are Aristophon and Hegesippus. In the autumn of 346 Demosthenes advised against immediate conflict with Philip, in V. *Peace*, and prepared to attack Aeschines for his part in the negotiations. However, the original attack misfired, as the main prosecutor, Timarchus, had an unsavoury personal record which made him vulnerable (Aeschin. I. *Timarchus*, of 346/5). After that, Demosthenes gained increasing support, and in 343 Philocrates was successfully prosecuted by Hyperides (Dem. XIX. *Embassy* 116–19, Aeschin. II. *Embassy* 6, Hyp. IV. *Euxenippus* 29–30); Proxenus was perhaps condemned for delay in conveying the second embassy to Philip (Dem. XIX. *Embassy* 280 with schol. [493 Dilts]); Demosthenes himself prosecuted Aeschines, while Eubulus and Phocion were among his defenders, and by a small majority Aeschines was acquitted (Dem. XIX. *Embassy*, Aeschin. II. *Embassy*; Eubulus and Phocion Aeschin. II. *Embassy* 184; Idomeneus *FGrH* 338 F 10 *ap.* Plut. *Dem.* 15. v, [Plut.] *X Orat.* 840 C). By then Aeschines was trying to distance himself from the peace, whereas in 346/5 he associated himself with it (Aeschin. II. *Embassy* 56 contr. I. *Timarchus* 174).

After 346 we can identify supporters of Demosthenes. Hegesippus, opposed to the peace, defended Timarchus against Aeschines (Aeschin. I. *Timarchus* 71). He also took an unproductively hard line when Philip offered to amend the peace ([Dem.] VII. *Halonnesus*), and served on one of Demosthenes' embassies to the Peloponnese (Dem. IX. *Phil. iii.* 72). Hyperides prosecuted Philocrates in 343 (Hyp. IV. *Euxenippus* 29–30), was appointed in place of Aeschines to defend Athens' control of Delos (cf. p. 340), and in 341/0 renewed Athens' alliances with Rhodes and Chios. Lycurgus, who is linked with Demosthenes ([Plut.] *X Orat.* 848 F) and was to be hard on alleged traitors after Chaeronea, served on Demosthenes' embassies, and so did Polyeuctus (Dem. IX. *Phil. iii.* 72 [Lycurgus not all manuscripts], [Plut.] *X Orat.* 841 E).

Demosthenes remarks on the solidarity of his opponents (XIX. *Embassy* 225–6). We come closer in this period than in most to party politics, with groups of men agreeing on distinctive policies over a range of issues, but the collision is at an angle rather than head-on. For Demosthenes resistance to Philip was all-important, but that conditioned his views on financial matters; for Eubulus financial recovery was all-important, but that conditioned his views on Philip. Attitudes to democracy were affected too: Demosthenes accused his opponents of being unpatriotic, and tended to identify democracy with freedom from an external master rather than with internal freedom, while they in response accused him of being undemocratic (cf. p. 340).

When war was declared against Philip in 340, Demosthenes reformed the trierarchic system; when Philip entered the Fourth Sacred War, in 339/8,

Demosthenes had surplus revenue diverted to the stratiotic fund (cf. p. 334). He was crowned for his services to Athens in 340, and again in the spring of 338; in 338 Hyperides was one of the proposers, and he was challenged but unsuccessfully in a *graphe paranomon* (Dem. XVIII. *Crown* 83, 222–3, 249, [Plut.] *X Orat.* 846 A, 848 D, F).

In the years after Chaeronea there were frantic swings of the pendulum. Hyperides and Lycurgus seem both to have been members of the council in 338/7 (Lucian, *Parasite* 42). Hyperides was responsible for emergency measures immediately after the battle (Lycurg. *Leocrates* 36–7, [Plut.] *X Orat.* 848 F–849 A, cf. Hyp. fr. 18 Burtt); and Demosthenes proposed measures after his return from the battle, perhaps through his friends (Dem. XVIII. *Crown* 248 contr. Aeschin. III. *Ctesiphon* 159, cf. Plut. *Dem.* 21. iii). Originally Charidemus, a man from Oreus who had been made an Athenian citizen and who was an extreme opponent of Macedon, was proposed as commander in chief, but the job eventually went to Phocion (cf. p. 340). On the other side Demades, a man from a poor background who was to be prominent among the friends of Macedon in the 330's and 320's, was captured in the battle, was liberated after reproaching Philip for his wild exultation (cf. p. 318), and then went with Aeschines to negotiate with Philip. Phocion also supported acceptance of the peace (Plut. *Phoc.* 16. v). Athens voted citizenship and other honours for Philip and Alexander ([Demades] *Twelve Years* 9, schol. Aristid. *Panath.* 178. 16 [iii. 297 Dindorf]).

In winter 338/7, as the new reality sank in, there was a change of mood. Aeschines was nominated but Demosthenes was appointed to deliver the funeral oration for those killed at Chaeronea (Dem. XVIII. *Crown* 285–8, Plut. *Dem.* 21. i–ii); and work on the fortifications continued, with Demosthenes as a member of the supervisory board (Aeschin. III. *Ctesiphon* 17, 31, Dem. XVIII. *Crown* 113). Demosthenes was elected theoric treasurer for 337/6 (Aeschin. III. *Ctesiphon* 24); Acarnanians were honoured who had fought with the Athenians as volunteers at Chaeronea and had fled to Athens after Philip's settlement (*IG* ii² 237 = R&O 77 ~ Harding 100); even Phocion had his doubts about the League of Corinth (Plut. *Phoc.* 16. v–vii). The rival factions took to the courts. Demosthenes was constantly under attack (Dem. XVIII. *Crown* 249); Aristo-giton was involved in prosecutions of him and of Hyperides (schol. [Dem.] XXV. *Aristogiton i.* 37 [16 Dilts]), [Plut.] *X Orat.* 848 F–849 A, cf. Hyp. fr. 18 Burtt). In return, Lycurgus prosecuted men for cowardice in 338 (Lycurg. frs. 9–10 Burtt, cf. Diod. Sic. XVI. 88. i–ii); and when Demades proposed honours for one of the men who had betrayed Olynthus to Philip in 348, Hyperides prosecuted him for that (Hyp. fr. 19 Burtt).

Early in 336 Ctesiphon proposed that Demosthenes should be honoured for a third time; but as Philip's Persian campaign got under way public opinion shifted yet again: honours were voted for Macedonians (*IG* ii² 239–40 = Tod 180–1), and even for Philip himself in connection with Cleopatra's wedding (Diod. Sic. XVI. 92. i–ii). Aeschines took advantage of this shift to launch a prosecution of Ctesiphon, on three counts: that he was proposing honours for

Demosthenes while Demosthenes held offices for which he was subject to account; that he was proposing proclamation of the honours at the Dionysia; and, above all, that he was making a false statement in a public document by claiming that Demosthenes always spoke and acted in the best interests of Athens (Aeschin. III. *Ctesiphon* 9–31, 32–48, 49–50). Then Philip was murdered. There was a chance that the succession would be disputed and all that he had achieved for Macedon would be undone; while Demosthenes led the rejoicing in Athens, Aeschines dropped the prosecution.

All too quickly, Alexander asserted himself and marched into Greece. When he reached Thebes, Athens panicked and sent a deputation to protest its loyalty; Demosthenes, though a member of the deputation, could not face Alexander and turned back (there were allegations that he was in touch both with Attalus and with the Persians), and it was Demades who made an agreement with Alexander (Diod. Sic. XVII. 4. v–ix, cf. 3. ii, 5. i, Aeschin. III. *Ctesiphon* 161, [Demades] *Twelve Years* 14). In 335, while Alexander campaigned in Thrace and Illyria, Demosthenes was allegedly receiving Persian money to support Greek resistance to Macedon (Aeschin. III. *Ctesiphon* 239–40, Din. I. *Dem.* 10, 18–22, Plut. *Dem.* 20. iv–v). Rumours that Alexander had been killed led Thebes to revolt, with encouragement from Demosthenes, but again Alexander quickly appeared, and Thebes was destroyed; and again there was a panic in Athens. Originally Alexander demanded that his opponents should be handed over to him: Demosthenes, Lycurgus and Charidemus appear in all versions of the list, Polyeuctus (and, less likely, Hyperides) in some. Phocion would have handed them over, but on Demades' proposal the two of them went to talk to Alexander, and Alexander was satisfied with the exile of Charidemus – who, with others, joined the Persians (Plut. *Dem.* 23. vi probably gives the authentic list; variants Diod. Sic. XVII. 15, Arr. *Anab.* I. 10. iii–vi, Plut. *Phoc.* 17. ii–x). Athens rewarded Demades with a statue and meals in the *prytaneion*, despite the opposition of Lycurgus and Polyeuctus (Din. I. *Demosthenes* 101, cf. Lycurg fr. 14 Burtt, Polyeuctus fr. i. 1 Sauppe).

By now the council of the Areopagus had attained a surprising prominence. At the beginning of the century Athens' new code of laws had been entrusted to the care of the Areopagus (decree *ap.* Andoc. I. *Myst.* 84), but there is no sign that this had any practical effect. About 354 Isocrates in VII. *Areopagitic* wrote of a glorious past of Athens in which the Areopagus had played an important role. In 352/1 the Areopagus, appropriately in view of its religious concerns, headed a list of those who were to take care of the Athenian sanctuaries (*IG* ii^2 204 = R&O 58. 16–23).

More strikingly, from the mid 340's we find the Areopagus on a number of occasions making an *apophasis* ('report') to the assembly (cf. Din. I. *Demosthenes* 50–1). In 345 Timarchus put forward a plan to clean up the area of the Pnyx: in accordance with his decree the Areopagus was called on to report, and it reported unfavourably (Aeschin. I. *Timarchus* 81–4). Two other episodes are probably to be dated *c.*345–343. A man called Antiphon, deleted from the citizen registers in 346, was charged by Demosthenes with intending to set fire to Athens' dockyards for Philip; Aeschines successfully defended him; but the Areopagus had the case reopened and he was convicted (Dem. XVIII. *Crown* 132–3 with schol. [245, 249, 252 Dilts], Plut. *Dem.* 14. v). When the Delians complained to the Delphic Amphictyony about Athens' control of their sanctuary of Apollo, the assembly elected Aeschines to respond, but referred the matter to the Areopagus, and the Areopagus substituted Hyperides – who convinced the Amphictyony (Dem. XVIII. *Crown* 134–6, [Plut.] *X Orat.* 850 A, cf. Hyp. fr. 1 Burtt). After Chaeronea, when some men wanted the chief command to be conferred on Charidemus, the Areopagus persuaded the assembly to appoint Phocion (Plut. *Phoc.* 16. iv). Dinarchus mentions a decree of Demosthenes authorising the Areopagus to punish offenders, and cites four cases including that of Antiphon (Din. I. *Demosthenes* 62–3); but probably he is confusing the issues, and these were all instances of *apophasis*, which as an exercise of the citizens' right to address the assembly may not have required formal institution. After Chaeronea the Areopagus condemned some of the men accused of cowardice or treason (Lycurg. *Leocrates* 52–4, Aeschin. III. *Ctesiphon* 252), and it is here that we should place Demosthenes' decree giving the Areopagus enhanced judicial powers.

Except in the case of Phocion's command, the Areopagus was consistently taking Demosthenes' side on controversial matters, and his opponents were alarmed and considered this undemocratic. This, I believe, is why, in early summer 337/6, when the mood in Athens was pro-Macedonian, a law was passed threatening the Areopagus with suspension if the democracy was overthrown (*Agora* xvi 73 = R&O 79 ~ Harding 101); similarly a powerful theoric treasurer was perceived as undemocratic when that treasurer was Demosthenes, and Hegemon's law on financial officials (cf. pp. 333–4) probably belongs to this same context. The Areopagus' prestige survived the attack: it was ordered to investigate allegations about Demosthenes and Persian money in 335, with no result that we know of (Din. I. *Demosthenes* 10), and the matter of Harpalus' money in 324–323 (below).

At this time there seems to have been a good deal of sensitivity about democracy, but a lack of clarity about what the essentials of democracy were. In Apollodorus' speech *Against Neaera*, of c.343–340, and Isocrates' *Panathenaic*, of c.342–339, we have praise of the democracy attributed to the legendary Theseus, which is represented as a democracy of a moderate kind ([Dem.] LIX *Neaera* 75–7; Isoc. XII *Panath.* 143–8). The relief at the top of the *stele* bearing the law threatening the Areopagus has been identified as showing Demokratia crowning Demos. In 333/2 the council set up a statue of Demokratia, and in the following two years the generals are recorded as sacrificing to Demokratia (*IG* ii² 2791; 1496. 131–2, 140–1); it has been suggested that the cult was instituted in 403/2 but was given new emphasis in the 330's.

After 335 politics entered a new phase: for the time being, Alexander was unquestionably in control, and Athens had to live with that; but there was still a chance that he would be defeated and killed in his Asiatic wars and that Macedon's supremacy would collapse, and Athens had to be ready to seize the opportunity if it arose. Demosthenes and his supporters kept in the background and his opponents ran Athens, except that Lycurgus took charge of the finances (though Demades was stratiotic treasurer, at any rate in 334/3: *SEG* xxi 552. 12). Attempts were made both to revive Athens' morale after the humiliation of Chaeronea and to maintain Athens' military preparedness.

In what has been called the silver age of Lycurgus (by comparison with the golden age of Pericles), Athens enjoyed its first major public building programme since Pericles' time (cf. [Plut.] *X Orat.* 841 C–E). Under Eubulus and/or Lycurgus the Pnyx was remodelled. Work in the agora included rebuilding the temple of Apollo Patroos, north of the council-house complex, and relocating to face that complex the monument of the *eponymoi* (the tribal heroes), whose base served as a state notice-board. A monumental theatre of Dionysus was built, and a Panathenaic stadium. Whereas the Periclean buildings had been erected largely at public expense ('public' including tribute from the Delian League: cf. pp. 50, 62–5), Lycurgus encouraged rich individuals to make contributions in exchange for inexpensive honours: a decree of Lycurgus honours a Plataean who helped with the theatre and the stadium (*IG* ii² 351 + 654 = Schwenk 48 = R&O 94 ~ Harding 118); in 321/0 Xenocles, the epimelete of the Mysteries, built a bridge on the Sacred Way from Athens to Eleusis (*IG* ii² 1191, 2840, *Anth. Pal.* IX. 147). There was a religious revival: festivals were reorganised, with specific items of revenue earmarked to finance them (*Agora* xvi 75 = Schwenk 17 = R&O 81, cf. *IG* ii² 333 = Schwenk 21); definitive texts of the tragedies of Aeschylus, Sophocles and Euripides were edited ([Plut.] *X Orat.* 841 F); Athens was assiduous in sending delegations to sanctuaries elsewhere (e.g. Hyp. IV. *Euxenippus* 22–4, Lyc. fr. 4 Burtt).

Athenians came of age at 18, and for two years were *epheboi*, 'on the verge of adulthood'. There had always been training opportunities of some kind for the *epheboi* (cf. Aeschin. II. *Embassy* 167), but about 335/4 a compulsory two-year programme was instituted for all young Athenians (probably, of hoplite class and above): the first year was devoted to military training, visits to temples and garrison duty at the Piraeus, the second to garrison duty on the frontiers (*Ath. Pol.* 42. ii–iv: inscribed lists begin with the *epheboi* of 334/3, *IG* ii² 1156). When Athens had been great, it had been a great naval power. An enlargement of the navy was begun in the time of Eubulus – Athens had 283 ships in 357/6, despite the Social War 349 in 353/2 (*IG* ii² 1611. 9, 1613. 302) – and under Lycurgus there was further enlargement and also modernisation, with the introduction of quadriremes and quinqueremes (ships with more than one man to an oar, more stable but slower: for the attribution of this development to Dionysius I of Syracuse cf. p. 280; quinqueremes were to replace triremes as the standard Greek warships) – 392 triremes + 18 quadriremes = 410 in 330/29, 360 triremes + 50 quadriremes + 2 quinqueremes = 412 in 325/4 (*IG* ii² 1627. 266–9, 275–8, 1629. 783–812 corrected). This was a larger navy than Athens had had in the fifth century, but the expenditure seems to have been futile: Athens could not find the oarsmen for so many ships, and there was now no rival naval power against which so many ships would be needed (in the Lamian War of 323–322 Athens used only 170 ships).

Charidemus and others had joined the Persians (cf. p. 339), and Iphicrates the younger along with envoys from Sparta and Thebes was found in Darius' entourage after the battle of Issus in 333 (Arr. *Anab.* II. 15. ii–iv). Alexander kept the Athenian contingent when he dismissed the rest of his fleet in 334 (Diod. Sic. XVII. 22. v), and took care to keep Athens loyal (Arr. *Anab.* III. 6. ii, 16. vii–viii). Despite the hopes of his opponents, he defeated Persian armies at the Granicus in 334 and at Issus in 333 (on his campaigns see chapter 24). In 331, as he was about to face the Persians in Mesopotamia, the Spartans took advantage of trouble in Thrace to rise against Macedon (cf. p. 345), and Athens, whose sea power could seriously have increased the pressure on Macedon, had to decide whether to join the rising. Demades helped to keep Athens out of it (Plut. *Praec. Ger. Reip.* 818 E), and this time Demosthenes played safe (Aeschin. III. *Ctesiphon* 165–7, Din. I. *Demosthenes* 34–6, Plut. *Dem* 24. i). However, Lycurgus' honours for the Plataean who supported the building programme praised him also for offering to make an *epidosis* 'towards the war if there were any need' (inscription cited above, 12–15): probably this is the war in question, and its mention indicates that Lycurgus would have liked Athens to take part. If the anti-Macedonian [Dem.] XVII. *Treaty with Alexander* is by Hyperides and is to be dated 331, perhaps he too was in favour.

But the rising was defeated, and the Persians were defeated at Gaugamela. In 330 Lycurgus made the anti-Macedonian gesture of prosecuting one more man for treasonable conduct in 338, Leocrates, who escaped by a tied vote (Lycurg. *Leocrates*, cf. Aeschin. III. *Ctesiphon* 252). Aeschines seized the opportunity to revive the prosecution of Ctesiphon, which he had dropped in 336 (Aeschin. III. *Ctesiphon*, Dem. XVIII. *Crown*), but he had misjudged the mood of the Athenians: although resistance to Macedon was not possible now, the jurors backed the man who had resisted when it was possible. Aeschines failed to obtain a fifth of the votes, and left Athens ([Plut.] *X Orat.* 840 C–E, Plut. *Dem.* 24. ii–iii).

From the mid 330's to the late 320's there were corn shortages in Greece, caused apparently by crop failures in and near the eastern Mediterranean, and known to us particularly from inscriptions. Heraclides of Salamis in Cyprus helped Athens in 330/29 and 328/7 by selling corn at a fair price, and by making an *epidosis* (*IG* ii² 360 = R&O 95). Demosthenes served on a purchasing board and contributed 1 talent ([Plut.] *X Orat.* 845 F, 851 B). In 325/4, to protect imports from the west against pirates, the Athenians sent a colony to the Adriatic, presided over by Miltiades, a member of the family which had been influential in the sixth and fifth centuries (*IG* ii² 1629 = R&O 100. 165–271, part trans. Harding 121). An inscription from Cyrene lists those to whom it supplied corn, with Athens as the largest recipient (*SEG* ix 2 = R&O 96 ~ Harding 116). There seems also to have been an attempt to bring more land in Attica under cultivation, and at the same time to raise money by selling off underused public land.

Athens received corn also from Harpalus, Alexander's treasurer (while it supplied him with women), and rewarded him with citizenship (Theopompus

FGrH 115 FF 253–4 and Python *ap.* Ath. XIII. 595 A–596 B, cf. 586 C–D). Subsequently, in 324, when Alexander returned to the centre of his empire and began punishing offenders (cf. pp. 357, 372), Harpalus fled, and approached Athens with thirty ships, six thousand mercenaries and a large sum of money. Demosthenes had largely remained out of the limelight since 330; but now he proposed the decree forbidding Harpalus to land. After taking his ships and mercenaries to Taenarum (cf. below), Harpalus returned to Athens as a suppliant with 700 talents. Various Macedonians demanded that he should be surrendered to them but, again on Demosthenes' proposal, the Athenians decided to surrender him only if demanded by Alexander himself, and meanwhile to place him under arrest and keep the money on the acropolis. Alexander's edict for the restoration of exiles threatened Athens' possession of Samos, and it was again Demosthenes who headed Athens' delegation to the Olympic games to raise the issue with Alexander's representative Nicanor (cf. Din. I. *Demosthenes* 81–2, 103). Shortly after this Harpalus escaped (to Crete, where he was murdered), and when the Athenians checked the money they found that half had gone (Diod. Sic. XVII. 108. vi–109. i, Plut. *Dem.* 25, [Plut.] *X Orat.* 846 A–B).

There was an outcry, and by a decree of Demosthenes the Areopagus was commissioned to investigate. After six months it produced a list of offenders headed by Demosthenes and Demades, and also including Polyeuctus and Aristogiton; there was inevitably a story that Phocion had resisted temptation. Public prosecutors were elected, who like the accused came from both sides of the old political divide: they included Hyperides and Menesaechmus. We have four prosecuting speeches, Hyperides V. *Demosthenes*, and Dinarchus (written for others) I. *Demosthenes*, II. *Aristogiton*, III. *Philocles*. Demosthenes was tried first, fined 50 talents and escaped into exile; Demades also was convicted; some men including Aristogiton were acquitted (Diod. Sic. XVII. 108. vii, [Plut.] *X Orat.* 846 C, Plut. *Dem.* 26. i–iv, *Phoc.* 21. iii–iv, Din. I. *Dem.* 45, 82, Hyp. V. *Demosthenes* col. 18, Dem. *Letter iii.* 37, 42). This was an explosion of anger in some ways comparable to the explosion after the battle of Arginusae in 406 (cf. p. 167); and shortly afterwards the nature of the world was changed by Alexander's death.

An Athenian called Leosthenes became leader of the body of mercenaries which began to assemble at Taenarum in Laconia when Alexander ordered provincial governors to dismiss their mercenary forces, and he was in touch with the Athenian council and also with the Aetolians (Diod. Sic. XVII. 111. i–iii, XVIII. 9. i–iii, Paus. I. 25. v, VIII. 52. v). There is a Leosthenes who appears as general 'for the territory' in an Athenian inscription (Reinmuth, *Ephebic Inscriptions* 15, l.h.s. 2–6): this second Leosthenes was the son of the Leosthenes who was defeated by Alexander of Pherae in 362–361 (cf. p. 238), and who went in exile to the Macedonian court (Aeschin. II. *Embassy* 21 with schol. [46b Dilts]). Often the ephebic inscription has been dated 324/3 and Leosthenes the general 'for the territory' has been identified with Leosthenes the mercenary commander; but more probably they are different men.

When Alexander died, in June 323, the old political alignments in Athens resurfaced. Athens led a Greek rising against Macedon, in what is called the Lamian War, since the main land campaign was fought near Lamia in Thessaly (in general, Diod. Sic. XVIII. 8–18). This rising was the work of Hyperides, backed by Demosthenes, who was allowed to return from exile (Plut. *Dem.* 27, [Plut.] *X Orat.* 846 C–D, 849 F–850 A), and it was opposed by Demades, who lost his political rights after three times prosecuting unsuccessfully in *graphai paranomon*, and by Phocion (Diod. Sic. XVIII. 18. i–ii, Plut. *Phoc.* 22. v–23, 26. iii). The influence of Hyperides is reflected in the fact that in 322 he was chosen to deliver the *Funeral Oration* (VI). But after a Macedonian victory at Crannon the rising collapsed. Demades had his rights restored, and he and Phocion negotiated with Antipater. Antipater's demands included the handing over of Demosthenes, who committed suicide, and Hyperides, who was sent to Macedon and executed. Though Phocion was not an enthusiast for democracy, in general the pro-Macedonians were neither more nor less democratic than the anti-Macedonians, but Demosthenes and his supporters had too often linked democracy with freedom. In the first of a series of changes over the next half-century, Athens was given not only a Macedonian garrison but an oligarchic constitution (Diod. Sic. XVIII. 18, Plut. *Dem.* 28, *Phoc.* 26. iii–28, [Plut.] *X Orat.* 846 E–847 B, 849 A–D). Demades and Phocion were both put to death in the upheavals of the next few years.

APPENDIX: SPARTA

When Cleombratus was killed at Leuctra in 371 he was succeeded by his elder son, Agesipolis II; but Agesipolis died almost immediately, in 370, and the Agid throne then passed to Agesipolis' brother Cleomenes II, who reigned until 309 but has left hardly any trace in the records. Of the Eurypontids, Agesilaus survived the battle of Mantinea in 362 and died in 360/59 on his way back from mercenary service in Egypt. He was succeeded by his son Archidamus III, who is commonly mentioned when Sparta was involved in foreign affairs: he was consulted by Philomelus before his seizure of Delphi in 356 (Diod. Sic. XVI. 24. i–ii, cf. Paus. III. 10. iii) and was appointed to command the Spartans in support of the Phocians in 346 (Diod. Sic. XVI. 59. i). When the Spartans did take part in the war, at Thermopylae in 352, Diodorus does not name the commander (XVI. 37. iii). From 353 to 350, while the Greeks were distracted by the Sacred War, Sparta tried to recover Messenia on the principle of *echein ta heauton* and attacked Megalopolis, and here again Archidamus is mentioned as commander (Diod. Sic. XVI. 39. i: cf. p. 305). In the west, Sparta had supported Dionysius I in Syracuse; and Spartan agents were active there in the mid 350's (cf. p. 288).

In 344 Sparta was fighting against Argos and Messene, which received help from Philip (Dem. VI. *Phil. ii.* 15, *hyp.* 2). Perhaps after that Archidamus went abroad: first to Crete, where he successfully supported Lyctus in a war against Cnossus, which was employing Phalaecus and his surviving mercenaries (Diod. Sic. XVI. 62. iii–iv, under 346/5); then to Italy to support Sparta's colony Taras against the Lucanians, where he was killed in 338, allegedly on the day of the battle of Chaeronea (Diod. Sic. XVI. 62. iv–63. ii, 89. iii–iv). He was succeeded by his eldest son Agis III.

The Spartans did not fight at Chaeronea, and they did not take part in Philip's common peace and League of Corinth. It appears that Philip invaded Laconia, and gave various border territories to Sparta's enemies; with or without a treaty, Sparta acquiesced. In 334 after the battle of the Granicus Alexander's dedication in Athens celebrated a victory won by him and 'the Greeks except the Spartans', and in 333 there was a Spartan envoy with Darius at Issus (Arr. *Anab.* I. 16. vii, II. 15. ii–v; cf. p. 352–3). An attempt to fight back in Alexander's rear had been begun by Memnon and was continued after his death by Pharnabazus and Autophradates: Agis asked them for ships and men to fight in the Peloponnese, but after Issus they could spare only 30 talents and ten ships, which were taken by Agis' brother Agesilaus to Crete. Agis himself in 332 joined Autophradates at Halicarnassus, receiving more money and 8,000 of Darius' mercenaries, and he took them to Crete: gratitude earned there might gain him more mercenaries for fighting in Greece (Arr. *Anab.* II. 13. iv–vi, Diod. Sic. XVII. 48. i–ii, Curt. IV. i. 38–40).

For what follows the exact dating is uncertain, but the essentials are clear enough. At some point in 331, if not before Alexander's victory at Gaugamela, surely before the news of it had reached Greece (contr. Diod. Sic. XVII. 62. i), the attention of Antipater in Macedon was distracted by a rebellion of Memnon, the Macedonian governor of Thrace, and Agis seized the opportunity to begin a rising in Greece. With support from most of the Peloponnese and Thessaly he had an army of 2,000 cavalry, 20,000 citizen infantry and 10,000 mercenaries, but Athens did not join in (cf. p. 342). After winning an initial victory, he began a siege of Megalopolis with good prospects of success. In the winter of 331/0, if the episode was over, Alexander did not yet know: he sent 3,000 talents to provide whatever Antipater needed for the war (Arr. *Anab.* 16. ix–x, cf. Diod. Sic. XVII. 64. v, Curt. V. i. 43). Antipater came to an arrangement with Memnon, raised an army of 40,000 (to which some League of Corinth states contributed) and marched to Megalopolis. Either late in 331 or early in 330 the Spartans were defeated and Agis was killed (Diod. Sic. XVII. 62–3, Curt. lacuna – VI. i, Aeschin. III. *Ctesiphon* 165–7, Din. I. *Demosthenes* 34). Cleomenes' son Acrotatus was beaten up for opposing the exemption from disgrace of Spartans who survived the defeat (Diod. Sic. XIX. 70. iv–v).

Antipater took hostages from Sparta and referred the matter to the League, and the League referred it to Alexander (Diod. Sic. XVII. 73. v–vi). We are not told the outcome for Sparta, but presumably it was required to join the League; Achaea and Elis were made to pay compensation to Megalopolis (Curt. VI. i. 20). Sparta is not among the states supplied with corn by Cyrene, but Elis is (*SEG* ix 2 = R&O 96 ~ Harding 116: Elis l. 34), so Sparta's absence more probably reflects lack of need than hostility. Agis' brother Eudamidas succeeded him: despite the wishes of some, Sparta refused to join Athens in the Lamian War in 323, and Eudamidas is associated with that refusal (Plut. *Spartan Sayings* 220 E–F).

NOTE ON FURTHER READING

On *eisphora* see G. E. M. de Ste. Croix, 'Demosthenes' τίμημα and the Athenian Eisphora in the Fourth Century BC', *C&M* xiv 1953, 30–70; P. J. Rhodes, 'Problems in Athenian *Eisphora* and Liturgies', *AJAH* vii 1982 [published 1985], 1–19. On festival liturgies see J. K. Davies, 'Demosthenes on Liturgies: A Note', *JHS* lxxxvii 1967, 33–40; on the trierarchy see Gabrielsen, *Financing the Athenian Fleet*. On the theoric fund and Lycurgus' office *epi tei dioikesei* see Rhodes, *The Athenian Boule*, 105–8, 235–40.

The suggestion that the *katagogia* of Xenophon, *Poroi*, iii. 12, are not hotels but brothels was made by A. J. Graham, 'The Woman at the Window: Observations on the "Stele from the Harbour" of Thasos', *JHS* cxviii 1998, 22–40 at 36–7.

On judicial changes see P. J. Rhodes, 'Judicial Procedures in Fourth-Century Athens: Improvement or Simply Change?', in Eder (ed.), *Die athenische Demokratie im 4. Jh. v. Chr.*, 303–19. On Eubulus see G. L. Cawkwell, 'Eubulus', *JHS* lxxxiii 1963, 47–67; on Phocion see Tritle, *Phocion the Good*. On changing understandings of democracy see P. J. Rhodes, 'Democracy and Its Opponents in Fourth-Century Athens', in a forthcoming Chieti conference volume. On the different lists of Athenians demanded by Alexander in 335 see Bosworth, *Historical Commentary on Arrian*, i. 93–5.

On the revival of the Areopagus see P. J. Rhodes, 'Judicial Procedures in Fourth-Century Athens' (above), 311–14; R. W. Wallace, '"Investigations and Reports" by the Areopagos Council and Demosthenes' Areopagos Decree', in *Polis and Politics . . . M. H. Hansen*, 581–95; J. A. Sullivan, 'Demosthenes' Areopagus Legislation – Yet Again', *CQ*[2] liii 2003, 130–4.

On the silver age of Lycurgus see F. W. Mitchel, 'Athens in the Age of Alexander', *G&R*[2] xii 1965, 189–204.

On Agis' war against Macedon see E. Badian, 'Agis III: Revisions and Reflections', in *Ventures into Greek History* ⟨ . . . *N. G. L. Hammond*⟩, ch. 13.

24

Alexander the Great: Sources and Outline

500	475	450	425	400	375	350	325	300

336 accession of Alexander
334 Alexander's entry into Asia; battle of the Granicus
333 battle of Issus
332 sieges of Tyre and Gaza
331 battle of Gaugamela
330 death of Darius
326 battle of Hydaspes
324 Alexander's return to Susa
323 death of Alexander

Sources

The works on Alexander by contemporaries and near-contemporaries have not survived. Of the five major accounts which do survive, that of Diodorus (book XVII), written in the first century BC, is the earliest. Q. Curtius Rufus almost certainly wrote in the first century AD and was known to Tacitus; if he is the Curtius Rufus of Tac. *Ann.* XI. 20–1, he was active in the second quarter of the century and held office under Tiberius and Claudius: he wrote, in Latin, a highly rhetorical history of Alexander in ten books (I–II are lost, and there are lacunae in what survives). Plutarch (first/second centuries AD) wrote a life of *Alexander* (the Roman parallel is *Caesar*; in this and the following chapter, references to Plutarch without further specification are to the *Alexander*), and his *Moralia* include two essays *On Alexander the Great's Good Fortune or Good Qualities* (which will be cited as *De Alex. Fort.* i/ii). Arrian, from Nicomedia at the east end of the Propontis, was active in the first half of the second century AD and held office under Hadrian: he saw himself as a second Xenophon, and hence his history of Alexander was entitled *Anabasis* (references to Arrian without further specification are to this); he also sought to celebrate Alexander the second Achilles as Homer had celebrated Achilles. Among his other works was the *Indike*, written in an imitation of Herodotus' Ionic Greek, which provides information about India and an account of Nearchus' voyage from the mouths of the Indus to the Persian Gulf in 325. In Justin's epitome of Pompeius Trogus (Latin, *c.*200–400 AD: cf. p. 294; in this and the following chapter, this will be cited simply as Just.), books XI–XII are devoted to Alexander.

Arrian's narrative has generally and rightly been regarded as the best. He was not a penetrating historian, and his reasons for trusting his preferred sources are naïve (cf. Arr. I, preface). Partly because of his 'Homeric' aim (for his aim of celebrating Alexander as earlier Greek writers had celebrated their heroes see I. 12. ii–v), he was too willing to see nothing but good in Alexander and to minimise Alexander's difficulties; but his sources were men who had served under Alexander, and were as well placed as any to know the truth even if it might not always suit them to tell the truth. These were Ptolemy (*FGrH* 138), a lifetime friend of Alexander and eventually a major officer, who after his death took possession of Egypt and founded the Ptolemaic dynasty there, and Aristobulus (*FGrH* 139), who held lower positions and had strong botanical and geographical interests; Arrian also used Nearchus (*FGrH* 133), the commander of Alexander's fleet in 326–325. Curtius has some material in common with Arrian; but much of the material in Diodorus, Curtius and Justin comes ultimately from a common source, probably Clitarchus (*FGrH* 137), who is not known to have served under Alexander himself but who wrote before the end of the fourth century: he had a taste for the sensational, but preserved a considerable amount of detail, not always favourable to Alexander. Plutarch, as always, used a variety of sources. Admirers of Alexander have been particularly disposed to accept Arrian's account; on the other hand, it would be dangerous to assume, as some revisionist historians have been tempted to do, that what is favourable to Alexander must be distorted by bias and what is unfavourable must be truthful.

Early writers whose accounts have been lost include Aristotle's nephew Callisthenes (*FGrH* 124), who accompanied Alexander in some sense as official historian, but who was put to death after the 'conspiracy of the pages' (cf. p. 371); Chares (*FGrH* 125), Alexander's chamberlain, who wrote about episodes at Alexander's court; and Onesicritus (*FGrH* 134), Nearchus' helmsman, who wrote a fictionalised account modelled on Xenophon's *Cyropaedia*. A 'source' of an altogether amazing kind is the *Alexander Romance*, falsely attributed to Callisthenes. Three very different Greek versions survive, and versions in Latin and in various eastern languages added further elaborations: Alexander's adventures include ascending into the sky in a basket borne by eagles and descending into the sea in a diving-bell. Towards the other extreme (in the opinion of some scholars), one of the sources cited for the end of Alexander's life (cf. pp. 351, 357) is a diary, the *ephemerides* (*FGrH* 117). Views of this have ranged from an official journal of the whole campaign, underlying much of what Arrian obtained from Ptolemy, to a hellenistic fabrication, fraudulently ascribed to Alexander's secretary Eumenes (on Eumenes cf. p. 374). A recent study suggests that it may actually be the work of Eumenes, not an official record or covering the whole campaign, but an account written up to emphasise Alexander's drinking habits and to show that Hephaestion's and Alexander's deaths were due to natural causes.

Accession and Consolidation

When Philip was killed, in July 336, Alexander, not quite 20 years old but already with military experience, was the obvious successor, though after Philip's marriage to Cleopatra he and his mother Olympias had quarrelled with Philip. Antipater presented Alexander to the soldiers as the new king. Two princes from Lyncestis and Amyntas the son of Perdiccas III, whom Philip had left alive, were officially blamed and put to death; Cleopatra and her infant daughter were killed, and so too was her uncle Attalus, who had gone with Philip's advance force to Asia Minor.

In response to rumours of rebellion in Greece Alexander marched south. Mountaineering was needed to by-pass opposition in the pass of Tempe (Polyaenus *Strat.* IV. 3. xxiii), but after that the Thessalians acknowledged him as archon for life in succession to Philip, and next the Amphictyony at Thermopylae recognised him; when he camped outside Thebes the Thebans acknowledged him and the Athenians, who had been in touch with Attalus, sent protestations of loyalty. Finally, at Corinth a congress of the League appointed him as commander of the Greek war of revenge against Persia (Diod. Sic. XVII. 3–4, Arr. I. 1. i–iii, Just. XI. 2. iv–vi, 3. i–ii, Plut. 14. i–v).

First, however, Macedon's other European neighbours had to be dealt with. Leaving Antipater in Macedon, Alexander campaigned first in Thrace as far as the Danube and then in Illyria. He was successful, but at one point he was dangerously trapped in Illyria (cf. p. 366), and rumours that he had been killed encouraged revolt in Greece – in particular, by Thebes, proposing 'to liberate Greece and overthrow the tyrant of Greece', supported by Demosthenes with Persian money and hoping for support from various Peloponnesian states too. All too quickly, Alexander arrived outside Thebes, and captured the city; Arrian blames the general Perdiccas for attacking prematurely, and the Greeks in Alexander's army for the worst of the violence, but Diodorus does not. The episode was treated as rebellion by a member state of the League of Corinth, and was referred to the League's *synedrion*, with the result that, with the exception of the fifth-century poet Pindar's house, the city was destroyed. Like Sparta's occupation of Thebes in 382, the destruction of Thebes shocked the

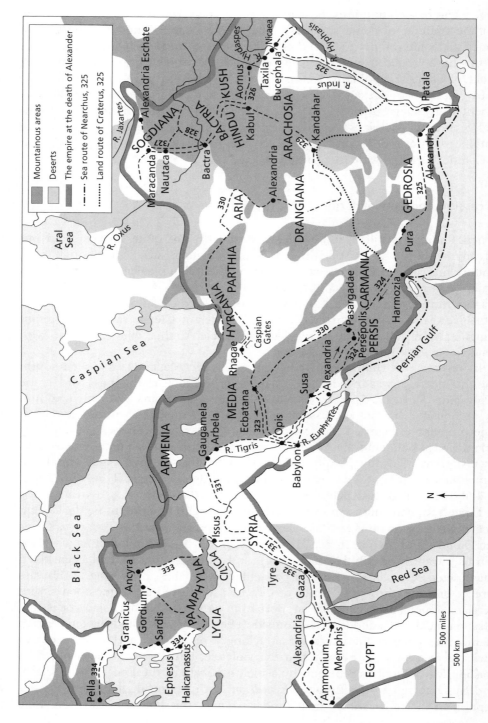

Map 8 The Persian campaign of Alexander the Great

Mountainous areas
Deserts
The empire at the death of Alexander
Sea route of Nearchus, 325
Land route of Craterus, 325

Black Sea

Caspian Sea

Aral Sea

R. Oxus

R. Jaxartes

Pella 334
Granicus
Ancyra
Gordium
333
Sardis
Ephesus
334
Halicarnassus
PAMPHYLIA
LYCIA
CILICIA
Issus
SYRIA
331
Tyre
Gaza
332
Alexandria
Ammonium
Memphis
EGYPT
Red Sea

ARMENIA
331
Gaugamela
Arbela
R. Tigris
MEDIA
Ecbatana
323
Opis
Babylon
R. Euphrates
Susa
Alexandria
330
334
Pasargadae
Persepolis
PERSIS
330
Rhagae
HYRCANIA
Caspian Gates
PARTHIA
ARIA
330
DRANGIANA
Alexandria
CARMANIA
324
Harmozia
Persian Gulf
GEDROSIA
325
Pura
Alexandria
Patala

SOGDIANA
Maracanda
Nautaca
321
328
Bactra
BACTRIA
HINDU KUSH
Aornus
Kabul
326
Taxila
Nicaea
Bucephala
R. Hydaspes
R. Hyphasis
R. Indus
325
ARACHOSIA
329
Kandahar
Alexandria Eschate

N

500 miles
500 km

Greeks (cf. Polyb. IX. 28. viii, 34. i). Thebes' place as the headquarters of the Boeotian federation was taken not by another city but by the sanctuary of Poseidon at Onchestus, to the north-west of Thebes. As for Athens, Alexander first demanded the surrender of the backers of Thebes, but was eventually satisfied with the exile of Charidemus, who joined the Persians (Arr. I. 1. iv–10, Diod. Sic. XVII. 8–15, Plut. 11. v–13, cf. his *Dem.* 23, *Phoc.* 17, Just. XI. 2. vi–x, 3. iii–4; for the Athenians cf. p. 339). In fact some other Athenians went to fight for the Persians also.

Alexander against Darius

In 336 Philip had sent Parmenio and Attalus to Asia Minor, and Parmenio was now left in command. They had landed at Ephesus in 336 and had won considerable support from the Greek cities, probably among the islands as well as on the mainland (cf. p. 367); but in 335 Memnon of Rhodes (on whom see pp. 325–6) led a Persian counter-attack, and Parmenio lost most of his gains and withdrew to Abydus to await Alexander's arrival (Diod. Sic. XVII. 7).

Alexander came in 334. Like Agesilaus in 396 (cf. p. 208), he represented the Greeks' war against the Persians as a continuation of the war against Asia begun with the Trojan War: he sacrificed on the European side of the Hellespont at what was said to be the tomb of the Trojan War hero Protesilaus; he sacrificed again while crossing and on landing in Asia; and he then went to Troy, sacrificed there and honoured the tomb of Achilles (Lysimachus, one of his tutors, had encouraged him to see himself as a second Achilles: cf. p. 374) (Arr. I. 11. v–12. v, Diod. Sic. XVII. 17. ii–18. i, Just. XI. 5. vi–xii, Plut. 15. vii–ix). Some texts allege that Alexander was in touch with Rome (Strabo 232. V. iii. 5, Plin. *H.N.* III. 57, Memnon *FGrH* 434 F 18. ii): the Romans are said to have made a dedication at Delphi after their capture of Veii in the 390's (Diod. Sic. XIV. 93. iii–iv, Livy V. 28. i–v), but contact between Alexander and Rome is probably the product of later wishful thinking (cf. Arr. VII. 15. v–vi, rejecting an alleged Roman embassy to Alexander in 323 – with a good reason, the silence of the best sources, as well as a bad one, that republican Rome would not have sent envoys to a foreign king).

The Persians had not challenged Alexander's crossing of the Hellespont. Memnon advised a scorched-earth strategy, but Arsites, the satrap of Dascylium, did not want to see his estates ruined, so Alexander had to fight his first major battle at the River Granicus, which flows into the south-west of the Propontis. Our sources give two very different accounts, which may be different attempts to conceal an initial defeat (cf. p. 362), but in the end Alexander was victorious, fighting in what was to be his standard order in a major battle, with infantry in the centre, Thessalian cavalry on the left, and himself attacking with the Macedonian cavalry from the right. Several Persian leaders were killed; but the campaign almost ended at this point: Clitus 'the black' was just in time to lop off the arm of a Persian who was about to bring his sword down on

Alexander's head (Arr. I. 13–16, Diod. Sic. XVII. 18. ii–21, Just. XI. 6. i–xiii, Plut. 16). At Dium in Macedonia Alexander commissioned statues of Macedonians who had fallen in the initial attack (Arr. I. 16. iv, Just. XI. 6. xii–xiii, Plut. 16. v); to Athens he sent three hundred Persian panoplies, to be dedicated with the inscription, 'Alexander son of Philip and the Greeks except the Spartans ⟨dedicated these⟩ from the barbarians living in Asia' (Arr. I. 16. vii, Plut. 16. xviii): the campaign was both an expansionist venture of the Macedonian kingdom and a Greek war of the League of Corinth.

Alexander was now free to receive or exact the allegiance of both Greeks and barbarians in western Asia Minor. Memnon was now placed in charge of the Persian defence, and sent his wife and children to Darius as hostages: he held out in Halicarnassus, and after the outer city had fallen to Alexander he took to the islands of the Aegean. Alexander, inferior at sea and perhaps short of funds, disbanded his fleet (apart from the Athenian ships, kept as hostages) and talked of defeating the Persian fleet by capturing all its harbours (Arr. I. 20. i, cf. 18. ix, Diod. Sic. XVII. 22. v–23. i). This was a risk, since Memnon was still at large in the Aegean, and he might have taken the war back to Greece and caused enough trouble to force Alexander to return, but it paid off (Arr. I. 17–24. iv, Diod. Sic. XVII. 21. vii–28, cf. Just. XI. 6. xiv–xv, Plut. 17. i–iii).

In 333 Memnon won over Chios and Lesbos (having to besiege Mytilene) and received envoys from the Cyclades – but he then died. Our sources claim that his death seriously harmed Darius' cause, but he could have achieved more if he had made for the Greek mainland. He was succeeded by his nephew Pharnabazus and by Autophradates, who had some successes, but their mercenaries were summoned to join Darius' army, and in the meantime Hegelochus assembled a new fleet for Alexander and in 333–332 recovered the Greek cities (Arr. II. 1–2, 13. iv–vi, III. 2. iii–vii, Diod. Sic. XVII. 29, Curt. IV. i. 34–7, v. 14–22, Plut. 18. v).

Alexander in the winter of 334/3 followed the coast of Asia Minor to Side and then turned inland to Gordium, the old capital of Phrygia. There a waggon was fastened to a plinth, and it was said that whoever undid the knot would become ruler of Asia: Alexander either removed the pin or impatiently cut through the knot. He then continued to Tarsus in Cilicia (Arr. I. 24. v–29, II. 3–4. vi, Curt. III. i, iv, Just. XI, Plut. 17. iv–18. v). He had proceeded through Asia Minor, but can hardly be said to have conquered it. Antigonus Monophthalmus ('the one-eyed') was appointed as satrap of Phrygia at the beginning of 333 (Arr. I. 29. iii; Lydia, wrongly, Curt. IV. i. 35) and retained that position to Alexander's death and beyond. Our sources do not tell us much about what happened except in the vicinity of Alexander, but in 332 Antigonus and others were to defeat contingents which had escaped from Darius' army after Issus (Curt. IV. i. 34–5, v. 13), and later he took control of Pamphylia and Lycia, in the south of Asia Minor (cf. Diod. Sic. XVIII. 3. i, Curt. X. x. 2).

In 333, when Alexander was delayed by a fever, Darius took a large army to the plain of north-western Syria, and in the autumn, while Alexander took the coastal route through the Syrian gates, Darius, impatient or misinformed, took an inland route towards Cilicia and reached the coast in Alexander's rear. Alexander turned back to fight in the coastal plain of Issus, where Darius could not benefit from his larger numbers: once Alexander was clearly winning, Darius fled, abandoning his chariot, his shield, his bow, his cloak and his family – and Alexander surprised his men by giving the family appropriate royal treatment (Arr. II. 4. vii–13. i, Diod. Sic. XVII. 30–8, Curt. III. v–xiii, Just. XI. 8–10. v, Plut. 18. vi–21, 24. i–iii). Others captured on the Persian side included a number of Spartans and renegade Athenians (Arr. II. 15. ii, Curt. III. xiii. 15, with different names). Also among the captives was Barsine, a daughter of Artabazus and widow of both Mentor and Memnon, who later bore Alexander a son, Heracles. In 310 Heracles was produced as a possible king, but in 309 he was killed (Curt. X. vi. 10–12, cf. Just. XIII. 2. vi–vii, Diod. Sic. XX. 20. i, 28. i–ii). After the battle we have the first of three alleged offers of terms by Darius to Alexander, this time an alliance and the ransom of his family, an offer which Alexander rejected (Arr. II. 14, Diod. Sic. XVII. 39. i–iii [where Alexander suppresses Darius' actual offer and publicises a fake, more obviously worthy of rejection], Curt. IV. i. 7–14, Just. XI. 12. i–ii).

Darius retired to the centre of the empire to prepare for another encounter. Alexander did not immediately follow him, but this should not surprise us: not only did he complete his plan of denying the Phoenician fleet any bases on land, but it would be natural for a man brought up in the Greek world to complete the conquest of the empire's Mediterranean provinces before pushing further east. In 332 (when the Greeks at the Isthmian games voted to congratulate Alexander) he moved southwards along the coast of Syria, where the other cities submitted but Tyre, on an island just off the coast, did not. For seven months Alexander besieged the city, building out a mole from the mainland on which to set up his machines. He finally broke down part of the city wall on the seaward side, with rams mounted on ships, and entered with great slaughter. The other city which had to be taken by a siege, lasting two months, was Gaza, on a mound a short distance inland: after its capture its governor was dragged round the city behind Alexander's chariot, as in the Trojan War Hector was said to have been dragged behind the chariot of Achilles (Arr. II. 13. ii–27, Diod. Sic. XVII. 39. iii–49. i, Curt. IV. i. 1–26, ii. 1–v. 9, vi, Just. XI. 10. vi–xiv, Plut. 24. iv–25). After the siege of Tyre Alexander is said to have received and rejected a second letter from Darius, offering the land west of the River Halys, i.e. western Asia Minor (Curt. IV. v. 1–8, Just. XI. 12. iii–iv).

Egypt had spent much of the past century and more in revolt against the Persians: the satrap surrendered without fighting, and Alexander was welcomed as a liberator. He founded his first Alexandria on the coast, on the west side of the Nile delta, and in the winter of 332/1 he visited the oracle of Ammon in the Libyan desert. In 331 he returned to Tyre, on the way putting down a revolt in Samaria. He delayed for some time, perhaps expecting Darius to come to Syria to fight, but eventually moved eastwards (Arr. III. 1–7. i, Diod. Sic. XVII. 49–52, Curt. IV. vii–viii, Just. XI. 11, Plut. 26–7; Samaria Curt. IV. viii. 9–10, Joseph. *A.J.* XI. 297–345). Darius is said to have made a third offer, this time of all the land west of the Euphrates: Parmenio said that if he were Alexander he would accept, and Alexander replied that if he were Parmenio he would accept (Arr. II. 25. i–iii [wrongly attached to the siege of Tyre], Diod. Sic. XVII. 54, Curt. IV. xi, Just. XI. 12. ix–xvi, Plut. 29. vii–ix).

Darius made his preparations in Babylon, and to force Alexander to approach by way of the Tigris Mazaeus, the satrap of Syria, burned the crops in the Euphrates valley. Darius waited for Alexander at Gaugamela, preparing a battle-field on which he would be able to use his large numbers. The battle was fought on 1 October (Plut. 31. viii with his *Cam.* 19. v); and, as at Issus, Alexander was more effective at exploiting a gap in the Persian line than were the Persians at exploiting a gap in his line. Darius fled through the mountains to Ecbatana (Arr. III. 7–16. ii, Diod. Sic. XVII. 53–61, Curt. IV. ix–xvi, Just. XI. 13–14. vii, Plut. 31–3).

Alexander proceeded to Arbela, where he found Darius' treasures but not Darius; to Babylon, where Mazaeus, who had commanded the right wing in the battle and then had withdrawn in good order, surrendered to him and in return became Alexander's first Iranian satrap; and to Susa, where again there was no resistance. As he continued through the mountains to Persepolis, his route through the Persian Gates was blocked by Ariobarzanes, the satrap of Persis, but he was shown a more difficult route which enabled him to attack Ariobarzanes from the rear. The palace at Persepolis was destroyed, either as a deliberate act of revenge for the Persians' destruction of Athens in 480 or as the climax of a celebration which got out of hand (Arr. III. 16. iii–18, Diod. Sic. XVII. 64–73. i, Curt. V. i–vii, Just. XI. 14. viii–xii, Plut. 35–8; on the destruction of Persepolis cf. pp. 374–5). Meanwhile the last round of opposition to Alexander in Greece occurred. If not before Gaugamela, before the news of Gaugamela had reached Greece, Agis of Sparta, who had been in touch with the Persian commanders in western Asia Minor, led a Greek rising and attacked Megalopolis; but late in 331 or early in 330 he was defeated and killed by Antipater (cf. p. 345).

Winter kept Alexander in Persepolis and Darius in Ecbatana. In spring 330 Darius withdrew to the east, and Alexander advanced to Pasargadae and then (according to Arrian) to Ecbatana. There the League of Corinth's war of revenge was officially ended, and the Greeks serving as allies were discharged (but many re-enlisted as mercenaries). He then divided his forces, leaving Parmenio behind with a part, and Harpalus to take charge of the treasures (Arr. III. 19; but in Curt. V. xiii. 1–3 Alexander by-passed Ecbatana to pursue Darius, and Diod. Sic. XVII. 74. iii–iv, Curt. VI. ii. 15–17, Plut. 42. v, cf. Just. XII. 1. i, link the discharge of the Greeks with Darius' death). With a smaller and lighter force Alexander went in pursuit of Darius, but about July/August, before he could catch up with him, Darius was first arrested and then stabbed to death by Bessus, the satrap of Bactria, who had commanded the Persian left wing at Gaugamela. Alexander gave Darius a royal funeral, and from this point increasingly represented himself as a legitimate King of Asia (Arr. III. 20–2, Diod. Sic. XVII. 73. i–iv, Curt. V. viii–xiii, Just. XI. 15, Plut. 42. v–43: cf. p. 375).

After Darius' Death

Bessus now claimed to be King (Artaxerxes V), so the pursuit of Darius turned into the pursuit of Bessus; but Artabazus, brother-in-law of Mentor and Memnon, refused to follow Bessus and joined Alexander. Satibarzanes, satrap of Aria, submitted but afterwards rebelled, so Alexander turned south-east from Hyrcania to deal with him: his capital Artacoana was captured, and an Alexandria founded at the present-day Herat, but Satibarzanes caused further trouble when Alexander moved on and was finally killed in 329 by a force which Alexander detached to deal with him (Arr. III. 23–8; versions of a significantly different narrative in Diod. Sic. XVII. 74–81, Curt. VI. ii–VII. ii). Alexander then surprised Bessus by travelling through the Hindu Kush to Bactria while it was still winter (330/29). Bessus withdrew into Sogdiana, north of the Oxus (Amudar'ya); Alexander pursued him, and Bessus was abandoned to Alexander by Spitamenes: a special court of the Medes and Persians was convened to condemn him for the murder of the King (Arr. III. 28–30, Diod. Sic. XVII. 81–3, Curt. VII. iii–v, Just. XII. 5. ix–xii).

Alexander proceeded to the Jaxartes (Syrdar'ya), beyond which were Scythians (it was still believed, as it had been believed by the Persians in the sixth century, that all the northern peoples from the lower Danube to this region were Scythians). On the river he founded Alexandria Eschate ('remotest': Khodjend) – which in recent times has commemorated another hero, under the name Leninabad. But Spitamenes rebelled, besieged Maracanda (Samarcand) and annihilated a force sent to defend it. Alexander now encountered his first serious local resistance since Tyre and Gaza in 332: he had to reorganise his cavalry in units which could be used independently in guerrilla warfare, and he received reinforcements in 329/8. Campaigning here continued through 328, but eventually Alexander gained the upper hand and Spitamenes was killed by his followers. In Arrian's account, in 327 Alexander had mountaineering successes at the Sogdian Rock, with a heavy snowstorm and capture by 'winged mountaineers' who climbed above the stronghold, and at the Rock of Chorienes, and he went back through the Hindu Kush. Early in 326 he captured Aornus (probably Pir-sar, despite recent challenges to the identification), the most spectacular of his mountain achievements, and then reached the Indus (Arr. IV). This version produces a very empty 328 and a very full early 327, so we should probably prefer the alternative. In this second tradition, instead of the Sogdian Rock and the Rock of Chorienes the same stratagems are used against the Rock of Arimazes and the Rock of Sisimithres, in the summer of 328, before Alexander's return to Maracanda and the killing of Clitus (below); in 327 Alexander leaves his winter quarters too early and suffers casualties from a snowstorm before proceeding to Aornus and India (Diod. XVII. lacuna–84–86. iii [cf. XVII. table of contents], Curt. VII. vi–VIII. xii. 3, *Metz Epitome* [another text in the Clitarchan tradition, available only for this part of the campaign], cf. Plut. 58. iii–iv).

Since the death of Darius Alexander had had increasing trouble with leading Macedonians and Greeks. In autumn 330 Parmenio's son Philotas was said to have withheld news of a conspiracy, for which he was executed, and emissaries were sent to kill Parmenio too. As legitimate King of Asia Alexander was increasingly using Asiatic troops, retaining Asiatic satraps and adopting aspects of Persian costume and manners: at Maracanda in autumn 328 Clitus 'the black' mocked Alexander in the course of a drunken argument, and the argument ended with Alexander's killing Clitus. In 327 Alexander married Roxana, daughter of Oxyartes of the Sogdian Rock (Arrian) or of Chorienes, a satrap who submitted to Alexander after the episode of the snowstorm (preferable restoration in Curtius, supported by the *Metz Epitome* – but some editors have restored Oxyartes). He then attempted to introduce the custom of *proskynesis* (prostration) to the European side of his court, but abandoned it after opposition, particularly from Callisthenes; and after that Callisthenes was condemned as instigator of the 'conspiracy of the pages' (cf. pp. 370–1, 380).

From the Indus Alexander moved on to its tributary the Hydaspes (Jhelum), beyond which a king called Porus was waiting to resist him. He managed to get his men across the river, and in the last of his major battles defeated Porus – but Porus, unlike Darius, was a worthy foe who did not flee when defeated, and he was reinstated as a vassal ruler. India was perhaps believed to be the easternmost part of Asia, and there were reports of a large kingdom, ripe for conquest, between the Indus and the Ganges. Alexander wanted to conquer this and go on to the end of Asia; but his men were demoralised by the thought of the large kingdom, by diarrhoea caused by the unfamiliar fruits, by the rain and mud of the monsoon season, and by the ever-growing distance from home. At the easternmost tributary of the Indus, the Hyphasis (Beas), in the autumn, the army mutinied, and Alexander had to give way. After building twelve large altars, he turned back to the Hydaspes and, using newly built ships, made his way to the mouths of the Indus. On the journey Coenus, who had been the army's spokesman at the Hyphasis, died; and Alexander was seriously wounded when he risked his life to spur on the army in an attack on the town of the Malli. In the summer of 325 they reached the Ocean and were startled by tides the like of which are unknown in the Mediterranean, and they made their base Patala (Bahmanabad) (Arr. V. 1–VI. 20. i, Diod. Sic. XVII. 86. iii–104. ii, Curt. VIII. xii. 4–IX. x. 2, Just. XII. 7. iv–10. vi, Plut. 59–66. ii).

After exploring the mouths of the Indus, Alexander set out to return to the central cities of the empire. Craterus was sent by an inland route with the veterans; Nearchus was to sail to the Persian Gulf; and Alexander went with the rest of the army through the desert of Gedrosia (the Makran), to respond to the challenge of what was reputed to be difficult and to explore the coast and make preparations for the fleet. The journey through the desert proved all too difficult and led to heavy losses; Alexander and the survivors reached Pura in late 325 or early 324, and spent several days celebrating their deliverance (Arr. VI. 28. i–ii rejects, and cites the silence of Ptolemy and Aristobulus on, stories of a Bacchic revel; but if the stories were true these authors could have chosen to suppress them). In Carmania, near the mouth of the Persian Gulf, they were joined by Craterus and made contact with Nearchus, and the army continued via Pasargadae and Persepolis to Susa (Arr. VI. 20. ii–VII. 4. i, Diod. Sic. XVII. 104. iii–107, Curt. IX. x. 3–X. i. 16, Just. XII. 10. vii, Plut. 66. iii–68. i).

The Final Year

Many must have thought that Alexander would not return alive, so it is not surprising that he found it necessary to assert his authority. Various commanders were summoned and arrested for misconduct, and some were later executed; the treasurer Harpalus fled to Greece with mercenaries and money (cf. p. 343). Nicanor was sent with orders to be proclaimed at the Olympic games that all Greek cities were to take back their exiles. There were also various festivities. Alexander and many of his officers married Persian wives (in Alexander's case, two); ordinary soldiers had their liaisons recognised and their debts paid. There was a parade of 30,000 *epigonoi* ('successors'), young orientals who since 327 had been undergoing training in the Macedonian style of fighting. During the summer of 324 Alexander went to the Persian Gulf, and then to Opis on the Tigris and to Ecbatana. At Opis (Arrian: in the alternative tradition Alexander seems still to be at Susa) he announced his intention of sending the European veterans home. This led to a mutiny; Alexander disbanded the army; the army asked for pardon and obtained it, and there was a great banquet of reconciliation; but Alexander persisted with his plan. Craterus was sent back with the veterans, while Antipater, who had been in charge in Macedon but had fallen out with Olympias, was to join Alexander (Arr. VII. 4. ii–13, Diod. Sic. XVII. 108–110. vii, Curt. X. i. 17–iv with lacunae, Just. XII. 10. viii–12, Plut. 68. ii–71).

In the autumn of 324 Hephaestion, the man closest to Alexander, died, apparently as a result of excessive drinking: this was a great blow to Alexander. In 323 he moved to Babylon: he had plans for expeditions into Arabia and to explore the Caspian, and there was talk of wilder schemes. Envoys came from Greece to pay Alexander divine honours, and there are allegations of embassies from more distant places including Rome (on which cf. p. 351). But there were various unfavourable omens. On 29 May Alexander was taken ill after a party, and on 10 June he died, not quite 33 years old. A pamphlet in the *Alexander Romance* (III. 31) alleged a plot by Antipater and his son Cassander to poison him – but it is not clear that slow poisons were available. The *ephemerides* gave an account of Alexander's last days, stressing his drinking habits and blaming his death on an incidental illness. Aristobulus denied his drinking habits, claiming that he went to parties only out of consideration for his companions. Probably the *ephemerides* are near enough to the truth: Alexander's hard fighting, hard living and hard drinking had weakened him, and a chill which a fitter man would have survived proved fatal. He left two sons, Heracles, born to Barsine in 327 (cf. p. 353), and Alexander, to be born to Roxana shortly after his death.

It was said that he was asked on his deathbed who was to succeed him and replied, 'the best' or 'the strongest' (Arr. VII. 14–30, Diod. Sic. 110–18 with a lacuna, Curt. X. lacuna–v, Just. XII. 13–16, Plut. 72–7).

NOTE ON FURTHER READING

General books on Alexander include Bosworth, *Conquest and Empire*; Green, *Alexander of Macedon*; Hamilton, *Alexander the Great*; Lane Fox, *Alexander the Great*; Stoneman, *Alexander the Great*. Collections of studies by different authors include Bosworth and Baynham (eds.), *Alexander the Great in Fact and Fiction*; Griffith (ed.), *Alexander the Great: The Main Problems*; Roisman (ed.), *Brill's Companion to Alexander the Great*; and 'Alexander the Great', *G&R²* xii 1965, fasc. 2.

For general discussion of the sources see Bosworth, *From Arrian to Alexander*; E. Baynham, 'The Ancient Evidence for Alexander the Great', in *Brill's Companion* (above), ch. 1. For commentaries on the surviving sources see Atkinson, *Commentary on Q. Curtius Rufus' Historiae Alexandri Magni*; Bosworth, *Historical Commentary on Arrian's History of Alexander*; Hamilton, *Plutarch, Alexander: A Commentary*; Yardley and Heckel, *Justin, Epitome of the Philippic History of Pompeius Trogus*, i. *Books 11–12: Alexander the Great* (introduction, translation, commentary). For Diod. Sic. XVII the Loeb edition (vol. viii, by C. B. Welles) contains some notes. The 'fragments' quoted from the lost sources are translated in vol. i of Robinson, *The History of Alexander the Great*, and discussed in Pearson, *The Lost Historians of Alexander the Great*. A translation of the *Metz Epitome*, by J. C. Yardley with commentary by E. B. Baynham, is forthcoming in the Clarendon Ancient History Series. On the *ephemerides* (diary) of the end of Alexander's reign see Bosworth, *From Arrian to Alexander*, ch. 7. On the *Alexander Romance* see Stoneman, *The Greek Alexander Romance* (translation with introduction and notes).

A. B. Bosworth, 'Plus ça change . . . Ancient Historians and Their Sources', *Cl. Ant.* xxii 2003, 167–98, uses Curtius as a test case to argue that historians followed their sources faithfully, presenting what they found in their own way but not irresponsibly adding material. The opposite had been argued for Curtius by P. McKechnie, 'Manipulation of Themes in Quintus Curtius Rufus Book 10', *Hist.* xlviii 1999, 44–60. Bosworth, 'Mountain and Molehill? Cornelius Tacitus and Quintus Curtius', *CQ²* liv 2004, 551–67, explores the use of Curtius by Tacitus but rejects identification with the senator of *Ann.* XI.

25

Alexander the Great: Topics

500	475	450	425	400	375	350	325	300

334 Alexander's entry into Asia; battle of the Granicus
333 battle of Issus
332 sieges of Tyre and Gaza
331 battle of Gaugamela
330 death of Darius
330 execution of Philotas and Parmenio
328 killing of Clitus
327 trouble over *proskynesis*
326 battle of Hydaspes
324 Alexander's return to Susa
323 death of Alexander

Military Matters

Traditionally the strength of the Macedonian army was in the cavalry, formed by the nobles who were the king's *hetairoi* (companions). At some stage the duty of guarding the king in battle was given to a unit known as the *ile basilike* (royal squadron); at the beginning of Alexander's Asiatic campaign the cavalry was a force of eight *ilai*, of which one was the *ile basilike* or *agema*; there were also four *ilai* of *prodromoi* = *sarissophoroi* ('forward-runners' = *sarissa*-bearers), last mentioned as a separate category in 329 and after that probably incorporated in the companions. Philip was the first to organise an effective infantry force, armed with the formidable *sarissa* (cf. p. 299); at the beginning of Alexander's campaign this was organised in six regiments known as *taxeis*, whose taxiarchs were important men. Anaximenes (*FGrH* 72 F 4) credits an Alexander with giving the names *hetairoi* to the cavalry and *pezetairoi* (foot-companions) to the infantry. Philip had *pezetairoi* by 349 (Dem. II. *Ol. ii.* 29), but according to Theopompus (*FGrH* 115 F 348) they were an élite body. Perhaps we should infer from Anaximenes that Alexander the Great gave the names *hetairoi* to the whole cavalry force (in the sources for Alexander that word can be used either of the cavalry or of the greater nobles who were more literally the king's companions) and *pezetairoi* to the whole infantry force. In a number of places Arrian refers to some of the infantry as *asthetairoi* (first in II. 23. ii), a word which editors for many years emended out of existence. The meaning of the prefix is unknown; possible guesses are that the *asthetairoi* came from Upper Macedonia and the *pezetairoi* from Lower, or (since the number of *taxeis* given this name by Arrian seems to increase) that it was a title of honour which could be conferred on a *taxis*. In addition to the six *taxeis*, Alexander had an élite infantry body known as *hypaspistai* ('shield-bearers'): this was perhaps a new name for Philip's *pezetairoi*; they were organised in three chiliarchies (literally, 'commands of a thousand'), one being the royal chiliarchy or *agema*. There has been much argument as to whether they were armed in the same way as or more lightly than the main infantry force: probably they were armed in the same way for major battles involving large numbers but could be armed differently for special duties. The title *somatophylakes* (bodyguards) is used sometimes of the *agema* of the hypaspists, sometimes of a small number of men serving as Alexander's personal aides, at first high-ranking but outside the general structure of the army, later usually cavalry commanders (Arr. VI. 28. iv lists seven existing and one new for 325).

Alexander inherited from Philip the use of a variety of forces in conjunction. His Greek allies in the League of Corinth provided him, in particular, with Thessalian cavalry, almost as good as the Macedonian, and with hoplites; he also had Greek mercenaries, light infantry from Thrace, especially Agrianian javelin-men, and engineers and *bematistai* (surveyors). Little is said about this in the sources, but the success of his campaign depended on considerable organisation for the conveyance of supplies and reinforcements, and for planning his advances into unfamiliar territory (there are glimpses at Arr. III. 6. viii, VI. 20. v, 27. i).

The force which he took to Asia in 334 probably comprised 4,500 or 5,100 cavalry and 32,000 infantry, of whom 2,700 (including the *prodromoi*) and 12,000 were Macedonians (Diod. Sic. XVII. 17. iii–iv, a detailed catalogue, cf. Arr. I. 11. iii); the higher figures of Anaximenes, 5,500 [or 6,100?] cavalry and 43,000 infantry (*FGrH* 72 F 29 *ap.* Plut. *De Alex. Fort.* i. 327 D–E), probably include the advance force of 336 (cf. Polyaenus *Strat.* V. 44. iv). Reinforcements reached Alexander on various occasions to 328/7, and again in India in 326 and in the centre of the empire in 324–323; but garrisons were left in various places, there were casualties in battle and from disease and other hazards, and for much of the time after 330 the army was divided and substantial parts of it were not with Alexander. The army which fought at Gaugamela in 331 is given by Arrian as 7,000 cavalry and 40,000 infantry (III. 12. v), and probably the force actually with Alexander was until 323 never afterwards as large. In 334 substantial forces were left with Antipater in Macedon, 1,500 cavalry and 12,000 infantry according to Diod. Sic. XVII. 17. v, and in 331 Antipater raised an army of 40,000 including loyal Greeks to fight against Agis (Diod. Sic. XVII. 63. i – but with difficulty, Aeschin. III. *Ctesiphon* 165). Some scholars have reckoned that by the end Macedon was seriously denuded of manpower; but others, taking seriously the fact that no Macedonian reinforcements are mentioned after 330, have resisted that conclusion.

On various occasions the nature and organisation of the army had to be changed. In 330, when he continued eastwards in pursuit of Darius, Alexander left substantial forces with Parmenio and with Harpalus, but Parmenio's men rejoined him in 329 (Arr. III. 19. vii–viii, Curt. VII. iii. 4). After Darius' death there was increasing need for the use of separate detachments and guerrilla fighting; in 330 (Curt. VI. vi. 15) or in 327 before entering India (Plut. 57. i, Polyaenus *Strat.* IV. 3. x) Alexander is said to have had the waggons and surplus baggage burned to produce a lighter army. Ships were built in 326 for the journey to the mouths of the Indus (Diod. Sic. XVII. 89. iv–v, Curt. IX. i. 3–4), and more ships, and dockyards, in 335 when he arrived there (Arr. VI. 18. ii–v, 20. i, v); but, except in the sieges of Miletus and of Tyre (p. 365), Alexander had no occasion for fighting on the water.

Originally the Macedonian cavalry were commanded by Parmenio's son Philotas, and the individual ilarchs seem not to have been important men; in 331 after Gaugamela each *ile* was subdivided into two *lochoi* (Arr. III. 16. xi). After Philotas' execution in 330 his command was divided between two hipparchs, the experienced Clitus 'the black' and Alexander's friend Hephaestion (Arr. III. 27. iv). Later the cavalry were reorganised in eight hipparchies, one being the *agema,* and the individual hipparchs (of whom Hephaestion was still one) were leading men as the ilarchs had not been (first mentioned in 329, Arr. III. 29. vii, but it may be that the first uses of the word are non-technical and the reorganisation followed the killing of Clitus in 328); for what was done in 324 see below. There was no comparable reorganisation of the infantry, except that by 327 there were at least seven *taxeis* (Arr. V. 11–12); before entering India in 326 the hypaspists were given silver shields and the title *argyraspides* (Just. XII. 7. v: earlier uses of the title by Diodorus and Curtius are anachronistic).

After Gaugamela Alexander started appointing oriental satraps (cf. p. 368), and later he started using oriental troops (first clear instance Arr. IV. 17. iii, in winter 328/7). At first these were organised in their own divisions and fought in their own manner, but a process of integration was begun at Susa in 324. There are problems with the text of Arr. VII. 6. iii–iv, where the manuscripts offer some outstanding orientals 'incorporated in the companion cavalry', 'a fifth hipparchy, not wholly barbarian', and the enlistment of barbarians in the enlargement of the whole cavalry force. Usually it is thought that after the losses in Gedrosia the eight Macedonian hipparchies had been reduced to four, a few orientals were designated *hetairoi* and were enrolled in these, and a fifth, largely oriental, hipparchy was added; but it has been suggested that the fifth hipparchy, 'not wholly barbarian', implies that four other hipparchies were created which were wholly barbarian, and that apart from the privileged few oriental *hetairoi* Arrian says nothing here about the Macedonian hipparchies. At any rate, there were now some orientals in the Macedonian hipparchies and one mixed hipparchy. As for infantry, in 327, 30,000 young orientals were set aside to be given a Macedonian training, and these *epigonoi* ('successors') were paraded before Alexander in 324 (Arr. VII. 6. i, Diod. Sic. XVII. 108. i–iii, Plut. 71. i, cf. Curt. VIII. v. 1, Just. XII. 12. iii–iv). Alexander's plan to send veterans home and rely on his new forces led to the mutiny at Opis (cf. p. 376); at Babylon in 323 in a sixteen-rank phalanx orientals filled all ranks except the first three and the last (Arr. VII. 23. iii, cf. Diod. Sic. XVII. 110. i–ii).

In his three major battles against the Persians Alexander placed the six *taxeis* of the phalanx in the centre and the hypaspists immediately to their right; Parmenio as second-in-command was on the left wing with the Thessalian and other allied cavalry and some light-armed troops; Alexander commanded on the right wing with the Macedonian cavalry and other light-armed, and attacked from there (e.g. Granicus, Arr. I. 14. i–iii). Inspiring leadership was important, but essentially it was the better army which won these battles.

For the battle of the Granicus in 334 the sources offer two versions, which differ so much that, whichever is right, it is hard to see how the other can have come into existence. Arrian gives the Persians 20,000 cavalry and 20,000 Greek mercenary infantry (with no mention of Persian infantry), Diodorus 10,000 cavalry and 100,000 infantry. In one version the Persians were stationed on the right bank of the river, with the cavalry in front with no room to charge and the infantry behind. When Alexander arrived Parmenio advised waiting until the next morning but Alexander insisted on fighting immediately; the *prodromoi* attacked the Persians' extreme left, and, when a gap appeared in their left centre, Alexander plunged in. There was a mêlée as the Macedonians fought their way across the river, until the Persians' centre caved in and their wings fled; the mercenaries stood firm but were massacred (Arr. I. 13–16, cf. Plut. 16). In the other version the Persians were camped beyond the river; Alexander did wait until morning, and crossed the river unopposed; the battle followed, with the Persians' cavalry in front and infantry behind as in the first version (Diod. Sic. XVII. 19–21, cf. *Fragmentum Sabbaiticum FGrH* 151 F 1. 1, Just. XI. 6. x–xiii, Polyaenus *Strat.* IV. 3. xvi). Most scholars have preferred Arrian's version, though some have thought that it makes the Persians too incompetent and have preferred Diodorus'; it is an attractive suggestion that behind the two versions lies an initial failure, which the two versions suppress in different ways, that Alexander first fought to cross the river and was defeated, but the next morning succeeded in crossing and then fought successfully.

At Issus in 333 Darius had reached a narrow coastal plain in Alexander's rear, which did not allow him to take advantage of his large numbers (but pre-

Ill. 14 The Alexander Sarcophagus (c.320), showing Alexander attacking Persian horsemen. Istanbul Museum/photo Art Archive, Dagli Orti

sumably not as large as alleged, from 310,000 by Curtius to 600,000 as hearsay by Arrian). Between the two armies the plain was crossed by the River Pinarus (which of three possible identifications is chosen does not greatly affect the general situation). Alexander had to fill the whole width of the plain, so as not to be outflanked. Darius commanded from the centre, where he placed his infantry; he massed his cavalry on the right, to try to force a gap between the enemy left and the sea; and he sent a detachment into the foothills to his left to try to outflank Alexander. Alexander sent some light-armed troops to deal with this detachment, and himself attacked the Cardaces, an élite infantry body, on the Persian left. In his phalanx a gap opened between the *taxeis* towards the right, moving forwards with him, and those towards the left, holding back with Parmenio, and Darius' Greek mercenaries pressed into this breach; but they were less effective than Alexander, who wheeled to the centre when the Persian left had collapsed. Darius led the Persians in flight, and Alexander pursued until nightfall (Arr. II. 6–11, Diod. Sic. XVII. 33–4, Curt. III. viii–ix. 15, Just. XI. 9. i–x, Plut. 20. i–v, Polyb. XII. 17–23).

At Gaugamela in 331 Darius chose his battlefield and made careful preparations: he arrived first, and levelled the ground for the sake of his cavalry and scythed chariots. Again the figures we are given are unbelievable: infantry from Curtius' 200,000 to Arrian's hearsay 1,000,000 (but they played no significant part in the battle), cavalry from Arrian's hearsay 40,000 to Diodorus' 200,000, but clearly more than the 7,000 given by Arrian for Alexander's army, and the sources agree on 200 chariots. On reaching a ridge from which the enemy could be seen, Alexander took Parmenio's advice and paused for reconnaissance, but rejecting the further advice to attack that night he then waited until morning. The Persians had cavalry on both wings, chariots and perhaps a few elephants in front of their line; Alexander, afraid of being outflanked, inclined both his wings backwards, and placed a reserve line of infantry behind the main phalanx. As he advanced, Alexander directed his whole army to the right, to put the Persians off balance and get away from their prepared ground. Bessus on the Persian left tried to outflank Alexander's right, and Alexander fed troops against him; in Alexander's centre the use of javelins and good discipline prevented serious harm from the chariots; on the other wing Mazaeus attacked Parmenio and sent a detachment to attack Alexander's base camp (successfully, but without serious effect). As at Issus, a gap appeared in the centre of Alexander's phalanx (some Persian cavalry broke through that, and perhaps through the reserve line too) and also between Darius' left and centre; and, as at Issus, Alexander was more successful at exploiting the enemy's gap. Again, Darius fled, and Alexander pursued until night. There are stories that Parmenio was in serious difficulty on the left and sent a plea for help to Alexander, who for that reason turned back from pursuing Darius; but in a mêlée of perhaps 200,000 men, with clouds of dust, it is unlikely that Parmenio could have got a message to Alexander, let alone that Alexander could have responded. The story helped to explain Darius' escape, and was no doubt elaborated when Parmenio was in trouble later (cf. pp. 370–1) (Arr. III. 9–15, Diod. Sic. XVII. 56–61, Curt. IV. xii–xvi, Just. XI. 13–14. iii, Plut. 32–3).

At the Hydaspes in 326 Alexander had to cross a wide and fast-flowing river, and then fight against the Indian prince Porus on the other side, and here he did have scope for tactical brilliance. Porus was waiting with an army which included chariots and elephants, blocking all the crossings, and expecting reinforcements. After a series of feints Alexander divided his army into three sections: Craterus was left opposite Porus with a substantial force; Alexander took his section several miles upstream, where there were islands in the middle of the channel; the third section was to use intermediate crossing-points. Alexander crossed under cover of rain and night, using boats and stuffed skins, and destroyed a force which Porus sent, too late, under his son; and the middle section crossed too. Porus left a small division opposite Craterus and faced Alexander with his main army, stationing infantry with elephants in front in the centre and cavalry with horses in front on the wings. Horses cannot face elephants unless trained, so Alexander had to deal with Porus' cavalry before his infantry attacked Porus' elephants and infantry. He advanced with most of his cavalry visible on the right wing but the rest, under Coenus, hidden in the rear;

when he charged from the right wing, Porus brought his own right-wing cavalry, perhaps behind his main lines, to reinforce the attacked left; Coenus then emerged and took Porus' right wing in the rear. After that Alexander's infantry attacked, and Porus' army was defeated with great slaughter; Craterus in the meantime crossed the river, and joined in the pursuit (Arr. V. 9–18, Curt. VIII. xiii–xiv; cf. Diod. Sic. 87–9, Just. XII. 8. i–vii, omitting the crossing of the river, also Polyaenus *Strat.* IV. 3. xxii).

Siege warfare was an area in which Alexander excelled (though he did also experience setbacks), taking advantage of technical developments which had begun under Philip and which continued under him (cf. p. 316). In 334 he attacked first Miletus and then Halicarnassus, the strongest walled city in Asia Minor, where Memnon was holding out. At Halicarnassus Alexander had towers, rams and catapults (this is the first mention of torsion-powered stone-throwers); the defenders had towers and arrow-firing catapults. At one point Alexander breached the wall, but the defenders had built a *demi-lune*, a semi-circular additional wall, inside; when some of his soldiers, the worse for drink, attacked that, the defence was so effective that Alexander had to make a truce to recover his dead. However, a three-wave attack on Alexander started well but ended badly; after that Memnon set fire to and abandoned the outer city, and Alexander moved on without capturing him or two citadels (Arr. I. 20. v–23. vi; Diod. Sic. XVII. 23. iv–27. vi, making Alexander's difficulties clear as Arrian does not); the citadels fell only to Alexander's commanders late in 333 (Arr. II. 5. vii).

In 332 most Phoenician cities submitted to Alexander (and their ships became available to him), but Tyre on its offshore island held out for seven months and hoped for help from Carthage. Under Diades of Thessaly Alexander's army used the most impressive range of machinery yet seen. Using stone from the remains of Old Tyre on the mainland, Alexander built a mole out into the strait, at the end of which he erected towers carrying catapults. When the Tyrians set fire to an old ship and used that to destroy the towers, he rebuilt them. The Tyrians would not fight at sea, so he blockaded them in their harbours; he set up new machines on the mole, and he mounted rams on ships to attack other parts of the city wall which were less strong (a development foreshadowed by the Athenians' mounting towers on a large ship at Syracuse in 413: Thuc. VII. 25. vi). However, the Tyrians fired missiles and dropped boulders in the sea to prevent the ships from coming close. When the Tyrians made a sortie from their northern harbour at siesta-time, Alexander was caught unprepared, but retrieved the situation. Ultimately the ram-ships made a breach in the wall on the seaward side while other ships fired missiles and attacked the harbours; Alexander's men used boarding-bridges to enter the city from ships (Arr. II. 16–24, Diod. Sic. XVII. 40–6, Curt. IV. ii–iv. 18, Just. XI. 10. x–xiv, Plut. 24. ii–25. ii).

Inland Gaza resisted too: it was on a mound surrounded by sand which caused problems for Alexander's towers and machines; he built a ramp for these (but not all round the city, as Arrian claims), and the walls were overcome by a combination of bombardment and undermining (Arr. II. 25. iv–27, Diod. Sic. XVII. 48. vii, Curt. IV. vi. 7–30, Plut. 25. iv–v).

Alexander's tactical ingenuity is apparent in a number of smaller episodes. In his Balkan campaign of 335, when he was not accompanied by any of Philip's experienced generals, he dealt with a waggon attack in Thrace by getting his men to open their ranks (to be done again at Gaugamela, above) or, where there was not room for that, to lie under the cover of their shields, and he stuffed skins used for tents to make rafts to cross the Danube (copied from Xen. *Anab.* I. v. 10; and to be done again at the Hydaspes, above). When dangerously trapped in a valley by the Illyrians, he frightened them off by a parade conducted in silence until it ended with a blood-curdling shout. He used portable catapults as field artillery (Arr. I. 1. vii–x, 3. vi, 5. xi–6. iv, 6. viii).

In 331/0, when he was on his way to Persepolis, and his route through the Persian Gates was blocked, he learned of a mountain route from his prisoners and followed that with part of his force, so that the Persians were trapped between this contingent and Craterus with the remainder (Arr. III. 18. ii–ix, Diod. Sic. XVII. 68, Curt. V. iv, cf. Plut. 37. i–ii). In 328–326 there were several spectacular exploits. The Sogdian Rock/Rock of Arimazes was captured by 'winged mountaineers' who used tent-pegs as pitons to climb above the fortress (Arr. IV. 18. iv–19. iv, Curt. VII. xi, Polyaenus *Strat.* IV. 3. xxix). To reach the Rock of Chorienes/Rock of Sisimithres a ravine was bridged (Arr. IV. 21. i–ix, Curt. VIII. ii. 19–28, Plut. 58. iii–iv). At Aornus guides showed how light troops could reach the ridge from the north, and a mound was built into a ravine to bring Alexander's catapults within range (Arr. IV. 28. vii–30. iv, Diod. Sic. XVII. 85–86. i, Curt. VIII. xi. 1–25, Just. XII. 7. xii–xiii, Plut. 58. iii–v). In 326 at Sangala, between the Hydaspes and the Hyphasis, the Indians' camp was protected by three lines of waggons in front of the city: a cavalry attack by Alexander failed to provoke a battle, and an infantry attack drove the Indians back into the city. Alexander built a stockade round the city and stopped two attempts at breaking out; finally he broke in by undermining the wall and using scaling-ladders, without needing the machines which Porus brought – but this was an expensive victory: Arrian reports 17,000 Indians killed, and on Alexander's side under 100 killed but over 1,200 wounded (Arr. V. 22–24. v, Diod. Sic. XVII. 91. iv, Curt. IX. i. 14–25, Polyaenus *Strat.* IV. 3. xxx).

As a commander Alexander was never at a loss, never conceded the impossible. He remembered successful devices, from his reading and his own experience; he was successful in various kinds of fighting (but never had to master naval warfare). He drove his men hard and fast, frequently surprising the enemy by appearing sooner than they had thought possible; and he took a personal interest in his men and set a personal example (e.g. Arr. I. 16. v, VI. 26. i–iii) – sometimes, as at the town of the Malli in 326/5 (Arr. VI. 8. iv–12, Diod. Sic. XVII. 93–95. ii, Curt. IX. ii–iii. 19, Just. XII. 8. x–xvii, Plut. 62), taking risks which even by the standards of ancient warfare a commander ought not to take.

Administration

The Greeks of Asia Minor had been subject to Persia since the Peace of Antalcidas, in 387/6, so they were now to be 'liberated' (cf. Diod. Sic. XVI. 91. ii [Philip], XVII. 24. i): in 334 Alcimachus was ordered to replace oligarchies with democracies, restore laws and remit the tribute exacted by Persia (Arr. I. 17. ix–18. ii). Alexander did not favour democracy as such, but inclined that way in Asia because the existing oligarchies had collaborated with the Persians. In various ways he claimed honours in the cities: in 333/2 Miletus appointed him *stephanephoros* ('crown-wearer', the eponymous official of the year: *Milet* I. iii 122, excerpted *SIG*³ 272, with editors' date corrected); at Priene, following a precedent set by the Hecatomnids, he became the dedicator of the new temple of Athena (*I. Priene* 156 = R&O 86. *A* ~ Harding 105, cf. Mausolus and Idrieus at Labraunda, *Labraunda* iii 13–14 and 15–19), but Ephesus is said to have rejected his offer to pay for and dedicate its temple of Artemis (Str. 640–1. XIV. i. 22). Parmenio and Attalus had added the island states to the League of Corinth (e.g. Chios: Tod 192 = R&O 84. *A* ~ Harding 107. 10–15). Probably the Greeks of the mainland were not enrolled in the League but were made allies on such terms as Alexander chose, and since at first Alexander was in need of funds they paid a *syntaxis* ('contribution', as in the Second Athenian League: cf. p. 233) to him instead of tribute to the Persians (e.g. Priene: *I. Priene* 1 = R&O 86. *B* ~ Harding 106. 13–15, probably modifying an original settlement in which a *syntaxis* had been required). The language was different, but in practice the Greeks were probably neither more free nor financially better off than they had been under the Persians.

Aspendus, perceived as Greek even if strictly it was not, was originally to provide money and horses, and after it revolted had to pay a larger sum and regular tribute to the satrap (Arr. I. 26. ii–27. iv). There is a story that at the end of his reign Alexander offered the Athenian Phocion the revenues of a city in Asia, as the Persian King had bestowed cities on his favourites (Plut. *Phoc.* 18, vii–viii, Ael. *V.H.* I. 25; for the Persian practice cf. p. 34).

Otherwise Alexander retained existing practice. The barbarians' territory was not to be ravaged, because it now belonged to the Macedonians (Just. XI. 6. i). Alexander began by appointing Macedonians as satraps in Dascylium and Sardis and claiming the tribute for himself. In Sardis he also appointed a garrison commander and a financial officer. This used to be seen as an innovation, but it is becoming increasingly clear that here too he was continuing a Persian practice: whatever the formal relationship between satrap, other officials and king, it was hoped that if one became disloyal the others would remain loyal. But for propaganda purposes the peoples of the western provinces could be 'liberated' too: 'He granted to the Sardians and the other Lydians to use the ancient laws of the Lydians and made them free' – which no doubt meant in practice that they too would be neither more nor less free than under the Persians (Arr. I. 17. i–vii). In Caria Ada, ousted by Pixodarus (cf. pp. 323–4) but holding out in Alinda, submitted to Alexander and was reinstated; but after her death he appointed a Macedonian satrap (Arr. I. 23. vii–viii, VII. 23. i). Sabictas ?= Abistamenes, in Cappadocia, was perhaps another native ruler rewarded for submission (Arr. II. 4. ii, Curt. III. iv. 1).

Syria, liberated by the Persians from Babylon, remained pro-Persian until Gaugamela (Arr. III. 11. iv, cf. p. 353 on Samaria); but Egypt, in rebellion for much of the time since the mid fifth century, welcomed Alexander (Diod. Sic. XVII. 49. i, Curt. IV. vii. 1–5, cf. Arr. III. 1. ii). Egypt was given tactful treatment: over the province proper were to be two Egyptian nomarchs (but one declined so the other took the whole), 'to govern their nomes as established since antiquity'; there were European army commanders, and two Egyptian Greeks were put in charge of the western and eastern frontiers; the one in the east, Cleomenes, was to receive the tribute from the nomarchs, and he eventually made himself satrap (Arr. III. 5. ii–vii, Curt. IV. viii. 5; Cleomenes as satrap [Arist.] *Oec.* II. 1352 A 16, Arr. *Succ. FGrH* 156 F 1. 5, Paus. I. 6. iii).

In 331 before leaving Tyre for Mesopotamia Alexander gave special appointments to two Macedonians: Coeranus was to collect tribute in Phoenicia, and Philoxenus in Asia 'this side' (i.e. north-west) of the Taurus (Arr. III. 6. iv). Because in Harpalus' absence (cf. p. 372) they had been in charge of Alexander's treasury, some have seen their new appointments as powerful posts with authority over several provinces, but more probably they were to collect money from regions not subject to satraps in the usual way: the cities of the Phoenician coast, and perhaps Caria, still in the hands of Ada, but where Philoxenus himself subsequently became satrap.

The first oriental appointed as satrap was Mazaeus, satrap of Syria under Darius, who in 331 burned the crops in the Euphrates valley and then commanded Darius' right wing at Gaugamela. After the battle he retired to Babylon, there submitted to Alexander and was made satrap, with a Greek garrison commander and a Macedonian financial officer (Arr. III. 16. iv, Curt. IV. xvi. 7, V. i. 17–18, viii. 12, cf. Diod. Sic. XVII. 64. v). He was the first of a series of Iranian satraps with European officers set beside them. Alexander could not claim to 'liberate' the heart of the empire as he had 'liberated' the western provinces; he was to represent himself as legitimate king (cf. p. 375), and to make his rule acceptable he needed the cooperation of the local aristocracy – but a Macedonian was appointed to the strategically important province of Arachosia, south of Bactria, centred on Kandahar (Arr. III. 28. i, Curt. VII. iii. 5). In fact, as Alexander moved further east, Iranian satraps and usurpers caused trouble, and they figured prominently in the purge of 324; most provinces were in European hands when Alexander died. In India Alexander reverted to appointing Macedonian satraps, but under them cooperative native rulers were retained and gained the territory of those who refused to cooperate. Porus is referred to as king and had no European troops stationed with him (Arr. VI. 2. i, cf. V. 29. iii; but called satrap Plut. 60. xv): after the abandonment of further eastward expansion, he was a vassal ruler on the edge of the empire.

According to Plutarch Alexander 'established more than seventy cities among barbarian tribes, planted Asia with Greek magistracies, and mastered their uncivilised and beastly way of life' (*De Alex. Fort.* i. 328 E–F). It has been generally acknowledged that the number is a great exaggeration, and the latest serious study is the most drastic, reducing the number of Alexandrias to six – in Egypt; in Aria (Herat); Alexandria Eschate (Khodjend); in Susiana, near the mouth of the Tigris; Bucephala, on the Hydaspes, where Alexander's horse Bucephalas died; in Macarene = of the Oreitae, between the Indus and Gedrosia – though there were other places, not founded as cities, where Europeans were installed in garrisons. Except in Egypt the cities were on the sites of older settlements: their purpose was primarily strategic and administrative, to keep garrisons in vital places and to act as a focus for the government of non-urbanised regions. Some seem to have been intended as trading centres too, but Plutarch's view of them as a means of spreading Greek civilisation is seriously mistaken: despite his own Greek education Alexander was not fond of the Greeks, and the settlements were in fact resented both by the native populations on whom they were inflicted and by the Europeans who were deposited in them. In 325, perhaps in response to a rumour that Alexander had been killed at the town of the Malli, 3,000 men left in Bactria set out for the Mediterranean (Diod. XVII. 99. v, Curt. IX. vii. 1–11); and after Alexander's death more than 23,000 men, 'thrown out in the remotest parts of the kingdom, longing for the Greek training and way of life', rose up in revolt, but were defeated and treacherously killed (Diod. Sic. XVIII. 4. viii, 7). But, although we should not attribute hellenising intentions or practices to Alexander, his conquests did in the end have a hellenising effect. Greeks and Macedonians became involved in government, and Greek became the language of government; the western and central provinces of the empire became part of a Greek/eastern Mediterranean world; and Greektype cities were founded later on a substantial scale by the Seleucids.

Alexander and his Subordinates

The commanders of Philip's advance force in 336 included Parmenio, his best general (cf. Plut. *Sayings of Kings and Commanders* 177 C), and Attalus, the uncle of his new wife. Alexander succeeded to the throne with the support of Antipater; he had no reason to love Attalus, and Parmenio acquiesced in his killing (cf. pp. 321, 349). In 334 Antipater was left behind in charge of Macedon, and Alexander began the Asiatic campaign with an army consisting largely of men who had fought under Philip and with Parmenio and his family well entrenched in positions of command. Parmenio himself ranked next to Alexander, commanding the left wing in the major battles while Alexander commanded the right; his son Philotas commanded the Macedonian cavalry, another son, Nicanor, commanded the hypaspists, and Nicanor's brother-in-law Coenus commanded a *taxis* of the phalanx (e.g. Arr. I. 14. i–ii). In addition to these,

Asander, possibly but not certainly Parmenio's brother, was made satrap of Sardis (Arr. I. 17. vii); and Coenus' brother Cleander fetched reinforcements from Greece in 334–332 and commanded the 'old mercenaries' at Gaugamela (Arr. I. 24. ii, II. 20. v, III. 12. ii; probably to be restored in III. 6. viii).

But before long Parmenio's family was in trouble. In winter 332/1 his youngest son, Hector, died in an accident on the Nile (Curt. IV. viii. 7–9). Asander was replaced as satrap of Sardis in 331, and no more is heard of him except that in winter 329/8 he brought reinforcements to Alexander (Arr. III. 6. vii, IV. 7. ii). In 330, after Darius' death, Nicanor died, and Philotas was left behind to attend to the funeral (Curt. VI. vi. 18–19, cf. Arr. III. 25. iv). Later that year, when Philotas had rejoined Alexander, there was a major crisis. A man called Dimnus formed a conspiracy, and his beloved Nicomachus asked Philotas to inform Alexander. Philotas did not do so, but the news reached Alexander by another route. Philotas' arrest was arranged by six men who were to be important subsequently: Coenus and Craterus, commanders of *taxeis* of the phalanx, Hephaestion and the Greek Erigyius, childhood friends of Alexander, and Perdiccas and Leonnatus, two of the killers of Philip's assassin (Diod. Sic. XVI. 94. iv). Philotas was arrogant and unpopular (cf. Diod. Sic. XVII. 66. vii, Plut. 40. i, 48), but here may have been guilty of no more than failing to pass on information which he did not take seriously. However, prompted by Craterus, Alexander demanded the death penalty, and the army voted it. Parmenio, with a substantial force and no longer with Alexander, might not be trustworthy after his son's execution, so Cleander and others were given the job of killing him. Various other men were put on trial, and some were condemned but others acquitted. A number of the soldiers were disaffected, and were put together in a unit of *ataktoi* ('unassigned', or perhaps 'undisciplined') (Arr. III. 26–7, Diod. Sic. XVII. 79–80, Curt. VI. vii–VII. ii, Just. XII. 5. iii, Plut. 48–9).

There is a series of stories in which Alexander benefited from not following Parmenio's advice: his advice to wait until morning at the Granicus (Arr. I. 13. ii–vii, Plut. 16. iii; but see p. 362); his advice to fight a naval battle when besieging Miletus (Arr. I. 18. vi); his warning against the doctor who treated Alexander in Cilicia in 333 (Arr. II. 4. ix–x, Curt. III. vi. 4–12, Just. XI. 8. v–ix, Plut. 13. v–viii); his willingness to accept Darius' final offer of terms (Arr. II. 25. ii [misplaced], Diod. Sic. XVII. 54. iv–v, Curt. IV. xi. 11–15, Plut. 29. viii); at Gaugamela his advice to delay for reconnaissance was accepted but his further advice to attack at night was not (Arr. III. 9. iii–iv, 10, cf. Curt. IV. xii. 21); his advice not to destroy Persepolis (Arr. III. 18. xi–xii). In each of the major battles, Parmenio had been in a defensive position on the left, while Alexander had attacked on the right; at Gaugamela, it was said (improbably: cf. p. 364), Parmenio had to send a message to Alexander, who turned back from pursuing Darius to help him (Arr. III. 15, Diod. Sic. 60. vii–viii [the message did not reach Alexander], Curt. IV. xvi. 1–3, Plut. 32. v–vii [Alexander rejected the appeal]). It has been suggested that Alexander had been scheming for a long time to escape from the clutches of Parmenio, and that in 330 his plans finally bore fruit; but Alexander was a man who reacted impulsively to crises rather than a patient plotter. Parmenio would not have been left behind with a substantial force if he had not been trusted, and the hostile stories may as well have been circulated after the crisis, to suggest that Parmenio had not been such a great man after all, as in preparation for it.

Immediately Philotas' cavalry command was divided between Clitus 'the black' and Alexander's friend Hephaestion. Coenus and Cleander backed Alexander and continued to prosper. But otherwise this crisis brought to the top a new group, men who were Alexander's rather than Philip's. Coenus, Craterus, Hephaestion and Perdiccas were all to be hipparchs when the cavalry were reorganised; Leonnatus held important commands (after as well as before the crisis over *proskynesis*, so if the mockery is to be attributed to a Leonnatus [Arr. IV. 12. ii] rather than Polyperchon [Curt. VIII. v. 22] it must be a different Leonnatus), as did Erigyius until his death in 327. Other childhood friends who had been exiled by Philip were to rise to prominence too (Arr. III. 6. iv–vi): Harpalus (cf. p. 372) had been treasurer from the beginning; Ptolemy held his first command in 330 and was now made a bodyguard (Arr. III. 18. ix, perhaps exaggerating; 27. v); the Greek Nearchus had been made satrap of Lycia in 333 and was later to command Alexander's fleet; Erigyius' brother Laomedon, being bilingual, was put in charge of the Persian prisoners. Meanwhile Antipater, who had backed Alexander as the new king in 336, was left in command in Macedon.

Further crises followed. In 328 Clitus 'the black', about to be left behind as satrap of Bactria, showed anger at Alexander's growing oriental affectations and denigration of Philip, and was killed by Alexander in a drunken argument. Alexander kept to his tent for three days, until he was persuaded to continue by the argument that the king's acts are by definition just or, according to Curtius, by the army's voting to condemn Clitus (Arr. IV. 8–9, Curt. VIII. i. 19–ii. 12, Just. XII. 6, Plut. 51).

In 327, when Alexander tried to introduce the custom of *proskynesis* to his European followers, the opposition was led by Aristotle's nephew Callisthenes (cf. p. 380). As well as being the official historian of the campaign, Callisthenes seems to have had some responsibility for the pages, the sons of leading Macedonians who were attached to the court to attend on Alexander. Led by one whom Alexander had had flogged, some of them, allegedly worried by Alexander's orientalism and his elimination of opponents, formed a plot, and news of it reached Alexander. They were tortured and executed, and Callisthenes was blamed, but Curtius maintains he was innocent, and Arrian says that although Ptolemy and Aristobulus considered him guilty most writers claimed that Alexander had already come to hate him and was ready to believe the worst of him. Disagreement about how Callisthenes died suggests something other than a public condemnation: the opportunity to remove him was no doubt convenient for Alexander but need not have been manufactured by him (Arr. IV. 13–14, Curt. VIII. vi–viii, Plut. 55, cf. Just. XV. 3. ii–vi).

So far Alexander had had problems with high-ranking individuals, but the army had supported him. In 326, however, the army mutinied at the Hyphasis, and Alexander had to abandon his plans to continue farther east. Coenus, who was connected with Parmenio's family but had backed Alexander against Philotas, and who could be described as 'among those most loyal to Alexander' (Arr. VI. 2. i), acted as the army's spokesman (Arr. V. 25–29. iii, Diod. Sic. XVII. 93. ii–95. ii, Curt. IX. ii–iii. 19, Just. XII. 8. x–xvii, Plut. 62). In the journey to the coast Alexander had to work hard to recover the army's loyalty, taking unnecessary personal risks until in the attack on the town of the Malli he was seriously wounded. In the course of that journey Coenus died, of an illness, as our sources agree (Arr. VI. 2. i, Curt. IX. ii. 20); and while this too may have been convenient for Alexander, we are not justified in suspecting foul play.

Neither are we justified in seeing the march through the desert of Gedrosia as an act of expiation imposed on the army. Alexander wanted to explore, and to support Nearchus and the fleet; stories that Semiramis and Cyrus had had difficulties there constituted a challenge, but he did send Craterus and the veterans by an easier route (Arr. VI. 24. i–iii). The difficulties were genuine; on reaching Pura Alexander blamed the satrap Apollophanes for failing to forward supplies, but we have to turn to Arrian's *Indike* to discover that Apollophanes had been unable to do that because he had been killed in a battle (Arr. VI. 20. v, 27. i, *Ind.* 23. v).

In his final years Alexander conducted a purge, particularly of Persian satraps and usurpers; but Cleander and his accomplices in killing Parmenio, who had remained in Media, were summoned and executed also, while Atropates, the Persian satrap of Media, had remained loyal to Alexander and survived, and Cleomenes, who in Egypt had enlarged his position and had offended the Egyptians but had done nothing to worry Alexander, had his misdeeds condoned (Arr. VI. 27. i–iv, 29–30, VII. 4. iii, 23. vi–viii, Diod. Sic. XVII. 106. ii–iii, Curt. IX. x. 20–1, X. i. 1–9, 30–42, Plut. 68. iii–vii). We need not be surprised that various men had assumed that Alexander would not return alive and had misbehaved accordingly (Arr. VII. 4. ii, Diod. Sic. XVII. 108. iv, Curt. X. i. 7). As always Alexander reacted impulsively to news of trouble, but we need not suppose that he imagined trouble where there was none, or had become neurotically afraid of anyone who might not be totally obedient: since we tend to hear only about men in high positions, we need not assume that those promoted to fill gaps were safe nonentities.

One man who expected punishment and did not wait for it was Harpalus, one of Alexander's childhood friends who was unfit for fighting and so made treasurer. He was said to have fled to Megara, in Greece, in 333 before the battle of Issus, but to have been persuaded to return to that position in 331 when Alexander advanced to Mesopotamia (Arr. III. 6. iv–vii). For Alexander to forgive and reinstate a man who had offended him would be unparalleled, and it is an attractive suggestion that Harpalus' flight was a cover for his going as a spy to investigate the trouble brewing in Greece. In 330 Harpalus was left in charge of the central treasuries when Alexander continued in pursuit of Darius (Arr. III. 19. vii); but he took to enjoying women and a notoriously luxurious life, in Babylon and in Tarsus (Cilicia). In 325/4 he fled, with as many mercenaries and as much money as he could take, and sought refuge in Athens, whose favour he had been cultivating; what happened after that we have studied in an Athenian context (Diod. Sic. XVII. 108. iv–viii, Curt. X. lacuna–ii. 1–3, cf. Just. XIII. 5. ix, Plut. 41. viii, and see p. 343).

It was Alexander's intention that when Craterus, who was ill, had returned to Macedon with the veterans, he would succeed Antipater there and Antipater would take reinforcements to Alexander. Some including Curtius have thought that Antipater was now facing trouble, but Arrian denies that. A possible explanation lies in the fact that Antipater and Alexander's mother Olympias had quarrelled. Not later than 331 she had gone to Molossis, where her daughter Cleopatra had been ruling in the absence of her husband Alexander (who went to fight in Italy in 334 and died there: cf. pp. 292–3), but Cleopatra had not welcomed Olympias, and had herself returned to Macedon to get away from Olympias. After that, Olympias and Antipater each denounced the other to Alexander. We cannot tell whether in planning to remove Antipater from Macedon Alexander believed Olympias and had therefore become distrustful of Antipater, or merely wanted to increase the distance between Olympias and Antipater. In fact Alexander's intentions were not carried out. At the time of Alexander's death Craterus had not gone further than Cilicia, while Antipater, who had perhaps recently been in contact on his own account with the Aetolians, had not himself left Macedon but had sent his son Cassander; and after Alexander had died Craterus and Antipater joined forces to defeat the rebellious Greeks in the Lamian War (Arr. VII. 12. iv–lacuna, Diod. Sic. XVII. 118. i, XVIII. 4. i, 12. i, 49. iv, Curt. X. vii. 9, x. 14–15, Just. XII. 14. iii, Plut. 49. xiv–xv, 68. iv–v, 74. ii–vii, Livy VIII. 24. xvii).

Diodorus links with Alexander's punishment of disobedient officials an order to the satraps to disband their mercenary armies (as Artaxerxes had ordered in 359/8: cf. pp. 224, 323). The intention cannot have been to remove all troops from the provinces; there is a suggestion that Alexander may have wanted to recruit the men into his own army; but the order created a flood of unemployed soldiers, many of whom found their way to Taenarum in Laconia (Diod. Sic. XVII. 106. ii–iii, 111. i, cf. Paus. I. 25. v, VIII. 52. v: see p. 343). Another order issued in 324 was that the Greek cities were to take back their exiles (Diod. Sic. XVII. 109. i, XVIII. 8. ii–vii, Curt. X. ii. 4–7, Just. XIII. 5. ii–v): exile was one factor which led men to take up mercenary service, and the order may have been intended to weaken the force taken by Harpalus and/or the force building up at Taenarum (which Harpalus' men joined). Athens was worried, because it had occupied Samos since 365 (cf. pp. 223, 236–7, and see *IG* XII. vi 17 = R&O 90. *B* ~ Harding 127); probably the order was a breach of the principle of stability underlying the League of Corinth (thus Curtius: cf. p. 319), and probably Alexander had long since ceased to care about the League's rules. Of inscriptions concerning the return of exiles, R&O 85 (*B* = *IG* XII. ii 6 ~ Harding 113), from Mytilene, is better associated with local arrangements in the 330's, but Tod 202 = R&O 101 ~ Harding 122, concerning Tegea, is rightly dated to 324–323.

Hephaestion, joint hipparch with Clitus and then one of the many hipparchs, but apparently not a particularly good military commander, was the man closest to Alexander (Curt. III. xii. 16). Probably they were lovers: at Troy in 334 he played Patroclus to Alexander's Achilles (Arr. I. 12. i); after Issus Darius' mother is said to have mistaken him for Alexander (Arr. II. 12. vi–viii, Diod. Sic. XVII. 37. v–vi, Curt. III. xii. 16–17). In 324 he became second in command, being described as 'chiliarch [the term used by Greeks for the Persians' grand vizier: cf. Diod. Sic. XVIII. 48. iv] in charge of the companion cavalry'; his hipparchy was called his chiliarchy, and it was still named after him after his death (Arr. VII. 14. x). No one really succeeded him, but technically his position was taken by Perdiccas (Diod. Sic. XVII. 110. viii, XVIII. 3. iv, Plut. *Eum.* 1. v, Arr. *Succ. FGrH* 156 F 1. 3). Hephaestion was on bad terms with the other leading men: as a supporter of Alexander's orientalising tendencies he clashed with those who disapproved, Craterus (Plut. 47. ix–xii, cf. Diod. Sic. XVII. 114. i) and Callisthenes (cf. Plut. 53. i); he quarrelled also with Eumenes (Plut. *Eum.* 2, cf. Arr. VII. 13. i, 14. ix).

Eumenes, a Greek from Cardia, had been Philip's secretary and became Alexander's (Nep. XVIII. *Eum.* 1. v–vi, 13. i, Plut. *Eum.* 1. iv, Arr. V. 24. vi, VII. 4. vi); after Hephaestion's death he was assiduous in proposing honours (Arr. VII. 14. ix), and when Perdiccas was promoted he took over Perdiccas' hipparchy (Nep. XVIII. *Eum.* 1. vi, Plut. *Eum.* 1. v). Eumenes may well be the compiler of the diary whose purpose was to stress the court's heavy drinking and the responsibility of that for the deaths of Hephaestion and Alexander (cf. pp. 349, 351, 357).

Aims and Ideals

Alexander was a Macedonian given a Greek education. His mother Olympias claimed to be descended from Achilles (Diod. Sic. XVII. 1. v, Plut. 2. i, cf. Arr. I. 11. viii); Lysimachus, one of his tutors, taught him to think of himself as Achilles (Plut. 5. viii); he read the *Iliad* with Aristotle, and treasured that copy of the text (Plut. 8. ii, 26. i–ii); he and Hephaestion were compared with Achilles and Patroclus (cf. above) – and in 335 Demosthenes called him Margites, the simpleton of a Greek epic (Aesch. III. *Ctesiphon* 160, Marsyas *FGrH* 135 F 3). For the Macedonians the war against Persia was a war of conquest, but Philip had already for the sake of the League of Corinth adopted the motif of a war of revenge for Persia's fifth-century invasion of Greece (cf. Polyb. III. 6. ix–xiv: see p. 320). Like Agesilaus before him (cf. p. 208), Alexander represented the enmity of Greece and Persia as a continuation of that between Greece and Troy, and he emphasised this in his sacrifices at the crossing of the Hellespont and in his visit to Troy. It was good propaganda, and he probably believed it himself.

But by 330 the object of the Greek war of revenge had been achieved: Darius had been defeated, and Alexander controlled the centre of the empire; Persepolis had been destroyed – whether as a deliberate act of policy, opposed by Parmenio (Arr. III. 18. xi–xii), or as the culmination of a drunken revel, incited by Ptolemy's future mistress Thais and afterwards regretted (Diod. Sic. XVII.

72, Curt. V. vii. 3–11, Plut. 38; and regretted later in Arr. VI. 30. i). The Greeks who had come as allies were discharged (at Ecbatana, Arr. III. 19. v; after Darius' death, Diod. Sic. XVII. 74. iii, Curt. VI. ii. 7). What was Alexander to do after that? The pursuit of Darius supplied an immediate aim as long as he lived; the pursuit of Bessus after that. And then – by the time he reached the Indus Alexander is unlikely to have believed that the eastern ocean was as near as is claimed in Arr. V. 26. i, Diod. Sic. XVII. 89. v, Curt. IX. i. 3, ii. 26–8, Just. XII. 7. iv; but he may well have believed that it was within reach and that he could conquer the whole of Asia. Our sources represent him as a man for whom beyond each challenge there arose another, a man driven by powerful impulses to see what others had not seen, to outdo the exploits of previous heroes and men. The expression, 'A strong desire (*pothos*, in Latin *cupido*) seized him', used frequently of Alexander (e.g. Arr. I. 3. v, II. 3. i, Curt. III. i. 16, Just. XI. 7. iv), is applied often enough to others too in classical literature, and there is no reason to think that this particular expression originated with him or referred to any particular drive which affected him distinctively, but it certainly appears true to the picture of his character which we are given.

From 330 onwards Alexander increasingly represented himself as a legitimate king – though as 'King of Asia' (Plut. 34. i, cf. earlier Diod. Sic. XVII. 17. ii, Arr. II. 14. viii–ix) he was not directly the continuator of the Persian Kingdom and its titles but the creator of something new. He was appointing Persians as satraps of the central provinces, and was to enlist oriental troops, at first in separate units and eventually in the same units as Europeans; he gave Darius a royal funeral (Arr. III. 22. vi, Plut. 43. vii), and punished Bessus for killing the King (Arr. III. 30. iv–v, IV. 7. iii–iv, Diod. Sic. XVII. 83. ix, Curt. VII. v. 36–43, x. 10, Just. XII. 5. x–xi, Plut. 43. vi). Worryingly for the Greeks and Macedonians, he adopted elements of Persian costume and customs, though not the precise dress and ceremonies of the Great King; he tried to extend the practice of *proskynesis* to his European followers (cf. p. 380); he married Roxana in 327, and he and his courtiers took Persian wives in 324; he showed a particular respect for the man who had made Persia great, Cyrus II (e.g. Arr. VI. 29. iv–xi, Curt. X. i. 30–5, Plut. 69. iii–v). To the disgust of his traditionally minded followers, Alexander was becoming an oriental monarch (Arr. IV. 7. iv, 9. ix, Diod. Sic. XVII. 77. iv–vii, Curt. VI. vi. 1–11, Just. XII. 3. viii–xii, Plut. 45. i–iv). On the other hand, he was far from gaining the approval of the Persians: he did not observe the cult of Ahura Mazda and the other ceremonies of the Achaemenid Kings or use their titles; the great capital cities were simply places to be garrisoned and/or looted; Iranian satraps with European officers set beside them are as likely to have felt humiliated as honoured.

How did Alexander perceive the various peoples who became subject to him in his kingdom of Asia? There are four texts on the basis of which it has been claimed that Alexander was the first person to conceive of the unity of mankind, but the claim does not appear justified. Plut. 27. x–xi (cf. his *Sayings of Kings and Commanders* 180 D) ends a chapter on Alexander's visit to the oracle of Ammon (cf. p. 378) with a conversation between Alexander and the suspiciously named and otherwise unattested philosopher Psammon: Alexander 'was greatly pleased at what was said, that all men are under the kingship of God . . . but even more Alexander expressed a more philosophical opinion about this, saying that God is the common father of all men but makes the best particularly his own'. This is surely non-egalitarian: what it stresses is that Alexander thought some of God's sons are more equal than others. Non-egalitarian again is Arrian's account of the banquet of reconciliation at Opis in 324, after Alexander had quelled the mutiny of the veterans (VII. 11. viii–ix): there was a great feast, attended by some 9,000 men;

> he was seated and they were all seated; around him the Macedonians, next in order to them the Persians; after them those of the other peoples who had precedence in rank or for any other quality; and he and those around him [presumably only those nearest to him] drank from the same bowl and made the same libations . . . and he prayed for various benefits including concord and partnership in rule for the Macedonians and the Persians.

We may compare Xerxes' council of war at Salamis in 480 (Hdt. VIII. 67. ii). This is hierarchical; it does not make a rigid distinction between Greeks/Macedonians and barbarians; but otherwise the most that can be said is that it recognises two master races rather than one (cf. Alexander's Macedonian and Persian bodyguard: Phylarchus *FGrH* 81 F 4, Polyaenus *Strat.* IV. 3. xxiv, Ael. *V.H.* IX. 3).

Alexander's Greek education will have taught him to make a rigid distinction between Greeks and barbarians. Isocrates claimed that the Athenians were superior to other Greeks as Greeks to barbarians and human beings to animals (XV. *Antid.* 293), and advised Philip to benefit the Greeks, be king of the Macedonians and rule over the barbarians (V. *Philip* 154). Aristotle regarded barbarians as innately inferior to Greeks and fit to be slaves (*Pol.* I. 1252 A 24–B 27; III. 1285 A 14–22, VII. 1327 B 18–38 distinguishes between the spirited barbarians of Europe and the submissive barbarians of Asia). In *De Alex. Fort.* i, after a chapter on Alexander's (doubtful: cf. p. 369) achievement in giving the crude barbarians the benefits of Greek civilisation, Plutarch continues (329 A–D): Zeno [active from the end of the fourth century, founder of the Stoic school] sketched the dream of the unity of mankind, but Alexander

> provided the fact for the theory: for he did not, as Aristotle had advised him, behave as a leader to the Greeks and a master to the barbarians, caring for the Greeks as his friends and kindred but bearing down on the barbarians as animals and plants [there is no confirmation that Aristotle went that far] . . . but thought he had come from God as a common uniter and reconciler of them all . . . bringing together from all sides as if he were mixing in a loving-cup their lives, their customs, their marriages and their ways of life. [In other respects there should be no difference between them, but] Greeks should be distinguished by goodness and barbarians by badness.

A slightly different slant is found in Strabo. 66. I. iv. 9:

> Eratosthenes [head of the library at Alexandria at the end of the third century] did not approve of those who divided the whole mass of men into Greeks and barbarians, and those who advised Alexander to treat the Greeks as friends and the barbarians as enemies. He said it was better to base the distinction on goodness and badness; for many of the Greeks are bad and many of the barbarians are civilised. . . . So Alexander, ignoring the advice, was able to accept and benefit as many men as were reputable.

Experience will indeed have shown Alexander that many of the Greeks were bad and many of the barbarians were civilised, and he no doubt came to appreciate aspects of Persian court life. He needed the cooperation of the Persian aristocracy, and there were advantages to be gained from intermarriage (no European women were married to Asiatic men; of the European men, only Peucestas, made satrap of Persis in 324, took to Persian ways with enthusiasm [Arr. VI. 30. ii–iii], and only Seleucus made a successful and lasting marriage [to Spitamenes' daughter Apame: Arr. VII. 4. vi]). Alexander's empire provided a context in which doctrines of the brotherhood of man could develop, as the world of the Greek states did not, but there is no evidence that Alexander believed in a mixed culture or that he philosophised about what he was doing. Plutarch made the essential point when he said in *De Alex. Fort.* i that Alexander provided the fact for the [later] theory.

At the end of his reign the Greeks were voting divine honours to Alexander. For a while it was believed by modern scholars that the Greeks made clear-cut distinctions between gods, heroes and human beings, and that if Alexander was indeed worshipped as a god in his lifetime that was startlingly new; but it is now coming to be seen that Alexander's deification was the natural culmination of a century or more of development. Descent from a god or hero was often claimed by kings and aristocrats (Alexander as a Temenid was descended from Heracles, and through Olympias was descended from Achilles), and comparison with a god of those who had outstanding achievements was a common literary conceit. Isocrates writing to Philip referred to those who had been judged demigods for their campaigns against the barbarians (V. *Philip* 137), and in the *Second Letter to Philip* said that if he conquered the barbarians nothing would be left for him but to become a god (*Ep.* III. *Phil. ii.* 5: authenticity disputed). Aristotle thought that in an imperfect world a plurality of men was better than one, but if one man really did surpass the others he would be like a god among men and would deserve total obedience (*Pol.* III. 1284 A 3–11, 1288 A 8–9, cf. VII. 1332 B 16–22). Callisthenes, who was to refuse to perform literal *proskynesis* to Alexander (cf. p. 380), was happy to write of him as son of Zeus, and of the waves of the sea as performing *proskynesis* to him (*FGrH* 124 FF 14, 31 – echoing Xen. *Anab.* I. iv. 18, of Cyrus in 401).

But there is more to it than that. While it was common for founders and benefactors of cities to be venerated as heroes after their death, as Brasidas was by Amphipolis after 422, it appears that before then the original founder, Hagnon, had been venerated during his lifetime (Thuc. V. 11. i: cf. p. 69). Outside that context, a hero cult is already attested for the boxer Euthymus of Locri in the mid fifth century (Pliny *H.N.* VII. 152, Paus. VI. 6. iv–xi, cf. Strabo 255. VI. i. 5, Ael. *V.H.* VIII. 18). Lysander, who won the Peloponnesian War for Sparta, was shown being crowned by Poseidon in the 'navarchs dedication' at Delphi, and at Samos there were games named after him and other honours normally reserved for gods – while Agesilaus is said to have refused divine honours in Thasos (cf. pp. 152, 205–6). In Sicily Dion, when he had at last got control of all of Syracuse from Dionysius II and his forces, is said to have been voted a hero's honours (cf. p. 288); and at the other end of the Greek world Clearchus, tyrant of Heraclea Pontica (on the south coast of the Black Sea) from 364/3 to 353/2, to have received *proskynesis* and 'the honours of the Olympians' (*Suda* κ 1714 Κλέαρχος). The most relevant precedents are provided by Philip, who if he did not quite become a god came very near to it. Early in his reign Crenides was named Philippi after him, and an inscription attests *temene* of Philip there, a word which could denote either 'properties' of Philip or 'sanctuaries' dedicated to him (*SEG* xxxviii 658 with xlviii 708, xlix 768; cf. p. 300). After Chaeronea the Philippeum at Olympia was built, to house statues of himself and his family (Paus. V. 20. ix). At Ephesus there was a statue of Philip in the temple of Artemis (Arr. I. 17. xi); the people of Eresus on Lesbos had a cult of Zeus Philippios (*IG* xii. 2 526 = R&O 83. γ. front = Harding 112. B. 4–5). As part of the celebration of his daughter Cleopatra's wedding in 336 a statue of Philip was paraded with the statues of the twelve Olympian gods (Diod. Sic. XVI. 92. v, cf. 95. i).

What of Alexander? When Olympias had fallen out with Philip, it suited her to claim that Alexander's true father was not Philip but Zeus (Plut. 2–3. iv). It was reported by Callisthenes (so well before the end of Alexander's life) that the sanctuary of Branchidae (Didyma) near Miletus, sacked by the Persians after the Ionian Revolt at the beginning of the fifth century, resumed operation and sent oracles to Alexander in Egypt about his birth from Zeus (*FGrH* 124 F 14. a), and Arrian states that Alexander went to the oracle of Ammon (identified by the Greeks with Zeus) to find out about his dual paternity (Zeus and Philip, as Heracles was son of Zeus and of Amphitryon) (III. 3. i–ii, cf. VII. 29. iii). So before Alexander went to the oracle, he was already beginning to think that he had a divine father. As pharaoh of Egypt he had become a descendant (but not son) of Ammon ex officio; if the priest did greet him as son of Ammon/Zeus (*pai Dios*, but Plutarch suggests that this might have been a misinterpretation of *paidion*, 'boy'), he may have meant no more than that. The consultation was private; Alexander was said to be pleased; and he said he would tell Olympias when he next saw her, which he never did. Later, at the mouth of the Indus, he was to make sacrifices said to be ordered by Ammon (Arr. VI. 19. iv, cf. *Ind.* 18. xi); the claim of Curtius and Justin that his followers were told to pay him divine honours looks like later embroidery (Arr. III. 3–4, Diod. Sic. XVII. 49–51, Curt. IV. vii. 5–30, Just. XI. 11. ii–xii, Plut. 26. x–27. ix).

Ill. 15 Treasury relief at Persepolis, showing the King receiving *proskynesis*. © The Oriental Institute Museum, University of Chicago

In 327 Alexander tried to extend the Persian practice of *proskynesis* – technically blowing a kiss (cf. ill. 15), which might be accompanied by a bow or full prostration – to his European followers. It was a Persian social custom to offer *proskynesis* to a superior and to kiss an equal, as those who had read Herodotus would have known (I. 134. i, combining *proskynesis* with *prospipton*, 'falling down'); Aristotle regarded it as a barbarian form of honour (*Rhet.* I. 1361 A 24–7). The Persian King was not regarded as a god, and those who performed *proskynesis* did not regard the objects of it as gods. Nevertheless some Greeks may have interpreted it in this way (cf. Isoc. IV. *Paneg.* 151); they certainly thought it a gesture appropriate only to gods and degrading if performed to human beings (Xen. *An.* III. ii. 13). There are two accounts of Alexander and *proskynesis*. One involves a debate among the intellectuals, in which Callisthenes expressed opposition, the Macedonians applauded him and Alexander agreed to abandon the idea (Arr. IV. 10. v–12. i, Curt. VIII. v. 5–21). The other is a story of a drinking party at which the guests performed *proskynesis* and Alexander responded with a kiss, but Callisthenes while Alexander was not watching refused to perform, and Alexander when told of it refused him his kiss (Arr. IV. 12. ii–v, Just. XII. 7. i–iii, Plut. 54. iv–vi from the chamberlain Chares). It is unlikely that both are true, and the experiment is more probable than the debate. Curtius, at least, thought that Alexander was claiming divine honours; some modern scholars have supposed that he merely wanted to unify court ceremonial and, since he was in Asia, to follow the Asiatic model. It is not credible that Alexander thought those who performed *proskynesis* were worshipping him as a god; but he was increasingly seeing himself as somebody special and as the son of Zeus; probably the east was going to his head and he liked being reverenced in that way, and to that extent the revulsion of the Macedonians and Greeks was justified.

In 323 the oracle of Ammon pronounced that the dead Hephaestion was to be venerated as a hero (Arr. VII. 23. vi, cf. 14. vii, Plut. 72. iii; worshipped as a god Diod. Sic. XVII. 115. vi, Just. XII. 12. xii, cf. Lucian *Calumny* 17); and 'at this point embassies came from Greece, and their envoys were crowned themselves and came up to Alexander and crowned him with gold crowns, indeed like sacred envoys coming to honour a god' (Arr. VII. 23. ii). Decisions are attributed to various Greek states: to Sparta, laconically, 'Since Alexander wants to be a god, let him be a god' (Plut. *Spartan Sayings* 219 E, Ael. *V.H.* II. 19, the only suggestion that the initiative was Alexander's). In Athens Demades proposed the recognition of Alexander as a thirteenth god; Demosthenes and Lycurgus are both said to have opposed it, but in 324/3 Demosthenes, perhaps sarcastically, granted that 'Alexander could be the son of Zeus and of Poseidon too if he liked' (Ael. *V.H.* V. 12; Timaeus *ap.* Polyb. XII. 12b. iii, [Plut.] *X Orat.* 842 D; Hyp. V. *Demosthenes* col. 31, cf. Din. I. *Demosthenes* 94); Hyperides in his *Funeral Oration* of 323/2 complained in general terms of divine and heroic honours paid to men (VI. *Epitaph.* 20–1). But Curt. X. v. 11 says the Macedonians refused, and the *Suda*'s entry on Antipater says that he was opposed (*Suda* α 2703 Ἀντίπατρος).

There is enough smoke for us to infer a fire: that the Greeks paid divine honours to Alexander at the end of his reign is likely. But it is less likely that they did so at his request – and we should reject the suggestion that, since he wanted to order the Greek states to take back their exiles but had no right to do so (cf. p. 373), he decided to become a god so that Alexander the god would order what Alexander the man could not: he was past caring about his legal rights, and although Greek states consulted oracles they did not receive and obey divine commands. There is no suggestion that any orientals, for most of whom it would indeed have been blasphemous, were called on to worship him as a god or did so, beyond the claim that since the (not yet conquered) Arabs had only two gods Alexander thought they should recognise him as a third (Arr. VII. 20. i, Strabo 741. XVI. i. 11). In a Greek context, after what had gone before, admiration or flattery would suggest that divine honours were a fitting tribute to the man who had so spectacularly surpassed the achievements of his predecessors, and it is likely that Alexander enjoyed this tribute to his achievements without any sense of blasphemy. Divine honours for rulers were to become standard in the hellenistic period, first attested for Antigonus at Scepsis (OGIS 6).

Alexander died in 323, shortly before his 33rd birthday. What might he have done if he had not died then? Arrian credits him in Bactria with intending to make an expedition from the Bosporus into the Black Sea, and at the Hyphasis with intending to circumnavigate Africa (IV. 15. v–vi; V. 26. i–ii, cf. Plut. 68. i [later context]). In 323 he ordered an exploration of the Caspian, and he began preparations for an expedition to Arabia, to which he had already sent explorers (VII. 16. i–iv; VII. 19. iii–20. x, Strabo 766. XVI. iii. 3, 778. XVI. iv. 19). There are other, less reliable, hints of further territorial ambitions (Arr. IV. 7. v, VII. 1. i–iv; Curt. X. i. 17–19 [the western plan to be mentioned below]).

After his death, at a conference in Babylon Perdiccas produced plans said to have been found among Alexander's papers, and persuaded the army to disavow all except the completion of Hephaestion's funeral monument, as 'over-ambitious and hard to achieve'. Diodorus gives as the chief of these: to build 1,000 ships larger than triremes, and to conquer the west by travelling along the north African coast via Carthage to the Straits of Gibraltar, crossing into Spain and returning through Europe, building harbours as he went; to build six temples costing 1,000 talents each; to arrange mass transportations of population between Europe and Asia, producing intermarriage and concord; to build a great pyramid to Philip (XVII. 4. i–vi). Alexander is no more likely than Lysander (cf. p. 205) to have made written notes of his plans for the future, but, whether authentic or not, with the possible exception of large-scale intermarriage and concord the plans are in character and credible as plans. But it is important that they were produced in order to be rejected, as after Julius Caesar's death it was decided – but not adhered to – that no decree of his should be published (Cic. Phil. i. 3, cf. Phil. ii. 91, Dio Cass. XLIV. 53. iv, cf. XLV. 23. vii): none of Alexander's generals was to be able to steal a march on the others by claiming, 'We must do X because Alexander told me that he intended to do X'.

At any rate, it seems that when Alexander thought of the future he thought in terms of further conquests and magnificent monuments. Yet large parts of the empire he had already conquered were still unpacified, and Greece was on the point of rebellion: his existing empire needed years of consolidation and careful administration, as according to Plutarch the Roman emperor Augustus had remarked (*Roman Sayings* 207 D). There is no indication that Alexander intended to turn to that, or that he had given any thought to a world which no longer contained himself.

Alexander had conquered the Persian empire; he had created a new kingship, and in his army he had done something to mingle Europeans and Asiatics; but he had not to a significant extent had either a policy of fusion or a policy of spreading Greek civilisation, and so it is hard to accept the picture of Alexander the dreamer painted by W. W. Tarn in the first half of the twentieth century. He had provoked, by his sympathetic reception of oriental ways, and had dealt with opposition from leading Macedonians and Greeks, but on the whole he had reacted impulsively as crises occurred, and it is equally hard to accept the picture of Alexander the schemer painted by E. Badian in the second half of the twentieth century. He was a military genius, clever in adapting to circumstances and inspiring as a leader of his own men, as military historians have long recognised; but (although on a smaller scale Greeks had been equally drastic in their treatment of defeated enemies) his military successes involved killing enemies on a scale not normally encountered in Greek and Macedonian warfare, as A. B. Bosworth has recently emphasised. He was a pragmatic administrator but not a patient organiser. Personally, he was a man who was eager to be up and doing, to discover new places and outdo the achievements of others; hard-living, like all the Macedonian nobility; impulsive rather than deliberate; and, especially towards the end, something of a fanatic. And in June 323 he died, with no obvious heir.

NOTE ON FURTHER READING

For general books on Alexander see the note at the end of chapter 24. A list of studies of particular episodes and problems would be enormous, and I limit myself largely to the more widely ranging works and to works which I follow on controversial matters.

Fuller, *The Generalship of Alexander the Great*, is a study by a professional soldier. Engels, *Alexander the Great and the Logistics of the Macedonian Army*, addresses important questions but is vitiated by the assumption that Alexander would not have used waggons. On military matters see also A. R. Burn, 'The Generalship of Alexander', *G&R*[2] xii 1965, 140–54; B. S. Strauss, 'Alexander: The Military Campaign', in Roisman (ed.), *Brill's Companion to Alexander the Great*, ch. 5. *Asthetairoi* are seen as the men from Upper Macedonia by A. B. Bosworth, 'ἀσθέταιροι', *CQ*[2] xxiii 1973, 245–53; as distinguished regiments by [Hammond and] Griffith, *History of Macedonia*, ii. 709–13. The view of the battle of the Granicus taken here was advanced by Green, *Alexander of Macedon*, 489–512 – but withdrawn in the 1991 reissue of the book, p. xiv, commenting only that recent studies had convinced him that it was 'flat wrong'. Darius' strategy for resisting Alexander is discussed by E. E. Garvin, 'Darius III and Homeland Defense', in Heckel and Tritle (eds.), *Crossroads of History: The Age of Alexander*, ch. 5.

On administration see E. Badian, 'The Administration of the Empire', *G&R*[2] xii 1965, 166–82, and 'Alexander the Great and the Greeks of Asia', in *Ancient Society and Institutions . . . V. Ehrenberg*, 37–69; W. E. Higgins, 'Aspects of Alexander's Imperial Administration', *Ath.*[2] lviii 1980, 129–52. An authoritatively minimalising view of Alexander's foundations of cities is given by Fraser, *Cities of Alexander the Great*.

Berve, *Das Alexanderreich*, ii, collects and discusses all the evidence for Alexander's subordinates; the most important are treated also by Heckel, *The Marshals of Alexander's Empire*; and see also W. Heckel, 'King and "Companions": Observations on the Nature of Power in the Reign of Alexander', in *Brill's Companion to Alexander the Great* (above), ch. 8. The view, here rejected, of Alexander as neurotically seeking to escape from the clutches of men who might be too powerful for him was advanced by E. Badian in several detailed studies and in his 'Alexander the Great and the Loneliness of Power', *AUMLA* xvii May 1962, 80–91 = his *Studies in Greek and Roman History*, 192–205; he has returned to the theme in 'Conspiracies', in Bosworth and Baynham (eds.), *Alexander the Great in Fact and Fiction*, ch. 3. That Harpalus' 'first exile' was a cover for a mission to spy on the Greeks was suggested by Lane Fox, *Alexander the Great*, 164 with 519, 411 with 542; Green, *Alexander of Macedon* (1974 Penguin edition), 222–3 with 538 n. 55, 281.

On Alexander as King of Asia see E. Fredericksmeyer, 'Alexander the Great and the Kingship of Asia', in *Alexander the Great in Fact and Fiction* (above), ch. 5; M. Brosius, 'Alexander and the Persians', in *Brill's Companion to Alexander the Great* (above), ch. 7. That Alexander believed in the 'brotherhood of man' was claimed by W. W. Tarn, 'Alexander the Great and the Unity of Mankind', *PBA* xix 1933, 123–66 = Griffith (ed.), *Alexander the Great: The Main Problems*, ch. 12, and his *Alexander the Great*, ii. 399–499 app. 25; and rebutted by E. Badian, 'Alexander the Great and the Unity of Mankind', *Hist.* vii 1958, 425–44 = *Alexander the Great: The Main Problems*, ch. 13.

A minimalising view of Alexander's deification was taken by J. P. V. D. Balsdon, 'The "Divinity" of Alexander', *Hist.* i 1950, 363–88 = *Alexander the Great: The Main Problems* (above), ch. 9; his divinity is taken more seriously by E. Fredericksmeyer, 'Alexander's Religion and Divinity', in *Brill's Companion to Alexander the Great* (above), ch. 10. On Euthymus of Locri see B. Currie, 'Euthymos of Locri: A Case Study in Heroization in the Classical Period', *JHS* cxxii 2002, 24–44.

That Alexander's posthumous plans were produced in order to be rejected is stressed by E. Badian, 'A King's Notebooks', *HSCP* lxxii 1967, 183–204.

26
Epilogue

We began in the aftermath of the Greeks' defeat of the invading Persians in 480–479. This was to be a defining episode for classical Greece, producing a greater and more self-conscious Greek unity than had been achieved before, and identifying the Persians (whose empire, despite the failure of this attempt to expand into mainland Greece, was in other respects as strong as ever) as the national enemy *par excellence*. Sparta, the strongest Greek state hitherto and the leader in the resistance to Persia, for a variety of reasons was not prepared to continue, so those who did want to continue the war against Persia were organised in the Delian League under the leadership of Athens.

In the second quarter of the fifth century Athens drove the Persians back from the Aegean as far as seemed worthwhile, until *c.*449 regular fighting against Persia was discontinued. During and after this process the Delian League was increasingly turned into an Athenian empire, in which the member states were made subordinate to Athens as Greek states had never before been made subordinate to a dominant state. Internally Athens took the final steps from a broadly based constitution to a democracy, in which basic political rights were extended to all free men of Athenian parentage, and the importance of the navy, whose ships were rowed by the poorer citizens, and of the empire meant that these rights were worth having and were proudly exercised. As democracy came to be distinguished from oligarchy, some other Greeks decided that they did not prefer democracy, and as Athens came to act as a champion of democracy in the Greek world Sparta, at the head of the Peloponnesian League, came to act as a champion of oligarchy. In this same period Athens came to be the economic centre of the Greek world, as the hub around which Aegean trade revolved, and the intellectual centre of the Greek world, with a large proportion of the best literature written by Athenians or by others living in Athens, and a large proportion of the best art and architecture produced for or in Athens.

Sparta had at first been unworried by the Delian League, but worries began as after *c.*460 Athens' power was extended into mainland Greece. Rebellions in 447–446 seemed to have reversed the growth of Athens, and the Thirty Years' Peace of 446/5 tried to establish a balance of power between an Athenian bloc based on the Aegean and a Spartan bloc based on the mainland. However, Athens' ambitions were unchecked, and it became clear that the growing power of Athens would not be compatible with the continuing power of Sparta. In the 430's Athens pursued risky policies which provoked, and may well have been intended to provoke, a confrontation.

In the Peloponnesian War, begun in 431, apparently but unsatisfactorily concluded in 421 and finally ended in 404, Sparta set out to break the power of Athens and 'liberate the Greeks'. Athens had the greater resources, and was largely invulnerable to what the mainland Greeks on their own could do to it; but Athens' resources were squandered in a misguided attempt to conquer Sicily in 415–413. Since the beginning of the war Sparta had been trying to gain the support of Persia with its vast resources, and Athens had been trying at least to prevent that situation from coming to pass; after 413 Sparta saw a possibility of victory and was prepared to pay Persia's price, that the Greeks of Asia Minor should not after all be liberated but should be handed back to Persia. That enabled Sparta to keep going until Athens' resources were exhausted, and in 404 Athens had to acknowledge defeat and the Delian League was broken up.

Athens was made subordinate to Sparta, though Sparta's allies would have liked to see it destroyed. Elsewhere Sparta began to follow Athens' imperial example, both among its allies and among states 'liberated' from Athens. As for the Asiatic Greeks, Sparta may before the end of the war have negotiated successfully for something less than total abandonment; in the event, when in 400 Persia laid claim to the Greek cities of Asia Minor, they appealed to Sparta and Sparta began fighting against Persia on their behalf. In Greece, with financial encouragement from Persia, a combination of Athens and Sparta's former allies began fighting against Sparta in the Corinthian War. In the Aegean and Asia Minor a navy commanded by an Athenian for a Persian satrap fought against Sparta, and paradoxically was represented as fighting for the freedom of the Greeks. But as the Spartans made no headway they turned to diplomacy, and in 387/6 the King's Peace or Peace of Antalcidas returned the Greeks of Asia Minor to Persia in exchange for a ruling that elsewhere all cities and islands were to be autonomous.

Sparta, which had obtained the treaty from Persia, proceeded to interpret it to suit its own interests, culminating in the occupation by Spartan troops of the major city of Thebes. In 379/8 Thebes was liberated with the support of Athens, and Athens then founded the Second Athenian League, aiming to defend the Greeks against Spartan imperialism and promising not to repeat the imperial practices of the Delian League. In 371 at Leuctra Sparta was overwhelmingly defeated by a Thebes which was already too strong for Athens' comfort, and within a few years Messenia had been liberated from Sparta and the Peloponnesian League had broken up. In the 360's, on the mainland Athens found it convenient to support Sparta against Thebes, while in the Aegean it could find nothing to do with the League except try to recover fifth-century possessions; and Thebes persuaded Persia that it was now the state most worthy of support, and set out to break Athens as it had broken Sparta.

Macedon, a marginally Greek kingdom in the north, had since the beginning of the fifth century impinged on the southern Greeks, but as an entity for them to exploit rather than one capable of exploiting them. But in 359 it gained in Philip II a king who was able to pull the country together, and to satisfy his ambitions by a clever combination of fighting and diplomacy. Between 356 and 346 he took advantage of the Third Sacred War, provoked by the attempts of the Thebans to use the sanctuary of Apollo at Delphi as a vehicle for Theban policies, to gain for himself a recognised position in Greece; and the Fourth Sacred War of 340–338 ended with his defeating a combination of Athens and Thebes, and creating the League of Corinth as a means of dressing his control of Greece in familiar and (to all but the most ambitious states) unworrying clothes.

Since the late fifth century, and particularly after the King's Peace, there had been those who complained that the Greeks had been at their best when united against the Persians, and that they ought to unite against the Persians once more rather than quarrel amongst themselves. After forming the League of Corinth, Philip planned to undertake a war against Persia at the head of the Greeks. He was assassinated in 336, but his son Alexander the Great undertook that war and conquered the whole of the Persian empire. But Alexander died in 323, contemplating further conquests rather than consolidation, and leaving no obvious heir.

What we call the hellenistic period, between Alexander's death and the Roman conquest, began as Alexander's generals started competing, at first in theory on behalf of possible heirs, and with the aim of gaining possession of the whole empire, later to carve out separate dominions for themselves. In 306–305 the various claimants started calling themselves kings; by the 270's three major kingdoms had been established, the Antigonids in Macedon, the Ptolemies in Egypt and the Seleucids in the near east. The Antigonids and the Ptolemies were both interested in Greece, the Ptolemies and the Seleucids were both interested in Asia Minor and the Levant. The Greek cities formed leagues and manoeuvred between the kings very much as in the past they had formed leagues and manoeuvred between the leading cities; in Asia Minor smaller kingdoms emerged, in particular that of the Attalids of Pergamum. The eastern provinces of the empire had been abandoned by Seleucus to Chandragupta, king of the Indian peninsula, in exchange for 500 elephants.

The rulers were Greek and Macedonian, and the whole area of the successors' kingdoms came to form an extended Greek world. Greek cities of a kind were founded, especially in Asia; but of course outside Europe there were large bodies of non-European subject peoples. The Romans were prompted to take a military interest in Greece by the activities of the kings of Epirus towards the middle of the third century and by the alliance between Hannibal of Carthage and Philip V of Macedon at the end of the century; and it is because the Greek world had been extended in this way that, once they had become involved, the Romans did not stop until they had taken over all of these kingdoms, ending with Egypt in 30 after the death of Cleopatra VII. And, among other consequences of the development which began with Alexander's conquests, it is because the near east had become part of the Greek world and then part of the Roman world that Christianity was to spread westwards into that Graeco-Roman world rather than eastwards into Asia.

Bibliography

The following list gives publication details of books mentioned in the Note on Further Reading at the end of each chapter; *Festschriften* are listed under the name of the honorand, after books by the honorand; where a book has different publishers in the UK and the USA, the UK publisher is named first.

Adams, W. L. and Borza, E. N. (eds.), *Philip II, Alexander the Great and the Macedonian Heritage*. Washington, DC: University Press of America, 1982.

Atkinson, J. E. *Commentary on Q. Curtius Rufus' Historiae Alexandri Magni*. Amsterdam: Gieben, 1980/Hakkert, 1994– .

Badian, E. *Studies in Greek and Roman History*. Oxford: Blackwell/New York: Barnes and Noble, 1964.

Berve, H. *Das Alexanderreich auf prosopographischer Grundlage*, 2 vols. Munich: Beck, 1926.

——*Dion. Abh. Mainz* x 1956.

Bevan, E. *A History of Egypt under the Ptolemaic Dynasty*. London: Methuen, 1927.

Bodel, J. (ed.), *Epigraphic Evidence: Ancient History from Inscriptions*. London: Routledge, 2001.

Boegehold, A. L. and Scafuro, A. C. (eds.), *Athenian Identity and Civic Ideology*. Johns Hopkins University Press, 1994.

Borza, E. N. *In the Shadow of Olympus: The Emergence of Macedon*. Princeton University Press, 1990.

Bosworth, A. B. *A Historical Commentary on Arrian's History of Alexander*. Oxford University Press, 1980– .

——*Conquest and Empire*. Cambridge University Press, 1988.

——*From Arrian to Alexander*. Oxford University Press, 1988.

Bosworth, A. B. and Baynham, E. (eds.), *Alexander the Great in Fact and Fiction*. Oxford University Press, 2000.

Briant, P., trans. Daniels, P. T. *From Cyrus to Alexander: A History of the Persian Empire*. Winona Lake, Ind.: Eisenbrauns, 2002.

Bruce, I. A. F. *A Historical Commentary on the Hellenica Oxyrhynchia.* Cambridge University Press, 1967.

Brunt, P. A. *Studies in Greek History and Thought.* Oxford University Press, 1993.

Buck, R. J. *Boiotia and the Boiotian League, 432–371 BC.* University of Alberta Press, 1994.

Buckler, J. *Aegean Greece in the Fourth Century BC.* Leiden: Brill, 2003.

—— *Philip II and the Sacred War.* (*Mnem.* Supp. 109.) Leiden: Brill, 1989.

—— *The Theban Hegemony, 371–362 BC.* Harvard University Press, 1980.

Buckley, T. *Aspects of Greek History, 750–323 BC.* London: Routledge, 1996.

Bury, J. B., rev. Meiggs, R. *A History of Greece to the Death of Alexander the Great.* London: Macmillan/New York: St. Martin's, ⁴1975.

Cambridge Ancient History², vols. v/vi. Cambridge University Press, 1992/4.

Cargill, J. L. *The Second Athenian League: Empire or Free Alliance?* University of California Press, 1981.

Cartledge, P. A. *Agesilaos and the Crisis of Sparta.* London: Duckworth/Johns Hopkins University Press, ²2002.

—— *Sparta and Lakonia: A Regional History, 1300 to 362 BC.* London: Routledge, ²2002.

—— *Spartan Reflections.* London: Duckworth/University of California Press, 2001.

Caven, B. *Dionysius I, War-Lord of Sicily.* Yale University Press, 1990.

Cawkwell, G. *Philip of Macedon.* London: Faber, 1978.

—— *Thucydides and the Peloponnesian War.* London: Routledge, 1997.

—— *Georgica: Greek Studies in Honour of George Cawkwell.* BICS Supp. 58, 1991.

Connor, W. R. *The New Politicians of Fifth-Century Athens.* Princeton University Press, 1971; reissued with new preface Indianapolis: Hackett, 1992.

Cornford, F. M. *Thucydides Mythistoricus.* London: Arnold, 1907.

David, E. *Sparta Between Empire and Revolution (404–243 BC).* New York: Arno, 1981.

Davies, J. K. *Democracy and Classical Greece.* London: Fontana/Harvard University Press, ²1993.

De Ste. Croix, G. E. M. *The Origins of the Peloponnesian War.* London: Duckworth/Cornell University Press, 1972.

De Souza, P. and France, J. (eds.), *War and Peace in Ancient and Medieval History.* Cambridge University Press, forthcoming.

Dover, K. J. *The Greeks and their Legacy.* (*Collected Papers,* ii.) Oxford: Blackwell, 1988.

—— *'Owls to Athens': Essays on Classical Subjects Presented to Sir Kenneth Dover.* Oxford University Press, 1990.

Eder, W. (ed.), *Die athenische Demokratie im 4. Jahrhundert v. Chr.* Stuttgart: Steiner, 1995.

Ehrenberg, V. *From Solon to Socrates.* London: Methuen/New York: Barnes and Noble, ²1973.

—— *Ancient Society and Institutions: Studies Presented to Victor Ehrenberg.* Oxford: Blackwell, 1966/New York: Barnes and Noble, 1967.

Ellis, J. R. *Philip II and Macedonian Imperialism.* London: Thames and Hudson, 1976.

Ellis, W. M. *Alcibiades.* London: Routledge, 1989.

Engels, D. W. *Alexander the Great and the Logistics of the Macedonian Army.* University of California Press, 1978.

Figueira, T. J. *The Power of Money: Coinage and Politics in the Athenian Empire.* University of Pennsylvania Press, 1998.

Finley, M. I. *Ancient Sicily.* (Originally published as vol. i of 3-vol. *A History of Sicily,* with vols. ii–iii by D. M. Smith.) London: Chatto and Windus/Totowa, NJ: Rowman and Littlefield, ²1979.

——*Democracy Ancient and Modern.* London: Hogarth Press/Rutgers University Press, ²1985.

Fornara, C. W. *Translated Documents of Greece and Rome,* i. *Archaic Times to the End of the Peloponnesian War.* Cambridge University Press, ²1983.

Forrest, W. G. *A History of Sparta, 950–192 BC.* London: Duckworth, ²1980.

Fraser, P. M. *Cities of Alexander the Great.* Oxford University Press, 1996.

Freeman, E. A. *The History of Sicily from the Earliest Times,* 4 vols. Oxford University Press, 1891–4.

Frézouls, E. and Jacquemin, A. (eds.), *Les Relations internationales: Acres du Colloque de Strasbourg 15–17 juin 1993.* Paris: De Boccard for Université de Strasbourg, 1995.

Fuller, J. F. C. *The Generalship of Alexander the Great.* London: Eyre and Spottiswoode, 1958/Rutgers University Press, 1960.

Furley, W. D. *Andokides and the Herms. BICS* Supp. lxv 1996.

Gabrielsen, V. *Financing the Athenian Fleet: Public Taxation and Social Relations.* Johns Hopkins University Press, 1994.

——*Remuneration of State Officials in Fourth-Century BC Athens.* Odense University Press, 1981.

Gagarin, M. *Antiphon the Athenian.* University of Texas Press, 2002.

Garnsey, P. D. A. and Whittaker, C. R. (eds.), *Imperialism in the Ancient World.* Cambridge University Press, 1978.

Gomme, A. W. *Essays in Greek History and Literature.* Oxford: Blackwell, 1937.

——*More Essays in Greek History and Literature.* Oxford: Blackwell, 1962.

Gomme, A. W., Andrewes, A., and Dover, K. J. *A Historical Commentary on Thucydides,* 5 vols. Oxford University Press, 1945–81.

Green, P. *Alexander of Macedon.* Harmondsworth: Penguin, 1974; reissued University of California Press, 1991.

Griffith, G. T. (ed.), *Alexander the Great: The Main Problems.* Cambridge: Heffer/New York: Barnes and Noble, 1966.

Grote, G. *History of Greece,* 'new edition'. London: Murray, 1869/84 (12 vols.); 1888 (10 vols.).

Grundy, G. B. *Thucydides and the History of His Age.* London: Murray, 1911; reissued as vol. i, with a second volume added, Oxford: Blackwell, 1948.

Guthrie, W. K. C. *A History of Greek Philosophy,* 6 vols. Cambridge University Press, 1962–81.

Hamilton, C. D. *Agesilaus and the Failure of Spartan Hegemony.* Cornell University Press, 1991.

——*Sparta's Bitter Victories: Politics and Diplomacy in the Corinthian War.* Cornell University Press, 1979.

Hamilton, J. R. *Alexander the Great.* London: Hutchinson, 1973/University of Pittsburgh Press, 1974.

——*Plutarch, Alexander: A Commentary.* Oxford University Press, 1969.

Hammond, N. G. L. (ed.), *Atlas of the Greek and Roman World in Antiquity.* Park Ridge: Noyes, 1981.

——*Collected Studies,* 5 vols. Amsterdam: Hakkert, 1993–2001.

——*Studies in Greek History.* Oxford University Press, 1973.

—— *Ventures into Greek History* ⟨*Dedicated to Nicholas G. L. Hammond*⟩. Oxford University Press, 1994.

Hammond, N. G. L. and Griffith, G. T. *A History of Macedonia*, vol. ii. Oxford University Press, 1979.

Hansen, M. H. *Demography and Democracy: The Number of Athenian Citizens in the Fourth Century B.C.* Herning: Systime, 1986.

—— (ed.), *Introduction to an Inventory of Poleis.* (Copenhagen Polis Centre Acts 3.) Copenhagen: Royal Danish Academy, 1996.

—— *The Athenian Democracy in the Age of Demosthenes.* London: Duckworth (Bristol Classical Press), [2]1998/University of Oklahoma Press, 1999.

—— *The Athenian Ecclesia: A Collection of Articles 1976–83.* Copenhagen: Museum Tusculanum Press, 1983.

—— (ed.), *The Polis as an Urban Centre and as a Political Community.* (Copenhagen Polis Centre Acts 4.) Copenhagen: Royal Danish Academy, 1997.

—— *Three Studies in Athenian Demography.* Copenhagen: Royal Danish Academy, 1988.

—— *Polis and Politics: Studies in Ancient Greek History Presented to Mogens Herman Hansen.* Copenhagen: Museum Tusculanum Press, 2000.

Hanson, V. D. *Warfare and Agriculture in Classical Greece.* University of California Press, [2]1998.

Harding, P. *Translated Documents of Greece and Rome*, ii. *From the End of the Peloponnesian War to the Battle of Ipsus.* Cambridge University Press, 1985.

Harris, E. M. *Aeschines and Athenian Politics.* New York: Oxford University Press, 1995.

Hatzopoulos, M. B. and Loukopoulos, L. D. (eds.), *Philip of Macedon.* Athens: Ἐκδοτικὴ Ἀθηνῶν, 1980/London: Heinemann, 1981.

Heckel, W. *The Marshals of Alexander's Empire.* London: Routledge, 1992.

Heckel, W. and Tritle, L. A. (eds.), *Crossroads of History: The Age of Alexander.* Claremont, Calif.: Regina, 2003.

Hignett, C. *A History of the Athenian Constitution to the End of the Fifth Century BC.* Oxford University Press, 1952.

Hill, G. F., rev. Meiggs, R. and Andrewes, A. *Sources for Greek History, 478–431 BC.* Oxford University Press, 1951.

Hodkinson, S. *Property and Wealth in Classical Sparta.* London: Duckworth and Classical Press of Wales/Oakville, Conn.: David Brown, 2000.

Hodkinson, S. and Powell, A. (eds.), *Sparta: New Perspectives.* London: Duckworth and Classical Press of Wales, 1999.

Holladay, A. J. *Athens in the Fifth Century and Other Studies in Greek History.* Chicago: Ares, 2002.

Hornblower, S. *A Commentary on Thucydides.* Oxford University Press, 1991– .

—— *Mausolus.* Oxford University Press, 1982.

—— *The Greek World, 479–323 BC.* London: Routledge, [3]2002.

Hurwit, J. M. *The Acropolis in the Age of Pericles.* Cambridge University Press, 2004.

—— *The Athenian Acropolis.* Cambridge University Press, 1999.

Jones, T. B. *Studies in Honor of Tom B. Jones.* (*Alter Orient und Altes Testament* 203.) Kevelaer: Butzon and Bercker, 1979.

Kagan, D. *The Archidamian War.* Cornell University Press, 1974.

—— *The Fall of the Athenian Empire.* Cornell University Press, 1987.

—— *The Outbreak of the Peloponnesian War.* Cornell University Press, 1969.

—— *The Peace of Nicias and the Sicilian Expedition.* Cornell University Press, 1981.

Kallet, L. *Money and the Corrosion of Power in Thucydides: The Sicilian Expedition and its Aftermath.* University of California Press, 2001.

Kallet-Marx, L. *Money, Expense and Naval Power in Thucydides' History, 1–5. 24.* University of California Press, 1993.

Kennell, N. M. *The Gymnasium of Virtue: Education and Culture in Ancient Sparta.* University of North Carolina Press, 1995.

Kraay, C. M. *Archaic and Classical Greek Coins.* London: Methuen/University of California Press, 1976.

Krentz, P. *The Thirty at Athens.* Cornell University Press, 1982.

Lane Fox, R. *Alexander the Great.* London: Allen Lane with Longman/New York: Dial, 1973.

Larsen, J. A. O. *Greek Federal States: Their Institutions and History.* Oxford University Press, 1968.

——*Representative Government in Greek and Roman History.* (Sather Lectures 28.) University of California Press, 1955.

Lazaridis, D. *Amphipolis.* Athens: Archaeological Receipts Fund, 1997.

Lazenby, J. F. *The Peloponnesian War: A Military Study.* London: Routledge, 2004.

——*The Spartan Army.* Warminster: Aris and Phillips/Chicago: Bolchazy-Carducci, 1985.

Lenardon, R. J. *The Saga of Themistocles.* London: Thames and Hudson, 1978.

Lewis, D. M. *Selected Papers in Greek and Near Eastern History.* Cambridge University Press, 1997.

——*Sparta and Persia.* Leiden: Brill, 1977.

——*Ritual, Finance, Politics: Athenian Democratic Accounts Presented to David Lewis.* Oxford University Press, 1994.

Loomis, W. T. *The Spartan War Fund.* (*Hist.* Einzelschriften 74.) Stuttgart: Steiner, 1992.

Luraghi, N. and Alcock, S. E. (eds.), *Helots and Their Masters in Lakonia and Messenia: Histories, Ideologies, Structures.* Washington, DC: Center for Hellenic Studies, 2003.

MacDowell, D. M. *Aristophanes and Athens.* Oxford University Press, 1995.

——*Law, Rhetoric and Comedy in Classical Athens: Essays in Honour of Douglas M. MacDowell.* Swansea: Classical Press of Wales, 2004.

McGregor, M. F. *The Athenians and Their Empire.* University of British Columbia Press, 1987.

——*Classical Contributions: Studies in Honour of Malcolm Francis McGregor.* Locust Valley, NY: Augustin, 1981.

McKechnie, P. R. and Kern, S. J. *Hellenica Oxyrhynchia, Edited with Translation and Commentary.* Warminster: Aris and Phillips, 1988.

Mark, I. S. *The Sanctuary of Athena Nike in Athens: Architectural Stages and Chronology.* *Hesp.* Supp. 26, 1993.

Marsden, E. W. *Greek and Roman Artillery,* i. *Historical Development.* Oxford University Press, 1969.

Marshall, F. H. *The Second Athenian Confederacy.* Cambridge University Press, 1905.

Matthaiou, A. P. (ed.), Ἀττικαὶ Ἐπιγραφαί· συμπόσιον εἰς μνήμην *Adolf Wilhelm (1864–1950).* Athens: Ἑλληνικὴ Ἐπιγραφικὴ Ἑταιρεία, 2004.

Mattingly, H. B. *The Athenian Empire Restored.* University of Michigan Press, 1996.

Meiggs, R. *The Athenian Empire.* Oxford University Press, 1972 (corr. 1975).

Meiggs, R. and Lewis, D. M. *A Selection of Greek Historical Inscriptions to the End of the Fifth Century* BC. Oxford University Press, ᵣ1988.

Meritt, B. D. *Φόρος: Tribute to Benjamin Dean Meritt.* Locust Valley, NJ: Augustin, 1974.

Meritt, B. D., Wade-Gery, H. T., and McGregor, M. F. *The Athenian Tribute Lists*, 4 vols. i Harvard University Press; ii–iv Princeton: American School of Classical Studies at Athens, 1939–53.

Mertens, D. *Der Tempel von Segesta und die dorische Tempelbaukunst des griechischen Westens in klassischer Zeit.* Mainz: von Zabern, 1984.

Meyer, E. *Theopomps Hellenika.* Halle: Niemeyer, 1909.

Michell, H. *Sparta.* Cambridge University Press, 1952.

Miller, M. C. *Athens and Persia in the Fifth Century BC.* Cambridge University Press, 1997.

Murray, G. *Aristophanes: A Study.* Oxford University Press, 1933.

Natoli, A. F. *The Letter of Speusippus to Philip II: Introduction, Text, Translation and Commentary.* (*Hist.* Einzelschriften 176.) Stuttgart: Steiner, 2004.

Nielsen, T. H. *Arkadia and Its Poleis in the Archaic and Classical Periods.* Göttingen: Vandenhoeck and Ruprecht, 2002.

—— (ed.), *Even More Studies in the Ancient Greek Polis.* (Copenhagen Polis Centre Papers 6; *Hist.* Einzelschriften 162.) Stuttgart: Steiner, 2002.

Nielsen, T. H. and Roy, J. (eds.), *Defining Ancient Arkadia.* (Copenhagen Polis Centre Acts 6.) Copenhagen: Royal Danish Academy, 1999.

Osborne, M. J. *Naturalization in Athens*, 3 vols. in 4. Brussels: Royal Academy of Belgium, 1981–3.

Osborne, R. *The Athenian Empire.* LACTOR Series i, ⁴2000.

Patterson, C. *Pericles' Citizenship Law of 451–50 BC.* New York: Arno, 1981.

Pearson, L. *Selected Papers.* Chicago: Scholars Press, 1983.

—— *The Lost Historians of Alexander the Great.* New York: American Philological Association, 1960.

Pelling, C. *Literary Texts and the Greek Historian.* London: Routledge, 2000.

Pendrick, G. J. *Antiphon, of Athens.* Cambridge University Press, 2002.

Perlman, S. (ed.), *Philip and Athens.* Heffer/New York: Barnes and Noble, 1973.

Piérart, M. (ed.), *Aristote et Athènes/Aristoteles and Athens.* Paris: De Boccard for Université de Fribourg, Séminaire d'Histoire Ancienne, 1993.

Podlecki, A. J. *The Political Background of Aeschylean Tragedy.* University of Michigan Press, 1966.

Powell, A. *Athens and Sparta.* London: Routledge, ²2001.

—— (ed.), *Classical Sparta: Techniques Behind Her Success.* London: Routledge/University of Oklahoma Press, 1989.

Powell, A. and Hodkinson, S. (eds.), *Sparta: Beyond the Mirage.* London: Classical Press of Wales and Duckworth, 2002.

—— *The Shadow of Sparta.* London: Routledge for Classical Press of Wales, 1994.

Pritchett, W. K. *Studies in Ancient Greek Topography*, 8 vols. i–vi (University of California Publications: Classical Studies) University of California Press, 1965–89; vii–viii Amsterdam: Gieben, 1991–2.

Raubitschek, A. E. *The School of Hellas.* New York: Oxford University Press, 1991.

Reinmuth, O. W. *The Ephebic Inscriptions of the Fourth Century BC.* (*Mnem.* Supp. 14.) Leiden: Brill, 1971.

Rhodes, P. J. *The Athenian Boule.* Oxford University Press, 1972; reissued with additions and corrections, 1985.

—— *The Athenian Empire. G&R New Surveys* 17 ²1993.

——(ed.), *Athenian Democracy*. Edinburgh University Press/New York: Oxford University Press, 2004.

——*A Commentary on the Aristotelian Athenaion Politeia*. Oxford University Press, 1981; reissued with addenda 1993.

——*Thucydides: History, II*. Warminster: Aris and Phillips, 1988.

——*Thucydides: History, III*. Warminster: Aris and Phillips, 1994.

——*'What Alcibiades Did or What Happened to Him'*. (Inaugural Lecture.) University of Durham, 1985.

Rhodes, P. J. and Osborne, R. *Greek Historical Inscriptions, 404–323 BC*. Oxford University Press, 2003.

Rich, J. and Shipley, G. (eds.), *War and Society in the Greek World*. London: Routledge, 1993.

Robinson, C. A., Jr. *The History of Alexander the Great*, 2 vols. Providence: Brown University, 1953–63.

Robinson, E. W. (ed.), *Ancient Greek Democracy*. Oxford: Blackwell, 2003.

Roebuck, C. *Economy and Society in the Early Greek World*. Chicago: Ares, 1979.

Roisman, J. (ed.), *Brill's Companion to Alexander the Great*. Leiden: Brill, 2003.

——*The General Demosthenes and His Use of Military Surprise*. (*Hist.* Einzelschriften 78.) Stuttgart: Steiner, 1993.

Ryder, T. T. B. *Koine Eirene*. Oxford University Press for University of Hull, 1965.

Salmon, J. B. *Pnyx and Parthenon: Public Building in Attica*. Oxford University Press, forthcoming.

Samons, L. J., II, *Empire of the Owl: Athenian Imperial Finance*. (*Hist.* Einzelschriften 142.) Stuttgart: Steiner, 2000.

Schachter, A. (ed.), *Essays in the Topography, History and Culture of Boiotia*. (*Teiresias* Supp. 3.) Montreal: Department of Classics, McGill University, 1990.

Sealey, R. *A History of the Greek City States, ca. 700–338 BC*. University of California Press, 1976.

——*Demosthenes and His Time: A Study in Defeat*. New York: Oxford University Press, 1993.

——*Essays in Greek Politics*. New York: Manyland, 1967.

Siewert, P. (ed.), *Ostrakismos-Testimonien I*. (*Hist.* Einzelschriften 155.) Stuttgart: Steiner, 2002.

Sinclair, R. K. *Democracy and Participation in Athens*. Cambridge University Press, 1988.

Sommerstein, A. H. *Aeschylean Tragedy*. Bari: Levante, 1996.

Sprawski, S. *Jason of Pherae*. Kraków: Jagiellonian University Press, 1999.

Stevens, C. E. *The Ancient Historian and His Materials: Essays in Honour of C. E. Stevens*. Farnborough: Gregg International, 1975.

Stockton, D. *The Classical Athenian Democracy*. Oxford University Press, 1990.

Stone, I. F. *The Trial of Socrates*. Boston: Little, Brown, 1988.

Stoneman, R. *Alexander the Great*. (Lancaster Pamphlets.) London: Routledge, ²2004.

——*The Greek Alexander Romance*. Harmondsworth: Penguin, 1991.

Storey, I. C. *Eupolis, Poet of Old Comedy*. Oxford University Press, 2003.

Strauss, B. S. *Athens After the Peloponnesian War: Class, Faction and Policy 403–386 BC*. London: Croom Helm, 1986/Cornell University Press, 1987.

Stylianou, P. J. *A Historical Commentary on Diodorus Siculus, Book 15*. Oxford University Press, 1998.

Talbert, R. J. A. (ed.), *Barrington Atlas of the Greek and Roman World*. Princeton University Press, 2000.

——*Timoleon and the Revival of Greek Sicily, 344–317 BC.* Cambridge University Press, 1975.

Tarn, W. W. *Alexander the Great*, 2 vols. Cambridge University Press, 1948.

Thompson, H. A. and Wycherley, R. E. *The Agora of Athens.* (The Athenian Agora, xiv.) Princeton: American School of Classical Studies at Athens, 1972.

Thomsen, R. *The Origin of Ostracism.* Copenhagen: Gyldendal, 1972.

Travlos, J. *Pictorial Dictionary of Ancient Athens.* London: Thames and Hudson/New York: Praeger for German Archaeological Institute, 1971.

Tritle, L. A. *Phocion the Good.* London: Croom Helm, 1988.

——(ed.), *The Greek World in the Fourth Century.* London: Routledge, 1997.

Tuplin, C. (ed.), *Xenophon and His World: Papers from a Conference Held in Liverpool in July 1999.* (*Hist.* Einzelschriften 172.) Stuttgart: Steiner, 2004.

Underhill, G. E. *A Commentary . . . on the Hellenica of Xenophon.* Oxford University Press, 1900.

Wade-Gery, H. T. *Essays in Greek History.* Oxford: Blackwell, 1958.

Walbank, M. B. *Athenian Proxenies of the Fifth Century BC.* Toronto and Sarasota: Stevens, 1978.

Weiskopf, M. J. *The So-Called 'Great Satraps' Revolt', 366–360 BC.* (*Hist.* Einzelschriften 63.) Stuttgart: Steiner, 1989.

Westlake, H. D. *Essays on the Greek Historians and Greek History.* Manchester University Press/New York: Barnes and Noble, 1969.

——*Studies in Thucydides and Greek History.* Bristol: Bristol Classical Press, 1989.

——*Thessaly in the Fourth Century BC.* London: Methuen, 1935.

——*Timoleon and His Relations with Tyrants.* Manchester University Press, 1952.

Whitby, M. (ed.), *Sparta.* Edinburgh University Press, 2002.

Wilson, J. B. *Pylos 425 BC.* Warminster: Aris and Phillips, 1979.

Woodhead, A. G. *The Study of Greek Inscriptions.* Cambridge University Press, ²1981.

Yardley, J. C. and Heckel, W. *Justin, Epitome of the Philippic History of Pompeius Trogus*, i. *Books 11–12: Alexander the Great.* (Clarendon Ancient History Series). Oxford University Press, 1997.

Index

Athens and Sparta are mentioned throughout this book: under their names topics are indexed but not events or individuals. Many entries are arranged chronologically, and for this purpose the fourth century ('C4') is treated as beginning in 404.

Abdera: in Second Athenian League
   233–4
Abydus: in Peloponnesian War   145
Acarnania: in Peloponnesian War   102–4
Achaea
   390's   211
   360's   199–200, 219–20, 254
Acragas
   tyrants early C5   72–5
   mid C5   77–8
   and Carthage late C5   275–9
Ada of Caria: daughter of Hecatomnos
   323–4, 367–8
Aegina
   in First Peloponnesian War   42–3
   430's   82, 84, 86–8
   in Peloponnesian War   101–2, 108, 110
Aegospotami: battle in 405   151
Aeschines of Athens   307–8, 309–13, 314,
   317–18, 336–40, 342; cf. 201, 295
Aeschylus of Athens, tragedian
   in Athens   39–40
   in Sicily   75
   in Aristophanes' *Frogs*   169–70
Aetna
   at Catana   75–6
   at Inessa   77, 279, 280

Aetolia
   in Peloponnesian War   97, 104
   C4   252
Agathocles, tyrant of Syracuse   290,
   292
Agesilaus II, king of Sparta   205–23;
   cf. 190–4, 200, 247, 250, 344
Agesipolis I, king of Sparta   210, 212–13
Agis II, king of Sparta
   in 418   127–9
   at Decelea   140–1, 143, 151–2, 163
   Elean war and death   205
Agis III, king of Sparta   345, 354
Agyrrhius of Athens   228, 262, 266, 268
Alcibiades of Athens
   early career   122, 126–30, 132, 155–7
   Sicilian expedition   132–5, 139
   religious scandals   133–4, 157–9
   later career   143–51, 160–1, 164–8
   in Aristophanes   169–70
Alexander I, king of Macedon   297
Alexander II, king of Macedon   253
Alexander III (the Great), king of Macedon
   347–83; cf. 189–90, 318, 319, 320–1,
   339–44
Alexander, king of Molossis   292–3, 314,
   321

Alexander, tyrant of Pherae 253–5;
cf. 199, 236, 238, 300
Alexandria: cities founded by Alexander the
Great 353, 355, 369
Alyzia: battle in 375 196, 215
Ambracia
in Peloponnesian War 102–4
garrisoned by Philip 202
Ammon, oracle of
and Lysander 205
and Alexander the Great 353, 378, 380
Amorges, Persian rebel 113, 143–4
Amorgus: in Second Athenian League
240
Amphipolis
Nine Ways 19–20
Athenian colony 69
in Peloponnesian War 111–12, 114, 183
360's 197–200, 236–7
in reign of Philip 236–9, 241, 299–300,
309, 311, 314
Amyntas III, king of Macedon 251, 297
Amyntas of Macedon, son of Perdiccas III
297, 321, 349
Anaxagoras of Clazomenae, philosopher
and associate of Pericles 66–7
Anaxilas, tyrant of Rhegium 72–3, 75–6
Andocides of Athens
on Peace of Epilycus 113–14, 143
and religious scandals of 415 158–9,
191, 267
on democratic restoration in 410 165
and peace negotiations of 392/1 191,
193, 268
speech *Against Alcibiades* attributed to
156–7
Andros: in second Athenian League 240
Androtion of Athens: governor of Arcesine
240
Antalcidas of Sparta
in 392 192, 210
in Hellespont in 387 211
Peace of, in 387/6 193–4, 211–12,
cf. 153, 185, 186, 196, 228–9, 247
suicide 199
Antipater of Macedon 311, 321, 344,
349, 351, 369, 373, 380
Antiphon of Athens: in 411 162–5
Arcadia
C6 4–5
470's–460's 22–5

in Peloponnesian War 98
C4 198–200, 217–21, 235, 237,
253–5
see also Mantinea, Megalopolis, Tegea
Archelaus, king of Macedon 131, 250,
297
Archidamus II, king of Sparta 26, 29,
85–6, 91, 101
Archidamus III, king of Sparta 344–5;
cf. 223, 308
Argaeus: claimant to throne of Macedon
299
Arginusae Islands: battle in 406 150, 167
Argos
470's–460's 22–5
in First Peloponnesian War 41, 42, 44,
51
in Archidamian War 95, 97, 99, 109,
114
later in Peloponnesian War 125–30,
133, 141, 156
early C4 192–4, 210–12
skytalismos in 370/69 217
360's 220
Ariobarzanes, satrap of Dascylium 222–4;
cf. 198, 218, 236–7, 254
Aristides of Athens 17, 31, 33–4
Aristophanes of Athens: comedian 84–5,
87, 118–19, 132, 159, 169–70, 180–1,
228, 267
Aristophon of Athens 270–1, 311, 336–7
Aristotle of Stagira, philosopher: *Athenian
Constitution* attributed to 8, 120,
161–5, 257–60
Arrian: historian 348
Artabazus, satrap of Dascylium 223–4,
239, 304, 325, 355
Artaxerxes I, King of Persia 34–5
Artaxerxes II, King of Persia 221–4;
cf. 191, 205
Artaxerxes III, King of Persia 323–6;
cf. 224
Artaxerxes IV, King of Persia 326
Arthmius of Zelea 43
Arybbas, king of Molossis 300, 314
Aspasia of Miletus: mistress of Pericles 66
Astyochus of Sparta: naval commander
144–5
Athenian League, Second
foundation and history 228–42; cf. 153,
185, 186, 195–6, 198, 248

Athenian League, Second (cont'd)
  introduction of *syntaxeis* 232–3
  after Leuctra 235–8; cf. 252
  Social War 239–40; cf. 200–1, 232
  Peace of Philocrates 310–11
  dissolved after Chaeronea 319; cf. 202
Athens
  external affairs 14–21, 41–52, 67–70,
    172–87, 226–42
  internal affairs 31–40, 54–67, 116–23,
    155–70, 257–71, 328–44
  buildings
    on acropolis 47, 50, 62–5, 83, 122–3,
      159–60, 170, 178
    in agora 38, 123, 170, 265
    long walls 41–2, 65, 151
    on pnyx 164, 170, 265, 341
  institutions
    archons 54–5, 58, 59–60
    Areopagus 35–40, 59–60, 258,
      339–40, 343
    assembly 57–8, 261–3
    council of five hundred 37–8, 56,
      57–8, 60, 162, 165, 166, 168
    epheboi 56–7, 341
    finance 45, 59, 68, 83, 91–4, 263,
      330–4
    Four Hundred 160–5; cf. 144–6
    generals 61, 335
    lawcourts 36–7, 55–6, 59–60, 260,
      262–3, 329, 335–6
    laws and decrees 166, 258, 260–2
    ostracism 33, 34, 35, 62, 65–6, 156–7,
      266
    probouloi 160
    proedroi 263–4
    prytaneis 37–8, 57, 263–4
    secretaries 263–4
    stipends 55–6, 162, 164, 262–3,
      329
    Thirty 257–60; cf. 204–5
  plague 430–427/6 98, 112–13, 122
  population of citizens and others 55–7,
    153, 260, 263
  see also Piraeus
Attalus of Macedon 321, 349, 351
Aulis: Agesilaus' attempted sacrifice at
    208–9

Babylon 354
Bagoas: grand vizier of Persia 325–6

Boeotia
  in First Peloponnesian War 44–5, 51–2
  in Peloponnesian War 97, 109, 110,
    125–7, 140, 142, 146
  imitation by Athenian oligarchs in 411
    162
  early C4 244–8; cf. 192–4, 205, 208–12
  370's–360's 248–56; cf. 196–7, 200, 216
  settlements in 338/7 and 335 318–19,
    351
  see also Orchomenus, Plataea, Thebes
Boeotius of Sparta: possible treaty of 149,
    185, 191
Bosporan kingdom (Crimea) 70
Brasidas of Sparta: army commander 98,
    103, 108, 110, 111–12, 174, 182–3,
    377–8
Byzantium
  470's 16, 19, 20, 26–7
  supports Samos 440–439 67
  in Peloponnesian War 145, 148, 151
  in Second Athenian League 229–32,
    237, 239, 254
  ally of Thebes 252, 304
  besieged by Philip 316

Callias of Athens: financial decrees of 83,
    91–2
Callias of Athens: possible Peace of 15,
    47–8, 68, 173, 185, 186, 226
Callicratidas of Sparta 150
Callippus of Athens: tyrant of Syracuse
    288–9
Callisthenes of Olynthus: under Alexander
    the Great 348, 356, 371, 377, 380
Callistratus of Athens 268–71; cf. 196–7,
    234–5, 236, 249
Caria: Persian satrapy C4 323–5; cf. 222
Carthage
  early interest in Sicily 71–3, 75
  in Peloponnesian War 122, 132, 133,
    135, 150
  in Sicily after 413 275–95
  Carthaginian *proxenos* of Boeotians 254
Carystus: in Delian League 19–20
catapults 280, 316, 365
Ceos: in Second Athenian League 199,
    237–8
Cephalus of Athens 267–9
Cersebleptes: Thracian ruler 238, 240–1,
    301, 304, 311, 315

Chabrias of Athens 200, 210, 214, 222–3, 227, 229, 233–4, 236–7, 239, 268–71
Chaeronea
  in First Peloponnesian War 51
  in Peloponnesian War 110
  battle in 338 318; cf. 201, 242, 249
Chalcidians see Olynthus
Chalcis
  c.446 51–2
  c.342 241, 315
Chares of Athens 237–9, 270–1, 301, 316, 318, 325, 336
Charidemus of Oreus, later of Athens 306, 318, 338–9, 351
Chersonese: C4 197–9, 236–7, 240–1, 301, 313, 315–16
Chios
  in Delian League 67, 173
  in Peloponnesian War 94, 95, 108, 109–10, 143–5, 174, 175
  in second Athenian League 229–32; cf. 195, 237, 239, 254
  and Mausolus 239, 323
  and Alexander the Great 352
Cimon of Athens 19–20, 28, 32–9, 44–5, 47, 55–6, 173
Cinadon of Sparta 206
Clazomenae: and Peace of Antalcidas 193, 228
Clearchus of Sparta 145, 204–5
Cleinias of Athens: tribute decree 50, 93, 174
Cleombrotus I, king of Sparta 213–16; cf. 229, 248–9, 251–2
Cleomenes II, king of Sparta 216, 344
Cleon of Athens 46, 67, 97, 105, 108–9, 112, 118–19, 120–1, 179–81
Cleonymus of Athens 92, 121, 159, 174
Cleophon of Athens 148, 151, 156, 166–8, 169
Cleruchies
  in Delian League 50–1, 176
  in Second Athenian League 199, 230–1; see also Chersonese, Potidaea, Samos
Clitus of Macedon: under Alexander 351–2, 356, 361, 371
Cnidus: battle in 394 192, 209, 210, 227
Coenus of Macedon: under Alexander 369–72; cf. 356, 364–5

coinage
  in Delian League 42, 50, 174, 176–7
  in west C5 76, 79
  in Athens late C5 150
  ΣΥΝ coinage 204–5
  in Sparta C4 206
  of Hecatomnos 323
  in west C4 237, 275–6, 280, 291
  of Philip 300
Conon of Athens
  in Peloponnesian War 147, 148, 150–1, 167–8
  C4 192, 207–10, 221–2, 226–7, 234, 268, 269
Corcyra
  430's 82–4, 87–8, 101
  in Peloponnesian War 95, 98, 103, 104–5
  in Second Athenian League 196, 215, 234–5, 238
Corinth
  in First Peloponnesian War 41–3
  430's 82–5, 87–8, 101
  in Archidamian War 97–8, 102–3
  later in Peloponnesian War 124–7, 130, 135, 138, 140, 142
  early C4 192–4, 205, 208–12, 227
  360's 199, 219–20, 237, 254
  and Timoleon's liberation of Syracuse 289–91
  garrisoned by Philip 202, 319
Corinth, League of 319–20; cf. 201–2, 242, 349, 354, 360, 367, 373, 374, 381
Corinthian War 209–11; cf. 185, 192, 227
Coronea
  battle in 447/6 51–2
  battle in 394 210
Craterus of Macedon: under Alexander 356–7, 364–5, 371–3
Crimisus, River: battle in 341 291
Critias of Athens 166, 167, 258–9
Croton
  C5 79–80
  C4 282–3, 285, 292
Curtius (Q. Curtius Rufus): historian 347–8
Cynossema: battle in 411 145
Cyprus
  in 478 16

Cyprus (cont'd)
  mid C5 43, 45, 47, 173
  C4 221–2; cf. 193, 325
Cyrus of Persia: son of Darius II 149–50,
  152, 191, 205, 221
Cythera: in Peloponnesian War 97, 110,
  141, 142, 152
Cyzicus: battle in 410 147–8, 165

Darius II, King of Persia 114, 148–50
Darius III, King of Persia 326, 351–4,
  362–4
Decelea: in Peloponnesian War 93, 135,
  140–1, 143, 151–2, 161, 163, 165
Delian League 14–21, 41–52, 67–70,
  172–87; cf. 25–6, 64, 91–4, 152, 158,
  204
Delium: battle in 424/3 95, 110
Delos
  in Delian League 18, 19, 45, 64, 173,
    177
  in Peloponnesian War 109, 156, 177
  C4 152, 227–8, 234, 319, 340
Delphi
  mid C5 44, 51, 79
  in Peloponnesian War 94
  and Jason of Pherae 252
  and Thebes 360's 201, 254
  Third Sacred War 302–5, 307–13; cf.
    201, 255
  Fourth Sacred War 317–18; cf. 201,
    242
  and Alexander the Great 349
  dedications
    serpent column 27
    Polyzelus' charioteer 74
    navarchs dedication 152
    dancing girls column 234
    360's 254–5
Demades of Athens 338–9, 342–4; cf.
  296, 318, 380
Demarete, daughter of Theron of Acragas
  72, 74, 76
democracy
  in Asia Minor under Alexander the Great
    367
  in Athens under Ephialtes 38–40; cf. 54
  in Athens second half C5 56–62
  in Athens 420's 126–7
  in Athens 415 157–9
  in Athens and Samos 411–410 143–6

  in Athens after Thirty 260–5
  in Athens in time of Demosthenes
    328–36, 337, 339–40
  in Boeotia after 379 248–9
  in Delian League 38, 46–7, 50, 175,
    179, 181–2, 184, 187
  in Peloponnese after Leuctra 217, 254
  in Syracuse during Peloponnesian War
    133–5
  in Syracuse under Timoleon 290–1
  polarisation of Greek world C5 123,
    125, 184, 187, 384
Demosthenes of Athens: military
  commander C5 98, 104, 109, 110,
    121, 138–40
Demosthenes of Athens: politician C4
  241–2, 301–2, 306–8, 309–13, 313–22,
    332, 334, 340–4; cf. 201, 295, 349,
    380
Dercylidas of Sparta 145, 192, 207, 210
Dinarchus of Corinth: orator in Athens
  296, 343
Diocles of Syracuse 274–6
Diodorus Siculus
  on Pentecontaetia 14–15
  on Sicily C4 72, 139
  contrasted with Xenophon on late
    C4–early C5 146–7, 167, 190–1, 257
  on Sicily C4 273–4
  on Philip 295
  on Alexander the Great 347–8
Dion of Syracuse 286–9
Dionysius I, tyrant of Syracuse 276–86;
  cf. 209, 215, 218, 227, 228, 232, 236
Dionysius II, tyrant of Syracuse 286–90
divine and heroic honours for mortals
  Hagnon and Brasidas 112, 377–8
  Lysander 152, 378
  rejected by Agesilaus 206, 378
  Dion 288, 378
  Philip 378
  Alexander and Hephaestion 377–81
drama, Athenian 39–40, 66, 117–19, 159,
  160, 168–70
Ducetius, Sicel leader 77–8

Egesta
  Elyman city 71
  mid C5 78
  date of alliance with Athens 45, 46, 68,
    78, 132

in Peloponnesian War   132–4
late C5–C4   275, 281
Egypt
  C5   43, 45, 56, 173
  rebellions against Persia C4   221–3,
    325; cf. 196, 200, 313
  and Alexander   353, 368
Eïon
  470's   19–20, 173
  in Peloponnesian War   112
Eleusinian Mysteries
  and Delian League   178
  scandal in 415   133–4, 139, 157–9,
    160
Elis
  470's–460's   22–5
  in Peloponnesian War   125–7
  C4   197, 198, 200, 205, 217, 219–20,
    226
Embata: battle in 355   239
Endius of Sparta   126, 143–4, 148
Epaminondas of Thebes   249–56; cf. 197,
    199, 218–21, 237
Ephesus
  in Delian League   178
  in Peloponnesian War   149–50
Ephialtes of Athens   35–40; cf. 28
Ephorus: historian   146–7, 190–1, 257,
    274, 294
Epidamnus: disputed between Corinth and
    Corcyra   82
Epidaurus
  cult of Asclepius   122
  in Peloponnesian War   108, 127–30
Epilycus, Peace of   113–14
Epitadeus of Sparta: alleged *rhetra* of
    206–7
Eretria
  in Delian League   51–2
  C4   241, 305–6, 315
Erythrae
  in Delian League   46–7, 173, 175, 178
  in Peloponnesian War   143
  Peace of Antalcidas   193, 228
  and Mausolus   239, 323–4
Etruscans   75, 284
Euboea
  c.446   51–2
  in Peloponnesian War   96, 143, 146, 164
  in Corinthian War   210
  in 370's–360's   233, 252

in time of Philip   239, 241–2, 305–7,
    315
  see also Carystus, Chalcis, Eretria,
    Histiaea
Eubulus of Athens   332–4, 336–7,
    cf. 306–8, 309–11, 314, 341
Eumenes of Cardia   349, 374
Eupolis of Athens: comedian   168–9, 181
Euripides of Athens: tragedian   117–18,
    132, 159, 169–70
Eurymedon, River: battle c.469   19–20
Evagoras, ruler of Salamis
  in Peloponnesian War   149, 151, 168,
    221
  C4   221–2; cf. 208–9, 211, 212, 227

Gaugamela: battle in 331   354, 361, 363–4
Gaza: siege in 332   353, 365–6
Gedrosia: Alexander's journey in 325   356
Gela
  tyrants CC6–5   72–6
  congress in 424   105
  late C5   275–9
Gelon, tyrant of Gela and Syracuse   72–3
Granicus, River: battle in 334   351–2, 363
Gylippus of Sparta   135–40; cf. 152, 274

Hagnon of Athens   67, 69, 112, 160, 162
Haliartus: battle in 395   192, 247
Halicarnassus: siege in 334   352, 365
Halonnesus: 340's   314, 316; cf. 241
Halus: in 346   310–12
Halycus, River: limit of Carthaginian power
    in Sicily   285, 292
Harpalus of Macedon   342–3, 354, 357,
    372–3
Hecatomnos, satrap of Caria   222, 323
Hegesippus of Athens   311, 313–14, 337
Hellanicus of Mytilene: historian   14, 28
Hellenica Oxyrhynchia   12, 146–7, 190
Hellespont
  in Delian League   19–20
  in Peloponnesian War   143–51
  in 387   193, 211
  in time of Philip   201, 296, 301, 315–16
  see also Chersonese
Hephaestion of Macedon: under Alexander
    357, 361, 370–1, 373–4, 380, 381
Heraclea, near Thermopylae   111, 209–10,
    250, 252
Heraclides of Syracuse   287–8

Hermocrates of Syracuse   105, 133, 135,
    138–9, 144–5, 274–7
Hicetas, tyrant of Leontini   289–92
Hieron, tyrant of Syracuse   72–6
Himera
    in 480   72
    in 409   275, 279
Hipparinus, tyrant of Syracuse   289
Histiaea (Oreus)
    in Delian League   51–2
    early C4   213, 214, 233, 250–1
    340's   241, 315
Hydaspes, River: battle in 326   356,
    364–5, 366
Hyperbolus of Athens   105, 121–2, 155–7,
    163
Hyperides of Athens   334, 337–40, 343–4;
    cf. 296, 314, 316, 318, 380
Hyphasis, River: mutiny in 326   356,
    371–2

Illyrians: and Macedon   297–300, 313,
    349, 366
Imbros: C4   185, 192–3, 212, 227–8, 231,
    319
inscriptions: problems of dating   45–6
Iphicrates of Athens   210–11, 215, 227,
    228, 234–5, 236–7, 239, 268–71
Ismenias of Thebes   213, 247–8
Isocrates of Athens   185–6, 191, 199, 220,
    240, 254, 295–6, 312–13, 339–40,
    376
Issus: battle in 333   352–3, 362–3
Italy
    C5   72, 79–80
    C4   282–3, 284–5, 292–3

Jason, tyrant of Pherae   250–2; cf. 153,
    215, 234
Justin: historian   257, 294, 348

King's Peace   see Antalcidas, Peace of

Lamachus of Athens   132–5
Lechaeum: in Corinthian War   210–11
Lemnos: C4   185, 192–3, 212, 227–8,
    231, 319
Leontiades of Thebes   213, 247–8
Leontini
    in Peloponnesian War   69, 79, 83–4,
        103, 106, 132

late C5–C4   277–9, 281, 288, 289,
    291–2
Leotychidas II, king of Sparta   16, 25–6
Leotychidas of Sparta: putative son of Agis
    II   205
Lepreum: in Peloponnesian War   98–9,
    125, 126–7
Lesbos
    in Delian League   19, 67, 173
    in Peloponnesian War   95, 108–9, 143,
        145
    in Second Athenian League   232–3
    and Alexander   352
    see also Methymna, Mytilene
Leuctra: battle in 371   216, 251–2; cf. 29,
    197, 235
Lichas of Sparta   144–5
literacy   3, 10, 16, 27, 205, 265
Locri (in Italy)   280, 283, 289, 292
Locris: C4   209, 252
Lycophron, tyrant of Pherae   250
Lycurgus of Athens   333–4, 337–9, 341–2;
    cf. 296, 329, 380
Lysander of Sparta
    in Peloponnesian War   149–52, 168
    C4   204–5, 207–8, 210; cf. 192, 247,
        258–9

Macedon
    C5–early C4   84, 111, 130–1, 234–5,
        296–7
    Philip II   294–326; cf. 189, 200–2,
        336–40
    Alexander III (the Great)   347–82;
        cf. 190–1, 300, 318, 320–1
Mantinea
    early C5   22–5
    in Peloponnesian War   95, 125–30, 133,
        152, 156
    in 385   194, 195, 212, 229, 247
    360's   198–200, 217–21, 255
Mausolus, satrap of Caria   323–4; cf. 223,
    239
Mazaeus of Persia   354, 364, 368
Megalopolis   218; cf. 198, 200, 224, 253,
    255, 305, 345, 354
Megara
    in First Peloponnesian War   41–3,
        51–2
    Athenian sanctions   82, 84–5, 86–8,
        177

in Peloponnesian War   96–7, 101–2,
   106, 110, 125, 148
in time of Philip   314
Melos: in Peloponnesian War   94, 109,
   131–2, 156, 179–80
Memnon of Rhodes   351–2, 365
Messana (earlier Zancle; in Sicily)
   C5   72, 76–7
   late C5–C4   279, 280, 282
Messenia
   460's–450's   28
   in Peloponnesian War   105
   liberated in 370/69   218; cf. 198, 220–1,
      253, 305
Methone
   in Delian League   177, 181
   captured by Philip   300–1, 321
Methymna
   in Peloponnesian War   108
   in Second Athenian League   230, 232
Miletus
   in Delian League   47, 67–8, 173, 174,
      175
   in Peloponnesian War   143–51
Mindarus of Sparta   145, 147–8
Molossis
   and Philip   300, 314
   and Italy   292–3
Motya   275, 281
Mytilene
   revolt in 428–427   98, 108–9, 174, 179,
      181, 182
   in Second Athenian League   229–32,
      236, 241
   and Alexander   352

Naupactus
   home for fugitive Messenians   28–9,
      44–5
   in Peloponnesian War   102–3, 104, 105
   C4   205, 209
Naxos
   in Delian League   18, 19–20, 35, 173,
      175
   battle in 376   196, 214, 233
Neapolis (in Italy)
   C5   69, 79
   C4   293
Nemea, River: battle in 394   210
Nepos: biographer   274
Nicias of Athens

in Archidamian War   109, 110, 120–1
Peace of   113–14, 124–6; cf. 93, 97,
   152, 197
after the Peace   126, 155–7, 158
Sicilian expedition   132–40
Notium: battle in 406   149–50, 167
Nysaeus, tyrant of Syracuse   289

Oenophyta: battle c.457   44–5
oligarchy
   in Asia Minor in 334   367
   in Athens 420's   116–17
   in Athens in 415   157–9
   in Athens and Samos in 411–410
      143–6, 160–5; cf. 93–4
   in Boeotia   244, 248–9
   in Delian League   179, 181–2
   in Greek world after Peloponnesian War
      153, 204–5
   in Peloponnese after Leuctra   217, 254
   in Syracuse 133–4, 135
   polarisation of Greek world C5   123,
      125, 184, 187, 384
Olympia
   in Peloponnesian War   94, 126–7, 156,
      205
   attacked by Sparta c.400   205
   and Dionysius I in 384   283
   360's   220, 255
Olympias of Molossis: wife of Philip   300,
   314, 320–1, 349, 357, 373, 374
Olynthus
   403's   84
   in Peloponnesian War   111, 125
   early C4   195, 297
   after Peace of Antalcidas   212–13, 215,
      229, 233, 247
   in time of Philip   240–1, 300–1, 305–7,
      309
Opis: mutiny and banquet in 324   357,
   362, 376
Orchomenus (in Boeotia)
   in First Peloponnesian War   51
   before Peace of Antalcidas   193, 210,
      245, 247
   after Peace of Antalcidas   215, 248–9,
      252–3, 318–19
Oreus see Histiaea
Orontes of Persia   222–3
Oropus
   in 411   146, 245

Oropus (cont'd)
  after Peace of Antalcidas   247
  in 366   199, 237, 254
  made independent by Philip   319

Paeonians: and Macedon   297–300
Parmenio of Macedon: under Alexander
  369–71; cf. 351, 354, 356, 362
Pausanias of Sparta, regent   16, 20, 25–8,
  34
Pausanias, king of Sparta   151, 205, 210,
  259
Pelopidas of Thebes   248–56; cf. 198, 199,
  215, 218
Peloponnesian League
  after Peace of Antalcidas   212, 215
  ends in 365   199, 220
Peloponnesian War, First   41–53
Peloponnesian War   81–115, 124–54
Perdiccas II, king of Macedon   84, 111,
  130–1, 297
Perdiccas III, king of Macedon   238, 297
Perdiccas of Macedon: commander under
  Alexander   371, 374, 381
Pericles of Athens
  to mid C5   31–2, 35, 38, 39, 44, 46,
    50–2, 55–6
  in Athenian democracy   57–8, 65–7,
    119–20
  after Thirty Years' Peace   67–8, 69–70
  causes of Peloponnesian War   84–5,
    86–8
  resources and strategy for Peloponnesian
    War   91–2, 96
Perinthus: siege in 340   316
Persepolis: destruction in 330   354, 374–5
Persia
  and Pausanias   26–7
  and Themistocles   34–5
  and Delian League   14–21, 41–53,
    67
  Peloponnesian War   93, 94–5, 99,
    113–14, 175, 183–4, 191
  early C4   191–202, 207–12, 221–2
  after Peace of Antalcidas   222–4; cf.
    199–200, 229–30, 236–7, 323
  support for Thebes in 367   198–9, 219,
    236, 254
  Artaxerxes III and successors   323–6; cf.
    313
  Greek desire for war against   202, 228–9

  war planned by Philip   312–13, 315–16,
    320
  conquest by Alexander   347–82
  see also Antalcidas, Peace of, and Kings
    and other leading men
Phaeax of Athens   106, 156–7
Phalaecus of Phocis   307–8, 309–10
Pharnabazus of Persia
  satrap of Dascylium   143–51, 168, 192,
    207–12
  later career   222–3
Pharsalus: C4   209–10, 215, 250–1, 253
Pheidias of Athens: sculptor   63, 66–7,
  178
Pherae: C4   199, 250–1, 300, 304–5, 313
Philip II, king of Macedon   294–322; cf.
  153, 189, 200–2, 234–5, 240–2, 253,
  336–9
Philip Arrhidaeus of Macedon   300, 320–1
Philiscus of Abydus   198, 218, 254
Philistus of Syracuse   274, 277, 284, 287
Philocrates of Athens   306–7, 309, 314,
  337
Philocrates, Peace of   309–13; cf. 197,
  232, 313–14, 337
Philomelus of Phocis   302–4, 307, 309
Philotas of Macedon   369–71; cf. 356, 361
Phocion of Athens   336–8, 343–4; cf. 306,
  314, 316, 322, 325, 367
Phocis
  mid C5   44, 51
  Corinthian War   209
  370's–360's   215, 249, 251, 252, 255
  Third Sacred War   302–5, 307–13;
    cf. 201, 241
  330's   319
Phoebidas of Sparta   213, 214, 247–8
Phormio of Athens   69, 102–3
Phrynichus of Athens: tragedian   39
Phrynichus of Athens: late C5   162–4,
  166; cf. 144, 160
Pindar of Boeotia: and Sicily   72, 75
Piraeus
  made Athenian harbour   32
  in Peloponnesian War   108, 151, 164
  in downfall of Thirty   259
  C4   210, 211, 227, 238
Pisander of Athens   159, 160–3
Pixodarus, satrap of Caria   323–5
Plataea
  ally of Athens   86, 244

in Peloponnesian War   86, 95–6, 102, 109, 245
C4   196, 235, 247, 249, 318–19
Plato of Athens   166, 274, 283, 287
Plistoanax, king of Sparta   29, 51–2, 113
Plutarch of Chaeronea
  on C5   14, 50, 64–7, 139, 156
  on C4   191, 274, 296, 347–8
Polyzelus of Syracuse and Gela   72–6
Porus, Indian ruler   356, 364–5, 368
Potidaea
  C5   82, 84, 86–8, 101, 111
  C4   237–8, 240
Priene
  in Delian League   67
  and Alexander   367
Pylos
  taken by Athens in 425   97, 105, 152
  afterwards   125, 127, 131, 148

quadriremes and quinqueremes   280, 341

religion
  in Delian League   50, 177–8
  scandals in Athens in 415   157–9
  in Athens C4   341
  see also divine and heroic honours for mortals
Rhegium
  early C5   72–3, 75–6
  Athenian alliance   69, 79, 83–4
  late C5–C4   280, 282–3, 289, 292
Rhodes
  390's   209, 211, 227–8
  in Second Athenian League   229–32, 237, 239, 254
  and Mausolus   239, 323
Rome
  and Carthage   71
  and Etruscans   72
  and Neapolis   293
  and Alexander   351

Samos
  in Delian League   45, 48, 67–8, 83, 92, 173, 174, 175, 178
  in Peloponnesian War   143–51, 160–4, 175, 183
  honours for Lysander   152, 378
  after Peace of Antalcidas   194, 199

Athenian cleruchy   237–8, 239, 319, 323, 343
Sardis
  battle in 395   208
  and Alexander   367
Scione: in Peloponnesian War   112, 125
Scyros
  C5   19–20, 173
  C4   192–3, 212, 227–8, 231, 319
Selinus
  in Peloponnesian War   132, 134, 275
  afterwards   275, 279
Selymbria
  in Peloponnesian War   148, 182
  siege in 340   316
Sicily
  mid C5   71–8
  in Archidamian War   94, 97, 103–4, 105–6
  in 415–413   93, 132–40, 174, 183
  late C5–C4   273–92
  see also individual cities and leading men
slaves
  alleged régime of, in Argos   57
  in Athens   57, 150
Socrates of Athens: trial   267; cf. 119
Sophocles of Athens
  civic career   160
  tragedies   39, 117, 169
Sparta
  harmosts   207
  population
    citizen numbers   216–17; cf. 29, 153, 207
    helots   4, 9, 27–8, 97, 207
    hypomeiones   206
    mothakes   135, 149, 150, 207
    perioikoi   4, 97, 194, 207
speeches
  in Thucydides   179–80
  in Xenophon   190
Sphodrias of Sparta   195, 214, 229–30, 248
Sthenelaidas of Sparta   85–6, 88
Struthas, satrap of Sardis   211
Sybaris   68–9, 73, 75, 79; see also Thurii
Syracuse
  tyrants C5   72–6
  after the tyrants   76–8
  in Peloponnesian War   103, 106, 132–40
  afterwards   274–92

Tanagra: battle *c.*457 44–5
Taras
  C5 80
  C4 292–3
Tegea
  early C5 22–5
  in Peloponnesian War 125–30
  360's 217–21; cf. 200, 255
Tegyra: battle in 376 215, 249
Tenedos: in Second Athenian League
    241, 242, 304, 316
Thasos
  in Delian League 19–20, 28, 35, 173
  in Peloponnesian War 149
Thebes
  in Peloponnesian War 86, 109
  404–360 244–56; cf. 189–90, 195–200,
    212, 214, 217–21, 229–33, 235–8
  sacred band 215, 249, 318
  in time of Philip 302–5, 307–9,
    311–12, 317–19; cf. 201–2, 239, 242,
    301, 304, 325
  destroyed by Alexander 349–51
  see also Boeotia
Themistocles of Athens 24–5, 31–9
Theopompus of Chios: historian 274
Theramenes of Athens
  in Peloponnesian War 147–8, 151, 162,
    164–9
  and Thirty 257–9
Theron, tyrant of Acragas 72, 75
Thespiae
  in Peloponnesian War 110, 140
  C4 248–50, 318–19
Thessaly
  C5 25–6, 41, 44, 167
  370's–360's 250–1, 253, 255; cf. 199,
    213, 215, 238
  and Philip 296, 300, 304–5, 313
  and Alexander 349
  see also Pharsalus, Pherae
Thibron of Sparta 207, 211
Thrace
  in Peloponnesian War 111, 150–1
  404–360 195, 229, 236, 238, 240–1
  in time of Philip 296, 299–301, 311,
    313, 314
  in time of Alexander 345, 349,
    366
Thrasybulus of Athens (of deme Stiria)

  in Peloponnesian War 145, 147, 149,
    163–8
  opponent of Thirty 259–60
  early C4 193, 211, 227–8, 266–8
Thrasyllus of Athens 145, 147–50,
    163–7
Thucydides of Athens (son of Melesias)
    65–6, 69, 120
Thucydides of Athens (son of Olorus)
  end of his history 146
  exile 111–12
  on Athenian politics and politicians
    105, 119–20, 126, 157, 161–5,
    180
  on causes of Peloponnesian War
    81–9
  on Peloponnesian War 96, 124, 126,
    132, 174
  on Pentecontaetia and Delian League
    14, 16–18, 175, 178–9
  on plague in Athens 112–13
  on Sparta and empire 152
  seasonal years 102
  speeches 179
Thudippus of Athens 92, 121
Thurii
  Sybaris to mid C5 68–9, 73, 75, 79
  440's 68–9, 79–80
  C4 283–4, 285
Timaeus of Tauromenium: historian 274,
    289
Timarchus of Athens 314, 337, 339
Timoleon of Corinth and Syracuse
    289–92; cf. 219
Timotheus of Athens 215, 223, 234–7,
    239, 269–71
Tiribazus, satrap of Sardis 192, 193, 211,
    222
Tissaphernes, satrap of Sardis
  in Peloponnesian War 143–9, 160–1,
    221
  afterwards 185, 191–2, 207–8, 221
Tithraustes, grand vizier of Persia
    208–9
Tolmides of Athens 44
Tyre: siege in 332 353, 365

women
  generally 9
  in Athens 56; cf. 55

Xanthippus of Athens 31–3
Xenophon of Athens
   Agesilaus, Anabasis 190, 348
   Hellenica 146–7, 167, 190–1,
     257

Ways and Means 240, 332–3
   Athenian Constitution attributed to ('Old
   Oligarch') 116–17, 180

Zancle *see* Messana

Also of Interest

A Companion to the Classical Greek World

Edited by KONRAD H. KINZL
Trent University, Canada

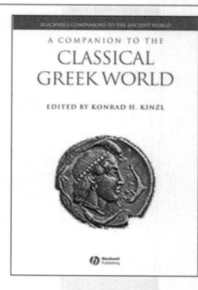

This **Companion** provides scholarly yet accessible new interpretations of Greek history of the Classical period, from the aftermath of the Persian Wars in 478 B.C. to the death of Alexander the Great in 323 B.C.

- Topics covered range from the political and institutional structures of Greek society, to literature, art, economics, society, warfare, geography and the environment
- Discusses the problems of interpreting the various sources for the period
- Guides the reader towards a broadly-based understanding of the history of the Classical Age.

Blackwell Companions to the Ancient World Series
648 pages / 0-631-23014-9 HB / **November 2005**
Order online at **www.blackwellpublishing.com/0631230149**

Ancient Greek Civilization

DAVID SANSONE
University of Illinois at Urbana-Champaign

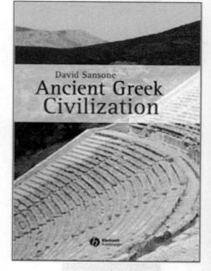

"Sansone's coverage and approach are fresh and distinctive, and his book richly informative, well-balanced, and engagingly written."
Stephen White, University of Texas at Austin

- Tells the story of Greek civilization from the Bronze Age to the transformation of Greek culture during the Roman Empire
- Surveys the impressive history, literature, art, and philosophy of the ancient Greeks
- Shows how the ancient Greeks used these forms of cultural expression to reinvent themselves and how Greek civilization has been continually reinvented to the present day
- Features include maps, illustrations, timelines, a glossary, a guide to ancient Greek writers and a bibliography.

256 pages / 0-631-23235-4 HB / 0-631-23236-2 PB / **2003**
Order online at **www.blackwellpublishing.com/0631232362**

 **Blackwell** Publishing

www.blackwellpublishing.com